D1639547

THE LETTERS
OF
LEWIS MUMFORD
AND
FREDERIC J. OSBORN

THE LETTERS
OF
LEWIS MUMFORD
AND
FREDERIC J. OSBORN

---

a transatlantic dialogue 1938–70, edited by Michael R. Hughes

---

BATH: ADAMS & DART

First published in 1971 by
Adams & Dart 40 Gay Street, Bath, Somerset
SBN 239 00099 4
Printed and bound in Great Britain at
The Pitman Press, Bath

INTRODUCTION

The origin of Lewis Mumford's and Frederic Osborn's friendship lay in their common interest in the ideas of Ebenezer Howard, the English originator of the Garden City concept. These ideas, expressed in *To-morrow* (later *Garden Cities of Tomorrow*) in 1898, had provided Mumford with important elements of his ambitious thinking on cities and town planning. Osborn was a disciple of Howard who had spent most of his working life developing Garden Cities. So when Osborn opened the present Correspondence in 1938 the two men were already friends in spirit.

Both were born in great cities, Mumford in New York in 1895, Osborn in London ten years earlier. Osborn's origins were lower-middle class, and he left a council school at fifteen for an office boy's job in the City of London. His adolescence was fairly typical for a bright boy of his time and background. He had a strong desire for knowledge and a great love of reading, which he indulged during work-time as well as leisure in a succession of undemanding clerical jobs. He attended night-school in a variety of subjects, developed an interest in politics and social reform and became a socialist. He started and acted as secretary of small clubs and societies, experimented in writing essays, plays and verses, and moved among like-minded people. Joining at the age of 20 the Fabian Society, from which he got tremendous stimulus, he discussed, argued and lectured about the issues of the day, edited *The Fabian Nursling* with St John Ervine and sat at the feet of his then heroes, Bernard Shaw and H. G. Wells.

A typical self-educated, metropolitan intellectual of humble origins, he might well have passed his years as a city clerk, company secretary or minor politician, had not a successful application in 1912 for a post as Secretary-Manager of the Howard Cottage Society in Letchworth altered the whole course of his life.

Letchworth, the first Garden City, founded in 1903 by Ebenezer Howard and planned by Raymond Unwin and Barry Parker, was a revelation for him. He had lived all his life in London and though taught to be proud of it deplored, and had often debated remedies for, its dreadful slums, overcrowding and squalor. Then overnight he was transported to a new environment planned on rational principles under a new form of land ownership,

v

graciously combining healthy homes and town and countryside, which offered a genuine community and a face-to-face culture no less rich than his metropolitan experiences. He immediately embraced it—not only the town, the people, his work, but the philosophy and principles which they expressed —and became a militant advocate of Garden Cities.

Osborn's work as housing manager, in which he personally collected rents, gave him a down-to-earth grounding in popular preferences and the practical consequences of planning and architecture which never left him. He played a full part in the varied life of the town, schooled himself in planning and sociological literature and became an accomplished exponent of the Garden City case. He was one of four Letchworth residents (including Howard, C. B. Purdom and W. G. Taylor) who associated themselves as the 'New Townsmen' to rescue Garden City ideals from the garden suburb distortion, and in consultation with the group wrote his first published work, *New Towns After the War* (1918). And when Howard in 1919 bought the land for Welwyn Garden City, Osborn went there with him as Company Secretary and Estate Manager.

For the next 17 years Osborn—one of a brilliant team—helped to create at Welwyn a town of world-wide renown, a second demonstration that man could plan and create humane, healthy communities of beauty and functional efficiency. Given the obstacles, Welwyn Garden City, the masterpiece of its planner Louis de Soissons, was a remarkable achievement, and in time was to add profitability to its many successes. But in the early days, when investors were deterred by the town's 'utopian' reputation and limited dividend, under-capitalisation was a permanent difficulty, and after a major financial reconstruction and change of control Osborn lost his job and left the Company in 1936.

He was immediately offered a Directorship in a local radio manufacturing firm, one which allowed considerable free time for other activities. Released from the day-to-day responsibilities of Welwyn, Osborn deployed his practical experience of town-building and political and propaganda skills into a wider agitation for a national Garden Cities programme. He became Honorary Secretary of the then named Garden Cities and Town Planning Association, a medium of potential influence, from which followed the events partly chronicled in this book. Its members already included such eminent planners and advocates of new towns as Raymond Unwin, Patrick Abercrombie, George L. Pepler and Richard L. Reiss, and during Osborn's regime many new recruits, among them Gilbert and Elizabeth McAllister,

Peter Self and Wyndham Thomas, were to make valuable contributions to its thought and propaganda.

In one of his letters Frederic Osborn describes himself as 'a specialist on things in general'; Lewis Mumford insistently describes himself as 'a generalist'. There is a similarity; but whereas with Osborn one suspects a rather neat description of his abiding curiosity in all things, with Mumford the term is a considered indication of a fundamental aspect of his philosophy and way of thinking. It implies not only the mastery of a multiplicity of subjects, which Mumford has, but an approach to problems which synthesises their different facets, including past, present and possible future, so as to comprehend them as a total unity. This ability, necessity even, to see things whole, came early through the influence of the many-sided biologist and town planner, Patrick Geddes, whose work Mumford absorbed in his formative years. Geddes aspired to unify the natural sciences with sociology, seeking a way of understanding the world as a totality rather than as fragmented experience. Mumford corresponded and met with Geddes, and Geddes' organic thinking and his original ideas on city history and planning became a seminal part of Mumford's own thinking.

Mumford's early manhood suggested a successful, conventional career as writer and critic. After study at the City College of New York and Columbia University, interrupted by war service in the U.S. Navy, he established himself as a writer and was an associate editor of *The Dial* magazine. Another of his mentors, Victor Branford, the British sociologist and colleague of Geddes, invited him to London in 1920 as Acting Editor of *The Sociological Review*. He returned to America in the same year and wrote for *The Freeman*, a journal of comment and the arts, in which he began to attract attention as a promising young critic. His first book, *The Story of Utopias*, published in 1922, signified interests far wider than conventional literature; in fact it dealt in limited terms with most of the themes which he was to pursue in his later works.

Throughout the next decade he worked on four pioneering books dealing with American culture. *Sticks and Stones* (1924), *The Golden Day* (1926), *Herman Melville* (1929) and *The Brown Decades* (1931) studied American architecture and literature with none of the usual deference to their European counterparts. When much of American art and criticism drew its inspiration and justification from Europe, these four books established a native American tradition with its own sensibility and perceptions, in particular revealing a post–1865 architectural tradition hitherto almost completely neglected.

His understanding of architecture and the environment was immensely deepened during these same years through his membership of the Regional Planning Association of America. This astonishing group, never numbering more than 20 people but including among them some of the most brilliant names of later years—Clarence Stein, Henry Wright, Stuart Chase, Benton MacKaye, Catherine Bauer—came together in reaction against disorders and inefficiencies in current urban planning. Throughout 1923–33 members met informally for wide-ranging exchanges and discussions, a group of greatly talented friends seeking and devising solutions for a revival of quality architecture and planning. The RPAA was an American bridgehead for the ideas of Geddes, Howard and Raymond Unwin, although its members brought to it and absorbed influences from many other sources, including Thorstein Veblen, John Dewey and Charles Horton Cooley. The new RPAA concepts found concrete expression, directly or indirectly, in Radburn, the Greenbelt towns, the Appalachian Trail, the Townless Highway and the 1926 New York Housing and Regional Plan. Less specifically, their demonstrations of the region as the basic planning framework constitute one of the most important, and still unfinished, chapters in American planning history, now world-wide in their influence.

Mumford's ten years at the heart of the RPAA, analysing with the best minds everything from regional theory to detailed street layouts, gave him priceless experience and insight of environmental needs and problems. From them he refined much of the understanding and perception which invaluably informed his later work. The member he credits as the most powerful advocate and planner of new communities was Clarence Stein, whose book, *Toward New Towns in America* (1951) is a classic.

His writings in the nineteen-twenties and his RPAA work were mainly concerned with American culture and experience. With his next work he made the first of his lifelong attempts to set down the essence of Western culture and history, as a prelude to understanding the present and controlling the future. *Technics and Civilisation* (1934) was not only a history of technology but was an analysis of how the development of tools and the machine had totally altered man's perceptions, transforming not only his technical surroundings but permeating his ideologies, his political and economic structures, his art and his morality. It was a brilliant, original book, covering ground (the relationships between men and machines) which Mumford was to make a central preoccupation.

It was planned as the first of a trilogy later entitled the Renewal of Life series, which would chart man's total past development and set out possibilities for his transformation and future growth. Its successor, *The Culture of Cities* (1938), instantly established Mumford as a thinker and social critic of major importance. In it he showed how the city, man's most complex social creation, had evolved in response to changing ideologies, reflecting in its layout and forms and physical priorities the cultural and spiritual beliefs of its inhabitants. He traced the spiritual heritage which had produced the degenerations of modern city life and set out a technical and moral framework within which the city could be rehabilitated. *The Culture of Cities* brought its author to world-wide notice, and became the most influential planning book of our time.

It also brought Mumford and Frederic Osborn together, although their friendship might well have developed without it. Their paths had run parallel for several years and their later work, particularly Osborn's on the British New Towns, would almost certainly have made them converge.

Both were happy in having life companions who were active collaborators in their work. Sophia Mumford and Margaret Osborn (who died in 1970) shared their friendship and did much to cement it through the many years of steadily ripening friendship which drew the two of them together in open intimacy: years when both would attempt and partially realise enormous tasks. In rich, varied lives, Osborn would play a main part in the establishment of a government programme for building New Towns in Great Britain; Mumford, as part of a wider vision, would alter world consciousness of what living in cities could mean. Frequently, and often maliciously, attacked for their ideas, their names would be linked throughout the world as champions of a new method of controlling urban growth and the deliberate organisation of communities, as two men who refused to be bound by the forms of the past; who saw that man could make his own forms, could create new cities and give millions the health and elementary decencies for a humane life. Two men who, having seen this, determined to bring it about.

M. R. H.

The Lewis Mumford/Frederic Osborn correspondence runs to some 450,000 words, which have been reduced by approximately half for the present volume. The omission of complete letters has not been shown but substantial omissions within letters are indicated thus: ...

For assistance in the preparation of this volume the Editor wishes to thank: Lewis Mumford and Sir Frederic Osborn, for much kindness and patient advice throughout; Rank-Xerox Ltd, Welwyn Garden City, and Mrs Anne Corrigan of Washington, D.C.; Hazle Carter, Tricia Fordham and Sheila Foxon; and my wife, whose help at all stages has been invaluable.

1938-1947

Although Mumford had visited Osborn at Welwyn Garden City in 1932 they had not corresponded; each was aware of the other's writings and activities during the nineteen-thirties, but it was not until he read The Culture of Cities *in 1938 that Osborn realised how close he and Mumford were in their attachment to the garden city movement initiated by Ebenezer Howard.*

The Culture of Cities is in effect a social and cultural history of Western Man interpreted through the evolution of the city from medieval times. Synthesising a vast learning in the arts, technology, history and philosophy, Mumford traced the development of city forms in the interactions of man's social, intellectual and spiritual life. It included a forceful, critical analysis of the industrial city and of contemporary megalopolis, relating their dehumanized environment, spiritual impoverishment and defects as organs of social transmission to a utopian faith in salvation by technology. The city's positive contribution to man's affairs was equally fully recognised, and the book ended on a note of qualified optimism: a way forward was pointed via the creation of planned, limited communities in a planned, regional framework, on the Social Basis of a New Urban Order.

In describing this New Urban Order Mumford paid high tribute to Ebenezer Howard, restating his Garden Cities idea as one of the bases for urban transformation. It was the most eloquent statement of this idea since Howard's book of 1898, and Osborn was excited and delighted by this brilliant and powerful fellow-supporter. His response was immediate. On 12 December 1938 Osborn wrote to Mumford, the first step in the thirty-two year and continuing friendship. The dialogue had begun.

In 1938 Osborn, whose practical involvement in building Welwyn Garden City had previously absorbed most of his time and energies, was on the threshold of the most active and influential period of his career. For two years he had been Honorary Secretary of the Town and Country Planning Association, which was enjoying new standing and influence. He had prepared and presented the Association's Evidence to the Barlow Royal Commission on the Distribution of the Industrial Population and was diligently working behind the scenes to stiffen its Report, when the outbreak of the Second World War transformed attitudes to planning and offered new scope for the ideas he stood for.

The planning possibilities presented by the First World War had spurred

1

Osborn and his fellow New Townsmen into renewed propaganda for the Garden City movement. Well aware how feeble their influence on postwar housing drives had then been, and having in the meantime acquired much hard experience of town building and political negotiation, Osborn determined from the start to ensure that history did not repeat itself. In this he was assisted by the fact that the Government had established, in the early years of the War, when victory was remote and doubtful, various bodies and committees to plan for the rebuilding of postwar Britain. One such was a Panel of Physical Reconstruction, set up in 1940 by Lord Reith, then Minister of Works and Building. Osborn became a member of the Panel and, as an unpaid, unofficial civil servant, moved into Whitehall for his first experience of the corridors of power from within.

Earlier in the same year the Report of the Barlow Commission had been published. It was a good analysis of the circumstances and problems of town planning and included important recommendations for a policy and machinery for national planning. It clearly bore the stamp of TCPA submissions and policies, especially in its more radical Minority Report, signed by Patrick Abercrombie, which advocated a Ministry of Planning with extensive powers to initiate city dispersal and build Garden Cities or satellite towns. Coming out when it did, with public and official interest strong, and providing a thoughtful, detailed review of the subject, the Barlow Report, and especially the Minority Report, clarified and directed planning discussion for the next decade.

Other influential wartime planning documents, on all of which Osborn as leader of the TCPA had influence, were the Reports of the Uthwatt Committee on Compensation and Betterment and the Scott Committee on Land Utilisation (1941–42), Forshaw and Abercrombie's County of London Plan *(1943), and* Abercrombie's Greater London Plan *(1944), which proposed satellite towns to relieve London's congestion. These were major statements which increased the pressure for comprehensive planning policies and which pointed the direction—towards planned dispersal and new towns—in which Britain was to move.*

In the consequent discussion and controversy Osborn played a part; played, in fact, several parts: as a Panel member he offered advice and drafted memoranda and reports; as TCPA Secretary he prepared evidence, appeared at tribunals and wrote endless documents; as discreet lobbyist he reasoned, chided and critically encouraged those whose support he wanted; as pamphleteer, writer, broadcaster and public speaker he kept issues alive and reiterated his policies incessantly. He was a member of the Labour Party Postwar Reconstruction Committee and advised informally the Conservative and Liberal Party equivalents. He organised and spoke at major planning conferences, prepared a new edition of Garden Cities of Tomorrow, *revised* New Towns After the War, *wrote, in* Greenbelt Cities, *the most developed argument for Garden Cities since Howard, and established, edited and contributed to an important series of booklets on Rebuilding Britain. He worked tirelessly to use every means and occasion to get the dispersal policies across.*

The 1945 General Election in Britain brought the Labour Party to power and Lewis Silkin, one time Chairman of the London County Council Planning Committee, became Minister of Town and Country Planning in the new Government. He quickly decided to implement Abercrombie's recommendations for satellite towns and appointed an Advisory Committee to prepare proposals. Lord Reith was its Chairman and Osborn a member. Working with tremendous speed the New Towns Committee produced three substantial Reports in only nine months. These recommended that New Towns should be established and built by Government sponsored and financed corporations, and set out the principles and methods of land acquisition, housing development and commercial and industrial policies. They suggested methods of finance, defined relationships with local government, made detailed proposals as to how the New Towns should be planned and the plans executed, and generally provided a remarkable set of blueprints for the creation of whole communities. The Reports were accepted and immediately embodied in Silkin's historic New Towns Act (1946) and Town and Country Planning Act (1947). Sites were designated and, with much opposition and many problems ahead, a Government-sponsored New Towns programme got under way.

The New Towns legislation was the triumphant culmination of the half-century campaign by the TCPA. Without Lord Reith's dynamic qualities the first New Towns would not have been founded when they were. Without Lewis Silkin's ministerial audacity and political ability they might never have been founded. But without Osborn history would also have taken a different path. He had dedicated his life to the cause of planned cities, had prepared the ground in so many ways, had helped shape the achievements along the way and, to crown thirty years' endeavour, had been a key person in the deliberations which finally brought them about.

Lewis Mumford was equally active in the pre-war years. From 1938 he enjoyed an international reputation for The Culture of Cities, *but even while that book was being written the values which it celebrated and sought to renew were crumbling before the advance of Fascism. This threat to Western civilisation and to everything which Mumford believed in was total and obvious, yet European nations seemed incapable of resisting it, while America considered it none of her business. But Mumford could not merely observe the destruction of civilisation: he wrote* Men Must Act, *a militant attack on Fascism which pleaded passionately for America to make a stand and impose a total diplomatic, economic and cultural blockade on Germany, Italy and Japan. This earned Mumford much unpopularity and criticism: friendships were strained and lost and he was attacked as a war-monger, even as a Fascist!*

With Men Must Act *should be mentioned* Faith for Living, *written in the bleak weeks of 1940 when it seemed that England must fall, and* Values for Survival, *a 1946 collection of wartime essays and addresses. This 'trilogy' gives us one man's response and reflections on the War, on its causes and prosecution, on the new world which had to be wrought from the peace. It typifies the polemical, journalistic, more directly engaged writing with which Mumford parallels his major works. And it demonstrated that he was no impotent philosopher paralysed by the consequences of action; but that he was both thinker and doer, a philosopher who would stand and fight for his creed, even if the price for it was war.*

Although he was one of the leading public figures against Fascism Mumford was not called to serve his country when America entered the War. He spent the years teaching and writing, unable to serve more directly in the struggle. He was Professor at Stanford University from 1942–44, in a new School of Humanities, but writing continued to be his main occupation. The South in Architecture (*1941*) *continued his study of American culture,* The Condition of Man (*1944*) *added the third volume to the Renewal of Life series. This was inevitably a sombre work, written under circumstances not envisaged when the ground plan for the series was laid down in 1930. In it Mumford traced the tangled spiritual history of the world crisis, hoping that if Man would understand and confront his collective past he could, like the neurotic unburying his personal past, conquer and transcend it.*

Mumford experienced some of the feeling and anguish of the War through his son Geddes, with whom he was more than usually close. On 13 September 1944 Geddes was killed on scouting duty on the Italian front at the age of 19. Green Memories (*1947*) *is the beautiful story of his son's life and brave death.*

Town planning continued to be a main preoccupation but Mumford played no active part in the Federal reconstruction programmes. For Osborn's 'Rebuilding Britain' series he wrote The Social Foundations of Postwar Building *and* The Plan of London County, *two penetrating applications of general beliefs which were reprinted in* City Development (*1945*). *He again joined with Osborn in writing an Introductory Essay to Howard's* Garden Cities of Tomorrow, *uncovering in the process a difference in their views on housing densities which in later years was to bring a controversial note into their correspondence. 1946 found Mumford engaged in a one-man campaign against the nuclear arms race, an issue with which he was to become passionately identified. In the same year he at last toured the principal cities of Britain as guest of the Institute of Sociology and received the Ebenezer Howard Memorial Medal for outstanding work in advancing Howard's principles. His meeting Osborn after a relationship by letter of nearly ten years was a milestone in their friendship.*

Mr Lewis Mumford,
per Messrs Martin Secker & Warburg,
22 Essex Street, London, WC2

Dear Mr Mumford
I have been wanting to get into correspondence with you for some time past,
by reason of interest in your writings on town sociology, which parallels much
more effectively what I have been trying to do over here. And now I have just
read *The Culture of Cities*,[1] and feel I must find time to thank you for a job
of work of first-class importance and fascinating interest. It is exactly the sort
of book I knew to be necessary but would never have had time to write, even
if I had possessed the energy and ability to do it. I have had a sense of complete isolation and ineffectiveness in pursuing similar lines of thought and
policy here, and it is immensely heartening to find that as a result of your
prolonged study of this really difficult and complicated subject, you come to
substantially the same conclusions and have developed the same enthusiasms
and precisely the same antipathies that I have developed. Of course I detected
when you and Catherine Bauer[2] called on me at Welwyn in 1932 (was it?)
that to some extent we were in tune, but I had no idea how far you had
adventured along these lines till I read your new book.

The old guard of town-planners in England have been as vague and inconsistent on fundamental issues as in America, but as a result of very persistent talking and writing in their small circle I have got most of the younger
planners, and some of the older ones, to accept in a general way the thesis of
decentralisation, control of size and density of towns, and state guidance of
the location of industry. And now I am engaged in a big effort to get this
general acceptance turned into a national policy—which of course is where
the fun really begins, because there is no doubt that there are colossal difficulties and many interests in the way in a closely settled country like this. At
a distance it seems that it might be much easier for the USA to give effect to
the policy, especially as you are only at the beginning of a national house-
building drive. On the other hand I think your political-administrative
obstacles are even greater than ours.

I have been going into the economics of British cities to some extent, and
I am sending you under separate cover the Evidence I gave on behalf of the
Garden Cities and Town Planning Association to the Royal Commission

---

[1] New York, London, 1938.
[2] Catherine Bauer Wurster, influential writer and political adviser on housing and
city and regional planning.

(now sitting) on the Geographical Distribution of the Industrial Population, and one or two other writings that will interest you as tracking the clues you also track, but with special reference to current British conditions.

You ought by the way to be aware, if it has not come before you, of the immense body of Evidence given by public Departments, City Corporations, and business organisations before the same Commission, about 26 volumes of which have already been published. The outlook is mostly pretty contemptible, but there is a vast body of important facts and statistics about towns and the location of industry. The discussion in this country began with my paper on Industry and Planning[1] at the Town Planning Institute, to which, if you remember, I invited you during your visit. At that time the idea of state guidance was regarded as fantastic. Now it is seriously contemplated, and the Commission is likely to report in favour of it. . . .

AMENIA, NEW YORK   14 January 1939

Dear Mr Osborn

I am very grateful for your letter and for the reports you were good enough to send along with it. The Garden City memorandum before the Royal Commission is a masterly document; and your sardonic picture of the disruptions of transport greatly delighted me, too. What you say about the weaknesses in my bibliography is altogether just: it arises partly out of the fact that I had planned, until within six months of the final date of publication, to make a hasty trip through Europe for the precise purpose of rounding up books that had escaped me and acquiring further documents and pictures: when practical necessities kept me here I was too exhausted to make the necessary efforts to get hold of these data by other means. So there is a great hole in my documentation here, particularly on the side where, until recently, I was best informed. As for my leaving out the *Journal* of the TPI and *Town and Country Planning*, that was another matter: it is an old joke in my experience that my bibliographies are usually pretty comprehensive except in their failure to list the books I have lived with all my life or have on my own shelf. That is what happened in this case. I shall take care to make amends if ever I can persuade my publisher to do a revised edition.

Since seeing you in Welwyn in 1932, much has happened in the United States one could not have predicted then: both housing and regional planning have taken on in an extraordinary way, though there is a great danger that the first, by being tied up to slum clearance, may miss some of its real opportunities. Last summer I made a brief tour of our West coast, and in the

---

[1] Published in the *Journal of the Town Planning Institute*, July, 1932.

Northwest I was the guest of the Pacific Northwest Regional planning groups. Though their thinking on the social and economic side is still unduly inhibited by fear of meeting public opposition, they are unusually receptive to ideas; and with a little outside stimulus, which they themselves seem to feel the need of, they may give the rest of the country something to think about. The Columbia Gorge, though scarcely anyone in the rest of the country seems to know it, is one of the finest pieces of scenery in the world: like a classic piece of Chinese landscape painting, unrolled on an endless *kakemono*. To prevent this from being ruined by the reckless setting of industry near the place where power is produced, instead of utilising the grid for decentralisation, is their prime problem at the moment. I have done a little memorandum on this for their Council: and I also—as the result of a short stay in Honolulu —did a report on re-planning Honolulu, naturally a sketchy one devoted to principles and approach, which I will send you as soon as I have copies.

The approaching stabilisation of population all over the world is already all-marked in such new parts of the continent, settled only fifty years ago for the most part, as in the Northwest; and this seems to me to offer special problems and special opportunities. I have emphasised this fact in both reports; and I wonder if there has been any special thinking on this subject in Great Britain. Industry was keyed during the nineteenth century to expansion: it will now have to be keyed to replacement, or rather, such expansion as may be possible will be only through increasing the amount of goods available *per capita*—not by increasing the number of heads. This is a radical change which seems to me to promise, among other things, large increments of capital at low rates for city building and regional reconstruction. Is not our chronic economic crisis partly due to the fact that the representatives of the old order will not face the implications of this change? Industrialists and business men with whom I spoke, unfamiliar with population figures and their implications, seemed to grasp the importance of these things as soon as one spread the facts before them.

I shall be very grateful indeed if you will keep me in touch with the work you are doing. During the last couple of months I have been busy on a book,[1] hardly more than a pamphlet, attempting to re-formulate America's attitude toward the international situation, particularly as regards fascism: apart from the fact that I necessarily speak here as an American I don't know whether what I have said here will appeal to you or not, but I shall send it on nevertheless when the book appears, for I think it is important that intelligent Englishmen should realise how intelligent Americans feel about the present posture of things. There has been a great deal of temporising and

---

[1] *Men Must Act*, New York, London, 1939.

mental fraud on both sides of the water; and the sooner it is cleared away
the better. Otherwise, my main task at the moment is to lay the foundations
for the final book in the series, which will give point to the other two and
perhaps even compel some revisions in them.

In a year or so from now I plan to get out a simplified version of *Technics
and Civilization*[1]: a small book, completely re-written, with certain things
added that I left out in the original. I had originally meant to deal with urban
utilities and the development of technics in building in the second volume;
but it proved impossible to do this except in the most sketchy way; so that
now I will restore those sections to *Technics*, where they belong. I will also
deal with agriculture, chemistry, civil engineering, and the more static sides
of technics in a more balanced fashion than I did in *Technics*. Eventually I
may make a parallel simplification of *The Culture of Cities*, too: this will
result in a sort of Aristotelian division into an esoteric and an exoteric
canon!

WELWYN GARDEN CITY   27 August 1939

Dear Mr Mumford
I have been trying to find time to write to you in appreciation of your
Honolulu booklet, and partially in appreciation and partially in criticism of
your extremely forcible *Men Must Act*. Now that we seem to be on the eve
of war, I am afraid I cannot carry out my programme of writing you fully
on both these subjects, but I feel I must send you a line or two as an opportunity may not occur again for a long time.

With your tremendous indictment of Fascism as a system I agree, and I
was filled with enthusiasm by the first part of your book, which stated the
case against the Fascist system more eloquently than any other book I have
seen. I am bound to confess, however, that I was disappointed and, indeed,
puzzled by your interpretation of Britain and the practical policy which you
suggest. You seem to me to be making exactly the mistake that many people
in this country made when Czechoslovakia was in question, and with less
excuse because you, at any rate, do understand what Fascism is. It is, perhaps, an exaggeration to say that you yourself were making the mistake, but
it seems to me that you went much too far in compromising with the fundamental American mistake on this point.

In September 1938, the people of Britain, if properly led, would have taken
exactly the line that they are now taking. I think half the population of

[1] New York, London, 1934.

Britain were convinced in 1938 that we ought to take a stand over Czechoslovakia. The other half were probably ignorant of what Fascism really is, and all sections were then considerably influenced by the belief that there were geniune German grievances arising out of the Treaty of Versailles. The belief of the dominant section of our Government, that an appeasement policy was practicable, was, of course, accepted by the majority of the people, but if the Government had decided in 1938 to take a stand they would have had the support of the vast majority of the population, though not perhaps the 99 per cent. that is in favour of their policy now. The reason for the increased solidarity is, of course, that last year it was only those who carefully studied foreign affairs who could see the significance of the sequence of events. The occupation of Prague was a conclusive demonstration to everybody, except a few pacifists and a tiny sprinkling of obstinate people who like to exercise their democratic right to oppose the stream.

In the policy you advocate it seems to me to be implicit that the first line of defence of democracy is in France and Britain, and it is difficult for us here to understand the view that America should wait until the first line has been taken before they join in the defence themselves. If we had all been solid together, and if we had all made a solid declaration together, it is obvious that war would not have come about at all. I personally took precisely the same view of Britain, in relation to the Spanish and Czechoslovakian crises, that I now take of America in relation to the French and British crisis. I realise, of course, the immense and natural strength of isolationism, because I have seen it at close quarters here at an earlier stage. Nevertheless, I think it is both short-sighted and morally wrong; the true logic of the situation for America to-day is exactly what it was for Britain in September, 1938. . . .

I have so often found myself in agreement with your way of looking at things that I regret the distance which prevents us from being in much closer touch, as I feel that we could have co-operated very effectively in the interpretation of democracy in relation to town planning, if not in regard to these larger issues.

AMENIA, NEW YORK   10 September 1939

Dear Mr Osborn
It was good of you to write me as you did; and I am answering promptly, though how soon this will reach you and under what conditions, heaven only knows. Events have been moving so rapidly that it is quite understandable that you find it difficult in August to understand the state of mind

in which I wrote *Men Must Act* last November. At that time it seemed to
me that if Europe kept on pursuing the Chamberlain policy it was lost: I
counted not only on the subjugation of Czechoslovakia but of France as
well. I saw no possibility for collective security by way of further appeasement: rather, I regarded the American government's acceptance of this coordinated action in the case of Spain, for example, as one of the things that
had helped give the Fascist powers the upper hand. The paradoxical isolationist policy that I urged was directed against accepting the Chamberlain
lead: it was aimed to produce action, even if the United States was forced to
act alone. It seemed to me that such democratic forces as were active in
Europe, active and resolute, might follow our lead: but that the one thing
that would be fatal for us would be to remain indifferent to the situation or
to share the delusive hope of 'peace in our time', whilst the irrational forces
that governed Germany and Italy and (potentially) Russia were uppermost.
My pamphlet was the first one to take this line; but it had a great inertia to
overcome, and I cannot pretend that I have been successful in lessening as
yet, to any significant amount, the forces that oppose all effort to act positively
in the present crisis.

Since I published my pamphlet the situation has altered; and neither my
original premises nor my proposals for mere non-intercourse apply. But up
to the March seizure of Czechoslovakia, indeed, up to the last moment
acceptance of the fact of war, there was no sure sign that the Chamberlain
government was not still seeking to give Germany whatever it demanded:
the betrayal of the Hudson proposals a little while ago made almost every
intelligent observer in America take the position that a sell-out would follow
—and it is quite conceivable that it had this effect on Hitler, too. So it is
very difficult to persuade the ordinary American that he has any real concern
in an enterprise that has been so badly mismanaged as this all-too-belated
stand against Hitler. The moral and political case against him has been built
up too tardily on your side of the water—as witness the more than diplomatic
unction with which Daladier addressed Hitler in his last important note
before the climax of the crisis. Needless to say, though I believe that the anti-
fascist countries have been supplying the chief incendiary with matches and
dry kindling, I know that the fire that has been lighted may prove quite as
dangerous for America as for England: hence I propose to waste no energy
on retrospective criticism and regrets. Indeed, I accept your own position
so completely that, when the Russian agreement with Hitler came over the
wires and two newspapers wired me for my opinion on it, I immediately said
that the entire force of the United States should be thrown on the French
and British side, as the only possible means of averting war. That was, I
believe, a sound proposal: it had no popular backing then, and it has no

popular backing yet; but it is one that I shall continue to push forward. I regard our present policy of neutrality as an extremely dangerous and cowardly one; and I shall do all in my power to transform it into active, military support of the anti-fascist powers—as the only act on our part that may help to shorten the war and avert the destruction of our common civilisation.

Now that England and France have struck, my original policy, which was based on the overwhelming probability that they would *not* strike, naturally must change from passive non-intercourse to active combat. I foresee some difficulty in putting my views into circulation in the early months of the war, for those who advocate war here are now as unpopular as pacifists were in the midst of the fighting during the last war: but I shall do my best. There are as yet only a handful of people who are ready to follow the logic of the situation: yet, in contrast to 1914, perhaps a majority, if one is to believe the Gallup poll, already believe that America will be drawn into the war if it lasts long enough. There is no doubt as to where popular sympathies lie: but as yet there is no sufficient sense of danger to overcome the reluctance to participate. And though the words and tone of Chamberlain's announcement of war moved even his opponents here—I was one of them!—I must tell you frankly that his presence at the head of the British government, after his record of muddle and self-deception and error, is a severe handicap from the standpoint of getting American policy reversed. A year from now that may not matter: at present, it undoubtedly has an effect. I may say that my own distrust of Mr Roosevelt, who almost always says the right thing and too often does the exact opposite, is hardly greater than my distrust of Mr Chamberlain: for I feel that Roosevelt's present 'canny' advocacy of neutrality, probably in an effort to allay Republican opposition, has given the country the wrong lead and will make more difficult the positive cooperation that we must inevitably give.

I will understand of course if the preoccupations of the war keep you from answering this letter.

WELWYN GARDEN CITY   30 May 1941

Dear Mr Mumford

I am not quite sure that I did not answer your letter of 10.9.39, but I can't remember doing so and will assume that I did not and apologise accordingly. I could quite sympathise with your first interpretation of the Chamberlain policy; it *was* very difficult to believe that our Government of those days could be so blind to realities, and therefore it was by no means a wild theory (at a distance) that they were either pro-Fascist or in the last stages of pacifist degeneration. The real key to the whole business was really to be found in the almost universal hatred of war. Chamberlain really represented the majority in his intense conviction that war must be hated in Germany as it is here, and that military bluster did not imply a serious intention of the Nazis to risk war ruthlessly in an aggressive policy. What I have never been able fully to understand is how he was able to maintain that outlook in the face of the Foreign Office, which must surely have been well-informed. Yet the whole story may prove to be one of a few determined and well-meaning boneheads in key positions, with a background of wishful thinking in the relatively less-informed circles in Parliament, and the universal and passionate desire for peace among the electorate. To this day we have a few people in this country who do not or will not believe that a wanton attack has been made on peaceful countries by a group of gangsters. I think the great toleration here of the back-pedalling of American democracy, in its progress to cooperation with Britain, is due to a recognition of some similarity in the situation there. You are further away, and though your political chiefs are well-informed and clear-headed they have had the same passionately-pacific and wishful-thinking background. Your criticism of Roosevelt is not an unfamiliar one to me; yet I am not sure that in the occupant of that position the world could conceivably have had better luck. A man does not rise to the Presidency without something 'canny' in his make-up; but he *can* get there without Roosevelt's intellectual and moral grip on great issues and without his power of utterances, which are acts in themselves. Suppose Coolidge or Harding were your President now?

However, it is not for me to tell *you* anything about these terrific matters. I have read *Faith for Living*,[1] which seems to me a magnificent stroke for the cause of civilisation. I think it is being read widely here, and I hope it has caught on in America. I am reviewing this book and pushing it in planning circles—the only ones in which I have any influence—because you are a god-sent reinforcement to my own sometimes desperate struggle for family living-space standards. We have here, as no doubt you have, a highbrow pseudo-modern aesthetic school of 'planners', (mostly young architects or old ones afraid of being thought back-numbers), who want to redevelop bombed cities at 40 or 50 dwellings to the acre. They make careful statistical calculations of the sizes of families, with a view to cutting down the space in each dwelling so that it exactly fits each family—the theory apparently being that you move house every time your family increases or declines by a birth, a departure of a young adult, or a death. They are now developing

---

[1] New York, London, 1940, 1941.

the theory, based on 'research', that if you provide group-heating every corner of a house can be used more fully all the year round, and therefore the space can be further reduced. Gadgets inside the house, nursery schools, school meals, crêches, and communal meals outside, will also reduce work and the need for space. Consequently, they say, there is no necessity to consider checking the growth of London and Birmingham: on the contrary, with the more 'scientific' use of space, you can get ever so many more people closer together and give them the wealth of city culture in more intense measure.

I have done a little to puncture these pretty theories, but they so suit the book of the urban landowners and the city corporations (who are pre-occupied with rateable value, rate revenue and aggrandising their own jobs and positions) that it is quite possible that we may be caught in two minds in our Reconstruction policy. If so the megalopolitan trend will be resumed at full swing—although the overwhelming lay sentiment in this country is really against it. Ninty-nine per cent. of our people really want the house-and -garden type of dwelling; but they hate the long journey to and from suburbs, and can be sandbagged into accepting the tiny well-equipped flat when they are told that long journeys are the only alternative.

I am very busy as a director of a factory manufacturing for the War departments and can therefore only give spare time to planning issues. But there is an immense interest in the subject here (for the first time) and I am therefore editing a series of short booklets setting out the planning issues clearly. The first of these is based on my 'Overture to Planning' in the enclosed Journal.

It would be of enormous service to our common objectives (for the controversy is really international) if you would write one of the booklets for this series, perhaps comparing the American and British city planning situation, and taking the line, if that is acceptable to you, that Great Britain, the classic land of the family house, should not think of deserting that standard because it cannot master the space-problem in its own cities. Rasmussen did a lot of good here by a somewhat similar appeal in his delightful book on London.[1]

Some continental architects here are influential in the space-cutting trend. But there are others (notably one from Vienna) who are imploring me to uphold the British family house, which they say is the envy of working-people in Central Europe, and the demand for which is the one strong card in the hands of the thorough-going city-planners. If it is thrown away, the main reason for controlling the growth of cities by control of the location

---

[1] S. E. Rasmussen, *London: The Unique City*, London, New York, 1937.

of industry (a thing under serious and realistic consideration here) disappears, and we merely get local architectural tidying-up as a substitute for planning. A big point these people make is the demand in cities like Vienna and Stockholm for a garden-plot in the environs, with a cheap shack on it, as a second dwelling place for week-ends and holidays—a confession of the unsatisfactoriness of city life in flats. . . .

AMENIA, NEW YORK   5 August 1941

Dear Mr Osborn

It was good indeed to hear from you and to learn how steadily you are carrying on your work. A few months ago my London publisher, Warburg, asked me to do a little book for a new series of his on city development after the war, with special reference to England. I was greatly tempted to do this; but my absence from your country since 1932, and particularly my lack of any firsthand acquaintance with the face of England today, made me finally say No; since I felt that an academic approach to the subject would be terribly unconvicing, even if it was sound. Your suggestion that I do a booklet for your new series is another matter however; and the only thing that keeps me from saying Yes to it at once is that I am just embarking on the first draft of the final volume of the series that began with *Technics*;[1] and I can't let myself during the next two or three months, be distracted by any other job. If you still should have a use for such an article toward the end of the year, I shall be happy to write it—as a voluntary contribution to a good cause. As soon as I have a little leisure I will write again and discuss the political situation. From the standpoint of material and production, despite many lags and weaknesses, we have made tremendous advances here: already registered in the higher prices of food and clothing and in the absence of many common articles which are in competition with army and navy needs. So the situation is immeasurably better than it was a year ago on both sides of the Atlantic. But much remains to be done before this war can be brought to a successful conclusion. Of that, more in my next.

WELWYN GARDEN CITY   18 September 1941

Dear Mr Mumford

Thank you very much for your letter of the 5th August. I am very delighted to hear that you will write a booklet for us, and it will be certainly quite

---

[1] The 'Renewal of Life' series, which ultimately ran to four volumes: *Technics and Civilisaton, The Culture of Cities, The Condition of Life* and *The Conduct of Man.*

useful if you could do it for us by about the end of the year. It is precisely because you are identified with the modern point of view and yet understand the human aspects of Planning that I particularly want a contribution from you as part of our British campaign.

I have been placed on the official Panel of Physical Reconstruction (under Lord Reith's[1] Ministry, which is an embryo organisation for National Planning) and on the whole it seems likely that the right standards will be applied in the initial thinking. There is, however, as you can imagine, a great deal of work to do in turning theory into practice, and there are many interests which are obstructive to Planning either consciously or unconsciously, among which the property interests in land and building are by no means the most formidable. There are, for example, the Government Departments who are handling pieces of administration which ought to be included in a Planning Ministry. There are also the larger local authorities, who may resist any attempt at the decentralisation of their cities for reasons of finance and prestige. To overcome these obstacles we have to invent a new Compensation technique, and we have also to do a great deal of hard propaganda work under conditions which do not permit of much expenditure or space in the newspapers. A very great asset on our side, however, is the immense public interest in Planning, and the expectation of better cities created by wholesale destruction and the hardships of war. I feel that the situation is quite hopeful if the Planners will think clearly, be resolute, and act unitedly. Planners, however, have been so miseducated by their unfortunate experiences of the past that it is difficult for them to be born again in this way. You will appreciate this from your knowledge of American Planners, whose literature I read fairly consistently. They tend to be satisfied with small successes in detail simply because no other opportunities have been open to them in the past, and their whole outlook has developed under these conditions. . . .

WELWYN GARDEN CITY   17 October 1941

Dear Mr Mumford
I am sending you with this a copy of the Report of the important Oxford Conference,[2] which will give you some idea of the thoughts of the Land-use

---

[1] Lord Reith of Stonehaven. Minister of Works and Buildings, 1940–42, Chairman of the New Towns Committee, 1945.
[2] The 1941 Conference of the Town and Country Planning Association. The papers were published as F.E. Towndrow, *ed.*, *Replanning Britain*, London, 1941.

Planners as to the shape of Reconstruction Planning. You will see signs that I, as a defender equally of the urban family dwelling with garden *and* the inviolate farmlands, am under two fires. The extreme countryside preservationist view, beautifully expressed by the prophetic Stapledon[1]—a great character whose books you must know—is a new thing and a good one; and its overstatement, even, is welcome as a protest against the suburban sprawl and the week-end bungalow. These are a menace in this small country, but the impulse to them is so strong (as a reaction from the hideous and congested towns) that they will not be easy to stop. Stapledon, to whom the town is a distant monster full of yahoos, doesn't realise that those yahoos govern him and me, and that their aspirations can't be met either by village industry or by closely built-up streets. In principle he's right in his outlook; but he's a bit under the influence of literary architects who, advocating dwellings at 30 or 40 to the acre because they like closed vistas and towering flats, back up the anti-decentralisation movement. Stapledon, not having knowledge of scale as applied to building, doesn't realise that a terrace or square at 6 to 10 to the acre is quite a different thing from a terrace or square at 25 or more to the acre. So, while contriving (as I always have, and with recent success) to oppose the complacency about suburban sprawl, I am now unexpectedly forced to conduct a campaign to re-assert the 'family space' standard, which between the two wars was almost universally accepted and crystallised in the Tudor-Walters Report's[2] (really Raymond Unwin's) practical formula of dwellings of a minimum of about 850 sq. ft. floor space, built at a maximum of 12 houses to the net acre—by no means an extravagant yet a workable and human standard.

Now, to apply even that norm of minimum, low as it is in relation to your ideal family home, means displacing some millions of people (I haven't yet been able to form a closer estimate) from the congested parts of cities. That sounds difficult, but at this period of history it could be done, because both the people and their workplaces have in fact gone out at least temporarily—through blitzing or anticipation of blitzing. We have the relatively practicable task of not encouraging industry and business to return; and much of it (as after the Great Fire of 1666) *won't* return unless it is coaxed and bribed.

So, if the stuffing isn't knocked out of all of us in winning this war (with the help of the gods and of America) we shall have the most extraordinary chance of retrieving some at least of the worst effects of the Industrial Revolution of 1750–1939.

---

[1] R. G. Stapledon, *The Land: Now and Tomorrow*, London, 1941.
[2] *Report of the Committee on Housing*, London, 1918. Chairman the Rt. Hon. John Tudor-Walters.

You will see in the Oxford Report the importance of the Barlow Commission's Report,[1] published in Jan. 1940. I worked very hard on the doorstep and behind the arras of that Commission, and the leading members of the three sections all tell me that it was my evidence and the examination on it that got them together on the essential policy. (This isn't publicly known in Britain, and it wouldn't do Planning any good if it became known at this stage—as I've been labelled as a 'fanatical' adherent of the Garden City movement, owing to my 16 years as estate manager of Welwyn. People can't understand that I came to believe in the small planned town as the result of thought about cities, and joined in the Welwyn experiment because I couldn't get the idea accepted in 1919 as part of the national housing policy. They think I was *born* with a belief in the Garden City idea—that it is a cause, not a result, of my analysis of the city problem! Now that opinion is sweeping round to my views, I'm in mortal danger of being canonised as a prophet of phenomenal foresight and insight—which is sheer idiotic mass nonsense. The same thing is liable to happen to you; but in two continents, which is much worse.)

Continuing. . . . We have to find somewhere to put the industries and dwellings of the de-congested millions. If Planners succeed (against spontaneous private tendencies and municipal intentions) in stopping both the spread of suburbs and rehousing at high densities in flats, the only course is to build new towns and extend the smaller towns. Here comes in the danger of the over-emphasis of rural preservation and the new political force centring on home food-production. I answer this, as you see in the Oxford Report, by an appeal for a balanced view. If houses are built at a maximum housing density of 12 per acre (about 40 to 50 persons at present sizes of families), with a normal proportion on larger sites, and with factories, shops, public buildings, streets and open spaces, the *over-all* town density in new development works out at about 20 to 25 persons per acre.[2] So if I displace 5 million people I only need 200,000 acres of 'rural' land for the purpose— and we still have 37,000,000 acres of land under cultivation in Great Britain.

It must interest you, and I think cheer you, to see Great Britain, in the midst of a life-and-death war, getting into factions about the proper size of towns and the right use of our limited land surface. Seven years ago, at a conference of economists, I twitted them with their extraordinary blindness in not seeing that the size of towns was one of the proper studies of mankind —and that while I had views about the appropriate size of towns for normal

---

[1] *Report of the Royal Commission on the Distribution of the Industrial Population*, London, 1940. Chairman Sir Montagu Barlow.
[2] This was a miscalculation. The overall density of a new town based on this standard works out at about 15 persons an acre.

industry, I was much less fierce about any particular formula than about the absence of controversy on the subject. I could die happy, I concluded, when the nation was divided into warring parties defending the 100,000 town, the 50,000 town, and other sizes. That has come about, sooner than I expected; but having heard many bombs fall, aimed as much at me as at anybody else, I have developed a desire to live to the next stage—which is the fascinating one of translating such theories into law and action.

So personally I'm making munitions most of most days in my home town, and sweating away at the problems of legislation and administration of national planning in the evenings and in odd half-days at the embryo Ministry of Planning in London, where Lord Reith has given me a room.

The background of public opinion, however, is still misty and uncertain. Hence the necessity for me to remain active (as far as I can) in the political and educational side of the subject. Hence, further, as a small start, the Rebuilding Britain series for which I am pressing you to write a contribution as soon as your work permits.

At the moment of writing the Battle for Moscow seems desperately critical, and though I write you of the future it is naturally of the present and the bitter experiences that Russia is going through, and which are inevitably ahead of *us*, that we are thinking most. Yet it is for the future, of our country and our children, and of Russia's and yours, that we are fighting; and we keep sane and courageous by thinking of that future in our night watches.

AMENIA, NEW YORK   23 November 1941

Dear Osborn

Your friendly letter of the 17th of October is a very welcome one, and in response I am first of all dropping the title before your name in the hope you will do the same.

I was on the point of writing you before your letter came because of the fact that the writing of the first draft of my book has prolonged itself beyond my expectations, and I wanted to let you know that it would be impossible for me to write the pamphlet before January. I will try to make up for lost time then by at least sending it over air mail. In one way this delay will be an advantage, for out here in the country I have no access to current British periodicals or books, and though the excellent papers in the Oxford Report which you were good enough to send me have been very useful, I think I would do well to immerse myself in all the available current literature for a while before attempting to set my own ideas in order again.

We are faced with a parallel problem in our own country, not because our urban areas have yet been blasted away by the Nazis, but because an almost equally ominous decay has been eating at the vitals of almost all our big cities: in some way our urban blight, accompanied by disuse and human desertion, has put our big cities in an even worse state than yours were before war broke out. There are various agencies at Washington that are aware of this problem, because it has left many of our cities practically bankrupt and without the means of keeping up the expensive physical plant which was needed in the days of their expansion. For the last three months a group of economists in the Federal Reserve System have been in consultation with me about a law they are endeavouring to frame which would provide for the large-scale re-building of our cities after the war. The immediate purpose of such re-building would be to provide immediate work for our industries, to tide them over the transition from war to peace; the ultimate purpose, of course, would be to replace disorder and blight with livable communities. But unfortunately, the men who are preparing the plan, though very able and far-sighted, insist on thinking of housing and city building more or less within the outlines of the existing city; and I find it very difficult to convince them that the essential pattern of urban growth must be altered, and that their problem is not to salvage the old order with values based on congestion and disorganisation, but to create a new order which will remain stable and self-renewing and which, above all, will be conceived in a fashion that will add to the real income of the inhabitants, no matter what happens to the existing financial structure.

I am trying to get them to see that the money should be allocated not for housing and building alone, and still less for the rebuilding of metropolitan slum areas on a pattern only slightly better than the existing one. The authority in charge of this development should be able to act at any point in the region, and should undertake any operation from highway building to park planning or reafforestation which may be necessary to create a new pattern for the urban community. I am still hammering away at this by long distance, but I think I shall be driven to make a last appeal in person a few weeks hence.

As for the general situation, I am happy to be able to report a real improvement over here. The substantial repeal of the Neutrality Act was morally an even more decisive action than the Lease Lend Bill, for the latter was based on the odious assumption that the people of the United States would do anything to win the war against Hitler except fight him, whereas the Neutrality Act was argued out in Congress on the basis that its repeal would mean actual participation in war and loss of American life. And having at last gotten over that hurdle, I think the country will be ready for what

follows: in some ways it is more ready for a decisive action, now that we
have gone as far as we have, than Mr Roosevelt has seemed to be. Already
the results of our war production are being felt throughout the country in
limitations on our choice of goods and in inability to get many articles of
common convenience. There is already very serious threat of inflation because
purchasing power and prices have risen while the stock of available consumer goods has decreased, and neither the President nor Congress has yet
shown the necessary courage to put a ceiling on advances in prices, though
the present scale of taxation will do something to retard inflationary tendencies next year, and perhaps before the situation becomes dangerous, a
more adequate law will be passed.

If this war has done nothing else, it has shaken all our complacencies, it
has disclosed the weak points in our daily routine, and it has made us conscious of weaknesses that might have been fatal to us if we had not been
challenged by an outside power. The fact that each nation has shown the
same blindness and has made the same mistakes, makes it plain that our
common scheme of life was somewhat at fault. It may still be necessary for
us in America to suffer some terrible reverse, like that you met at Dunkirk,
before we face the real facts of the world situation and throw ourselves into
the conflict with all our might and main. The one thing that I dread, to
speak frankly, is a peace participated in by an unawakened and unchastened
United States. But that is a matter beyond any mere human provision.

WELWYN GARDEN CITY   17 December 1941

Dear Mr Mumford
So after all, your country, like mine, had its mind made up for it by outside
events while it was seriously debating whether it should make up its mind
or not.[1] Your personal foresight, at least, is vindicated; and I'm sure you
find it, as many of my friends here did, a very melancholy satisfaction.

I never have time to write to you as I should like. But there is one point
of immediate policy you might consider. We have marginally lost some
efficiency here by not planning the location of the miscellaneous factories
that are needed for war-production—the building of which goes on very
actively for at least the first two years of a war.

I tried, without much success, to get a National Planning Set-up with a
section for industrial location, and in particular to press the building of
sectional all-purpose factories in advance in the smaller towns and in places

---

[1] The Japanese Air Force attacked Pearl Harbour on 7 December 1941.

scheduled as suitable for expansion. If this had been done we should have been saved much additional congestion in large cities and much unnecessary daily movement of workers. And the building industry, partially unemployed at the start of the war, could have been got fully to work without waiting for the rush of demand for space which, when it came, couldn't be met without much delay. Further, considered placing of factories will help a lot at the end of the war, for the same reasons that make it a factor of efficiency during the war. It can be related to housing and communities. . . .

WELWYN GARDEN CITY   16 January 1942

Dear Mumford

Possibly the most exciting event in this mechanical age, for anyone with a sense of history, was to listen in an English living-room to a perfect trans-mission of President Roosevelt's declaration of war speech while it was actually taking place in Congress. I try *not* to get used to these miracles, and therefore did for a moment get a dramatic thrill out of the occasion. Since then we've heard Churchill in Congress and at Ottawa—a little distorted by atmospherics, which, oddly enough, helped the imagination a little towards the appropriate awe. I have some criticisms of Churchill, as you have of Roosevelt. No man can be adequate to the situation in which each of these is placed. Yet, counting our blessings, it is something that they have the power of expression to document history as it happens. With every instinct to be captious, I think back to Baldwin, Chamberlain, Hoover, Coolidge, and marvel at our luck in not having the dumb to speak for us.

Don't hurry about the booklet. Just do it when you easily and conveniently can. I am sending you, by concurrent post, one or two more of our publica-tions which will show you some of the points where we think it is necessary to give or threaten battle. You will, I am sure, realise that at the moment I am having to attend mostly to other planners. Generally we are in spiritual agreement as to what we want and in our assessment of what our 'clients', the masses, want. I differ from most of the rest in my accent on clarity of policy for example in treating as worthy of full respect, and not for easy compromise, the need of family living space and the almost universal popular demand for the one-family house. My reason is that I am sure technological conditions could be reconciled with that demand. But most planners are too much cowed by the City-in-Being; they can't really conceive that there isn't some deep law or necessity at work producing intense business-concen-trations. Perhaps you have to be actually *in* business and industry (as I am) to realise the invalidity of that supposed law. I think I shared the doubt, perhaps, until I had negotiated with 1,500 or so firms who were locating new factories and saw how their minds worked, and how much they themselves were dominated by uncriticised assumptions and distrust of their own judgement. But planners are not business men; and business men very naturally fall for the economists' canonisation of them as high priests of dialectic necessity. I think there's a taint of Herman the German in all of us, not merely in Hegel and Marx. It took forty years of boardrooms, public-house bars and Rotary Clubs to cure me of identifying Babbitt with historical determinism.

Our great strength, if we can arm it, is the solidarity of mass opinion on the family-house and nearness-to-work issues. Every official interest tends to be against us, as in your country. My hope is that in 1942 I can get started a popular campaign, and at least immobilise any serious counter-campaigns. I repeat, we have just a ghost of a chance of success here, where mass opinion, if it is intense, does count, and where (strange company for me) the highly-placed religious and patriotic influences (which you can see at work in the tone of the BBC, *The Times*, etc.) are very conscious of the importance of the family issue just now. The Labour movement *was* a force in the same direction, but I feel it has got into the hands (a) of the old-guard institutional trade-unionists and (b) of a rather urbanised, feminist, 'neo-technic', middle-class type who prefer nursery schools to babies. The latter supply the ideas and the former backpedal on them without producing substitutes or effectively representing their clientele. The Communists here, influenced mostly by pictures of Russian buildings during the old Bauhaus period, are all steel-and-glass and Metro and communal cocktail bars in blocks of flats. I fear that now that we are likely to be in closer touch with Russia (for which may fate be praised) the uncritical friends of Russia will follow the Soviet's return to traditional architecture and want to put onion-bulb pinnacles on tractor factories. The great majority of architects here, and the semi-cultured section of the public, remain traditionalist or even nostalgic for Old England; but a vastly larger number of the public are completely indifferent, except that they associate simplicity of design with cheapness and with 'Council houses', and therefore tend towards a degree of elaboration without taste when they are well enough off to buy their own homes. England has great merits (having been brought up on Wells and Shaw and the world-minded who sneer at this country, it has taken me a long time to realise the unique sanity, balance and capacity of my own people), but England has among its defects a very deep-rooted social snobbery, which operates at every income-level right up the scale; and income is not the only element in it, though it is, as in all countries, the easiest rough test of standing. I am pretty sure that this national characteristic will last a long time, though its value is much less in these days of mechanised armies, and the prestige of the 'governing class' as such has almost disappeared.

However, that's too large an issue to pursue. Important factors to watch are (a) that the graduated income tax is wiping out hereditary wealth slowly but surely, (b) that as one symptom the great 'public' schools are all facing bankruptcy and can only survive by a deal with the State, which will radically change their clientele and status, and (c) that an extension of the school age to 15 and a great development of state secondary education is now a certainty after the war; the school age may even go to 16, though that can't be regarded as certain. Don't overlook, though, that Churchill is a flicker-up, and something of a justification, of the aristocratic tradition against the belief in a great industrialist (Baldwin and Chamberlain). While the 'technocrat' types don't count here in politics at all, mainly because they are simple-minded and are prone to fall for currency panaceas and anti-Banker complexes, and for the general view that universal welfare would happen at once if it were not deliberately sabotaged by anti-social interests—really a very silly view. To you I may seem merely 'English' when I say I would prefer to be governed by the hereditarily-trained political class than by the scientists and technicians; but my observation is that the intense concentration of their examination-passing phase deprives them of the knowledge needed for the equally difficult business of politics, quite as much as their training in accuracy unfits them to argue with the masses. Where the future political leadership is to come from is still an unsolved problem. In the meantime, however, we have developed a huge, well-trained bureaucracy, which is capable of political technique more or less adequate to the changes in society, but cannot provide the political leadership or function well without it.

I am at present unrepentantly reformist and Fabian. I want, in town planning, as well as in these industrial matters, to develop the *rules* by which social interests are safeguarded, rather than to plan in detail from a centre. I want to leave as much play as is possible for free initiative, choice of type of dwelling and layout, and so on; rather extending the area of social control under proved necessity than allocating the exact function and scope of each agency of production and service. I don't claim to see the final boundaries of control and freedom; but I regard freedom as an end in itself. So in regard to the siting of industry I take the view that we must put geographical limits on it to prevent cities becoming too large and too dense, and that we may load the choice in certain directions by inducements or by building towns, factory estates, and so on. But we haven't, and can't have, the 'science' to produce a complete national pattern of population-distribution in a changing world. The socially-necessary 'rules' for city-development have been missing in all history; we now have to devise and implement them.

2

My own belief (which I have never yet written about at all) is that what is missing in the modern set-up is a 'church' in which an intelligent man can believe; an organisation and personnel, that is, specialised on personal conduct and with practical wisdom derived both from a liberal education, specially centered on that interest (instead of 'theology'), and from close and intimate contact with all sorts of men and women in every kind of personal crisis from childhood to old age (in other words a 'priesthood'). I think (you may well disagree) that the church is an ancient necessity which needs a 'protestant' reformation every now and then; and if it is incapable of that it steadily loses ground. But the needed reformation this time is so drastic that I see little chance of its happening. On the other hand, new starts in humanistic and ethical movements all fail because they have no endowments, no specialised and dedicated 'priests', and hence cannot add wisdom and experience of men in all kinds of mental and physical distress, to goodwill and sound thinking. I sometimes think the family doctor is the nearest thing we have to a functional priest today—and he spends the best seven years of his life learning the names of bones and nerves etc., and must tend to a behaviourist rather than a psychological analysis of his patients. What I can't believe is that these valuable functions of a church and priesthood, in keeping us in touch with the eternal verities and helping us through personal vicissitudes, can only be exercised on the basis of beliefs in conflict with intelligence. Realisation of the threatening nature of the world and of its magical possibilities, stimulus to knowledge of other men and other countries, independence and brotherhood, courage and duty; surely we'd accept reminders on such matters more readily from men whose intelligence we respected as well as their dedication? But, as I say, I've never been able to pursue thoughts on this subject.

WELWYN GARDEN CITY   4 April 1942

Dear Mumford
I send you a copy of *New Towns After the War*, a new edition of a little book I wrote in 1918. It has interest as an early statement of the case against metropolitan concentration, which has now been developed much further— and also as a forecast all too painfully exact of what would (and did) happen between the wars if we failed to plan. I should write a very different book today, but I think there is some value in the simplicity of the analysis, which I couldn't now recover.

WELWYN GARDEN CITY   27 April 1942

Dear Mumford

Your letter of 14 February arrived on April 25th. It is good of you to struggle
to write that pamphlet for us. I hope you don't have to scrap it; I would
rather wait a while than not have it, though it would have much interest
just now. If you can't do it after all, naturally it is a case for regret and not
reproaches on my part. But please do it, when you can.

I have been trying to write a book on certain aspects of the town-country
pattern for 2 years, but have made little progress with it. I support my
family by being Finance Director of a Radio Company, and the relatively
short-term issues of the planning movement take all my spare time and
leave me none for formulating certain wider ideas that have been germin-
ating (and probably mostly getting killed off like spermatozoa) for a quarter
of a century. I console myself with the thought that one can't really live two
lives, and that probably the non-existence of that book is more of an irritation to me than a disaster to civilisation—though I shouldn't be trying to
write it if that were the whole story.

In view of the obviously critical state of American thought on the big issue
of democracy and economic control, I look forward to your next book with
much interest. Essentially the same crisis is in progress here, as everywhere,
but the balance of forces and the general academic background is really
different in this country. Here, while the intelligent socialists are in doubt
about the boundaries to which they should expand, the vocal capitalists (with
quite insignificant exceptions) are in doubt about the boundaries they will
defend. At our Cambridge Conference in March, for example, several
academic agricultural experts, (including one University Professor who is
also a College bursar and estate manager), calmly and objectively advocated
complete land nationalisation as a commonsense expedient for town and
country planning; while a peer who owns many thousands of acres and is
Chairman of one of the chief land-owners' organisations, opposed it quite
mildly, though as it happened not very cleverly. Both these people are
members of the Town and Country Planning Association, and they and all
the others who spoke argued the matter without referring to Bolshevism, or
to our equivalents of Jefferson and Hamilton, or God, or 'rights', or the
Anglo-Saxon dream or anything of that sort.

One interesting thing is that few people see the likelihood of the Labour
Party getting a clear majority soon after the war, nor is there a hint of the
emergence of any new party. In practice, therefore, the left seems faced with
a choice of continued coalition government for the Reconstruction period,
or going into opposition and leaving the big initial decisions and the peace

settlement to the Conservatives. The more clear-cut left people are in the fix
in that they don't really think the Labour Party (still controlled and likely
to remain controlled by non-theoretical Trade Union leaders) would be
more imaginative or decisive than the Conservatives; in fact the Conservatives, with a Labour opposition, would probably cut some knots and be
more radical than a Labour Government with a Conservative opposition. So
I assess that the Labour Party managers will, unless the political climate
changes with further war experience, work for a continued coalition in
which they will probably hold the key positions for social policy. But the
Conservatives learn by war experience too; and as you are well aware,
while big business may have put a party in power, the politicians gain true
dominance in war-time, and they are quite capable of kicking away the
ladder by which they climbed if they can get solid mass support for a 'radical'
policy. So you may say either party is capable of fairly drastic planning, but
the Conservatives will find it easier.

AMENIA, NEW YORK   16 May 1942

Dear Osborn

I have been delinquent in my correspondence with you, more out of a
sense of guilt, probably, than because of a better reason; though of course
I have been working hard ever since my return from California in March.
But I had very real hopes of being able to complete and revise the manuscript of my pamphlet, long before this; and I simply have not gotten around
to it. What is worse, I cannot predict when I will be able to; for I have just
received an appointment to a Professorship in the Humanities, to give the
basic courses about which a new school of Humanities will be built at Stanford University, in California, forty-five miles south of San Francisco; and
between preparing these courses, which begin at the end of next September,
and trying to finish my Volume 3 in time for publication next year, I shall
be more busy during the next six months than I dare to imagine. Fortunately,
I know from past experience that when one has little work to do, one sometimes doesn't do even that little; and that when one is keyed up to high
activity, one sometimes does three times what one ordinarily is capable of;
so there is still a chance that I can send you the ms. before another few
months are out—especially since I have more than three-quarters of it
written. Whether it is what you want is another question: for it is an attempt
to take a very long view of the changes that are now going on, and to work
out, more closely and specifically than I have yet done, my general theory of
stabilisation.

It is unfortunate for me that though I stated the general notion about the present transition from a period of expansion and rapid change—15th to 20th century—to one of stabilisation, balance, internal rehabilitation, and in some respects *material contraction,* in both *Technics* and *The Culture of Cities,* I did not fully grasp its historical implications and its connection with the birth-rate, until I wrote my report on Honolulu in 1938. This is all very directly bound up, however, with the kind of city that we are planning to build; since wherever metropolitan conditions prevail, the net rate of population increase not merely drops toward zero but shows signs of becoming a decrease. Theodore Roosevelt saw the significance of this and sounded the alarm a generation ago; but he was looked upon as old-fashioned and hysterical, I well-remember, and I probably shared this attitude toward him: whereas now, it is plain, he spoke like a true statesman; and much more was bound up with his campaign against 'race suicide' than mere jingoistic self-assertiveness. I have been pressing this whole point of view with the two men in Washington who are helping to map out a policy for post-war building, Messrs Greer and Hansen. The latter, you perhaps know, is our equivalent of Maynard Keynes; and though they are both enlightened, in the main, about the need for making constructive activity have priority over the profit-producing motive in the transition to peacetime work, they still cling to the notion of rebuilding the existing mass-cities—though any large programme for doing this will result in automatically raising the price of land and thus curbing the programme itself before it has properly gotten under way. On the basis of a rational population policy, however, I don't think that adding to cities of more than 50,000 people can be justified.

I appreciate your thoughtfulness and generosity in sending me, not only the excellent pamphlets in your series, but your *New Towns After the War,* which came but the other day. Your book is so astonishingly fresh in this revised form that there is no doubt you were guilty of writing a classic; and its original failure to influence those who should have been influenced has a certain parallel to my own failure with *Men Must Act*: in both cases, the mournful honour of being correct in our analysis hardly makes up, even subjectively, for the deplorable result of not being listened to! Your new introduction is admirable, and the letter from Shaw was good enough to awaken memories of the clean, courageous dramatist whom I worshipped in my youth—a figure who for me has been badly muddied by the muddled old man who has so often wagged his beard from the pulpit since his last great play, *Saint Joan.* Your book should get attention now, and I wonder if you would have any objections to my seeing whether it would be possible to have it published over here—if your publishers haven't taken any steps. It may be quite impossible, and I will offer it to only two or three houses where I have friendly connections; but I should like, for our sakes as well as yours, to try. I was dismayed, when I looked up the bibliography of *The Culture of Cities* to see what I had said about New Towns, that the book was not even listed. This is the old sad story of my often omitting the books in my own library, the ones that have become so much a part of my mental furniture that I never notice them. But I got your book soon after it was published, I well remember, and was much impressed by it; as I was—I discovered a little while ago on going through some old numbers of the *Journal of the American Institute of Architects*—by your article on how garden cities had been sacrificed to the building of Welwyn. I wrote a long review of that article in the *Journal*: our first bowing acquaintance with each other. That must have been in 1923. Your forbearing comments on Howard's *coup* were very fine: I am glad I saw something of him here in 1925, the time he tried to convert Henry Ford to garden cities!

The war is being waged like an advertising campaign, in which the customer is being wheedled and cajoled into accepting a particular product: whereas war, by its nature, admits of short cuts that the ordinary psychologists of business, whose advice so widely prevails, have no conception of. No one knows what our general staffs have up their sleeves; but everyone with intelligence hopes that they have *some* definite plan of their own which will be unleashed by the 15 June: something far more definite than merely waiting for the Russians to do the dirty work for us, whilst we disperse our forces in defensive operations that are doomed, by their very nature, to defeat, since they leave the initiative to our enemies. The notion that defense is the only morally justified form of warfare partly accounts for our long paralysis; and from the behavior of our army and navy leaders during the last year, I can see why my original plea for bold action met with universal denunciation.

I don't know whether I ever properly answered your January letter; but I want you to know how deeply interested I was in your comments on religion; and I hope that my next book will be able to carry the argument you advanced a little further. If I didn't feel that some sort of answer, which dealt with the whole structure of ideals and purposes, was important for framing even our day-to-day plans in industry and city development, I should hardly have the temerity to absent myself, at this critical moment, from active war duties. The latter will probably come in any event, surely will if the war lasts as long as I expect it will; and meanwhile I want to have my book ready for the printer by next January.

As for the dilemma of collectivism versus voluntary initiative, I think it needs a general re-thinking in view of our actual experience with collectively patterned institutions, both private and public. We have made a great mistake, I believe, in thinking that the issue has something to do with ownership and profit; that is a very minor part of it. I made a stab at defining the respective territories of the collective, the uniform, the automatic, the socialised, and the individual, the voluntary, the adventurous, in the last chapter of *Technics and Civilisation*; but I very much want to amplify this chapter, in the light of both public experience and my own further reflections. There is so much that needs fresh thinking, so much that needs fresh doing, that I almost feel as if Shaw's prescription in *Methusaleh* is about the only thing that will save us!

This letter has grown unconscionably long; but it is a poor return for all your patience and courtesy, and I want you to know how warmly I appreciate the comradely interchange that has grown up between us. If only we had realised what sort of people we were when we so briefly met!

WELWYN GARDEN CITY   26 June 1942

Dear Mumford

First, congratulations on your Professorship. It sounds as if you are evolving a new university subject, and I would like to hear more about this when you have time.

Next, I am much encouraged by your appreciation of *New Towns After the War*. I did not understand how strong your own anti-Metropolitan tendency was until I read *The Culture of Cities*. Your way of dealing with town history makes mine seem very thin and unlearned. In the course of a busy life I have never been able to give day-time hours to study or writing, and my 'leisure' pursuits have been discursive and undisciplined. So if I had not been simple minded and Babbitish by nature, I should have had to pretend to be so as a literary pose. Nothing is worse than half-digested history or imperfectly-cooked criticism. Because I find that a large part of the intelligent public is taken in by allusive writing based on quick reading and an eye for the significant, I have not always been able to refrain (in occasional articles) from playing this easy game, with a temporary gain of prestige that makes me laugh. But I suppress any such tendency as soon as I notice it.

I share your feelings of regret about Shaw, though I think *St Joan* was the first clear sign of the decline, rather than the zenith, of the old power. For me his last great play was *Heartbreak House*. Yet the vices in *St Joan*, which become unbearable in the subsequent plays, now seem to me to be latent in a great deal of his mature work. He had no philosophy; and he was irresponsible as a reporter. His strength was that of a great comic dramatist and satirist. Doesn't drama survive because things of equal apparent validity violently clash? If the clashing things are persons the dramatist may present them both (or all) with sympathy based on deep intuition, and still be a philosopher with a clear set of values. Example: Goethe. If the clashing things are ideas, then the dramatist, if a philosopher, must take sides; and there is a propaganda element in the play (as there was in some of Shaw's most characteristic masterpieces). But if the dramatist is primarily a dramatist there will not be a 'philosophy'. Good case: Ibsen—a born dramatist whose personal philosophy included ideas on social complexes, as well as individuals, and for that very reason no clear philosopher. On the major modern issues—individualism versus collectivism, dictatorship versus democracy, intellect versus animal optimism, etc.—Shaw does not know what he thinks. He isn't even capable of grappling with the issues tentatively. As a politician he makes reckless statements with great wit and apparent conviction. Looking back I can see now that he always did, even when I first heard him tearing up Wells in their famous Fabian duel (was it in 1908?); and when he tore me up in a paternal way as the great Mogul visiting the Fabian Nurslings. Such is the prestige of wit that we all consented to be torn up. But reading through some of these incidents now, I find we were taken in. Even my own reasoning, in one case I have on record, was clearer and sounder than his, and within a space or two he was saying what I had said with prodigious effect; but I never noticed it. What made Shaw possible to work with was his personal friendliness and generosity. Everybody agrees about this. He was always looking for material for his sensational utterances, and picked it up from Webb and dozens of others, sometimes unconsciously as we all pick up many of our ideas; but if he were conscious of taking anything from anybody, he would overwhelm his contributor with credit. He didn't and doesn't know the name of meanness in such things. But as a philosopher, as a wise man, as a student of state affairs, he was a fraud; and to-day he is pathetic, because his instinct for plausibility has deserted him.

And now about your booklet for my series. Seeing that you have written three-quarters of it I feel justified in urging you to complete it, as total economy of work. You have a strong following here and it would be a reinforcement to my group to parade a token of your support, as well as to have another contribution from you to the very active discussion now proceeding. So please polish it off!

I write at a moment of depression following a wave of unjustified optimism for which people are blaming our leaders. Tobruk fell some days ago and the Axis tanks are fifty miles inside Egypt. Sebastopol seems in grave danger. The organisation for total war, however, is getting very complete in this country, and there are now very few who are not coming under the various conscription and man-power laws. It is difficult to realise what a revolution has occurred. A tiny symptom. Our town is a new industrial centre three miles from the ancient palace and country town of Hatfield—the core of aristocratic England in which you can still feel continuity from the great Burleigh and the incredible Elizabeth. Imagine it: that my wife, a Labour Party JP, together with the wife of a railway trade-unionist, were sitting on a tribunal here before which the millionaire descendant of Burleigh came to plead that he might retain one of his *two* remaining maidservants. Graciously, and in all fairness and responsibility for the war effort, the tribunal, having ascertained that the maid was old and feeble and useless for making aeroplanes, allowed the appeal. Perhaps in America that doesn't seem to signify much. It means nothing here either, because though it is happening all the time we don't really know it. It isn't in the papers, and therefore isn't truly happening. But gradually we shall understand that it *has* happened. My wife and I hadn't noticed it until, with great objectivity and effort to get historical perspective, we pieced together, over our last tin of Canadian fish, what she had been doing this afternoon. We saw she was a Commissar, a Tricoteuse being merciful to future princes. And there are still more proletarian Commissars for whose mercy I as an industrial director have to plead daily. Yet the shop stewards still say Sir to me, and I say My Lord to the Most Noble Marquess. And sincerely and without irony. This is England in Revolution.

WELWYN GARDEN CITY   30 July 1942

My dear Mumford
A copy of the enclosed *Town & County Planning* has been sent you from the office, but as an insurance I am sending you another copy. There is much in it about US planning—some of which I hope may interest you. I have been a little more violent than usual in a review of Giedion's book[1]—chiefly because I found the book had impressed some of the architectural nitwits here. One reviewer had treated it as a more serious and weighty work than *The Culture of Cities*, and a complete answer to the Decentralisers! As Giedion's book is almost unobtainable here some of the architects would have taken this valuation on faith; so, while giving credit to the merit of the book as a gallery of pictures, I put it in its place as a contribution to planning and aesthetic theory. Our Journal is now, I am glad to say, read eagerly by the intelligentsia.

I write just after the fall of Rostov, so you can imagine we are all feeling a bit grim, and the urgency of after-war planning is somewhat in recess.

---

[1] S. Giedion, *Space, Time and Architecture*, Cambridge (Mass.), London, 1941.

The American 'occupation' is becoming noticeable everywhere, and it will be interesting to watch the effect on the relations of the two peoples. I think there is more tension than with the other 'foreigners' here—chiefly because we don't regard Americans as foreigners (though of course they are) and there is a curious clash of superiority complexes at first. Admittedly there is a touch of unjustified and unconscious loftiness in our tolerance of other nationals. On the other hand we are far from 'effete'. Our toughness is that of rubber rather than (as we suppose) granite. But it does stand up to high explosive fairly well. Anyway, we are likely to share experiences that will be a far severer test of visitors and hosts than either has yet known—including shortages, very hard for rich peoples to bear, and horrible doubts. Let's hope we shall earn each other's respect.

STANFORD UNIVERSITY, CALIFORNIA   27 November 1942

Dear Osborn

Your letter of the eighteenth arrived a week ago, in very good time indeed, since our own time for receiving mail from the East has been lengthened by from one to three days, because of the congestion of our transportation system. I am pleased to learn that you are going on with the publication of my pamphlet; for I have not been able to find an American magazine that would take it, though I offered to reduce its size to the usual requirements here. The thesis itself shocks a great many people, who do not see as clearly as Mill did that the conditions for stabilisation are precisely those for increasing human welfare: that our new 'expansion' will be a vertical expansion, which will give more real wages to the common man, and enable the industrial system itself to achieve some sort of durable order and stability without the halts of periodic crises and liquidations. The whole thesis is implied in both *Technics* and *Cities*; yet I now wish I had seen it as clearly as I now do, when I wrote those books. If there is a fallacy in the argument I hope this publication will bring forward the criticism it needs.

I still have not been able to persuade my publisher to make up his mind about your *New Towns After the War*; and I have just written him another letter to prod him into a decision. It will be a hard book to get published in America, I am afraid; and yet it is just the sort of thing we need, and if only a thousand copies were sold I still think it would justify the effort; because those who have been doing the thinking and planning of our current housing are still operating on an extremely superficial basis, and a large part of their work, consequently, is incredibly dismal, because of a cheese-paring policy in the wrong places. The war has begun to jolt our daily living habits; but it will take much longer, I am afraid, to jolt our ideas and loosen them sufficiently from the context of our pre-war customs and expectations to enable us to take the positive steps that will be necessary, alike in city building and in world organisation. Here in America the young people have been taught during the last generation by cagey, disillusioned men, who have disciplined themselves in the scientific and statistical methodology, but who have no belief in the human will and the imagination: hence they have been so pathetically unready to deal with the plans of our enemies, who at least can boast an inhuman will and a dehumanised imagination—but at least will and imagination of some sort are not lacking. Though I cannot pretend that the courses we are working out here in the School of Humanities are what I would like them to be—for apart from my own weaknesses, I must train three assistants before we shall all be able to play the same music—nevertheless my lectures have proved even better than I had hoped, by reason of the contrast they afford the student with the usual fare. I liked the comment of one student: Mr Mumford hasn't taught us anything new, but what we already knew now begins to come together, so that we can use it.

My presence here on the West Coast is still somewhat unreal to me. My wife has been ill pretty steadily since we came here, my seven-year old daughter is deeply homesick for her country surroundings (for this is really suburbia), and I myself have been harried by an infected tooth: so that none of us has yet the sense of having taken root, or of really belonging to the region. All this has been increased, doubtless, by the fact that the war has at last fully come home to America; and our universities, with the lowering of the draft age, are in for a stiff bit of reorganisation. It is doubtful if the courses that we have planned for the School of Humanities will be given beyond June, if even that long; and those of us who have no aptitude for teaching mathematics, chemistry or physics will, if we stay on at all, probably find ourselves with only girls to teach. This shaking up might be a great boon to the universities, if their own staffs would use it as a means of creating a more vital routine of study; but since it has been accepted reluctantly, and since it goes too far in emphasising only the mechanical part of a soldier's preparation, the losses will probably counterbalance the gains.

But of course the situation is full of incalculable elements. The grand news from Africa, the blows now being struck by Russia, all seem to point to the possibility of a much earlier German collapse than anyone could have counted on even three months ago. Though I expect Hitler to use torture as a form of blackmail for 'peace' when the going gets worse, and though I don't think the next ten months will be easy ones for any of us, from what I know of the Germans I expect them to crumble up completely as soon as they lose the hope of victory. But the mopping-up process will be a long and tedious one; and at the moment when victory seems assured for our side, it will be doubly necessary to guard our tongues and exercise a forbearance and understanding beyond the usual human requirements—a matter on which our own journalists and politicians need a good deal of schooling—and a great practise in humility and self-criticism.

Did I ever tell you how much I enjoyed your review of the Giedion book, and how sound I thought your criticism was? I have known Giedion's work for a long time and know what an effort it has cost him to move away from the purely abstract esthetic position he once occupied; but the fact that he is a good historical scholar gives authority, in the minds of many people, to his very shallow pronouncements on the nature and task of modern city planning. This is true of the whole school: the most recent publication of the CIAM (International Congress of Modern Architects) is a handsome brochure called *Can our Cities Survive*, by J. L. Sert, the Spanish architect: a very decent fellow. But when I saw the book in ms. I discovered that, though it dealt with recreation, it had no other reference to the civic and social functions of the city: hence I refused to give it the blessing of an introduction. They have made a few pallid efforts to meet this criticism; but the lesson they failed to learn from Howard they are not likely to learn any more effectively from me. Part of their failing is due to a chronic weakness in plans for urban improvement: beginning with evils that must be corrected, instead of with the city as a whole, in all its functionings. The over-emphasis of housing as mere building was one of the bad results of this.

WELWYN GARDEN CITY   23 March 1943

Dear Mumford

I am glad to say *The Social Foundations of Post-War Building*[1] is at last published. I am sending a copy with the ordinary mail copy of this letter, but not with the Air Mail copy. I have also asked our London Office to send you by book post half-a-dozen copies. Please let me know if you want any more.

The more I read this essay the better I like it. Opinion here, among the intelligentsia, is just getting ripe for this particular dose of thought. I think your essential thesis will be understood by more people from this short statement than from *The Culture of Cities*. Many were vastly impressed by that; but as you know, few read a long argument attentively; and you gave

---

[1] London, 1943, reprinted in *City Development*, New York, London, 1945, 1946.

your readers such a mass of illustrative material, of such an interesting kind, that they were a bit dazzled.

My very pedestrian foreword is calculated, whether successfully or not, to draw attention to the main argument. I have a low opinion of the basic seriousness or capacity for real thought of the cultivated public in England and America, who are as subject to momentary fashion as the cinema public. But our line of thought has nevertheless to be *made* fashionable, as a stage in its progress. And you have registered here as an indispensable article of the furniture of just the sort of household you most deride. Whereas I am, and will probably remain, regarded as a Victorian survival, and am patted on the head by Archbishops, who smile at my declared atheism as a form of unconscious Christianity, like Mrs Humphrey Ward's.

The immediate planning situation is bad. The Ministry responsible for housing has told the local authorities to go ahead with one year's programme without waiting for major Town and Country Planning decisions, which are held up by party machinations on the land compensation question. My association has issued a manifesto which I think will cause some hard thinking in Government circles, as the local authorities are seriously worried by the old dilemma of suburbs versus flatted tenements—both of which are now fiercely unpopular with women's organisations and men in the services, who have been systematically canvassed on the housing issue. The outcome can't be predicted, but I have still a good deal of hope for a Decentralisation policy, which is just practicable in this country.

STANFORD UNIVERSITY   24 April 1943

Dear Osborn

I am months behind in all my correspondence, for it has now reached a point that requires the services of a non-existent secretary; but I am particularly ashamed not to have answered yours of 19 February before your letter of March twenty-third arrived, and then, the other day, the first copy of the new pamphlet. As to the last, I am wholly delighted by your Introduction and reasonably pleased with the total effect of the argument itself in print, though it was only by the narrowest margin that it escaped the wastebasket last spring. I am not sorry now that you urged me or that your interest made me give my foundling thoughts another chance. You are right, of course, in saying that I have been premature in announcing the end of the mechanical life-theme: as a matter of fact, as I pointed out in *Technics and Civilisation*, I don't look for it so much to be abandoned as to be transformed from within: the over emphasis is the sort of thing that inevitably happens in controversy, when one is attempting to challenge views which seem more solidly entrenched than the practices which they sanction. As in most sicknesses, people have a life-conserving way of minimising the nature of the crisis through which they are passing: of attempting to interpret its unfamiliar choices in terms of the past with which they are familiar. That is why we all, myself included up to 1933, had a far too favourable interpretation of the last twenty years, and even treated some of the most serious signs of decay as the marks of a progressive civilisation. Heaven knows I can claim no originality for asserting that a nation that doesn't produce enough babies to replenish its losses is on the downgrade, no matter how admirable its infant mortality rates: Theodore Roosevelt was saying that, with strenuous earnestness, almost forty years ago. But I can understand his probable feelings at being treated as a bellicose reactionary for saying these things, for the chapter which reiterated them, in *Men Must Act*, led to my being branded as a fascist.

You are quite right about Sir Ernest Simon and the New York speedways. I had a very good chat with him when he visited Stanford, but it was mostly on education and I didn't have any chance to put him right about that particular type of showy public work. The New York express highways would be admirable if they were related to anything except the desire, on the part of the more prosperous, to get out of New York as fast as possible; actually, their function is to increase the planless decentralisation of the metropolis and thereby pile up such a load of decaying properties in the centre as to hasten the final exodus. As city planning they are weakminded even in terms of the existing metropolis; though they satisfy the metropolitan sense of show. It is easy to confuse these highways, however, with another type that has been created in the back-country: one-direction roads sometimes separated by a strip as wide as a quarter of a mile: townless highways that deliberately by-pass all the existing villages and towns, and are admirably fitted for cross country travel. These could be more modestly done than our present examples and would serve a programme of planned decentralisation on garden city lines. Our present highway schemes serve, alternatively, to congest and depopulate the big cities: to congest the metropolitan district and to depopulate the central areas. The road has become an end in itself: chiefly because any fool who can handle a square and a triangle fancies himself capable of planning one.

I find it hard to report about the general state of mind in America because my own nose has been so very close to the grindstone, and except for a brief visit to San Diego, which is an anthill of naval activity, the most warlike looking city in America, I have had no opportunity to talk to anyone except my immediate friends here. We have had no such verbal leadership in this war as Wilson gave us in the last one; and many of us are exceedingly suspicious and critical—even those who voted for Roosevelt and have no venomous feelings about him—over the policy of Vichy appeasement that has been carried out in North Africa and which, we fear, may also be applied to Spain and Italy. The President, like your typical Englishmen, holds contradictory opinions and performs contradictory actions: so his reassurances as to his honest ultimate intentions do not reassure us. Good leadership would, I think, tighten popular support for all the necessary measures of war and put the civilians on a more equal footing with the fighting men in seriousness of purpose; but this has been lacking, and all the vices of our peacetime radio and advertising have been reproduced and magnified in our propaganda, which errs on the sugary side; while the mass of our people, used to treating all propaganda as lies, is impervious to the most honest statements and the most salutary truths, even when, occasionally, they are offered.

A large part of my colleagues are already teaching mathematics and physics to incipient soldiers and sailors, instead of their usual subjects; and within a few months the lads in military uniform here will vastly outnumber the handful of the halt, the blind, and the infirm who will remain. My own programme will thus be curtailed for the duration of war for lack of students; so I shall let two of my staff stay on to take care of the few who remain by tutoring them and guiding their readings, while I myself will take a leave of absence, between June and January, so as to finish the book on which I have now been working for the better part of five years. In January 1944 I expect to come back here to teach for the Army, unless I am needed more urgently elsewhere. They doubtless have need for people with my all-round capacities and habits of coordinated thinking at Washington; but the very departments that need me most are probably least conscious of their own deficiencies: so I remain unused. It has been hard to reconcile myself to such a modest role as I seem destined to play in this war; but it matches my influence before it broke out, which was of course nil. My consolation is my book; for now that I have started on the third draft I feel confident about both its solidity and its originality. In the end, it will be my heaviest contribution to the post-war period. I have promised myself, incidentally, to revise and simplify the latter parts of *The Culture of Cities*, for an Argentine edition that is in prospect; but I frankly don't know when I am to get the time to do this.

WELWYN GARDEN CITY   7 September 1943

Dear Mumford
Your letter of the 24th April has lain on my desk for many months. I get further and further into arrears with my writing programme, and correspondence becomes nearly impossible. I think I told you that I am a Director

of a Radio manufacturing company, the work of which under present conditions is absorbing as well as important. The campaign of the Town and Country Planning Association for a post-war policy takes another large slice of time; in the course of it I write many articles and lectures, which are widely published as ephemera. Lack of time to produce more considered writings is a progressive exasperation, and failure to keep up with such correspondents as yourself a deprivation. I haven't learned, as you have, to retreat from the daily war and make a more solid contribution to thought —or rather, to put my contribution in a form that will impress the academic world; for in fact I do put a lot of thought into my ephemeral writings, and the results do get into currency. So there's no real loss, except a loss of the personal satisfaction of being able to find what I have thought in a few convenient volumes.

I am sending you with the ocean-going copy of this a few reviews of your booklet. Papers in this country are now very small, and short booklets are rarely reviewed. But they get into circulation, and yours has been widely read by the right sort of people. I am encouraged by what you say of the state of mind of the younger people. Actually I wonder whether any large number were caught in the depravity and pessimism of the twenties and thirties—and whether in moving from New York to Stanford you found a more representative sample of people. In England the film of society really touched by the poetry and precious literature associated with that period was an extremely thin one, though important because it probably contained a large proportion of those with sensitivity to creative art. Therefore one worried about it, because by all the rules the influence should have ripped right through society; but I don't think it did. I left the London cafés for Letchworth in 1912, and from 1918 I happily engaged in the big constructive job of building Welwyn, and came into touch with manufacturers and technicians doing jobs of work and liking it. But I never lost touch with the cafés and the literary and politically 'advanced' circles. They produce in me a Chestertonian mood or pose; I scoff at them rather than argue with them; and the result is, I think, that I am regarded as a lost soul, a Metropolitan gone bucolic, a revolutionist who has sold out, or a rationalist who has gone soft and been converted. The truth, as I have told them, is that they are the victims of the propaganda of commercialised and syndicated art, and that they are the worst type of 'provincials' (this gets under their guard)—the Provincials of Piccadilly. Middletown is less provincial really, for it does know that London exists. These people don't know that Middletown exists. However, there are times when it is quite useless to argue. Lately this impermeable world (perhaps you are responsible) has been infected by a craze for the 'neighbourhood' idea; and from being a complete outsider and philistine I am in real danger of being canonised—though that hasn't happened yet, and there is a good chance that I may escape it through the appropriation of your and my ideas by some café-lounger who hits on an acceptable new literary trick. In any case, however, it doesn't make much difference what the metropolitan coteries think. They don't think anything long enough to affect action. I go to a lot of conferences of municipal councillors and officials and serious-minded people who run practical affairs in big cities and small. It is a fact that if at such a conference I quoted a line from any of the best known poets of 1919 to date, not a soul would recognise it.

The nearest *popular* thing to the spirit of the decadent Anglo-American literature is a certain type of music, banned during the war by our BBC, usually sung by female crooners. To my surprise, because it doesn't give me even a morbid type of pleasure, this does make a definite appeal to a minority of ordinary young people, though the appeal *may* by one of fashion, since the BBC ban seems to have ended its popularity even at dances. In England this 'slush' music, which seems to me in spirit rather like some of the poetry of the twenties, and having the same large percentage of spoof or sham in it, has never appealed to a majority. But it has come back via the programmes for the American forces here, and I must confess hearing some of these with shocked amazement. It is difficult to believe that Roosevelt and these sex-vitiated crooners express the same civilisation. I feel as if I am ninety-nine and an aged female ape were lamenting my impotence. (That indeed is a drastic bowdlerisation of what I feel, for the sake of my stenographer.) I wish you could explain this. Because there is every sign that this music evokes some strong response; it suits something in its vast audiences. Also I feel it is American. But it is American in the way most alien to me. To a minority here, it seems, it is not so alien, but rather interestingly 'foreign' and thus attractive.

The County of London Plan[1] is a profound disappointment. It talks the language of 'decentralisation' and plans to slow up the process as much as possible. Having paraphrased my views of it several times in articles and lectures, I'm too weary of it to do it again in this letter; but you will see a short statement of my views in the Summer *Town and Country Planning*, which you should have received some time ago. Abercrombie had the chance of a century. Great pressure was put on him by the LCC, but he was in a position to stand out. Early on in the preparation I had an evening with him and Forshaw, and many times I pointed out to him that the cities of the whole world would be influenced by this Plan, if it were really sound and

---

[1] Patrick Abercrombie *and* J. H. Forshaw, *The County of London Plan*, London, 1943.

logical. But, as you well know by the example of Thomas Adams, planners have been conditioned to compromise by their whole history; and, after all, it is rather much to expect an architect-technician-writer-university professor to have the drive of a bull-dozer. I was too confident about Abercrombie, who is intelligent and has had a good education in the issues (he was a member of the Barlow Royal Commission). I kick myself that I didn't sit on his doorstep at County Hall as I did on Barlow's doorstep during the sittings of the Commission. But I could not have believed that any planner could state in full detail the case for Decentralisation, and then produce a Plan that doesn't do the main thing necessary—permit the majority of people to have decent family homes. It's all the more extraordinary because we have had, in the last year or two, every conceivable kind of opinion survey on the type of dwelling desired—housewives, men in the services, women in the services, factory workers, rural workers, and cross-sections in every direction—and they all show that 90 to 95 per cent want houses and gardens and don't want flats.

The LCC is led by middle-class Labour Councillors right out of touch with popular opinion but very close to the transport and public service interests, and terrified of a drop in rateable value or of a loss of their slum electorate. The Plan, which contemplates 75 per cent of London families re-housed in flats, and a merely 'token' decentralisation of people, and a brake on, rather than an encouragement of, decentralisation of industry and business, is impracticable anyway; because Londoners will get their houses by continuing the suburban sprawl, and presently the spontaneous move-ment of industry to the suburbs (following the workers) will produce 'blighted areas' in the centre. I continue to point out that planning the centre at much lower density is in the long run a wiser financial policy, and that new towns are in every way better than a continued suburban sprawl. But it is a bit late to start the old argument all over again, and to fight a Plan drawn by our most eminent colleague in the Decentralisation move-ment! Nevertheless, I am continuing the battle, which even now is not lost, because the public starts, as I do myself, from the housing standard. There is no danger of the Plan being carried out. The real danger is that Housing, as in 1919, will run away with everything and simply expand every centre of population in proportion to its present size.

AMENIA, NEW YORK   24 October 1943

Dear Osborn

I would have written you long before this had I not, after leaving Stanford in June, plunged into the writing of the final draft of my book, which is to be called *The Condition of Man.*[1] Merely in order to get the 214,000 words typewritten took no little part of my time and energy this summer; and since I had to add some two hundred pages to the draft I was re-writing I was thoroughly busy, and kept pushing my correspondence to one side in such a ruthless fashion that I will have to pay the penalty for months, making apologies! I cannot persuade myself that any book is worth the time and effort I have spent on this one; though there are perhaps a few things in it that need to be said. In the last chapter, partly out of weariness and inability to think things out freshly, I had to fall back on a dozen pages from the Faber and Faber pamphlet; and I would like to have your and their permission, formally, to use this material.

Your letter mightily interested me and gave me much to reflect upon. I find the fact that I haven't been in England since 1932, and got around all too little then, is increasingly a handicap: which makes me more eager than ever to get the feel of the place next summer. Strange as it may seem on the surface, I think the processes of decay that have become apparent throughout our whole civilisation have perhaps gone farther in America than anywhere else. Don't be deceived by our appearance of youth and vitality: the Civil War killed many of the roots of our deeper culture and since that time we have fostered all those forces and mechanisms which have detached people from the essential life of man. Even though England led the way in the paleotechnic revolution and depleted itself badly, it never completely succumbed to the machine: your roots remained in contact with your own soil and your own nourishing past: so that you were capable of being rejuvenated in your extremity, by threat in the summer of 1940, that would have crumpled up a weaker people forever. The decadence which even the older ruling classes showed in the 1920's and 30's in England was not irreparable: for there was still something underneath it—if nothing more than family memories and regimental prides. Our weakness goes much deeper; for though a whole generation, led by Van Wyck Brooks, has tried to replant itself, as it were, in our past, resuming the continuity which the Civil War and the rise of corporate industrialism had broken, the dominant institutions of our day have been against this effort. Our young intellectuals —and I was one of them!—were more disillusioned by the First World War than the weakest spirits in Europe: and the drivel of our radio programmes, the whine of self-pity in our popular music, are symptoms of a formidable kind of escapism which gives me great concern: for whatever has happened or may still happen to our soldiers at the front, the American people today still show little signs of any change in their characteristic ideas and attitudes

---

[1] New York, London, 1944.

—even though their weaknesses contributed to our critical humiliation at Pearl Harbor.

Our good and our weak qualities are both embodied in Roosevelt: that is the secret of his popularity and his apparent success. At a distance you see Roosevelt's best side: and I would not deny his great qualities: there have been moments during the last three years when he acted with alertness and even heroism, incomparable alertness, genuine heroism. Perhaps his most daring act was one for which he has never been given sufficient credit in America: his taking the responsibility of sending you what was practically our entire supply of rifles and ammunition outside what was actually in use by our handful of regular soldiers; and of course his audacious conception of Lend-Lease was another such act, although we will all finally have to pay a certain price in misunderstanding and eventual bad tempers, for the cagey vagueness which he characteristically enshrouded these transactions in. So much for his good side: there are many other evidences. But essentially, he expresses the same civilisation as the 'sex-vitiated crooners' you properly are repelled by: he has the same incapacity to face reality and the same desire to dodge responsibility.

Had he any of Churchill's greatness in 1940, Roosevelt would have seized Pearl Harbor as an occasion to confess his own sins of hesitation and weakness and temporising, and he might, by being generous enough to attack his own weaknesses, have succeeded in bringing home to his country-men the disastrous nature of their own: instead he covered over our disgrace by blaming it on the 'treachery' of the Japanese; he attempted to cushion the shock of war, refused to face the rubber plight until it was finally forced down his throat by the Baruch report, and permitted the army and navy representatives to soften every blow and every weakness, so that our people should not feel the hardships and brutalities that faced us, too keenly: the unctuous drool of the advertising man and the publicity expert stands between us and reality, as a result of this policy; and since we haven't, like you, had actual bombs and devastation and death to bring us to our senses quickly, we are bound to make bad partners, because of a disparity in our experience. Like the American people, Roosevelt has not grown with the war: it was symptomatic that a few months ago he could actually boast, in his speech from Canada, that we had not entered this war by any choice of ours. Indeed, he clings so pathetically to that sad boast that he even did the British the injustice of including you in that statement: although the fact is that your actual *choice* in September 1939, re-enforced the following summer, was what saved the world from complete Nazi domination for at least another century, perhaps longer.

I have gone into this because I think it important that on both sides of

the water our judgements of our leaders should be accurate as well as generous. The weaknesses Roosevelt has consistently shown in his dealings with
Vichy and in his complaisant view, indeed his active collaboration, with
catholic Fascism, are going to prolong the war and make the tasks of peace
much more difficult: if indeed they do not lay the fuse for another war.
Having said this much on our own shortcomings, I should perhaps in candor
add what I think about Churchill:

As a leader, from the 1930's onward, he seems to me to stand high above
Roosevelt in essential strength; if one man deserves the world's gratitude for
rescuing it from Mrs Lindbergh's 'Wave of the Future' it is Churchill: hence
I well understand the admiring unanimity with which his countrymen regard
him; and I think this view is shared by the majority of Americans, if one
excludes the despicable minority of isolationists and the more vengeful Irish.
But Churchill's strength lies in his connections with the past: this very
historic sense helped restore England's greatness at the moment she desperately needed it: but the seeds of the future are not in him, alas! and his very
skill in dealing with the hard problems of the moment have robbed him of
the ability to think of a different kind of future. With Churchill's principles,
Roosevelt's utter lack of principle, and Stalin's ruthless contempt for any
arrangement that does not re-assert and re-enforce the power that is concentrated in the Kremlin, I see little immediate hope of laying the foundations for a better international structure. Whatever is done, it will take
decades and generations to work out the terms of an essentially peace-willing
world order. But bad leadership may postpone even the beginning by giving
play to the truculences and antagonisms that are generated in the very act
of fighting; and by their cowardice and their false 'realism' they may increase
the moral devastation and disillusion and social disintegration.

AMENIA, NEW YORK   2 December 1943

Dear Osborn

Since writing you I have been devilling over the finishing touches to *The
Condition of Man*; and when inspiration failed me I had to make up for it
by sheer dogged effort and craftsmanship—which I think I did, though not
without reaching the perilous limits of exhaustion. Fortunately, I have a
week or ten days before me, while the revised galleys get under way; and
I am taking my first real vacation since 1940. I need at least a month of
idleness before I shall really be back in fighting form; but I won't get it,
since I am due back in Stanford University by 10 January: same address
as before. Once I am back there I hope to get busy over the LCC planning

book and write a comprehensive criticism of it; but as yet I have been too tired to glance at anything that really required attention and understanding.

You were very good to send me that *Weekly Review*, with its generous criticism of my pamphlet: thanks again. The copy of *The Story of Utopias*[1] which I am asking the publisher to send you is but a poor return for all your many gifts. Fortunately it was reprinted from photographic plates last year: there has been a small persistent demand for it, if only as a pony in sociology classes on Utopias! The book was something of a *tour de force*, such as only a very young man could attempt; for the entire work on it, including 'research', was done in five months. My work at Stanford promises to be interesting, despite the fact that there will probably be only a dozen or two students, girls and 'disabled' boys in my humanities courses; for we have a new President, and he is entrusting to a group of us the re-planning of the university—a job which, if done well, may have a wide influence. I am keen to add a school of planning to the existing schools in the university: one which will give the same basic courses in geography, economics, sociology, psychology and history to everyone engaged in planning, whether he be an architect, an engineer, or an administrator, and which will allow at the same time for the necessary professional specialisation. If we can work out the right pattern for such a school, we may find a means of giving a unified approach to the other professions, too, and so bring them into some sort of working harmony, the lack of which, the lack of any basis for which, is one of the main obstacles, as I see it, to intelligent action. Now that most of the conventional courses are scrapped in favour of the army and navy training programmes—which incidentally have taught the universities many valuable things and will have, on the whole, a salutary effect—we have a fine opportunity to make a fresh start. There is both justice and irony in the fact that I am now having thrust into my lap, despite great personal reluctance, the very job that old Geddes[2] wanted above all others all his life: it is up to me to deliver the goods! I am still looking forward to being in England next summer; but the plans for the great offensive against Germany are being so tardily executed that it seems possible to me now—as it did not last spring—that every available bit of space on ship and plane may be needed for military purposes next June: so my fingers are crossed. More about things in general presently. In the meanwhile, my warmest greetings for Christmas and the New Year: may this be the last War Christmas, at least on your side of the water.

---

[1] New York, London, 1922, 1923.
[2] Sir Patrick Geddes, biologist, sociologist, historian and town planner. Exerted strong influence on the young Mumford.

Dear Mumford

I am looking forward to the new book with much pleasure. My own book on planning makes no progress. I have only spare time for writing and the work of the Town and Country Planning Association, and we are hotly engaged in the controversy on post-war policy, now reaching crisis and decision, so I have a considerable output of memoranda for parliamentarians and bureaucrats, press articles, booklets, and letters to the newspapers. These have a more immediate influence on coming policy than any book could have; but all the same the necessity exasperates me, because I am all the time simplifying and reiterating, whereas I feel I have a more solid and permanent contribution to make to the subject on which, by accident, I have specialised for twenty-five years.

The London Plan has at last crystallised the issues which I have vainly sought to get discussed—namely those of the standards and general direction of future city development. I have for years worked very closely with Patrick Abercrombie, and it was largely through him (and Mrs Hichens)[1] that we were able to get the Barlow Royal Commission to come down on the side of decentralisation, limitation of city growth, and the national control of the location of industry. Abercrombie is the only philosophic or sociological planner in the country; and as he is also (since Unwin died) the recognised head of the profession, his prestige has, with the new fashion for planning, risen to great heights. He was able, therefore, to get the urban issues that you and I know to be important more comprehensively stated, in the Preamble to the London Plan, than has been done before in a planning report. He was, however, as Consultant, associated with the Architect of the LCC, and the work was done, not in Abercrombie's private office, but in the LCC office, with the maximum daily influence of the old point of view and at very close quarters with the housing and planning schemes already on the table and in the files in 1939. Though I was, having expected one of the great historic documents of planning, bitterly disappointed with the Plan when I first studied it, I now think that in the circumstances Abercrombie did as well as any man, of the type who can survive in planning practice, could have done. But it was quite impossible for the TCPA or me to bless the Plan unreservedly. We applauded its general boldness and frame-work, and in very plain terms objected to its housing standards and to its 'back-pedalling' on industrial and business decentralisation.

The LCC has a Labour majority rather more than ordinarily under the

---

[1] A member of the 'Barlow' Royal Commission.

thumb of a party junta—partly because of its precarious position and of a very poor rank and file personnel—which, again (as you will understand better than most people here) is due to the filtering out from the County of London (our Manhattan) of the prosperous and enterprising elements of society and the best of the intelligentsia, who have moved to the outer suburbs. Such intelligentsia as is left is, as you would expect, of the over-urbanised café-lounging, quasi-communist, quasi-technocrat type—right out of touch, not only with the sanity of the countryside but with the psychology of ordinary home-centred urban workers. They mistake the highly organised and commercialised theatre etc. for culture; and mass-meetings of unrelated people for democracy. And being right inside a huge city, they cannot see it as a whole. Moreover, and this is very important, town planning and town structure is a subject entirely neglected by the left movements, as well as by everybody else. So the issues which have suddenly come into promin-ence are unfamiliar to them, and they are at the mercy of fashionable literary attitudes—most of which in this country are concerned either with country-side preservation or with a poor type of modernist architectural theory, nominally functionalist but actually what I call 'constructivist', that is dominated by the possibilities of new materials as a means to architectural escapism. The *Architectural Review* is one of the centres of this outlook. I wouldn't so much mind their constructivist motive of functionalism if they didn't back it up by pseudo-sociology—the idea that we are passing into an age when buildings express the communal life which is to replace, rather than supplement, the family life.

I have been at war with these people for years, and I think their annoyance with you is that up to a point they had misread you as a modernist *tout simple*, and nothing could annoy them more than to find you in essential alliance with my school of thought *and* a defender of the out-of-date and despised cult of the family. I have written little on aesthetics, though I have in due course much to say on that subject, and their wishful thinking has therefore led them to class me as a philistine, or at best as a neo-Elizabethan or neo-Georgian romantic. (Welwyn happens to be built mainly in an honest and functional continuation of the Hertfordshire tradition, with life and freshness of detail, and the use of the local brick was economically and structurally entirely justified—indeed inescapable unless one wanted to be funny just for the sake of being funny. Letchworth, begun in 1904, was of course in the Morris–Voysey–Barry Parker current, and its use of Fletton brick covered with cement plaster was dictated by the conditions over the whole region within reach of the Peterborough brickfields.)

Now apart from the TCPA, which has the biggest following of any plan-ning impetus in the country as a whole, and is gaining influence very rapidly, this modernist-technocrat school is the only one with any following, and its hold on the smart publishing houses and the coteries of London have given it some pull with the Labour people, who want to be in the swim but have no knowledge of planning themselves. Abercrombie is free of the influence, and its really wholly with us. He has not resigned from the Association, and indeed I remain in full understanding and contact with him, despite our difference on the strategy of London planning. Our objectives are wholly the same, but he has compromised for the moment at a level which I think mistaken and strategically unwise.

Behind the whole issue is the pressure, in which we and the London Labour caucus are at one, for the national adoption of the Barlow policy of decentralisation and control of industrial location. The majority of the London Labour Party are inclined to take the view that they could have adopted a bolder policy of decentralisation if the Government had come to a decision, and this is the climb-out that I am leaving them. But the chief leaders are playing up to the interests by taking the line that further decentralisation would disembowel London. The machine, so far, goes with the main spokesmen, and for them therefore I am Public Enemy No. 1. The *Architectural Review* crowd have seen their chance and opened a violent (but very incompetently-conducted) attack on me and the TCPA. This sounds like a sad dispute among planners in the face of the real enemy. And I am being blamed for that. But actually we have said a great deal more in praise of the Plan than against it, and we have made planning a political issue, and a subject of universal discussion, for the first time. The intensive newspaper controversy which has resulted has already made decentralisation and the restoration of a good family housing standard one of the main issues of reconstruction policy. I think we shall succeed in forcing the hands of the Government on the Barlow policy. And I think the LCC will soon be saying that of course, they have always wanted to do what I want, but couldn't unless they had the backing of a national policy.

Now as to your visit to England. I hope you will speak at some sort of meeting or function of the TCPA. Would you kindly consider (I write for the Executive on this) accepting the Howard Memorial Medal? The idea of this, instituted five or six years ago, is to keep Howard's memory fresh, and it is given only to people who have been, in a broad sense, consistent supporters of Howard's essential idea and have made a distinctive contribution to its development. So far it has only been awarded to Raymond Unwin, Barry Parker[1] and Patrick Abercrombie. It will be a small matter to you, but we hope you will accept, and allow the presentation to be made

---

[1] Unwin and Parker, the first planners of the Garden City movement, planned Letchworth Garden City, New Earswick, Hampstead Garden Suburb etc.

when you are here. I am working on a new edition of Howard's book, which should be published about the middle of 1944. I hope to do an Introduction characterising the man and shortly putting his work in historical perspective. Faber will publish the book in as worthy a style as is practicable in war time.

Your summary of America and Roosevelt gives me much to think about; I feel still ignorant of America, and wish my reading and contacts could be supplemented by a visit there. I wonder sometimes if you don't expect of people a breadth of historical knowledge, a prescience, and a world-consciousness that they never will and never could have; whether you are not struggling to find a way of avoiding periodical cataclysms that never can be avoided; whether indeed you are not trying to round off the human novel by a happy ending that would be not only unconvincing but inartistic? You struck a chord in me once by saying the world can only be understood as a tragedy. Without accepting that otherwise than in a very subtle sense, I do sometimes wonder whether you are not complaining of the tragic weft in things that is essential to any pattern at all. The mystery remains why whole masses of people, who after all have plenty of notice of the tragic weft in their own lives and the lives around them (apart from war), can become in their general tone and culture so devastatingly superficial, trivial and maudlin. I sense that it is due to the successes of mechanism, the idea of progress extrapolated to infinity, and also (this is King Charles's Head, of course) to the divorce of the urban masses from the phenomena of growth and decay, from the struggle for survival as an eternal reality rather than as a defect of capitalist society, and from the prolonged quiet satisfactions that fill in the texture of the tragedy.

The absence of priesthood with real prestige, taking an honoured place in a real community, is related to these shortages. The Churches have lost the power of Reformation (in England they seem to me on the verge of recovering it), and the literary fathers (of whom you and Sinclair Lewis—*horribile dictu!*—may be different types) wait vainly in your confessionals for clients. I have thought of going into the priest business myself, as the BBC want me to do Sunday night postscripts, but I am scared stiff of million-audiences and of my own tendency suddenly to see myself and all else in the comic light. *La Trahison des Clercs* may thus be due to modesty or to the irresponsibility of the comic spirit.

As to your judgment of Roosevelt, I am not in a position to contest it. But knowing something of the scale of government in proportion to the scale of men (even the biggest possible men), I wonder whether you allow enough for the fact that a man may be clear as to the necessary thing to do, yet realistic in his judgment that he cannot do it until the waters have risen to a certain level. It doesn't seem to me necessarily wrong for Roosevelt to claim that a war he wanted, but America plainly did not want, was thrust on him. Nor is he to blame, I think, if your national publicity takes some of the habitual tone of the advertising men who are the only available instruments to run it. In the last war we had the same thing here. How can a leader make himself a full substitute for bitter personal experience? Judged by his own statements, Roosevelt looks to me a bit bigger than you make him—in fact, in all the circumstances, surprisingly near the adequate.

WELWYN GARDEN CITY   13 January 1944

Dear Mumford

It is kind of you to have told your publishers to send me *The Story of Utopias*, which I shall be very glad to have. I have kept random notes for years of the physical planning proposals (more often assumptions) in such Utopias as I have read; but knowing your methods I feel sure your book will have superseded all my notes. My reading anyway has been very sketchy, as I have spent my life mostly in counting-houses, board rooms and committee meetings; and of the millions of words I have written, more than half must have been minutes and business memoranda. Bacon didn't say so, but Minute writing maketh a drily accurate man. Now that, in connection with war-time political advocacy of planning, I have to write for the press 2,000-word articles in 750 words, the training is not without value. Even my self-destructive habit of writing satirical verses (about once in three months over thirty years) has proved of utility—because even one's vices become part of one's personality in late middle age.

I congratulate you on the most interesting job of replanning the University. You will no doubt weigh carefully the advisability of trying to give architects and engineers a sociological background, and the danger of making them bad architects and amateur sociologists. The temperament of most men drawn to architecture (by its delusive similarity to creative 'art') seems to me to disqualify them as advisers on town structure. Geddes and Unwin do not strike me as of the 'architectural' type. But presumably you aim to select men with a new conception of architecture? Over here, we suffer from the pseudo-sociology of men with the 'aesthetic' preoccupation.

STANFORD UNIVERSITY   19 February 1944

Dear Osborn

The honour which you so casually broached to me in the midst of your December letter gave me immense gratification, it goes without saying, although there is only one man to my knowledge who really deserves the Ebenezer Howard medal—and indeed a whole series of them—and that is yourself. When I was young I affected to despise honours and dignities of all kinds—and very possibly I did despise them then—but now that I am within two years of a half century I discover that my feelings towards such things have more than mellowed. The esteem of one's fellow-men, whether deserved or undeserved, is about the only reward of work that is substantial and lasting; and in middle life it comes at a time when one's native self-esteem is beginning to diminish through the natural growth of one's critical faculties, and in that fashion external honours fill up what might otherwise be a deplorable vacuum. So I accept the honour your Executive proposes with becoming gratitude and humility.

At the same time I should warn you that the event on which it hangs— my actually coming to England—is still highly uncertain of fulfillment. Up to January I had been led to believe that all the arrangements for the journey were being made by Mrs Farquharson in England. Unfortunately, the original plan was side-tracked because of the well-meaning but unfortunate intervention of an American official, Victor Weybright, who is in charge of American visits to England at the English side. In the middle of last summer this gentleman entered into correspondence with the State Department for the purpose of having them underwrite my whole journey, as they have done with hundreds and perhaps thousands of other Americans on semi-official missions. Mr Weybright had apparently forgotten that I have been an outspoken and unrelenting critic of the State Department's foreign policies since the Spanish Civil War, and that in more than one instance my criticism has gotten under Mr Hull's skin.[1] I know this from at least one letter he addressed to a publication in which I had written. The State Department, accordingly, not merely refused to sponsor my trip, but also refused to allot me plane accommodation so that I could reach England by the end of next June—I finish up here on June 26th. Upon being told about this in January I made application for passport and steamer accommodations, but I have still to hear from the State Department whether they will grant me one or the other, and there is a very real possibility that they may delay matters so long that without actually saying No to my application they will prevent me from going over next summer. Apart from this, it would not be hard for them to give very plausible reasons that would prevent a civilian who was not actually on a government mission from making this journey at the end of next June, when every available inch of space may still be needed for military personnel.

---

[1] Cordell Hull, US Secretary of State, 1933–44.

STANFORD UNIVERSITY   10 March 1944

Dear Osborn

This is just the hastiest of notes to give you the latest news. My State Department handsomely lived up to my expectations by pretending to be unable to act on my passport application till next June. This would not have cancelled my trip because, with the backing of the Local Government Board and perhaps Lord Halifax, I think I could have made them change their mind quickly enough: but something more decisive intervened. My body, deprived too long of its natural rest, seriously revolted; and in order to avert any permanent injury to my heart—which still is organically sound—it is necessary for me to cancel my British journey, or at least postpone it till I have become fully restored.

WELWYN GARDEN CITY   24 March 1944

Dear Mumford

Forgive me for delay in answering your letter of February 19th. We have had almost a Parliamentary crisis over the relation of our Planning proposals to Housing, and this has given me a lot of extra work. It is by no means over, nor is the work. At present it looks, superficially, as if Planning has gone down before the urgency of Housing and as if we go back to the policy of 1919–39, accelerated by the advance of collectivism in the Housing field and national enthusiasm for a Full Employment policy. Churchill and his immediate circle do not understand the city-development issues at all, and the one Ministry which partially understands them (the new one of Town and Country Planning) has been grudgingly equipped with charming but weak men unable to fight for the necessary powers and supremacy over other departments in the matter of land-use. The public certainly wants Planning in a vague way, because it senses things went wrong between the wars and because of our propaganda; but only a few really understand how or why things went wrong, though we now have the public ear and education is proceeding apace. Time, however, is against us. The municipal housing schemes are crystallising all over the country, and the pressure for houses from the bombed-out and newly married couples, plus the pressure from the building industry for definite prospective jobs for which they can prepare, is producing schemes for extensions of big cities, and for over-dense central rebuilding, on a large scale. If these schemes all go on, industry and transport and public services will all develop just as in the past, and the opportunity of the 'pause' will have been lost.

I am bound to add that the 'social scientists' contribute to the confusion by their equivocations and uncertainty as to whether they should be descriptive or prescriptive. They often describe accurately within a studied field of reference, and then prescribe under the influence of background assumptions outside the field, where they are really only laymen. And their quite unscientific prescriptions come out with the trade-mark of the academics. I am getting really annoyed about this. An outstanding example was Dr Gutkind's *Creative Demobilisation*[1]—a most pretentious and pseudo-scientific affair issued under the Editorship of Karl Mannheim, who is himself a genuine thinker and a formidable one, but apparently not critical of the quality of work under his aegis. All these people regard me, of course, as a shameless one-track propagandist. And I am certainly a propagandist of policies which emerge from thirty years of experience and study in my own field. Yet I try not to make assertions outside my knowledge or to proceed on uncriticised assumptions, or to treat abstract objectives such as 'maximum productivity' as paramount, or to treat my own preferences as mass-preferences—all of which things the 'scientists' do constantly without a shiver of shame.

However, gradually the battle which we have waged on about six fronts is gaining ground. If it proves useless, it will not be because people can't be convinced, but because by the time we reach the objective the Housing Army will be in possession, with its vast energy and no interests in planning.

I have discussed with Faber and Faber your offer to write a preface for *Garden Cities of Tomorrow*, and a letter I had from F. V. Morley on the subject, saying Harcourt Brace are much interested in the idea. Faber and I both think that if you write an introduction it ought to go in the English edition as well, along with mine. I am sure an introduction by you would be of interest to English readers, and as I am also writing one you need not consider, more than would in any case be natural to you, the double audience. What do you think about this? I have left it to Faber & Faber to consider whether they will negotiate with Morley or with their own American connections. If I can get my own introduction written, as I hope, in the next few weeks, I will send it to you. We should like the English edition published in the autumn, if possible; so if you can give me any idea of the time you would want for writing the introduction it would be helpful.

AMENIA, NEW YORK   11 June 1944

Dear Osborn

Your letter of 28 March came in the early weeks of May; and I found myself putting off answering it from week to week, because of the hope that your

---

[1] London, 1943.

introduction would in the meanwhile arrive. It hasn't come yet but, like much other mail, it may have been held up through the extra precautions of censorship before the invasion. I have improved my time by re-reading *Garden Cities of Tomorrow* and making notes toward my own introduction, which I am rather loath to write till I see yours, since I don't want unnecessarily to duplicate some leading thought of yours. The re-reading has left me more full of admiration for Howard than ever: his equable mind, his really statesmanlike insight, his sense of the whole situation, give the book even now a force which has not been diminished by the practical success of the Garden Cities: rather, it tempts one to recover more of the essential idea he broached and to wipe the idea clean of many accidental associations which attended its translation into practice.

What strikes me perhaps for the first time—though I read the book first some twenty-three years ago and have read it at least two or three times more since—is how little he was concerned with the form of the new city, and how much he was concerned with the processes that would produce and extend such communities. His ideas about the future city are distinctly Victorian, by H. G. Wells out of Buckingham, as it were, as in the conception of the Crystal Palace: yet even that conception is little more than a doing over of Princes Gardens in Edinburgh, with the park strip on one side and the shopping strip on the other, plus a little extra glass! He was a statesman in the great sense of the word: a statesman in the same sense that the early Cooperators at Rochdale were statesmen; and he illustrates the equable good sense of English state-craft at its best, for with all his fine sense of the moment he was not, like too many of our contemporaries, afraid of rational plans and long-term commitments.

The critics of the Garden City have obviously neglected the book completely and read into the movement all their pet dislikes. When they think they are criticising Howard, they are criticising Unwin: not the Unwin who helped plan Letchworth, but the official who lost sight of the essential garden city principles in his promotion of housing, at twelve houses to the acre, whereas Howard's proposed lots are approximately the same size as New York's, 20 × 100, or 130! The very building of Letchworth and Welwyn, while it immensely helped the idea, by bringing it down to earth, also limited it; for admirable though each of them is, they each have weaknesses in plan and execution which people too easily identify with the original idea, instead of realising that both the improvements and the lapses from the key proposal are the inevitable price one pays for transposition into actual life. You see I am all primed to write my share of the introduction; and as soon as I get your draft I will sail in. Incidentally, I am naturally pleased at your suggestion that it should go into the English edition, too.

My book[1] came out punctually on May 18, and I trust that by this time you have received the copy I sent you: it will appear in England, probably, in the autumn. I timed the book for this particular moment because, two years ago, I had the fatuously optimistic notion that the war would just be entering its last phase this spring; but considering that everyone's mind is preoccupied with the movement now under way and with the fate of his friends, relatives, or associates on the other side, it has done very well: 4,000 copies by the end of the second week, despite the fact that it received an even more hostile handling in the New York press than *Faith for Living* or *Men Must Act*: hostility and neglect being the price one pays for doing one's best work. The poor devils of reviewers, who haven't the patience or the wits to read the book, likewise lack the charity to give me the benefit of the doubt or to admit that I may know my own business better than they do; so, because they do not wish to swallow the bitter medicine of the book as a whole, they complain because I do not promise them a pink pill and a quick recovery in the final chapter. They are right in thinking that volume III is only the first half of *The Condition of Man*, and that a fourth volume is to follow. But if they are not strong enough to swallow the purgative, they won't be ready for the treatment in that final volume, which I have a superstitious reluctance to announce before it is actually in a state of gestation. I do not expect you, dear Osborn, in the midst of all your pressing and important work, to do more than glance at the illustrations in *The Condition of Man* until your own affairs are less urgent: but eventually I look forward to your criticism, whether by letter or face to face, if I manage to get over next year, as I hope and intend to do.

We came back here at the end of April; and so badly did I need the rest that has followed that I *still* haven't written a word of my criticism of the London plan for the *Architectural Review*, though from week to week I keep putting it on my calendar, and from week to week the planting of my vegetable garden, or bouts of sheer lazy rambling over the countryside, with my sketchblock in my knapsack, takes my mind away from its intellectual obligations. But the rest has been very good for me: I can now work for hours with a spade or a hoe; and if I can down my conscience long enough to continue it for a few more months, I will be completely whole again, I think, and much more ready to embark on the big jobs that lie before me. Since I am not naturally a lazy man or an irresponsible one, I am taking my present inertia as a sufficient sign that, whether I like it or not at a time like the present, it is the best use I can make of my time. Our son, who will be 19 in July, is now in North Africa, heading for some yet

---

[1] *The Condition of Man*, New York, London, 1944.

unknown destination; and so for my wife and myself there are now two important fronts, the big one in northern Europe and the other one, wherever it is, in which he will have a part to play. He is a rifleman; and when I picture what he is facing, I keep on hoping that in a pinch his youthful experience as a trapper and a hunter will stand him in good stead. (With a little luck for good measure!)

As for the war, the better our technical handling of it becomes, the worse the political manipulation appears: the lack of moral principles and intelligent social ends, which I have tried to indicate in *The Condition of Man*, is now showing up on a great scale on both sides of the Atlantic and threatens to blight the fruits of our victory. One of my friends in Washington, a good man in an important place, writes that he is afraid that the peoples who are fighting will not demand enough of their statesmen, and as a result will get nothing by way of solid achievement on the positive side. As soon as victory seems assured, I hope to bring out a pamphlet on this situation, 'Antidote to Disillusion'. But of that more later.

WELWYN GARDEN CITY   19 June 1944

Dear Mumford

This is a brief note to thank you for sending me *The Condition of Man*. I have only dipped into this as yet, but it is evident that I am going to enjoy it greatly. Already my amazement at your capacity for assessing significant personalities and relating them freshly and convincingly to their background of time and place is renewed. Old Wells (whom I once read with slavish devotion and whose current productions, alas, I can hardly be bothered to open), struck a chord in me recently by a remark that 'life is too short for learning, anyway'. It takes me days to get to the heart of a writer of the past or present, and the days (or weeks) in which I could write justly and out of my own experience in elucidation or criticism of his thought, simply don't exist. How you do it, therefore, is a mystery to me—because I am convinced intuitively that you do it adequately. You have on me the effect that the schoolmaster produced on Goldsmith's villagers.

I have just read, and briefly reviewed, Saarinen's *The City*,[1] which lacks your responsible profundity and documentation, and is in fact a rather wordy but sincere elaboration of two or three simple and strongly-held ideas; but which I hail as significant because it shows the first strong bridgehead of the conception of physical decentralisation in the modernist architectural camp. It is refreshing to me to find an architect getting the human values

---

[1] New York, 1943.

3

into perspective; and, as you will see, I have seized on this as a tactical gain to consolidate. In this country the advanced architects (the *Architectural Review* following and others) are not particularly intelligent and cannot state the aesthetic case without falling into sociological absurdities. On the other hand the traditionalists just splutter. One or two of them, like Professor Richardson,[1] can be amusing and spirited; but the best of them are (as perhaps they should be) mostly inarticulate with their pens and tongues, Abercrombie being the one outstanding exception.

I don't know if it is the ten years in the difference of my birth-date and yours, or sheer ignorance, or a considered opinion that a finally analysable rhythm and overall shape is a necessary constituent of all 'art', and a certain gravity essential to great art, that makes me sceptical of some of your acceptances. I don't know if this will arise in a review, which under present conditions is likely to be absurdly short. But (to take instances) while I couldn't have any doubts about *Ulysses* or *Recherche du Temps Perdu* or your selections from Van Gogh, I cannot place these Picassos, or *The Waste Land*, on the heights even of virtuosity. The passage of years and the chorus of criticism don't, I find, modify much my first reactions in these cases. Which may prove to you that Britain remains an island. On the evidence that works of this period give of the state of soul of urban civilisation, I am wholly with you. The decay of Joyce into *Finnegan's Wake* wholly suits my spiritual as distinct from my aesthetic valuation of *Ulysses*; it interests me all the more because he carries into his nonsense the highly-decorated and elaborate rhythms against which the staccato and documentary schools revolted, besides their arrested-adolescent nihilism. One can't, of course, escape the consequences of one's own course of mental development. I myself reacted definitely with outward violence but inner mildness from the Victorian bourgeois atmosphere when I was 17, and for five or six years I was thoroughly taken in by Bloomsbury and its absorption in ephemeral movements and its scorn of stability. Letchworth (which is utterly despised by the urban mind, and which certainly seemed to me to have a backwoods air when I went to it fresh from Post-Impressionist exhibitions, first nights of Shaw and Strindberg, political theorising, emotional experimentation and social irresponsibility), cured me of Bloomsbury and of contempt for plain humanity; and when Prufrock, Hecatomb Styrax, Sweeney (poorly chosen names they seemed) and the female smells in shuttered rooms broke on the scene, they seemed to me to come from the dead world of the nineties rather than from the contemporary age.

---

[1] Professor A. E. Richardson, Professor of Architecture, London University, 1947–.

That Ezra Pound became the hireling of Roman Fascism, therefore, gave me malicious glee. That Eliot found what I thought his needlessly lost soul in the socially powerful but intellectually negligible Anglican Church did nothing to incline me to take his verse more seriously. He remains mostly outside my range of wave-lengths, except for his occasionally super-hetero-dyne echoes of the masters. Perhaps the job I accidentally dropped into, of building new towns, (and, incidentally, of collecting the rents of people battling with older and more perpetual problems), exempted me both from the sense of futility of the twenties and thirties and from the futile reactions against that futility. At any rate I am now disposed (maybe this is becoming my King Charles' Head) to be as scornful of the urban oscillations, aesthetic and intellectual, as I find what is left of my old Bloomsbury world is of me.

At the time of writing it is twelve days since the Allied landing in France, and a few days after we have become acquainted with the signature tune of the pilotless planes, which hit the headlines as a novelty rather than as a scare. The revolution in policy implied in the White Paper on Employment Policy has not therefore yet produced its full effect on opinion. With long hours of work and Civil Defence vigils at night, people are slow to get into complicated subjects, though there are thousands of study circles. Our own attempted revolution in physical planning policy suffers not so much by lack of current interest as by the neglect of the subject in the inter-war period. The Departments are moving so very slowly in our direction that the chances are that temporary housing will restart on the old lines, before the far-reaching implications of the Barlow Report are sufficiently widely under-stood and accepted to produce the necessary administrative machinery and legislation. Full employment and social security have the discussions and passions of a generation to influence policy; town and country arrangement the mere arguments of an intelligent minority. I am getting tired of stating and restating my ideas in articles, lectures and memoranda, and beginning to wonder whether I would not have better spent my limited time and energy on one well-documented book. But I haven't the apparatus or the capacity for things like *The Condition of Man* or *The Culture of Cities*. Yet I doubt if, in these days, it is effective to go to war with my primitive arma-ments. All the more do I value your formidable intervention.

WELWYN GARDEN CITY   11 July 1944

Dear Mumford
Your letter of the 11th reached me late in June. Since then all my available time has been taken up with memoranda and articles on the Government

Town Planning policy, which has begun to crystallise after years of shaking test-tubes. There is a Bill giving city authorities powers to buy up 'blitzed' and 'blighted' areas, a cumbrous affair but showing a movement of thought in the right direction. There is at last a formal acceptance of the main ideas of the Barlow Report for decentralisation of the congested cities—but in rather equivocal terms, and springing from their concern for unemployment in industrially declining regions rather than from the need of living-space in the big cities. The government have decided (this is a revolution in policy) that they will in future influence the location of industry. Lastly, the Government has produced a watered-down version of the Uthwatt proposals[1] for land-value compensation and betterment under national planning; this concedes the Uthwatt analysis of the problem, argues that the Uthwatt solution is technically impracticable, and makes weak proposals which are just as difficult. But I am reluctant to accept a solution that won't do the trick. In such a case I feel the thing to do is to go on ruthlessly expounding the necessities of the case, in the hope that the compromise, when it comes, will be nearer what is needed than it would be if we accepted the first thing offered.

I like your draft of your introduction to Howard's book. I have not yet written mine—but it is the next job. I am perhaps a bit handicapped by having lived at too close quarters with Howard in his later years, while not having known him during the first fourteen years of his campaign. I am inclined to rate Unwin's part in the garden city movement higher than you do—in fact to doubt if it would have got far without him. Howard believed in the family house and garden, but he had not a measuring mind, and when he wrote his book his calculations were a bit primitive. Actually his housing density was not 130 (as your letter says, but I don't think means) but sixteen per acre, including access roads. Having lately gone very thoroughly into the whole question of an acceptable housing density, I find considerable scientific validity in Unwin's twelve per acre, which was based on a coincidence of a lot of factors. In Welwyn Garden City our average density has fallen much below twelve, and tends to fall further. Indeed, I find that the maximum compression possible in the long run, taking full account of the existing set-up of big-city industries and population, is about twenty families per acre (including as large a proportion of multi-storey buildings as will be permanently acceptable). If you go above that density, the suburban trend will continue. It's a long story to demonstrate this; but I am very sure of it now. Unwin, as a working architect actually carrying out schemes, arrived

---

[1] *Report of the Expert Committee on Compensation and Betterment*, London, 1942. Chairman Mr Justice Uthwatt.

at conclusions substantially in agreement with mine as an estate developer. I think at one time he did not fight hard enough against the suburban solution, but he always saw it was wrong, as Howard did.

Howard always supported my efforts to turn decentralisation into a national policy. But his mind didn't really run that way, as I showed in my introduction to the 1942 *New Towns*. He believed, more than I did, in the power of cooperative initiative and example. I suppose I have always really felt that the centripetal tendencies of industry and population were too strong to be countered by voluntary effort. The truth may lie in between. If Howard and Unwin had succeeded (as they did not) in setting a fashion of thought among industrialists and in the political movements, more might have been done by private initiative. I think after this war, fashion and the policy of governments will be set in the same direction. It would always be difficult for national policy in a liberal democracy to work against private fashion. But private fashion in this case needs national policy before it can be fully effective.

I did not know you had a son in the army, but can understand how much your thoughts must be with him. He is very young to be on foreign service. Neither of our two children is in the fighting services. Our son is in the last year of the medical course, and expecting soon to be called on for work in a casualty unit, which is being used as a form of last-year hospital training; and our daughter (21) is in the Ministry of Information. Both are in London during the day, but now come down here at nights to be a bit out of the centre of the 'doodle-bug' attacks, of which Churchill's speech will have given you a fair measure. We are all a bit under fire in Southern England, but seeing and hearing our thousands of bombers going out day and night we know just enough of what their activities mean to realise how fortunate this country has been compared with France (and Germany).

AMENIA, NEW YORK   29 August 1944

Dear Osborn

I am writing you with a great feeling of tardiness and guilt, since your letters of June 19 and July 11 should have been answered long ago; and doubtless they would have been, had I not wanted to accompany my note with the promised Howard Introduction. That Introduction is at last written; and it will go forth to you just as soon as my wife finds it possible to transcribe it into typewriting that the printer can read: meanwhile accept my apologies for the inertia which has dogged me ever since I finished *The Condition of Man* and *it* finished me. This American introduction is unconscionably long, as it turns out, not because I have dwelt very long on the American application of his contribution, but because I wanted to straighten out certain misconceptions of Howard's work I find on both sides of the water. Doubtless you have been doing the latter in your Introduction, too; so I herewith give you permission to cut out any part of mine that you are disposed to. You will note that part of my fire is directed against the *Architectural Review* crowd, though I don't mention them by name: they have, of course, their equivalents in this country. What you say about Unwin's contribution is just; and I think you'll find that I make that plain enough in my Introduction. But if Howard never followed his own advice of going on from the first experiment to broad legislation, Unwin's use of his strategic position to make twelve to the acre a substitute for real decentralisation was a serious weakness, though of course he did it with the best of intentions.

I have made very clear where I stand on the issue of open versus closed planning; and you will find that I have reached almost exactly your conclusions, though I haven't all of your experience to justify them. I stuck entirely to Howard's ideas themselves and didn't deal at all with the modification of them that took place, naturally, in building Letchworth and Welwyn, partly because this was particularly up your alley, and partly because I didn't like to say anything about two towns I had last seen in 1932.

The meagreness of my current English background accounts for the unconscionable length of time I have taken in doing my critique of the London Plan for the *Architectural Review*. I brooded over that all spring; then I reached back into all my memories and read a number of collateral books about England and London; then I went back to Abercrombie's text and combed through it carefully; then I brooded some more. The results of all this incubation will undoubtedly fill the editors of the *Architectural Review* with consternation and horror; for, though it has still be to decently typewritten, it comes to some 12,000 words; and I should not blame them for throwing it out the window, even apart from the fact that they will want to take issue with me on all my leading ideas. Mine is perhaps an even more damning criticism of Abercrombie's work on London than you have made: though I go to great pains to appreciate his many fruitful suggestions and proposals. My main criticism is on a line that none of us has developed sufficiently: the relation of planning to population and in particular to births. And one of the worst oversights in *The Culture of Cities* was my failure to say anything about this. At that time I welcomed the approaching stabilisation of population, if only because it would give the lie to people who predicted the endless expansion of the great metropolises, but what I should have pointed out—and what I do with some impressiveness, I hope, in my criticism of the London Plan—is that the big city not merely devours population, but, because of its essential animus, prevents new babies from coming into the world. Accordingly, the one extravagance England cannot afford after the war is repopulating its big cities at anything like the pre-war standards. The main lines of this argument are simple, but the demonstration is somewhat complicated; for although there is plainly a relationship between the size of a city and the number of births per thousand, a mere reduction in the unit cannot be counted upon to have a salutary effect. Hence the need to put the case for the small city, and for decentralising London into small cities, with a certain amount of circumspection.

Your June letter throws up all sorts of interesting points about our respective backgrounds; but I think you are inclined to exaggerate the differences between them, for I am an atypical member of my generation, having reached a precocious sort of maturity before 1918. I left the Navy, where I had been trained as a radio operator, to become editor of the fortnightly *Dial* in 1919, when I was 23, and therefore did not participate so heartily in either the illusions or the disillusions of my contemporaries. I, too, had grown up on Shaw and Wells, which is why I find the living corpse of the first even more repulsive than the repetitious mummy of the second: through Graham Wallas[1] I touch the Fabian Society directly, and if I lived in Pimlico in 1920 and in Bloomsbury in 1922, I didn't absorb their intellectual atmosphere or follow their fashions. My judgement of Picasso was a sober one; but it is more devastating to his admirers than almost anything else I said; for it implies that, with all his natural gifts, his main significance for the future will be as a symptom, a symptom of our corruption from one who made it visible. My relations with old Geddes were never intimate; he was too old and I was too young for there to be any real partnership between me and that old Bull of the Herd, until he had died; but he turned my mind into fruitful channels and made me ready to bridge the gap between city and country, though I moved out here later in my life than you did. I wish now I had made the break five years earlier than I did, so that my boy would never have had to endure the misery of journeying long distances to school in the city, as he did. But unfortunately, Amenia is no Welwyn or Letchworth; and though its farms are fairly prosperous, I lack the stimulus that a garden city would give. But I have learned much from the country and when I come to re-write *The Culture of Cities* it will, I trust, have a sounder rural bottom than the original book did. For years I was tied to New York because I depended upon magazine writing to support me; and unless editors saw my face often they tended to forget me. I am just now at

---

[1] Sociologist, contributor to the seminal *Fabian Essays*, London, 1889.

the point where I can stay away from the city without its affecting my income; but I still have to solve the problem of finding a good environment for both my family and for my daily work. I have rambled along about these matters to show you, I suppose, how natural it is for us to be so close together in our thinking: a fact I appreciate, not only from your letters, but from the series of admirable articles of yours which I have been diligently studying the last couple of months. I have said hardly anything on the London Plan that you didn't say better in a number of other articles, and not least in your *Planning of Greater London*[1]: a *great* job!

As night by night the war news improves on the continent, I am tempted to exult; but the edge is taken off one's joy by the devilment you continue to suffer from the doodlebugs. It will take generations, I fear, to remove that gangster mentality in the Germans. Except for his historic excursions into Germany's dim past, I find myself pretty much on the side of Vansittart,[2] and very fearful lest people will again be more tender of the Germans than of the peoples they have tried to mutilate and exterminate. My son is now fighting in Italy: he spent his nineteenth birthday dodging machine-gun bullets. Though his usual letters are as laconic as Caesar's *Commentaries*, I finally got him to describe his six days of combat in an 'ordinary' battle: a grim account that brought the war very close to home indeed.

WELWYN GARDEN CITY   6 October 1944

Dear Mumford

I had to go away for a fortnight to shake off the effects of overwork; hence I am only now acknowledging your Howard preface which I received just before going away. And now I also have your long and most interesting letter of August 29th.

On the whole I agree with your assessment of Unwin. But the present revival of the housing-versus-planning dilemma does remind me of the enormous power of the suburban trend; and while I made the same criticism of Unwin (and of the whole leadership of the Garden City movement) in the 1920's, I doubt whether, in the then state of opinion, anybody could have stemmed the tide. I have made a bit of an effort since 1938, when I gave some scientific-looking evidence to the Barlow Royal Commission, and an impression has been made on responsible opinion here; but I doubt if this would have been possible had it not been for the Barlow Report itself

---

[1] London, 1938, with Preface by Raymond Unwin.
[2] Lord Vansittart of Denham, diplomat, who advocated stringent post-war measures against Germany.

(published Jan. 1940) and the coincidence that the big air-raids occurred in 1940–41, making people planning-conscious for the first time. Barlow tells me that he accepted the thesis of the Association, and added to it the idea of regional diversification of industry, which we did not much develop in our Evidence. Even now the public is vague on the subject, and the pressure is for houses, houses, anywhere, so long as they are built quickly. Unwin was swept away by the suburban flood, like all the other architects; but he alone of them knew it, and kept up a bit of a protest. He got no support from anybody, except Purdom[1]—whom nobody could work with for long—and myself. And I did next to nothing, after writing *New Towns After the War*, till about 1936 when Welwyn had been safely established. Still, your criticism stands; Unwin was always regarded as a bit 'long-haired'; his analysis did not keep pace with economic and sociological thought; and he was not thought much of by business men, any more than Howard was.

I have read most of *The Condition of Man*, and admire it greatly, but I still feel incompetent to evaluate it. It certainly causes *me* to examine my own presuppositions. I suppose I had better wait for the English edition before attempting a review; I hope it won't be too long delayed.

While in Scotland I met Mears, the Farquharsons, and Patrick Geddes' geographical son, who is working for the Scottish Government on a scheme for National Parks in the Highlands. I raised again the question of a reissue of *Cities in Evolution*[2] but they are all undecided about it. Some editing is certainly needed in that case, and a new set of illustrations. But if the work were well done, and someone wrote a lively new introduction, I should think there is a public for the book in Britain and America. I regret not having met Geddes; indeed I only heard him once, when he visited a school in Welwyn Garden City and gave a rambling, untidy, yet stimulating lecture. Very much the sort of lecture that Mears still gives; or so it seems to me in a rather vague recollection.

One odd thing about the situation here is that I, a lifelong, almost instinctive anti-clerical, find myself in alliance with the Anglican Bishops. Partly, I think, as the result of my own work, the Church here (which has influence far in excess of the numbers of its congregations), has clearly seen and stated the connection between housing-planning and family idealism; and it is a most valuable ally. It is all the more odd because there is no real chance of a revival of large-scale church-going. But people who don't accept the theology of the Church, and have no intention of deserting the prevailing

[1] C. B. Purdom, who played important part in the development of Letchworth and Welwyn Garden City. Author of *The Building of Satellite Towns*, London, 1925, 1949.
[2] Sir Patrick Geddes, *Cities in Evolution*, London, 1915.

agnosticism, do somehow accept the Bishops as guides in this sort of issue. And just now, for reasons difficult to explain, the Bishops are intelligent and wise. Both the Archbishops are strong supporters of our decentralisation policy.

My wife (to whom I showed your letter) is as much touched as I am by what you say about your boy's fighting experiences. He is really too young to be in the front line, and it must be a source of constant anxiety to you both. At the moment we are reacting from the wave of optimism as to the speedy end of the war caused by the collapse of the Germans in France. It was not unfounded. But it now looks possible that something like a Western Front is being stabilised. The Arnhem episode caused much grief here— coming as it did at a time when it seemed that everything was going with electric speed and certainty. But pauses are in the regular rhythm of this war; and the liberation of France and Belgium by this date is more than we dared to hope for in June.

I hope you are feeling well again. I am in a bad patch at the moment, and a bit deterred by the mountains of work ahead. But I feel the effort of the last four years has not been wasted. The real planning issues are at last being discussed seriously, and one has to realise the genuine difficulties and to be patient.

WELWYN GARDEN CITY   25 October 1944

Dear Mumford

I have received your article on *The Plan of London*,[1] and if I can arrange for its publication in booklet form I would like to accept your offer of it. I told Abercrombie I was thinking of this, and that your review is pretty critical of the Plan; and though he said little at the time I sensed that he was not exactly delighted; he has since written me sending a copy of his review of *Culture of Cities* in the *Manchester Guardian*, which I did not see at the time, and which he now thinks was unfair. (I agree with him about this). In spirit and principle I feel very close to Abercrombie; he is the only planner of standing in England who has a reasonable grip on both the socio-logical and technical elements in planning, and I don't want to discourage him or lose such influence on him as I have. He is reasonably tough and reasonably understanding, however, and he took very well my severe criticism of the London Plan, while the LCC leaders opened a violent personal attack on me as a misleader of the Association as well as a poisonous anti-planning

---

[1] Published as *The Plan of London County*, London, 1945, reprinted in *City Development*, New York, London, 1945, 1946.

reactionary. This rocked the boat for a few weeks, but of course I kept the course and the attack quickly petered out.

It was a great help to me that Abercrombie wouldn't yield to pressure on him to resign his Vice-Presidency of the Association; the issue was not fundamental enough for that, he rightly said. A working planner must compromise to some extent with the authority for whom he plans. I was very disappointed in this case, because it was the first big plan of this period and was advisory (not a statutory plan), and therefore I thought Abercrombie should have run the flag to top-mast—or at least nearly to top-mast, not two-thirds down. Because he really agrees with me, though he can't admit it even to me, and because I don't accuse him of anything worse than making the best compromise he thought he could, after fighting for better things, we have maintained cordial relationships.

I tell you all this because I may find it desirable to preface the booklet by a short note supporting its thesis, but hinting at the reason why a planner like Abercrombie takes a half-way course. The real reason is that so few people understand and back up the planning principles he would like to apply. In other words, the current state of public opinion must affect current plans. I am not yet sure I shall strike this note. But if I do, you will realise that I must do all I can to maintain intellectual unity among the few advanced planners, and to maintain their credit with the public: because our battle with the philistines is by no means won.

AMENIA, NEW YORK   11 November 1944

Dear Osborn

What you say about Abercrombie disturbs me in one particular only; and that is that he should have the impression that my unfavourable criticism of *The Plan of London* is connected in any way with anything he may have written or spoken about *The Culture of Cities*. The one and only time I ever subscribed to a British clipping service was to get reviews of my *Herman Melville*[1] in 1929 or 30; but for some strange reason, which I still can't fathom, that book was utterly ignored in England, the one place where I should have thought it would have a royal reception, since the English kept Melville's name alive when it was forgotten in America. Since then I have never tempted fate by trying to get hold of the British reviews; though occasionally one or another may drift my way. I have learned a lot from some of my bitterest critics, perhaps from them particularly; so I shall not

---

[1] New York, London, 1929.

hesitate now to look up Abercrombie's review at the first opportunity. For no matter what he may have said, it will not change my opinion of his work as a whole, and that is that he is the most intelligent and the most capable, in all ways the most fruitful of planners—if one leaves out of account the older generation of Parker, Unwin, and Schumacher of Hamburg.

I share your admiration of him, and none of my praise, either in the introduction or elsewhere, was perfunctory or meant in a Pickwickian sense. Though there are various technical matters on which, there being more than one possible solution, I might differ from him, I deliberately eliminated most of these points from the discussion, not merely because his own judgement might be better than mine, but because they were relatively unimportant. (One passage, on the possibility of roofing over part of the goods yards of the railroads, to serve as landing fields for helicopters and to canalise that form of traffic to keep it from being an infernal nuisance, I may restore in my American version of the article because I want to press the point on my American colleagues.) But my criticism, you will note, is far less of his detailed proposals than of his major assumptions: not of his technical skill but of his urban statesmanship. There I think he succumbed too easily to the short-sighted views of his clients, the LCC, who, because of their very 'enlightened' and 'socialised' policies, have been far too uncritical of their own assumptions and the results that have flowed from them.

But above all, dear Osborn, please assure Abercrombie of my complete innocence of his views about myself or about *The Culture of Cities* when he wrote his report. My bias was entirely in his favour: indeed, was I not the one American, though nameless, whom he quoted in his report, and did I not even see the effects of some of my own thinking, well-digested but still visible to my partial eye, in other parts of his work? These very facts made it difficult for me to trust my own judgement when I found myself opposed to him, and it accounts for the unconscionably long time I took in getting to the bottom of the matter. . . .

And please don't apologise for the kind of review you may do of the book: I shall be honoured and flattered to have any review at all from a man whose opinions I respect as much as I do yours. If the book doesn't carry most of its own evidence with it, I have partly failed, and you should say so. But I hope that volume IV, if I live to write it, will clinch the argument; though it may be two or three years more before I shall have it finished. Volume III is purgatory; volume IV will be what is left of Heaven! I am in the same predicament as you are, and most intelligent men are, with regards to the Church: I accept the wisdom that survives there, but not the worm eaten supports, which the clergy seem to value often more than the living plant. Some of them have jumped to the conclusion that I am more in their camp than I actually am; but *The Condition of Man* should have rectified that too benign error!

We were grateful for you and your wife's words about our son; but they came just a few days before we learned that he was killed in action on 13 September. Merely by living in England you doubtless have a more intimate sense of death and grief than we in America, no matter how keen and willing our imaginations, can have, until death actually visits our household: then one finds out how sluggish the imagination was, and how the loss of a dear son is not just a loss but an amputation, which will leave the nerve endings exposed to the end of our lives, long after the visible bleeding has stopped. He went into action with a good heart; fortunately, he was more mature than lads of his age usually are, for both the mischances of life and his own education had toughened him, and what life had begun his work in the army completed; for the letters he wrote after being in combat showed that, faced daily with death, he had learned some of the best lessons about comradeship and love that life offers any of us. A month before his death he had gotten transferred from a communications company to a line company, where he was first scout: the solitary human tentacle thrust forth in every advance. He felt that his luck had changed for the better then; his whole life had prepared him for just that job: his life as a hunter, a trapper, a solitary roamer of these woods and fields. We do not yet know how he met his end; may never know; but I am sure he gave a good account of himself; and we who remain can only hope to live up to his example, and the example of the thousands upon thousands like him. Death may do something to the spirit of my country that success and prosperity could not do: the results of the last election, sweeping away the isolationists, seems to indicate that the lesson of the dead and the maimed will not, this time, be wholly lost.

WELWYN GARDEN CITY 30 November 1944

Dear Mumford

My wife and I are deeply shocked and distressed to hear of your loss, which by reason of the intellectual and moral sympathy we feel with you, comes to us as a personal one. We ask ourselves how we could possibly stand up to such an event in our own lives, and we really don't know the answer. Philosophically I tell myself, and I think I believe, that a vivid and happy life is its own justification and completion, no matter how long it lasts; but the death of the young fits into no acceptable pattern, and I can think of nothing consolatory to say to a mourning parent. One's helpless instinct is to demonstrate, if one can, a sharing of the grief, knowing all the time that the sincerest, sympathetic feeling is an ephemeral thing beside the personal loss that remains with those who suffer it.

It may surprise you that even here the war can seem remote, and that we have to stimulate our imaginative realisation of what the men in the fighting forces are going through. It is true we have lived for years under sporadic air bombardment, and at times with a sense of very imminent peril—when perhaps the whole sky over us has been lighted with flares, the air filled with the drone of hostile bombers, shells bursting high over our garden trees, and bombs exploding near by. Again and again I have stood in my garden, or by my ARP[1] post, and watched the terrific exchange of lethal power. Even to-day we get occasional warnings and hear V1's go over and see the flashes and hear the bangs; and this brings back something of the initial perturbation of 1940–41. But though frequently we hear of friends being killed or injured—it seems as often at home as abroad—and though we know a V2 may descend without warning at any time in this part of England, we have learned to discount the minute mathematical probability that such things will happen to us individually. Above all we have our comfortable beds and heating and a routine that is arduous but rarely unpleasant. We do not feel in the battle line at all for the greater part of the time. And although many have lost their homes, and one third of our houses have been damaged, the less imaginative of us, here no less than on your side, sometimes get tired of war news and cease to be preoccupied with the hardships and greater dangers of the men in the air and in the line. Such is human nature. It is well that animal optimism rides above imagination and balanced vision, and even recent experience of calamity. Yet one fights against the complacency into which it so easily develops. News like yours comes, by some queer trick of the mind, almost as a rebuke to us for remaining unscathed in these tragic times.

Coming to our projects. I have at last drafted my Editorial Foreword to Howard's book, and I am sending it to you for your frank comments. It is as long as your Introduction, which I want to include (if the publishers agree) in the English edition, and though a little of the content perhaps overlaps, my presentation is so entirely different that, apart from the propriety of two prefaces, I think they can live together in the same book. As to the propriety, I intend to be somewhat guided by Faber as to what we should call the two essays—whether they should both precede Howard's text, or whether one should go in as a Postscript. My present thought is that the English edition should be described as 'edited with a foreword' by me, and that my foreword should be immediately followed by your introduction.

---

[1] Air Raid Protection.

Whether you want my essay in the American edition is a matter on which guidance may come from the American publisher; I hope it may be of sufficient interest but shan't be hurt if it isn't thought appropriate.

AMENIA, NEW YORK   13 December 1944

Dear Osborn
Your letter of 30 November has just come, and I want you both to know how deeply my wife and I are touched by your sympathy. Our son's death has, in a way we could not anticipate, shaken our lives to their very foundations: a private day of judgement, even as the war is in so many ways a public day of judgement on the lives of the nations and on the values by which they have lived.

Your emendations to my Howard Introduction are more than welcome: I not merely accept them but am incorporating them in the shorter version *Pencil Points* will publish in February or March. Please refer to me as *Mr* not Professor. The latter title covers but a year of my life; and if anything, I am an *Anti*-professor in all my ways and works. In the old Germany one used to get better hotel accommodations at low rates if one bore the title of Professor: but that Germany is hardly even a memory now and I can't think of any other reason for sporting the title.

WELWYN GARDEN CITY   13 December 1944

Dear Mumford
. . . Your response to my vague hint of a visit to America is encouraging. At present it is only a wish or a background thought; I doubt if what I stand for is well enough known on your side for an invitation to emerge naturally; though I have no doubt of the advantage to myself, or indeed of the mutual value of an exchange of ideas and experience, if I could meet the right groups. I couldn't in any case come before the summer of 1945, and I don't want to be away when you are over here. But I would be glad of any advice. Barlow, Scott, Uthwatt and others would certainly give me credentials as an 'influence'.

We have just had a Conference, mainly of local authorities, on 'Decongestion and Overspill' Planning which is now the fashion as a result of the TCPA campaign. Many cities are at last preparing long-term plans for reducing density down to a tolerable level, and studying how to relocate the 'overspill' in country towns and new towns rather than in suburbs. That involves relocation of industry. The Government have accepted control of location of industry, but the Department to administer that control is to be the Board of Trade, which so far is only concerned with getting industries to the pre-war 'depressed' areas with a view to forestalling regional unemployment. Legislation is due on this control fairly soon, and our next battle is to get the terms of reference widened out to include priorities for industrial development in garden cities and country towns in prosperous as well as unprosperous regions, and to get the Board of Trade to exercise its locational influence within a pattern laid down in principle by the Ministry of Town and Country Planning.

I think our prospects of success are good, in view of the fact that 'dispersal' planning has become the 'only wear'. But the Board of Trade is an obstinate body, and senior in prestige to the Ministry of Town and Country Planning. And there are many cross-currents to be watched; one of which is that popular opinion is still much more alert on quantitative housing than on planning, and a big push on housing suits the Government's Full Employment policy, and is relatively easy. Our warnings about the dangers of continuing old forms of city development can be, and are, represented as academic frills that may delay rebuilding. The areas of potential unemployment are, as a result of the bitter experiences of the inter-war period, very strong in Parliament. Some of the big cities (unwisely, I think) are still backpedalling on dispersal and loss of rateable value. So we have only the smaller towns as a definite political force to back up the growing instructed opinion in favour of national planning, plus a few enlightened big towns who see they must 'disperse' or decay.

The smaller towns are fairly strong in Parliament, being represented by County members who are mostly Tories; but municipally they are disheartened and weak; we have been trying to organise them through our Country Towns Committee, which is certainly creating an impression. Till recently we could make no headway with the County members as they were organised by the 'Save the Countryside' (Aesthetic Preservationist) planners, who were in tacit alliance with the Architectural Planners. These contended that you could rehouse town populations where they are, in multi-story flats, and thus conserve England's precious agricultural land. As our campaign has developed, however, it has become clearer to the countryside people: (a) that the flight from congestion can't be stopped and had better be canalised as we have argued; and (b) that a countryside starved of secondary industry and gradually declining in population through advances in agricultural mechanisation is not really being 'preserved'. So there has been a consolidation of all the planning forces on our policy, and the architects have changed their note.

The Preservationists, however, have their value for us. For they are really the strongest Tory core of the demand for Compensation-Betterment legislation. They want to preserve green belts from ribbon development and sprawl, and they also want the owners to be compensated for their development rights. Hence the interest in Uthwatt. I have to keep reminding everybody that there is also a Compensation problem in lowering city density— my view being that your and Howard's strategy of drawing off the pressure and letting central land values decline would produce a political opposition to the whole dispersal policy and a determined effort to continue city development at high density, which is practicable for a limited period.

I agree with you that we probably can't in practice, and ought not to, compensate fully for inflated central values. But in this country it is best to go as far as we can in compensation. It won't be *politically* practicable unless we also collect betterment on increased values elsewhere—with our taxation system it won't really matter if the Compensation-Betterment doesn't balance (as it won't); but to get planning accepted here by both the Right and the Left you have to compensate reasonably, and you have to make some effort to collect Betterment. I still remain of opinion that the Landowners made a mistake in not embracing Uthwatt as their saviour. The new pattern of planning is getting accepted, and if there is no settlement of the Compensation and Betterment issue, relocation of industry (by licensing and restriction) will in fact reduce urban values without much Compensation. I have always been in favour of a square deal with established interests; but I am not going to put myself out to save them from their folly, based on a rather crude selfishness. I don't know how the battle about Comp. and Bett. is going behind the scenes, but it is an interesting situation, and the position of land-owners is not getting stronger.

WELWYN GARDEN CITY   20 December 1944

Dear Mumford
Abercrombie's *Greater London Plan*[1] has now been circulated to authorities and reviewed in the press, but will not be available to the public for three or four months. It is a far better statement of the problem than the LCC Plan, and he has gone a little way to meet our criticism by giving alternative decentralisation figures if the LCC density is reduced to 100 instead of 136. Also he proposes eight or ten new towns twenty to thirty miles out, designates a lot of small towns in the outer areas for expansion, severely limits further

---

[1] London, 1944.

suburban growth, and studies methods of industrial decentralisation and community development. I am supporting the Plan, while maintaining the criticism of the redevelopment density proposed. It is so great an advance on any other big regional plan that one must be enthusiastic about its general pattern. I hope copies are getting over to America for those specially studying the problem; and I presume you will have seen a summary already. I will refer to it in my introduction to your booklet.

AMENIA, NEW YORK   30 December 1944

Dear Osborn

I don't know how, even in a short note, I could have forgotten to mention with how much pleasure and profit I read your Introduction to Howard. Among other things, I hadn't known that he was an inventor or that he had made so many trips to America in the early days—the only time I met him was on his last trip over here in 1925 to attend the International Town Planning Congress, in which I had a hand. Morley, of Harcourt Brace, relies on me for advice about matters like this book; and you may be sure that I would insist on your introduction remaining in the American edition if there were any question about it. Don't bother about the matter of re-numeration for my very small contribution; its publication in *Pencil Points* independently well pays me for the time I spent on it. I hope I made myself equally clear about the criticism of *The Plan of London*: in that case, my only compensation will be indirectly through the sale of *City Development*[1] in both countries: actually, since I was 'resting' at the time I prepared myself to write it, I spent far more time on it than the most extravagant of American magazines would have paid me for it; in other words, it was a labour of love; and at the present strained moment in international relations in general, love is perhaps the only valuable thing one can contribute to the easing of our difficulties.

What you tell me about the present planning situation, with the possibility of getting the Tory preservationists on your side, seems to me genuinely hopeful; and I trust that Abercrombie, in his advance from the County to the Greater London plan, will think of my criticism of the first as giving further backing to his improvements in the second. I have taken the outsider's privilege of being more intransigent in my proposals than those who are immersed in the practical details and personal alliances that are necessary toward getting any programme fulfilled, would be justified in being: the better to clear the air of clouds and false hopes.

---

[1] New York, London, 1945, 1946.

I have not written you about general political matters for a long time, but this is not to say that I have not been greatly exercised over them; for the mistakes both our countries have made, alike in military strategy—the failure to cross the Channel in 1943—and in political planning, are now coming home to roost in the form of sheer war weariness, which you as a people legitimately suffer from, and in a failure to hold together along the lines of common principles and common policies. Our President's Eliza-on-the-ice-floe policy, of jumping from expedient to expedient, offering the worst of precedents in his Petain–Darlan misalliance, has now brought its own terrible retribution; and if we should be weak enough and stupid enough to fall apart now, our enemies will win the peace once more, even if they lose the immediate military decision. The end of that will be the wholesale disintegration of our civilisation, in which we will all go down together, because we had not enough discipline at the critical moment to work the ship together, and not enough sailing ability to read a plain chart and head for a commonly agreed destination. If ever there was a grand opportunity to make use of the goodwill and determination of the people of the United States to achieve a durable structure of peace, that time is the present moment.

Churchill's Tory Imperialism is almost as short-sighted as Chamberlain's appeasement of Hitler, in that it seeks to secure an insignificant and meaningless gain—the lifeline of the Empire—which will be worthless if we withdraw our interest from Europe, at the expense of a really major measure of security: American participation in a plan of world cooperation. Churchill's greatness when defeat threatened the world is matched only by the pettiness of his conceptions at the moment when our very victory is near enough to be postponed indefinitely or be nullified by a critical error. If a new understanding is not forged between our countries in the face of this threat, it will be a dark day for all of us. Forgive me, dear Osborn, if I address you as if you were a public audience.

WELWYN GARDEN CITY   2 January 1945

Dear Mumford

During the Christmas holiday I have at last been able to complete the work of editing Howard's book, and the material should go to the publishers this week. I do not think you will object to the very slight revisions I have made in your essay, but I mention them so that you can challenge them if I have overstepped the discretion you gave me.

I have deleted your reference to Garden City, Long Island, because Howard always said that he did not know of that use of the term when he chose it himself (see on this Unwin's chapter in *Town Theory and Practice*, edited Purdom, 1921; Howard also told me he hadn't heard of the Long Island scheme when he wrote his book). He may have heard the name and forgotten it, of course. See my note on definitions, which I propose to add to my Preface. . . .

I enclose a copy of the proposed Select Bibliography. I have avoided all books prior to 1898. Of the immense literature directly or indirectly inspired by the Garden City movement, I have included only those which have made important and surviving contributions to the elucidation, development and working-out of the essential Garden City idea, or are most typical of a class. I don't want to expand the list much, but will be glad of suggestions from you, especially of American and foreign books which have made a substantial contribution, not to urban study or town planning as such, but to the Garden City line of thought. I think you will approve this limitation.

I propose to put on the title-page 'Edited with a Preface by F. J. Osborn. Introductory Essay by Lewis Mumford.' I have titled your essay: 'The Garden City Idea and Modern Planning.' This could be altered if you don't like it.

I have revised the index, working into it references to all the names and the main topics in your introductory essay and my preface. I have slightly amended my preface, merely to clarify some of the more congested passages and to meet suggestions by Howard's family and some of the Old Guard of the Association.

WELWYN GARDEN CITY   13 February 1945

Dear Mumford

Your letters of 13, 29 and 30 December all arrived between 4 and 6 February. They catch me at a moment when I am struggling with uncompleted programmes in at least three fields of activity or sub-activity—planning politics, publications on planning, and preparing for the change-back from 100 per cent war production to peace-production in the industrial firm of which I am a director. I fear that by being inescapably embroiled in all these three things I don't do any of them as well as I would wish; and as to the arts and graces of living, they have disappeared from my ken. It is a relief that Civil Defence has been reduced almost to a token service; I am on duty every ninth night still, but remain in bed unless there is a siren warning; and it is an advantage of the V2 weapon that it only announces itself by explosions, which don't concern you unless they are near enough to do damage in your sector, whereas the V1 can be observed *en route* and causes people to be

called out over a wide area with only an off-chance that it will drop near
by! War-production, however, goes on at full intensity; peace production is
only in the paper stage, but is beginning to occupy the minds of manage-
ments still heavily engaged in immediate work also. So there is an intensi-
fication rather than a release of pressure, despite the demobilisation of much
of the Civil Defence force.

It must be inexplicable to you that it has taken me six months to read
The Condition of Man, which has been my companion on many train journeys,
which I have greatly enjoyed, and which fills me with admiration for the
scope of your learning and power of synthesis. I don't feel able to make a
valuation of your judgments of the key-personnel of Western history that
would be of the slightest use to you; but I still hope to send you some random
notes when I have more leisure. My review of the book should appear in the
Spring *Town and Country Planning* (in about two months' time), but it will
attempt no more than to interest planners in the book without revealing
the full extent of my own incompetence to review it. I shall not class you,
as a Sunday paper reviewer (who was otherwise very cordial) did, as a
Socinian heretic—not only because I don't gather that you are, but also
because my mind is a sieve that will not retain even the crudest notion of
what a Socinian is, even if I look up the animal in the Encyclopedia. This
to you must be a pitiful revelation, though as a philosopher you must have
reconciled yourself to the fact that it takes all sorts (including the vague
and woolly) to make a Western world.

The Howard book[1] is in the press, and I think proofs should be available
in another month; they will be sent to Harcourt Brace as soon as they are
corrected. I am glad you think that both the introductions should go in the
American edition, and I am grateful to you for waiving any question of
royalty on yours. As a by product of the work I did on the book I have
written (also for the next *T & CP*) a brief sketch of the history of the Country-
belt idea which may interest you;[2] it is very slight, and will tell you nothing
that is not familiar to you; but one of my purposes is to get young historians
to see that there is a field for research and assembly in this subject—physical
grouping having been much neglected in history in view of its profound
effects on political, economic and social thought and events. Another is to
get the planning circle, which is in the main opportunist and technical, to be
more interested in the historical background; by following one thin strand

---

[1] Ebenezer Howard, *Garden Cities of To-morrow*. Edited, with a Preface, by
F. J. Osborn. With an Introductory Essay by Lewis Mumford. London, New
York, 1945, 1965.

[2] 'The Country-Belt Principle: Its Historical Origins', *Town and Country Planning*,
Spring, 1945.

I make it easier for them to begin this interest. I hope this is a justification for what must seem to you nursery-school simplification; but in any case I don't know enough to present a fuller picture with any confidence.

Town Planning has gone off the front pages and Cabinet agendas with the passage of the Planning Act. The new Ministry shows no sign of taking definite steps towards the accepted dispersal policy. Some local authorities are trying to get together on the subject; but I fear they will find the difficulties too great without constant drive from the centre. Many authorities will go the old way, and I don't see the Ministry pulling them up. I feel our Association ought to be all over the country fanning the spark; but we haven't the people or the organisation to do it. So I feel a bit in the doldrums, and don't quite see how to get into the breeze again.

I don't habitually come to precise conclusions on international happenings as they happen, because I don't have to write about them. But I am a bit disturbed by your view that our leaders are losing the chance of Anglo-American cooperation for peace by relatively simple wrongnesses of policy or outlook. I didn't understand the US Petain–Darlan policy, but surely its motive was expediency on the military rather than the economic-political plane? And did it not in fact stall off the complete German control of French Africa and make our landings there easier? Churchill, I am pretty sure, has no interest in the political colour of the groups contending for power in other countries; his one idea (it may well be too simple an idea) is military victory at the earliest moment. But I think he is in agreement with every party that US cooperation with Britain is vital to us after the war; it is a universal and passionately held wish here. Such difference of opinion as there is in Britain on this matter, is between those who think we can count on whole-hearted American cooperation in a peace system, and those who think we cannot count on it. The doubt may be wrong, but you can't say it is without any foundation at all.

The truth is we suspect ourselves (rightly) of a tendency to facile optimism about the future; and just because we so passionately want to believe that America will in fact be wholehearted in the peace system, on a basis of principles rather than of narrow self-interest, we discipline ourselves to scepticism on the point, in order not again to enter a fool's paradise. It is a dangerous mood, because it can easily lead to the conviction that, weak as the British Commonwealth now relatively is, we have nothing better to rely on; whereas we ought to bank on a world-organisation of which the US and ourselves are a solid and united core. Great leadership is needed on both sides of the Atlantic to make that cooperation real. I am sorry to note your impression that Churchill seems to be backing the Imperial horse, and thereby weakening the American impulse to join in a world system. If so, there is a vicious circle at work. I am sure that British opinion is almost 100 per cent for the fullest cooperation with the U.S.A. The doubt is solely as to whether the U.S.A. will, when the war is over, see the necessity of it from your point of view as we saw it from ours. We must attach the first importance to U.S.A. cooperation, just because we cannot be sure what Russia's real policy will be. Everybody wants friendship with Russia, but we can't get clear evidence as to what Russia wants, and this is a perpetual worry, which may or may not be cleared up a little later.

AMENIA, NEW YORK   19 February 1945

Dear Osborn

I can hardly believe that I haven't yet answered your letter of 2 January; though when I recollect the state the Mumford family has been in the last six weeks, with a succession of illnesses that has knocked us down like the proverbial row of ten pins, I can partly account for my dilatoriness. By all reports this has been a severe winter throughout the world; the sub-zero weather here has been prolonged and the snow by now has heaped up by the roadside higher than one's head; and if we, who are well fed, have staggered under it, it doesn't require much imagination to picture how you have fared in England and on the Continent. We have been so isolated here this winter, for days and weeks at a time, that for our own mental health we have decided to move to *Hanover, New Hampshire*, the seat of Dartmouth College, where I used to be a visiting lecturer, since we have many good friends there. We will be there only for the next three months; and since all our plans have gone astray this year and this one may, too, you had better continue to use the above address.

As for the Howard introduction, all your changes of course have my blessing. I particularly like your note on Definitions: it is needed. The definition of *Satellite Town* made me wonder whether the idea had taken on independently in England, or whether it owed its existence to a book Graham Taylor had written in 1915: *Satellite Cities*, though in that book the name refers only to the quasi-independent industrial suburbs of the big city. I have always been reluctant to use the term, because it seemed to convey the notion that the solar central city would remain unaltered, and that it would remain a controlling influence. But I have spent twenty years trying to find a better name for the Garden City and haven't succeeded. Your book list is excellent; and as I think I told you already, your preface on Howard and his work was very enlightening even to one who had followed him as closely as I had.

My own little book on *City Development* was ready for publication by
March; but the government suddenly commandeered all the paper destined
for the spring batch of Harcourt books, and as a result I won't be able to
send you a copy till April. I have been eager to find out what the English
reviewers would say about *The Condition of Man* and I was delighted to find
a long review in *The New Statesman*—only to discover that the writer was
a compatriot of mine, David Coyle; so I am still none the wiser. One of the
penalties of writing a long work in separate volumes, published at wide
intervals, is that by the time one reaches volume III the reviewers have forgotten, if they have even read, what was in volume I, and they reproach one
for leaving out of the third book something one has dealt at length with in
the first.

AMENIA, NEW YORK   18 March 1945

Dear Osborn
You don't know how pleased I am that your own plans for coming over
here are maturing, as your letter of 25 February told me yesterday. By now,
you probably know, any academic arrangements we could make would
probably have to be for next autumn—though if other invitations should
bring you over before that we might be able to squeeze in a few university
invitations at the last moment. I am herewith writing to Catherine Bauer's
husband, William Wurster, the dean of the School of Architecture and
Planning at the Massachusetts Institute of Technology, to whom I have
already tentatively broached the matter of your coming; and if he can make
any definite offer now he will probably write you directly. Once I have settled
with him I will write to my friends in Princeton and Yale.

Under separate cover I am sending you a reprint of the Howard Introduction, just to show you how *Pencil Points* played it up. The contrasting
photographs of the pallid Howard and the sardonic, saturnine Mumford
are merely funny; but the respectful treatment itself is a good sign and I
think it will clear the air. Unfortunately I had to cut the article down in
order to fit their space requirements, and the only part I could lift out of
the argument in a body was that on open planning. I regretted that; but
there was no other course. Incidentally, by one of those shifts in fashion
with which I don't sympathise the *typography* of Howard's diagrams awakens
a sympathetic echo in our bright young men: you will note how faithfully
the editor took them over.

I haven't received a comment from anyone on the *Architectural Review*
article, excluding of course yourself; and I am wondering whether the views
I set forth have become so commonplace that no one cares to dwell on them.

Except for calling me a Neo-Spenglerian[1] and herding the young away from me, the *Review* did itself proud. Never was an adjective more mischosen than that one: If I am not an anti-Spenglerian I am nothing. Unfortunately, most of the people who reject Spengler make the mistake of forgetting that his predictions of what would happen to Europe have proved dismayingly correct; and they make the further mistake of thinking that to acknowledge this is to become his disciple.

The flattering London *Times* review of *The Condition of Man* was as helpful to my ego as a timely bottle of Scotch: an American friend passed on the review to me, so I trust you didn't bother to get hold of a copy, though the impulse to do so was a very friendly one. If ever a writer had an opportunity to cash in on his reputation I suppose I have that chance now in England, precisely at a moment when my acceptance—I will not say my circulation—in the United States is at its lowest. Some of those Bloomsbury followers with whom you threaten me would doubtless be an embarrassment: or rather, I would be an embarrassment to them if I actually made my appearance: so if I want to keep my star above the horizon I had better, perhaps, remain at a distance.

Seriously, the problem of my coming to England this summer has become more, not less complicated, with time. By now I have spent a year in practical idleness, consuming the royalties that should have gone to my support whilst writing my next book; and my decision now has to be formed by compounding three uncertainties: the physical state of my heart, still erratic and 'tired', more as the result of mental anguish, I am sure, than because of any physiological disabilities; second, the state of my work, how much I can get done on my book before summer; and third, the state of my bank account.

In a few weeks I hope to have advance copies of *City Development*, postponed for a month because of a government raid upon our paper stock; and I'll send you off a copy as soon as it comes to hand. With a not altogether innocent intention, I have omitted my own foreword to the Social Foundations essay and have used only your own all-too-generous words. Rarely does an author get a chance to print a puff right in the middle of his book!

WELWYN GARDEN CITY   28 March 1945

Dear Mumford
Letters take a time just now: yours of 19th February got to me on 23rd March. I regret the record of the Mumford family health; may the move to Hanover put you all right! We had one longish spell of snow here but no

---

[1] Oswald Spengler, German Philosopher, author of *The Decline of the West*, English trans. 1926–28.

abnormal degree of cold, and the winter as a whole has not been a severe one. As I write the weather here is perfect—early June in March—and as in England the spring is the time for trees and gardens, it is hardly possible to imagine the external world behaving itself better anywhere than at this moment here. The thought of the Anglo-American advance over the Rhine puckers one's brows as one enjoys the immediate scheme; but as the weather also suits this distasteful yet necessary work of wholesale destruction, the sense of satisfaction is at the highest possible in these terrible times. I share your feeling that Whitman stands up to such situations. We are reminded several times daily of the non-dominance and non-permanence of the personal consciousness in the universe by the more or less distant 'plonks'of rockets and flying bombs, which shake our house but not our animal faith; we don't feel here (as we do when in central London) that these formidable intruders are searching particularly for us. A 9,999 to 1 expectation of life is our conviction of immortality.

Proofs of the Howard book are now expected in a week or two, and once they come I shall press on the remaining stages in order to get the material over to Harcourt Brace and yourself. I am now convinced that everything is set for a world-wide revival of interest in the 'Garden City' idea; and therefore the sooner the new edition of Howard is out the better. This time it will be taken as a proposal that must be seriously entertained, and I think the work we are doing in technical and academic circles precludes the confusion with garden suburbs that occurred last time.

Editing the book set me digging into my notes on the pre-history of Howard's ideas, and setting out what I knew of the after-history. Besides the short, and (by comparison with your sort of work) narrow, study of the country-belt idea which I am publishing in the Spring *T & CP*, I have written a very polemical but I think essentially sound analysis of the chaos of sectional planning enthusiasms of the 1920's and 30's, which I am delivering as an address to the Town Planning Institute on 5th April (The Garden City Idea: A Revaluation). It is fiercely critical of the muddled thinking and bad advocacy of 'planning writers'—few names are mentioned but everyone will know 'the individuals who happen to be meant'—and after the first heaving of rocks about I feel sure what I say will be accepted, though not admitted. Thirdly, I have written a very bare and factual account of what we did and learned in building the two garden cities—with reasonable candour about our failure or doubtful successes; though on the whole I think we made few that could have been avoided; and at the end of this some proposals for using the experience more widely. I propose now to put these three pieces of work in a book with some such title as 'Green-belted Cities: The British Experience'.

As to the term 'Satellite Towns'. What decides me to use it freely is that Abercrombie's Greater London Plan 1944, which is the first complete working-out of the Garden City idea for a Metropolitan Region, proposes eight or ten new towns with this name for the London Region, with no possibility of confusion with the Industrial-Suburb or Wythenshawe type. The history of the term is this. Taylor's book, *Satellite Cities*, was published here in 1919, but is practically unknown: so the fact that he meant the Pullman type (a continuation outward of cities of industrial suburbs) doesn't interfere with our use of the term here. Welwyn Garden City, 1919, advertised itself widely as 'a Satellite town for London'—very clearly defining itself as a true Garden City in Howard's sense, catering for industrial dispersal from a Metropolis and having some economic linkages therewith, but independent of London in the work-dwelling relationship, and socially. Abercrombie's adoption of it, because the Greater London Plan will carry very great authority, coupled with the violent attack I am making on imprecision in planning literature, will I think fix the meaning as much as any meaning can be fixed in this muddle-headed world. Whether uniformity of terminology can be extended to the USA I don't know. Perhaps you can do something about this.

If you query the title 'Green-Belted Cities', I reply that here I use the term (and I shall say so in the book) as meaning *both* Garden Cities (with true Country Belts) and the re-nucleated communities inside the big cities, which possibly won't be separated by more than narrow Park-Strips or Park-Belts, when redeveloped. Of course I agree with you that Garden City does not etymologically cover Howard's idea; but it is in itself a pleasant term, we haven't found a better one, and if we did it might still be perverted if planning writers remain inefficient. So I've set myself to correct the perversions and restore the term to its original clear meaning, while accepting 'Satellite Town' as an alternative in the case of Garden Cities and genuine Country Towns in the region of a large Metropolis or regional capital.

As to an American visit, I gather our Planning Ministry would facilitate it if some convincing unofficial invitation were received; but wouldn't regard me as a suitable 'semi-official' missionary. Not having thick enough pants to sit on ice cold doorsteps, I am not actively (or sedentarily) persisting in the suggestion. I have lots of other things to do; and the idea is perhaps luxurious in my time-starved state. When are you coming here?

WELWYN GARDEN CITY   24 April 1945

Dear Mumford

This is a hurried note in acknowledgement of your letter of 18 March, to hand to-day, with the cutting from *Pencil Points* of your Howard essay. I detest that photograph of Howard—he wasn't smug and he wasn't the elder of a nasty little tin chapel—but your Mephisthophelean smirk (no doubt equally untrue to life) does something to redeem the Garden City movement from the Little Bethel atmosphere which Howard's first name and portrait suggest.

Thanks for your work with Wurster; I have already had a cordial invitation from him. It seems likely that one may also come from the National Housing Agency; and what was a pleasant idea to play around with when bored with work is now becoming a rather frightening prospect—since I really don't quite see how I can spare the time for an American trip. Just now I am concentrating on completing a small book on our Garden City experience, and this is piling up arrears of other work all around me. The planning situation here has deteriorated; and I ought to be running about the country, lobbying members of both Houses of Parliament, and pouring out press articles and letters to influence the immediate present. I did this for the four years from 1940, with some effect; but I was irritated all the time by the fact that I had not stated my case anywhere fully and could not get academic and professional circles to see the issues in right perspective. Therefore I have lately been trying, very inadequately, to write books; and now I am even more irritated, for anything serious I could write would not have much influence for years, and in the meantime legislation and the schemes of local authorities are crystallising. If you find in some of my writings a tendency to be savage with planning writers—who ought to have been doing this work but in fact write books of contemptible vagueness and opportunism—you will perhaps understand that I am annoyed with my own slow speed and lack of judgment as to where it is best to concentrate my own attacks. My present view is that a visit to the USA would be so much of a stimulus that it might be a good investment of time; but that I won't go unless there seems to be a genuine desire from somewhere that I should do so, and it doesn't cost me anything but the time.

HANOVER, NEW HAMPSHIRE   5 May 1945

Dear Osborn

Your letters of 28 March and 24 April now cry aloud for an answer; and here is the beginning of one; though there are so many things to talk about, from Roosevelt's death to more personal matters, that I hardly know where to begin.

Your dilemma about what you should be doing to promote planning finds more than an echo in my own heart; for, except for the writing of *The*

Condition of Man, I find it hard to justify the course of my own life during the last three years, or to understand why it has taken a turn so remote from the interests that had, for the previous six years, been uppermost in my mind. If I were sufficiently pious I might conceive that the Lord was saving me for more important matters, and was deliberately putting me at a distance from the war itself; but I haven't the bent of mind that takes comfort in such mysteries, so I feel rather like a fish that has been tossed by a storm onto the beach and can't flop back into the water.

For me it is even a little irritating that the essays in *City Development* should have no recent essay on planning in the United States; but the reason for this is that my own countrymen, who have an unholy respect for the 'expert', never think of calling upon me for my opinions in the fashion that you or the *Architectural Review* did: hence I lack the necessary external stimulus. Philosophically speaking, I am a deliberate anti-expert; and I have spent no small portion of my life exposing the inadequacy of the single-track thinking of the expert: so there is plenty of reason for their suspicion and hostility. The only public body over here that has ever shown any interest in my work is the TVA; but that came on the brink of the war and at that moment I wasn't able to respond to it. . . .

I am glad you are developing further your ideas about *Green-Belt Cities*; and hope, as soon as the manuscript is ready, you will show it to me and let me in turn show it to Harcourt Brace. The so-called progressive planners and architects have lived within a very narrow circle of ideas; and they show an ignorance about the nature of city development before our own day which is almost as complete as Hayek's[1] apparent ignorance of the evils that accompanied the Elysium of competitive freedom of which he dreams. Their tendency to date progress as 'before and after Le Corbusier' is nothing less than pathetic. Did I tell you that Sert, a very fine man, had in accordance with CIAM[2] instructions written his whole book, *Can Our Cities Survive?*, without a single reference to the functions of government, group association or culture in the first draft? For these progressive architects the whole life of the city was contained in Housing, Recreation, Transportation and Industry. His amended version at least made verbal acknowledgement of these other functions, though the original four-cornered structure remained, as an indication of the sociological superficiality of the CIAM analysis.

President Roosevelt's death made a profound impression upon all of us; though those who were in New York and Washington tell me that the real

---

[1] F. A. von Hayek, political and economic philosopher.
[2] Congrés Internationaux d'Architecture Moderne, founded in 1928 to promote the 'New Architecture'.

depth of feeling was more visible there than elsewhere; and the current newsreels seem to confirm this. As you know, I loved him considerably this side of idolatry; but I don't think any other man embodied so completely, in such a representative manner, both the virtues and the weaknesses of my fellow countrymen in the mass; and they loved him because he symbolised their own being so completely, on both sides. His great achievements are beyond anyone's dispraise: the TVA, Lend-Lease, and not least, the swift courage which permitted him to send you practically all our World War stock of arms and ammunition, leaving us weaponless as late as 1941, when our first large scale army manouevres began. But our position of neutrality on Spain, our playing with Petain, our reluctance to arm convoys, our unreadiness for Japan's attack, can all be traced to the weaker side of his character: like his countrymen, he tried to face both ways.

His death is not as fatal a blow to the good causes for which he stood as, at a distance, it might seem. As a King he was a more effective ruler than as a Prime Minister, so to say; what he symbolised was more important than what he did. His death makes his symbolic leadership all the stronger, and it puts his cause above the very real possibility that he himself might, in a fashion that happened too often throughout his administration, betray in practice what he advocated so eloquently in words. At the present moment it is perhaps better to have a firm little man, rather than a weak great man, at the helm. At least, this is the only consolation I get out of his death. Truman lacks Roosevelt's imagination, and that is a serious lack today; but he seems to be clear-headed, courageous, and pertinacious; and best of all, he will not meet with the automatic opposition from other little men that Roosevelt, by reason of his very greatness, so constantly met. If there is enough political courage and wisdom to lay down the framework for an International Constitution, I should say that Truman will have a better chance of carrying the Senate with him than Roosevelt would have had. There is no doubt where the American people stand; except for minor pockets of isolationism the desire for cooperation on a grand scale, to avoid friction and abolish war, is universal. Whether we are tough enough to keep to this course during the first few years of bickerings and disappointments is the only real question.

I forgot to mention one of the most profound tributes to Roosevelt that his death brought forth: our highly commercialised radio chains somehow overcame both their cupidity and their infinite capacity for bathos for four whole days; and gave themselves over to as complete and dignified a response to this event as was conceivable: indeed, rather more than was conceivable to me. Such a break with a bad tradition records the depth of the shock. Even D-Day did not meet with such a complete response here.

WELWYN GARDEN CITY   12 June 1945

Dear Mumford

Your letter of 5th May gives welcome signs that your health is returning. I hope this will enable you to get ahead with volume IV. After all, things do move after phases of apparently eternal suspense: the German War is over, and I have read The Condition of Mumford (as it is disrespectfully known in my family). Alas, my mind is like a photographic plate under too little developing fluid; I can't keep the plate all flooded at once, and by the time I reach the last corner the rest has dried up. I have done a very short review for our *Journal*. The length of the review has nothing to do with my assessment of the value of the book; it merely reflects the fact that the *Journal* is specialised on physical planning. Nor has it to do with my genuine feeling of incompetence for the assessment; for when ever did that deter any reviewer? It was a big handicap to me that a life-long habit of literary browsing has not been accompanied by a habit of deciding what I think about what I read—except in narrow spheres of technical interest. Your book made me want to read Thomas Aquinas, Dante, Luther, Rousseau and all the rest as carefully as I once read Fourier, Owen, Marx, and Mill.

I have one serious doubt about your position—or the expression of it in this book. You seem to reject a struggle for survival within the species, though (not I think quite explicitly) accepting it as between species. I haven't read Kropotkin's *Mutual Aid*[1] for so long that I forget if he admits any inter-species struggle at all. I must say I don't see how one can wholly reject it, though I have certainly not thought out its exact relation to the Mutual Aid weft in the pattern. As a gardener (at the moment of a neglected garden) I can never forget the determination of every plant to grow into the space occupied by other plants. Society (or what I understand you to mean by the super-ego) may act as the gardener and by weeding or replanting (and destruction of plants outside the gardener's sympathy) prevent an injurious clash; but surely the basic natural fact is the tendency of all individuals to encroach on space also wanted by other individuals, even of the same species? Measured limitation of population might be one way of social gardening. But we are a long way off having a world-gardener.

Roosevelt's death caused us all deep grief; it came so close to us that we could not quickly realise it, and so much has happened since that we can't get the loss in perspective yet. I feel he was a big man; the only world-states-man we had. We shall never know whether he could have succeeded in the major task of bringing about some confidence and some common policy between Russia and the West. The descent of the iron-curtain on half

---

[1] P. A. Kropotkin, *Mutual Aid*, New York, London, 1902.

Germany as well as all the Balkan States is ominous, and we are watching
Czechoslovakia with anxiety. Roosevelt might have dared to say that some
Germans may still be human; which would be far-sighted politics. As it is,
the Western Allies will undoubtedly behave with the humanity of a decent
jailer, but no one may declare they will do so for fear of being classed as a
dupe or sentimentalist.

I don't expect to come to the US this year. The NHA[1] pursued Jacob
Crane's verbal invitation with a very cordial written one to give them as
much time as possible in Washington if I come. But our MOI[2] find a visit
on planning outside their scope—which is that of explaining our war-time
effort to Allies. I would really rather wait till 1946, but the NHA, being in
the middle of a study of British planning methods, want me to go this year
if at all. Like you, I don't get much encouragement from state departments
in my own country.

WELWYN GARDEN CITY   26 July 1945

My dear Mumford

I am rather ashamed of my incompetent review of *The Condition of Man* in
the forthcoming *T & CP*, which you should receive in a fortnight or so. But
the fact is that, by your standards, I am uneducated in history and philosophy.
If I had read more carefully your *Technics & Civilisation*, before the later
books, I might have reviewed you more intelligently. You mustn't mind if
one of the reasons people read you is that they have so much to learn, and
if their reviews are consequently of little value for your own thought.

At the moment planning policy discussion is in suspense, awaiting this
week's election results. There is an undoubted swing to Labour, and before
you get this you will know far more than I know now. The most the Conservatives really hope for is a clear majority of fifty to seventy. Labour
hopes to be the largest party, but is not confident of a working majority.
Both might be wrong either way; the electoral experts are baffled by the
long interval since the last election. In any case the position of our sort of
planning will be somewhat stronger, and the Association will have a few
MP's making the subject their first interest—which will greatly help me in
organising a Parliamentary group of all parties. The Ministry of T & CP are
plucking up courage a bit. The Minister has given a clear lead to dispersal
policy in a speech at Manchester. He has also disapproved the reactionary

---

[1] National Housing Association.
[2] Ministry of Information.

City of London Plan[1]—to everybody's astonishment, especially the City's. It is an interesting situation in the City. The chairman of the TP Committee is a personal friend of mine[2] and a member of the Association. He is a youngish man who two years ago was lost in the dumb ranks of the Common Council; but he has just been made Sheriff-Elect, which means he automatically becomes Lord Mayor after a number of years. I don't understand City politics, but one of its characteristics is that no *person* seems to count, and there is no real electorate and nothing resembling ordinary local democracy. I suppose someone somewhere decides policy, but even the Planning Officer of the City (another friend and supporter of mine) cannot tell me who it is! It is an unprecedented situation for a Government Dept. to check the City, and everybody seems to assume it is the most daring and dangerous action ever taken. But it may be the end of the world's greatest bluff, since where there is no opinion there cannot really be power. I am going for the first time to the Common Council meeting tomorrow (oddly the meetings are in public, but no one ever goes, and I have never seen a report). It amuses me that the two men whom I would have supposed to have most influence on City Planning (the Chairman of the Committee and the Planning Officer) are dead against the Plan and pleased that the Ministry has objected to it. But I suspect the Ministry's objection is on grounds that won't appeal to me much more than the Plan itself; they will have been carefully chosen for some obscure reasons of strategy. Behind it all, however, is the dispersal issue.

No one in Welwyn Garden City or the City yet realises it, but the Committee Chairman and Sheriff-Elect was for a short period on the Urban District Council of WGC when I was the Clerk, which is the source of our contact. I don't propose to embarrass him by advertising that historical fact at present.

The LCC has accepted Abercrombie's County Plan, and is putting a large chunk of it into operation. The housing standard is still bad, but I don't worry much about that at this stage—it is quite unacceptable to popular opinion and will have to be amended as operations proceed. While maintaining my criticism, and yours, I am supporting the acceptance of the essential principles. A lot of work is being done by the LCC and some outer boroughs on schemes for the satellite towns, though I hear there may have to be further legislation as the Act of 1944 does not give all the powers needed. It is so important that the principle of dispersal is now fully accepted by the LCC, and the difficulties are so great and genuine, that it would

---

[1] *Report of Improvements & Town Planning Committee on Post-war Reconstruction in the City of London*, London, 1944.
[2] Sir Frederick Tidbury-Beer.

clearly be a mistake to make a song about the inadequate quantitative scale of the dispersal. It is a twenty years job anyway, and the argument as to standards will proceed for years—with more and more public understanding as the first areas are redeveloped. At present, as I always expected, the public mind is dominated by the housing shortage. In the last few weeks there has been organised squatting in empty mansions, with enough public approval to force the Government and the authorities into more active requisitioning —a score for the anarchists.

There is a dim-out over Europe, and though the Pacific War is given priority on the BBC and in newspapers, it is not possible for people here to hold it in the forefront of their consciousness as they did the War in Europe. We are astounded at the advance of the front almost to the Japanese main-land, and at the scale of the bombing of Japan—but try as we will (and I speak for myself here) we cannot bring it all home to ourselves. It is really the same with the European situation. We know the situation is appalling, we feel it is not being well handled, we sense that new sowings of dragons' teeth are being made broadcast, we are worried about Russian policy, about relations with France, about the huge questions of future international alignments and world economic policy—but for the moment we cannot crystallise any passionate attitude. The absence of Parliamentary debates, and the uncertainty as to who is to govern this country, makes suspension of opinion seem somehow justifiable to ourselves. It is a 'waiting' period, during which we pursue small business and personal objectives provisionally and as in a dream. But everybody feels it is temporary, and that before long we must force ourselves to think and act. I may be extending my own mood to others; I am very tired, and perhaps need a holiday which I cannot resolve to take. I hope you are continuing to improve in health. What are the pros-pects of your visit over here?

AMENIA, NEW YORK   5 August 1945

Dear Osborn

Your first letter was written on the heels of Roosevelt's death. Most of us here have been pleasantly surprised over Truman, who, while he lacks Roosevelt's audacious political imagination, has many qualities our great president lacked, including candor and a capacity to conciliate his political opponents; so the change seems, on the whole, almost providential. The sweeping Labour victory in England seems to have placed Truman's opposite number in office; and there again there is, I think, some advantage at this particular moment in having a man like Truman to ease the shock for our

American conservatives, who are already, in their panicky way, picturing Downing Street as a suburb of the Kremlin, and who would let their imaginations run in an even more licentious manner but for Truman's moderating influence. My own sleep would be a little quieter at night, incidentally, if by some magic a Russian counterpart to Truman and Atlee should take Stalin's place. But that seems almost as far in the distance as it was in 1935; and we will all probably have to manoeuvre the political applecart over a very uneven and rocky road for the next generation.

Now as to planning matters. I first must record my admiration, if I haven't done so already, for your article on *The Country Belt Principle*. You have gone further into this matter than I had done and have taught me several things I didn't know before; if anything should clear the air, it is precisely this article—though I suspect that many of the people who oppose us do not in the least want the air cleared. Your tribute to Thomas More was no more than his due; and it established, among other things, the essential continuity of British thought here. Since you have brought in many contributions I have never suspected, you may perhaps forgive me for wondering at your neglect of Evelyn's *Fumifugium*, which added to the notion of a country belt the typically Renascence suggestion that it should be planted with pleasantly odoriferous shrubs, to perfume the inner airs. Surely it is a good principle, even in a labour-governed England, to have the gentry on one's side!

As for the American reviews of *City Development*, they have proved more than favourable: I feel, when I read some of them, as if I were having an early peek at my obituary: I behold my reputation lying in state, embanked in pious flowers and wreaths. My not altogether innocent strategy of publishing the essay I wrote in 1921 had precisely the effect I wanted it to have; and my barefaced printing of your praiseful introduction to the first pamphlet, instead of contributing my own, undoubtedly awed a few people, who regarded me rather as a local nuisance than an international figure. Yet with all the praise *City Development* has received, its sales were less than half of those of *The Condition of Man* during the same period. So it turns out that my 'popular' books are unpopular, and that books which are difficult to read are easy to sell. One must reconcile oneself to the fact that we live in a paradoxical world! Maybe that is why Christianity, the most paradoxical and self-contradictory of religions, has prospered so long.

During the last few months I have been partly preoccupied with a little task set me by the Office of War Information: a series of letters, addressed to various Germans, real and imaginary, to tell them what an American thinks of their present condition. This has caused me to spend some time delving into the German mind; and the conclusions I have reached about it are pretty discouraging, if one is impatient for any quick reformation and improvement. So far as I can discover, if one excepts an exile like Heine or Friedrich Forster, there is no literature of self-criticism in Germany: hence Germany has never had its egoism and complacence reduced by the astringent medicine that your countrymen and mine have swallowed, administered by its greatest writers, from Milton and Cowper onward. I had not dared to imagine that the decisions Potsdam reached about Germany would be as tough as they actually are; but, on the basis of my own observations, my letters, as it happens, have hewed very close to the Potsdam line. I can't imagine any young German wanting to read what I say for another ten or twenty years; but maybe the reaction to Nazism will come quicker than I anticipate, once the Germans realise that there is no way out merely through the re-building of their old establishment. Once they are desperate, they may finally come to grips with themselves and eventually come to terms with their situation. It will be long before dawn really breaks over Europe again, and there will be many false dawns before that happens; but I think that even such a reserved optimist as myself might say now that there is a faint glimmer of light at the horizon's edge! (Let us hope that this light comes from the sun, and not from the flashes of distant guns, beyond earshot!)

I haven't half covered either of your letters; but today is one of those rare Sundays this season when the sun is shining fiercely and a clear breeze has driven all the clouds away; and I feel the same pull of Bank Holiday that the radio tells me your own crowds feel, so I will go off with my box of sketching crayons for a walk on the hills, where the lavender bergamot has, for the first time in my memory, covered acre upon acre of the pasture land, through some freak of seeding and the weather.

WELWYN GARDEN CITY   14–17 August 1945

My dear Mumford

There is no particular occasion for this letter: for the record, I last wrote you on 12 June and 26th July, and the last letter I had from you was dated 5 May. If I were, like a journalist, in the habit of being stimulated to writing by events, I should have plenty of reason for shooting off my pen; but I am never ready with a comment on the passing show. The first Atomic Bomb announced itself just nine days ago, Russia declared war on Japan a week ago, and at the moment of writing rumours of a final Japanese acceptance of the surrender terms seem to be boiling up to actuality. I realise dimly that it has been a Week of Destiny for the human race; but journalistic emphasis on this fact produces (by habit) a doubt—in this case quite un-reasonable—as to whether anything important has really happened.

In the nearer field of Town and Country Planning I am trying to assimilate that fact that there is a new and entirely different Government with a man-date to crash through interested obstructions, that Lewis Silkin[1] (the agent of the unsatisfactory elements of the LCC Plan, but a man of some ability and knowledge and—as a friend puts it—'mental mobility') is Minister, and Fred Marshall of Sheffield (whom I have regarded as a supporter of 'my' policy) the Junior Minister, and that several real enthusiasts of the TCPA are now MP's.

The Greater London Plan is published in full to-day, and a feature of the Exhibition to celebrate its birth is a huge, and I am told, most attractive model of one of the proposed satellite towns, prepared by the Ministry itself. Also, this week (after vainly trying to do so for two critical years) I have given up my daily executive work in industry and have become, except for certain not onerous directorial functions, a full-time free-lance nuisance in the planning world. I should feel that things are at least happening. I should be running around asserting that what I have been fighting for for years is becoming real, and insisting on taking part in the constructive work that plainly is now going to be done. Instead, I want to go to sleep. I have been for some time, in a number of mild and uncertifiable ways, ill; but I only realise this because suddenly I find myself free of pain and clear-headed. But after such a spell I am surrounded by a hundred unfinished jobs, and I neither want to do any of these nor am disposed to start new ones. I have managed, with a painful effort, to write a short manifesto which has gone to the new MP's. And in a day or two I must really restart the wearisome business of rolling logs uphill. But for the moment I can do nothing but write easy letters in reply to correspondents who have probably forgotten their queries to me. I imagine this is the sort of state you were in after finishing *The Condition of Man*; but I have no such excellent consola-tion to fall back on. *Green-Belt Cities* is no justification for a nervous break-down, so I cannot indulge in one.

A by-product of the election is the necessity of writing dozens of letters of congratulation to colleagues and personal acquaintances who have been elected—among these are no less than five residents of WGC, besides the Labour candidates for both divisions in which the estate is situated—to friends who (mostly quite unexpectedly) have reached the pinnacle of their ambition by being appointed Ministers, and to Tories and Liberals who have lost office and seats and all hopes of influence for years and perhaps

---

[1] Lewis Silkin, 1st. Baron Silkin. Minister of Town and Country Planning, 1945-50, when the principal New Towns legislation was passed.

for ever. I console these last by expressing my own view, deliberately arrived at after many temptations, that there is a lot to be said for not being in Parliament. Yet even I, who am resolute on the point, feel in a way bypassed when so many acquaintances of quite moderate ability reach positions of apparent power and dignity; so it is not easy to condole effectively with those who have banked on a parliamentary and ministerial career, and are suddenly deprived of it.

The Labour Party are at least as clever as any dominant party we have ever had (which perhaps is not saying much); it is possible that they are in for twenty years. Predictions on this however are meaningless till we see how the world situation shapes. I see no opposition group in sight which can popularise a policy clearly distinguishable from that which the Government will pursue (much of which is common ground among people in all parties). The opposition will need a lot of luck to find such an issue and consolidate upon it within five years. Their historic suit, that of realistic nationalism against fluffy pacifism, is no longer trumps, and the Labour Party now hold as strong a hand in it as they do. Moreover, they are far more deeply divided than the Labour Party is on the issue of the correct limit of state intervention. Though we were hesitant to realise it, all the evidence should have led us to expect this landslide; we still suspected that the 'silent voter' would support Churchill, as he did himself. In the event, the accession of the Labour Party to real power now seems to have been inevitable. Even many of those who voted the other way half wanted it, and the figures of total voting understate the drift of opinion towards Labour, or at any rate away from Conservatism. But Churchill could have reduced the turnover by more intelligent electioneering. The magnitude of his catastrophe is due to his relying on the incredibly bad advice of Beaverbrook and the Tory die-hards. He entirely failed to sense the national mood.

What has happened is a very big step in the British revolution—a shift of power to meet new conditions and new ideas. Britain will not willingly go far towards Communism; it will remain at heart a free-enterprise nation; but like every other nation it consists mainly of wage- and salary-earners, and it is determined that the public interest shall prevail over money-interests. No more than America, however, has it yet faced the dilemma of the trend towards monopoly. It does not accept the state-monopoly solution, despite Laski and Aneurin Bevan; and sooner or later it will revolt against the facile solution of state ownership and be driven to expedients of entirely new kinds, which Labour philosophy at present scornfully scouts.

Next day (*15 Aug.*): VJ Day, the Japanese have swallowed their bitter pill overnight. Columns and columns in the papers on the inexplicable attachment of the Japanese to the mystical descendant of the Sun-God. And

George VI going in his gilt landau, with my old friend Walkden[1] of the Railway Clerk's Association behind him dressed up as Captain of the Yeoman of the Guard, and wee harmless Charlie Ammon[2] alongside in the uniform of the Corps of Gentlemen at Arms, and a huge crowd shouting 'Banzai' or making noises to that effect. I am, I suppose, a loyal supporter nowadays of constitutional monarchy, which has some practical advantages, but I have never understood the mental mechanics of its evident profound appeal to my normal fellow-countryman, who in this respect are as mysterious to me as Japs. I rather think Hirohito could be replaced in practice, if the real rulers wanted it, as easily as Edward VIII, and that makes me indulgent to the institution; but in that case why all this hoo-hah? Why the incessant efforts to make a useful political fiction seem based on emotional reality? And what are the real thoughts of my lords Walkden and Ammon as they take their places behind the Throne, as the intelligent but unforcible Lord Chancellor Jowitt, on his knees, gives His Majesty his script for the King's Speech, written by a principal Civil Servant and vetted by the inner Cabinet, and the Lords and Commons hang upon his slowly delivered words? I am sure they *think* they are taking part in the greatest joke left on earth; but I am also sure they feel like the angels on the ceiling of the Sistine Chapel— which is what I would feel, too, and wonder at myself for consenting to be cast for a part for which nature had not physically endowed me, in a show at which I had scoffed all my life.

Both Walkden and Ammon are sincere and simple men, who have given a lifetime of service to the Labour movement without seeking prominence or privileges; that, no doubt, is why Attlee has chosen them for this curious honour. Behind it all is something of partisan glee in seeing unassuming friends in positions that in the past were coveted by people of the greatest wealth and bluest blood. They imagine thousands of true snobs gnashing their teeth at the dreadful sight. But whether anybody gnashes to any appreciable extent I have no means of knowing. Sea-green incorruptibles of the Left will probably have the strongest feelings; they will go about saying that these once faithful proletarians have sold out for the chance of titles and attitudising in fancy dress. But Attlee's choice is astute in that few would really think Walkden and Ammon would accept such grandeur in any other than a spirit of historic irony. By so doing, of course, they give new life to our ancient institutions. I cannot feel alarmed about that, because they work, and do not nowadays obstruct democracy. The symbolic value

[1] A. G. Walkden, 1st. Baron Walkden. Trade union official and Labour Member of Parliament, Captain of the Yeoman of the Guard, 1945–49.
[2] C. G. Ammon, 1st. Baron Ammon. Labour Member of Parliament, Captain of the Gentlemen-at-Arms, 1945–49.

is obvious, but all the same, I repeat that I cannot really understand their hold on the nation.

The King's Speech promises early legislation for compensation and betterment and further control of the use of the land, which is reassuring. I had a fear that this very difficult issue would be postponed, and all the emphasis put on speed in housing. Our work does not appear to have been wasted.

Against the competition of all this other first-class news, the Atomic Bomb has had a majestic press, scores of scientists being paid good fees to write the same limited story over and over again. I found one could not have too much to read about it, no matter how many times the same matter was repeated. What will be the political effects? I rather think the Bomb strengthens for the time the world-wide tendencies towards organisational centralisation. It is so clear a case of development on a scale that only Governments could undertake, and the collectivists will legitimately exploit it as their type-case of future industrial development. In the USA where perhaps state intervention is under-appreciated, that may do good. Here and in Europe it may further discourage the free-enterprise side of political philosophy. At the moment, however, it is the international-military aspects of the discovery that dominate discussion. There are suggestions that Anglo-American priority in it may strengthen the diplomatic position vis-a-vis Russia; but no one knows if our statesmen dare, or would think it wise in a war-weary world, to play their card. Looking a year or two ahead, it must I think be assumed that at least the USA, the British group, and Russia will all have plants for producing the new type of bombs. But who can believe that these three nations can agree on their own respective positions in the world sufficiently to act as a triumvirate world-government, and to deny the use of Atomic Bombs to the rest of the world? Or that they can agree to hand over a monopoly of it to the United Nations Organisation? Or that if they did, whether the solidarity of the Big Three inside the UNO could be perpetuated?

If one were capable of cosmic detachment, one would forecast that there must be one more world war, in the course of which Britain becomes the 49th state of the USA, and world-power finally passes to the new organic combination. The USA is far and away the most powerful nation, but is it in sight of the political maturity and the mood to take on world-rule or decisive world-leadership, with all the cost and trouble that must entail? I have seen Great Britain tire of a much smaller burden, and all our tendencies (witness Ireland and India) are towards not merely decentralisation but towards encouraging absolute independence. World-government would be possible on the basis of the acceptance of a status quo for the distribution of population and the limits of state-power. But there is no possible permanent status quo. I begin to wonder (still in the character of the cosmic observer) whether we may not have to pass through a phase of world-tyranny before a democratic world government becomes possible. But you may think I am still suffering from the concussion of that much-publicised bomb. . . .

I don't think philanthropic housing people anywhere realise the irresistible strength of the impulse towards the family house and garden as prosperity increases; they think the suburban trend can be reversed by large-scale multi-story buildings in the down-town districts, which is not merely a pernicious belief from the human point of view, but a delusion. Many of our 'practical' people, including our Mr Silkin, share the delusion, and I am sure they compare notes about me and decide that I am a well-meaning but wrong-headed idealist. In my present mood of cosmic detachment I am inclined to think the multi-storey technique will have to have its run, and that the best I can do is to make portentous prophecies that it must fail. In a few years, the multi-storey method will prove unpopular and will peter out, and the mechanism that must be set up for partial dispersal will have found its feet and will be more consistently operated. It is a pity we can't go straight for the right policy. But it takes a long time for an idea, accepted theoretically, to soak through the whole of an administration; and the conflicting idea of good multi-storey development has enough enthusiasts to claim a trial in some cities on a fairly large scale. Damage will be done to society by the trial; but probably all I can do is hasten the date of disillusion. If I have underestimated the complacency of the urban masses, the damage may amount to a disaster.

P.S. I had forgotten what I think was the one thing I definitely meant to refer to when I started this letter; the further development of the bout between the Planning Ministry and the City of London. I went to the Common Council meeting and listened to a very boring and amateurish debate, in which one member after another protested against the Ministry's unparalleled insult to the ancient City and ended by supporting the proposal that the City should do exactly what the Minister asked—scrap the plan and get a consultant planner to start all over again. The Minister, in a most sweeping letter, had told the City that it was the heart of the greatest Capital in the world, a centre of world trade, commerce and finance, and the work place of considerably more than half a million persons. It lost a great opportunity in 1666, and it must not lose this even greater one. The City should ask itself: 'What sort of Place should the centre of a world capital, with an ancient and glorious history and a thriving and growing modern life, be?' The City should be 'visibly the capital of a world-wide community of great nations', and such a result was 'unlikely to be achieved by the Plan now presented'. The Plan appeared to be 'dominated by the desire to avoid the

purchase of land, and to interfere as little as possible with existing ownership boundaries'. (Bear in mind that this came from the Conservative
Caretaker Government). As to transport, 'the fundamental requirement has
not been grasped'. The provision of open space was inadequate. The total
accommodation allowed in the Plan was stated to be 50 per cent in excess
of previous accommodation, 'but is probably nearer double that figure', and
the Plan advances 'no justification for such an increase'. The Plan 'is poor
estate development'. It is 'not the way to recreate values'. And there were
many other radical criticisms. What sort of revised plan will now emerge
it will be interesting to see. It is likely the new Government will compel the
City and the LCC to give their planning powers to a regional planning
committee.

AMENIA, NEW YORK   26 August 1945

Dear Osborn

Your splendid letter of 14–17 August has crossed the one I wrote you a
few weeks ago; and since I am about to settle down, I hope, to a bout of
work, I shall answer it at once. At the time I wrote you only one bomb had
fallen, the bomb which brought the Labour Party into power in England;
and if I am not mistaken, I said that this would improve relations with the
United States. Alas! for my optimism. In the long run I think this is true;
for the majority of Americans will be more sympathetic to a socialist England
than to a Tory England; but I had reckoned without our financial rulers
and had underestimated their influence on President Truman. His abrupt
ending of the Lend-Lease arrangement was nothing short of brutal; and
being so, it also seems to me sinister: a deliberate attempt to embarrass your
new government. For the first time in four years, I sent a telegram of protest
to the President: a meaningless gesture unless a thousand other Americans
had the same impulse and obeyed it. I never expected that Truman would
have Roosevelt's imagination; but up to the time the atomic bomb was
used I had looked with increasing favour on his actions. Now, I feel that
we are in the hands of a small man; and unless our own labour union leaders
are big enough to exert pressure on the government, in order to save themselves eventually—it would really be the merest prudence on their part to
come out on the side of their British comrades—the dearly won harmony
between our countries will have been seriously compromised, if not broken,
by our own acts; with what results, in this disordered world, no one can
know.

When the atomic bomb was used, I had the same impulse to share my hopes and fears with you as you have shown in your letter. Not that the bomb came as a surprise. I had not known of the experiments that were being conducted on it but I had accepted Henry Adams's theorem as to the increasing acceleration of power, and had referred to it again and again in various essays; latest, perhaps, being the first section of the last chapter of *The Condition of Man*: a chapter I re-read, in the light of the atomic bomb, with a grim satisfaction not unmixed with sadness at finding once more that my worst anticipations have come true. (As a prophet I have been no better than anyone else; my good fortune has been due to the fact that I kept my optimistic predictions to myself and published only the pessimistic ones, which turned out about 75 per cent accurate.) Most of the benign anticipations of the extensive industrial use of intra-atomic energy seem to me premature and probably baseless: the question is whether we have the intelligence to devise the necessary controls and the moral strength to cooperate in enforcing them, before we blow the human race off the planet. On the basis of our immediate reactions, those of my own country's political leaders above all, I should say that the outlook is black. Our use of the atomic bomb, even once, was, I believe, a suicidal act. I do not take exception to its invention: once the discovery was made that was unavoidable in view of our enemy's intentions. But its use, without warning, is quite another matter. That showed to what extent the practice of obliteration bombing had made us the same kind of moral nihilists as our enemies. I have been struggling the last fortnight to put down on paper my complete reactions to this terrible challenge, and I confess that it taxes my utmost powers, for I don't think we have much time to recover the ground we have lost and to reach a new, high level in political organisation and social control; and, on the most optimistic view I can take of the situation, only a miracle will save us. The only encouraging fact to me is that so many other people, here as well as in your country, share my pessimism. That alone may pitch our efforts to the intensity the situation demands.

I forget whether I told you in my last letter of the book of political and educational letters I propose to publish next spring:[1] my essay on atomic disintegration will be the climatic one in that volume; and the strange but encouraging fact is that all the other essays look as if they were intentionally directed toward the same target. If I manage to get this essay published in a magazine, which is very doubtful, I will send you a copy in advance of the book itself. Somehow, the dangers that impend in every direction one faces spoil whatever fresh taste for life the moment would otherwise offer me:

---

[1] *Values for Survival*, New York, 1946. An abridged edition was published as *Programme for Survival*, London, 1946.

recently many little things have happened that would, ordinarily, give me no small pleasure—such as learning, from the Dutch publisher who wants to translate *The Culture of Cities*, that the book was used as a basis for secret lectures during the war. But there is too much sand in the spinach. I must, however, record the real sense of reward I got when I read your introduction to the County of London Plan pamphlet, which came, a bundle of 'em, yesterday. I thought that you hit just the right note; and I am glad, too, that my own essay will sound much more cogent with a Labour Government in power than it possibly could have had the Tories been returned.

I can understand very well your feelings with regard to old colleagues who have come into power. I felt much the same myself during the prosperous days of the New Deal, when the things I had worked for during the twenties came to a head in Washington and in the Tennessee Valley, without myself or any of my colleagues being given a chance to work in any of the strategic positions; while other, less capable people fumbled and muffed the opportunities which they were only partly prepared to handle. I hope, however, that your own health recovers sufficiently to enable you to play your active part as the intellectual cutting edge of this administrative and political advance. Now is the time to bring the main efforts of your planning life to a real head.

There is, incidentally, one point that I wanted to make about the re-planning of bombed areas which I left out of my original paper, but still think should be considered: for the immediate task of housing, it will be a tremendous economy if temporary shelters could be laid down on the same pattern as the ultimate housing will take, so that where new utilities must be built, or where, in time, the land is improved by trees and gardens, it will contribute from the outset to the amenity of the community. If tall apartment houses are to be built eventually, there is no relationship between the temporary shelter pattern and the final one; but if family houses are built, the improvements that are instituted now will be part of a continuous operation, in which every ounce of individual effort will finally show. The houses may be temporary, in other words, but all other forms of surface or subsurface improvement should be instituted at the beginning, with a view to the final shape the community is to take. There will probably be temptation to crowd the temporary quarters and to pay no attention at first to the final form; and I think that both expediency and long run prudence should combat this. Forgive me if I am talking at a distance of something that has been considered and disposed of a long while ago.

Our views as to the political and economic changes that are in store for both Britain and the United States are very close. You will call those changes Socialist in England; and the press, at least over here, will cling to the slogan of Free Enterprise; but actually we will both be creating mixed economies, in which the ends will be increasingly socialistic, that is, in the direction of equality, as De Tocqueville predicted a century ago; but in which the means will be as varied as the situation demands. These economies, it seems to me, will be in contrast to that of Russia, in which the ends are no longer in the direction of equality, but in which the means are rigorously unified.

Unfortunately, the world is ruled by catchwords, and even people who should know better refuse to look beneath the labels long enough to find out what is going on. In any other country but the United States, at least in any socialist country, the Tennessee Valley Authority and our various other state power projects would be hailed as a triumph, instead of being rather shamefacedly concealed as a flaw on the fair face of free enterprise. My own state, New York, has during the last twenty years advanced so swiftly in social legislation that its provisions for the aged, for widows and their children, and for handicapped children, compare favourably with those in any other country in the world. A large part of the land of the state, in the Adirondack forest area, has been socialised, and the Saratoga Springs are likewise run as a state enterprise, not merely providing medical treatment but selling bottled water. Add to this all our municipal housing on a large scale, not merely in New York but in many smaller cities all over the state. Yet because the people who have instituted these measures have not changed their party labels, the fact of the change and the significance of the change have both been overlooked.

WELWYN GARDEN CITY   3 September 1945

Dear Mumford
Proofs of Howard's book have at last begun to come in, and I propose to send you them (for Harcourt Brace) as soon as I get a complete set. There may be no letter with them, so will you take this as the accompanying note? My Preface may need a little amendment; I find for instance, in checking Bellamy's *Looking Backward*,[1] which I had not read for over thirty years, that I was wrong in thinking he anticipated the garden city 'pattern of town and country' *in that book*. The Boston of 2000 AD still had 300,000 population, and Julian West was impressed by its monumental grandeur—though there were of course spacious squares with trees, statues and fountains. It was not until *Equality*, which I think was only published in England in 1908, that

---

[1] Edward Bellamy, *Looking Backward*, Boston, London, 1888, 1889. A book which strongly influenced Ebenezer Howard.

Boston was dropped to 75,000 in order to have a decent density, and Manhattan was reduced to 250,000. As Bellamy died in 1896, *Equality* must have been written before Howard published *Tomorrow*, and it is possible that Howard had seen the American edition of *Equality*. Howard was instrumental in getting *Looking Backward* published here, I think in 1888. He told me he had never met Bellamy, but I did not ask him if he had corresponded with him. It is almost certain he did, but unhappily his papers were destroyed by Lady Howard, and though he wanted me to have them and to write a biography, I was never able to see them. It is at least possible that Howard tried out his ideas in correspondence with Bellamy, and that on the town and country arrangement the influence was the other way round—but I shall say nothing of that conjecture, of course. What Howard got from Bellamy was, he told me, the enthusiasm for a socialist community, and it was as a socialist community that he first thought of the ideal town. From the first he conceived it as having a belt of rural land associated with it, every industry, as in Bellamy's dream, being carried on by the community, including agriculture. Then he saw the great difficulty of municipal agriculture, so he thought 'Why not let agriculture be carried on by private enterprise, the land being owned by the public and the increments of urban value thus being secured?' From that he extended the principle to the factory industries, shops, etc. Knowing that Howard was a voluminous and easy letter writer, I think it is almost certain that he would write to Bellamy to express enthusiasm for his book and to put up these variants of his ideas. But it is pretty clear he did not get the rural belt idea from Bellamy. He had not read Owen or Fourier, but 'knew vaguely about them'. He had read Richardson's *Hygeia* in 1875, when in America, and (characteristically) wrote to him, but had no reply.

When I have time I will write down for private circulation the still unpublished data I have on the influences on Howard, and the history of the Green-Belt idea. They are not important, but they will interest a few students at some time. For instance, the fact that Howard first reacted from the simple communism with which Bellamy had overwhelmed him by reflecting on the difficulty of agriculture (the only 'industry' of which he had had personal experience) is really significant. I had overlooked this till just now, when I re-read a note I made in 1918 of a talk with Howard.

Your publishers did not after all send me *The Story of Utopias*.[1] Don't trouble any more about this. After the transatlantic efforts to get it, and after combing out the London libraries in vain, I found it this week in the WGC Public Library, which is housed at No. 9 Guessens Road opposite

---

[1] New York, London, 1922, 1923.

my house! (A moral story.) I like it very much, and it is of great interest to me because for once I find my reading has covered most of the ground. You will have seen from my article on Green-Belt History that on one or two points I have taken a slightly different view. For instance I rank Owen higher than you do, and give him priority over Fourier in their particular wave of the community-founding idea. I will check this again, but I am inclined to stick to my guns on the point.

Green Belt Cities[1] is only just starting its course through the press. It begins with an account (polemical and bright, I think) of the planning controversies since 1900 and especially since 1920, showing the re-emergence of the garden city idea in British planning. (There are references to American and Continental influences and I treat the British urban situation as typical of that of Western civilisation.) The bulk of the book is a discussion of the actual experience of town-building *ab initio* at Letchworth and Welwyn, followed by some practical consideration of the current problem and the application of this experience. I close with an appendix on the History of the Green Belt Idea—a slightly revised version of the article you have read. The bulk of the matter refers to the British experience, and the question is whether the book is strong enough, coming out with or after Howard's, to make it of real interest in the USA. I can't honestly say that the book will have the appeal of seeming difficult to read. I would much rather write such books, but have conditioned myself to writing for the moderately-intelligent reader who has no knowledge of my subject, and only a weak desire to acquire it.

Yes, I think it might be wise to write a new introduction to your *County of London Plan* in your English book, dealing briefly with the Greater London Plan. This latter is causing much popular discussion all over the London Region—though not in Central London, where there is no local public opinion. The Exhibition has been well attended, and probably for the first time tens of thousands of people are beginning to understand and take as seriously meant the idea of Dispersal, Green Belts and Satellite Towns. It is a brilliantly planned Exhibition and includes a model of a projected new town of 60,000 at Chipping Ongar, Essex. I ought to be irritated that Letchworth and Welwyn are not mentioned in the Exhibition, and that the term 'Garden City' is studiously avoided (Abercrombie's Report is not guilty of this): also that, while we have an excellent model of Welwyn that could have been shown, the Ongar model, produced by the Planning Ministry, shows a very amateurish lay-out by student architects subject to fashionable crazes but with no practical experience—the curse of all exhibitions. But on

---

[1] London, 1946. Second edition 'with Prefatory Afterthoughts', London, New York, 1969.

the whole these things don't matter. The broad principle of the Plan is what we have been fighting for all these years, and the practical defects in the model would not 'register' with the public on that scale. 'Everybody' is talking Dispersal, Satellite Towns, Green Belts, Location of Industry, etc. (Everybody, that is, except the much larger everybody, who is still talking Housing, as in 1919.)

AMENIA, NEW YORK   18 September 1945

Dear Osborn

I have always admired the practices of our great mail order house, Sears Roebuck and Company, which maintains no files of its vast correspondence; and though I keep all the interesting letters I receive for the benefit of posterity —like most things that are done intentionally for posterity this will probably miss-fire—I keep no record of my own correspondence; and I am even a little surprised to find from your letter of the third that I wrote you on August fifth, although I am quite sure that I wrote you later when Truman terminated the Lend-Lease arrangements so abruptly. On that matter, after due consideration, I think I can recognise more than one motive on his part: the influence of some of his anti-British advisers, like Leo Crowley, who have a grudge against the British as such; the influence of a financial group who are alarmed at the prospects of Socialism in Our Time in Britain; a desire on his own part to placate and disarm criticism in Congress, by taking the initiative quickly in terminating Lend-Lease; a desire to show that he sticks by his principles, for he had given the casting vote in Congress which decided that Lend-Lease was to terminate as soon as the war came to an end—though the President had plenty of leeway in deciding when that date was to be fixed. Along with these obvious influences, his peremptoriness may have been due, in addition, to being in a spot over some aspect of British foreign policy, as it has developed perhaps in the Potsdam conference. All these, of course, are guesses on my part; and the last is a wild guess. But the hard thing to understand is how Truman, whose political moves have if anything been left of Roosevelt's, was moved to carry this act out in such a sudden and brusque way. That the American trades unions, now very powerful, did not see through the attempt to discredit the British labour government and come to the rescue, only shows the low quality of their political thinking: low and shortsighted.

As you will see, I have corrected the accompanying proofs; and thank you, to begin with, for saving me from mis-statements. My own memory of *Nothing Gained by Overcrowding*[1] would have made me swear that it dated

---

[1] Raymond Unwin, *Nothing Gained by Overcrowding!*, London, 1912.

back to around 1903 or 1904. I am therefore staggered to find that you date
it as 1912, and that the edition I consulted, when writing *The Culture of
Cities*, was 1918. That pamphlet, incidentally, had a decisive influence on
Stein and Wright, the planners of Radburn and Sunnyside: Unwin's economic
demonstration, plus their visit to Letchworth Garden City in 1923, were the
foundation stones for their work, though Wright had been one of the designers
of American war housing schemes before that date, for our Shipping Board
houses. Did you ever meet either of them? They knew Howard well. Wright
died in 1936; but Stein is still living, and his influence is visible in one of the
best of our large housing developments, Baldwin Hills in Los Angeles.

You remind me of a long neglected duty: namely that of dunning the
publisher who got out a photographic edition of *The Story of Utopias* and
finding out if he is still in business, and if so why he hasn't given my royalties
on an edition that has been sold out. The fact that you didn't receive a copy
seems to establish that conclusively, for I ordered twice from my bookseller
but never checked up with my wife, who pays the bills in this household,
to see if it had gone out to you. I am as amused as you are over where you
finally found the book. The book has some of the charm of youth as well
as its callowness, I suppose. I probably told you that it was a sheer *tour de
force*: I got the idea of writing it in January, got a contract with the publisher
in February, spent six weeks reading the utopias—up to then I had read
only Plato, More, Morris, Bellamy and Wells—wrote the book between April
and June, and corrected proof before I sailed for Europe in July. I was a
little exhausted by the effort, but on the whole no other book of mine ever
came more painlessly. In order partly to confound people who fancy, because
they don't like my present ideas, that my style has become unduly involved
and tortuous, I used whole pages from *The Story of Utopias* in *The Condition
of Man*. It may be a sad commentary on me that my style hasn't noticeably
improved in twenty years; but I defy my critics to pick out, without having
read *The Story of Utopias*, which is the old and which the new text! (The
other reason for using that section was that I was fresh from England and
my first experience of the Country House; so what I said then I just couldn't
improve on later.)

What you say about the exhibition of the Greater London plan reminds
me of Catherine Bauer's explanation of why the younger architects and
planners have such a loathing for the very name and idea of the Garden
City. She knows those boys and girls better than I do, partly because she is
ten years younger and partly because she has spent more time in England
since 1932. She interprets their reaction simply as snobbery: a combination
of communist snobbery and old-fashioned upper class snobbery, which has
affixed the label of 'middle-class' to the Garden City idea. It is really a

disgraceful kind of isolationism; and it shows, too, a curious effort of dis-attachment from a significant national tradition, which made England, before 1914, the Mecca for every intelligent German and French architect or planner. (This has its parallel in the attempt on the part of the fashionable moderns to look down the nose on William Morris; whereas every continental typographer, furniture designer or architect, no matter how far he has moved away from Morris, recognises his decisive influence in initiating the whole modern movement.)

On the matter of Germany I hope to talk at length in another letter. The danger at present seems to me to be that of repeating the mistakes made after the last war: to assume that the honourable and intelligent minority in Germany speak for the whole population, and to give more aid, comfort, and sympathy to the Germans than to the people they have victimised. I know the Germans quite intimately, not merely because I speak and read their language, but because, on my mother's side, I have nothing but German ancestors, chiefly from Hanover. This being the case, I naturally repudiate the notion that there is something wrong biologically in the German strain! But I do think that one large element in German culture, since Luther's time—probably aggravated by the disruption of the thirty years war—has set the German character in a mold hostile to international cooperation, as between equals, and has made the Germans rely upon the soldier and the soldier's methods more than any other country: warfare has become for them a medium of life, and all their leading thinkers—except those of the Enlightenment, when English and French ideas prevailed in intellectual circles—have, instead of repudiating this barbarism, confirmed it and deepened it. The most human and European mind in modern Germany, Thomas Mann, wrote two books during the last war that express the German worship of the soldier, which is not confined to a reactionary class, to per-fection. I have gone into some of these weaknesses in my letters to the Germans; and maybe if I wait till they are published next spring I will present my own attitude more persuasively. . . .

AMENIA, NEW YORK   19 September 1945

Dear Osborn
Yesterday, when the copies of *Town and Country Planning* you were good enough to send me came, I said to myself: if I'd only waited to answer Osborn's letter for a day, I could have thanked him for the review,[1] too.

---

[1] Of Mumford's *The Condition of Man.*

Fortunately, I wasn't so precipitate yesterday, being busy with a spade and a wheelbarrow redeeming my ancient flower beds from the jungle that crept in on them this summer; and today your letter of 14 September just came by air mail: which is getting back to pre-war schedules again, or something better.

I wish all reviewers came up to your standard of understanding, insight, fairness and perspective. There is nothing that could flatter a writer so much as having his words taken in the serious fashion that you have taken mine: such a review outweights a barrowload of compliments of the ordinary kind. I am highly pleased with what you have said and what you have implied. You could differ from me in a far more radical fashion than we yet seem to have differed on any subject, and that would not abate a particle of my present pleasure. Thank you for taking the pains to write this review. Did I tell you how disappointed I had been—wanting to know what the *English* would think of the book—to find that the *New Statesman* gave it to an American, a very decent fellow whom you may have met, named Coyle; but all he could think was, I hadn't mentioned the TVA. An American abroad is always a sort of caricature of his countrymen, no matter how normal he may seem at home; and that review was in our best foreign tradition. (He had forgotten that in the *The Culture of Cities* I had devoted two whole pages to the TVA, writing in 1937 when there still wasn't very much to see or report, except that things were going well and a good beginning had been made!)

As a matter of fact, the TVA *is* one of those rare institutions that is all it is cracked up to be. In fact, it was one of Roosevelt's most masterly strokes. I class it with Lend-Lease as an act of statesmanship, and I contrast it with his National Recovery Act, instituted at the same time as TVA, which would have, in practice, clamped an almost fascist monopoly, with government sanction, on every part of the industrial world. Because it was regarded as a Democratic measure our government has never been able to give the TVA the publicity it really deserves, except *outside* our country. But gradually Americans are getting to be proud of it and to want more public works on the same pattern: this appreciation came first from the people in the Tennessee Valley itself, and that was the result of the excellent administration of the project from the start. They always kept in close touch with the farmers and the manufacturers and, while ready to take the initiative, never imposed measures one-sidedly from on top. A totalitarian government would have played the whole project up to the skies, as an example of how their particular nostrum surpasses all others. Our nostrum being democracy, we are almost ashamed to confess that we did it!

As to the tactical matter, of achieving socialism without using the word itself or waving all the banners that go with it, I am entirely at one with you. In any particular situation I am not merely ready to go as far as a socialist or a communist, but possibly a little further; but I do my level best to avoid prejudicing the issue by using the current catchwords: the only time I lapsed from this, as far as I can remember, was when I used the term 'basic communism' in *Technics and Civilisation*; and there I was more intrigued by the reference to basic English than to Communism, and I promptly redefined the word in a fashion to withdraw the allegiance of any communist. My private opinion is that the British Labour Party would get along much better, at the present moment, if they had an instrument or apparatus for smothering the voice of Harold Laski.[1] Old Geddes used to say that one should imitate the political practice of the Catholic Church: keep one's purpose definitely in view but never announce it beforehand or boast when one has achieved it.

Some day we must sit down and have a talk about Howard. I had forgotten the episode of his wife's destroying his papers, though I think you or someone else mentioned it once upon a time to me. All that you have written about him fascinates me; it's a shame that you were denied the data that would have made a biography possible. Heaven help England when the noncomformist streak that Howard represented, with a sort of quaker gentleness and humility, disappears.

WELWYN GARDEN CITY   21 October 1945

Dear Mumford

I look forward to meeting Frank Morley here, and I may have proofs of *Green-Belt Cities* to show him. The book is being speeded up if possible, as the subject has become more topical because of the Government's setting up a New Towns Committee to advise on definite action. (I am on this Committee, and I should want to add a lot to the book if the Committee's Report came out first.) Steps are already being taken for the starting of three of the eight satellite towns for London, and our Committee has been asked to advise on necessary legislation as a matter of urgency. This certainly looks like some success for the TCP Association's campaign: though it is a pity we did not reach this stage two years ago before the emergency housing programme crystallised.

I am flattered by your offer to write a preface for my book if Harcourt Brace will publish it, and would of course much like you to do so; but I am

---

[1] Harold J. Laski, Professor of Political Science, London University. Important influence in Fabian Society and Labour Party.

also scared of being 'placed' by you. Over here a few people think I have had more effect on the planning situation than I have. The vast majority (of planners) think I have had none at all. I am human enough, therefore, to hear with pleasure of a plot which Abercrombie and others are now hatching to throw me a public dinner this winter, fastening on me some responsibility for the drift of opinion. I know well enough that I am merely one link in a multiple chain, and am doubtful of the morality of accepting credit for being at the point where the chain passes over the pulley. Yet at my age, with much still to do before a nominal policy becomes a reality, I can't afford to disdain any accession of prestige that will help me in the job. All the same I feel it is a weakness to take pleasure in praise; and also a lot of humbug always creeps into these affairs, since some people have to come to them who do not in their hearts agree with the valuation they imply. I shall feel at my own dinner what I often feel at other people's funerals.

When you next write, will you tell me if and when you are visiting this country? There is a scheme on foot to institute a periodical Howard Memorial Lecture, with a reasonable honorarium, in Welwyn Garden City, and I am informed privately that you would be asked if a date could be arranged when you are here. The proposal has not yet been definitely accepted, however. No more has happened about my visit to the US, and this New Towns Committee seems to put it out of the question for at least six months, and perhaps a year.

I think Catherine Bauer is largely right about the architectural reaction against the garden city idea. But the Le Corbusier outlook never affected more than a few schools and years here. More serious was the antipathy of street-picture traditionalism as represented by Thomas Sharp; and this was only influential because for a time the countryside preservationists had the mad idea that they could stop the explosion of the cities by building houses at forty or more to the acre. Architects under this influence, and their countryhouse following, idealised the gardenless street as more 'social' or 'communal' than the suburban villa. It never was a hopeful movement since all English people really want (rightly or wrongly) to live in a free-standing house, to which the semi-detached house is the nearest attainable economic approximation; and the people who idealised the built-up street mostly lived themselves in free-standing houses—often right out in the counties around the big cities. More important even than this aesthetic reaction (which had much justification in the bad architecture and lay-out of the suburbs and ribbons), was the reaction against one-class suburban housing estates starved of public buildings, and the verbal confusion between 'garden suburbs' and 'garden cities'. This verbal confusion is by no means dead. But so far the term 'New Towns' is clear of the confusion, and the public do seem to understand (as I always thought they would if the Government accepted the policy) the real meaning of the terms of reference of the new Committee.

I had evidence of the new understanding at a big public meeting at Barnet this week. Barnet, an old town almost but not quite engulfed in the suburban sprawl, is scheduled in the Greater London Plan to remain at its existing population of 23,000. The town council continues the 'automatic' ideal of rising to 60,000, and is fighting rather feebly for its municipal ambition. The public however, have clearly seized the issue, and I had no difficulty in carrying the meeting with me in favour of the Abercrombie Plan, despite the opposition of Councillors present. It is certain that they would be turned out at next year's election if they persisted in their view; they are therefore now conducting a Dutch auction—they have offered 45,000 as a compromise, and at the meeting said 'Of course this is only a bargaining figure!', but the public, realising that Barnet is on the edge of the vast mass of London, wants to keep every acre of open land as part of its own and London's green belt. I do not think till this year there has ever been anywhere a large public meeting on a practical issue of planning. I was able even to make the meeting understand the vital issue of Compensation for 'Sterilising' the Green Belt land, and of the collection of Betterment on other land elsewhere as a set-off. Further proof that difficult problems will interest the public if the issues come closely home to them. Such meetings are likely soon to occur all over the country.

Catherine Bauer is right also in seeing that snobbery is a big factor in England. Among both the upper and middle classes, though, the word 'garden city' stands more for a working-class housing estate, with perhaps just a touch of philanthropy. It has therefore been something to approve but on no account to live in. Welwyn has done much to kill this prejudice, but not all that is necessary. Good social enterprises here always tend to be looked on as philanthropic—providing what, as I once said, 'Good people think is good for people'. We never had this atmosphere in Welwyn, largely because the leading personalities in the scheme went to live in the place from the start, and assumed they were producing a town for themselves in *collaboration* with the rest of the population, which is the attitude I am trying with much difficulty to get understood. On the New Towns Committee, which is an able body of successful industrialists and professional men, I shall have a job to correct the assumption that we are providing for 'the people', but I feel sure of being able to do so in the actual wording of our Reports. Still, there is a long life ahead for British snobbery. Howard was entirely free and unconscious of it; and Unwin very largely free though not so unconscious. I think possibly what puts you against Owen and Ruskin is that they were both ingrained snobs and philanthropists. So was Octavia Hill. And you must admit they had reason when you think of the quality of the urban mobs produced by the Industrial Revolution, as described in the Hammonds' books for example, with whom Owen and Octavia had to deal in detail.

We feel here that Truman does not get larger as his personality becomes clearer, and I daresay you feel the same about Attlee. Attlee is, I think, at heart a rather over-simple Socialist or Collectivist, but he is sincere and must have much ability in committee. It is a big drawback that he cannot say anything of interest in a speech; there is no salt at all. I don't know him personally. Morrison[1] I know well; he is intelligent, extremely able, and more likely than any other labour leader to look for ways of reconciling individual enterprise and initiative with essential social controls. I had a message from him recently that he still cordially supports the New Town policy, for which (under my direct influence) he was about 1918–24 a great enthusiast; this will be helpful, as he is in a key position. He favours socialism operated by public bodies with some degree of autonomy, and I am sure that is a line we have to work upon, in order to get diversity and avoid over-centralisation. Dalton[2] on the other hand is a rather mechanical collectivist, and he also is in a key position. Cripps[3] is the same. There is a high degree of sincerity in all these men, and Attlee probably prefers sincere doctrinaires to self-seeking opportunists. It is a big question which is the greater danger to democracy.

As to Germany and Eastern Europe, we are just drifting and, I feel, leaving things too much to entirely unqualified generals. In the end I don't see that there is any possible policy but to foster a revival of Social Democracy in Germany, and to do this we simply must modify the moral excommunication of some Germans. I would not question your analysis of the German political tradition. But we have a limited time over which we can control the whole country in detail, and surely we must choose the least poisonous Germans and give them some degree of trust? As to how this is to be fitted in with the Russian policy of communisation and economic sabotage I simply don't know. I cannot believe there is any hope in the policy of sabotage. It just impoverishes us all. There is no doubt a terrible historic justice in the fate of the millions of displaced persons and of the German masses facing a lower standard of living; but the individuals suffering cannot be expected to see it as it appears at a distance. Their conception of history will start with

---

[1] Herbert Stanley Morrison, 1st. Baron Morrison. Labour politician, held many Ministerial posts and was Deputy Prime Minister, 1945–51.
[2] Rt Hon. Hugh Dalton, Minister of Town and Country Planning, 1950–51.
[3] Rt Hon. Stafford Cripps, Chancellor of the Exchequer, 1947–50.

their own situation. The world badly needs a voice, audible from San Francisco to the Urals, to restore its sanity. I have no hope that such a voice will emerge. Despite all criticisms of Roosevelt, I feel he was the one man who could on occasion speak for and to the best side of humanity. It is impossible to know whether he would have risen to the present situation, but what he might have done is a pointer to the sort of lead the world needs.

WELWYN GARDEN CITY   4 December 1945

My Dear Mumford

. . . My own book, *Green-Belt Cities*, has moved faster than I expected, and may be out in February. I have no spare set of proofs, but will try and get an advance copy for you. My contentious but I hope sound discussion of urban development policy concerns all countries, but the description of Letchworth and Welwyn necessarily elaborates details of technique special to Great Britain. While the book may appeal in Britain to some of the general public interested in planning, it is possible that outside this country it will only specially interest planners and sociologists. And some of these may be put off by my insistence on preserving a non-expert approach. I am not displeased with the book at the moment, but I have focused on it rather intently and no one has seen it but myself, not even the Letchworth and Welwyn people; I may therefore be oblivious of some major defects of form or content. I feel well able to stand up to any possible reactions to it by town-planners, but not so confident of those of economists, sociologists and historians, into whose folds I make temerarious raids. I send you a review of Boardman's book on Geddes[1] from *Nature*, a leading journal of science. There was also a mention of your *Culture of Cities* in a long study of architectural literature in the *Times Literary Supplement* a few weeks ago: did you see it? If not, I will send you my copy. The article took a view of the subject that I really do not think will be possible after *Green-Belt Cities* is published—if anybody reads it.

Prospects of the two books may be helped by the existence of the official New Towns Committee on which I am serving, and also by the private plot which I am told is being hatched to throw me a public dinner in February. This is getting a bit alarming, as the 'committee' for it now includes the Archbishop of York, the Lord Chancellor, the Lord President of the Council, the Lord Privy Seal, the Minister of Town and Country Planning, an ex-Viceroy of India, several other ex-Ministers, and the Chairman of the

---

[1] P. L. Boardman, *Patrick Geddes, Maker of the Future*, Chapel Hill, London, 1944, 1946.

Barlow Royal Commission. Justices Scott and Uthwatt consulted and delivered a High Court Judgement, that they cannot indulge their personal desire to take part, as that might be intervening in 'politics', and 'Justice must not only be done but must seem to be done'—their letter (which I have seen) will be one of the most amusing in my personal archives if I can steal it. You must be amused by the portentous names we give to our state officers; so are we at times, and we pass around such remarks as that Greenwood[1] is 'neither a Lord, nor a Privy, nor a Seal',—he is still 'Uncle Arthur'. Inside the Cabinet, and indeed among all members of the House, Ministers are always Clem, Herbert, Ernest, etc., and so they were in the Coalition Cabinet. But still something of the historical magic clings around the archaic titles, and thus a queer duality of personality is produced. It has a certain charm, perhaps a certain value, and one comes to accept it. It also helps to make one realise that Smith, Jones and Robinson, with whom one spoke at street-corner meetings in one's ignorant youth, are now for good or ill persons of enormous influence in the world. And an episode like the formation of this dinner committee reminds a writer that his work, of which he has no evidence of notice for years and years, is in fact passing into other minds and producing some impression all the time. I can, of course, see that very clearly in a case like yours, but nobody ever comments on my work—no doubt because very little of it is in published volumes. Having had little time in my life for writing, I have deliberately concentrated what I have done on the rather small public exercising political leadership. Probably I would have been well advised to write more books for the wider public while the subject was fluid. I let the architects and the aesthetics pure and simple get away with it between 1920 and 1936 while I was absorbed in Welwyn Garden City. It is indeed fortunate that you didn't.

I understand the Goverment's Land Compensation Bill is in draft. I do not know its terms, but I think it is impossible that it should not cause a first-class political row—unless it is so weak a Bill as to be useless. Discussion of it will bring a much greater consciousness of the Green-Belt issue. I am not so sure it will raise so effectively the other issue of excessive density in redevelopment. We are not out of the aftermath of the single-minded countryside preservationism of the 1930's.

WELWYN GARDEN CITY   27 December 1945

Dear Mumford
Your letter of 11th December came on Christmas Eve, and this may reach you early enough for my family's good wishes to yours to operate over all

---

[1] Arthur Greenwood, Labour Member of Parliament. Lord Privy Seal, 1945–47.

but a day or two of the new year. I wrote you last on 4th December, so we are out of phase; but no matter. I am glad to hear of the foreign editions of your books. And I am reassured in my opinion of the Greater London Plan 1944 by yours, which I will of course make known to Abercrombie. It is true that the credit of the Garden City idea, despite the efforts of the newer men to ignore Howard (and myself incidentally) and to dissociate you from Howard's 'movement', is reaching an 'all-time high'. The difference between Abercrombie's first and second London Plans is at least partly due to our criticisms of the first. Great efforts were made to induce him to resign from the Town and Country Planning Association and to fasten on me the disrepute of a wrecker of planning; but I knew that Abercrombie was unhappy about his compromise with the leaders of the LCC, who wanted no dispersal at all; and I maintained a strategy of critical encouragement, which succeeded just when I had begun to doubt whether I had been mistaken in refraining from an all-out attack. You will see, perhaps, why I wrote that apparently unnecessary introduction to your *Plan of London County*; it was to cover myself with the minimum backwash on you. The controversy became very dangerous at times; but fortunately our opponents handled it clumsily and gave me an opportunity to make one or two public statements jointly with Abercrombie, which diverted the lightning.

I had read Lloyd Rodwin's article[1] just before your letter came. I get copies of that journal because I am writing an article for it on British Planning thought, and was rather surprised that the Editor had not drawn my attention to Rodwin's outburst. But I don't think I shall make my article a direct reply; I can deal with him quite adequately by referring to exponents of the same point of view here. Despite a lot of reading he has not got either his history or his planning philosophy into right perspective. Like Sharp and all the younger school here he is building up a synthesis and a policy that is almost the same as that of the Garden City 'proponents', but it is important to them that it shall be new and their own work. That does not annoy me a bit, really, though I get a certain amount of fun in pointing out that they are re-digging the same canal. It is amusing that he makes so much of municipal ownership and leasehold planning, and of the marriage of community-building with regional planning, without seeing that Howard anticipated the first and his followers here have taken the lead in the second. More amusing that an American in 1945 rebukes Howard for not being a national planner and reorganiser of local government boundaries in 1898. I am surprised that he is so unaware of the Town and Country Planning Association work on

---

[1] Lloyd Rodwin, 'Garden Cities and the Metropolis', *Journal of Land and Public Utility Economics*, August, 1945. Replies by Mumford and Catherine Bauer were published in the following issue of February, 1946.

machinery and planning standards in recent years; he does not seem to have read anything but Sharp, Liepmann and PEP since 1940.

Though we are, by reason of our political structure, more likely to apply dispersal planning as a national policy than you are, it is by no means certain that we shall not be defeated, partially by the housing shortage and the opportunism it prompts. Our Government will have to be more courageous than Governments commonly are if we are to avoid a continuance of the 1919–39 drift. A talk I had a fortnight ago with Herbert Morrison, who is the second in command, showed me that the situation is understood and the desire is there. But I doubt the strength of the personnel in the next layer below the top. So though I cannot refrain now (having the access) from direct pressure on the powerful few, in the main I still place more reliance on the slower process of the spread of sound ideas among the groups actually responsible for practical development. The pen, I think, is still mightier than the lobby. And I resent the time I have to spend pulling the tangled wires.

Now about programmes. When you are in England the Town and Country Planning Association will probably want to present you with the Howard Medal at a dinner, at which a carefully prepared address by you will not be called for. But we should like something from you, and I will let you know later whether we prefer a Memorial Lecture or a special meeting in London. And I am hoping you will have time for a stay with us in Welwyn Garden City, where we cannot entertain you in luxury but you can be as free as you choose, since we are all busy enough not to be impelled to absorb your time.

The New Towns Committee has just drafted its interim Report (on Agencies for Building Towns) after two months of intensive work. I have to reconcile myself to the compromises in content and style of collective authorship. No one else on the Committee combines experience in town-building with experience in the philosophic and political warfare on the subject—so you can imagine the torments I have gone through and the restraint I have had to exercise. The task was made no easier by the fact that, while wanting endless refinements in the draft (for which those unfamiliar with the controversies could not see the reasons), I also wanted maximum speed, since legislation is being deferred for the Report. I got the speed but not always the precision. But I think the Report may help the process of political crystallisation. . . .

HANOVER, NEW HAMPSHIRE   19 January 1946

Dear Osborn

Your last two letters both bear a December date, and it is high time that I answered them: all the more because of the very welcome news that they contain about the double honour—if an honour with an honorarium does not become, in fact, triple—that you are proposing to bestow on me. I will be very happy indeed to give the lecture under the terms you outline, and will say so whenever the official announcement comes. Meanwhile, it would be a great help to me if you would suggest what, from your side, would be the most advantageous topic I could handle in the lecture. I don't say that I will be able to do it; but it might at least give me a useful clue which I could apply to whatever theme I finally hit on. I write my books without any thought of their audience: I write for those who are capable of understanding me, or who find it worth while to make the effort. But I look upon talks and lectures in quite another light; for unless one meets the audience half way, unless indeed one takes something out of the audience, the lecture itself, however well it may go when it is printed, seems to me to fail of at least half its purpose. To combine the two ends, evocation and printed exposition, is one of the hardest tasks in the world; and there are only two people who succeeded here, to my own taste: John Henry Newman and William James. My little book on *The South in Architecture* (1941) is the nearest I have ever come to it.

As to date, I have just received a letter from the Farquharsons, dated 12 January, giving me a tentative schedule for my two months abroad. The Farquharsons I am afraid, have decided to reward themselves for the original effort they have made to bring me over by treating me as a personal possession, not to be handled without the written consent of the owners. They can do this, with a sense of perfect righteousness, on the ground that they are protecting me from being run to death through too many engagements and too much hospitality. I have been both tactful and firm on this matter; but at a distance it is a very difficult matter to handle and it has already left me with a very unpleasant sense of irritation. If the whole business of getting over this coming summer were still not so complicated, if it did not need the active aid of Pepler[1] in getting steamer priorities for me, and all that kind of thing, I should be tempted to throw all the arrangements over and make the trip entirely under my own steam. This of course is a very private confession, not to be used in dealing with Farquharson or Pepler; but just to explain what the difficulties are. I have told Farquharson, who is allowed to reimburse The Institute of Sociology by fees for the expenses of the trip, that the proceeds of the Howard lecture are to be mine. On a separate page I am giving you the schedule as it has been tentatively made out. Since I am now in robust health I have no objection to having conferences of an

---

[1] Sir George Pepler, Chief Technical Adviser to the Ministry of Town and Country Planning, 1943–46. President of the International Federation for Housing and Planning, 1935–38, 1937–52.

informal sort with other groups of planners; and since I share your respect for the Manchester report—indeed I did a review of it for *The Guardian* a few weeks ago—I have indicated to F. that I'd be particularly happy to have an informal meeting in that area.

I think I sent you the criticism of the Garden City idea that a young man named Rodwin wrote. After writing him a long personal criticism I was finally persuaded to put it in the form of a letter, and my reply, along with Catherine Wurster's, will be printed in the next number of the *Journal of Land and Public Utility Economics*. You may be interested to know that in the first number of the architectural journal, *Metron*, which our people are publishing in Italy, my introduction to the Howard book was published. Morley is supposed to be on the high seas now, in a tramp steamer, bumping from crest to trough; and in another week I shall find out directly from him what, if anything, has been done about your books.

WELWYN GARDEN CITY   28 January 1946

Dear Mumford

This replies to your letter of 19th January, containing the news that your tour is arranged for June–August 1946. Mrs Farquharson proposes Thursday 27th June for the Howard Memorial Medal presentation, and from then to 3rd July for your visit to Welwyn. We are arranging accordingly. Probably the Welwyn lecture will be on 28th June (evening), and certainly it will be in that period. To the extent that you don't want to be elsewhere we are reserving a bed and a quiet room for your use in this house during that six days, and you needn't fear being 'entertained'. This applies at any other time during your trip if you wish. I mentioned before that Margaret and I are too busy to be more than civil to you; but I do want a few hours exchange of views with you while you *are* in England.

I understand the Welwyn Company are not specifying the lecture subject closely, but that they would like it to have to do with garden-city creation or something arising from or contributing to that sort of planning. What we know least about here is the thought of other countries parallel to our own thought. You can assume an intelligent audience, mostly living and working in the new town, mostly not specially informed on the philosophy of which it is an outcome, but certainly disposed to be interested in any elucidation of that philosophy and in a friendly way to come back at you with practical experience—as if the frog would lecture the anatomy professor. A fair number will have read some of your books and your introduction in the Howard book. Though Welwyn is 75 per cent manual, and 25 per cent white-collar, I should expect the percentages in the audience to be the other way round—as it is indeed when the speaker is Laski or a Labour Minister; yet it will be 75 per cent or more Labour in national politics. Like all semi-high-brow English and American audiences, this one will lap up and be impressed by psychological and sociological subtleties, but will not really carry much away from these except an enhanced awe. They and the subsequent wider public who will see the lecture in print will be touched more closely by things going direct to their experience of life in persuasive language. In saying this I have told you nothing. I try myself to lecture at once intelligently and intelligibly, and fall far short of what I aim at. I find one must never 'talk down' to an audience, and yet that one can never sufficiently assume ignorance of one's own assumptions and specialised knowledge. You can completely satisfy five per cent of the audience and earn the dazed respect of the rest; or you can interest the five per cent reasonably and gather the others to your fold. I lean to the latter policy, for my own talking. But I strongly advise that you do what seems natural to yourself, even if it means making assumptions not wholly justified about the average intelligence of the audience. I share your admiration for William James's methods; I am not so sure about J. H. Newman.

Advance copies of Howard's book[1] have now gone out, and I presume six have been sent to you by Messrs Faber & Faber. I asked them also to send one to Harcourt Brace.

I am glad to hear you and Catherine Bauer replied to Rodwin, whose article I had seen before your copy came. I have not had time yet to write for the same *Journal* the article the Editor asked me for months ago, but I did not intend a direct reply. The New Towns Committee has kept me very busy these last three months, and will do so for another three or four months. And I have had a bad phase of intellectual constipation. I never felt less effective, and the public dinner to me on 21st March clashes more violently with my feeling about myself even than it would at a time of normal productivity.

HANOVER, NEW HAMPSHIRE   10 February 1946

Dear Osborn

My last letter to you, expressing my bad temper over the way my hosts have been handling my trip, seems to have operated in a mysterious way before you could have received it; for my recent letters from the Farquharsons have been much more cooperative and considerate in tone, and with that change

---

[1] Ebenezer Howard, *Garden Cities of To-morrow*, edited, with a Preface, by F. J. Osborn. With an Introductory Essay by Lewis Mumford. London, 1945.

my own malaise over the situation has vanished. Let me thank you at once for your generous offer of putting me up while I'm at Welwyn; I should be grateful for it even if the housing and hotel situation were not as drastic as it actually is, and, things being what they are, I must express a beggar's gratitude as well as a friend's gratitude for the prospect. I have always liked the 'let-alone' quality of English hospitality: so don't feel that I will want to prey on your time or will feel neglected because you and your wife have your own work to keep you occupied.

I have not seen Frank Morley since his return from London for, being eight hours north of New York, I don't go down there more than once a month or so. I am hoping he will show me your book, for the sake of my professional opinion. As to the Introduction, my own inclination would be to side with Morley and to say that ten convincing words of praise on the jacket are worth a thousand words of appraisal inside; nevertheless, if your book were coming out at the same time as the Howard book there might still be something to be said for an American introduction, which would tie up your English approach with our own special conditions and problems. I will discuss this further with Morley after I have read your book. You cut such a very wide swathe that perhaps it is not really necessary.

The reports of your own re-doubled activities and of the honours that are naturally and properly at last topping them are very gratifying. I wish I could give such a good account of myself; but since I am not part of a decentralised order, I feel myself very much stuck off in a corner; and I realise more and more how much my own political and perhaps even intellectual effectiveness is dependent, at the moment, upon my being near to New York. Since one cannot find living quarters there except under intolerable black market conditions, I must resign myself to being out of it; something that is more easy to accept when one is actively writing a book than when one is still in the preparatory phase.

I have been dismayed recently by the precipitate, amateurish way in which the Site Committee of the UNO has gone about trying to select a site without any clear-cut notion of what they were selecting it for, and without any notion that they were incapable, without the aid of a climatologist and a sociologist, of making any rational decisions. If the UN holds up the selection of a permanent site long enough, so that my words would not merely whistle down the wind, I might devote my RIBA[1] lecture to a discussion of what such a programme should be and lead up to the suggestion of a world capital conceived on garden city lines.[2] I have some fresh ideas about the actual

---

[1] Royal Institute of British Architects.
[2] Mumford did so, proposing a site in a blighted area of Manhattan between Washington Square and Bleecker Street, with Fifth Avenue as its axis.

process of planning and building which neither the right nor the left wing groups in the planning movement have paid any attention to.

Did you happen to see my review of the Manchester Plan in *The Manchester Guardian*? Since I have never been in Manchester I was forced to take refuge in generalities. One of my best reasons for going to England this summer is that it will enable me to be much less vague on matters where, through my long absence, I have been losing my grip. Your handling of Abercrombie, incidentally, I regard as admirable in every way; for you applied the right sort of pressure upon him without causing what would have been a most disastrous rupture. Remembering what you had told me of his feeling that I might, heaven forbid, carry over any animus on account of the review of *The Culture of Cities* he had written—which I still haven't read!—I went out of my way to praise him in the Introduction to the Manchester review: all the easier because every word was entirely honest.

Presently, I will be sending you a copy of my collected essays, *Values for Survival*. The main item in that is my essay on the atomic bomb, a matter over which my own anxiety grows steadily, as the sense of alertness and danger in my countrymen diminishes. We now have enough bombs to blast out of existence, according to reports from the scientists, the states of Illinois and Indiana; and we are still making them. These are the actions of madmen, whose madness consists precisely in the fact that they regard their conduct as normal, sane, prudent, tending toward national self-preservation. When I raise my voice to say these things, as I am now doing, I will be treated in the same fashion I was when I wrote my *Call to Arms* in 1938: for which reason, indeed, I am reprinting that otherwise quite obsolete and unimportant article. Your paper shortage has hit my publisher so hard that my book probably won't be printed till 1947 or 48 in England.

WELWYN GARDEN CITY   19 February 1946

My dear Mumford

First: family gratitude for the 'candies' which, with your New Year Greetings, came last week. A highly-pleasurable addition to our small ration of standardised sweets.

Second: acknowledgement of your letter of 10th February, received yesterday. I shall no doubt see you at some function soon after you reach London, when you can tell me when you want to stay in Welwyn. I see the Welwyn Lecture is announced for Tuesday July 2nd. The Howard Medal Luncheon is in London on Thursday June 27th, and the provisional expectation is that you come to Welwyn that evening till the following Wednesday.

Howard's book was duly published on 8th February, and so far there are only local reviews, but the book is being reprinted at once, so the publishers' caution is slightly rebuked. (They only printed 2,000.) *Green-Belt Cities* appears on 8th March. This is twice the price, and whether it will equally survive the ordeal of birth remains to be seen. You should get a copy as soon as anybody; so should Morley.

I have had to defer my American articles to analyse the proposed subsidies in the Housing Bill, 1946, which put a heavy bonus on flat-building. But the promoting Ministry has made what I think a prodigious slip. I am able to prove conclusively that, for every 100,000 people rehoused, if half of them were rehoused in two-storey houses at eighteen an acre on the most expensive land in cities, at least £5,000,000 could be saved as compared with housing all of them in flats at thirty-six an acre on the same area, after allowing for the cost of housing half the people (50,000) in a new town. In addition the whole 100,000 would have 900 sq. ft houses instead of 750 sq. ft flats.

I won't bother you with the arithmetical details, but the demonstration, which I have now documented fully, is as sensational in its way as Unwin's *Nothing Gained by Over-Crowding*. The Bill comes up for first reading next week, and I hope to brief a few MP's in the meantime. I had a letter opening the barrage in *The Times* three days ago, but so far there is no come-back. Since then I have doubted whether I could be right (the figures seem so crazy), but after all possible checks I find I am. It is almost certain that, using American building costs and land costs, the same demonstration could be made for American cities. But to do that I should want:

(a) The building cost per sq. ft (excluding site costs) of an apartment in a Metropolitan or large-city centre, as compared with the building cost per sq. ft of a house in a small town in the same region (say within twenty or thirty miles).

(b) A reasonable estimate of the cost per sq. ft of a terrace house (not a flat) in a central Metropolitan area. (It is unlikely that any have been built recently, but an estimate of cost should be possible. It is probably less than that of a flat in the same district, but it would not destroy my argument if it were the same.)

(c) Scale of site costs per acre of land used for block-apartments in cities and for houses in small towns or suburbs in the same region.

Have you any comparative figures? If so I would like them.

I think nothing could be better for your RIBA lecture than a proposal for the world capital conceived as a garden city, with a discussion of the siting. The arguments which prevailed with the old League for having the capital in a town in one of the West European states were in my view all valid, except the tactical one of weaning the most powerful nation from its

5

infantile isolationism—which I agree may turn the scale in the present world situation. But whatever it is, the capital should be a demonstration of organic planning and of the proper relationship of town and countryside. A grand subject. I fancy it will still be in time in June.

WELWYN GARDEN CITY   ·   12 March 1946

Dear Mumford

. . . My analysis of the finance of multi-storey high-density housing, arising from the subsidies in the Housing Bill now before Parliament, is arousing much discussion, after a lull of three weeks during which, no doubt, experts behind the scenes were making desperate efforts to upset my figures. It is a heaven-sent opportunity to explode the theory that high density has an economic justification. I must confess I had not realised how overwhelming the case is on mere financial grounds. The figures issued by the Government gave me all the data necessary; I did not have to make any debatable assumptions. The battle is now raging in Parliament (where McAllister[1] presented a fully-documented case based on my analysis) and in *The Times*. I enclose with the book a copy of my memorandum to MP's. As I said in my last letter, I hope some American economist will make a parallel study for American cities, where the figures are different but the ratios must be much the same.

HANOVER, NEW HAMPSHIRE   5 April 1946

Dear Osborn

For the last six weeks my wife and I have been conducting, almost single-handed, a campaign to get our government to take more decisive measures to relieve the present international tension by desisting from our unlimited production of atomic bombs, and dispelling Russia's very legitimate fears that we are planning a wholesale attack upon her when we are ready. Given our past history, Russia's past history, and the bias of our respective ideologies, I don't know if we can persuade the present leaders of Russia to talk and act reasonably, provided that we set them a good example; but I think that the experiment is worth trying. Indeed, I believe that our present sleepwalking progress toward atomic war is plainly suicidal, and since that

---

[1] Gilbert McAllister, Labour Member of Parliament. Secretary of the Town and Country Planning Association, 1936–38; editor of the TCPA Journal, 1936–42.

is so we must take bold measures to call off the atomic armament race, at a moment while we still, from the standpoint of the atomic bomb, have decisively the upper hand. Once Russia catches up with us in this department of extermination it is Britain and the United States, not Russia, that will be vulnerable. Our present Churchillian complacence here is fantastically stupid. I tell you all this only to explain why I have been such a bad correspondent lately; and, since I am now deeply in arrears for time, why I will probably remain so until I appear in person in England.

Meanwhile, *Green-Belt Cities* has come, and I am filled with admiration over both its form, which is remarkably handsome for these threadbare times, and for its content, which makes you stand out as Howard's one and only true continuator. Morley has been so sunk in work since returning from England late in January, in a ship where the passengers fared worse than cattle in a cattle-boat, that he hasn't yet had time to read the book; and we therefore haven't put our heads together yet over what is to happen to this and to the Howard book. I am writing him today to jog him along on this matter. Meanwhile *Values for Survival*, which I sent you early in March, can't be published by Warburg for lack of paper: instead, he proposes to bring out the long essay on the Atomic Bomb by itself.

If during the next month or so you are visited by Szymon and Helena Syrkus, two Polish architects and planners who have been over here, they come to you with my blessing. He spent three years in Auschwitz; she was a leader in the abortive insurrection; both of them are part of the new Polish regime and are therefore oriented toward Russia and correspondingly suspicious of British policy; but for all that, and for all the difficulties of talking freely with him unless you speak German or French, you will find them, I think, a rewarding pair. They designed and built a cooperative housing project in Warsaw before the war, at which time they were probably only social democrats; and what is better, they lived in their own houses and discovered by experience and discussion with the workers there what was wrong with them. They made studies of the greater Warsaw area before the war—that was how I got into correspondence with them in 1938 or so— and their present plans for the city's development are an interesting variant on Abercrombie's plans for a decentralised metropolis. They have more to learn from you in England than they have from us in America.

Spring has come early here and the red alder outside my study window already shows green buds; down in Washington, where I spent last week, the magnolias and cherry trees were in fullest bloom. I suppose the gorse will be gone by the time I reach England, the cuckoo will be throaty and harsh in his notes; but maybe there will be red poppies growing among the wheat!

WELWYN GARDEN CITY   16 April 1946

Dear Mumford

The last letter I received from you was dated 10th February (but see below) since when I have sent you mere bulletins dated 19th February and 12th March. You should have received six copies of Howard's book, and a signed copy of my *Green-Belt Cities*. The former went out of print before publication, and the latter has gone well enough to justify reprinting at once; both have had friendly press notices but not many really intelligent reviews. I begin to think that, outside *belles-lettres* and economics, reviewing is a dead art in this country. Admitting that town planning is a minority topic, I feel that the number of people who would be interested in what I write is several times as many as the number who in fact come across it. By starting with compensation and other technical branches of the subject I have got myself into a high and dry pigeonhole, and there I shall remain until some abnormal reviewer reads the text of a book by me as well as the publisher's blurb. Still, I must sympathise with the reviewers, who are all handicapped by lack of space. I have just written 600 words on the English edition of your *City Development* for *The Spectator*, and by the time I had indicated briefly what the book is about, talked it up so that people would buy it, drilled one or two holes in it just to show my critical independence, and made one joke for the sake of readability, I had no words left for a carefully-balanced judgement. My complaint is that most reviewers don't tell the potential reader what is in a book—an elementary necessity.

Thank you warmly for sending me *Values for Survival*; I have not yet had time to read it. I am in arrears with a lot of journalistic commitments owing to concentration on the work of the New Towns Committee, which has now submitted two interim reports (the first of which is published and has had an unexpectedly good press) and is completing its longer final report. We go to Sweden next week, for inspiration on the aesthetic rather than on the organisational side of our subject, and also perhaps for a joy-ride at Government expense with an entirely comfortable conscience, since we deserve it, and the joint experience will certainly improve our report. I opposed the trip with purposeful inefficiency. It will be more valuable to me as an individual than to the Committee as a group; I am excessively insular in experiences, and am aware of it.

The Government is introducing a New Towns Bill in a month or two— the first unmistakable legislative result of the ten years' campaign of the Town & Country Planning Association since I became its Hon. Secretary. The obstacles have been formidable, and having become adapted to the function of airy-fairy town-building from an ivory tower, I am alarmed at the probability that I shall be forced to take part in the practical work once more. It was a shock to me when I had to start Welwyn at 34. At 60 the prospect is a nightmare. If only one could be an irresponsible stream trickling over a virgin plain, instead of a river clamped between built-up banks!

As I write there arrives your letter of 5th April, and I resolve to read at once your chapter on the Atomic Bomb. Agreeing wholly about the *necessity* of an understanding and arrangement with Russia, I am pessimistic about the possibility. Such evidence as there is goes to show that the Russian rulers are realistic and nationalistic to the point of complete indifference to the interests of the rest of the world. I confess I cannot accept this judgement unreservedly; it is too indigestible. But neither can I dismiss it; successive waves of evidence will not allow me that complacency. I can even entertain the idea that because in the atomic age Russia will not be as vulnerable as Britain and America, the Russian Government are not interested in any agreement to avoid an armament race. I find it difficult to believe that they fear an attack by the Western Powers. They have the means of being informed about opinion in the West, and it is at least possible that they are seizing the opportunity given by the inherent pacifism and isolationism of the democracies to strengthen in every way their hard-won military position. It seems to me that everything they have done in Germany, the Balkans, ersia and China is consistent with that interpretation: even the tactical withdrawals when they find there are limits to what a war-weary democracy will stand. If your chapter swings me over to another view I shall be grateful. I do want life and happiness for Russians as well as for Americans and Britishers; but if Russians are unable to see why, I think it is a bit difficult to discuss with them on the basis of common human sentiment. One is driven then to argue on the basis of mutual economy in corpses.

Our garden, neglected during the war, puts up a flicker of its old self in the spring, but will be nothing at all any other season until I have time to think about and refurnish it. When that will be I don't know. I make resolutions, and forget them in the pressure of affairs. We have one superb magnolia which excelled itself in this warmest of recent springs; but was suddenly desolated by a sharp frost. And grass is beginning to grow where we had war-time cabbage because even the continuing food-shortage could not make me tolerate my own inefficient vegetable growing any longer. I find, as I have said before, a basic reassurance in magnolias and grass; they are not deterred by inexorable fate. This is not quite the Wordsworthian reassurance, but I expect less of the universe than he did, or at any rate something different.

HANOVER, NEW HAMPSHIRE   12 May 1946

Dear Osborn
For the last two months I have been in something of a whirl, and I am not
out of it yet: so I don't even remember if I thanked you adequately for the
two copies of *Green-Belt Cities* that reached me, especially that with the
(I hope not entirely ironic) inscription.

When I first made arrangements for my trip the British government still
exercised some authority over travel and some of the best ships were still
on the seas. All this has changed during the last two months, and I now
find myself scurrying around for an air passage, for which my Town and
Country Planning ministry sponsorship is quite worthless, since British
Airways is not yet in operation. I still hope to come on schedule; but it's
all very tentative: quite disturbing to a too sedentary person like myself.

This atmosphere has been the worst possible one for writing my lectures
in and I have to make up for much lost time. Maybe I will still be revising
the Howard lecture after I have given it. As to your book and the Howard
book I am, to speak confidentially, in an even more embarassing state; for
I am now having a very formidable argument with Harcourt, Brace and
Company, which may end in a complete breach, over their treatment of my
books; and for me even to mention your books now to Frank Morley would
only be to lessen their prospects. Do write him direct!

WELWYN GARDEN CITY   20 May 1946

Dear Mumford
Your air mail letter of 12th May arrived on 16th May. It is to be hoped the
problem of your passage will be quickly solved. Having seen the itinerary
worked out for you by the sociologues, I fancy you could claim that your
non-arrival will not only endanger foreign relations but disrupt the programmes of most of the educational and technical institutions in Great
Britain. I am conscience-stricken at having myself entangled you in two public
appearances. Of these however only the Welwyn lecture need require prior
thought. At the Howard Medal lunch you just listen and (if you can stand
England's post-war grub) eat. I could almost draft for you the simple necessary response (strike out words you think inappropriate to the experience):

'My lord chairman, my lords, ladies and gentlemen: It is with genuine
/strange pleasure that I have shared this Trimalchian/impressive meal, the
nature of which justified the doubling/withholding of the Dollar Loan, with
so many supporters/dupes of the Town and Country Planning Association,

none the less/particularly because our contact has been so brisk and brief. I am gratified/dismayed to think that such a body as yours should select me as one of the series of recipients of the Medal commemorating the life-work of that modest genius/antiquated Ebenezer Howard, and I shall treasure/file away this characteristic sample of craft-work with mixed/profound feelings of melancholy/satisfaction.

I'm sorry to hear you are in dispute with your publishers, since I had been under the impression that they were looking after your interests well. Don't however think about the Howard book and mine. I will write to Morley myself about these, for what the effort is worth. The reception of my book here has been neither as bad as I thought possible, nor as good as I thought conceivable. I overlooked what I regard as a first principle of composition, having learned it from Edgar Allen Poe's famous essay; and that is to get in the first verse or paragraph the style and rhythm of the piece. I have realised since that I begin with solemnity and conventional quotations, whereas the real tone of the book is meant to be my personal blend of tolerance and irascibility, of fundamental assurance usually masked by a pose of deference, but coming into the open against exponents of ideas that I think half-baked or mischievous. Only the reviewers who already know my atmosphere seem to have detected what I was at. I forgot that reviewers don't read books, and must be told at the start how to look at their job.

I have just got back from a visit to Sweden, when I got in 12 days a fairly good idea of the urban situation, since I was with the New Towns Committee and met the relevant people. The suburban exodus there is in the phase that it was in here between 1900 and 1914, and they do not realise that it is likely to accelerate very rapidly. They are interested in our ideas, and they are reading your books; but except for a preoccupation with community centres, in suburbs, and with road-planning for safety, a policy has not crystallised. I realised there the sensational interest of the British New Towns policy for other urbanised countries.

WELWYN GARDEN CITY   21 June 1946

Dear Mumford

That you may see how we see ourselves, whether you chide or pat, I send you some Town and Country Planning Association printed matter. The Association has 2,000 members, including 300 local authorities. Most are laymen, but we have the pick of the technicians. There are affiliated Associations in Scotland and Victoria (Australia) and I am trying to start others.

Since 1936, when I took over responsibility, we have restricted membership to people in express agreement with our policy, which some thought suicidal at a time when the garden city idea was out of fashion. But we have greatly increased our membership, and even those who disagreed with us admit that we have been the major force in producing the new planning policy now accepted.

The literate planning movement has been almost wholly against us, and still is—though the professionals accept new towns as they accepted suburbs and flats, because they never quarrel with their bread and butter. The best-written books are by countryside preservationists, who (mistakenly) detest us. The architects' books are bad in all respects; none of the good men can write or speak. Abercrombie is the one conspicuous exception; he wavered a little on the garden city policy during the desert campaign inside the Barlow Commission; but ever since the Report he has been grand. Some of the old TCPA supporters, like George Pepler, have their hearts in the right place, but lack the awkward obstinacy necessary at times.

You will soon sense the attitude of planners outside the TCPA towards it and me. Generally they do not realise that we have been a factor in the position, because they do not understand that planning is political as well as technical; they think, as architects think, that they are given increasing functions as a reward of virtue. Instead of feeling gratitude to lay enthusiasts, they suspect them of wanting to muscle in to a promising new profession. Actually, I never knew a body of people less actuated by the motive of personal gain or ambition than the Association group. Some of the literate and semi-literate technicians have resented my own reviews of their books, all the more because the defects of thinking I spotted were really there. Inside the technical bodies there is no academic criticism; bad and good books are treated alike. Genuine reviews therefore come as a shock, though I have always been much milder than scientists and medical men are about each other's books.

MALVERN, WORCESTERSHIRE   6 July 1946

Dear Osborn

Your incomparable kindness and thoughtfulness and hospitality, to say nothing of your wife's delectable cooking, thrown in for good measure, have invoked in me a sense of gratitude which I fear it would be 'un-English' for me fully to express. Nothing would please me more than the ability to accept your wife's invitation for another day or two in your friendly household; but I will have to count my minutes when I finally come back to

London, and so I will have reluctantly to say no to that. I am setting aside the evening of 6 August for seeing you and any people you may be bringing together, and shifting the *New English Weekly* people from that date to the preceding Saturday. If for any reason this does not suit you, either now or later, please tell me as soon as possible. After 11 July the Institute of Sociology, Malvern, will be my forwarding address.

WELWYN GARDEN CITY   18 July 1946

Lots of people are away in August, so I don't quite know the composition of the small party on the 6th. So far there are Julian Huxley, Donald Tyerman (former Acting Editor of *The Economist*, now on *The Times*), and possibly Ivor Brown (of *The Observer*)—all very well-informed people. Lord Beveridge will be in Germany, Sir Arthur Salter in America, Lord Samuel at an Oxford Conference, and George Orwell in Scotland; but all send messages to say how much they would have liked to meet you.

EDINBURGH   22 July 1946

Dear F.J.

Long before this, as you must have guessed, I have had more than my fill of parties. If the party for 6 August had arranged itself easily I would say go on with it; but since it hasn't, since I must see Julian Huxley previously anyway, and since I'd like very much to see you privately once again, I suggest calling it off. Then you and I might meet for lunch or tea that day if you were in town. This seems to me a much better arrangement.

I hear echoes of your wife's voice in the street around me, especially in the Glasgow people who came to last Saturday's conference, and I have fallen in love with Scotland all over again.

WELWYN GARDEN CITY   31 July 1946

The little party next Tuesday is at the Hungaria Restaurant, Lower Regent Street, at 7 p.m., and I will be there at 6.45. The others coming are Miss Barbara Ward, Donald Tyerman (a very able economist-journalist who is assistant-editor of *The Times*, and a strong supporter of our planning policy), Ivor Brown (editor of *The Observer* and a member of the New Towns Committee), Julian Huxley, and my wife. I had to go on with the party because Barbara Ward and Tyerman, both I think key people here, proved most anxious to meet you; apart from the fact that I was anxious that you should meet them before you leave. . . .

I broadcast for five minutes last night on the Final Report of the New Towns Committee, and the BBC told me they regarded this as linking up with your own broadcast (the second one, on Sunday) which I shall hear with much interest. The Report is a much better and more interesting document than *The Times* leading article would suggest; I don't know who wrote this, but it certainly was not Tyerman. You ought to look at the Report before your talk; and lest you have not seen it I enclose a copy. Some of the things *The Times* say we omit were dealt with in the Second Interim Report, which I think you have had.

The Ministry are proceeding, so far, with new towns at Stevenage (extension 6,000 to 60,000), Hemel Hempstead (23,000 to 60,000) (both in Hertfordshire), Three Bridges, Sussex (new town), and Harlow, Essex (new town). For Manchester, Mobberley in Cheshire seems a serious intention. Others are under active consideration, but have not yet been announced. No definite scheme has yet been announced for Scotland. The Government have said they intend to start at least twenty schemes. I am meeting Silkin to-morrow and may get more news. The New Towns Bill should be passed this week. It is a pretty remarkable development, which I should hardly have believed possible in 1939.

RMS *Queen Mary*   12 August 1946

Dear F.J.
We have stopped at Halifax to disgorge almost 3,000 Canadian wives and children; and since that will add an extra day to my voyage, I have decided to fill it up with writing some of the letters I had planned to write when I was finally back in America. So this first note will carry no reports of Sophy and Alison; but will say something I hardly need, I hope, to put in words: namely, how happy I am at the thought of the hospitality and friendliness with which you and Margaret surrounded me all the while we were together. That final dinner carried generosity far beyond the normal bounds of friendship; but it was the perfect farewell touch, and the company could not have been better picked to my taste and interest. I had many vivid moments on my trip; but that dinner ranked with the best of them. There are many things about what I saw and discussed in Britain that I want to comment further on when I write you later; but all that can wait till I can use my typewriter more conveniently. I go back to my country with immense

confidence in your capacity to carry to fruition all the great enterprises that have been projected—provided the international situation does not worsen, but gets better—your educated youth seem to me extremely good and with an excellent grip on themselves and plenty of confidence—once sadly lacking in the twenties and thirties. As for myself, the whole experience has been a stimulating and refreshing one, so that I bless Sophy again for almost pushing me into it at a moment when—after a two year interval of idleness—I was once more absorbed in my work. But not the least reward of the trip was the satisfying of my hitherto 'ghostly' relations with you and your family. What you gave me and did for me is beyond mere thanks.

WELWYN GARDEN CITY   20 August 1946

Dear Lewis

I write this on the 10th August but it is typed on 20th August when my secretary returns from holiday. Primary theses: congratulations on the shining success of your visit, and thanks for what you did to reassert human principles in planning. You came in the midst of, and contributed to, the registration of Dispersal and New Towns as a national project. I hope the sense of taking part in something of historic importance compensated you for so much travelling and talking. I and my family were glad to get closer to your personality, which more than stood up to their exacting (and I think onerous) standards.

For the Town and Country Planning Association group it is a bewildering moment. We are not used to being agreed with by Ministers, down to inverted commas and semi-colons. We feel there must be a 'catch' in it. We realise that there are two tragedies in life: the one, not to get what you want; the other, to get it. I have real anxiety as to what the new towns will be like. Everyone assumes they will be as great an advance on Welwyn as Welwyn was on Letchworth. But knowing the nature of the job and the attainments of the available personnel I cannot feel assured of that. Contrary to received opinion, Welwyn's circumstances were uniquely favourable. The team had experience, imagination, clarity of thought, enterprise, and courage in translating thought into action; and above all it had cohesion and ample time to work its problems out. That will not occur again by chance. The powers that will promote the new towns do not fully understand the nature of the job. And I am not confident of getting them to understand it in time; though I shall make some effort. Unless they can be got to see it, the new towns will not be even as good as Welwyn; they will be like the great housing estates of 1919–39, with the mechanical addition of neighbourhood-unit structure (an ideal only half-truthful) and a few standardised frills. And socially they may embody, as I have said before, 'what good people think is good for people'. This is my headache; I keep the possibility in mind in order to drive myself to the continuance of an unpopular critical attitude which may help to avoid it. I have learned in the last twenty-five years that I cannot impose a point of view without being hated for it by the majority. But I have also learned that you can impose it by being conciliatory in spirit and implacable in thought all the time.

I have just read your address to the Town Planning Institute. It was spiritually sound, but I think it suffered tactically by your unfamiliarity with the audience. You must have fired good trains of thought in some of the younger people. But some of the planners will absorb only what appeared to support their own prejudices. Thus some believers in high density will seize on your criticism of twelve houses an acre, as Silkin did at the meeting. These will ignore your plea in the same address for more space. You told me you want frontages of 30 ft, but you did not say this to the TPI. An average frontage of 30 ft, with backyards of the just tolerable depth of 35 ft, would mean a maximum density of fourteen an acre; but you said you believed twenty or a little more can be satisfactory. It would not matter if planners in general were familiar with practical site planning, but strangely enough they are not. They are subject to fashions and reactions to fashions, and Sharp,[1] for instance, constantly says that you can place twenty-five houses or more on an acre, without saying what component standards he has to lower in order to do it.

Raymond Unwin is in disfavour at the moment, and I was sorry you added a wisp to his cloud. His work was thoroughly scientific, though he was not an ideal expositor. The last time I discussed a scheme with him we were planning to build fifteen or sixteen houses an acre, to concentrate development to the maximum; and while approving our experiment he knew exactly what we had to sacrifice to do it. I have since regretted this scheme. It meant frontages of 17 or 18 ft. The houses are so good that the scheme passes muster, but the architecture suffers considerably and it is a constant criticism that the frontages are cramped and the gardens on average too small to be justified in a new town.

In redevelopment, I think, we have to work to the highest tolerable density, and I have studied this very carefully in the last few years, both for myself and as a member of the Ministry of Town and Country Planning's Density Committee. The latter has come to no conclusions, but my latest published views are in my chapter 'Space Standards in Planning' in the McAllisters'

---

[1] Thomas Sharp, architect, planning consultant, writer.

Homes, Towns and Countryside (Batsford, 1945). Using 850 sq. ft as the average floor-space, 22 ft as the minimum frontage, 15 ft depth of fore-court and 35 ft depth of garden, and allowing for variety of lay-out, you get a maximum density for family houses in terraces of about eighteen-and-a-half to an acre. Including 20 per cent of multi-storey flats at forty an acre, you get a 'mixed' density of twenty-one. No one has replied to this very precise demonstration, which I think cuts space standards to the bone. Sharp still talks of twenty-five cottages an acre; I do not think he has ever built an actual housing scheme, and studied its reception. I have not only built many, but managed them for years afterwards—a chastening experience which architects escape.

I regret also your questioning of the zoning of factories, just when we are getting the idea accepted. I discuss this in *Green-Belt Cities*. Wansbrough's[1] letter in *The Times* was nonsense and Holford[2] disposed of it the following week. A few small workshops distributed about a town may seem unobjec-tionable, even advantageous, but even these must not adjoin houses. Busi-nesses grow: small workshops expand into factories; Birmingham is the classic city of this phenomenon. No one disputes that there can be more than one factory zone even in a small town; and Abercrombie's LCC Plan provides for many well-distributed factory zones in inner London. The industries at Welwyn are as clean and noiseless, and many of them as small, as you will get anywhere. But I can say from close observation that the arguments against mixing them up with houses, or having a lot of small zones, are overwhelming. And it seems wrong to me to suggest that carefully-considered views on matters of this kind, evolved and tested in practical development, are mechanical prejudices. Wansbrough was in error in saying that in 'new towns' there is a tendency to put factories in remote quarters; they will all be within walking or cycling distance of the houses. In Letch-worth and Welwyn the workers normally go home in the lunch hour, and so they will at Stevenage if the provisional plan is accepted. There are no other 'new towns' plans yet. So I could not see what you were tilting at.

After hearing Julian Huxley, I am rather inclined to hope Planning will be handled by the Economic and Social section of UNO. His is a very lively mind, but he seems to me incorrigibly affected by the germs of Marxism, Megalopolitanism and uncritical Modernism. But I may be wrong, and I would be glad of your views on the UNO question. I am more and more inclined to look for the best growth in technique and culture in selected breeding from known reliable species, rather than in sudden mutations.

[1] George Wansbrough, industrialist and financier, Joint Treasurer to the Fabian Society, 1936–37.
[2] Sir William Holford, architect and town planner.

One must admit occasional exceptions, but a love of revolutions seems to me a perversity. I am very bored with the current mechanical Leftism in politics and art. Agreeing that some political integration of the world is a necessity, whether or not in itself regrettable, I can see no possible stability in it unless (a) the futurists come to terms with the traditional values, and (b) there is the maximum possible devolution of power and of the exercise of initiative within the minimum framework necessary to avoid outbreaks of violence. The movement towards collectivism and world-government is moving so quickly that I think much of the world's best intelligence should be given now to the consequential problems.

Underlying my view is an inability to believe in the elimination of biological competition—which seems to me the fundamental predicament of living and, therefore, growing things. I do not see clearly the form this will take when, as seems to me essential, world-wars have been abolished. In the garden, a man is the god who kills and selects. In the world, some day, a human government will be that god. I don't yet see its structure, its sanctions, and its principles of selection. And I am distressed and alarmed that the best minds are resolute to set up that god without giving him any rules for facing the grim realities of his task. The Palestine problem gives a faint hint of the dilemmas of a world government.

Unsolved problems of the ultimate would never seem to me an excuse for not tackling the soluble problems of the proximate. And I do not despise those who say the more distant future must take care of itself. But if people preach and want me to share enthusiasm for a Wellsian world state, they must convince me that they see, at least in principle, a set-up and a policy for it. The belief that the obvious next stage is better, and must be hurried on because we are Partners of some vague Life Force, exasperates me. I am as little enticed to climb on the Juggernaut Band-Wagon as to lie down under it. It is more philosophical to go aside with an ephemeral book of verse, jug of wine, and Thou; or to cultivate an ephemeral garden. Because these are the two typical English reactions, we are thought by Germans, Jews and Irishmen to be incapable of serious thought. But I begin to doubt if anyone will begin to understand the unintelligent English except ourselves. Knowing our propensity to shy at cliff-edges and mirages and the spirits that haunt the fringes of the road, we put on blinkers. More 'philosophical' races drive over the cliffs, chase the mirages or worship the spirits. And those of us who are emancipated from the national blinkers seem to want us to do the same. But sooner or later they find a new kind of blinkers; 'in spite of all temptations he remains an Englishman'. The world will, I now think, have lost much by the recession of England, unless something of its racial genius survives through the United States, which I fancy is unlikely.

I was intrigued by your parable of the wall and the 'haha'. The latter is in fact intended to give a view from the mansion over the meadows, while preventing the cattle straying into the pleasure garden. The wall is a means of securing in a thickly populated country the essential family privacy that in a sparsely populated one is secured by distance. Don't you yourself preach privacy as a right of man? And isn't the desire for opportunities for it universal? I found in Sweden, a thinly populated country, the garden fence beginning in the middle-class suburbs. In Welwyn fences are lower, and doors more usually open, than in the crowded parts of London. If people can have privacy when they want it, and if there is no habit of trespass, doors come to be left unlocked, as they always are in rural England. A bunch of young American officers, whom I cross-examined at Southampton University last year, told me the American back-yards are unfenced because no one would dream of crossing anyone else's boundary. (I confess I doubted this, but they insisted, and made me want to test the point when, if ever, I visit your country.) Russians shut themselves up in their flats, and have not even the equivalent of our public houses or the French cafés. So I am not sure the wall is evidence of an English peculiarity. A Tory candidate, calling on a Communist voter, asked him what was his first want in life. He answered: I want a house to myself, with a garden, and with a wall round the garden, and with spikes on top of the wall; and it is because Capitalism will not give me this that I am a Communist.

Now I (F.J.O.) have always had the privacy I want, and as a young man in a city I had no communal life at all and found my family life a bit boring. I therefore naturally accentuated (too much perhaps) the value of communal life. I moved among people who did the same. And I found many idealised the communal life and even wanted to abandon the family idea altogether. There is always a tendency to this exaggeration among urban collectivists— you have it in Owen, Engels, Wells, Bellamy, etc. In Welwyn, where every-one has a house and a garden, we find a moderate desire for social and communal life; but it is not carried to the length I would have expected as an unmarried youth in London. The demand has definite limits; I am more communal in my habits than most people are. I find many women dislike the idea of nursery schools and crèches; they want to look after their own children. And young men and women prefer lodgings to hostels. We have more than once had to convert nursery schools and hostels, started with enthusiasm and subsidised, to other uses. Even during the war, when we had hundreds of young women transferred against their will, they would not continue to live in the hostels we provided, at considerable expense, to meet their expected needs. They drifted away to lodgings as soon as they could get them in congenial families. They did not save money by this.

They liked it better. This surprised me, but I had to take notice of it. I think probably many girls would like to live, usually in pairs, in convenient small flats if they could get them at rents as low as lodgings. But this gives the privacy they want; hostel or communal life does not. Is it not the same in the USA? Is the closed door and the wall distinctively English?

AMENIA, NEW YORK   23 September 1946

Dear Osborn

I still must call you that, because 'Eric' belongs to Margaret, and 'F.J.' sounds too American, in the gregarious Rotary Club manner; but I use your surname only in a Pickwickian sense. Conveying, I hope, a warmth and intimacy which our meeting sealed if it did not establish. These lines are just to say that I have a long letter cooking, in answer to your generous epistle: but the last three weeks I've spent writing a book at a desperate pace—some 4,000 words a day—and on top of that my poor mother, suddenly invalided and disabled, possibly dying, has presented an immense problem of nursing, housing and care which still has not been solved. The shortage of housing space and help here magnifies all one's difficulties in such an emergency. But I want you to know that I've been thinking of you and will write presently.

HANOVER, NEW HAMPSHIRE   10 October 1946

Dear Osborn

If I don't sit down and write you this minute, at the beginning of the morning, before I have done any work on my book, I may not get a chance to write you before Christmas, because at the end of a day of writing three or four thousand words I am as dry as a squeezed orange: so here goes.

You are wrong, dear Osborn, in thinking that I am one of those who disparage or belittle Unwin's work: it is the one point I would take exception to in *Green-Belt Cities*; for the confusion between open planning and garden cities was not, to my mind, Unwin's fault. If he made any serious error it was that of sliding into the policy of expediency in furthering town extensions, rather than balanced communities. No: his work, particularly his analysis of land costs and site planning, was extremely fruitful in its day and still has to be assimilated by many of the people who criticise it. But I don't think that the standards he arrived at were final ones, any more than the standards of the earlier bye-laws, which he helped to overthrow, were final ones. Experimentally, enough town extensions and garden cities have been built on this open basis to prove, it seems to me, that there is a good case against setting this as an overall standard. In parts of a town where large families are to be encouraged to settle, a standard of twelve or even eight houses to the acre seems to me proper. But I have gradually—certainly not hastily—come to the conclusion that we sacrifice too much in the way of social convenience when we spread a town of even 30,000 people so widely that walking distances become excessive even within the neighbourhood unit of five to ten thousand people. I would throw less land into the private garden and forecourt, and more into neighbourhood greenbelts.

Your mixed density of twenty-one families to the acre seems to me admirably to meet my requirements; though I should be inclined to lop 5 ft off your forecourt. Where permanent public open spaces, in the form of parks and playgrounds, are assured, there is less need of maintaining a suburban standard of private open space. On this matter it seems to me that both thought and practical design have become prematurely stereotyped. Likewise, now that public power can be exercised positively and not merely through restrictive legislation, I think it becomes less important, on public schemes, to fix the exact number of houses per acre: even with an overall density of twenty-one one might have a larger number in one part of the estate and a smaller number in the other. The legal standard seems to me a clumsy alternative to positive design.

I don't think that Unwin, or even perhaps—dare I breathe it?—you, have yet realised how, unconsciously, the standard for ample private space was based upon the assumption, genuine enough in the days of old-fashioned town extensions, that the country would always tend to get farther and farther away from the townsman. Actually, the garden city principle changes this condition; and even before the New Towns Act the legislation Unwin had helped to further tended in the same direction, to the extent that it 'sterilised' agricultural land. If permanent access to the countryside is assured, and if it is close at hand, one needn't depend so much on the private garden to satisfy one's need to be close to growing things. If one is a gardener, well and good, one will want a big garden, perhaps; but even a small patch for cultivation will often satisfy, by challenging one's ingenuity. Unwin wanted to have the garden big enough to let a family grow its own potatoes and cabbages; but except in the case of marginal families that might be handled in other ways, as by the more convenient location of special allotment gardens. There is, I think, an adjustment to be made, in every particular case, between the need for open space and the need for community, just as there is within the house between the need for mechanical utilities and the need for rooms. If one treats the open space standard as an absolute one, one may sacrifice too much in other directions.

As to my remarks at the TPI, they were badly reported: you wouldn't guess, from the lame printed version, what a good talk it was. But unfortunately mere patching couldn't recapture what I said; and I didn't have time to re-write it thoroughly. What I was challenging in that talk was not zoning, but the practice, again, of making zoning an absolute. I think our living quarters, even in model towns, might become unnecessarily dreary unless we tolerate, in the design of the neighbourhood units, workshops as well as stores such as you have wisely provided in Welwyn. I have already said this in *The Culture of Cities*: and by workshops I mean the inoffensive small light industries or crafts, not factories. What I was doing was taking for granted the validity of the zoning idea, as I take for granted the validity of open planning; and then making a plea for not treating it as absolutely inviolable. There is a lot to be said for Samuel Butler's dictum that even the most unquestionable virtue should always be mixed with a little of its opposite. That is true even of beauty and order, as I found by experience on the campus of Stanford, which is handsome in the same way that so much of Welwyn is, with comely houses and lush gardens. When I walked to the university I found myself, every now and then, following the back alleys rather than the streets, in order to recover, in the disorderly plants that had escaped the gardens, in the piles of bush clippings or of manure, in an occasional workshop or dishevelled garden house, a sense of the earthy realities and fundaments. Without that touch of homely workaday activities, our all-too-perfect front lawns and gardens were in fact a libel and a lie. By pretending to be above such activities, as much as the Renascence Palace was above them, the middle classes have created for themselves something that is below them. Life, real life, is better than that. One should be able occasionally to smell the sweat! That is my reason for not wanting all a town's normal industrial and business activities put completely out of sight and out of mind.

By writing like a madman for three weeks whilst I remained in Amenia—Sophy having come up here with Alison to start school—I managed to do the second draft of my memoir on my son;[1] which turns out to be a much bigger and wider-ranging book than I intended it to be. It now satisfies Sophy's exacting eyes, as the first draft did not; but I still don't know if I should publish it in my own lifetime, or indeed publish it at all; and if I do, whether to do so in America, or perhaps show it first to my English publisher. If I don't publish it I'll send a copy over for your private reading, as the next best thing to a family visit. My mother, who is now almost 82, suddenly lost most of her mental faculties whilst I was away; and the problem of getting

---

[1] *Green Memories. The Story of Geddes Mumford*, New York, 1947.

her adequately looked after has plagued us up to now, but is momentarily solved, or in process of being solved. This throws a formidable expense on the family budget; but fortunately my royalties have kept up to their usual level the past six months; and I should, with good luck, be free to plunge at last into volume IV before the winter is completely over.

WELWYN GARDEN CITY   17 October 1946

Dear Lewis

This is not a letter but a bulletin to tell you a little of what happened at the International Housing and Town Planning Congress at Hastings last week. It was a real event: 350 delegates came from other countries and altogether there were 1,250 from twenty-three nations. A surprise to me was that there was a delegation of a dozen or so from Poland. Representative parties came also from Belgium, Holland, Denmark, Sweden, Norway, Switzerland, France, Portugal and the United States; smaller parties and single delegates from Indonesia, Australia, Bolivia, Czechoslovakia, Greece, Hungary, India, Luxemburg, New Zealand, South Africa, Uruguay, Spain and Austria. Russia, despite many telegrams, was not represented. But it was a much more representative gathering than I had expected.

It was essentially a 'Garden Cities' or 'Dispersal-and-New Towns' week; and probably the peak of prestige for British planning; all the other countries just now seem to be watching us and trying to adopt our policy to their purposes. Several spontaneous eulogiums were delivered on Howard, and Rasmussen pronounced a fervent oration on Raymond Unwin in proposing the sending of a telegram of greetings to Lady Unwin. You and Catherine Bauer and I were bracketed as the world's propagandists of light. All this was sobering to me, but good for the solid phalanxes of British municipal councillors and officials, who did not know they had been entertaining angels unawares.

I had some good talks with Catherine Bauer, who lectured me severely and at length on my supposed antagonism to modern architecture; an implied rebuke to you for thinking I had better be left in my state of ecstatic darkness on the subject. But in the end I think she felt you had been right.

WELWYN GARDEN CITY   12 November 1946

Dear Lewis

I told Barry Parker you had nearly referred to him in your BBC Talk, and in reply he writes so glowingly of your 'instinctive niceness and refinement of feeling' that it is clear that you have quite cheered him up by having hesitated before not mentioning him. But you are already as well aware as I am of his saintly sweetness.

Catherine Bauer has passed through London on her way from the Continent to the USA without having time for another talk. She finds Britain ahead in planning, but gives Sweden better marks for architecture. My own opinion is that architecture has lost its way in Sweden, even more than in England; but Sweden has not the mass of thoroughly bad stylism in commercial buildings, or of slummocky non-architecture in domestic buildings, that we have. Modern Swedish architects, gazing with me at seven-storey Point Houses and detached suburban houses, and grappling with my alien lay queries as to what principles of line or mass inspired them, replied: 'We have not solved the problem of the exterior'. Their interiors are not only functional but often exquisitely beautiful.The Philistine is with them in caring little for external design. But whatever the justification for that, I say it is an abdication of Architecture.

I didn't have time to get at the springs of Catherine's religious passion for modern architecture, nor even to find what she means by it. I find I respond to some 'modern' buildings here aesthetically, but not to most—in percentages the pleasure is not greater than I get from town buildings in general. And when I do get the thrill I can detect the observance, in a vague way, of some of the principles of good traditional design. But I haven't formulated any principles clearly, and don't at present intend to try. I don't, however, gladly accept Ahren's view that architecture is lost for the time being, and that the date of its return is unpredictable; that therefore we should for the time being concentrate on planning, where principles can be agreed. In England some of the younger architects seem to me capable of beautiful external design. And I would have thought that was true in the United States, unless the pictures I like are disreputable in the eyes of the true gospellers. I confess I haven't much confidence in the taste of people who can't see merit, and vitality, in the best parts of Welwyn Garden City. The architects here, who are not out of the living English stream, have no thought of making a complete break of style in the newer parts of the town. But there will certainly be subtle changes. I think the modernists here are modifying more than the traditionalists. Some at least confess to reconversion.

New Towns are encountering a lot of organised opposition on the designated sites, much of it of course mere manoeuvring for compensation terms. We are taking counter-measures, and I do not think the opposition is formidable, though the situation has not been well handled by the Ministry.

WELWYN GARDEN CITY   26 November 1946

Dear Lewis

This is to let you know that I shall probably arrive in your country about the middle of December for a six weeks' visit on an itinerary to be arranged by the National Housing Agency. As they are paying my travelling expenses and a *per diem* allowance while I am there, they will make all arrangements, with 'time out' if I want it for my own purposes. I know you are absorbed in your writing programme, and as we have met so recently we shan't have accumulated a 'head' of ideas demanding exchange, so I won't *expect* to meet you this time. The National Housing Agency plan is that I go to Washington first and meet Wyatt and his circus; then go on tour, and come back to Washington for the last week—which it seems likely will be at the end of January. I have no idea yet what happens in between. . . .

HANOVER, NEW HAMPSHIRE   2 December 1946

Dear F.J.

I was on the point of answering your two November letters today, if indeed I do not still owe you an answer for that of 17 October, when your surprising and altogether delightful announcement of your visit to the United States came this morning. I could wish that your visit were to be made at a more seasonable time of the year; for the long, soft, mellow autumn has suddenly, overnight, changed into roughest winter, and of course the landscape is never as attractive in winter as in the growing season: you might even think, without my present warning, that Americans don't cultivate gardens, because a good part of them will probably be under snow while you're here. But never mind: it is good that you are coming under any circumstances; good for us if not for you. I hope that the National Housing Agency will route you right out to the West Coast, for no one really knows America who does not know that part of my country, as well as the East—and at least the geraniums will be in flower in California. They will probably work you good and hard, in return for their *per diem* allowance; but I want you to know that our all-too-brief meetings in England by no means exhausted my own desire to see more of you, if we can possibly arrange it, and no pre-occupations of mine will stand in the way of our meeting if you are within hailing distance. Best of all would be if you could spend a day or two with us here, or if possible more, in this relatively ideal New England town, which is almost a garden city in spite of itself. I should even like to arrange for a lecture here, if you aren't too fed up. We are four hours from Boston and eight from New York; and if you *can't* come here, I'll make every effort to meet you at one or the other places.

I lectured for a week at MIT just before Catherine Wurster came back, so I haven't yet had a chance to hear at first hand what she saw and did and said: it might even be profitable for us three to put our stubborn heads together if you manage to get to Cambridge. Until the 6 February, when I leave to give a few lectures in California, I shall be at the above address all the while—except for a dash to New York on Sunday, 22 December, to give a lecture. . . . You will find plenty to eat and drink here, and if you should need an overcoat you can also get that, though I warn you to be sure that it is an English one. But unless the coal strike is settled in short order you may find yourself as underheated as you would be in England. On the other hand, that may prove more tolerable than our chronic winter overheating indoors: a relic of the days when there was actually 'wood to burn'. Enough for the present: this is by way of a preliminary embrace. We only wish Margaret were coming with you!

HANOVER, NEW HAMPSHIRE   11 December 1946

Dear Osborn
I am ashamed once more that your letters of 21 and 29 October should have remained so long unanswered. I can only plead that I had a great many little additions to make to the proofs of the book of political and educational essays that is coming out next spring; and on top of that I was suddenly called upon, not only to make corrections in the text of *The Culture of Cities* for the French and Dutch editions[1], but also to write a fresh preface, weed out and add to the bibliography, and what is worse, gather illustrations for three plates that had gotten lost in the course of their pilgrimages the last eight years. These niggling jobs take as much time as an important one would; if anything more.

I am glad to have had at last a belated opportunity to rectify the gross injustice to your name which I made by unaccountably leaving you out of *The Culture of Cities* in the first edition; and I crimsoned to discover that I had consistently given *Garden Cities of Tomorrow* the wrong title: this being one of those cases where one is so sure—for some obscure reason— that one doesn't bother to check. Not least of my changes, I was able to throw out the last plate on Frankurt Romerstadt and substitute two plates on the planning of Greater London. Having had Abercrombie's second effort in my hands for the last three weeks, and having at least partly digested

---

[1] Neither of these editions was published.

it, I completely share your enthusiasms for it. Indeed, I look upon it as the best single document on planning, in every aspect, that has come out since Howard's book itself: in fact it may almost be treated as the mature form of the organism whereof *Garden Cities of Tomorrow* was the embryo.

I have saluted the book, in words as unqualified as this, in the letterpress; and I even hope it may have some influence in both Holland and France upon those fashionable souls who still worship at the shrine of Le Corbusier, without realising that even the fashions have changed! I don't know which to admire more about Abercrombie's work: its intellectual penetration, its political skill, its beauty of presentation, or its all-round comprehension of the planners and the citizen's job. If you ever have occasion to speak to him, please convey him my very respectful compliments: for in breaking out from the constrictions of the LCC plan he actually answered my criticisms before I had formulated them.

In going through *The Culture of Cities* I find little I should like to revise in the first five chapters: with the last three, on the other hand, I have many kinds of dissatisfaction: they lack focus and they lack bite: even the part on the Garden City is not as good as my introduction to your reprint. I had hoped to re-write the last chapter, but by the time I had done my minor revisions I realised that even this would require a couple of months of fairly solid work if I were to do it adequately; so I have postponed this till I shall have visited England and shall have finished volume IV. My next job is to revise *Technics and Civilisation* for a Swedish and Dutch edition,[1] and here, I regret to say, I simply cannot leave the text alone. Not merely have my opinions become more strongly moulded during the last dozen years, but a book on Technics today that does not refer to atomic fission, as we now so politely, almost mincingly, call it, would be more obsolete than is seemly at the present juncture.

From the reports of what is now going on in England, from the evidence of the Greater London plan, you must now feel that the tide has at last set in your direction. The original job of making the ideal credible has been performed, and the main task now is to master the political methods that will most effectively translate it into a reality. We have not yet reached that stage here. Even as good a person as Catherine Bauer stands only half way between young Garden City critics like Lloyd Rodwin and myself, so we are far from having reached the political stage. And I fear the results of our immaturity here once the post-war building boom, now held up by high prices, shortage of skilled labour, and hopes of even higher prices, gets under way.

---

[1] These revisions were never made.

As for my personal life, I now have begun to spend half a dozen hours a week, in an informal tutorial capacity under the sponsorship of the Dartmouth College library, acting as a cross between a Socratic interlocutor and a father confessor to any students who may have need for this. I value the opportunity because it brings me closer to some of the best of the younger generation, not a few of whom are veterans home from the war, tough, steady-eyed, sober for the most part, and pathetically eager to unlimber their minds again and to master all that college can put before them. Meeting some of them in groups I have had very keen discussions with them: their maturity as persons makes up for any lack of academic preparation. One of the best of these lads, it turned out the other day, was the pilot who had flown MacArthur out of the Philippines in 1942: today he is a major. Not having my own son to cherish, I do my best for his comrades. I have discovered that one of the things they find hardest to face is the awareness of how many of their generation did not come back. While they rejoice in their own survival, they have a deep conviction that there was no justice in it—no justice, that is, in any visible human sense.

WELWYN GARDEN CITY   11 December 1946

Dear Lewis
Alas! your letter of 2nd December arrives just after I have heard that Wyatt's resignation from the National Housing Agency indefinitely postpones my visit. It is rather a nuisance since I had cleared the next six weeks of all engagements, and I seem very likely to be involved in heavy commitments in the rest of 1947, and if the invitation is renewed it may be difficult to find the time. However, I shall still hope to see America before I die. And of course if I ever do come, I shall want to have some good talks with you, wherever you may be at the time. From your own experience you will understand that there is an element of relief as well as disappointment in the cancellation of the trip. I am very busy and not very well, and I am not at all sure that I could stand up to the itinerary by which the National Housing Agency would have to justify its *per diem* allowance to the Treasury, and remain alert and interesting to the experts I should encounter.

HANOVER, NEW HAMPSHIRE   1 January 1947

A happy New Year, dear F.J., to you and Margaret and Tom and your daughter. I am chagrined over the fact that the inconstancy of our government, which has always been specially marked in the matter of housing, keeps me from uttering these wishes in person; for, as I wrote you in a letter that may not even have been forwarded from Washington, the few days we had together last summer were all too brief for my taste, and there are many things we might have talked about that we didn't even skirt on. Those days together have remained as sunny in memory as they were in fact; and the breakfasts in your garden have almost indissolubly mingled in my mind with the kind of morning fragrance that William Morris put into the opening pages of *News from Nowhere*, so that I feel that I have actually had a foot in utopia at one moment in my life; a feeling that I never had as a mere *visitor* anywhere else before, except perhaps on the terrace of my friend Lester McCoy's house in Honolulu.

Looking back on the year, my English trip naturally dominates every other part of it, and my stay with you, coming in the very middle of it, is the apex of my personal contacts with England. Ever since coming home I have been wanting to write about it; but my preoccupation with the biography of my son, the third draft of which I finally finished a few days ago, kept me from writing even a line for my private satisfaction. I used to toss my stray reflections and soliloquies into the *New Republic*, which was quite glad to print them; but there is no magazine now to serve as an outlet for my private trivia, even if I had the time to give to their writing. But I think I told you in my last letter or so that I have been lecturing on planning affairs in England at MIT and at Yale, so I have not been completely bottled up; and the young listened to me, tracing the triumph of Howard's and your ideas with close attention not unmingled with envy. I keep on emphasising to them the importance of long term plans and ideas, instead of playing more timidly for immediate tangible gains; and the triumph of the New Towns idea is a beautiful concrete illustration of what I mean.

Actually, both thought and practice in housing in this country have been *going backward* since the middle thirties; and some of this is due to the fact, I fear, that people like Clarence Stein[1] and myself and the group we worked with in the twenties have not been feeding the housing movement with fresh ideas and objectives. The Greenbelt Towns,[2] though half baked in their conception at Washington, were the direct outcome of our thinking; but so far backward have we gone in the meanwhile, thanks to the leadership of reactionary opportunists like Robert Moses,[3] that New York City's municipal housing is the most prison-like and congested that can be shown anywhere, and has become worse during the last seven years. How far our

---

[1] Clarence S. Stein, architect-planner. Important member of the RPAA. Very active in the promotion of American New Towns.
[2] New Towns sponsored by Roosevelt Administration in 1935 at Greenbelt, Maryland, Greendale, Wisconsin and Greenhills, Ohio.
[3] City Parks Commissioner, New York, 1934–60.

thinking has gone back you can gauge from the conclusions of Charles Abrams' recent book, *The Future of Housing*, an extra copy of which I am sending on to you, though you will doubtless get it for review in the ordinary course of things. If I were in New York or Boston I should be tempted to gather a group of the younger people together and take up the thread where Stein and Wright[1] and I laid it down in the middle thirties; but for the moment, settling down in a big city under present housing conditions, it is a wilder hope than your coming to the United States with the aid of our housing administration!

When I wrote my paper on *A World Centre for the United Nations*, I little thought it would have such an ironic aftermath as the acceptance of one-two-hundredth part of my proposal, in the shape of fifteen acres hastily snatched at the first bid from the philanthropic but peremptory Rockefeller. The way in which the whole decision was arrived at was a caricature of decent public policy, to say nothing of scientific judgement; and even if three thousand acres had been offered, the manner of reaching the conclusion would have been offensive. Unfortunately, I can hardly even plan a campaign to extend the area to be used by the United Nations, for they have taken a site that is by nature far too hemmed in to exist as an independent unit, in contrast to the vast acres that could have been redeemed in the lower part of Manhatten, in the heel of our stocking shaped island. Someday the United Nations will repent of its haste; but I am glad that I shall not live long enough, in all probability, to have the temptation to say: I told you so.

Between now and next April I have a series of small jobs to finish up, three lectures on Christianity in a Time of Troubles, which I shall give in California in February, and a long article on the urban community for an encyclopedic book on architecture the Columbia University Press is going to do: also two little articles on cities for Chambers' Encyclopedia. After that, if my luck holds, I shall get to work in good earnest on volume IV of my series: practically the foundation of all my other works, and my last will and testament. After *that* the only graceful thing to do will be to die promptly at the height of my private glory if not my public fame, before I become an embittered old man.

WELWYN GARDEN CITY   7 January 1947

Dear Lewis

I wrote you a few days ago, but your letter of January 1st has come since and I must send you a short note to say, first, how delightful my family and I find

---

[1] Henry Wright, architect, pioneer of low-income housing, important member of the RPAA.

your warm expression of feeling about your English trip. We ourselves, being English, could not say the sort of things you say about the atmosphere in this town; but Margaret and I, having lived in big cities, and moving in congenial circles in a new one, see what you mean and very much agree with it. If you could have got into the industrial life of the place, as of course I have, and could compare it with the equivalent in paleo-technic industrial areas, you would not think of William Morris but you would feel that something new had been created. You will have detected in *Green-Belt Cities* my confidence that the Howard formula has been vindicated; but when you live close to many people whose lives have been affected by it without any intention on their part, you are too conscious of their scepticism and minor complaints to stress your satisfaction. Further fields are greener even as seen from the greenest. It requires a very balanced knowledge of the needs and wants of human beings, from the cradle to old age, to judge what sort of environment gives the greatest good to the greatest number. There are plenty of people in Welwyn Garden City who are more conscious of its drawbacks than of its merits. They do not know, and no one can prove to them, that all but a tiny percentage of them would, in any other place, find the surplus of consciously-felt drawbacks even greater. It is those who live mainly for some one interest that cannot be found here that would be better-placed somewhere else.

I am sorry to hear of the setback to housing in the United States. Sooner or later, as happened here, the impossibility of providing low-rented dwellings for city workers must drive the political machine to a big expenditure on subsidies; but so long as middle-class building booms, and there is 'filtering' by the occupation of cast-off middle-class houses, that may be stalled off. In the meantime much damage will be done to planning by the further spread of suburbs, since the down-town areas cannot be rebuilt more openly without subsidies, and even high-density redevelopment is very slow without them.

Don't you think you need in the United States a persistent group like the Garden Cities Association, plugging away at a simple-minded advocacy of dispersal and small towns? I think it was the persistency with which our group stuck to one objective, and even over-simplified it, that lodged the idea in the political mind. When I took over the Secretaryship of the Association in 1936 I re-stated the objective in all kinds of ways, and I pursued the ramification of Howard's critical analysis into fields appealing to different interest groups, ideologies and scientific specialism. It was what Sidney Webb called 'stratified electioneering', but it all led up to one simple objective. I would have thought some sort of Howard Group or New Towns Association, bringing in as many different sorts of interest and skill as possible, but held together by the key principle, could, seeing there is no other solution of the urban problem, get your public to understand it and accept it. Methods are secondary, and the society should not make them an article of faith.

WELWYN GARDEN CITY   4 February 1947

Dear Lewis

. . . I am immersed in writing about the Planning Bill, which amounts to a revolution in land tenure. In principle it is dead right. As in other fields, our semi-socialisation policy is *not* out-running a good theory of the correct boundaries between public control and personal initiative. If we went slower or less far we could not meet the needs of a mechanised and highly integrated economic system, and would incur the danger of inflation and chaos. If it were not for the organisational importance of the ideological Leftists in local branches of Labour Parties and Trade Unions, no doubt the Government spokesmen would say much more about the problem of making Socialism or semi-Socialism work, than they do. The ghost of Ramsay Macdonald haunts the Cabinet table and every Minister's chair; none dare be suspected, or suspect himself, of faint-heartedness or weak conciliation on the principle complementary to collectivism—freedom of initiative and enterprise. The institutional guardians of that principle, with the exception of the small shopkeepers, are more completely disfranchised than any functional class has been since the Feudal system.

Big business is in fact cooperating in the new system with surprising completeness. Only late at nights, and in secret conclave, do they express resentment or doubt. These are of course latent, and politically the Right will seize on and capitalise any breakdown of the machinery or irritating use of bureaucratic power—things that must occur in greater or less measure. Even now most of the spokesmen of the Right don't see what a chance that is going to give them. Many of them are disposed to play the card of Christianity, duty and other-worldliness—of a moral renascence and higher standards of endeavour in manual work and management—as the alternative to 'Marxist' materialism and a solution by governmental control. That is not a good party card here, because the Labour movement is not spiritually Marxist and a revival of Christian idealism, if it came (which is possible), would go through all ranks and could not be made a party monopoly. On the whole, therefore, I think the reaction against the sufficiency of organisational control will occur within both Left and Right. It should not menace the Labour Party at the election of 1950 provided the leaders have the courage to attack the belief on the Left that the benefits of the Age of Plenty (30 hour week etc.) can be paid for by the further elimination of unearned incomes. They have 50 years of their own propaganda to correct, but they are so well aware of the true situation of this country that before long they must go all out to make it clear to their supporters.

I think also there is enough intelligence and philosophy in this country to make the masses and the politicians realise that the whole future of civilisation may depend on the system Britain and the smaller democracies can evolve at this critical period. If the Neo-Technic order goes down in disaster, instead of evolving to a better order, historians may say that we failed to develop the governmental technique and the subtle ideology necessary for its survival. But if this group of nations fails, I wonder what others can succeed. It does require both an acceptance of government to a high degree, and a practice in the working of highly-organised governmental institutions, that I cannot see (at my distance) on the horizon in the USA, Russia, China or India. This is why I can't at present believe in an 'integrated' World-Government, but tend to think on the lines of a United Nations Organisation guaranteeing (on the whole) existing national units against attack and providing a machinery for negotiating (not determining) conflicts of economic interest. I put it this way: if I am only just convinced that institutionally Britain (or Sweden) with its gradual evolution and long practice, can solve its internal problem of control versus freedom, how can I begin to believe in a World-Government at this stage? Prove to me that the choice is World-Government or downfall, and I write off Civilisation as lost. If I see a ghost of a chance in one direction, and none at all in another, I choose the ghost. Actually my animal optimism tells me it is not a mere ghost, but I cannot prove that.

Catherine Bauer wrote me an interesting letter a few weeks ago, giving me her own variant of the familiar dilemma of the woman wanting to combine professional with family life. In full measure they are obviously no more combinable than my three alternatives of business man, political writer and comic poet. I chose (or allowed chance to choose for me) a double role that precluded full effectiveness in any, and reduced me to mere amateurism. In a sense I have made many such choices: between staying in England and emigrating to a richer country; between a bachelor life (which suits quite a big section of my temperament) and marriage; between being relatively rich and mortgaged to business and being relatively poor and free to develop my intellectual interests; between a diffused impact on a large society and a concentrated impact on a small one; and so on. I don't really see that the woman's dilemma, real as it is, differs in kind from any man's. Which is not to say that I don't sympathise with it. Some people seem to 'get it both ways' by reason of extraordinary energy or exceptional luck; but they don't really; the same energy employed in a single direction would have taken them further. Naturally I am all in favour of freedom for everybody to make such domestic arrangements as facilitate their own choice or compromise, if they can find partners who agree with such arrangements. But it is no real grievance against society that it offers us choices. The complaint, if any, should be lodged in higher quarters. . . .

HANOVER, NEW HAMPSHIRE   6 March 1947

Dear F. J.

. . . Last week I returned from three weeks in California, a little ruefully because my lectures, which were not, I suspect, very good in the first place, were further weakened by an inconvenient attack of laryngitis, and instead of meeting people at the Pacific School of Religion, where I lectured, I spent most of my waking moments over a croup kettle, which was the best that an eminent young throat specialist could do for me. The joke about this treatment was that it did nothing to relieve my voice at all, so on the last day, having no voice, I went around to the local chemist shop—which I had happened to notice as a good example of modern architecture—and from the proprietor got a special throat lozenge with a long chemical name, probably quite poisonous, which restored my voice in one hour: precisely what I had hoped to get from a specialist. The experience, coming after that horrible January, left me feeling rather desperate; but I spent a week among my old friends and colleagues at Stanford, which is a very pleasant place, and I used my time profitably there, acting as consultant in the laying down of future plans for the 7,000—yes, seven thousand—acre campus.

The last letter I had from Catherine a month or so ago told me that she is still making efforts to get you over here; and since too many cooks spoil the broth, I shall keep out of this effort until I can be of some special use. We are not really ready for you at the present moment: only the young would understand what you are driving at and would sympathise with your premises. You are right in saying that we need a persistent organisation to push the whole business of planning and city development here. I forget whether, when we were together or otherwise, I ever discussed the old Regional Planning Association of America, which flourished between 1923 and 1933; for there *was* such a group, and it laid the foundation for the positive work of the Roosevelt administration, including TVA[1]. Unfortunately, we broke up, partly because some of the members went to Washington or the TVA, and though we kept a pro-forma existence we failed to attract new members, particularly the young, though we made Catherine Bauer secretary just for this purpose. Because of our defection, I believe—and because no other group took on the

---

[1] The history of the RPAA is told in Roy Lubove, *Community Planning in the 1920's: The Contribution of the Regional Planning Association of America*, Pittsburgh, 1964.

job—the housing and planning movement has been going steadily backward. If I were able to live in New York I might try to rally the younger men; some of them in Cambridge and Washington have begged me to do this; but Hanover is eight hours from New York and fourteen from Washington; and that is too great a degree of dispersal: a single day in New York costs me three actual workdays, and that is a heavy tax.

What you say about the practical impossibility of World Government is true; and in ordinary times I should bow meekly to your judgement. But in the present situation I am tempted to quote the sign that someone saw in one of our military headquarters: the difficult we do immediately; the impossible will take a little longer. I admit that world government will take a little longer; but the nature of our present crisis is such, with respect to the powers of destruction we now command, that if we don't make serious steps toward world government immediately, if we continue the present jockeying for military position and advantage—and by 'we' I mean particularly my country and Russia—the results will be far more disastrous than the worst mess that premature world government could conjure up. I confess I don't know fully how to make the Russians see this, still less how to get any home pressure exerted on the Russian government; but I do think that my own countrymen, by failing to take positive measures to disarm Russian suspicions and by persistently using wrong symbols—like the ex-Wall Street shark, Baruch—have raised obstacles that could have been avoided and have made the situation more difficult. Our greatest weakness, which is a universal one, is the failure to realise that we are facing a situation that is without precedent, therefore without practical guidance of any sort in history; and that we must attack it with a continued vigilance that even war itself doesn't usually command. We are still asleep; as much so as when I wrote *Gentlemen You are Mad;* and I am as much asleep, as much paralyzed, as anyone; for if I were really awake I couldn't feel myself doing the things I actually do do from day to day, like re-planning the Stanford campus. . . .

WELWYN GARDEN CITY   30 April 1947

Dear Lewis

I had your letter of 6th March on my return from Northern Europe. My tour proved interesting and I think worth while from my point of view, if not from that of my audiences and contacts. But I made no new generalisations, which rather suggests to me that I was mentally in an inert, unreceptive state. Perhaps some will dawn on me in retrospect. My mind needs stimulus by inspired exaggerators or people who discover and concentrate intensely on half-truths, which I take a joy in debunking and getting into balanced perspective. Meeting sound, ordinary, wise people leaves me dead and nearly dumb; and there are all too many sound, ordinary people in planning circles, wherever one goes. Hardly any planners have any breadth of culture or diversity of interests. And neither have I, I find, when long in their society. So I listen at inordinate length to technical dissertations, answer plain stodgy questions on law and practice, and now and then complete new sets of pictures of quiet lives. And I know that just out of reach were tensions and passions and extravagant ideas that would interest me and start my sluggish brain and emotions working. Of course I did run into some interesting households and heard some varied war experiences (especially in Holland). But in the main I lived in hotels, gave lectures to audiences meeting just as English audiences do, and met people in their houses only long enough to wish to know them, not to understand them or to sense their real predicaments.

As to world-government, will you answer for USA acceptance if I answer for Britain? And do you think France and the other European countries, the South American states, India and China, will come in, to the extent of cooperating in coercing a recalcitrant Russia? I agree with your logic, but it won't come real to me. I see just a hope for the UN type of organisation, based on mutual defence of *status quo* boundaries, with ticklish future negotiations and threats when it is essential to make necessary changes and adjustments from time to time. If that fails, we are in for another World War, which might lead to the unified government of an impoverished world. What you say about failure to realise the situation is unanswerable. But there are things of which human beings, in their present state, are incapable. I just can't convince myself of a jump at this stage to world-government. I admit the corollaries. But what deity has offered us universal order and peace, and at what date? Which is no reason at all for your desisting from your demonstration.

I have accepted a combined invitation by the Institute of Planners and the National Housing Agency to visit the USA in the fall, which I suppose means September–October, and I now await a definite date. They want me to visit four universities and a dozen cities at least, but I have asked them not to rush me around on a conveyor-belt, since I shall seem more intelligent if I have a little time to look at things and reflect. This is all Catherine Bauer's doing, but the sponsors say the idea has evoked spontaneous interest in a lot of places. I will let you know my itinerary so that our paths may cross somewhere. Paul Oppermann of Washington is handling the arrangements.

WELWYN GARDEN CITY   9 July 1947

Margaret and I are most grateful to Sophia and you for sending us that most thoughtfully-selected parcel of foodstuffs. It is more than kind of you both, though I feel a little ashamed to learn of it on my return from Sweden, where I have been living for a fortnight in the utmost luxury—even though there were many foods I had to avoid, and I abstained entirely from the four or five varieties of alcohol offered me at each of the nine official banquets. But Margaret and Tom, who were not with me, are in a position to appreciate your gift without this troubling of conscience.

I had a memorable tour, perfect weather on both sea journeys by the beautiful and comfortable *Saga*, sunshine all the way in Denmark and Sweden, and a princely reception everywhere. At one point the shade temperature rose to 36·5 C (98·4 F) which is far higher than we ever get here even in August; but we were not much distressed by it, even when travelling in motor-coaches. We had time for long talks with a lot of planning people, and I consolidated many existing friendships and made many new ones. My party of fifty-four was not very distinguished, but it was a good cross-section of the provincial councillors and officers concerned with planning, so we had many useful exchanges of views. I would not choose, except as a matter of duty, to travel with so large a party; but on the other hand its presence draws out many people one would not meet otherwise, while one can search out one's own friends in the free intervals. So I enjoyed the tour immensely, and incidentally benefited by it in health.

AMENIA, NEW YORK   31 August 1947

Dear F.J.

Your letter of the fourteenth confirmed, happily, what I had heard from Catherine Bauer: that your stay would be extended a little and you wouldn't be rushed so hard. I am relieved to learn that you are coming by the *Mauretania* and I trust that you will put your foot down hard on any attempt to shoot you around swiftly by plane in this country. Apart from anything else it is the worst way possible to see the country, since except when you are approaching a port the good planes maintain a very respectful distance from the land below. You will probably be happier staying at a Park Avenue apartment than you would at any New York hotel that I can think of. The real difficulty, of course, is meeting people outside the social strata that will entertain you. I know how that problem always devils me when I travel; though to my sorrow, I also realise that it is only when travelling that my intelligence and my conscience regards this matter as a problem: ordinarily one trusts to the thinnest sort of contact to understand what is going on in other strata of society. (In such matters Sophy is a great help to me; and I perhaps tend to rely too much on her graphic reports of conversations).

I was plagued about this very matter when I was in England, though on the whole I had a better opportunity to talk with working class people than I had ever had before. The one contact I really regretted missing was with a Lancashire working girl whose husband, in the air force, read my books: she and her girl-friend (her husband was away) offered to show me the interior of their Manchester home and give me a glimpse of what ordinary life there was like. It was impossible for many reasons to accept that proposal, which came by mail: Sophy berated me for being a scared-cat when I showed her the girl's letter, but she didn't regret that missed opportunity any more than I did. I don't know any way of overcoming this handicap.

As to Clarence Stein, I was perhaps unfair to him in warning you beforehand; for people who have seen him recently say that he is now in better shape than he has been for a long time. Should he have his guest room free and ask you to stay with him you'd find him the best of hosts. As for the New York planning office, it is headed by the reactionary Robert Moses; and the only thing I should perhaps warn you about in connection with him is that it would not be wise to mention my name, let alone allude to our friendship, in front of him. He is a gifted administrator, but it is hard for an honest man to tell whether he has done the city more harm or more good, on a balance of considerations, by his past performances. There is no doubt about the competence of his staff or the high quality of their technical ability: what is lacking in Moses is social insight. His influence has mainly been responsible for the fact that all our recent New York housing developments since 1938 have been in the form of thirteen-storey skyscrapers.

What you say about England puts the whole case very vividly. Your lack of 'imagination'—I always wince when I say this about a country that produced Shakespeare and Lewis Carroll—saved you from being beaten by the Nazis, and it may save you again. Fundamentally, I still feel that my country, which is rolling and wallowing in a perfect pigsty of inflation prosperity, is in equally serious condition and, since it does not realise its peril, will take far longer to get on its feet once its present course drags it to the depths, national and international, to which it is heading. I may be unreasonably apprehensive; but I publicly doubted the existence of our 'prosperity' in 1928; and I see the same symptoms of anesthetic hilarity now. But in some ways you should, as a visitor, find even our sins, or the temporary results of our sins, a diversion from the stoic diet of Old England.

WELWYN GARDEN CITY   6 September 1947

Dear Lewis
I have just had your letter of 31st August. I leave on 24th September and may not have time to write again.

I realise the probable difficulty of getting outside the circle of one's hosts, but I hope I shall be able now and then, without seeming discourteous, to follow up introductions I may have to different circles. For instance, in New York I have introductions to some of the Labour Union people through their opposite numbers here. No equivalent of your lost Lancashire lass is likely to invite me to meet her, but if she did I should certainly want to accept. Dickens on his second visit to the US refused all home invitations and insisted on staying in hotels, probably because he wanted to do some unsponsored prowling. I am not following that policy, because I shall only be a short time in any place, and I would much rather get the feel of one sort of home life than of none at all. It would help me to meet and go round with one or two low-level housing administrators who actually go in and out of dwellings to collect rents or supervise repairs; much of my own knowledge of everyday life came from doing that for many years. When on tour as a young Labour propagandist I stayed a good deal in working class homes; but I shall not have the chance to do that in America.

I am getting very worried about the impracticability of the refresher course in facts, figures and policies, on both sides of the ocean, that I had planned. I concentrate very much on one or two issues on which I think at a given moment official policy or public opinion is wrong. I hammer at these for years, and though I read everything as it comes I do not carry a balanced picture of the whole subject of planning and its economic background in my mind. So when an issue on which I am vague comes up, I get out a lot of books and notes to refresh my memory and document my arguments. I cannot carry my study around with me in another country, and again and again I know I shall be stumped by people with more detailed memories, though I may know they are wrong because they have not got all the data in balance. I wanted to bring a big notebook of statistical and other data, but there seems small hope of writing one up. This is a real headache. No one who engages in public discussion ever had a worse memory than I have. Every fact and figure I read goes to correct my views, but they do not remain accessible to me in impromptu discussion. I should have been a woolly, suggestive minor poet rather than a political journalist.

T. S. Eliot broadcast his *Four Quartets* here last night, in good voice and with the exact rhythm in which I read them in print, and I envied his advantage in being able to dodge all the difficult stages in his argument, and thereby to seem much more profound than he is. Mind you, I think a poet is entitled to dodge in this way when he is seized with some idea on the very margin of the capacity of the human mind. Eliot's effects remind me of a cotton wool snowstorm in a children's pantomime, where the management will not allow the property man enough cotton wool to last out the scene. But that is a discursion.

I hope before I come to get inside the Ministry of Planning for a day or two to see how the administration is tackling the new Act, and I may be able to give a fairly clear picture of what is happening in that field as well as of the policy controversies and their results. But on the general economic and political field I am far from clear. Herbert Morrison has been very helpful in arranging for me to see his economic advisers in the Cabinet Office; but in this sphere, as in aesthetics, I suffer by too much intake and not enough expression, so that I remain in a state of suspended decision that is mentally injurious. I wish I had, as you seem to have, a hard-working Unconscious that would cough up useful results when required. If I have one at all, which I sometimes doubt, it is no better than a very bad filing system.

HANOVER, NEW HAMPSHIRE   15 December 1947

Dear F.J.
That was an all-too-brief and tantalising glimpse of you Friday; and as usual it has left a hundred things unsaid. Never mind: may we meet again soon, and, if heaven will grant it, with a little more leisure for idle discourse. This note is just to wave you on your voyage and to bid you a Merry Christmas when you get there—give Margaret our affectionate greetings. May the New Year restore your health and many happy days!

1948-1959

By 1948, when Osborn had returned from America, the New Towns concept was firmly established in British government policy, and as the programme moved forward Osborn's role became more that of guardian of its principles and general conscience of the Town and Country Planning Association. He didn't work on any of the New Towns, having declined the offer of the Chairmanship of Bracknell because of his age and for technical reasons. The TCPA continued to absorb most of his time and energy; he worked for it harder than ever, frequently lamenting the absence of able, younger men to take the reins from his hands.

The Association was still a voluntary public-spirited body, badly lacking money for adequate administrative and research facilities, and carrying on its work was a heavy strain on its small but very enthusiastic staff and on Osborn himself. He led TCPA study-tours to over a dozen foreign countries and conducted reciprocal Swedish and Russian planning parties around Great Britain. He organised the TCPA criticism of the County of London Plan, his Evidence vis-à-vis his friend and colleague Abercrombie—as described to Mumford—being a model of his tactics on such occasions. He worked tirelessly for the Green Belt policy which the Government adopted in 1956. He conducted a resounding campaign against tower-block flats, belabouring short-sighted officials and fashion-bound architects with his statistics of popular preferences and the anti-social effects of differential subsidies. A property company's take-over of Letchworth Garden City, and the abandonment of its limit on dividend, found him rallying an opposition which eventually secured an Act of Parliament to restore the public equity in the town estate. And from 1949 he did some of his most effective work as Editor of the Association's monthly journal Town and Country Planning, in which for 16 years he expounded the New Towns philosophy and crusaded for humane, gimmick-free planning based on known needs and preferences.

During these years he often felt that he and the Association had failed in their mission: that the New Towns achievement was minimal when compared with the ever-rising tower blocks and the ever-expanding cities. In 1956 he was knighted for his services to town planning; an honour which pleased him, because in England a title increases the recipient's influence, but the irony of his elevation was not lost upon the lifelong socialist, and he was far from complacent about

155

the continuing trends in urban development in England, America and other countries.

1951 was an important year for Mumford for with a fourth, originally unplanned, volume of the Renewal of Life series, The Conduct of Life, *he concluded his massive testament. Teaching at the University of Pennsylvania and MIT occupied some of his time but he continued to produce books.* Art and Technics *(1951) was his Bampton Lectures' exploration of a favourite, central concern;* The Human Prospect *(1955) was an anthology of his work, by other hands. And in the same year the* Transformations of Man *outlined his new interpretation of civilisation, developed in detail in* The City in History *(1961) and* The Myth of the Machine *(1967).*

Writing books was, as always, Mumford's primary activity, but he was also involved with public affairs. There was a fight in 1949 to prevent the Greenbelt Towns, the fruits of the RPAA activities, from being turned over to private hands. He inevitably found himself opposing McCarthyism, and his timely denunciation of American nuclear military policy was expressed in In the Name of Sanity *(1954). Mumford had always been concerned with man's misuse of his environment and natural resources. In the Wenner-Gren Conference on Man's Role in Changing the Face of the Earth (1955), of which he was Co-Chairman, he presented a paper on the Natural History of Urbanism, which, backed by many other papers, was of importance in sounding the alarm against ecological suicide. And throughout this period, in fact from 1932 to 1962, his Skyline criticisms in* The New Yorker *carried his thoughts to a wider audience.*

Mumford visited England in 1953 and 1957, where first-hand observation of British New Towns led to differences with Osborn over housing densities. Mumford thought the New Towns were generally too open and wasteful of space and lacking in variety and experimentation. His criticisms provoked a strong response from Osborn and their exchange of letters on the subject provide the only discord in their relationship.

Mumford was also sharply critical of American planning: public housing and urban renewal were turning into gross caricatures of their great intentions, while in many respects the big American cities were on the brink of a disastrous breakdown. Against this background he began to revise The Culture of Cities, *to incorporate into it his thoughts of the past 20 years. But his thoughts were too original for a revision; a new and different book came forth. So in the excitement of new ideas and discoveries Mumford began work on* The City in History, *the book which was to usher in possibly his most creative decade.*

It is now almost three months, dear F.J., since we saw each other in New York, and if I have been silent all these months it is not for any lack of thinking about you but only because I know from my own experience how busy you must be in trying to catch up with your affairs, and because I knew from Margaret, what you yourself confessed here, that you would need a thorough physical overhauling when you got back. By the same token, of course, I have understood your silence; but was glad to see from the announcement in *Town and Country Planning* that you have, at least, not been idle, even if you've spent some part of your time lying on your back. I knew, alas! that we'd worked you hard; and still I was a little staggered when I saw, in cold print, the figures in ton-miles that measured the extent of our brutality. I have only been to New York once since I saw you, yet even in my casual contacts then I had a sense of the impact you had made on people; and though Stein may have proved trying to you at times, your visit seems to have accompanied his complete rejuvenation for he has never been in better health mentally or physically for over ten years. You were just the prescription in psychosomatic medicine that he apparently needed; and I find that my chief function is in acting as a wet towel on his proposals and reminding him that any organisation dominated by such ancients as himself and myself is bound to have little influence, unless we have younger people in it from the start.

How have I spent these last three months? I came back from my trip with a lame back which made me walk around like a really old man for four weeks, and a mysterious growth on my soft palate which sent me to the doctor for a checkup, since our knowledge of the importance of getting hold of cancer early makes me treat the minor disorders of the body far more respectfully than I once would have done. So far it seems benign, and since the doctors aren't worried I, too, am at ease; though there were a few moments when I found myself speculating as to how I should behave if it were bad, and concluded that I should be one of the world's worst examples of a philosopher in distress.

Finally, in January, I sat down to the serious revision of *The Culture of Cities*, and found that instead of it being a minor operation it was a major one, even though most of my changes fell within the last 150 pages. I was tempted to work in some of the fresh thoughts I'd put together in the introduction to Howard and in the Rebuilding Britain essays, and then found that this just wouldn't work. But I had to excise not a few prophecies that had come true, and to change into the historical tense the passages that led directly up to the adoption of the New Towns policy. The thing that gave me most satisfaction about the revision is that it at last does at least do a semblance of justice in the bibliography to your own work.

Having finished my annual article on the Atomic Bomb, again for *Air Affairs*, my desk is now clear, and if my demon can be dragged from the cellar where he has been sulking for the last few years, I shall, within the month, begin work on volume IV. But I have made so many false starts here that I hesitate to mention the matter, even to a close friend like you, and the least said about it the better. If I find myself stumped once too often I shall solace myself in my frustration by returning to the novel I began in 1939, only to have the war halt me in mid-passage: though I suspect that even there I shall have to begin over again, so much having changed in the last ten years both in the world and in myself. Meanwhile, the skies, which looked dark enough already, are growing darker once more; and my atomic bomb article was addressed to the problem of what measures we in America and England might take to help the light break through again. We have told ourselves so many fibs and half-truths, and in America we have worked up such a phobia against Russia, that I doubt if we have the courage and insight to carry through the only measures that to me seem promising. Still, I have tried to suggest what they might be, and if the editor dares to print the article I'll send you a copy of it presently.

WELWYN GARDEN CITY   16 March 1948

Dear Lewis

I have now decided, after good advice following a very exhaustive examination, to have the operation called Gastroenterostomy, for which I go into hospital in about a fortnight's time. It means being a further eight weeks or so out of action, which is a nuisance just at present, but if the job puts me completely right, of which there is a good prospect, it will have been worth the capital investment of time. I am taking two weeks 'on' to clear up my more urgent arrears of work. I hope I may be able to write a little in this time about my American observations; but I shall not be able to do that with the amount of documentation it properly calls for. I hope my American friends and sponsors are not going to be annoyed with me about this. I think they might have a grievance against me for travelling in a slightly lamed condition; but I really thought the interest and excitement would enable me to 'snap out' of the malaise. You must dismiss any idea that the journey was an excessive strain or did me any harm; I really had quite a leisurely time. If I had been in normal health I should have rushed around a bit. It annoyed me slightly that I couldn't, but I had determined to be philosophical about that and on the whole succeeded. Now I console myself with a thought of coming again when I am fully normal and active.

I meant to tell you in my last that the military people whom I met in

Washington showed that they had been immensely impressed with your lecture to them some time before. It had undoubtedly set them off on a train of thought that they regarded as of major importance. As it chanced, I was at my best in the impromptu talk I gave to one or two of them—the key point of which was the need of balancing high productive potential with defensibility, which of course points to grouping, but not massing, of industry and population. I said it was just a coincidence that the social and military considerations at present point to the same kind of planning; but it was a coincidence of great political importance. I said I thought this is realised in England, though not yet quite logically followed up, partly because the military factors can't be much discussed politically. They surprised me by saying that until your address no military influence whatever had been exercised or even mooted on the distribution of industry. It was now, however, being actively considered. This of course was a bit secret. You may not hear much from me for the next two months.

HANOVER, NEW HAMPSHIRE   29 March 1948

Dear F.J.

When your letter of the sixteenth came I had the impulse to write you immediately. To be sure of saying a cheery word before the operation created, as is the habit of operations, that state of detachment, indifference and general loathing for the banalities of life which is the reward for either the exercises of the mystic or the surgeon's knife. I won't speak lightly of your ordeal, if it is still before you, because I know that it will take resolution, patience and fortitude; but since, apart from your stomach, you possess an astonishingly youthful vigour and buoyancy, I count upon these qualities to see you through, till the moment your energies return in sufficient quantity to promote an equally youthful rebellion. I can't think of a better time to court the 'wise passivity' of convalescence, sloughing off all the cares and responsibilities of a wicked world, than precisely this moment. Since neither of us achieved the rank of Prime Minister there is probably nothing we can do to turn the world away from its present wicked and destructive courses; indeed, there's probably precious little we'd find to put our hands to if we *were* prime ministers. This is a moment for high resignation; and there is no more decisive form of this than a prolonged period in bed. While the world itself continues to go from bad to worse, I trust you will go from good to better. If there's any way in which the Mumfords can help in that recovery, I trust Margaret will promptly call upon us.

As for myself, after grinding away for a month at what purported to be volume IV, I realised—here I suddenly change the figure—that a second mis-carriage has taken place; if, indeed, conception had actually ever occurred! This is a strange plight for me to be in, the first time I have ever faced it; for the beginning of my books usually proceeds without a hitch, once the first draft is done, however difficult may be the eventual writing of them. So at the moment I am convalescing from my little spiritual malady, to speak about it in less gynaecological terms; and for a while I felt bleak and empty. But the other day, when I was feeling most desperate, I suddenly found myself over-taken by the idea for a quite different kind of book, nothing like anything I—or for that matter anyone else—had ever written; and I can hardly bear to let the idea incubate a little before starting work on it. But I plan now to go back to Amenia a little earlier than I would have ordinarily, possibly the last week in May, in order to begin work as early as possible. I don't dare tell you what it is all about until I put it on paper; indeed, I shall scarcely dare to tell you then, lest the good idea shouldn't survive a searching outside look or the second draft of it. But there is an unmistakable feeling in a writer when he has con-ceived: when, instead of willing to do this or that he finds himself the glad victim of something outside himself, greater than he is—like an Amorous Shavian swain in the toils of the Life Force—and by all the subjective symp-toms this will be a real book, possibly a towering one, fortunately far simpler than any other work of mine in style, though still perhaps a little complicated in method. But there: I must shut up or the idea will pop out of my mouth whilst I am gaping in wonder at it.

And by now—even if Margaret has let you read this—you must be tired; so I'll sneak out, only stopping to say over my shoulder how pleased I was over your account of my 'influence' over military circles in Washington. Fantastic as it might seem, my *Air Affairs* article helped to cure them of their faith in the almighty atom bomb and thus, indirectly and by many devious turns, may have been partly responsible for Truman's demand for a larger army: some-thing that I regard far more hopefully than many of my other friends do, in-cluding Catherine Bauer. But the Army hasn't asked for any more lectures so I fear I have turned out a military, as well as a political, butterfly.

HANOVER, NEW HAMPSHIRE   6 May 1948

Dear F.J.

I haven't at this moment the leisure and the grace of mind to answer your letter of 26 March, though I've read it and enjoyed it to the full a second time. Your writing, incidentally, which looks at first glance so neat, so clear, so transparent, is one of the most devilishly hard scripts to decipher I've come across: though I thought I had broken the most difficult case of all when I translated Herman Melville's handwriting, which had quite baffled his first biographer. Actually, yours is more teasing, and I pride myself that only one word in your last letter escaped me. Don't hesitate, when finally you are able to write me, to do so by hand, for I've mastered it. I can speak freely on such matters, I trust, not merely because of our friendship but because my own handwriting is so monstrously bad; and yet, as the years go by, I find myself, particularly at the end of a day, recoiling from the typewriter with its clatter and taking refuge in the quiet, if undecipherable, pen.

All this is by way of prelude to my main reason for writing: to hope that you are, by now, well past the worst stage of your ordeal and beginning to feel the first waves of vitality *creep*—I will not mock you by saying *surge*—through your body. It may be long before either you or Margaret can spare me a line; but be assured that I am thinking most affectionately of you even if, during this next month, I will be too busy planting a garden, packing, moving, preparing some lectures I must give in June, to put my feelings in so many words. I was touched to get your admirable guide to *Town and Country Planning*, with its nicely balanced conspectus of the literature and its more than generous reference to my own work—on which I, incidentally, look back with an ever-more-jaundiced eye, wondering what weaknesses or inadequacies in me kept it from being better than it was. As I see them, the little essays in *City Development* will probably prove more durable than *The Culture of Cities*, even though I've tightened and thinned and simplified that a little for the new edition. Up to now I've written nothing, except perhaps *Green Memories*, paradoxically enough, that is likely to be read by anyone except a PhD fifty years from now; and to be read only by PhD's is nothing short of a second burial. Solemn thought; and a bad one to wake up with in the middle of the night, for after more than forty years of professional writing, one should have something more to show for it than this. There is much to discuss with you further, when you get to the discussion stage: but this you must consider as nothing more than a tap on the door and a friendly smile of sympathy.

WELWYN GARDEN CITY   1 June 1948

Dear Lewis

. . . I was amused to have from David Williamson an extract from a letter you wrote to him characterising my incursion on the American planning scene. All too flatteringly, of course. It will be just good luck if my visit was at the right moment to 'enthuse' planning leaders ripe to come together for a new endeavour—which, from the many letters I have had, does seem a possibility.

What you say to Williamson, however, does make me wish that we could have opened out a bit more to each other. It interests me much that you think, indeed take it as obvious, that you are 'radical' and I am 'individualist', and also that you think there was a brilliant planning lead in the USA in the 1920's, which (apparently for no fault of its own) lapsed. Is that last a correct historical analysis? Had you really then the critical armoury and the political realism to create a dispersal movement? I think back to the new start that Howard, Purdom and I tried to give our movement in 1918–20. Howard had prestige and moral force; but his appeal was to an almost infinitesimal public, and to rather a sentimental, impractical section of that. Purdom had practical experience and a good deal of business realism; but he has never shown any sense in politics, even to this date. I had political and propagandist intuition, but almost no relevant experience. *New Towns After the War* (1918) interested a handful of realistic people and a few hundred vague idealists; it did not influence the Government Reconstruction Commission or the party programmes at all—except that I got (uncontested and therefore nominal) acceptance of the policy at the 1919 Labour Party Conference; which the Executive could ignore. Indirectly our influence began to work, of course, but on very long term processes—e.g. Neville Chamberlain's Unhealthy Areas Committee of 1921, whose Report fell dead but left Chamberlain so much a convert that when he became Prime Minister in 1937 he appointed the Barlow Commission. But the direct political effect of our New Towns Movement was nil. Its only real direct issue was the foundation of Welwyn Garden City; a *tour-de-force* on Howard's initiative.

New Towns After the War put a very complete and convincing case for our policy. But there was no real *experience* behind it; and the economic and political arguments, though fairly complete, were undeveloped and thin. Nor did our movement produce other writers who would reinforce and fill in the obviously sound arguments. Purdom did a bit towards this with the TCPA Journal and the books he wrote and edited between NTAtW and about 1934, when he dropped right out of the movement. I really think the first document to touch the effective people—in politics, business, economics etc.—was the Evidence of the TCPA to the Barlow Royal Commission in 1938. I prepared that; and it is a very different document from NTAtW—because in those twenty years I had had a real grounding in the hard schools of town building and municipal politics. Once the statesmen, the intelligent press and the business world began to take our arguments seriously, and contest them seriously, we were able to develop the case in an altogether realistic and persuasive way. We were also forced to go fully into all the problems of law, finance, local government, compensation, standards, densities, architecture etc. that our policy raised.

This phase of the controversy was entirely different from the fundamentalist-argumentative-idealist stage of 1918–20—when we failed, very understandably. The suburban movement, on the other hand, succeeded riotously, as it did in the USA, and for the same reasons: for every realistic, experienced person who could put the case for Garden Cities or true Dispersal, there were thousands of realistic, experienced persons who could put the case for open, well-planned suburbs. . . . All that time, of course, I spluttered ineffectively about the mistakes being made, equally in the middle class suburbs and the public housing estates. But if I had known in 1918–20 what I knew by 1938, and still more if I could have worked out a practical, legislative policy as we had worked it out by 1942, I should have put the case very differently with, I think, real results.

Can you say that that is not true for the leaders of planning in the USA also? Doesn't the experience of actually building the Greenbelt Cities, and the further documentation of the case against big cities, and even the British precedent (with its utility as well as its warning) make all the difference? I feel it does. I really don't think that the failure of the movements of the 1920's is due to national 'cussedness' in either country. In our case it was just due to our own inexperience and inadequacy. . . .

AMENIA, NEW YORK   18 July 1948

You would hardly guess from my tardiness in replying, dear F.J., what a great relief it was to me to get your letter, and to have news, directly, of the success of your operation and your progress in recovery—slow and irksome though that process may often seem to you. I have no doubts as to your essential physical energy and fortitude; but it was a great joy, nevertheless, to see your handwriting again, and yourself back in your old form. Speaking of your handwriting, as you did in the letter itself, I must add an interesting observation: that I read it swiftly and without a break till you reached the point when you began to talk of city planning activities and your own work: at that point, I had occasionally to pause, to re-examine, to interpret, very possibly because at that point you unconsciously began to write faster.

Meanwhile, since getting your letter we have moved down here from Hanover; and though we all along had the impression that we were merely camping there it took us two whole weeks to pack up our household goods, which mounted to forty boxes and cartons, to say nothing of extras like beds; and we have not, though we've been here more than a month, unpacked very much of it: for the addition of two or three hundred more books, to a library already as tight as mine, means the building of book-cases, for which I haven't had time. Shortly after coming down I went out to Iowa (the University) to give a lecture; and incidentally I visited one of the few successful utopian communities on record, the Hutterite Amana community: a group of some five or six villages, separated by a few miles from one another, but within sight. The houses and public buildings—which look so domestic they are scarcely distinguishable—would do credit to Clarence Stein's best work at Sunnyside; and from the beginning the elders tried to balance agriculture and industry, so that even today, while their original communism has turned into mere cooperation—a change that took place during the early depression of the thirties— they both raise their own beef and pork, and build refrigerators and furniture. Their communism prospered for a long time and they supported a community of some fifteen hundred people; but after a while the absence of incentives lowered their efficiency, and to save themselves when they reorganised they had to introduce a hard-boiled business manager and throw out some two hundred drones. The place is worth a closer study than any one has yet made of it; for their communism was for them, not an end in itself, but a vehicle of their religion, which rested on the belief that 'inspiration' did not end with apostolic times, but was still at work in rare individual souls, and from generation to generation they seek and listen for such in their own community— although on their own confession the voice of God does not speak very often, indeed has not been heard since the eighties. Failing the voice, they do the best they can with the wisdom of their elders. Being German in origin, and being isolated, they still remain German even in language; and they have a reputation for curing their excellent hams in the Westphalian style. Each village, incidentally, has its own slaughterhouse and smokehouse; and they send their bacon and hams over the whole country.

As you must know from correspondence with others over here, the repercussions from your trip continue to be felt: recently the Regional Plan committee came out in favour of ten garden cities for the New York region, precisely the sort of policy we had tried to persuade Thomas Adams into backing when he wrote his original report back in the twenties —though I hear some of the present New York group have not yet got it fast in their minds that a garden city is something different from a commuting suburb. Stein has been reactivating the Regional Planning Association of America; and when I get back in the autumn I will probably take some active part in this because I have the ears of the younger group to an extent that the members of Stein's generation haven't.

AMENIA, NEW YORK   19 September 1948

Dear F.J.

I am writing you this before I receive from Clarence Stein some of the old
stationery of the Regional Planning Association of America: that little organisation with the mighty name about which I probably have told you much at
one time or another. But it is only fitting that this friendly note should accompany the formal one. Our revival as an association is the result, more than of
anything else, of your visit; for more than once during the last decade and a
half I have tried to bury the old Association under the sod, on the theory that
a dead organisation should not lie around and moulder publicly. Somehow,
Clarence couldn't bring himself to snap this link with the past, and I am glad,
in view of his renewed health and our possibily renewed activity, that we
didn't. We are at last doing something that we didn't do very successfully in
the past—that is, enlist younger people in the Association; and if we actually
manage to revive, we should, in a few years, have renewed ourselves from top
to bottom with a new set of younger officers. I think I shall try to institute here
your admirable practice of having a group of honorary vice presidents, in
order to preserve continuity and, at the same time, give over the reins to those
who are, or should be, doing the work. On the garden city side we didn't do as
much as your group did in England; but in making regional planning a conceivable political subject and in elaborating the first programme for such work,
a very different task, we did perform a useful function; and when I came to
write a brief history of the association, as an incident in our revival, I realised,
better than ever, how much weight our small group had actually carried.

As for the political situation, about which we haven't had a serious discussion for a long time, I can't say anything very hopeful. I fear that the Republi-
cans will win by such an overwhelming majority that it will leave the more
liberal members of the party, including Dewey himself, in a hopeless position,
the victims of the reactionary bosses who will regard the victory as a mandate
for reaction, if not for isolation; so I may very well vote for Truman, a peanut
politician, as we say contemptuously, just in order to stem the tide. Wallace,
fortunately, has lost ground steadily; so at least in international affairs we
shall probably present a fairly united front. My own fears about the present
situation are not shared by many people; but I suspect that Russia is playing
with us over the Berlin situation in order to force a military showdown; not
immediately, but as soon as the bad weather settles over Europe, say in
November right after the election. If they have decided that war is inevitable
that is the best time for them to act, since the longer they wait the worse their
military position will get. If they can occupy the continent, or even France and
Germany, by the opening of spring, their position will be good and ours will be

relatively weak. It sounds mad, of course; but I am getting used to living in a mad world; and I suspect we shall all have to, before sanity declares itself again.

P.S. Clarence's secretary never did get around to sending me any of our own RPAA stationery; but I finally managed to dig up a sheet from my own files and I trust you'll convey what's on it to whomever it most concerns. The allusion to a 'garden civilisation', incidentally, harks back to the very first article (still unprinted) I ever wrote about Garden Cities, probably in 1916. I happened to stumble upon it a few months ago going through my files, though I have a dim impression I may have mentioned it to you before. Its title was: Garden Civilisations.

WELWYN GARDEN CITY   2 November 1948

Dear Lewis

Please look on this as an interim note just to maintain contact and to thank you for your latest letters. I am getting stronger and less troubled physically, but my capacity to work has not returned, and I begin to wonder whether it will do so or whether I am truly the victim of the 'senility' the US Immigration doctor diagnosed without looking at me in September 1947. Work was always against nature with me—entirely an acquired habit and generated by business or other environments that thrust activity on me. The habit continued after I had retired from such environments, but it has been broken by my illness; and I doubt if I can reinstate it from inside myself. All through my life till this last period I have found myself writing something or other whenever I could make an occasion or was not distracted by some other passion. Much of this writing was fragmentary, or did not reach completion because I was always stopped by outwardly imposed work or activities; much of it was in letters to people who replied perfunctorily; but I did not mind about this—the effort was a satisfaction in itself, and a useful means of crystallising my thoughts and observations. Now, however, I generally find writing a distasteful effort. I have no ideas I particularly want to crystallise. I browse in books of all kinds; and this reading passes through my consciousness without leaving much behind. In other words, I am extinct or sadly demoralised; I am not yet sure which. I am fit only to take chairs and steer discussions and make minor adjustments between more active minds.

In the chair at the Howard Jubilee Dinner I read to a large and friendly company your letter on behalf of the Regional Association (now I hear re-named Council). I am glad to hear that this is making a new start, and especially that you have drawn in, as enthusiasts for Dispersal planning, some of the younger planners. Don't let the older ones go, though. Over here they have, despite a lack of drive, proved useful because somehow they have (possibly from Unwin and Howard) a better grip on human fundamentals and a deeper faith than our younger men, who seek novelty rather than sound standards.

NEW YORK   25 December 1948

Christmas dinner is over, dear F.J., and in the spirit of the festive day I've been thinking of you and Margaret, wishing you, by telepathy or whatever other mode will do the trick, the joy of the day and all possible blessings for the New Year. Fortunately, I had two cups of coffee at the end of the meal and that will keep me awake till Sophy's relatives, some sixteen or eighteen of them, foregather here at the end of the afternoon. We had the usual ritual of the Christmas tree and the exchange of presents just after breakfast this morning; and a little while ago we had the traditional Christmas goose, a little tough as it turned out, but redeemed by Sophy's inspired stuffing and the wine that went with the course. Now we are in that state of blissful torpor which is, at times, a useful substitute for more dynamic kinds of happiness.

Nothing could have rejoiced us more than the news, in your last letter, that you were at last beginning to feel your old self again. I didn't expect this to come about much sooner than it did; and I know how hard the intervening period must have been to bear; but I am glad, we are both glad, that it finally happened in nature's own good time. I have had no time for reading all fall since my schedule is a desperately crowded one, with absences of from a week to a fortnight, and then a perpetual drive and flurry to get half the letters answered and half the work done that has accumulated on my desk in the meanwhile. So I envy you, more than a little, your chance to mull over things; and especially to re-read Wells's *Autobiography*, which I value greatly too: both for what it gives and for the things absent which, curiously, it points to. I suspect, dear F.J., that one of the great bonds between us is the fact that we are both, so to say, children of Wells and Shaw—to which I add, in this multiple parentage, for myself, likewise Chesterton. These men dominated my adolescence; and stayed with me, sometimes with very bad influence on my sexual and marital life, right into maturity: particularly Shaw, with his cool rationalism and his cerebral sort of sexuality. I have grown, during the last fifteen years, actively to dislike Shaw, both as a man and an ideological influence; though I would have given my hand to have met him when I was young.

As for Wells, he seemed priggish to me when I was young; and his lack of a sense of the tragic, his failure to understand the irrationalities in man and nature, seem to me terrible weaknesses, still; yet he has for all that diminished less in my consciousness, and I have far less a sense of having been betrayed by his inadequacies, which I outgrew, than I was betrayed by Shaw. Toward the end of his life, as I perhaps told you, something prompted me to write a letter to the deserted old Wells to express my admiration and my gratitude, and I got a very humorous and friendly reply back from him; so I regret that I never met him before he died. But he was only half a guide; and one of my own missions has been to give to my younger generation some of the dimensions of human experience that both these great figures left out of their vision of life. The clue to Wells' strength and weakness was in his over-reliance on science and education: he never realised that there were depths to man's character that needed to be touched before these could have their desired effect. All that religion describes as 'grace' and conversion was absent from his outlook; although the failure of his own doughty pen, widely read, to produce the changes he had hoped to bring about should have warned him of the limitations of his own method. It was typical and pathetic, I think, that he should have valued so highly the South Kensington degree in science which in his old age he finally achieved. . . .

Our newly named Regional Planning Council of America is meeting at regular intervals and has already begun to take an active part in politics. Our first job is to combat the inertia and folly of the bureaucracy at Washington which, having in their mind fully capitulated to Dewey and reaction, now find it hard to adjust themselves, in their plans for housing, to the strong leftward swing which the whole election, not merely Truman's re-election, indicated: so they are opposed to taking anything like the bold steps that the present situation calls for. Stein is fighting bravely to save the Greenbelt Towns; and the housing group that recently met the President, advocating new towns instead of slum replacement, met with a favourable reception from him: so perhaps we shall overcome the lazy minds in the bureaucracy and in Congress. If I weren't so infernally occupied this winter, with obligations I can't throw off, I would probably try to apply my mind to the simple sort of statement of aims you so wisely suggest. But we are all working together and it is, I think, a good group; though I find myself sadly disappointed in my old disciple and colleague, who has become so used to sidelong and indirect approaches, in order to get something done, that she is almost an obstacle when the time calls for a strong frontal attack, which is what I think is now needed. This is one of those situations where our old intimacy, of eighteen years ago, is still a handicap to my opposing her without appearing, to her, to be doing it from buried motives, or without awakening in her buried responses of quite factitious antagonism which has nothing to do with the merits of the case. The moral of that is never to have a love affair with anyone one may reasonably expect to work with in future!

Once more, dear F.J., I am astounded and chagrined to see the date on your unanswered letter, to say nothing of the Christmas greeting that followed it. But the fact is that I piled up more work this winter and particularly more travelling than I could handle comfortably; and there have been times when I've felt like a beaten, winded dog, with his tongue hanging out of his mouth and his feet limping, chasing a fox that is hopelessly out of sight and out of reach.

This month, March, is the first period during which I can look forward to as many as four consecutive weeks at home: so once more, as usual in our winter moves to the city, I find myself with the winter nearly at an end without my having seen a play or listened to a concert, except one or two of the most minor order: as destitute of the advantages of the great city, thanks to my frequent absences, as though I'd lived all winter in Raleigh of Chapel Hill: perhaps a little more so. But the winter has had its compensations, for the challenge of having to give my lectures on the Future of Western Civilisation has sharpened up certain lines of thought I intend to pursue further in my book; and I have found my Southern students both eager and responsible: far better than I had dared hope they would be. As for the people of North Carolina, for all the poverties and crudities of their life—it has the highest rate for murder of any state in the Union—they are essentially a sweet lot of people, and they've given a very warm reception to the Westerners and Northerners who, for the most part, have replaced the mouldy native stock in the school of architecture. I've given them of my best and have felt amply rewarded by their response. But of course I shan't repeat this experience next year, for it is very disruptive to family life and to consecutive work of any other character.

A little while ago I received an invitation to sit on a UN commission that is to meet in Paris next autumn; and I was tempted to say Yes, if only because of the chance it would give me to see Europe with all my expenses paid. But as I plan things now I shall still be working at volume IV next autumn, indeed, right into the middle of the winter and perhaps even beyond; so I had to say No, though my refusal tore my daughter's heart for she had dreams of seeing Paris. As a compromise, I've promised, if enough funds are available then, to go with Sophy and Alison to Europe late in the spring of 1950, when, I trust, my book will be done and my mind could well do with an airing; and with those far prospects before us we settle down to the intervening fourteen months or so! I am telling a few people like you in advance of my intentions, because it is a way of planning ahead for doing a few lectures which I've been asked to do at various times the last few years, without being able to comply. (Canon Demant recently asked me to take part in a Christmas Summer School, for example, though what this heathen should be doing there I wasn't quite sure: there is a vast difference between a professing Christian and a practising one, and while I trust I sometimes succeed in being the second I have no claims to being the first!) Volume IV will settle all doubts on that score, and will probably result in my being torn limb from limb by all the groups, ecclesiastical and political, that have kept on hoping they could some day absorb me and claim me!

Your reminiscences in your last letter, about Shaw and Wells, awaken kindred memories of my own, though of course I never set eyes on either of them: the influence they both had on us originally is probably one of the underlying ties in our friendship, dear F.J. I still wish I had at least seen them and envy you the occasions when you did: or rather, the youthful part of me still stirs with envy, though in the course of time I outgrew both of them, continuing my own development beyond the point where each had become self-arrested, mainly out of complacency and the soporific effects of outward success, I suspect. Having had a much more modest amount of success and acclaim and publicity than either of those writers, it was perhaps easier for me to keep on growing: I've not been chained to an earlier stereotype. But I share your admiration for Wells's *Autobiography*; and there have been times when I've wanted to do a long essay on his life and work. Some day, with leisure and opportunity, I may still do it.

You ask about the regional Development Council. We have been meeting regularly and applying ourselves to our self-education; and there is at least a nucleus of younger people in the group who may carry on the work. But something of the dynamism we used to have in the twenties has vanished with old age; and unless the young ones supply it I don't know if we will be once more the influence we originally were. Stein's health has improved steadily ever since you left America; and he has been the backbone and organising force in the whole enterprise. But I have been away too long and too often to back him up; and he needs the intellectual stimulus and, if I dare say it, guidance which I used to supply. Not as an association, but as a group of people meeting opportunely, we have, I think, been of some little help in reframing the housing bill: for at one time it looked as if there would be no provisions in it for new communities or for anything except the usual slum replacement, on site that is, usually with another potential slum. By prodding Catherine Bauer pretty hard we got her to prod the housing officials in Washington; and I think something has been written into the bill. The great obstacle in Washington now is that the top officials all through the bureaucracy were so convinced that Dewey would be elected and were so eager to hold their jobs, that they had adapted all their plans and expectations to his rule and had abandoned even the very timid measures they used to frame. Unfortunately, these cagey gentlemen haven't *yet* taken in the fact that Truman won the election.

WELWYN GARDEN CITY   6 March 1949

Dear Lewis

Since I have restarted thinking about planning it is being borne in on me that our campaign to stop the big cities expanding and increasing their density has so far failed. We have had a *succes d'estime*. But the city fathers and powerful elder brothers (like your Moses and London's Cyril Walker, who really run the business) have not the slightest intention of changing their course. I am not yet at all clear whether and how I can work to redeem the situation. I am even contemplating a book which is just a sheer critique of the great city—a sort of amplification of the sort of violent lecture I have given on the subject in a number of countries. This seems terribly like beginning all over again as I did in 1918 and in 1936, as if no one had ever heard of the limitation and dispersal idea. The danger is that the intelligent readers would say 'this is what everybody knows already'; and that I shall fail to reach the wider public as I did before. But really I think a book of the Great Illusion or Road to Survival type is wanted, with overwhelming documentation (which I could now provide). I wonder however whether I can again give it the bite it needs, or whether the amytal has finally inhibited the pointed phrases and illustrations that once seemed to come to hand fairly freely.

In the meantime I am plodding on with organisational work for the TCPA, and trying to gather a younger group and prod them to write sense effectively. The sort of writer needed, however, does not grow on every gooseberry bush. The subject requires a lot of knowledge in a lot of fields; and also a controversial wariness that I have not been able to teach the younger men. The most literary of them seem invariably to come under the dominance of those in the community that I know to be unrealistic. There exists in their minds a sense that the family home is a dying institution, and that we are on the threshold of a new world in which, somehow, man will be born again as a social animal in a way different from the present and past ways. When I was a young member of the Fabian Society I was surrounded by people who felt like that; and I scoffed at it then as I do now, though I had no means of knowing then how deeply right I was. All that has happened since is that new layers of half-educated and experience-starved people have swallowed the same fallacies,

The more originative layer, the *avant garde*, tends now to be religious like Eliot, or to preach political despair like Aldous Huxley; or, like dozens of New Writers, simply to *constate* psychological atmospheres instead of doing the same for social situations as Arnold Bennett and Upton Sinclair did. If I get cross enough about this, I may burst out in a more or less effective protest. I may have to change my name and pretend to be a wild young native of Bali or Porto Rico who in about five years has acquired all that is known at the London School of Economics and the New School of Social Research, and mocks at it remorselessly. As F.J.O. I am once for all an old Victorian fossil, though I have written so little in book form. Where are our allies? Why did G.K.C. become a Roman Catholic? And why did he die? The world is out of joint, and I wasn't born to set it right.

I am pretty sure the answer is to forget the highbrow and literary world and focus on the far more numerous and far more intelligent people in industry, business and politics, who have blind spots and yet are running the world. I know they are not in the least as Huxley, Eliot and Auden see them. I am the victim, after all, of my early Bloomsbury associations and values. All I have to do is shake them off. I shall have to shake off Freud, Jung and Adler too, because they don't know the people I know. A shocking mood, I fear you will think; in that case I have to shake off you as well, or get you round to my Victorian scientific attitude.

Here is a symptom of what I am up against. You know about the Abercrombie plans, and my discretion in supporting them with some mild criticism. Well, the LCC has announced a new housing project at Roehampton, an open suburb six or seven miles from Charing Cross, where in 1921–27 they built an estate of 1200 houses at about twelve houses an acre (maximum at one point was fifteen). This is one of the best and most attractive interwar schemes, only to be criticised on the ground that suburban extension was the lesser of two evils. In my *London's Dilemma*[1] I deplored the choice between houses with gardens plus straphanging, and flats near work. This new scheme will house 21,000 persons at twenty-eight dwellings an acre in a suburb; so we have got to multi-storey flats *plus* straphanging. The LCC Labour Party are furious with me for attacking this project. I am obstructing the housing of Londoners, playing the Tory game on the eve of the election, etc. etc.

My dilemma is that I can spend most of my time raising hell about these symptoms of metropolitan policy, and get reported in the press and write articles for technical papers and perhaps create some immediate effect; or I withdraw from the scene for a year and write a book which convincingly demonstrates that we are going in the wrong direction, and after it has been reviewed as an excellent restatement of what everybody realises already, find

[1] London, 1949.

that about 2,000 copies of it are sold. Or I can try to do both, as I did in the past, and then wonder whether I should have done better to concentrate on one of these courses and spend a day a week in the garden and live a year or two longer.

I envy your capacity to withdraw yourself from current affairs for long periods; yet I am not at all sure I ought to imitate it, even if I could. Things like the TCPA do have some running effect on the national situation; and I am absolutely certain that if I dropped the Association at present it would cease to have any definite effect. I am always in hope that new leaders will emerge, with some substratum of implacability under their tacticity. But in fact after Unwin no one arose but Purdom, who had implacability without political talent; and after Purdom there was no one till I jumped in. And I have less of some sorts of ability than these two had. And all those I can see in sight, or have patiently tested, seem to have less still, or no sense of direction at all. At times the TCPA seems to me too like the Voysey Inheritance. Yet I am constantly amazed at its prestige all over the world, as in this country. Inside its mantle my sheep's bleat becomes a lion's roar. It will pain me to hear the lion roaring with not even a meaning in the underlying bleat. So I am caught in the trap; and I am even taking on the job of Hon. Editor of the *Journal*.

Possibly the UN Commission of which you speak is the central body for the Working Parties being set up by ECOSOC in various countries. I have been asked to be chairman of the one for GB, with half a dozen weirdly assorted young men supposed to have ideas and some training in sociology, landscape design, surveying and architecture. There is a delicate suggestion that, after all, my generation did something for planning in our time, which I suppose means that I am a sort of restraining hand on the wild brilliance of the young. By God! I wish I could see the wildness or the brilliance; they all seem to me to be patiently researching into the obvious; counting trees to see if there is really a wood; and catching ideas from fools with a gift for expression (like Corbusier) as the young catch measles. I can almost believe, in spite of what I said above, in Jung's division of humanity into people who have direct feeling and derivative intelligence, and people who have direct thought and derivative feeling. Except that many of the young in our field seem to be derivative both in thought and feeling. If Jung is right, their feelings are outside the public picture. The extraordinary unanimity with which they parrot catch-words and catch-ideas would make me angry if it did not make me laugh. If I could only recover the slight gift I once had for making people laugh with me something might be done. Maybe I shall have to stop taking amytal and let laughter and acidity rip.

No; I don't think our Wells–Shaw influence has much to do with our friendship. Its beginning was adventitious. My King Charles's Head is the limitation-dispersal idea; and I seized on you, as I seize on anybody whom I think I can exploit for the advancement of that idea. It helps to maintain interest between us that we look at things utterly differently and do not understand each other one bit. You are a really good and nice man (I am sorry to say this, because I feel the judgment will shock you, but I know Margaret would understand exactly what I mean), whereas I am fundamentally unscrupulous, except mentally. You have a good memory and a capacity for self-discipline; I have neither. You are an articulate philosopher and trained student of thought. I am impressionistic, yet ceaselessly critical inwards and outwards.

Shaw never influenced me; Wells certainly did, for many years. Both entertained me inexhaustibly, and though I read them less, they still do. I think Wells has the prettiest gift for epithet in English literature, and that Shaw is the next wit to Voltaire. But Rebecca West's criticism of both, that they had no sense of process, is entirely valid. It is the handicap of writers to be out of the daily business of human organisation; and a mystery to me that even one or two, Balzac for instance, were able to write really good novels of business and politics—the two really important social activities. Shaw claims to have learned what he did know from Webb; the answer to that is Webb's *Soviet Communism*, with its credulous innocence. Voltaire was going somewhere; where is Shaw going? Does anybody know, or care? Wells was going somewhere; it was to Totalitarianism, and he pushed on long after any sensible person could have seen it. And then he wrote a last despairing book that was sillier than his faithful ones. What fascinated me in these two men was their literary gift. It took me a longer time than it takes most people to see that men can write superbly and write nonsense. I am still all too easily taken in by people with this gift. Shaw was for a time a pungent critic of society, on the basis of its own assumptions, as most good satirists are. Some of his early prefaces are, in this kind, great. But the more sure of himself he became, the more he talked nonsense. It is always, right up to now, brilliant comic nonsense. For which he deserves to be buried in Westminster Abbey.

I spent last week in Northern Ireland, trying to start a planning society there. One third of the state is Roman Catholic, and the majority Protestant and Unionist. I saw something of the two civilisations in open conflict there. And I cannot doubt for a moment that I am on the side of Voltaire in *that* issue. This is salutary, as I am very much inclined to an alliance with the churches on the family home issue, and one cannot help being on its side in Eastern Europe, where it is the only outpost of resistance to the Totalitarian state. The Unionist Government of NI is far to the right of our Tories here. I found liberal minded people confronted with the choice between the two reactionary types, and voting Unionist-Protestant. Without doubt in that situation I would have to do the same. I did detect where the resolution of the conflict will come from: a new generation is already present which will change the parties from inside. But having read the Catholic Archbishop's Lent Ordinance—a logical, legalistic document threatening the Faithful with the penalties of mortal sin for marrying non-catholics, or sending their sons to Trinity College, Dublin, or eating meat on Fridays, or reading books not published by the Catholic Truth Society—I just wondered how long the infiltration of saner ideas will take in that community. The strangle-hold is of unbelievable strength and rigidity. The compulsion that children of mixed marriages (for which a dispensation is rarely given) must be brought up as catholics succeeds to the extent of 100 per cent. This ordinance occupied two columns of the principal news page of the leading daily paper of Dublin. The techniques of institutional and state control have made great advances since the days of Voltaire and Tom Paine. Which fact has to be accommodated in our philosophies.

AMENIA, NEW YORK   9 June 1949

My intuition, when I got your letter of 6 March, dear F.J., was to sit down and answer it immediately, as you had done with mine; for, I said to myself, it will probably be months before I get around to it otherwise. And alas! how right I was—as the date of this one proves. In the meanwhile, however, I've had the pleasure of reading your letter more than once, and chortling over it, particularly over the parts at which Margaret, quite wrongly it happened, thought I would take offence. I've never held that agreement or likemindedness or even literary admiration, a more touchy matter with authors, was an indispensable pre-requisite of friendship; probably because my oldest friends used to deride my ideas and dislike my literary style when I was young; and I just got used to it. Even now there is a certain undercurrent of *hostility*, which amuses and doesn't disturb me, between me and my best American friend, who happens to be a psychologist, and a very good one at that; though not about his own personal relations where he shows—and I think he knows my feeling about this and resents it—a sublime unconsciousness of what he has actually done to the people around him.

As for understanding, I think we understand each other quite sufficiently: always allowing that there are plenty of mysteries that remain even after the most extensive self-exploration. I am probably much less highbrow and sealed-off than you imagine: in fact my Rorschach examination, a psychological appraisal I went through for the fun of it a couple of years ago and possibly even told you about, shows an almost even balance between the intellectual, emotional, and practical parts of my nature: something I had been aiming at, but had no objective evidence of having achieved. If I were a real intellectual, my column denoting that would have towered up above the other two. When I was on the Board of Higher Education I found I even had a talent for working with people on committees and getting things done administratively; so much so—and this again I've probably told you—that I said to Sophy, 'I'm getting so good at this and I find it so fascinating, that if I don't resign soon I'll probably be running for Governor of New York'.

As for our fundamental philosophies, yours might be more hedonistic than mine in emphasis, because for me the great end is not to be happy but to be *absorbed*, and pain and grief are as capable of effecting that as pleasure; but your saying that your creed would 'take account of as many different ways of life as would be consistent with the stability of society' is precisely what I am trying to state and work out in my final volume—though you may not recognise the results, when you are confronted with them, as in any sense similar to yours. As for my being a 'good' person, I smile wryly at that; for I shall probably spend my old age attempting to expiate sins which, even at this early date, seem to me unthinkable: not vulgar sins, perhaps, in every case, but such as to make me ask myself, a little wonderingly, was I really that kind of man, and what could have made me so blind, at that period, as not to realise it. My special admiration for Dostoyevsky, which developed late, is due to his capacity for telling in some detail the truths that I have found out about myself—not, I hasten to add, lest your imagination jump about too freely, that I've ever tried to rape little girls, like him, or even for that matter to rape big girls: since the real curse of my life is rather that big girls, too often for comfort, have tried to rape me; and as you must well know, that cannot be done.

But the book I am now writing[1] is one in which I deal, from beginning to end, with the eternal platitudes; and it would be sickeningly impossible to read did I not embellish my conclusions with such modifications as my actual experience of life suggests: before each monumental truth, respected for ages, I have as it were to plant the tiny living sapling of my own experience, which will cast its shadow on the monument. To do this with a certain degree of honesty will be the test of my abilities, not as a writer, but as a man. In the chapter on marriage and the family, for example, I must say all that I believe and actually live by on that subject, and yet admit not merely what everybody knows, that it is possible to fall in love outside of marriage, but even that someone with whom one was once deeply in love, twelve or fourteen years ago, from whom one has been separated physically and emotionally, on the surface, for many years, can nevertheless remain an integral part of one's life.[2] There's no use

---

[1] *The Conduct of Life*, New York, London, 1951, 1952.
[2] Although written, this chapter was omitted from *The Conduct of Life*.

writing the book at all unless I can acknowledge the contradictions that life presents even during the periods of highest concentration and integration!

But this is not the time for me to be telling you about the book; except that I've had the old experience of finding that the hard parts, about religion and love, have come relatively easy, and that the easy parts, on which I am now working, those dealing with economic and political facts, bringing forth arguments and principles that I know by heart, have proved to be the hard parts. The book is already about 150,000 words long; and it will probably be 200,000 in this first draft, before I begin to condense and re-write it. I have been up here the last three weeks, no, by now it is four, working on it: leading a solitary life, keeping house for myself, with no one but the cat for company; and even she sometimes deserts me or is exiled indignantly when she climbs up our big kitchen chimney to bring down a swift. Sophy and Alison come up for weekends; but I find the life, somehow, a little lonely and grim.

There was a time, as late as 1937, when I loved being alone here; but somehow my son's death seems to have changed this feeling, in some queer way; so that my attention is never quite concentrated upon my work, and one ear is always cocked, as it were, for a footfall: a footfall that never sounds.

I've managed to put enough money by this last winter, money which I thought at first would cover our expenses to Europe in good part, so that I shall be able to continue writing on the book until it is done, unless some unexpected catastrophe overtakes me. With luck, I should be finished by the first of the year. But now that I've reckoned seriously with my financial state, especially with the fact that my royalties have at last begun to fall, since I've published no successful book since 1944, I realise that it will be quite impossible for me to come to England again in 1950. My consolation is that if volume IV seems as good as the earlier ones it may very well be possible to come in 1951, the year of the great exhibition; and once I realised that this was afoot I almost voluntarily set the date forward another year to include it. By that time, of course, many other things may have happened, but I refuse to anticipate too many of heaven's inscrutable plans.

WELWYN GARDEN CITY   8 July 1949

My dear Lewis
Your letter of 9th June arrived last week when I was on tour with forty-five Swedish planners around our Midland cities. Margaret read it with much interest before I returned, and I have suggested that she should take the next shift in writing to you. But to the loss of others she uses up all her letter-writing time in letters to the family. I exhaust such literary energy as I still possess (it

is less than it was) in correspondence of the organising type for the TCPA and its journal and in replying to reactionary architects and agriculturists in the London *Times*. So I write few letters in which I can take a real interest, and scarcely any solid articles. And my mind is becoming as dry as a sucked orange that has been left out in the sun for a summer. Just before I left for the tour I wrote an article on residential densities that is in its way a restatement of Unwin's *Nothing Gained by Overcrowding*. But I got less fun out of doing it than I would have done had I not felt I was recapturing trenches that had been consolidated thirty years ago, and lost again only by sheer wicked neglect and callousness by professional planners and philanthropic housers. To have to go over this ground again at this date seems to me an expense of spirit in a waste of shame. However, I did it, with a number of diagrams that I hope may be effective, and the article appears in the forthcoming *Town and Country Planning*,[1] of which journal I have now, with misgivings as to time and competence, taken up the Editorship. I think of amplifying the material in the form of a pamphlet.

I do not understand why the fashion just now among the intelligentsia has set so strongly in the direction of cutting down family living-space—which I am sure they in their own lives, and men and women in general, regard as one of the most important of the social mimima. I remember that in one of your books you wrote of a queer hatred of the family home, taking the form of enthusiasm for exterior facilities and mechanical gadgets in lieu of space. Publicly and privately I have pointed out again and again the statistical fallacy they have fallen into: a family is not a static unit—it begins with two persons, rises to four or more, and then falls on two again. Its principals do not wish to move house every time a baby is born or a grown child leaves home. Therefore the normal family home should provide for the normal family at its peak, and if there is sometimes a spare room or two, for a parent or visiting child to stay in, that is not a social or economic disaster. At times they will wish to move house; at times, if the family is specially big, they *must* do so. Changes of job, city, or income are good reasons for moving—when the family does so of its own volition. 'Decanting' people, as it is called, so as to keep each house exactly filled and no more, would not be human if it were practicable, which it is not in a country that still values freedom. I say all this, but the statisticians take no notice. Even in the Population Report, of all unsuitable places, the same idealism is stated—and I know the idea comes from one of the statisticians who is deep in the highbrow planning circle with whom I am always at loggerheads. I think by persistence I shall be able to debunk

---

[1] 'Town Cramming: The Art of Maximising Densities', in *Town and Country Planning*, Summer, 1949.

this queer enthusiasm. But I wish I could understand why it has gained such a widespread hold.

In London just now the authorities are building eight and ten storey flats, intended for families, with an average floor area of, in some blocks, 650 square feet. The current two-storey house, with an outbuilding, has 1,000 or 1,050 sq. ft. The public subsidy of the house, which costs about £1,600 including the site, is £600. What the flat costs is not yet disclosed, but in one case in Holborn I find the *subsidy* (for 650 sq. ft) is £2,900 a flat! As the rents come to about the same, the cost must be something like £3,800. The difference in land cost accounts for only about £550 in this case. Royal personages open these wonder-flats, admire the gadgets, the central heating and hot water, the automatic lifts etc. Mayors wear haloes, women's columns write as if the millennium of the housewife had arrived; and until I started to do so this week, no one mentions the 650 sq. ft in lieu of 1,000 sq. ft, or the extra public loss of £2,300 in giving gadgets instead of living-space. I wonder if anybody cares, or if there is any common sense left anywhere . . .

Going round England with the Swedes, I found suburban housing going merrily on. The houses are better than between the wars—larger and better fitted—but worse architecturally and less skilfully laid out. The architectural revolution has destroyed what was good and produced nothing in the least pleasant in its place. One has to realise, however, that in this country as in yours, only a tiny minority cares for architectural shape as it is understood by the schools. Everybody cares about the size and quality of houses, and in these there has been a considerable advance, though at a great financial and labour cost. Prefabrication, though still experimental, has been very injurious to external design and variety of layout. The joke is that in most cases the pre-fabricated or semi-prefab. houses have cost more than the traditional construction. One or two systems are now costing very slightly less, and may survive, but the architects have not found out how to make them look good and interesting in groups. However, I am sure the occupiers are pleased with the new houses as a whole. They still do not notice the spread of suburbs, longer journeys to work etc., because these are lesser evils than having no separate home. Thus planning has lost in the struggle so far.

AMENIA, NEW YORK   12 September 1949

Dear F.J.
On the matter of the proposed overcrowding of New Towns 'to save the land' I would like to continue the discussion that we begun, I suppose, when you were editing *Garden Cities of Tomorrow*: For though I do not find myself in a midway position between you and your opponents on this subject—heaven

forfend that I should ever be caught advocating the middle course as a way of appeasing (*read* infuriating) both sides—and am much closer to your position than to the people who would cut down family space and amenity, I am concerned lest you put the case for open planning in too absolute a manner, without admitting many variations that no one as yet has tried. For the people who suggest re-housing densities of over 100 people an acre I have nothing but reproach: I am willing to make that an upper limit, and would treat any attempt to break it down as suspicious and as requiring an overwhelming proof even for a single exception. On the other hand, remembering the kind of city I've liked to live in and work in, I am more favourable to the upper level, which means twenty-five or thirty houses to the acre, than you are, because what one loses in one kind of amenity one may gain in another kind, like accessibility of neighbours and closeness to meeting places.

Some of the ways of getting higher densities, which you list in the Summer number of *Town and Country Planning*, seem to me quite tolerable if the planner knows what he is doing. Windows not less than 20 ft from public ways is a quite new requirement in city building, which came in with the suburb: I'd be ready to omit it on occasion in order to get more rear space. So again with roads not less than 40 ft between fences: far too much housing seems to me to be done *on* such roads, and too little on narrower cul de sacs. Even the facing window not nearer than 70 ft seems very far from being an absolute rule: with planting to take care of the lower levels view and horizontal windows, starting four feet from the floor, on the second storey, sufficient privacy can be achieved at half that distance. As for the back garden, the reason there is so little space in the rear at twenty-seven houses to the acre, in the Dutch examples you illustrate, is the fact that an absurd amount of space has been reserved for a large number of unnecessary streets, far too wide for any traffic such a community is likely to have. My point is that you can't, except very extravagantly, *legislate* good planning, though in a period of wholesale building such as happened after 1920 in England, and as will happen again, there is undoubtedly a very strong temptation to do so.

The trouble at present is that the field is divided between two stereotypes: the suburban type of open plan, in which each house makes a pretence to a self-sufficiency it cannot in fact afford till the standard of living is much higher, and a barbarous Le Corbusier/London County Council type of overcrowding, which pays no attention whatever to the desire of families to have a house and land visibly their own, in intimate relationship. I should like to see the Town and Country Planning Association hold a prize contest for ideal designs of a different pattern from the current ones: designs in which every part of the development, from the house itself to the street system, would be re-thought for the sake of finding alternative solutions to fit special conditions.

Take the matter of not using good soil for housing sites. I don't think that the statistical answer, even if it is sound, is a sufficient one. It may be that there *is* plenty of good land left, and plenty more, even in England, that might be redeemed. It may also be that some of the good land, if used for a housing estate, might be well-used to produce domestic garden produce. Still, I should also like to see plans prepared, on the basis of actual soil surveys, indicating how the very good land would still be preserved for market gardens, and the siting of the houses so arranged as to take the maximum advantage of the open space thus kept as working gardens. Am I not right in remembering— it's twenty years almost since I last saw Hampstead Garden Suburb—that Unwin and Parker provided allotment gardens running *behind* the private gardens in some of the blocks. That's one of a number of arrangements that I'd be working to perfect if I were a planner and not a mere writer. Though I think that Dr Kenneth Barlow's group in Coventry made an unwise decision when they proposed to build a many-storey apartment house in their family unit, situated on their farm, you have to reckon with the fact that this came from a very sensible man, in love with family life, who was one of the original Peckham experimenters. And people like that won't be convinced by anything like a general rule that doesn't seem to do justice to their needs. So much for my friendly and sympathetic amendments to the case against cramming.

WELWYN GARDEN CITY   25 December 1949

Dear Lewis
The last letter on my file is yours of 12th September. At least you cannot say that I am distracting you much from work on your book. This is not however due entirely to my thoughtfulness for you. In October I was visited by a meaningless virus disease called Shingles, around half the waist; harmless to the point of laughableness but extremely painful. This immobilised me for four weeks just when I was beginning to look at my arrears of work and to speculate on the ideal of overtaking them. Now my desk is like Hiroshima after the bomb explosion, and infected in the same way with dangerous radiations every time I turn over part of the heap.

As it is Christmas Day I have dug down to your letter, and recover the shock I felt when I first read your really frightening views about urban density. It seems that like Roosevelt I have everybody against me but the electors, and in this case they are disfranchised by the technical mystery of the subject. You are so hatefully, assuredly and unexpectedly wrong on this subject that I will not harden this sentimental season by arguing with you now about it. I must just seek, probably vainly, to mobilise humanity against you and all the other architectural theorists who are unwittingly destroying the belated revolt against urban squalor. You know not what you do. But as long as I have a breath left in my body I will fight against you.

We are having a quiet Christmas, as we always do; and I spend most of my time in my study being oppressed by my neglected tasks. We had Colonel D. L. R. Lorimer, the expert in almost-unknown languages, with us for Christmas Day; his equally distinguished wife Emily, also an intimate friend of Margaret's and mine, died a few months ago, and his daughter having married a South African he is left entirely alone. Though he does not talk 'shop' much it is a bond between him and Margaret that she, though by fate a housekeeper and a perfect one, is by true vocation a linguist and philologist; no matter how pre-occupied she is (and she always is) she never fails to be roused by a comment or query about a word or a phrase. I share this interest, though I am not so good at it as these two. Col Lorimer has already fully documented several Persian dialects and an unrelated language spoken only by a tribe of 5,000 in an inaccessible valley in the Himalayas. He has the material for still more funny languages, and a publisher for one of them; but at 73 is beginning to be doubtful whether he can complete his work now that his wife (who with extraordinary discipline and energy translated lots of books from German, wrote a lot, and yet functioned as his secretary and kept him at the job) is no longer there to help. He has a curious airy pessimism that both worries and fascinates us. I suppose his reading public consists of about twenty people, scattered all over the world. Therefore his books, which require special phonetic type and cost thousands of pounds to produce, can only be published when some learned society in Norway or somewhere has funds to spare for pure and profitless science. He has a fine collection of folk-tales that could find readers, but being a disinterested scientist he does not exploit them.

There are many things I would like to write about, including my worries about the planning situation in this country. After my illnesses and absences I go back into the political struggle with misgivings and doubts of my own grip and effectiveness; also with increasing bitterness at *La Trahison des Architectes*. But I have to go back, much as I want in my few remaining years to write on other things. I could do both if I had your discipline and energy, but I have neither. Thank God Duhamel, the most planning-conscious of all novelists, has never met or heard of me! I could not bear either a physical or literary portrait of myself by a truly discerning artist. Lately, as you will have noticed, I have looked too much at myself. I must get back into my old habit of looking outward, and resume my normal optimism.

A letter written on Christmas Day is a very special kind of letter indeed, dear F.J., and I have long been meaning to answer it; but the suspicion you uttered in your latest letter a few days ago, that I might be ill, was in fact true for the better part of two months . . . two months that I badly needed for the finishing of my book were blasted away, and instead of being ready for fall publication I shall be lucky to have it written in time for the spring of 1951.

It's a great nuisance, for if I had known that I couldn't finish the book this winter I'd have taken on more lectures and had a little put by, towards another bout of leisure, for later in the year. Well: that's life; and I can at least be glad that the leisure gave me time to look at the book critically—a most dismal, depressing sort of look in the circumstances—with the result that I have decided to cut its size down drastically, merely in order not to bore myself when I have to read it!

Your admirable biographical essay on Ebenezer Howard gave me great pleasure; and I think it was fitting and helpful that it should moreover have appeared in *The Times*. But what shall I say to your refusal even to discuss any further the matter of urban densities?[1] There is nothing that should be beyond discussion between reasonable men; and in matters so open to fallible decision and diverse purposes and interests as urban densities I am astonished that you, of all men, should take a position that would be hardly becoming to a Roman Catholic discussing transubstantiation. You can make out a very good case in many circumstances, dear F.J., for a density of twelve to the acre; and in making it out you would frequently have me on your side. But when you say that anything above this is a vote for urban squalor, you are simply talking nonsense; and nonsense so stark and staring that one begins to wonder whether the case for twelve houses to the acre is as good as it has seemed. For why should anyone make a dogma of such a figure if there weren't something shaky and irrational about it? At some point, I would agree, one must set a limit of urban density for residential areas; and I would put that at 100 people to the acre, favouring much lower densities for people with families, for people who loved gardens, for people who liked and could afford a sense of detachment and isolation; but being willing to go up to a hundred on behalf of special social facilities and conveniences that come with closer living, or when bachelors, with no special liking for the amenities of home life, were to be provided for. Why should you not merely oppose such a standard as a matter of personal choice—which of course you have the right to do—but confuse reasonable and intelligent people like me with people who recklessly would increase the densities beyond any human measure, and seek to make all of us

---

[1] FJO had not said that he would *never* discuss the matter further.

your enemies. I refuse to be locked up in that Warsaw ghetto; and I call upon you openly to withdraw from your highly unsound position—or I shall write a satiric verse about it in your own best manner and pillory you in the stocks of the comic, which, as long as you hold this premise of undiscussability, is where you belong.

WELWYN GARDEN CITY   6 March 1950

Dear Lewis

This is the briefest note to commiserate with you in your health troubles, and to hope that they are blowing away. I would have thought it a good plan to accept the Hawaii offer, since it would enable you to combine a useful job of work with a change of scene valuable to you and the family. I know that I would accept it, despite the perpetual call of my local activities in England. But I confess that one factor in my case is an entire disbelief that my presence anywhere is of importance to the world; which I do not find inconsistent with a habit of feeling that while I am on a job I must do the most I can with it. My scale is however different from yours. I suppose I might conceivably write a book of 250,000 words; in fact I do the equivalent in articles, lectures and letters, I suppose, two or three times a year. But I am sure I could not face rewriting such a thing once it were more or less in shape. I might correct it in a wholesale manner and have it re-typed; but I could not pull it to pieces and do it again. Your calmness in face of such a prospect fills me with awe; but of course so do your books when you have finished with them. Also I could never plan leisure ahead. I take it just when I should not—when articles are unwritten and lectures unprepared and letters unanswered and the garden full of weeds, by sitting and dozing for hours over a meaningless book. And if ever I go away, it is when I cannot spare the time, and I work harder (at irrelevant things) than when I am at home. Which is why millions of words of mine lie about the world, but there is no row of books with my name. A far from admirable story; but I have had a lot of fun.

I don't see the force of your tirade against my density principles, seeing that you yourself, objecting to my rigidity, propose another limit which seems just as decided. You know about most things, and I know about few—one of which is density. On Christmas Day I merely said I would fight your heresy; I never said I would not argue with you. How else can one fight error except by argument? When I have time I will explain to you where you are wrong, both in your statement as to what I stand for, and in the components on which you base your own standard. But for the moment I have temporarily exhausted my almost inexhaustible capacity to repeat myself. I would only say that you considerably exaggerate even my intransigent rigidity. If you will look at the

February *T & CP* (Leading article) you will see that I support the density of 100 persons an acre for redevelopment with the reservation 'not to be lightly exceeded'. I make clear at the same time what are the sacrifices of important amenity it involves as against the 'decent maximum' of twelve houses an acre, which by the way includes small open spaces and reservations for allotments. I do not ask for detached houses, nor for the 30 ft frontages you once said should be the standard. Such components would in practice reduce density to something like nine or eight an acre. Perhaps in your calculations you ignore what Abercrombie in the LCC Plan called the margin for inefficiency; which I prefer to think of as the margin for human variety and architectural interest?

WELWYN GARDEN CITY   28 April 1950

Dear Lewis

I have so much work and worry here just now in connection with the TCPA and the *Journal* that I feel I ought not to be making the American trip so soon. And it is not going to be easy to decide what to say, when I am there, about our situation. My honest opinion is that for the time being the dispersalist movement is losing out, as it clearly is in Canada and the USA also. But one has to be very careful how one puts this. The city situation is so desperate that if we were starting afresh we ought to be able to start a forest fire of determination to make a radical change; but we are not starting afresh, and there is a strange impression in the public mind that we have gained everything we want and might as well retire into honourable seclusion. I do not publicly blame the professional planners; but in this private letter I can say that they are as hopeless as ever. They have none of the social passion of Unwin; all the passion is for Architecture, National Parks and Silhouettes—and even the aesthetes are torn between a childish 'Modernism' and a nostalgic Mummificationism.

Here the Modernists stand for multi-storey flats and the Mummyfiers for terrace houses and closed vistas. The speculative builder's name is mud; but he stands far nearer to the ordinary man. The contrast in standards can have a big effect in diminishing the prestige of public housing and planning. My dilemma is that I will not join in the popular criticism of planning, with which I greatly sympathise.

The Director of the TCPA, Donnelly, got into Parliament (the only Labour gain), so in addition to editing the *Journal* I have had for several months to run the Association office, and to interview candidates for a new appointment. I am in the last stages of this hazardous process just now, and not very happy about the choice available at the rewards we can offer. This is about the sixth time I have had this situation since I took over responsibility for the Association, and I am getting slightly tired of it.

AMENIA, NEW YORK   14 June 1950

Dear F.J.

I've been up here for the last three weeks, finishing the planting of my garden, transplanting bushes and making new flower beds, and tidying up my books and papers, which every few years get into a positively ruinous tangle; and generally getting things tidy so that, as soon as the spirit really moves me, I shall settle down to the final re-writing, as I hope, of my book. As long as the weather remains fairly cool it is hard to tear myself away from my garden; and I sometimes work harder than a man of 54, with a somewhat erratic heart—if still a sturdy one—should do; but presently the humid days of July will be here, and I find them almost as conducive to literary work as rainy weather is: in either case the temptation to be outdoors, working or walking over the hills, is removed.

Sophy has lately sent you from New York, I think, two back numbers of *The New Yorker* in which I have criticised our present housing standards and presented the general case for lower densities and decentralisation. The articles have awakened a good deal of interest; and Ross once more feels, as in the case of the famous Moses attack, that he is performing civic duty by publishing them; and since I have convinced him I have probably convinced a lot of other people, as he is a very able and hard-headed fellow. Stichman, the State Housing Commissioner, came back recently with a letter defending the Commission's—and so the local Housing Authority's—policy of building ten and fourteen storey buildings. Instead of basing his defense on the fact that it is hard to acquire land within the city, difficult to rehouse the slum dwellers at any time and especially in a period of general shortage, and finally, on the fact that the national housing bills gave aid only for slum clearance, (and until last year gave no encouragement toward building in outlying areas or wiping out the excessive costs of slum land), he delivered himself up to me by making out a much weaker case. Namely, that if my standards were followed there wouldn't be enough land available this side of Hartford, and anyway, New Yorkers like high buildings rather than low ones. That was easy to answer, for even at 50 people per acre New York could house three million people on its present land; at 100 per acre, six million, leaving only two million of its present population to be settled elsewhere. While at the density rate of Harlem Houses, 220 per acre, we could accommodate the entire prospective population during the next sixty years without going outside the present territory. I'll send you the Sky Line with this final answer to Stichman.

Dear Lewis

How youthful it sounds to me to be 54! Between that age and 60 or so is I think the prime of life. The advantage of being 65 is that I have been able to draw my post-war credit of income tax, which will go a long way to pay our fares across the Atlantic. I *feel* as I did at 30, but I think I am much slower in the uptake and in getting things done; and memory for new impressions is much less lasting, in the sense that the impressions are not available. They are all there, I find, but a layer or two down, and have to be elicited by notes or by some accident of association. This makes writing on any subject comprehensively and in balance a much more laborious process.

I received *The New Yorker* of May 20 with your very telling criticism of high density—better written than my criticisms of London, but on the same lines. And I remember standing in the core of the city of London about 1912, when I think I was first clear about the evils of high density, noticing the rebuilding at still greater heights then going on, and wondering what force could possibly stop it. I had precisely the same feeling in 1947 in the Rockefeller Centre: that of a boy with a pea-shooter in the line of route of a thousand tanks. In 1912–17, when I was an idealist social-democrat, it seemed to me the only potentially equivalent force was the army of the awakened multitude whose lives were depreciated by the city trends. And in fact the subsequent British acceptance of dispersal in principle *was* part of the social revolution that ultimately placed Labour in power (though the revolution passes far beyond party boundaries here). What I could not foresee was the confusion of mind of the city multitudes—their inability to seize, or having glimpsed to hold, a true picture of the city process and how it affects their lives.

In the engineering and chemical techniques the experts on the whole serve their public well, though the public do not understand how they do it. In architecture and town planning they do not; the lines of communication of popular desire are crossed. So the power, whether adequate or not, is not brought to bear on the point of action. I still do not see just how we can correct that situation; it is always on my mind. Howard's answer was the simple one of small scale example, in which in thirty years he succeeded. But he was wrong in thinking it would be spontaneously or commercially followed. We have had it politically accepted here. But in the cities I can still stand and feel that the real forces are still pressing in the wrong direction. A vast movement of ideas and passion could alone reverse the trend; we have not yet by any means created it, have we?

AMENIA, NEW YORK   20 August 1950

Dear F.J.

You are only, I reckon, about six weeks away, and the thought of your so early appearance—along with the pleasant distraction of finishing my book—will reduce this letter to the briefest of notes: a mere wave of the hand to wish you a good voyage. I shall be in New York on the 27th September and we hope you and Margaret will have an early lunch or tea or dinner with us.

If you could manage it so, we'd love to have you weekend with us in Amenia from 14th to 16th October: if your own schedule should be too crowded for comfort, we hope that at least Margaret would come for a taste of the country. (But you owe it to yourself, too, to see some of our *real* country!)

So much for immediate arrangements. Next—welcome!

WELWYN GARDEN CITY   27 February 1951

Dear Lewis

. . . The tour was a wonderful experience, and so many people tell me what we said was useful that I must believe it; but I don't feel in my bones that I was able to make any contribution of weight to the well-informed criticism of cities and advocacy of dispersal planning that you and others in your group are putting out. Over here, since I got back, I feel even less effective. The TCPA seems to me to be losing ground to the agricultural lobby and to the town-cramming theorists with whom that lobby is in alliance; and I have not the sense of argumentative power to maintain the townsman's side of the case that I had in 1936 and again in 1942. The fact is I cannot do what Unwin did so successfully—say exactly the same thing in speech after speech for years—and yet this is the only way to be effective politically. I have done this, of course, to a less extent—but I hate it, and because I bore myself with necessary reiteration I refrain from taking part in the national controversy on many occasions when I know I ought to break in.

What is very disappointing to me is that no one else here takes up the campaign with any passion or persistence. After fifteen years of it, I could fairly have expected some real reinforcements. Unfortunately, while I know I am only pottering with the political campaign just now, I cannot resolve to disentangle myself from it and concentrate on some writing projects that would interest me intensely and perhaps have long-term value. So at present I am not properly doing anything, and am beginning to wonder whether I shall ever be of any use again. Of course, as you will see at once, mine is a plain case of discouragement, which might be cured at any moment by something or other 'coming-off'.

In the last month Margaret, as Chairman of the local United Nations Association, and I as a rank-and-file member, have been involved in trying to deal with a small but mischievous anti-American 'Peace with China' movement. The *New Statesman* group has persuaded many people here that the USA is in a state of 'War hysteria', and that we are in active danger of being dragged into war with China. This has brought into an unholy alliance all the fellow-travellers of Communism and the innocents who tend to believe that the Korean incident is due to some sort of misunderstanding for which the Atlantic powers are to blame. They use McArthur's pronouncements, of course, some of which are a gift to them. And they parade Nehru—carefully concealing, if they remember, that he approved entirely the UN resistance to the North Korean aggression, from which all the trouble at this moment stems. Many people simply do not follow foreign events closely, so confusion is caused by this sort of campaign, the energy of which comes from communistic or quasi-communist opinion, backed by a certain number who think there are 'faults on both sides' and that peace can be promoted by a middle group of the truly pacific and wise. . . .

I was shouted down at a Peace with China meeting at which an anti-American resolution was carried, entirely without any speeches except those of the mover and seconder. (I send you a copy of the report.) Some reputable observers do say that there is or was a section of US opinion in favour of a preventive war; but in the course of our tour we did not meet a single person of that opinion; nor did we happen to come across a leading article of that tendency in the chance selection of papers we bought daily. During the Korean reverses we certainly found many people who cursed Washington for getting into that war, and said 'we must come right out of Korea immediately'—a point of view that was more politically expressed later by Taft and Hoover. We also met people and read columns that bitterly criticised British social policy, quantum of effort in the UN resistance, and so on. All that is to be expected in a free democracy. But that the USA is to any appreciable extent 'war-minded' seems to me complete nonsense. . . .

Postscript. Ten days after the Peace with China meeting the UNA held a larger meeting, much more normal and representative in its attendance, at which Professor J. D. Hicks (History, Univ. of California, visiting Professor at Cambridge Univ. for a year) gave a most admirable lecture on American foreign policy. He was extremely candid about the cross-currents of opinion in a large democracy, and he threw a lot of light on the development of American policy from the Monroe point of view up to the current general acceptance of world responsibility, and the doubts of it by those who still hanker after the traditional isolationism. With far greater and deeper knowledge he confirmed the impressions that Margaret and I had come back with.

Significantly, most of the moving spirits in the Peace with China movement, who had been accusing the UNA of not giving opportunities for study of the situation, stayed away from this meeting, and so did most of the Quakers who voted for the anti-American resolution, but were very uncomfortable about its having been taken without discussion and about the suppression of my own attempt to speak. If I could have obtained a hearing I could not have succeeded in getting a different resolution; but I think it very likely I could have prevented any resolution being passed at all—which was probably why the chairman (a Marxist who claims not to be a Communist) would not let me speak. I was, however, quite satisfied with the course of events, because it undoubtedly destroyed the moral effect of the meeting. . . .

NEW YORK   4 March 1951

Dear F.J.

. . . The final concentration on my manuscript, before it at last went to the printer in February, got me down; and I am only beginning to crawl out of the fatigue and the depression which naturally follow such a prolonged and intense effort of the will as one must make on a big book. There is no remedy in the doctor's kit for this disease, as I have long known: the real cure is idleness, frivolity, irresponsibility; but though that seems like a sugar-coated pill, if indeed it can be called a pill at all, there is something in the very nature of the disease itself that resists its administration; and that must first be overcome.

Despite all my self-admonitions I began a few weeks ago to write out my Bampton Lectures; and threw myself into such a deep state of hopeless fatigue after a few mornings' work that I finally surrendered, to the point of saying to myself that it would be better to give the lectures extemporarily, with some lack of perfection and finish, than to attempt to produce them in a written version and then find myself without the presence or the energy even to read them—if they do not, in that state, prove too awful to read. With that decision made, I feel better; although I had to make still another decision before I could finally be at ease.

This had to do with our going to England in early summer, about which you may have heard rumours. I found about a month ago, after talking with Ross of the *New Yorker*, that it would be possible for us to go as a family if I did as few as three Sky Lines while abroad; and I figured that, with a few extra supplements earned in advance, our expenses could be comfortably paid. We were all gladdened by this prospect, until I finally brought myself to confront the grim fact that this would mean not merely my working at top speed up to the time I climbed on the ship, but would mean having to work further after I got there, when every nerve in my body would be begging me to quit work altogether and relax. That would be a very good way to head into a general nervous breakdown, something that I have studiously tried to avoid, however sorely tempted! So we have decided to abandon our plans for spending the summer in England. If my advance royalties should be covered by advance sales on *The Conduct of Life*, and everything else were propitious, I might make a short visit to England and the continent some time in early September, if only to escape the sense of desolation I always have when the reviews begin to come out. . . .

I've just gotten halfway through Harrod's biography of John Maynard Keynes;[1] and would dearly like the opportunity to discuss it with you at length. It has been extravagantly praised today in both *The Times*, and the *Herald Tribune* by people who are equally respectful of the author and the subject. Actually, the book seems to me a very competent and just estimate of the man, though lacking in the kind of psychological insight I find essential in a good biography; but I find that Keynes himself is far from attractive to me as either a man or a thinker. Even after Harrod's well-reasoned plea on behalf of *The Economic Consequences of the Peace*, it strikes me as a presumptuous and shallow work which probably did more to unsettle the world's judgements and to prepare for the Nazi counter attack than any other single book— though doubtless there were many facts other than books that must be taken into account. Keynes was wrong in thinking that the economic situation was more important than the political one; and that bias led to a persistent misinterpretation of everything the military party and the Nazis in Germany planned and did. The greatest blunders of the Treaty of Versailles were political ones, fostering an isolationist nationalism among the small states without providing any counterbalancing mode of political cooperation, and failing to prevent German remilitarization, though this had begun as early as 1928 under the Republic and had been denounced by Carl von Ossietzky.

For me, the great merit of Harrod's biography is its analysis of the Bloomsbury group and the sort of intellectual and moral atmosphere that produced a man like Keynes.

What silly, clever people they were, that set; and how absurd it was that they should have assumed that they were the cream of England when they were in fact but a sort of curdled and addled residue of the Victorian milk they rejected! In the very qualities on which they prided themselves, their intellect and their feelings, they were extremely shallow people, inflated by the curious notion of greatness that exists in Oxford and Cambridge, people for

---

[1] R. F. Harrod, *The Life of John Maynard Keynes*, London, New York, 1951.

whom that word is reserved for obscure dons and conceited fogies, transformed by local mirrors into world figures! People who took Moore's
Principia Ethica as serious thought. Good heavens! I know better now why
you jabbed so often at the Bloomsbury group. Their brilliance was just the
phosphorescence of decay; and though Keynes was saved from complete
corruption by more solid qualities derived from conservative and traditional
England, too much of Bloomsbury remained in him.

AMENIA, NEW YORK   12 June 1951

. . . Is it actually almost the middle of June, dear F.J.? I can still remember
with such vividness my pleasure over the fact that our February letters
crossed that I can hardly believe that more than three months have passed
since then. But this fore-shortening of time always happens when one is
intensely preoccupied: I remember Von Baer's remark, in the year when he
discovered the process of fertilisation: 'When I started work, the fields were
bare, and when I raised my eyes again, I was surprised to find that the rye was
standing knee-high!' The writing of my Bampton lectures and the final
corrections of *The Conduct of Life* have occupied me so completely this spring
that everything else is as a dream; and there were times of such pressure
when reality itself was a nightmare. But I have happily got through this long
chore without breaking down in the middle of it, as I sometimes feared I
might; and at this moment Sophy, in New York, is busily finishing the Index,
so my task is almost ended. . . .

Whether I can go to Europe next Spring, as I now plan and hope, depends,
to put it brutally, on how well *The Conduct of Life* sells; and I can have no
preliminary opinion about that. If I trusted in statistical demonstrations I
could prove by a graph that since *Technics* sold 5,000 the first year and *Cities*
7,500 and *The Condition of Man* 11,000, *The Conduct of Life* should sell about
12,500, in which case, despite the fact that I've had to draw $4,000 in advances,
I should be able to go! But one can't tell in advance what is going to help or
hinder the sale of a book and this one, instead of climbing over *The Condition
of Man*, might easily fall below *Technics and Civilization*, in which case I'll be
in a pretty pickle. My English publisher, Warburg, is enthusiastic about the
book and I have a notion that it will do very well indeed in England; I hazard
that much by way of prediction. But it won't come out there till next Spring
and my present publishers, despite their seemingly generous advance—it's only
seeming because it is covered by my annual earnings on other books—show
every indication that they are going to sabotage the book, for purely human
reasons that have nothing to do with their business interests. If only business
men acted the way that Ricardo and Marx say they do!

But the fact is that the people who are now left in Harcourt are all strangers to me who, in the course of time, have driven all my friends out of their posts, the last of whom was Brace, one of the original partners. They identify me with the people whose places they have guiltily usurped, by all sorts of machinations; and though I begged them not to publish the last volume of the series, in a conference last year, unless they accepted my own estimate of the series, and of the book's importance, they are now dishonourably going back on promises they made then; and their lack of enthusiasm will certainly hurt the book's chances unless there should be an unexpected and overwhelming response from the public. Forgive me for going into these tedious details of an author's life. It is fast becoming a sort of King Charles' head with me: all the more because my position is so helpless. At this moment I cannot even express my anger in person to them, lest anything I say only decrease by that much more the chances of the book.

As for your trip here, dear F.J., I have heard nothing but enthusiastic reports about it; and you may be sure that it did *us* a lot of good, whatever it may have done you. And as for your frustrations at home, well, I can understand and sympathise with them because I am in much the same kind of situation. For all our renewed activity, the Regional Development Council hasn't been able to stir the initiative we had hoped in other parts of the country: people are willing to follow our lead but not to develop leads of their own. Like Ulysses, Stein, MacKaye and Mumford are 'not now that strength which in old days moved Earth and Heaven', and the people who should be taking over our posts and functions have not yet appeared—or won't take responsibility till we fade out of the picture altogether. We have a good attendance at our meetings; but somehow the burden remains mostly on our shoulders. Your own position is a little different in that you are partly a victim of your own success, just as Stein was when the Roosevelt administration took over housing and regional planning. He should at that moment have been one of the first people summoned to Washington, as you should have been invited to Whitehall: yet the net result of all his early efforts was that he didn't even get a minor job, apart from his consultations on Greenbelt. There is some strange human propensity here that I haven't yet analysed satisfactorily to myself. probably a covert resentment on the part of those who inherit a policy against those who originally formulated it. In similar fashion, I never was asked to do a single thing for the Roosevelt administration during the war, though I was the leading advocate, or at least one of the earliest advocates, of taking positive action, and would have served anywhere my capacities could have been used. . . .

WELWYN GARDEN CITY   16 July 1951

Dear Lewis

. . . One thing on which we seem to differ is in our respective degrees of acceptance of the 'psycho-analytical' interpretation of others' actions. You may think it is due to my having been born ten years too soon—a thought I entertain, of course—but I don't think so. Even if of your generation I would still have been disposed to look first for simpler explanations of such phenomena as the displeasing behaviour of your publishers. Is it not more likely that these business men simply find it difficult to believe, even with past evidence before them, that large numbers of people will really want to buy a book they can't understand themselves? I recall my own experience with *Greenbelt Cities* and the 1942 edition of *New Towns After the War*. I am pretty sure Faber and Faber were advised by a reader of the super-aesthetic countryside-preservation school, rather precious also in his literary tastes, who did not really like my somewhat brash humour and controversial ferocity. On the other hand my book was topical, and in its own unfashionable way was rather well written; so they saw they could sell one or two printings and published it, without any real hope of building me up. Dent published the other book because their Chairman, W. G. Taylor, was involved in its first publication and had a personal interest; but when it could have been sold they held copies back, and later it had to remaindered—though they told me they were holding back because it would easily sell out in due course. As an author I naturally think more could have been done with both books if the two publishers had taken more interest, but I don't think they had any complexes. The books were very small fish in their catch, and they naturally concentrate on those with obvious business possibilities. However, you may have good reasons for thinking there is a complex in the minds of your publishers. I do not doubt, though, that business men, in 999 cases of 1,000, act on Ricardian motives plus the motives of satisfaction in their kind of craftsmanship (which includes production and selling and the pleasure of upward curves on their charts), and that this is usually distorted rather by their own favourable enthusiasms and desire for prestige than by self-destructive complexes. If your case is an exception, I would say it is extraordinarily bad luck for you and should produce no generalisation about business men. It is not in my experience that business men do not want to be thought well of by both their suppliers and customers—a non-economic motive ignored by Marx, which has survival value but is not to be accounted for by the conscious pursuit of self-interest alone. . . .

I have a half-day at home in the midst of the International Federation Conference at High Lea, Hertfordshire, where . . . I was amazed, and momentarily encouraged, by support from all the French housing and planning people present, whose spokesmen not only brilliantly exploded Le Corbusier's mad 14-storey glass-house at Marseilles, but expressed astonishment that England, the envied country of the family home with garden, should be increasingly piling houses on top of each other. (The latest fad here is the 'maisonette' block, in which 2-storey houses are built on top of each other up to eight storeys—which as the French rightly said is combining the disadvantages of flats and houses). The high officials of our own housing and planning ministry were undoubtedly impressed by these attacks, which were really unanswerable; but the drift of things is simply too much for them. I am more and more convinced that we must lose unless somehow we can bring the force of popular opinion to bear—and I just don't see how to do it I can't get the money, and I can't get together even a dozen passionate enthusiasts to splutter along with me. I feel spent and futile, and can take no pleasure in dialectical triumphs that are just throwing the sand against the wind. Your way is the only way: to write books that build new foundations of thought. But that is a twenty-five year process, and therefore not for me at my age. And I shudder at what will happen in the meantime. And so I pursue the short cut route which isn't open.

In such circumstances one blames oneself. I have not done the most or best I could. If I am an 8-cylinder engine I have never fired on more than three at a time; and I have mistaken this for balance and the golden mean—in which I came to believe early in life. My view was that you should live as well as do, be as well as act. It is true that my diversity of interests did prove useful, in the absence of a good formal education, in enabling me to concentrate to some extent, in such activities as I have pursued, on a new combination of subjects of importance. But I went on with the diversity of living after I had found my mission. Probably I am so made that I had to; but it is suspicious that I have had an almost consistently happy life—happy I mean on all the normal planes; not the unconscious happiness of the devotee. That sets a problem. I want people in general to know my secret of happiness; it would be better if people at large could balance fairly work and leisure, absorption and productiveness. But what was right for me as a man was not right for me as a missionary, and I have no gift of self-immolation, only a desire for fair play all round, on which on the whole I think I have acted. I can defend myself as a philosopher, but as prophet I am a washout because it isn't in me to be more than consistent; I cannot be single-minded.

AMENIA, NEW YORK   31 July 1951

I was on the point of writing you, dear F.J., even before your letter of the 16th came, prompted by the July number of *Town and Country Planning*, which, as it turned out, was almost a Mumford number, what with various quotations and the report on Dispersal, which was largely, as you may have suspected, my handiwork. I'm not sure but that I'd have had a better winter if I had rested in December and January, instead of pushing myself hard to get that report written; but there's no use crying over spilt milk, especially over spilt milk in a worthy cause. Unfortunately, though Clarence Stein got the report into C. E. Wilson's hands in person, there is no one in Washington capable of taking in our proposals, still less of acting upon them. The House of Representatives, being composed largely of small town lawyers, are the natural support of the Real Estate lobby; they do not even have to be brought up to oppose public housing or town building of any kind, for they are of the very class that hopes to make a little extra money in realty speculation of one sort or another. As a result, even the kind of public housing program a conservative like Senator Taft supports is voted down by a large majority in the House. This is all the more fatal at the moment because Congress in other ways has shown itself singularly inept and unrepresentative: with all his faults, Truman is far closer to the best intentions of the American people as a whole than their more intimately chosen representatives. One of the many paradoxes of our republican form of government.

I must have been a little careless to have given you the impression that I believe that business men usually act on non-Ricardian principles. I wouldn't even say for a moment that Harcourt Brace does not act *usually* with a single eye to business profit. 'Irrational' factors do, I think, often cut across practical business judgement in all enterprises: certainly we have a massive example of this in the general hatred of most American business men for Franklin Roosevelt, the man who bolstered up capitalism and saved them: this animus has now been transferred to Truman for much the same reason, though never have corporate profits been higher or incomes so lush as in the last few years....

Your present mood about your own work is one that from time to time I succumb to about my own, but I don't think it is seriously justified in either case. As a rule, people under 30 are likely to be too favourable in their judgements about their intentions and their accomplishments; and people over 50, like you and me, are likely to be too hard on themselves, and to write down as inconsequential a full career and a happy life . . . You will find a full justification for your career when you come to read *The Conduct of Life*. For yours has been a balanced life, with everything you have done in due proportion to the whole; and though such a life seems to leave less of a mark than a highly concentrated, specialised existence, whatever it does do is usually sound and will show great lasting powers, with little need for radical amendment and correction . . . In either kind of life there is a sacrifice, but the kind you have lived is,

I believe, the better choice, and the more exemplary one for our age. I made the same choice myself with eyes open. I might have risen to eminence in one of four or five careers; but as soon as I decided that balance was more important than specialised facility—and that this balance included my emotional life, my relations with women, my family and parental responsibilities—I knew that even in the fields where I had made original contributions I would not, in all probability, have more than a modicum of recognition in my own lifetime. But if our civilisation doesn't continue fatally on a course that can only end in Robotdom or Wasteland, those who have sought for balance rather than success will be hailed as the saints and prophets of the new age, who taught the mechanical monsters of the machine age how to be human. You have an honourable place in that company, and much solid work behind you that will remain solid, without further protection: so it is no time to be downhearted, even if the currents and winds of fashion are blowing for a moment from the wrong direction—as they indeed are.

WELWYN GARDEN CITY   11 September 1951

Dear Lewis

Incredible that your letter is dated July 31st; the world spins with such acceleration that at times I think I can detect the precession of the equinoxes. A sixteen-day tour in Austria, the first five days of which seemed as long as a happy childhood, now contracts to a flash; and I have been back a week, with only two weeks to complete about six solid lectures and Encyclopaedia articles, and I have done, as far as I can see, nothing—except that, out of sheer physical strength and moral weakness, I rebuilt about 6 sq. yds of my rockery and discouraged by premature movement a lot of hopeful spring-flowering plants. My garden is indeed the symbol of my life; it is always going to be worth looking at next year or the year after. . . .

Probably I should have been more effective if in the last few years I had been able in some way to continue combining practical work with writing; for example as chairman of one of the New Towns or even as a member of a central advisory committee. My friends are as puzzled as I am that I was not brought into this work somehow—more puzzled, because in fact I was not sure I wanted to push uphill again the logs I pushed from 1919 to 1936 at WGC, and I gave Silkin some excuse for leaving me out of the work. But it is also true that for reasons that, like your publishing experience, verge on psychological complexes, he wanted that excuse. He sees himself as the Edward I of the twentieth century—a view I astutely encouraged in him at the right time—and is even a bit jealous of the noble Howard. I know he is troubled in his conscience about me, through reports of things he has said to others; but really he need not be. The main contribution I had to make was made long ago; and though I could have directed one or two of the New Towns more efficiently than they have in fact been directed, simply because of past experience, that would only marginally have affected the success of the whole scheme. In the main so big a job had to be carried out largely by new men, who had to learn by their own experience.

Silkin really was the key man in the series of events. If he had been as subtle or sensitive to true dynamics as a normal politician, he would never have started in a couple of years a dozen or more new towns or brought about the revolution in land tenure of the 1947 Act. No one at present sees this more clearly than I do. I think Silkin's twinges of conscience about his treatment of me are partly stimulated by his gradual discernment that I see the magnitude of his personal achievement, which he is all the more keen on having recognised because he has been kicked upstairs into the House of Lords and can't ever be in a similar great position again. He could never understand that I chuckle secretly and with complete satisfaction that he did what I had been trying persistently to get done for twenty-five years, and that though I have a weak liking for credit and flattery when they come my way—because they do give one a glow for a few minutes—I regard the quest for credit and status as almost as low a motive, notwithstanding Milton, as the quest for lots of money. But anyone who wants things done in the world has to realise that these are powerful motives with business men and statesmen, and he has to be more tolerant of them.

They are less harmful than the Hitlerite motives of domination and cruelty, which I would never encourage even for the greatest objectives.

My doubts about your interpretation of the motives of your publishers seem to me now offensively disrespectful to you; I could only (half-heartedly) stand by my objection to your generalising them to business men as a class. I have a soft spot for business men—holding them to be, both as a group and at their best, more admirable than politicians, artists, authors, shopkeepers pure and simple, or wage-earning mechanics. They carry more responsibility, have less vanity, are more resilient and provide more recruits to unselfish social work, I think, than any other group except perhaps little women and good wives. One day (in my next life) I am going to write a great work in Defence of the Business Man. I class him with Upton Sinclair's Jimmy Higgins (whom I have also inordinately admired in many incarnations) as the salt of the earth to whom justice has never been done—just because he is sometimes fairly well off . . .

It is opportune to mention here that I have been re-reading some of your *Condition of Man* and *Values for Survival*, and my admiration for your sound learning and force of expression grows so strongly that I really feel quite inadequate to corresponding with you. I am sure I have in my life read as much and as variously as anybody ever did. But I have no memory and no power to assemble and organise what I have read, so that I am always at a loss both as a conversationalist and as a writer for facts and illustrations. To be really frank, I think I abstract something from every single thing I read or hear; I constantly correct my outlook, or what stands for my philosophy, by any new information or thought that in the least conflicts with my built-up view. But I am not sure that considerations are not leaking out of my store as fast as they come in, so that while as an elderly and thoughtful man I must on main issues be reasonable and wise, I doubt if I gain in wisdom. I never sit down and sort out and weigh up what I think and know, except in one very narrow field. You evidently do; your knowledge is far better held; and your reading has been resolutely of the really important books. Thus you are really educated, whereas my assembly of knowledge and thoughts is a disorderly ragbag. By accident it was useful at a certain stage for my purposes of synthesis in the town-country field, but the study has run past me; more efficient writers have taken the subject up, and any contribution I can in the future make will be polemic rather than philosophic. . . .

WELWYN GARDEN CITY   26 October 1951

Dear Lewis

A brief flash this time, mainly to thank you for having had sent to me *The Conduct of Life*,[1] the arrival of which this morning is of course quite an event in our household. Always in a sense here as a member of our larger international family, you were at breakfast more actively present than usual. And Margaret and I will read the book with special expectation and respect. Glancing through it, I chance on a passage or two relating to town planning that give me an excuse for quotation in the December *T & CP*, on which I am now working; I telephoned Secker and Warburg and found I could say they are publishing the book, probably in Spring 1952; and though it is on the fringe of our speciality as a journal, I should be able to review the book then as one by a writer important to planners. . . .

With just over half the returns in, the Election shows at this moment a loss of twelve seats by Labour, so that it is pretty certain the Conservatives will have a small majority—rather smaller than I expected. I voted Labour myself, but have sufficiently mixed feelings not to be upset by a change of Government that is not a landslide. Both parties are uncertain, not only as to the handling

---

[1] New York, London, 1951, 1952.

of current difficulties, but as to where they want to go next. The responsible Labour chiefs have probably the soundest political philosophy, but the 'drive' in the party is mechanically socialist in the old sense, and cynical party managers think this myth is the only key to enthusiasm and votes, and they and the childish idealists are a disabling influence on the leaders, who can't neglect the constituency parties in which Bevanites and Fellow-travellers (often middle-class high-brows in minor industrial and public jobs) tend to be the most vocal in rather small working cliques. On the other hand the Tories are being very slow in moving towards a modern economic policy, and a lot of their supporters believe that salvation lies in cutting annoying controls and expensive services. With a large majority they might be pressed to do very silly things; with a small one they will have to face every issue in detail; and if they put some good men in the important ministries the change may be healthy. The real difficulty on both sides is that we are not getting men of quality adequate to the problems; a lot of very poor fish rise rapidly in politics, as they can't in industry. Perhaps that is the toughest problem for democracy.

I have a difficult time ahead with planning politics, as neither party showed the least interest in planning during the election, and a lot of Mohawks are out with tomahawks. A Tory landslide would have made things more difficult for me. But now much depends on who happens to get the job of Planning Minister. Just because planning has no following its minister has an exceptionally free hand; and because so few people or organisations know anything or say anything about the subject, we can probably get ourselves listened to if we have anything to say. I confess myself utterly weary of repetition after all these years; tired especially of the superficiality that the conditions of the market-place compel me to. The TCPA undoubtedly needs a new figurehead and spokesman; but not a candidate is in sight. So for me, at present, there ain't no escape.

NEW YORK   8 December 1951

. . . That rich and copious letter you wrote me early in September, dear F.J., has long been waiting for an answer, to say nothing of your more recent acknowledgement of *The Conduct of Life*; but my own life has been too copious—though in no wise rich—to let me do this in my usual time for letter-writing, at the end of a day; so now I seize a vacant Saturday morning to write you, possibly because I feel a little too sad to write my overdue Sky Line for *The New Yorker*. My sadness is due to the fact that Harold Ross, the editor of *The New Yorker*, died the day before yesterday. We were not close friends, but we were very solid ones; and the longer I knew him the more I respected him. He was a hard, driving, awkward, demonic man, with a passion for accuracy that would have made a great scholar and with a ruthlessness in his personal relations that sprang out of his desire for perfection in the one thing he really cared for: his magazine. There are not too many people like that around today, or probably any other day. When he knew he could rely on a man he put unlimited faith in him and backed him up fully and generously in all matters, including financial ones, for he fought for more generous shares of the profits for his authors and his staff, against the habits of the business department. He died at 59 of an operation on his lungs . . . His going will probably not make any immediate difference in the paper, which may coast along on the momentum he gave it for another five years; but in the long run it will have its effect—and even before that it may have results in my own life. Year by year the leaves of my generation are falling from the tree; and since I am a poor hand at making new friends I find myself facing the usual blight of old age, which I watched in the case of my mother: loneliness and desolation. All but two of the closest friends of my youth are now gone.

Enough of that: hence loathéd melancholy! Your reflections on your own life have recalled to me a certain parallel I may have mentioned before between your own career and Clarence Stein's: for Roosevelt treated him, when he came to the White House and undertook housing and planning, precisely in the fashion that Silkin treated you, and with similar damage to the movement he was advancing. In your case I hope that there comes a belated flowering, like that of the Aloe in Melville's poem, such as has recently happened to Stein: for the Aluminium Company of Canada has called him in to help plan a new town they are creating in the wilds of the Northwest, chosen because of its abundance of electric power since the ore comes all the way from the West Indies. Perhaps you've heard the story, or part of it; but it almost stands a re-telling since it is such an edifying and moral tale. The Alcan people had compiled a list of about thirty planners, English and American, who were asked for preliminary interviews about the project. Clarence's name was not on the list. The young Executive in charge, consulting Holmes Perkins, was asked by him why he had not included Stein, and it turned out that he had never heard of him. The other planners had, many of them, made strenuous efforts to get the job, had made hasty climatic surveys, topographic surveys, etc. Stein got it because he was the one person who showed that he had any grasp of the political and administrative realities in founding a new town; and because he said that before he did anything he would consult on the spot the people who could give him the best advice. Very wisely he refused to accept the planning job itself, which he turned over to Albert Mayer. He remains a consultant and is having a very good time. In fact he is now, once more, at the top of his powers; almost the same man I knew in 1925 though he is now

almost 70. That kind of opportunity is better than a magical injection of hor-
mones to promote rejuvenescence! . . .

WELWYN GARDEN CITY   29 January 1952

Dear Lewis

Your letter of January 12th comes when that of December 8th, an important
one, still remains unanswered. Let me first thank you for letting me read your
unpublished article of 1917 on Garden Civilisations, which certainly ought to
have been published at the time. I am sure I should have welcomed it; but I
am also sure that I would have seen in it the heresy that it was my mission in
life to crush at that time—the application of the name *garden city* to industrial
or residential suburbs. How bad-tempered I was with all sorts of good people
who would *not* see the difference between open development and detached
development—between a well-planned addition to an over-large city and a
new town isolated by an agricultural belt! How right I was; and yet how
ineffective I must have been as a speaker and writer not to be able to get
responsible people to see the difference for another twenty to twenty-five
years! Unwin was quite clear about the difference; but he was a bad propagandist on this side of the planning campaign; nothing could have been more
unwise than his famous demonstration that you could put double or treble the
population at decent densities by expanding London only a few miles in radius.
As he didn't want to expand London by even half a mile I never could see why
he used that illustration! But every single exponent of 'garden cities' in Europe,
except Howard, Purdom and myself, fluffed this fundamental point. And so
far as I met them or read them, so did the Americans who were at that time
regarded as planners. I remember saying about 1920 or early in the twenties
that I would die happy if I could see people seriously fighting each other for
different ideal sizes for a town; it was their complete inability to take an
interest in the size question that infuriated me for years.

However, I did live to see people battling about theories of size; and am I
dying happily? No, sir. I am in better health than at any time in my life; and
less happy about the campaign I have spent so many years on than at any time.
Which doesn't of course, mean a thing; tomorrow, or next year, I may be dead
or full of enthusiasm for some new development. . . .

I've just spent three days in a hospital ward full of the most shocking cases
of head injuries and diseases; men who have been smashed up in accidents, or
whose bones are crumbling; and who have been pieced together with metal
screwed into unlikely parts of their faces or coming out of the mouth or ears.
And do you know, though I am quite childishly susceptible to the horror of

such things, after a few hours I got used to them, and was thereafter impressed by the extraordinarily good social atmosphere of the ward. It is a temporary community, of which the oldest inhabitants may have been there five or six months, most for two or three weeks or months, and some, like me, for a few days only; but really it would be worth a serious sociological study. The most advanced surgery and medicine is practised in such a hospital, and the prestige of the top surgeons is not less than that of popes and emperors (and far better deserved). The hierarchy of nurses and specialists is very complex; but throughout there is a standard of work, and of enjoyment of work, that is magnificent—at least it dazzled me in my brief transit, in which I was examined very thoroughly by a team, operated on for a minor affair (comparable to a thickened toe-nail) with miraculous efficiency, and discharged without formality before I had been out of bed long enough to know the names of all the pretty little nurses and the gargoyles in the beds. The patients, some of them with the scaffolding I have described, did, with great gusto, all the sweeping and many odd jobs in the ward; and it was very clear that there was a decided social order of distinguished personalities, passengers, and village idiots; I am not sure I got beyond the village idiot stage—though one patient of 30 or so called me 'Pop'. A most interesting, a reassuring experience. Since I was last operated on, for a much more serious affair, methods have very considerably changed; I was anaesthetised by two injections, revived by injection (I believe), and stitched with stitches that dissolve and don't have to be pulled out. And I was out of bed at 6 a.m. the morning after the operation. Maximum commonsense, minimum fuss, and yet great care at every stage to ensure the right treatment and regimen. And not a cent to pay. (This I didn't quite like; one feels a certain desire to reciprocate, and doesn't know how) . . .

I have not written much about the neighbourhood, but you will have noticed from my occasional notes on the subject that I do not really believe in the Village within the Town; I mean that I do not believe it can be created by the physical structure of a neighbourhood and its centre.

I do think that the social structure of a town of 10,000 or 20,000, isolated from other towns by agricultural land, is different from that of a neighbourhood of 10,000 or 20,000 which is part of a continuously built-up million city. It is, however, the isolation—or rather the distance from other large groups of people—that produces the more concentrated interchange between people in a village or small town; not its internal physical lay-out. As a resident for thirty years in WGC, which has grown from 400 to about 20,000 in that time, I am conscious of various groupings: my family in its one house; the over-the-garden-fence community of the immediate neighbours (perhaps six to ten families); and then WGC as a whole; then Greater London; and then Great Britain. Inside WGC I have no consciousness of a larger neighbourhood than the six to ten houses; but of course I am conscious of lots of such communities as the factory in which I work, the political party to which I belong, the Chamber of Commerce, etc., etc. I draw my friends more from WGC than from outside—that is, I see my WGC friends more often—but from any part of WGC and from other parts of GB and the world; not particularly from a neighbourhood within WGC. I do not believe much in attempts by organising community centres to make people especially ward-conscious; they will naturally be so to a slight extent; but unless there is an obstacle or an interval of distance they will not be neighbourhood-conscious to any important extent. . . . .

The fact is that I am much against the superior-person theory that is at the bottom of many community-centre projects. Highbrow types are always seeking new opportunities of showing common people how they should live and what should interest them; and I think they have already plenty of scope in the schools and (here) on the radio. I suppose I am a bit untidy in my mind about this, since in some vague way I do accept the hierarchy of education. But I am influenced by a strong and rather bitter feeling that in recent years social science, as it impinges on planning, has gone very wrong; and the architects even more wrong—indecently, inhumanly wrong. Here they have captured the BBC Third Programme and television; and they are driving me into a belief in commercially sponsored programmes—a horrible but less inhuman alternative. There was a lecture on Le Corbusier a few weeks ago on the Third Programme, that reached the last degree of precosity and treason to human standards; it was given by an architect who was for years, till a year or so ago, the head of an architecture school in England. It appals me to think that our young architects are being *taught* by such men; no wonder they produce such shocking schemes. We have a lot of them in the TCPA Students Group; charming young people, but as herd-minded as lemmings. Now that academic authority is passing into the hands of the Corbusierites, apparent support is given to the opportunist leanings of the LCC and other housing authorities, and the Ministry, and more and more block flats are being built, and density is gradually being increased in normal housing estates and in the new towns. The tacit conspiracy between the countryside preservationists, the city authorities and the architects, of which I wrote in *Green-belt Cities*, has now succeeded, and generations of town-dwellers will suffer for it. And I am now too tired of the sound of my own voice to protest with the necessary vigour. . . .

When in France in March I took the occasion to go down to Marseilles and have a close look at Le Corb's fantastic Unité d'Habitation. I collected all the data necessary to show its economic and social absurdity, and with less amplitude its technical absurdity; but in six weeks I haven't been able to put my material together—or it would be more honest to say simply, I have not put the material together. I have spent most week-ends in the garden. I have sat a number of hours pleasantly talking, and I have read very many books and hundreds of newspaper columns. All justifiable; but the fact is they seem, looking back, less worth doing than writing an article to debunk Le Corb.

I spoke to a crowd of architectural and planning students in London on the Marseilles scheme. Their state of mind would interest a really profound psychologist; it is one of deep obsession that is as irrational as an inconvenient fashion in dress: in a sort of way important, because fashion is a fact that leaves a permanent mark on many things; but not in my view to be respected simply because, like the King's Evil, it is a phenomenon of Nature. When my mother wore leg-of-mutton sleeves and hour-glass corsets, I can remember both hating the fashion and seeing that, being the fashion, it was somehow smart and irresistible. When the fashion changed to short sleeves and natural corsetless waists, the feeling of smartness was accompanied by a rich glowing feeling of rightness as well. Clearly there can be genuine fashions (whatever fashion is) that are bad. I am sure Le Corbusier is such a fashion. He has passed in some regions; but he is raging in the Architectural Association School in London now; and the young men under his influence are completely impervious to economic or human considerations. I have no doubt I undermined the orthodoxy of one or two; but it was curious to note the intensity of feeling of the majority—it was just as if in my youth I had, in a Methodist bible class, questioned the divinity of Christ. I had the same impression of animal unreason.

Have you written anything about fashion? Is there any penetrating study of it? I have not discussed it with anyone but a typical Hermann-German who saw deep significance in every manifestation of it, and just made me laugh—as Freud's early works did—by a sort of systematic credulity. I may be odd in this matter; I have a strong sense of what *is*, or even is becoming, *the fashion*— which I have not succeeded or much tried to succeed in analysing; and at the same time a kind of scorn or non-acceptance of the fashion when, as it often is, it is silly or arbitrary. Non-acceptance rises to irritation or anger when the fashion is injurious to health or real beauty—but I think I am still conscious of some sort of wave of stupidity that it isn't much good to argue about. The present use of lipstick is a case in point. Most young girls look less pretty with it, and most older women turn soft sweet faces into vulture-like masks; but if you discuss the subject the eyes of young and old go fixed and glassy as if you were rifling the ark of the covenant and they did not wish to notice such delinquency in a friend. Most of the architect-students' eyes went glassy when I described Corb's Marseilles fantasy; a few only went emotionally amok. . . .

I suppose you have detected that we have a very strong revival here of the

Malthusian scare, coupled with grave doubts about Britain's ability to maintain sufficient export sales to buy food. The farmers' lobby, about the best-organised pressure group in this country, is exploiting this fashion for all it is worth; and the industrialists, who stand for 90 per cent of our living, are not asserting their own position or claiming ability to keep Britain going. There is of course reason to be anxious about the sufficiency of the world's food supply; there always has been, and probably there always will be. But this is more than the normal worry; it is, again, a fashion of thought. Whereas a few years ago all highbrows had to be worried about the distribution of wealth, and at another time all had to be worried (simultaneously, that is the point) about more industrial output; now they all have to be worried (simultaneously) about starvation the year after next. If we don't starve the year after next, therefore, the fashion will change, though the fundamental world situation will not have altered that much.

You see I am getting an anti-fashion complex!

Young men and women in thousands are still obliviously getting married and wanting a house to live in and a garden to grow things in; but farmers, food scares and architectural fancies are forcing them into flats. I ask myself: why is a fashion, and a mere minority fashion, so powerful against my commonsense and the unaltered wish of the mass of customers? . . .

AMENIA, NEW YORK   10 July 1952

Dear F.J.

Rain set in the night before last and this morning it is raining harder than ever: one of those steady rains that come, in these parts, from the sea and usually last for two or three days. Naturally, it didn't come in time to save my pea-vines from being burned to a crisp, nearly, during an unseasonable hot spell, when I was down in New York and could neither mulch the ground nor water it; but still it has brought enough water to keep the garden going well into August, even if we have one of our usual droughts; and best of all, it encourages me to stay close to my desk today so that I may catch up with my long put-off correspondence, and so that later I may begin to put my files in order.

On the thirtieth of June we turned our backs to New York and moved all our household rubbish up here; since which time we've been busily at work amalgamating two households—which in this instance meant building two extra book-cases and falling back upon two spare-rooms, an attic, and the attic of our old carriage house, to take care of the excess of domestic goods. Spohy has been working like the proverbial beaver; and even I acquired housemaid's knee toting heavy boxes of books upstairs and down: the first time that this ever happened to me, so that I am full of surprise, dismay, and chagrin! . . .

The first part of your paper on Le Corbusier[1] was admirable, written with a kind of equability and generosity which is truly English; and I am very eager to see what you say in direct criticism. The Marseilles habitation seems to me a monstrosity, and a belated one at that, for it is a Fourier phalanstery without the psychological insight that that queer genius often exhibited. You are right in thinking that it is a product of fashion, in which the irrational factors play a larger part than rational ones, though the latter are often paraded as a mask. So that in this country housing officials, who have barely heard of Le Corbusier, nevertheless imitate his Voisin Plan in every new project between New York and Los Angeles, with only a few lone voices, like Catherine Bauer's and mine, to protest against it. That the intelligentsia of Britain should have gone in for the same absurd formula is sickening. I should have had a lot of fun this summer attacking them; indeed, I had planned to begin the attack with an address at the annual meeting of Abercrombie's Rural Preservation Group. I trust all goes well, so that I may join you, in more ways than one, next spring . . . One of the reasons for my wanting to go to Europe is that I want to collect fresh illustrations of recent work, mainly in England of course. If this new edition of *The Culture of Cities* turns out well, I shall follow it through with a revised *Technics and Civilisation* and with an amplified and illustrated *Conduct of Life*. But that takes me into rather a remote future; since I have two fresh works I want to finish during the next few years; one on Love and Marriage—a deleted portion of *The Conduct of Life*, and the other a contribution on Religion and Mankind to a new series of rather small tracts that Harper and Brothers is going to publish here.[2]

Only one thing is lacking for all these projects, apart from time; and that is any kind of public response, at least among my own countrymen. As I have told you, I think, *The Conduct of Life* was only perfunctorily reviewed in the general press and many papers neglected it entirely; *Art and Technics* has met with an even colder and stonier shoulder: no reviews at all in any important newspaper, almost a boycott in fact, if not in intention. Even I am a little puzzled as to why this should be. It would be easy to say that this is just one of the consequences of the maudlin hysteria that now afflicts so many of our countrymen, panicky not merely over communism but over anything savouring of criticism of the established order, in which they are abetted by a disreputable crew of ex-communists, who are even more disruptive

---

[1] 'Concerning Le Corbusier', in *Town and Country Planning*, July and August, 1952.

[2] This became *The Transformations of Man*, New York, London, 1957.

reactionaries than they were as revolutionaries. That would be an easy explanation, and a colourable one, up to a point; yet it doesn't explain the facts satisfactorily to my mind, since even papers that are favourable to me, like *The Saturday Review*, have behaved in the same fashion. Yet on the other hand, just yesterday, the publishers of *Art and Technics* came forth with a decent-sized advertisement of it in the *New York Times*, which means either that it is selling well or that the manager of the Press is out of his mind. A queer world!

Your experience in getting people to understand the garden city, dear F.J., parallels that of Stein and myself, though you've devoted far more effort to the cause and have, on the whole, worked in a more favourable environment. That back in 1917 I should have confused the Garden City with open development generally is, I think, excusable in a lad who had been studying cities consciously for only two years: what struck me, on looking back on it, was that even at that early point I should have realised that the transformation from one urban type to another involved our civilisation as a whole. . . .

What you say about the succession of model industrial schemes is extremely interesting: as so often happens, an incomplete account of an historic movement, that gets into print, often keeps people from searching out the earlier or parallel transformations that had remained unnoted. Thus people would have regarded the superblock as a modern invention, if I had not had the good fortune to have lived in Cambridge in 1918, and to have had enough of a town-planner's eye to recognise the existence of early nineteenth-century superblocks all over this region. Even now, when I recently referred to such blocks, a Cambridge official city planner sent me a plan of the city and asked me to point them out—and there they were, visible to the naked eye, more numerous than I had remembered. Yet she was unable to identify them. (Her reply: Oh, is *that* what you mean?) So, too, the row-house, planned not around the periphery of a block but in parallel rows, was a nineteenth century contribution in Manchester, New Hampshire; done rather better than in most Federal housing developments today.

NEW YORK   12 August 1952

Dear F.J.
I write to record, with prayerful hosannas, the fact that I had, nine days ago, an uneventful operation and an 'uninteresting' recovery—to my surgeon's delight as well as my own. This is my first major experience of surgery—apart from a brief tonsillectomy—and it turns out to be one of those things that, on reflection, it would be a pity to have missed. I approached the operation in a

spirit of yoga-like tranquillity, not to be accounted for by the drugs I later received; and if I can preserve some of this detachment once the immediate challenge is gone my life may enter into a new phase! All in all, I've been lucky: not merely in this luxurious hospital very well run, with a desire to please rather than to intimidate and frustrate the patient, but I even have, as a last touch of good fortune, a room that overlooks the Hudson, giving me a view of the George Washington Bridge with the Palisades behind it—at night a veritable Whistler nocturne. . . .

NEW YORK   14 August 1952

The main purpose of this note, dear F.J.—since you already have heard about my physical state in the letter that crossed yours—is to tell you that if 1917 is the date on the Garden Civilisations ms. that is the right date—though my memory would have put it a year earlier—if only to make it easier for my pride to accept its juvenilities! Heaven knows it needs annotations; but despite the youthful vagueness as to what constitutes the Garden City I *had* actually read *Garden Cities of Tomorrow* and grasped its significance; and this early self-indoctrination formed the basis of my friendship with Clarence Stein (who had also read it) and led to our making this the core of our housing and planning program in the Regional Planning Association of America we founded in 1923. You know all this probably: but it is as well, perhaps, to have me bring it back again before you proceed to the much-needed annotations. Please make clear that this is a specimen of unpublished juvenilia—of interest only to sympathetic antiquarians.[1] . . .

AMENIA, NEW YORK   11 September 1952

Dear F.J.

Your note from Bart's Hospital was something of a bombshell. I trust that by the time you get this you will be over the worst hurdles of this operation. I am relieved to find you are in a hospital with such a fine reputation, for in this particular operation I've concluded that the hospital is almost as important as the surgeon. It will be fun to compare notes with you, for as I may have said before, there seem to be as many schools—full of self-righteousness and theories—on the technique of a prostate operation as there are in esthetic dancing. You've had experience of a major operation before, as I had not, so you probably don't need the only advice I can give—namely, that the second

---

[1] 'Garden Civilisations' was not in the end reprinted in *Town and Country Planning*.

stage of recovery is more difficult than the first. The operation is now six weeks behind me and I have regained the 13 lb. I lost at the hospital and *look* healthy. . . .

Good heavens! . . . The usual exclamation of pained surprise, dear F.J., at finding that your November letter is now at least two months overdue for a reply. During those two months various things happened: we came back here for the Christmas holidays and found ourselves more grateful than ever for this simple rural dwelling, after living on the eighteenth floor of The Drake in Philadelphia with a feeling of remoteness and insulation that no radiant, fog-lavendered sunset ever quite compensated us for. After that I wound up my courses at the University of Pennsylvania, addressed two civic groups—one of them, the Farmount Park Art Association, honoured me with a medal for nameless services—and then, just a few days less than four weeks ago, we came back here to be enfolded once more in this very satisfying life. I told you, I think, about my sleepiness and lethargy all autumn, a state I too thoughtlessly attributed to my operation. It turns out that I got over the operation in good fashion, but fell prey to a slow infection, caused by the too quiet demise of one of my teeth. Twice before this had happened in my life—each time with the same sleepy symptoms; but my operation threw me off the trail. Now I feel like my old self once more, though I shall have to endure a dismal round of dental work . . .

I don't know if I said anything about the election in my last letter to you. What has happened since has only confirmed my most dismal fears. Despite Eisenhower's immense personal triumph, which freed him from the need of any subserviency to McCarthy and Co., he has neither the courage nor the insight to take a stand against this native form of fascism: on the contrary, the State Department, already demoralised, has truckled under to the Senatorial inquisitors; and unless the schools and colleges who are coming in for investigation for 'harbouring communists' stand up more manfully, our constitutional liberties, already badly undermined by security precautions and the cold war, may disappear entirely before we waken sufficiently to the danger. The confidence I had in 1940 about our ability to fight fascism without being infected with it has proved unsound. Though at least two-thirds, probably three-fourths, of the country is as decently democratic as it always was, a sufficient minority has been given enough power in Congress to terrorise and browbeat the rest of us.

The other day Mrs Agnes Meyer, an owner of *The Washington Post*, delivered a stinging attack against the Senatorial inquisitors; but there have not been enough people of her courage willing to speak out at the certain price of being branded by Goebbels-McCarthy as a communist. When I made a similar declaration at a public celebration at Cooper Union Institute the other day, the audience was entirely with me but not a paper reported my words; so neither the press nor the radio—for this is not a lone example—give a true picture of America or give an indication of the opposition both to the way we are fighting the cold war and the way we are forfeiting our constitutional liberties. My worst fear is that Eisenhower's free market policy may cause a break in prices within the next year sufficient to cause a depression; and when that happens the scapegoats will not be just the Jews but everyone associated with the New Deal, by that queer kind of logic whereby fascism appeals to the irrational by its habit of calling white black.

Altogether the outlook—barring a miracle—looks pretty black here. Perhaps that's why I devoted a whole section of *The Conduct of Life* to the possibility of miracles!

WELWYN GARDEN CITY   2 March 1953

Dear Lewis

... Margaret and I hope to go to Spain in April, but will certainly be back, if we go, before you arrive in England on May 11th. We would be glad to have you here for as much of your stay as you wish; you know of course that we are forty minutes from Kings Cross, within easy car drives of the new towns of Stevenage, Harlow, Hemel Hempstead, Basildon, Bracknell, and Corby. Hatfield is next door and Crawley can be reached in 2½ hours, by train or car through or round London. I may be free all the time, but there is a possibility that I may have to lead a TCPA Tour to Scotland, including the two Scots new towns, between May 16–25, unless I can get some other known planner to lead it . . .

The Annual General Meeting of the TCPA is in London on May 13th at 2.30 p.m. The Archbishop of York presides, and it would be grand from our point of view if you could be our principal guest on that occasion as it would undoubtedly be widely reported.

Letchworth celebrates its fiftieth anniversary on September 1st, with a local exhibition. I consider they are not making nearly enough fuss of a really important occasion (they have no idea of their international fame), and have been bothering them to get the TCPA, TPI and RIBA together for a celebration in London also: for the reason that a far more influential and distinguished company can be got together in London—say for a luncheon—than at the Letchworth celebrations. But they have dithered over this and so I have not pursued the matter. I am tired of being the one person in England who knows the importance of the garden city movement and will take any initiatives to keep it in evidence. If, however, I could say that you would be available on Tuesday, September 2nd—the day before you go, which seems very cruel— I feel sure we could really make something of a London occasion, with representative bigwigs.

We have just had a conference on Dispersal at Leamington at which several conurbations and about 100 country towns were represented; and at the moment this is regarded with more favour than new towns, as the fourteen already started are now going as fast as is practicable, and yet everybody sees that they are not enough to deal with congestion or rebuilding. There is still a need for a few more new towns but the present Minister (Macmillan) is against them, though he is pushing on housing in those already started. A central reassertion of the major principle is appropriate just now and it could be tied on to the Letchworth Jubilee. . . .

I'm better in health than ever before, but acutely aware of my own ineffectiveness as a politician of planning; and even claiming failures in public— which of course produces Pecksniffian reassurances from nice kind people who don't care a damn, but don't like to see an old chap moping.

AMENIA, NEW YORK   14 March 1953

Dear F.J.
This letter will be even briefer than yours of the second, but it will have the virtue of promptness. As to giving a talk on May thirteenth. Though I tremble at making such a commitment, lest the Gods again interfere with my plans, I'll be happy to talk at that meeting but doubt if it is wise to make me the principal speaker. For I shall have been in England, at most, only two days and will not yet have been able to see anything or even to have gotten the feel of things. Perhaps I can raise a few good questions, but what I will have to say will be more tentative and circumspect than it might be at a later date. (Remembering how useful your advice was last time, I must ask you how, exactly, one addresses the Archbishop of York, both in conversation and on the platform!). If your meeting on September second is held in the afternoon I have no objection at all to talking; it would be, in the old fashioned terms, both a duty and a pleasure. An evening meeting, though, would be a little rough, and if you find you have to set it then, then leave me out. . . .

AMENIA, NEW YORK 18 March 1953

Dear F. J.

If I had been in a little less haste to answer your note of 2 March I might have been a little tidier in mopping up the details. First, I have no intention of visiting all the New Towns. For my *New Yorker* articles it is important that I deal with the one or two that are most near to being finished, or otherwise most significant. Would that be Harlow or Hemel Hempstead or is Stevenage far enough along? I should like to make my first visit there alone and without any official courtesies, much though they might facilitate the work. But it would be a help, of course, if I knew what people to see and talk with after I had taken in the town by myself. When I go back again for a check-up I shall be glad, indeed grateful, to have you as a guide and mentor, whatever first-aid may be locally forthcoming. Before I go I'd like to know, too, what areas of London have gone farthest in rebuilding. Stepney? Lambeth? Where? For I shall do an article on that phase of housing and planning, too. In August, when we go up to Scotland, I shall probably visit at least one of the Scotch towns and even, on my own, the Durham towns.

I don't know how I am going to pack all the things I want during the August sojourn, especially since it is so difficult to go places spontaneously with any hope of a night's accommodation. (Bad enough if alone, I suspect, but hopeless with four people seeking lodgings at once!). My tentative plan is to get cheap lodgings in London for at least the first two weeks, and then make excursions. . . .

WELWYN GARDEN CITY 30 March 1953

Dear Lewis

I blush for the week's delay in answering yours of the 18th. The funerals and sickbeds of my vanishing contemporaries, mounting now to their peak of frequency, only partly account for it; for I also have had some difficult drafting to do on statements and reports for TCPA. The Minister of Housing has been stampeded by the agricultural lobby (powerful in the Tory party) into a campaign for high-rise building, and the British people must become 'flat-minded'—which amounts, of course, to a reversal of the dispersal and new towns policy the parties accepted a few years ago. He is pushing housing in the new towns already started, because they are there and can help his drive towards 300,000 units a year 'no matter where'. But he has stopped the one new town (Congleton) that had been designated but not started, and is not likely to start any more . . . So in view of the fifty years campaign of the TCPA I had no alternative but to submit to my Executive a pretty strong protest, reciting the essential arguments again. Unfortunately, I had a year or two ago eased up on my war-time policy of making sure my Executive contained only genuine enthusiasts for our policy, thinking the all-party acceptance of that policy made it wise to broaden our basis for carrying out the policy. And now two or three of the inner ring prove to be party men before they are TCPA men; and I had a tremendous fight last week to get a sufficiently clear statement agreed by the Executive—every line and figure being contested. To my surprise, when they were defeated (with English courtesy of course) they did not resign; and I am bound to see that this means that they are on my Executive to hamstring our fighting potential. It's bad enough to have the political world against us or indifferent, without having to fight every word of a statement inside the Executive.

I tell you this because you will see I don't want you to preach Christian tolerance of big-city and high-rise addicts when you come to our annual meeting on May 13th; though of course I'm not expecting you to be my St George and rescue me from the dragon. Be yourself, and it is sure to help. You know how important the British lead has been in the world at large. These Ministers think all the wisdom is in Sweden, France, Germany and other distant countries of which, like Chamberlain, 'we know nothing'. They won't believe me when I say (from personal contact) that Continental housing men envy British standards.

Now your queries. Of the new towns, Crawley, Hemel Hempstead and Harlow are neck and neck in the lead. The best, soundest and least novel is Crawley. The most interesting architecturally, and the least sound functionally, is Harlow. Hemel Hempstead has patches of extremely sound and architecturally decent work and patches that are experimental and, I think, doubtfully good. You must, I feel sure, see both these. Stevenage is the unlucky child and much behind, but you may wish to evaluate it. Basildon is a gallant attempt to bring some design into a district almost ruined by bad commercial building. . . .

WELWYN GARDEN CITY   10 April 1953

Dear Lewis

This lets you know at the earliest moment that we want you to speak (as principal guest) at a dinner in honour of the fiftieth anniversary of the foundation of Letchworth, the First Garden City, on the evening of September 1st— not at lunch on the 2nd, as I at first suggested to you. I hope you have not in the meantime fixed up anything else for that date. There are events at Letchworth at midday on both days that preclude a London lunch.

A special committee has been formed, representing the five main organisations concerned—the TCPA, the RIBA, the Chartered Surveyors Institution, the Town Planning Institute and First Garden City Ltd. The Right Hon. Viscount Samuel has been asked to preside; and if he cannot we next ask in succession the Speaker of the House of Commons (a former Minister of Town and Country Planning), the Master of the Rolls (Sir Raymond Evershed, who was on the Uthwatt Committee) and Sir Eric Macfadyen (Chairman of First Garden City Ltd.). We have to have a long list of alternatives, because September 1st is a bad date for a public dinner, Parliament and the Court being on vacation and perhaps a third of the bigwigs of London away. But we must coincide with the Letchworth Jubilee Fair; and the Committee feel that with five organisations taking part, having between them many thousands of members, we must be able to assemble a reasonably impressive party.

The probable order of proceedings will be: a speech by the Chairman; speeches by you and another in honour of a toast to the First Garden City; and a reply by Sir Eric Macfadyen. If we can all agree on fairly short speeches, and there is no elder statesman in the chair, I would like to include one or two more speeches, so that in one way or another the speeches represent housing, architecture and planning, as well as humanity and the social sciences—for all of which, however, you would be regarded here as an admirable spokesman.

I am chairman of the organising committee, and have been asked to speak myself, after you; I am, as it happens, the only surviving person (except Purdom, who is not acceptable to First Garden City Ltd.) that was actively connected with the development of both garden cities and with the garden city movement. (I was housing manager at Letchworth for five years—1912–17—and was fully involved in its social and political life.) Whether I speak or not depends on the composition of the speakers' list; I regard myself as in reserve if required. . . .

AMENIA, NEW YORK   12 April 1953

Dear F.J.

Thank you for all your helpful guidance, which was prompt enough so far as my end was concerned. There is no fight in which I could participate with a better conscience than one against the current irrationality of 'high-rise' apartments: the very name sticks in my gullet; and I shall enter into that fight without any of the sort of embarrassment one sometimes feels as a visitor in a family squabble, since the insanity is such a universal one and I've already made my position clear over here. The very fact that my approach to the subject is a little different from yours will save it from being a mere echo and add strength, I hope, to our combined forces. Moreover, as an outsider, it is easier

8

for me to praise your past accomplishments in establishing human standards of housing. After living on the nineteenth floor of the Drake all autumn, I am well equipped to speak by the book on the subject. My own experience has been that prepared statements, though a guarantee of accuracy, often miss the most important things one says when the occasion actually comes, and are treated by editors as a license to neglect the speech, to boot. So I will stick to my usual method of the 'spontaneous' delivery. . . .

WELWYN GARDEN CITY   8 June 1953

Dear Lewis

Your note with the two notes duly arrived and is noted and the notes placed in sanctuary till your return. I trust you are enjoying your visit to Europe and imposing on yourself more relaxation than you did in England. People here, I am sure, only worked you as hard as you encouraged them to work you; but I know too well the temptation to see everything within reach of a once-in-a-lifetime orbit. Unless you can be grimly resistant, your family, when it joins the caravan, will work you harder than any of your hosts. So pile up some reserves while you can—*if* you can!

More than ever, since I got back from Spain, I am in a state of half-complacent futility. With a stack of unanswered letters and claims for work on my desk, I have just spent a week preparing my evidence for the public inquiry into the London County Plan on behalf of the TCPA. My evidence, given last Friday, was I suppose the only one, of many thousands, that dealt with the issues of policy in the Plan as a whole. But the national and London press, still pre-occupied with the Coronation, royal peregrinations around the schools, and the Derby horse-race between the Queen's horse and a horse ridden by Britain's most popular jockey, whom the Queen (a racing fan herself) had just knighted, could not be bothered with the future of Britain's capital city. Not one reporter was present, and no newspaper, so far as I know, published a word of the short 'handout' which I sent it. The court-room contained nine persons: the Ministry's inspector, counsel representing the LCC, one minor planning official, Professor Sir Patrick Abercrombie, myself, one member of the TCPA Executive, and three lost souls dozing on the public benches—who had probably dropped in for a rest after waiting many hours to see the Queen go by.

Abercrombie is professionally retained by the LCC to defend the Plan against objectors; so he had on this occasion to defend it against me—an amusing situation, since I am Chairman of the TCPA Executive and he is one of our Vice-Presidents.

I think the strategy of the LCC representatives was to deprive the occasion of any possible drama; but they need not have worried, since my own strategy was to be utterly mild in manner, congratulatory of the completeness and clear thinking of the analysis in the Plan, and arithmetically unanswerable in my demonstration of what the plan means in living conditions for future Londoners. Both strategies succeeded. They had decided to let me make a considered statement without breaks, which I did to the extent of twenty-five minutes. But they also decided, cleverly I think, not to let counsel cross-examine me, but to ask Abercrombie to follow me with a counter-statement, led by counsel to help him to the chosen issues. After this I was to be invited to question Abercrombie, which was odd, but pretty safe, since I have neither any experience in cross-examination nor a liking for extorting confessions of inconsistency or muddled thinking. The LCC would not have minded if I had gone on to weaken the authority of their most advanced adviser, because all along the line their instinct is to soften and blur the original proposals of the 1943 Plan so that their commitment is as vague as possible. But I wasn't going to fall into that trap. I knew that Abercrombie's real position is nearer to mine than the Plan's, though he had committed himself in 1943 to a compromise that I consider too low down in the practicable scale. So in my questioning, which had to be completely respectful and polite, I could do no more than try to pull him a little more in my direction than, as official defender of the new plan, he was disposed to go. In this I succeeded to some small extent. But the truth is that his statement in reply to mine was largely vague and irrelevant. Neither he nor the LCC counsel had the figures from which it would be possible to judge what proportion of flats to houses the plan will mean. Nor had the planning official who was present, and the figures are not in the published plan, though they must have been prepared for the purpose of estimating the ultimate population aimed at.

So Abercrombie could neither accept or repudiate the 'guesstimate' I hazarded, from my own 'shirt-cuff' calculations, that ultimately 2 millions would have to live in flats, as against only $1\frac{1}{4}$ millions in vast expanses of houses with very small gardens, and that all the present more spacious residential districts in the County would have to be redeveloped at seventy persons an acre to get this population in. He did admit, however, when I pressed the point, that if my figures were roughly right the proportion of flats was most regrettable. Everybody present agreed, moreover, that the public were entitled to know the correct figures; and no doubt, as a result, some figures will be produced. But I fear they will be presented in such a way as further to confuse the public, who cannot interpret density calculations. Abercrombie's main weakness is that he does not really know what such densities as 136, 100 and 70 persons an acre mean in terms of practical layout. He said, for instance, that at 136 persons an acre one third of the people can live in houses; and as soon as we went into this it came out that half the 'houses' were double maisonettes (two storey houses on top of each other), which are, of course, only four-storey flats differently partitioned. It is appalling that a distinguished planner can be so confused; but I had to refrain from any hint to that effect. I wonder sometimes whether I am wise to be so restrained and gentlemanly in view of the terrible importance to humanity of the matters at issue. However, my statement, which I shall publish in full in our Journal, makes the essential points with clarity as well as politeness. The subsequent backchat did nothing to weaken my arguments or figures.

The television broadcast of the Coronation was superb, and it may have incalculable consequences for the future of the monarchy and the established church. I had not intended to watch the whole proceedings, but they held my interest—for seven mortal hours! It may well be that nearly half the total population was looking in. I had mixed feelings, among which was certainly a strong sense of the history of power and faith stretching back into lost ages, and of the compelling irrationalities of an organised society. It would be idle to deny that the vast majority of my countrymen were completely swept away by the experience. David Low had a cartoon next day called 'The Morning After', satirising in King's Jester vein the '100-million spree' with its fairy princess dreams. The outburst of indignation which followed was enough to rock the *Manchester Guardian* to its foundations. One has to take notice, even if one can't understand—and I admit I can't.

Churchill in his Garter robes, the real ruler overlaid by the pictorial mediaeval knight, was curiously out of it; the politically and economically functionless heralds and hereditary nobility and maids of honour all over it. And yet somehow it strikes deeply into a world-wide, common consciousness, and for that reason has importance. I must have been born with a blind spot.

WELWYN GARDEN CITY   9 June 1953

Dear Lewis

I am replying at once to your enquiry of the 7th, by-passing a long letter in my nearly legible handwriting, which awaits completion and should be posted tomorrow. It is mostly about the proceedings at the London Plan Enquiry when I gave evidence in 'objection' to the Plan last Friday. If you have time to read it you may find it some slight use. My guess in that evidence that the new London Plan means that 2 million of the ultimate population of the County will have to live in flats, and $1\frac{1}{4}$ million in houses with very small gardens, was not contested; because neither Abercrombie who appeared for the LCC against me, nor the members of the planning staff present, had the figures for the various density zones or from the total; but my estimate cannot be taken as authoritative. Ling[1] told me a week ago that he thought the ultimate proportion was about half and half, but I cannot understand how that is possible. In any case there must be grave doubts whether a population known by surveys to have a 90 per cent preference for garden houses, would in the long term accept 50 per cent of flats. Taking into account the advantages of a metropolitan situation, I would guess the true tolerance at about 30 per cent of flats. And anyway I think that is a reasonable aim when you are dealing with several millions.

As a result of my guess, which has to be taken notice of until it is officially corrected, there is no doubt that the LCC's own estimate will have to be produced.

I don't remember what article I gave you on the question of the costs of flats and houses, but I enclose a one-page memo with the essential figures. I have no recent figures of the actual contract costs for flats. The figure for the cost of houses is an up-to-date Welwyn figure, and that for the cost of flats is derived from the difference in the actual capitalized subsidy after allowing for the difference in the cost of land. It must be right within plus and minus £100. The figures for the subsidies are most certainly right—and this gives you the comparative cost to the public, which cannot be contested.

I concentrate on this figure because the LCC do not disclose the actual total costs of the flats alone and the houses alone in a mixed scheme, and enough dust is thrown to make the comparison of like with like extremely difficult. A subsidy scale is always the result of fierce horse-trading between the Government and the local authorities, and they, the authorities, must have convinced the Government that flats cost about £1,100 more each than houses in order to get that subsidy fixed. . . .

PARIS   2 July 1953

Dear F.J.

. . . I find myself, on the basis of the few New Towns I have seen, occupying a midway position between you and your opponents: or rather, not midway but essentially different from either. I reject high buildings and high densities for family living: but I also find a certain inflexibility in your definition of good housing and planning standards, which I think damages our common cause. Gordon Stephenson has just done some housing in Wales that comes to

---

[1] Arthur Ling, Chief Planner to the London County Council, 1945-55.

around 100 people per acre; and it seems to me to have qualities for family living which a mere addition of garden space on a more conventional pattern would not create. There are many potential forms for a modern community besides the open (suburban) pattern you advocate and The High Paddingtons the *Architectural Review* people admire, and I find that issues that have caused the two sides to lock horns are unreal to me; unreal and stultifying to the imagination. The planners of the New Towns seem to me to have over-reacted against nineteenth century congestion and to have produced a sprawl that is not only wasteful but—what is more important—obstructive to social life. I prefer Fresh Meadows or a somewhat modified Lansbury: though I think there are dozens of other variations to be tried. If I succeed this coming winter in writing a new book on urban problems—I have almost given up the hope of revising *The Culture of Cities*—I will go into this more thoroughly. We must talk this over at length when we meet.

GENEVA   16–27 July 1953

Dear F.J.

I am writing you this from the bourgeois tranquillity of Geneva—whence we beat a hasty retreat, skipping Provence in order to recuperate from the noise and heat of Rome. We have had a remarkably good time, sometimes unbeliev-ably good; but we have about reached the point where one more work of art, one more building or one more place of historic interest would have the effect of a final mouthful of sweets on an overloaded stomach.

I write now to say that I am happy over your thought of reprinting my words on Howard and the GC from *The Culture of Cities*, but unhappy over the fact that they are so inadequate. If there is time, I'd be grateful for a copy of what you want to print so that I might make a few slight revisions to tighten it up. . . .

AMENIA, NEW YORK   23 September 1953

. . . Greetings, dear F.J.! Your farewell party with your family sent us away from England with a smile of happiness on our faces which lasted well over the Atlantic, till we encountered the tail end of a hurricane a day or so out of New York. The ensuing thirty-six hours were almost as tedious as a New York customs inspection; but at all events we escaped the dreadful heat wave which prostrated the Eastern coast for two weeks before our arrival and did not abate till the third of September.

We came back here to find the countryside more browned off than we could ever remember its being in the very worst droughts of the past, so desiccated that on the poor soils at the crest of the hills the leaves of the trees had turned dun, as in November, and in some patches had already fallen away. The one particular weed that is the usual pest of our garden, with a tiny daisy-like flower and a heavy root system, had fortunately disappeared; but as if to offset this boon the golden rod had shot up to six or seven feet, something I don't remember from before either, and despite a prodigious scattering of mole poison in the spring, those pests had dug up the whole lawn, probably searching for moisture nearer the surface. Still, our house looked good to us, even though there was a barrel, actually a barrel, of second class mail to throw away; and the grapes showed no sign of blight though they had not received a drop of bordeaux mixture. By now we have unpacked and I have tidied up the wilderness outdoors; but—such is our fate—we have begun packing again, and after taking Alison over to the New Haven railroad for Boston tomorrow, we will start off for Philadelphia the following day....

I am sorry that, with one thing and another, we didn't see more of each other; yet I am grateful, as ever, for what we did have of each other's company. I have sent you, by slow mail, a copy of *The New Yorker* with my first London Sky Line and will follow it up with the other two. My subscription for the *Architectural Review* expired while I was abroad, but I have renewed it and will look at Richards' piece as soon as they send me my back numbers. I wish I knew some way of making possible another visit to America for you and Margaret. Give her our warmest greetings; and our thanks to you both for the gracious hospitality in which you enveloped us. This letter is just a stopgap till I catch my breath.

WELWYN GARDEN CITY   18 October 1953

Dear Lewis

Your letter of 23 September was waiting for me on our return from our 'busman's holiday' in France—which turned out to be thoroughly enjoyable, if less fruitful as a study tour than any I have led since the war. The French, like the English, hold their own language to be sufficient—so, though we had a dozen very cordial official receptions, there was nothing like the amount of technical interchange of facts and ideas that we have had in other countries— even in Spain, where the architects turned out in large numbers for whole evenings and there was time to worry out meanings in bits of three or four languages.

The others saw for the first time, and I for the second time, the 'Corbusier' at Marseilles—and had to agree that it is an impressive monstrosity. Crowds of sightseers visit it daily, and there is a charge for admission and a continuous service of guides; it is a tourist asset to Marseilles—at Government expense. But it was difficult to get any information about it: the guides are not technical nor managerial. The only fact added to what I had already obtained on my much more useful first visit with technicians was that the cost is believed to be nearly £3 million. When I was there in March 1952 the cost was up to £2 million. Most of the flats are now occupied, half having been sold and half let as intended, and I was told that people are quite pleased with their accommodation. The three large passenger lifts (fifteen persons a time) for 350 flats were said to be too few; long queues develop three or four times a day. None of the shops and offices were yet occupied; and the problem had emerged that when they are the lifts could not cope with shoppers. So outsiders, it was contemplated, would have to walk up to the seventh floor—plus the 25 ft of the pilotis. Children were actually running about in the roof-playground, the fitments of which seemed well calculated to kill them off quickly if there were any romping. Magnificent views from the windows remain the one great asset.

The fundamental criticisms are inescapable. The 75 ft depth and 7 ft ceilings produce bedrooms the shape of a potato chip; 7 ft by 6 ft by 20 ft or more long. The centre of the block is dark and must become smelly. The central corridor 'street' is very dimly lighted because Le Corbusier thinks people move more quietly in the dark—a wonderful example of his propaganda powers. The access, by the lifts and long corridors, must have an imprisoning effect—Margaret said the Howard League for Penal Reform would condemn the building as a prison. The architecture and decoration are powerful and whimsical, and I think with time will seem oppressive and tiresome—the latter because you cannot see impressionistic decoration day after day with continued pleasure; you want to rub out the graffiti or add some of your own. Or so I feel—but this is a matter of taste.

As always, when you went off in that taxi, I had the feeling we had again missed our chance and duty of a real heart-to-heart talk; and yet perhaps that isn't in our stars. Perhaps I am doomed always to talk to you as Gladstone talked to Queen Victoria, 'as to a public meeting'. And maybe the cause is the same: shyness in the presence of the mighty. Shyness, anyway—an unrecognised Londoner's characteristic. I boast of being 'an escaped Londoner'; but perhaps I have never really escaped. The charming self-disclosure of a good American is as impossible for us as the sensuous unblushingness of a Spaniard. Yet consciousness of inhibition doesn't prevent us from a deep sense of superiority to those who are more natural and frank.

My work is in a truly awful state. I have a great deal of writing to do, and can't do it. When I do write I am constipated, matter-of-fact, and deadly dull.

I am tired of my limited subjects, and bored by the necessity of saying over and over again what needs to be said, but should now be more freshly said by others—who however, don't appear. I am, in the literal meaning of the word, discouraged. Because I am conscious of being regarded by bright spirits as being a repetitive bore, I lose opportunities of saying, as I know I could quite forcibly and effectively if I would make the effort, things that I ought to say— in the press and elsewhere. This gives me a sense of being traitorous to my purposes. I read when I should be writing, and potter in the garden when I should be reading or collating my immense mass of notes. I know by past experience that some little success or adventitious opportunity enables me to snap out of such a futile mood; but for a long time no such outside aid has come to help me. I have taken on too much and I am mentally tired, and in that state I always do the wrong things first. For instance, I write a long letter to an American friend, which after all could have waited—because writing a letter is easier than writing an article. And then I reflect that after all we are as God made us, and I shut up and go to bed. I can natter at myself, but I can't worry. Which is why, at the age of 68, I am a cheerful, irresponsible youth. And why I shall die with all my sins upon me.

The three of my family very highly enjoyed our little dinner party, and it was a great pleasure to all of us that all of you seemed to enjoy it too. As you saw, I fell in love with your Alison, who seemed to me to have come out of the chrysalis to the butterfly stage (though this is a quite depreciating image) and to have just the right sort of awakening interest in unknown people; I was sorry she was snatched away just as the light was glinting on her wings. Sophy too came alive to us more than was possible on our previous short meeting in New York; and made us wish we had been able to get to know her better.

PHILADELPHIA   27 October 1953

Here, dear F.J., is the last installment of my observations on planning in England. How it came out in an American periodical I don't know, for I fear that the greater part of it could be understood only by one who lived in England; and it is obvious that it is meant more for those who are immersed in the movement than for an American spectator, standing on the side lines. As a matter of fact, it falls with a bump between two stools, because under the limitations of *The New Yorker's* space and treatment I have omitted many illustrations and concrete points that would be necessary to carry conviction on your side of the water. Not that I can hope that I shall, on the matters where we still differ, win you to my side. Indeed, there are parts of this article where our differences may, in fact, cause you pain, although they are merely a more concrete example of matters I pointed out in my essay in Howard's book.

Much as I love gardening myself and much as I'd like to share this joy with other people, I don't think that the garden city idea should be tied up to the notion of providing a garden for everyone sufficient to grow vegetables and even potatoes: human wants are more various than that, and many people would be well content, as indeed you are, with a patch big enough to grow flowers, provided other facilities and amenities necessary for family life were also provided. The other mistake I feel that you've made, in answering Richards—whose criticism I purposefully refrained from reading till after I had written my own—is that you defend, not merely twelve houses to the acre, but the wasteful laying out of residential roads with wide verges and deep setbacks of houses in the New Towns: often, I suspect, in obedience to arbitrary requirements of the Ministry of Transport. The result is that you are identifying the Garden City with one type of town and one type of planning; whereas it is not merely conceivable, but it seems vital to me, to conceive of maintaining garden city principles in towns that represent wide variations in design and considerable differences both in residential density and in the manner of layout—though I would always keep an upper limit of a hundred people per residential acre as the highest permissible top.

I know we have talked about all these things before, without being able to close up the space between us; but I go over them now only to make clear the points where I feel your own approach leaves you most vulnerable.

My work here at the University of Pennsylvania has proved more interesting than last year, if only because I am less sleepy; but it demands so much of my time, since I am giving a wholly new course which goes over the ground I covered almost thirty years ago in *The Golden Day*,[1] that I am not getting all the time I had hoped for the revision of *The Culture of Cities*. Despite all my reluctance, since I 'd rather be writing fresh books, I feel a sort of duty to keep that book in existence by making a very thorough revision, in the light of all that I have been learning the last fifteen years or so. Whether it will justify the effort, by claiming the attention that would be accorded to a new book, is a problem. But I must take my chance with that. . . .

LONDON   6 January 1954

Dear Lewis

You will have received the New Towns (January) issue of *Town and Country Planning*, which I think gets this great social experiment in better perspective than anything yet published. If you know of any people who ought to see it please let me know, and I will send copies.

---

[1] New York, London, 1926, 1927.

In it I make a slight reply to the *Architectural Review* attack; I hadn't time or space for dealing with all its errors and fallacies. When I came to summarising what it said, I found it so absurd that I left some statements to answer themselves. If there is a comeback I may have to be more explicit. The *AR* attack was a strategic mistake which will cost them a lot of prestige.

You will see that I collected a lot of personal impressions from residents in the towns. I suppressed no criticisms, though I reduced to summaries two that were obviously party-political in inspiration, dealing with a high-rent agitation that is well-known and is not special to the new towns—the truth being that old rents here have simply got to be raised to meet, at least substantially, the great change in money values, which creates anomalies between all old and all new houses.

The Ministry are delighted with the issue; it has been prominently noticed in *The Times* and other papers, and will do more good all round than I had dared to hope. The most satisfactory thing is that we have maintained our own criticism of the tendency to debase housing and density standards without being written off by the Ministry; they are uneasy about this themselves. Also about the lag in social amenities, which can be corrected.

WELWYN GARDEN CITY   9 June 1954

Dear Lewis

As if to quiet your conscience (though I am sure you know it already) I must record that there was no letter from me unanswered. Nowadays I am behind with letters to all the (very few) people I correspond with from home; except one old boy whom I knew in my youth who lives alone, is physically in an appalling state, so that he is turned out of most cheap restaurants, and is a misery to meet, but has a passion for serious literature which he assuages by sitting two-thirds of every day in a public library and about which he writes me many shortwinded but really quite interesting notes—sometimes on several successive days. For some years I have fitfully responded, with comments on what he has been reading and sometimes with quite long dissertations on what I have been reading myself. It is a queer correspondence, in which a lot of half-digested views on books appear. One of my recurrent themes is that a great deal of contemporary literary criticism is bad (I mean by the standards I respected when I was young enough to have some judgment—those of Johnson, Matthew Arnold, Russel Lowell, Bagehot, Saintsbury etc.); I overstate, and he gets really angry, because though not stable in taste he is really very sensitive and appreciative and always widening his range. He is a quite futile person, and cannot write more than 200 or 300 words at a time; but if he had got into the right groove when young, instead of becoming for forty-five years an accounts clerk in the Post Office, he might have been a good critic, because of his sensitivity and high accuracy of expression. He is a sort of literary Bartleby; and I haven't the heart, nor the wish, to shake him off. After all, the waste of time and mental effort is no more than that of a weekly hour of unbuttoned chat in a pub—in which I don't indulge.

I have no other intelligent correspondents except your good self; but please don't assume any moral responsibility for me as *your* Bartleby! I have a vast number of intelligent friends in a lot of countries, with whom at very long intervals I exchange letters, all short and on specific points of fact or information. And I have one or two ancient friends, non-literary and non-political, to whom, at even longer intervals, I write in various laboriously maintained conventions for reasons of sentiment, affection or loyalty—which sounds more cold-blooded than it is. I believe in and am emotionally adapted to friendship; but I have no gift for it. I forget birthdays, and procrastinate for years in arranging meetings. . . .

Wanting now to write on other subjects, or in a more synthetic way on the major urban development issues, I find myself tied down to the daily controversy, with almost no support for what I think the necessary corrective accent to the damaging combined influence of our agricultural and preservationist groups, architectural theorists of 'urbanity' (a word most misleadingly used), and an 'economy' drive unwisely directed to the reduction of floor-space in houses below a formerly accepted minimum, but very cleverly presented in official publications. I am continually involved in press discussions; lately with some success in cities like Glasgow and Birmingham, which (partly for political reasons to retain party electors in particular areas, largely at the expense of the State subsidies, which are much larger than the local tax subsidies) are beginning experiments with multi-storey flats. My figures have made a serious impression in Birmingham; and a similar press correspondence is now in full swing in the leading Glasgow paper. In that case some local people are coming in with weighty support, but this has been rare; and I have felt isolated and in danger of becoming regarded as a public bore. (Certainly I am boring myself by saying the same thing a hundred times in different words).

You did my campaign some harm by the article quoted in the *Architectural Review*. Even the LCC are now worried about the prospect of generalising the density of 100 persons (thirty dwellings) an acre over vast areas of the county, because it means about 56 per cent of the families in such zones in multi-storey flats; whereas there are already huge areas zoned at 136 persons (88 per cent multi-storey flats) and pretty large areas at 200 persons (all flats). Taking all the zones together, you get something like 75 per cent flats in a city of 3,300,000 people—the true tolerance probably being about 20 per cent, and the real *preference* not more than 10 per cent or so. For this reason the LCC (it is our biggest success in principle) has now gone completely round and is making the most strenuous efforts to use the Town Development Act for systematic dispersal to a great many small towns up to 100 miles from London. The Ministry is half-hearted about this great project and is being very mean about the necessary State grants, simply because of the agricultural-country-side-preservationist opposition and the decadent idealism of the architectural profession. When you say 100 an acre is all right, you gravely undermine my argument and encourage the Minister in his reactionary tendencies. All he really cares about is getting up the maximum number of houses—because the mere number has become the effective political counter. He is not interested in the overall cost in subsidies since the extraordinary subsidy scale, which now gives £1,456 more for a flat than for a house (£2,301 as against £845), being on the statute book, does not get questioned by the Treasury, but (this is literally true) only by my single voice. It is not part of my tactics to attack the Minister. The real source of the terrible mistake we are making is in the minds of the planning technicians, and it is there that your influence is potent. May posterity forgive you!

While I give no public signs of discouragement, the moral strain of this long fight has I think told on me to some extent in a loss of energy. I have always depended on occasional driblets of partial success for encouragement, and find when I get it I can do more. And what is more important, flashes of success encourage my very small band of supporters, which is now at its minimum. The income of the TCPA does not at present permit me to engage a full-time Director, and this is a nuisance, because I spend far too much time on mere administration and organisation. However, the brighter side of things is that since the prostate operation I have returned to almost perfect health, and with luck I may be able to keep on with the business for a few more years. . . .

AMENIA, NEW YORK   23 September 1954

Dear F.J.

. . . Till the middle of August, when I knew that some sort of calamity was bound to happen, so full and rounded and idyllic was this life of ours, everything had gone well. I got the first draft of two books written, a big one that may take me years to write and a little one that I must polish off next spring; and in addition, I had written two new lectures that form the climax of a little book of essays and lectures I have sent to you: *In the Name of Sanity*.[1] If in England it seems irrelevant or over-anxious in many parts, as my publisher

---

[1] New York, 1954.

Warburg seems to think, the fact that there is at present such a difference between the mental climates of our two countries is significant, though, as for the matter of anxiety, I think we have all plenty of cause for concern over the unthinking uses of the new energies we now command. Nations that pollute the air as foully as yours and mine do—I speak with especial vehemence as a part-time resident of filthy Philadelphia—have good reason to fear even the peace-time dangers of atomic energy; for while a good strong wind can wipe away the effects of even a lethal smog, there is no way of disposing safely of the by-products of fission, except by shooting them into outer space.

How right you are about the paucity of good town planning literature: if I were a younger man I would plan to write at least two more books on the subject, though as it is I am a little shamefaced about not having yet revised *The Culture of Cities*—or I would be, if I hadn't, in spite of myself, been learning so much during the past ten years. Even in my course on Civic Design I found it hard to use Unwin's book,[1] much though I admire many parts of it; and I was grateful to Gibberd for having done such a good job in furnishing a modern successor.[2] You yourself, if you weren't too active in the daily battle, should write the kind of all-embracing book about The Garden City that Purdom failed to do in his revision. Why shouldn't you emulate Stein's example in tackling this task?[3] A person who writes so felicitously as you do should toss off the definitive work, on the idea and the practice of the Garden City, in six solid months.

Your remarks about the harmful effect of my article quoted in the *Architectural Review* puzzled me: so much so, indeed, that I went back to the original and read it carefully—and now I am puzzled more than ever. I can only account for your thinking that I had attacked low density housing, or had weakened your case, by remembering that words have no meaning of their own but act like a Rorschach ink-blot to bring out the meaning that is in the mind of the reader. As you have long known, for I expressed the idea in my introduction to the new edition of *Garden Cities of Tomorrow*, I have never held that twelve or fourteen houses to the acre was a sacrosanct figure, never to be violated: on the contrary, I have felt that to fit all the needs of all the various kinds of inhabitants, there should be a range of densities from twenty or less people to an acre up to 100; and as long as the planning continued to be strictly in terms of human needs, carefully examined and appraised, I would even, in small patches—especially if they adjoined a considerable park or greenbelt—permit a slightly higher density. That every inhabitant of the city should have a private garden and that every garden should be of the same

---

[1] Raymond Unwin, *Town Planning in Practice*, London, 1909.
[2] F. Gibberd, *Town Design*, London, 1953.
[3] C. Stein, *Toward New Towns for America*, New York, Liverpool, 1951.

size, big enough for a vegetable crop that includes potatoes, as Unwin urged when he established the twelve to an acre principle, has never seemed to me a sufficient ideal for urban planning; though many parts of residential neighbourhoods might well have fourteen per acre as their uppermost limit. This is my position in general.

But I was so conscious of the lineup between the high-density group and your own when I wrote that article on New Towns, that I did not question the low all-over standard of residential development. I challenge you to find a line in which I say that the density should be higher than it is—or even imply this. What I was challenging were what seemed to me two defects, quite serious ones: first, the lack of variety in the layouts, the failure to see new possibilities in grouping; and second, the absurd wastage of space in acres of unnecessary streets, too wide for any probable or tolerable traffic, with the houses set too far back from the street—as if there were not any other way of ensuring privacy. I admit that the standardisation is at a high level, but the fact is that it is wasteful and dull, and these qualities in themselves draw discredit on the principle of twelve houses to the acre in residential areas. The overall density I certainly consider too low, and the various neighbourhoods of the New Towns are too widely scattered to fulfil the social purposes of living together in an urban community. This is not something that can be remedied by any simple formula. . . .

You may not agree with this criticism—of course I know you don't. But I can't see how you can confuse it with an attempt to break down the low-density principle for residential development. In any quarrel between you and the fashionable school that has gone in for high apartment houses and high densities, I shall always be fighting shoulder to shoulder with you; but you give an unusual advantage to the enemy if you range me, against my own judgement and practice, on *their* side. Please consider this whole matter carefully. We can ill afford to misunderstand each other in a world that has a sufficient number of misunderstandings, of a less national nature, on its hands. . . .

WELWYN GARDEN CITY   24 October 1954

Dear Lewis

F.J.O. is distinctly discouraged and conscious of inadequacy and the absence of collaborators and successors in the work that seems to him desperately necessary to retrieve the planning situation. I make desperate resolutions to reorganise my affairs and concentrate on the things that matter most, and daily fail to operate them; moral inadequacy aggravates the real difficulties. Evidences, that ought to be impressive, in Sweden and Norway and at the

Edinburgh Congress of the International Federation, of wide influence of TCPA persistence, fail to give me the needed encouragement. I read too much, ruminate too much, worry too much, and don't do the obvious jobs, hoping that someone else will take a hand—and nobody does.

The one thing that keeps me making the resolutions I don't properly pursue is the complete certainty that the policies I am identified with would have, if they understood them (and it is my neglected business to ensure that understanding), the passionate support of the urban population at large. I always address, however, the experts, the politicians and the small articulate groups whose bias and personal interests are not those of the planned millions. Everybody is against me except the 49 million electors—as someone once said of Franklin Roosevelt—but I can't, as Roosevelt could, get contact with my supporters, though as it happens I am better at their language than at technical jargon or 'cultural' eloquence. The indications for my proper tactics are therefore obvious; but I am inextricably tangled in my present position and routine and don't see any way to relieve myself of my accidental responsibilities, which must somehow be kept going by someone. To get that relief, particularly in the organisation of the TCPA, seems the only practicable course; and I am trying to do it, so far without any prospect of success.

To be specific: I can't drop the daily routine work of the TCPA, which is the only body doing anything at all to resist the drift away from sound policies, until it can appoint a full-time man able to keep it going. Its income does not now permit of that; and there is no one in the very able membership of its executive who could possibly become chairman unless there were a director to do the daily work; and hardly anyone who is free to express in the controversies the point of view on which we all agree. Those who understand the position are all men who have to think of their own jobs or potential jobs and could not, without serious danger to themselves and their families, be conspicuous in what is a most difficult political campaign (though not at present a party campaign). One or two consultants, like Pepler and Abercrombie, are the most free; but they are not independent, as I am, while they are extremely busy and are all men of my own age. Some younger man, in business or a free profession, might take over if there were someone to do the daily work; and these two men are what I am looking for; the prior condition being a sufficient increase of income. A succession of Hon. Treasurers have so far failed to solve that problem.

So now you see why I don't do the obvious and write the books and pamphlets that are called for in the present situation. If I had more discipline or energy I could—hence the daily resolutions and daily lapses.

End of wail. I was very glad to hear from you; and one resolution added is that someday I will write you about your serious error on the density question.

Dear F. J.

We came back here from Philadelphia a few days ago, to find the very cheery picture of you and Margaret waiting for us among our otherwise horrendous batch of accumulated letters and advertisements and magazines. (Between sixteen and twenty magazines, about half of them paid for, come into this house regularly, and I seem to spend at least half my time merely getting rid of them). I haven't yet settled down to work, for there is the usual accretion of small chores to be done before I can execute any larger intentions; but I hope by March to begin work on a little book, the first draft of which I did last summer and probably told you about: an attempt, naturally impudent and possibly unprofitable, to say something about human history in fifty thousand words that Toynbee alas! didn't manage to in ten volumes.

But before I do that I must write a paper for an interesting conference that will be held at Princeton next June on Man's Role in Changing the Face of the Earth. It hasn't been publicly announced yet, but the news of it has gotten around and many people fancy that it is on some highly secret matter. Besides being chairman of the section dealing with Man's Role in the Future, I have been given the task of writing about The Natural History of Urbanism; and since no one quite knows what this really means, and even if they do no one else has had the temerity to treat the subject, I have kept putting off my assignment to the last moment and in the end will be driven to write an apology for not doing any more than outlining the problem. The geographers should have done the job a long time ago; but as far as I can discover have not even nibbled around the edges. This is part of the general neglect of the city which was so obvious during the nineteenth century and still holds in very respectable circles. . . .

What I want to know about ancient cultures is how many of them followed the Chinese practice of using nightsoil in the farms around the city, but so far I haven't had luck in running this down though I have at my hand a copious tome, just published, which professes to be a History of Technology. Our conference at Princeton is to be a true symposium for the papers will have been printed, and presumably read, before we meet. Our great difficulty is in getting someone to present a paper on the possible result of fissionable materials on the earth and the atmosphere, for people who know any authentic data on this subject are prevented, in my still very benighted country—despite the exit of McCarthy—from saying anything about it, particularly if they make any quantitative estimates; though it is precisely on how much radioactive material would do how much damage that a rational judgement must be based.

From this little item I might pass without any jump to a discussion of the present international situation, which has suddenly become very dismal and potentially dangerous. Last summer Eisenhower in large part atoned for his appalling weaknesses and ineptitudes by holding his own, almost single-handed, against the large war party among his advisers, who were ready to have a showdown over Indo-China even if it meant war with Soviet Russia; but his latest pronouncement on Formosa makes it seem that he has at last given in to them, at the worst time and in the most damaging way. It would need someone of Roosevelt's large capacity and astuteness in manipulation to manage a retreat from our untenable position about Formosa—which should be given to the *Formosans*, under United Nations protection—and about the Chinese generally. No one of his calibre is visible in Washington today; no one, that is, capable of framing a more positive strategy than the one followed since 1945, which has put ourselves and the whole world in a state of total insecurity. The paper I wrote on the Atomic Bomb in 1946, the one which resulted in my invitation to the War College by General Gruenther, has turned out to be the one really sound prognosis that anybody made; yet when I included it in the book I published last fall, *In the Name of Sanity*, not a single reviewer here commented upon it even by way of rebuttal, though there was indeed nothing to rebut.

Here we are talking about International matters again, in the very vein in which our correspondence originally began in 1938 or 1939; and the world situation, so far from having improved with the removal of the infamous Hitler, has merely disclosed that all of us, granted the weapons and the opportunity, are ready to be imitation Hitlers for lack of imagination capable of conceiving the humane alternatives. I forbear to pursue the subject any further for I find little solace in contemplating the present posture of things, even when I comfort myself with the thought of all the time and effort I've expended, fruitlessly it turns out, to prevent this dark situation from developing. As Thomas Lamont once remarked, 'the hardest words to pronounce in any language are: "I was wrong". But the most insufferable are: "I told you so!" '

WELWYN GARDEN CITY   5 February 1955

Dear Lewis

Your highly-packed letter of 31 January reminds me in a lot of ways of my inadequacy as a correspondent. I spend more time apologising for not answering letters than in answering them; and it is due to sheer inefficiency (a sort of laziness) rather than to overwork—though overwork is another symptom of the same thing. I really will try to write you a decent letter soon; but this again must be a rushed interim affair. . . .

Of course I did receive your book *In the Name of Sanity* and, in fact, read it.

I found it very eloquent and the Caliban and Prospero chapters moving, and the whole thing deserving and indeed necessitating a thoughtful comeback—which I will not attempt to vamp now because I made no notes and have to read the book again to be clear what I wanted to say. I do remember, however, my main reaction, which may show you that I share the general demoralisation of standards—though I really don't accept that. I just can't go with you in your view that there is a moral collapse in the general support of the decision to make atom and hydrogen bombs. It seems to me to be part of the frightful logic of war, or collective defence; and I see no possibility of any nation refraining from creating the most powerful weapons it can create, so long as it knows that others (possible enemies) can do so. I think nations and groups never stuck at any means whatever of saving themselves and those dear to them from an outside enemy—anything, that is, that seemed *necessary* to avoid defeat or subjugation. It is too long a job for me to amplify this just now; but I indicate just where I find your powerful argument does not carry me with it. The solution must be, I think, in an *agreement* by all parties not to commit reciprocal suicide; I see no other way—unless you consider world conquest by a super-Napoleon a way. I just can't believe either in the practical possibility, or even in the rightness, of a unilateral resolve not to have atom bombs while potential enemies have them. . . .

We live and learn. A month or so ago I had not heard of the Tachen Islands or of the eye disease glaucoma. And today the world is at war about those islands; and tomorrow I go (it is a small thing but close at hand) into Barts Hospital to have an operation on my left (and fortunately less important) eye.

Time, I see, takes a different view of Eisenhower's line from yours; it shrieks that he has fallen for the British policy of appeasement. I feel pretty sure, despite *Time*, that the American people no more want war with China over Formosa than they did over Korea. But I think they may well be, as we are, profoundly worried by the outward pressure of communism, and see Formosa as its next aggression. The old dilemma! Here we can't see why the USA wants to keep Chiang in the UN; and many are shocked that he is using US planes to bomb the Chinese mainland. No doubt the USA sees that as part of the defence of Formosa, and Formosa as strategically important to US defence. But the entanglement with Chiang weakens British solidarity with the USA—though we feel the necessity of solidarity.

AMENIA, NEW YORK   20 February 1955

I didn't mean to let more than a week elapse, dear F.J., before answering your letter of the 5th of February; for though letters may be a burden when you have to answer them this one would have been—and possibly still is—in the category of those which one does not even have to read, let alone respond to. My first thought, of course, is commiseration over your extraordinary bad luck: extraordinary, somehow, in proportion to your general appearance of robust health and youth; for it would seem as if Emerson's law of compensation was mischievously at work here and that you have been getting, in recent years, more than your share of physical trials. I have no temptation to be a Job's comforter so I had better extend you my sympathy as silently as possible and let it go at that. I trust you are recovering rapidly and are in good spirits and are enjoying your enforced idleness, instead of feeling apologetic over what I suspect is your mythical laziness, which probably exists in contrast only to some mythical Osborn of monstrous dimensions that you conjured up in your youth, when you were reading H. G. Wells.

At the moment I am pushing through with some odd chores before getting down to my book on *The Transformations of Man.* I have re-read the first draft of that manuscript, incidentally, twice since last December; and each time have been surprised to find it is one of the most lucid, perhaps even the most brilliant statements that I—or perhaps anyone else—has made in summarising human history. It came so easy last summer that I distrusted it and tossed it aside without daring to examine it carefully; but unless I am quite out of my wits now, it will turn out, I think, to be an important job—provided that the last chapter, which deals with future possibilities, has any of the qualities of the earlier chapters. So far it is the most ragged chapter in the book so I think that I will begin the re-writing with that chapter, while my energies are fullest. But I am still a few weeks away from this because other matters detain me: chiefly the need to get ahead with a few *New Yorker* articles, so that I won't have to think of finances till next June at earliest. And there I find myself in a comic predicament, for I began by writing one Sky Line, prompted by recent proposals to place sixty-storey skyscrapers atop the Grand Central and the Pennsylvania Stations, in areas that are even more overcrowded, with high density office buildings, than they were when you were last in New York; and before I knew it that article led to a second, on the causes of congestion, and a third, on what to do about it in New York, and a fourth, on how to handle it in the outlying region: all of this amounting to a re-statement of the case for decentralisation we first made in the Regional Planning number of the *Survey Graphic* in 1925, now effectively reinforced, for purposes of illustration, by the New Towns policy of Britain.

The editors of the *New Yorker* hadn't bargained for anything like this and neither had I, so I am not at all sure that they will want to go beyond the first article; but in the very act of stating the problem I found myself being challenged to give a concrete and specific, not a merely general, answer to the problems that are now before us.

On top of that, I must finish the paper on the Natural History of Urbanism, a subject that frightened me at first when I found out just how little had been done, but that now begins to open up a little, with increasing excitement on my own part, as the trail widens; for I confess it is an aspect of city development that I was more interested in as a young man than I have been these last twenty years. The difficulty is that the geographers have been more concerned, in the past, to find out what geographic forces have done to mould cities, than to discover what cities have done to remake the earth. This is partly because a general change in the scale of cities, with every townlet in Texas threatening to become a second London or New York, did not become visible, or technically feasible, till half a century ago. To my great delight I discovered that the great George Perkins Marsh, in the final revised edition of *The Earth and Man*, published in 1907 after his death, inserted a footnote on the effect of cities in modifying the climate, and that is one of the few avenues for research that have been effectively followed up. But there has been no serious investigation on the effect of uncontrolled urban growth on the water supply, or on the general ecological balance; and the need for this is one of the things that my paper may open up—with, fortunately, just the right people in my audience. Griffith Taylor, who was extravagantly kind to me in his acknowledgements in *Urban Geography*, sometimes even attributing to me ideas Geddes had first formulated, has been of little use because he is primarily a geographic determinist and hasn't much of an eye for things that originate in man. The best sustenance I have found is Brunhes' book on *Human Geography*, but that too is very sketchy and so relieves me of a little embarrassment over the sketchy and provisional nature of my own paper, which answers nothing. What you found out about the Levite Cities, as published in *Greenbelt Cities*, seems, according to Childe and other archeologists, to have been common in Mesopotamia and possibly even in Egypt: the God owned the lands surrounding the city, and since they were worked for the benefit of the Temple they probably continued in existence till faith faltered or the God was overthrown by a rival deity—unless, of course, the pressure of land rents from within finally inundated the agricultural domain with building lots. You've published a string of admirable quotations in *T & CP:* have you ever used this from Aristotle's *Politics*—'All cities that have a reputation for good government have a limit of population.' I stumbled upon this the other day, while looking for something quite different. . . .

I am sorry that my arguments about the use of the instruments of extermination have not convinced you on either moral or practical grounds; but since I realise that most of the clergy are also in your camp, I must set down my own moral position as the minor aberration of an otherwise sound mind, or treat those in the opposing camp as the victims of a far more awful aberration since by their very numbers they multiply the sin—and should I be right in this, I might nevertheless be damned on Christian grounds for my pride! But by now I am shifting my ground to practical matters, since my own critique of the ethics of extermination, as being as repulsive to civilised man and as unusable as cannibalism, finds so little assent. The practical grounds seem to me overwhelming by now. We are in a position in which inadvertently, once we resorted to nuclear weapons, we might render this planet uninhabitable. There are both political and military answers to the possibility of an enemy using the one-sided possession of such weapons for bloodless blackmail. But the 'ability to retaliate' is no guarantee against either war or complete annihilation; and it seems to me that we are swiftly piling up fears and hatreds to a point at which the prudent Eisenhowers will be overwhelmed by their Chiefs of Staff, who will set in motion forces that will be uncontrollable in action and unextinguishable in result. . . .

WELWYN GARDEN CITY   23 February 1955

Dear Lewis

When I last wrote you I was just going into Bart's Hospital for an operation on my left eye. I am out again after about a fortnight, and have to admit that my plan to re-read and comment on your *Sanity* couldn't be carried out. For much of the time I had to remain supine and motionless, and though I could see quite a lot of the ward happenings with the other eye I could not read with any great continuity, and note-taking (without which I cannot now organise what I read) was impossible. So that task is a pleasure still to come, and it may be a month or so further delayed.

The operation seems to have done what was urgently necessary in relieving internal pressure and saving what is left of the visual field (retina), but a complication that occurs in 2 per cent of cases fell due on my day: an opacity in the lens that will, probably in the course of a year, have to be dealt with by another operation. In the meantime this eye is obscured, and though I have never used it much for reading its obscuration is a nuisance in getting about and interferes at present with reading and writing also—though I have quite a hope that I may get used to it and reduce the nuisance value.

Till today the surgeon thought I would have to cancel our projected holiday in Sicily—which Margaret badly needs and we were both anticipating with pleasure. Now, however, I am told I can go, and we leave on March 3rd and return on 25th. You can guess that the time in hospital and the intended three weeks absence cause me much pressure of work in this next week; among other things I have to prepare two issues of *T & CP* and to complete an article on housing subsidies for *Lloyds Bank Review*.[1] This last will interest you, I think, and I will have a copy sent to you in due course. . . .

Dear Lewis

Whether it is your turn to write or mine I don't know, but I am conscious of being a very bad correspondent nowadays. I have been reminded of you by the pleasurable task of voting, as an Hon. Member of the American Institute of Planners, for your election (which should have long preceded mine) in the same class; and by writing a very short notice of *In the Name of Sanity* for *T & CP*. I find in this a noble restatement of the religion of all sensible men, and can rejoice that you have not kept it to yourself like other sensible men. But I still have not had time to read and evaluate your book up even to the limit of my small capacity. I have a dim and diminishing conviction that I know where I stand in these high matters and a languishing hope that I may some day sit down and try to formulate my own working philosophy, in the course of which I should have to try to understand what you and others with whom I feel a deep sympathy really say. But time flies, and a lot of work arising in fields of immediate policy keeps me occupied, with a growing feeling of inadequacy tending towards futility. Considering my calendar age I do not *feel* old. But I went to a Scottish society's dance last night with Margaret and joined with her in an eightsome reel, a thing I hadn't done for years; and I was interested to note that my feet would simply not move at the speed required for the steps of which I remembered the shapes perfectly well. They just *wouldn't* obey my instructions! And though I am unconscious of it, I can suspect that my mind behaves in the same way when I am reading serious contributions to thought. . . .

We have been in seven of the chief countries of Europe in the last 14 months, and these travels and the vast amount of printed matter that descends on me from all parts of the world ought to make me very well informed on the developments in town planning. But again, my inability to sit down and think consecutively about what I know, is an obstacle to generalisation—though I am intensely irritated by the clearly inadequate generalisations made by a large number of architectural writers and talkers on our radio programmes, who judge everything by their peculiar aesthetic pre-occupations and desires and almost all overlook the immensely more important effects of building design and planning on the life and work of the millions.

---

[1] April, 1955.

One very serious thing is becoming more and more plain to me: the sins of the fathers in crowding towns are going to be visited on many more than the third and fourth generation. The jealous gods may have showed mercy unto thousands when they permitted the vast suburban expansions of the first half of this century; but this has been associated with a further concentration of employment in the city cores that ties other thousands of the less mobile or prosperous more tightly to their wretched tenements; I think of Paris, Lyons, Berlin, even Amsterdam, for all its visual charm. The tenth generation of the denizens of the immense rabbit-warren of Lyons see a flat on the tenth floor in a new modern building with trees and gardens below as paradise, and are told that in any case the more perfect paradise of the one-family house cannot ever be for them. Thus governments who are too shortsighted, too weak or too lazy to deal with the relocation of over-centralised employment, have good opportunist reasons (with popular acceptance) for falling for the gracious-*looking* multi-storey flat which is pressed on them by architects and the defenders of agriculture and the countryside.

The very powerful counter-argument of cost and subsidies that by luck has been presented to me in England is less effective on the Continent, mainly because the standard of space and of equipment accepted there in flats is far lower than ours, and only their well-off middle classes have had a taste of the combination of space and good fittings in family houses. One effect of the small production of the latter class of dwelling there is that they have not learned, as England has, how to produce it at minimum cost. For comparable quality these other countries can produce flats about as cheaply as we can, but they can't produce houses as cheaply as we can. Everywhere, of course (except as in Holland and Sweden in certain areas where foundations are excessively costly), flats are dearer per square metre of floor-space than terrace houses, but whereas in England the difference is of the order of 175:100, on the Continent, by reason of inconsistency of quality, the difference is only of the order of 130:100, or even 120:100 where there are no lifts, as in Germany and Holland, for four or five storey tenements. The system of subsidies everywhere masks this difference of cost, which would otherwise be influential in personal choice. But only in England, so far, is the difference so great as to be usable in political argument—since it is very difficult to use the other difference, that of the sheer quality of the two products. . . .

Howard came too late in history; and I do not deny that Unwin and his colleagues, though he was sound in understanding, were not insistent enough on the regional aspect of planning and not astute enough in their propaganda to see how the idea of low density could be misused in favour of the suburban solution—now I notice, paralleling in the USA what happened here in 1900–1939. (It seems to be the same in Canada.)

Unwin at least had a human basis for his ideas. It disquiets me greatly that the issue of the standard of housing and family environment is everywhere far less influential in the dynamics of planning than the issue of car-parking, and in England, owing to our peculiar hierarchy of effective public opinion, the silhouette of St Pauls. At any rate this is so in 'intelligent' discussion as it protrudes itself in the press and on the BBC; it is not quite as influential as this would suggest when you trace the motives of the uncultured nobodies who run local government. Their prepossessions are with the local housing-shortage lists, and in England they build flats because our ridiculous system of subsidies puts a heavy differential cost on the state exchequer.

You can take as entirely accurate my figures on this subsidy question in our *Journal*. The Ministry and local authorities read what I say, and are very uncomfortable about the facts; but the whole question of rents is political dynamite here, and they don't know how to deal with the increasingly absurd distribution and scale of subsidies. The present Government, by raising the rate of interest on housing loans at the same time that it asserts its intention of reducing subsidies, seems to me to have got itself out on a limb. I fear for the position of our new Housing Minister, who is wholly in favour personally of my policy, but is not, I think, riding the whirlwind and directing the storm. . . .

WELWYN GARDEN CITY   5 December 1955

Dear Lewis
It is a really lovely December so far, with little rain and bright sunny days, and I have been reconstructing my badly neglected garden, which I have always been in terror some lizard of the architectural press might one day inspect and report upon to my discomfiture. I have spent three mornings excavating a huge hole across my rockery with the intention of building a stepped path across it; I have never moved so much earth in my life and for the first time in seventy years I feel therefore that I could, in a post-cataclysmic age, grow and boil myself potatoes, and in due course tidily dig my own grave—though someone else would have to fill it in. At present there are mountains of clay and tons of flints retrieved from all over the garden during my autumn campaign, all waiting to be put back under the proposed path, topped with cultivable soil and planted for spring flowering. My garden is entirely a spring garden; I have never had both the time and the energy at the right seasons to produce anything like as good an effect in summer and autumn—an ambition that remains and that becomes ever more unlikely of fulfilment. I have planted this autumn well over 1,000 bulbs, one by one, and people say I look well. By gosh, I ought to. But in the evenings I write Planning Notes and edit

the illiterate articles of earnest planners, and often this keeps me up till midnight.

It is a terrible life; for most days I attend the TCPA office, where activity is at an all-time peak. My notoriously charming staff, for which I am envied by an increasing number of tycoons and technicians whose own enthusiasm for planning has been remarkably aroused by their existence, are working time and a half (in spasms of weeks on end) and obviously enjoying it. The latest spurt was in connection with our annual conference last week, which attracted unprecedented press attention, and ended with a House of Lords reception by Lord Beveridge and a House of Commons Dinner for the presentation of the Howard Memorial Medal to Elizabeth Mitchell of Lanarkshire—the real force in the Scottish section of the TCPA, which has just scored a success in the Government's decision to proceed with the fifteenth New Town, at Cumbernauld, for the overspill of industry and people from Glasgow. We have also issued an important Memorandum to our Minister on Green Belts, the result of a committee representing all interests, including speculative builders, who agreed on unanimous and strong recommendations. The Minister had requested this advice, so the Memorandum has almost official status. He is far more respectful to the TCPA, and in fact also to me personally, than Macmillan was; indeed he accepts fully our whole gospel, though whether he has the strength to carry it out in present very difficult economic conditions remains to be seen. . . .

The TCPA situation is extraordinary. Our influence is very high just now, owing to the energy of my staff and the recent adhesion of the best group of young men we have ever had, including one, Peter Self,[1] who is making real contributions to thought on dispersal policy in a most constructive and effective way. The thing is now intensely alive. But we are running at a loss of £2,000–3,000 a year, which we can only do for another year without a drastic cutting down of the organisation; and we just haven't solved the problem of how to increase resources, though much work is being done on the problem. Hence I am more worried than I am elated.

In the New Towns issue of *T & CP* for Jan. 1956, now going to press, I have the most remarkable series of impressions of the new towns by visitors last year from about a dozen foreign countries—all evidencing the almost sensational effect on world opinion of the new town adventure. There are plenty of detailed criticisms, some justified, some I think not. But there is no mistake about the general astonishment at the enterprise and wistful approval of the dispersal aim. It is quite as big an impression as that originally caused by the garden city idea—but this time it is not in the least misunderstood. We really

---

[1] Professor of Public Administration, University of London, 1963. Subsequently Chairman of the Executive of the Town and Country Planning Association.

have this time succeeded in starting a world movement, and I really think there is a chance it may be effective—though it is far too late in time.

We have both been bad correspondents, dear F.J., and so can without excessive unction show charity to one another—as indeed you must now, for this will be a poor answer to yours of the 8th which reached me as a sort of greeting for my sixtieth birthday: that milestone. . . .

As for me, like a fool I tried to finish a book, and so emerged, in September, so tired that I wanted a vacation but instead found myself saddled with a new course in the University of Pennsylvania, which has added to my general debility, indeed exhaustion. I am supposed to take on another visiting professorship at Brandeis University this spring, and dread it—though as yet I see no honourable way out, short of falling seriously ill! My plans for Europe are also somewhat indeterminate, though we have a Cunard passage for early July: partly because Alison may want to get married, partly because I haven't decided whether I can so arrange my affairs that I might stay on, in Italy say, through the winter of 1956–57, revising *The Culture of Cities*. The shifting of the date of the Vienna Congress to July I find highly inconvenient for all my plans this year—though in other years it was the late September date that kept me from attending!

Meanwhile I've sent you a little Anthology of L.M. that needs no acknowledgement, and presently there'll be a more interesting work, that I was tasked with last summer: *The Transformations of Man*. ('Presently' means next spring!) The success of good books in paperback editions is giving my old books a new lease on life: *Sticks and Stones*[1] and *The Brown Decades*[2] are now available and *The Golden Day* will follow. Unfortunately the cheapness of the paperback lies not in its simple form and its large printing order: most of the economy is taken out of the hide of the author: so I hesitate to let The Renewal of Life series go the same way, lest I have too scant royalties in my old age. Forgive this quite inadequate letter: I am still tired.

Dear Lewis
This is to thank you warmly for sending us *The Human Prospect*[3]—a very convenient and admirably got-up Essence of Mumford, which Margaret and

---

[1] New York, 1924.
[2] New York, 1931.
[3] New York, London, 1955, 1956.

I are most glad to have and will certainly enjoy reading, including, and perhaps especially, the pieces we have read in other forms. In fact, I have already read much of it while staying at some friends' farmhouse residence near Bishops Stortford for the first part of Margaret's convalescence. As always in your writings, I find many thoughts with which I am in very great sympathy, stated with a learning, a force and a documentation that I couldn't begin to emulate. I am sure this collection must send many readers to your longer books. Again, many thanks. . . .

I have been suffering from a minor but troublesome affliction which is probably fibrositis, and may be due to a little over-exertion in the garden a week or two ago. Of course it had to coincide with several planning engagements, the most compelling of which was a select conference at Swindon of metropolitan city authorities and councils of small towns, to discuss the working of the Town Development Act. It was for me a remarkable occasion, because we had councillors from London County, Birmingham and Manchester falling over each other to proclaim their passion for reducing their populations and industry, pressing the Ministry of Housing and the Board of Trade (who were strongly represented there) to do more to make the dispersal Act effective, and pleading with the small towns to take financial chances to help them by accepting their overspill. These men all talk as if the programme is obvious and as if they have been wanting it all their lives, and as if they are glad the TCPA at last sees the problem in perspective and gets people together in this helpful way. But secretly I was thinking of the many occasions over the last twenty years when I have attended meetings of city bigwigs and spoken at conferences and public meetings in these big towns, and been disregarded or dismissed as an unpractical, starry-eyed idiot. But in my concluding speech from the chair, for which with a painful effort I managed to stand up for the only time in the day, I made a speech which fell in with the current theory that it is the big cities that are the prime movers in a new and vastly important reconstruction movement. The change in the climate of opinion here is amazing. But the Town Development Act is not making any very rapid headway, and the new subsidy scales in the Housing Subsidies Bill do not seem to support dispersal sufficiently, though they are certainly intended by the Minister to do so. We are therefore keeping up our pressure on the Minister and on Parliament during the debates on the Bill—with what success remains to be seen. It is quite a new sensation for me to be fighting *with* the big cities and the country towns capable of and desiring planned expansion, vis-a-vis the Government Departments which completely accept the dispersal policy but are not operating it with sufficient courage or vigour. . . .

Coincidentally, we are arranging a wide distribution of the TCPA Memorandum on Green Belts, which I had prepared by a special sub-committee on

which we had the advice of all the interests affected by this equally revolutionary innovation—including speculative builders (who want to know where they
can build private houses kept out of the green belts to be reserved around all
towns), building societies (who finance that sort of building), industrialists
(who are concerned that factory and mineral developments shall not be unduly
obstructed), and lawyers and planners concerned with administrative methods.
It is a short but I think practical document; and it has the status of having
been prepared at the special request of the Minister. Fortunately, the bulk of
the work on all these things was done before I ran into this tiresome temporary
disability. Fortunately also I now have for the first time since I took over the
TCPA in 1936, three or four very able young men who are really keen on our
policy and will soon be doing the job better than I have been able to do it. I
am hoping they won't be discouraged by the still formidable difficulties and
resistances. . . .

WELWYN GARDEN CITY   4 January 1956

Dear Lewis

I wrote you on the 20th Dec. in reply to your welcome letter of the 11th, but I
don't remember if I mentioned, as I meant to, the special New Towns issue of
T & CP for January. I have just had my first copies (the issue is late), and I am
really rather conceited about it. I feel that for interesting people newly in the
subject of dispersal planning it is as good as a systematic book on it—which I
have never had the time or energy to write. The twenty comments from visiting
planners and sociologists are well-informed and intelligent, and at the same
time prevailingly enthusiastic about the whole principle as a lead to international practice. . . .

Arising from the recent Government decision here to reserve green belts,
and my reprint of a historical study of the green belt idea in the December
T & CP, one or two students have written me for further clues and this caused
me this week to have another look at your *Story of Utopias*. I didn't find much
about the green belt principle in it, but I am reminded of its great merits as a
study of the wider subject. And I noted that in the bibliography you mention
Pemberton's *Happy Colony*, which curiously enough I had not mentioned,
though there is a summary of it in the notes I made in 1918—the last time I did
any real research on the subject of 'community' planning. It seems to have had
a green belt as an integral part of the idea, though the plan is not otherwise
very realistic. I think I must have regarded it, as I regarded Buckingham's
book, as one of the many variants of Owenism—on which point I see you take
a different view. . . .

CAMBRIDGE, MASSACHUSETTS   4 February 1956

We moved up here this week, dear F.J., and while the weather has been grim—
though not so bad as what you are experiencing in England—we are delighted
with our new surroundings: not least with our apartment, still set in trees at
the edge of the old Common not far from the spot where stood the old elm,
which I can remember, under which George Washington assumed command
of his rebellious army in 1775! A few days after I sent you my hasty scrawl on
the New Towns, Albert Mayer published an enthusiastic article on them in
the Sunday Magazine of the *New York Times*. There I discovered, to my
personal chagrin and public delight, that the 'Common Rooms' I advocated
in lieu of big centralised community centres had already been installed, at
least in Harlow. (We had them in Sunnyside, through the accidents of some
leftover space, which Stein and Wright took advantage of.) Mayer said:
'The New Towns are certainly not distinguished as yet for stimulating or
challenging architecture; but these one or two-room centres are often striking
architecturally'.

WELWYN GARDEN CITY   10 February 1956

Dear Lewis

. . . Albert Mayer, whizzing through London from Israel to USA, dropped in
on me a copy of his *New York Times* article, about which he took a tremendous
amount of trouble in our office earlier and by many letters and telegrams; and
which I think a really fine job—practically 100 per cent correct, and that
is rare in foreign assessments. He doesn't say, by the way, that the little
'common rooms' in the NT's act as neighbourhood centres; and I find on
checking my own WGC experience with that of NT social organisers that they
function as committee-meeting places for a variety of groups over quite a
wide area—not just the immediately surrounding houses—and not as a near-
neighbourhood focus. Letchworth and WGC had about as many dispersed
small halls, which are immensely useful in any community and of which no
community has enough; but none of them function as just near-neighbour-
hood centres or bring together the neighbours as a geographical social group.
The only thing that ever did that in WGC was the air-raid warden service
during the war.

I have often thought that we need some street-group political function to
enable us, or compel us, to associate with our accidental neighbours; but I
can't think of one. Community life in a new town is of the interest-group
pattern, not the neighbour pattern—except in the very earliest days, when
everybody is uprooted and willing to let the accident of being co-pioneers

determine their associations with others. Very soon the interest-group pattern reasserts itself. The only 'community' you are then conscious of is the whole town, and that consciousness, though it diminishes with size, continues to some extent because the town is separated from other towns by a green belt of some width. I doubt if you can create in a town strong neighbourhood-consciousness, though you can provide neighbourhood convenience, and that produces just a little such consciousness. People gravitate towards others of like social class and interest. The only group, as Chesterton saw, in which you meet people you don't naturally like or understand or share interests with, is the larger family group—cousins, brothers' and sisters' spouses, aunts, uncles, nephews, nieces etc. It would be good if we could somehow replace this enforced association, but no one has shown how. The old persons' homes, in small pockets, might help, again just a little.

WELWYN GARDEN CITY   14 March 1956

. . . I am amused at your disillusion about immunity from common colds; I am under the same pleasant illusion so far. For many years I have had no more than one-day colds with salvos of terrific sneezes and copious outflows of fluid—and these are so rare that I think for years they won't ever come again. Samuel Butler thought, as I do, that the incalculability of fate is one of the gods' best ideas. I find I plan and replan daily on the assumption that I shall live for ever, and that I shall die tomorrow—and I do both with the utmost inefficiency, as my living associates know and my executors will find out.

I have promised a book on New Towns for March 1957; and though I resolve daily to prepare a syllabus I haven't in a month even started that. The daily press of events and tasks fills all the hours for which I have any energy. The latest is a real worry about First Garden City Ltd. (Letchworth), the directors of which have suddenly asked the stockholders to abolish the limits of dividend and to take to themselves the entire equity. I am so shocked that I tend to splutter ineffectively. The TCPA Executive has to decide tomorrow whether it will declare war in defence of a principle it has committed itself to for fifty-seven years; and my deep hatred of civil strife is at the moment struggling with a no less deep conviction, overlaid by long-undisturbed moral cowardice, that there are occasions when men and societies must risk all to retain anything. Of course this over-dramatises the immediate crisis. I may find it right to be as politic as usual and exculpate myself and the TCPA by reasoned (and ineffective) objections to the betrayal, instead of carrying the fiery cross through the streets of Letchworth. The TCPA may think it is folly to take the field unless you have at least a chance of victory; and I have to tell them (after enquiries) that the Letchworth UDC—the only institution that can be said to represent the Town and its inhabitants—has consented to the selling of the vital pass. My personal trouble is that I know the TCPA would, however tremulously, follow any strong lead I give, telling each other behind my back that the old man has always been right, but is probably wrong this time. I can't be sure many of them wouldn't desert in the heat of battle . . . I will send you the papers about this as a contribution to your study of the philosophy of history and of social and business ethics.

WELWYN GARDEN CITY   25 March 1956

Dear Lewis

I promised to send you the papers about the Letchworth affair, but I have only my own statements in duplicated copies. The scheme of the Company is in a printed Notice of Company Meetings of which we have only one copy. I found I had to advise the TCPA Executive to make a fight for the principle of the limit of dividend and the use of surplus profits for the benefit of the town. They agreed (with one cautious lawyer's abstention from voting); and simultaneously the Local Authority of Letchworth (UDC) decided unanimously to oppose the Directors' scheme. It has been a very hectic week—rather like an election campaign, with letters going out to all stockholders, telephones ringing all the time, press reports, promises of support and disappointing refusals etc. etc. It is a tragedy for the Letchworth idealists, including Norman Macfadyen, who was on the Executive with me for years and is really sincere. But he doesn't understand company business and had been got to believe that the Directors are saving *something* from outside financial sharks, who are just on the point of getting control and ousting the present Board. (This is a fantasy; it would take years for anyone to get control.)

The trouble is that the shareholders *can* change the structure of the Company if they get a 75 per cent majority. The Directors are working like mad to get in proxies in favour of the scheme from the more idealistic holders (to 'save' the Company); and these will vote on the same side as the commercially minded group who want to destroy any limit on the dividend. We are trying to get votes against the scheme, but the pathetic thing is that the shareholders who would want to preserve the principle just can't believe Directors like the Macfadyens would sell the pass. A few will take the trouble to read what we say carefully, and if they do they will vote against the scheme. But I think it is likely we shall not succeed. There is no question at all that we had to do what we could to stop the scheme, which is a betrayal of trust of an outrageous character. I am handicapped a bit by the fact that three of the Directors are officers of the TCPA, and by my dislike of Lutheran language—I should rather say, my inability to utter phrases in that language that spring to my lips. In any case where financial interests are at stake you have to be very careful what you publish. It is interesting that the financial papers this week report only briefly the opposition, but do not comment—though last week they were accusing the Directors of not giving the stockholders enough. The Directors had not done anything to inform the holders of their public obligations.

Lord Pethick-Lawrence, still alive at 85, is the only surviving signatory of the Memorandum and Articles of FGC (in 1903). He replied to our letter that he had given the Directors his proxy in favour of their scheme. I wrote him again, and he has now withdrawn it and is attending the meeting himself; he had quite misunderstood the ethical position. If I could get other shareholders to study the thing properly I am certain we could at least prevent a 75 per cent majority, which would be enough to kill the scheme. Unfortunately the Bournville Trustees, of all people, are supporting the Directors. They are the largest holders. I am trying to shake them. You will wonder if I am right. I wish I were not; but there never was a clearer case. I should have to write a novel to explain the situation on the Board and in the administration of the Company that has led to such an indefensible line of action. . . .

WELWYN GARDEN CITY   5 April 1956

Dear Lewis

Several things. First, warm thanks for sending us your new collection of *New Yorker* essays.[1] I have read one or two already, and see we are going to enjoy them very much. It is also a book I can review for the TCPA journal, whether or not copies are on general sale in this country. We will try to get some copies for our own bookshop. It is very kind of you to send us so many of your publications. I wish I wrote more books and could reciprocate, though with less impressive works.

Second, the Letchworth scandal. I went to the Company's meeting today, when the proposal to remove the dividend limit and make the company purely commercial was duly carried by proxy votes collected by the directors; but we did put up a most vigorous protest which is certain to get into the press, and is likely to lead to legal efforts by the Letchworth Urban District Council to claim its rights. I made a speech almost in the terms of the enclosed summary for the press: you will see it is pretty strong—and it visibly troubled the

---

[1] *From the Ground Up*, New York, London, 1956.

consciences of the directors arranged in a row along the platform. Effective speeches were also made by Lord Pethick-Lawrence (an original signatory of the Company's constitution in 1903 and still at 85 forceful and lucid), C. B. Purdom (who has a special position as an original member of the Company's staff and the historian of Letchworth), by a barrister on behalf of the Letchworth UDC, by a son of an early Chairman of the Company (a distinguished literary critic and poet—Iolo Aneurin Williams), another barrister who resides in Letchworth, and two or three others who had consulted with us about the presentation of the case. We had all the arguments, but we could do nothing against the proxy votes the directors, by stating the case incompletely, had gathered together, and the speculators with whom they were in unavowed alliance.

Great efforts were made by the officials, on the pleas of a technical defect in my letter of appointment as representative of the TCPA, to stop me speaking or even being present, but we overcame these by protests and threats that they might invalidate the meeting. Sir Eric Macfadyen in the chair made a lamentable apologia for the betrayal, saying at one point that he had been under a wrong impression of the Company's constitution, because he had read my preface to Howard's book and Purdom's big book instead of going to the original documents. I had to ask him if he was accusing me and Purdom of misquoting (both of us are very careful on such matters); and he had to shuffle out of the innuendo very quickly. Altogether he put up a very poor show.

I took Pethick-Lawrence to lunch afterwards, and he said the affair is the most infamous thing in his business experience. Yet because of the way the Directors had stated the case originally to the stockholders he had at first given his proxy to the Directors, and had only withdrawn it and attended the meeting himself when I had given him all the facts in true perspective. The unhappy part of the whole thing is that three of the directors are members of the TCPA Council and Executive. I am hoping they will all resign as I do not want to work with such men. I am sure that all the rest of our distinguished Council will agree with me. It won't do the TCPA any harm to have taken this stand, but the Letchworth Board is hopelessly discredited. I am very glad I decided to register this protest. It has meant a lot of work; the office for the past two weeks has been like the headquarters of a presidential election campaign. And certainly the last has not been heard of the affair. . . .

Pethick-Lawrence, a Labour Peer who was Secretary for India and with Stafford Cripps negotiated the independence of India and Pakistan, and a lawyer of much business experience, takes the view that this incident is quite untypical of London business standards, which are high; but I fear a lot of left-wing people will see it as another instance of the habits of capitalism. It will discredit many honest business enterprises which are introducing an element of public interest into private enterprise; this is perhaps the most regrettable consequence. Don't ask me how a Board hitherto regarded as reputable got into such a state of mind; I can't at present clearly answer. Some are unhappy, but none had the courage to resign. They had worked on a rather inexperienced Urban District Council by delusive promises of little gratuities to the town in place of its birthright; and until I met the Council myself they had not seen the proposals in perspective. Now they do, but whether they will have the courage to take legal action remains to be seen. The TCPA has done all it can. . . .

CAMBRIDGE, MASSACHUSETTS   20 April 1956

Three letters of yours, dear F.J., have piled up in my file this last month; and it is high time that I began to answer them. . . . Your series of notes on the situation in First Garden City Limited were indeed shocking, if only because they reminded one again of the mutability of all human institutions and how difficult it is to pass on good ideas and principles from generation to generation, though bad ones have an odd way of being toughly self-perpetuating. I am glad that you stept into the breach for I think it's important to keep going and renew these old idealisms. The fact that it is necessary to make such a fight gave me the same melancholy feeling I got back in 1946, when I talked with a group of British co-operators who wanted some help or counsel on how to retain the old co-operative spirit, that is, some of the original Rochdale essence, brewed as it were in the primaeval tea, when all the present members seemed to want was a bigger 'divie'. I am eager to know how your campaign has turned out, though even if you win you are old enough to know that such battles are never safely settled but must be fought repeatedly—like, I suppose, everything else in life.

My own news continues to be pleasant. At the end of the month, the fact that I am getting a renewal of my old Guggenheim Fellowship will be publicly announced; not a great sum ($3,500) but enough, together with three free months at the American Academy at Rome, to enable me to spend eight months in Europe without any serious strain, even if I don't write an article, and even to come back here with a not-too-depleted bank account. It's almost too good to be true. . . .

WELWYN GARDEN CITY   23 April 1956

Dear Lewis

. . . The Letchworth affair did produce some strong press comment—notably leading articles in *The Times* and the *New Statesman*, taking the view I took of it. We also had some good letters in *The Times*—to which the company did not reply. The Letchworth local authority is now taking legal opinion from a very eminent Queen's Counsel, and so I hope there will be a legal action. The TCPA Council, to whom I reported the very vigorous action I took, unanimously endorsed what I had done—but the three members who are also on the Letchworth Board discreetly refrained from attending. The only bright feature of the whole disgraceful affair is that it draws prominent attention to the financial soundness of the garden city method of town development; it has produced surpluses well worth stealing by the stockholders. . . .

I have declined an invitation to visit Australia this next fall—so our round trip won't be for another year at earliest. I can't yet shake off the TCPA shackles.

WELWYN GARDEN CITY   30 April 1956

Dear Lewis

The summary of the Letchworth affair to date is that the commercially minded shareholders got their way at the company's meeting, but the local authority is now taking legal opinion as to whether the town's rights can be restored. There is a tiresome delay, owing to the engagements of the Q.C. instructed, and I am trying to keep a discussion going in Letchworth in order to stiffen up a rather apathetic local opinion. I am still at a loss to evaluate the motives of such directors as the Macfadyens, who have been closely identified with garden city idealism; I find it difficult to measure the degree of indifference to principles and of mere weakness. I can make no secret of my disgust with them, whichever it is. The TCPA is supporting me in my action—though I know that some members (only a few) would prefer to let the affair slide. There are always some people who join a society like ours because it has influence with Ministries and local authorities and because they like to be on any accessible band-wagon. They don't realise that we only have influence because we stand for something definite, and that if we always took the complacent line we should soon be ignored. It happens that at the moment our status with the Ministry and Government is exceptionally high, largely owing to my personal conversion of the present Minister[1] to the new towns philosophy when he was out of office and Parliament in 1945—a piece of sheer luck. I couldn't have foreseen that one day he would be the Minister for the subject. He has an exaggerated idea of my personal part in establishing the new towns policy—and tells everybody, publicly and privately—which is gratifying, no matter if it gives me too much of the credit.

---

[1] Rt. Hon. Duncan Sandys, Minister of Housing and Local Government, 1945–57.

AS OF AMENIA, NEW YORK   14 May 1956

Dear F.J.

At last the fatigues of this oppressive year, which began for me with Sophy's falling ill a year ago in April, have caught up with me; not too seriously but sufficiently to make a fortnight at Amenia seem like a promise of heaven. There was no let up in my duties at any moment. I needed a month's vacation at least when the summer was over, and all I got finally was part of a week in bed in February! I am more than resigned to the bout of idleness that now looms ahead for the summer, though probably, as soon as I have recovered my tone and energy, it will not be quite so empty of work as it now so invitingly promises to be. This will explain, at all events, why the article I had meant to write for *T & CP*, expanding my remarks on New Town planning and the superblock, is unwritten and may, I fear, long remain unwritten. . . .

By now, or shortly, you should have a copy of my *Transformations of Man* in your hands. I promise to overwhelm you no further with books for the next few years; but don't think that this book involves any embarrassing duties of reading or commenting upon it, unless you turn to it in the mood you might to any such production if Tom, Dick or Harry had written it. As I've told you, I think it is one of the best things I have done but I doubt if any reviewers will find this out; and I am even prepared to have my best friends overlook its virtues, as one of them in Cambridge has already done. The book, in its quiet, unassuming way, overthrows, or at least badly tilts at, many well-established assumptions in history and philosophy, and repairs the damage, I believe, with a better interpretation. Yet it may well be ignored or dismissed for a long time to come, as Henry Adams' prophetic essays back in 1909 on the coming crisis due to atomic power were ignored. I feel very serene about its eventual fate, though I don't promise not to curse picturesquely when I find, as I have every reason to anticipate, that it meets the same blank wall here that most of my recent books, since 1944 in fact, have met.

One of the things that makes it easy to be nonchalant is a marvellous piece of good luck that has befallen me. MIT up here have promised to appoint me a Bemis Professor for the autumn semesters of 1957 and 1958, after I get back from Europe. My only duties will be to sit down and think: no classes, no lectures, just casual associations and a seminar once a week to deal with some aspect of my own thinking. It's both an honour and a windfall, and I welcome it doubly because I find this Cambridge milieu highly stimulating intellectually, and rewarding in the social life it offers, though we may not be so lucky as to again have an apartment as charming as our present one.

P.S. What a bitter ending, that defection from the old Garden City ideals. I can easily understand how painful in both personal and impersonal ways it must be for you. If Howard didn't live to see the full fruition of his ideals he at least escaped this! . . .

WELWYN GARDEN CITY   21 May 1956

Dear Lewis

. . . Thank you for your latest book, *The Transformations of Man*, the first chapter of which at least restores my belief that my own mind is normal and still capable of being newly informed and guided by superior knowledge and reasoning powers. I like very much the scheme of the book, and will read it attentively to see whether I can accept your view that Man is on the way to a fresh great transformation; and also whether you are restating with your extraordinary wealth of data and knowledge of past philosophies the religion of my sort of 'sensible men', or formulating a new one that I have to consider accepting. You wouldn't want me to be other than sceptically receptive at this stage; and anyway, what else could I be within six days of my seventy-first anniversary? I (and Margaret too) appreciate very highly your habit of sending us your books as they come along; and we hope your second sentence doesn't mean that you are not going to write any more for years. . . .

The tiresome job I mentioned is a review for *Land Economics* of Lloyd Rodwin's book[1] on British New Towns. It assembles an immense mass of information, misses an immense mass that is equally important, and somehow gets the whole thing wrong, owing I think (but this is what I have still to define) to something defective in the academic approach to a practical political and constructive business. Having started on the job, I was a bit disconcerted by receiving a publisher's circular in which you are quoted as calling the book a 'masterly analysis'—since that is just what I am disposed to say it isn't. Are you fairly quoted? Did you express no reservations? The position, as I see it, is that the garden city and new towns pioneers set out with a perfectly correct analysis and prescription to do a very big and very difficult thing, had to contend with innumerable obstacles, foreseen and unforeseen (but even the latter not unexpected), and have had a partial success so far and hope for more success. They know they could not *command* any success at all; therefore they are mildly gratified at such success as they have had. But also they wanted (perhaps even at times hoped) for more: therefore they are mildly disappointed. But Rodwin seems to trace any shortfall in their wildest hopes to lack of foresight or defects in their proposals; and that seems to me quite unjustified by the documents in which their proposals are made—with the exception

---

[1] Lloyd Rodwin, *The British New Towns Policy*, Cambridge (Mass.), London, 1956. Osborn's review appeared in *Land Economics*, August 1956.

that there was a little of Utopianism along with a great deal of plain practicality in Howard's book of 1898. The men who took up his ideas and applied them experimentally were entirely realists. There was no Utopianism in my book of 1918, or in the First Garden City prospectus of 1903, or the New Towns Committee's reports of 1946, or in the propaganda of the TCPA since 1899. I am not saying that a touch of Utopianism is a vice—but in fact it was not present, except in Howard, and in him it was not very important save as an element in his own personality that probably enabled him to do his very remarkable work. . . .

AMENIA, NEW YORK   27 May 1956

Dear F.J.

I have fifty final exams to correct before I can resume work on my garden, and your letter, which came just yesterday, gives me a welcome excuse for neglecting my university work a few more minutes. In going through *The Transformations of Man* please don't confuse the author's opinion with those expressed by the writer of the blurb. The kind of transformation I broach at the end must seem, if my analysis has any substance, to be a probable consummation of all that has gone on before, but it certainly won't take place, except in minute amounts, in our lifetime, and the alternative, which I broach in the 'post-historic' chapter, seems alas! a more likely possibility. In getting an outside view of this work, I have much more regard for your opinion than for specialists in various departments who will find that I have stept on their toes or neglected their favourite idols. If my main theses weather your scepticism I shall be much more comfortable about them; and if they do not, I'll value all that your hard common sense will bring to bear on them to reveal their weakness, beneath the plausible covering that I have, no doubt, given them. This book will come out in England, by the bye, next winter or spring, so it might be worth while holding off the publication of a review till then. . . .

As for your judgement of Rodwin's book, I suspect it is far sounder than mine, for I have an indecent way of being too kind to my enemies, especially my intellectual enemies, and from the time I first answered his attack on the garden city idea in *Land Economics* I have always so regarded him. His weaknesses are those of the academic mind. Though praise of his New Towns book was not unqualified—I don't know what part of it they quoted—I was so pleased and astonished that he had made as favourable a presentation as he did that I leaned over backwards to commend the job, believing that he would do far more to bring about an appreciation of the New Towns achievement, despite his often superficial and niggling criticisms, than I would be able to do.

He was as surprised at my favourable response as you were and as a result has been very friendly; all the more because he knew I had refused to recommend him for the post at Manchester he finally held. But he learned a lot in England: he even found out that my picture of the industrial town in *The Culture of Cities*, which he had dismissed as 'subjective', erred if anything on the favourable side. So sail into him, and even into me, in your review, if you are so inclined! The 'disappointment' about the success of the New Towns does not seem to me other than the normal disappointment that attends the translation of any ideal into practice: certainly it is far less than our legitimate disappointment in the Christian Church, say, or in Parliamentary government! . . .

WELWYN GARDEN CITY   2 June 1956

I feel I ought to let you know at once, my dear Lewis—however dissonantly the news will fall on Republican ears—that in the Birthday Honours List of two days ago it was announced that The Queen has been graciously pleased to bestow upon me the dignity of Knighthood. If I survive the flood of congratulations so long, I shall on 10 July next become to the outside world Sir Frederic and my spouse will become Lady Osborn, but we hope that to everybody who really matters to us we may still be thought of and addressed as F.J. and Margaret. I must add that we had no hesitation at all in accepting this honour; it is beyond question that in England, and also in many countries overseas, a title, however illogically, adds to one's authority and therefore to one's influence. People ask: Why the hell is he a 'Sir'? What the hell has he done? They look him up in *Who's Who* and are disposed at once to believe that he probably knows something about the subjects on which he talks and writes. And his Lady appears to be (what in this case people ought to have seen without the appellation) a person of distinction. And this despite the known fact that men are awarded honours for almost any sort of 'successful' activity, good or bad or socially valuable or innocuous or even harmful. We accepted, not only for the very real fun of the thing—the congratulations are nice to receive—but also because there are still things we want to get done in our few remaining active years, and this will undoubtedly help.

Incidentally, this is the first purely Garden City honour since Howard was knighted in 1927; I am cited as 'Chairman of Executive Committee, Town and Country Planning Association'. It is thought that this recognition will give a fillip to the Association: in fact, to my amusement, one or two people have already joined who should have signed up years ago, but hadn't troubled.

The week of the Welwyn Drama Festival, which I started twenty-seven years ago, begins on Monday. It is this town's most remarkable annual social occasion. Twenty-two one-act plays of diverse types are played by amateur companies, four of them societies in the town and others from near and far; and the theatre, which holds 1,100, is filled every night, more than half of the audience coming for the whole week and treating it as a get-together. Very pleasant in a town that is now so large as to have grown out of the stage when you know everybody you meet in the street or the shops. There is also a very high standard of appreciation of the merits of plays and of production and acting, due to our practice of having each year a first class adjudicator who holds forth after the performances on each evening, first publicly and then at a private party for the players of that day. In a town like this the drama is one of the best social binding forces, since people of all classes and kinds do things together. I have to go every night as chairman, and it is very enjoyable—but a bit of an interference with other work. ·

I have read *The Transformations* but am not ready to say anything about it, except that I am dazed by the assurance with which you size up the philosophic developments of our species. My ignorance seems abysmal; you make me feel a very simple-minded anti-Fundamentalist who hasn't a clue as to where he got his own 'spiritual' assumptions. No doubt at all this is good for me, but I must belong to the blind generation that you despise. I had supposed I and others who take things seriously and feel responsibility for advancing human welfare, did so because it is our nature as family animals. I have to think about your view that we derive this state of mind from 'axial' prophets who promulgated a view of God that, while we can now see it as a delusion, is somehow intuitionally right or philosophically essential. I can't say more yet than that I have to think about it.

CAMBRIDGE   8 June 1956

Dear F.J.

Your letter came only an hour ago and greatly rejoiced us: in witness I now sit down, mid all the untidiness of household packing, to send you our felicitations. Indeed we are pleased, though privately I had accorded you the honour in 1946 and was chagrined that the Labour government did not agree with me then. As you doubtless have found out, as one grows older 'honours' are the only rewards that give satisfaction.

WELWYN GARDEN CITY   12 June 1956

Dear Lewis

Margaret and I have found it both a duty and a pleasure to acknowledge the hundreds of messages of congratulation we have received, and therefore you are let in for an additional (one-sided) round in our correspondence. We thank you (both) for your charmingly expressed letter of 8 June.

Though I am always troubled by the slowness of the progress made in apply-ing the planning principles with which I have come to be identified, I do not feel that the efforts I have made have ever lacked appreciation. Both nationally and locally lots of people have thrown bouquets at me that have been quite embarrassing; they are simply impressed by the fact that I have done a certain amount of public work without financial reward. They don't seem to realise what a colossal piece of luck it was that I found myself, in the last twenty years, in an economic position to do what I wanted to do for most of my time, and that I happened to have just the right knowledge and experience (again by pure luck) that was required for doing it. I have never acquired the discipline for really hard work, nor have I made any sacrifices at all. I have ambled easily along a road that always seemed obvious and open. Fortunate coin-cidences occurred at all the appropriate moments. My course through life, so far, certainly bears out the proverb that it is better to be born lucky than rich. Yet I lap up appreciation just as if I deserved it morally.

Therefore I am again discomfited, though admittedly with a complacent gratification, that I received this morning an invitation to a dinner to Margaret and me on the day of my investiture as a knight, at which the chairman will be Lord Salter (President of the TCPA) and the speakers are to include Duncan Sandys (Minister of Housing and Local Government), Herbert Morrison (Deputy Prime Minister in the Labour Government), Clement Davies (Leader of the small Liberal Party in Parliament and the Chairman of the Greater London Regional Committee that applied the Abercrombie Plan), Sir Thomas Bennett (Chairman of Crawley New Town and the architectural successor to Unwin) and Gilbert McAllister (who was Secretary of the TCPA when we started the campaign in 1936). I don't know who are the moving spirits in this frightening compliment, but it is not the TCPA staff, who were solemnly instructed by me that a dinner was unnecessary and inappropriate in all the circumstances. (In all conscience, the knighthood is compliment enough.) Margaret is mainly disturbed by the thought that, having been seen in the same frock at functions for years and years, she will have to get a new one for this solemn occasion!

The best thing about the whole strange business is that it really strengthens our hands in the campaign, which is at another critical stage but still goes on. I have just put to bed a fighting issue of *T & CP* with some very solid arguments about the means of making a greater success of the Town Development Act, and an article by Bennett on Housing Standards that I think is the most weighty contribution to the subject since Unwin's Tudor-Walters Report. Bennett is one of the most successful British architects, with a power of exposition equal to his knowledge (a very rare combination), and his experience as chairman of Crawley has brought him 100 per cent into our camp on housing and planning standards.

So I am a bit encouraged at the moment.

AMENIA, NEW YORK   27 July 1956

Dear F.J.

. . . My *Transformations of Man* was neglected by the publisher here and ignored by the press: so its fate will probably be similar to that of *In the Name of Sanity*, which sold three hundred copies less than the advance sale! Plainly I must face the fact that whatever the merits of my work, I am unable to speak to my own countrymen: what I say is by now so foreign to their ways of thinking and their general way of life that they will not even bother to read it, much less to discuss it. Partly it is the penalty one pays for having been on the scene too long; and that is an old and inevitable mischief, which can't be remedied; but even more it's because the present generation doesn't want to consider any ideas that would lessen their blind assurance that all is going well, or if it is not going well, can't at all events be remedied by any positive act of their own. Yet this literary neglect has a paradoxical side to it: for never have there been more calls, from a wider variety of sources, for my personal services or my personal appearance: so that I now command what once would have seemed to me fabulous fees for whatever I choose to do. Face to face with me a lecture audience will greet my words with great enthusiasm: left to read the same words in a book they turn aside, with positive antipathy.

AMENIA, NEW YORK   26 August 1956

Dear F.J.

About a week ago I despatched to you a bulky and weighty book, one of the kind that would dampen almost any human soul on first sight; so I had better explain promptly, before you get it, that there is no need for any personal acknowledgement of it. Indeed, I would have been better advised, I have no doubt now, to have sent it to your *T & CP* office since the chief claim it has on your attention is as a subject for review. The subject of it is *Man's Role in Shaping the Face of the Earth*[1] and as such it has at least a dozen papers that your readers ought to know about. But perhaps the main interest of the book is that an international conference on the subject did take place; and that, for

---

[1] Chicago, Cambridge (UK), 1956, *edited by* W. L. Thomas.

those of us who were involved in it—if not for the reader struggling through the pages that ensued—it was a very exciting event. I have extra copies of my own paper on the Natural History of Urbanism; so if you know of anyone who might be interested in that theme I'll be glad to send him a copy directly. There is almost no literature on *that* subject, unfortunately; and such digging as I actually did barely scratched the ground.

I've had a first hand report, both about yourself and the Vienna Congress, by one of my Pennsylvania students, who was rather more impressed with the former than the latter, though he valued the opportunity for at least viewing the great menagerie of planners assembled in Vienna. I myself have mixed feelings about my having missed it and will probably long continue to harbour them. As for your extremely friendly suggestion that we join your delegation to Russia (presumably as Hon. Brit. Subjects, a flattering thought), I am very grateful for it; and Sophia, with her Russian background, is positively excited. But I doubt whether, after a whole winter of travelling and interviewing and studying, I shall be good for any fresh impressions by next May; and I hesitate to tie us to a program we may not, for either psychological or practical reasons, be able to carry out. You are an old hand in such matters and will doubtless get more out of those two weeks than I would be able to in as many months. So I'd better say now, albeit with reluctance and reserve, that you'd better count us out.

As for my immediate plans, a variety of reasons have impelled me to postpone sailing till the seventeenth of October, and may even cause me to put the date off till the middle of November. The purpose of this is to spend more time in Europe, and particularly in England, in May, when the weather has a better prospect of being fair and suitable for gadding about than it has in October or November, combined with my doubts, after a very barren and depressing summer, about my being able to spend all the time I had planned to do in Rome on literary work, since at the moment I find myself empty. I realise that this may unexpectedly give way to just the opposite state, but I can't count on it; and therefore I am trying to shorten my trip a little in order not to deepen my sense of futility and frustration. I have never yet spent even six months abroad; and I have always begun to feel a certain restlessness, a certain eagerness to return to my native land, around the end of the third month. I daresay that if one stays longer one may get one's second wind, but it is chancey . . .

What you write about *The Transformations of Man*, even tentatively, is extremely enlightening to me; all the more because your difficulties arise from matters that I have so long taken for granted that I am hardly aware that for anyone else they would *be* difficulties. What you say may account for the massive reluctance of my own American contemporaries to have anything to do with my whole thesis. My position here becomes more and more puzzling to me: Cooper Union, about to celebrate its founding, has offered me the highest lecture fee I've ever received, to wit a thousand dollars, to give the principal address on that occasion. The subject they suggested is—*The Transformation of Man!!* Which would seem to imply that my face, not my pen, is my fortune: or perhaps I should say, my 'platform presence'. . . .

WELWYN GARDEN CITY   28 August 1956

Dear Lewis

. . . It is very clear to me that all over the world planning conceptions are at a critical point; the dispersalists and the agglomerative idealists are running neck and neck. We should have hit harder in the 1920's, or we should be young men now. Our successors are numerous, but they seem to me to lack the necessary simplicity for a powerful impact on popular opinion. I am getting very contemptuous of the pathetic cry for 'more research'. We make millions of maps and never look at the compass. The whole road is obstructed by a forest of signposts, and all the drivers wail for more signposts, to guide them out of the forest. . . .

My simple mind looks to the plain human quests that cause the 'trends'. It is so very obvious that families want family houses and also want motor-cars so that they can go where they wish when they wish. They also must have work to get incomes, and they must be able to buy all sorts of things. Also they must have schools for their children. After that they *like* to have accessible a lot of other facilities, but their desire for these varies greatly in composition and intensity. Any urban directory indicates the list of institutions etc. for which a demand exists. The planning problem is to arrange these things, along with dwellings and workplaces, in such a way as to place them in reach of people— keeping as short as possible the more frequent types of journey, and not impossibly long the less frequent types. I know you have to have a lot of information and experience to plan a layout that meets the requirements; but in the end the job is a practical one, and can never be reduced to an exact science. As to putting it over, fundamentally you say to people: Here is a nice, pleasant, convenient arrangement don't you think?—which we propose, or which we are building. We take into account your responses, as the public, while we go along; in fact, we have to, because we are under your orders, either as consumers free to buy or not to buy, or as electors governed by your fashions and fancies (which we seek to influence by what we think attractive ideas, but which when your fancies are definite and steady we respect). . . . No entrepreneur ever acts on more 'trends'; he seeks to produce what he has reason to believe will be saleable. In my experience the most successful business men have an almost uncanny intuition as to popular responses, to new ideas as well as established ones. They employ research workers, mostly to answer questions they ask; but the research workers are often surprised at the decisions their bosses take, which have to be positive. . . . However, you know all this: I am just doodling. . . .

I think planners have to decide what sort of towns to propose; but they won't usually be the developers, so their method must be to set *limits* to what the developers can do. I am inclined to think it is more important for planners to decide what is wrong than to prescribe what is right—certainly they can't do that in all detail.

WELWYN GARDEN CITY   5 September 1956

Dear Lewis

I think I acknowledged receipt of the chunk of platinum entitled *Man's Role* before I had your letter of 26 August; I did highly appreciate your sending it to me. I have only been able to nibble at bits of it, but I am putting a short 'review' of it, saying just what it seems to be about, in *T & CP*—mentioning your chapter on *The Natural History of Urbanism* as one that planners should read. . . .

Of course there are, as always, new connections and analogies in your article; and on this, as always, I compliment you. In saying that there is almost no literature on the subject I suppose you meant nothing on the criticism of urbanism as destructive of important values and resources—e.g., your very interesting point that the baths of Rome ate up the surrounding forests. But I would have thought the broad picture of urban development was fairly well described by geographers: I seem to have a fairly clear mental picture of it, and I must have got it from somewhere—Pirenne, Vidal de la Blache, Mumford, Geddes, Fleure?—and there is what seems to me an intelligent short summary in Smailes' *Geography of Towns* (1953). But isn't the need more a matter of impressing a moral or ethical view of the facts of urbanisation than that of getting the process more clearly defined?

I contribute to this criticism in my random way; see for instance my observation that the wealth of cafés and wine gardens etc. in Vienna (as in Paris) reflects the inhabitability of its family dwellings (cf. Carcopino on the necessity of public baths in Rome). It was a joke against Letchworth that you only saw people in the town centre up to about 10 p.m., when both of them went home! The fact is that home-centred culture, which is healthy, does to some extent conflict with the 'Bloomsbury' type of culture—theatres, ballet, lectures, eating, Johnsonian coffee-house cerebration etc.—and that most people value more highly the former if they can't have both. I wonder sometimes whether the radio and TV are not enabling people to have it both ways—with some obvious danger of lack of diversity, of mass-fashion, of clique dominance.

Two little points on your essay. Surely cities always tended to grow first where there is some concentration of population; that is, where good quality land facilitated agriculture? The reflex effect in improving nearby agriculture is surely secondary? Orwin said that market-garden land was found near because the market was near. When this land was built on the market-gardeners went further out and repeated the improvement of the land elsewhere.

Then you don't query Dudley Stamp's ramshackle figures of urban encroachment on farm land which, after a long controversy, I have discredited. The latest development of this is a Wye Agricultural College pamphlet that confirms my contention that the best way to increase food production is to lower the density of housing from 14–16 to 8–12 an acre. (I will send you this publication.) You give my friend Geoffrey Block the credit for the garden-produce argument, which he got from me. No matter! . . .

WELWYN GARDEN CITY   4 October 1956

Dear Lewis
Lloyd Rodwin is very angry about my review of his book in *Land Economics:* the Editor has sent me a copy of a rejoinder that she is inclined to think too bad-tempered to publish—but I am inclined to encourage her to publish it, with a counter-comment by me in which I will try to make clearer where I think he went wrong. I reject entirely his contention that the 'proponents' of the new town idea were oblivious of some very important considerations, such as the cost of scrapping capital in the old cities. It is pretty evident that he has very little acquaintance with the economics of development. That perhaps is excusable in a social scientist; but he ought to have a better idea of the things that matter to ordinary working families, as well as of the complexities of political procedure in a democratic country. I, like you, have spent most of my life trying to impress on a preoccupied world the importance of a particular issue and the practicability and need of a particular kind of enterprise. I resent being told that when I cannot get society to act quickly in the way I propose, the reason is that I did not myself understand what I proposed and the obvious corollaries that it would involve. . . .

M.P.O. and I have just got back from a very pleasant 10 days in Wales. We stayed some days at Portmeirion, a hotel estate developed in the last twenty years in an utterly romantic architectural style by Clough Williams-Ellis, who has loaded it with antiquities and curiosities and fanciful decorations and yet hardly fails at any point to make the effect charming as well as amusing. I would not have believed it possible in these days of austere aesthetics; but it 'comes off' completely. Moreover the hotel is extremely well run and one of the most comfortable I have been in. The rest was good for Margaret. She goes to a sort of clinic for treatment in three weeks' time, and we have some reason for hope that she may get a bit of relief.

I went to speak at a conference at a Lutheran Evangelical Academy in Germany a few weeks ago. The atmosphere was quite surprising—as liberal as that of a Fraternity House in the USA, while at the same time the discussions were incredibly patient, earnest and frank. The thesis was Planning and Freedom, and I had been asked to go by the Foreign Office here because they think the new assertion of the supremacy of the personal conscience against the state by this church is internationally important. I don't know whether they understood my attempt to explain the philosophy of government held by a race that is averse to exact formulations of philosophy! . . .

The academic boys for once have done a good job: the pamphlet *The Garden Controversy*[1] by two of the staff of the Wye Agricultural College (London University). They examine in detail the argument that I have put up for years that the produce from gardens at low density is greater in value than that from the whole area of agricultural land taken for development, and leaning backwards in the approved scientific manner all the time they find unequivocally that I was right. Their conclusion is that the best way to increase food production in England is to build houses at ten or twelve an acre, and that some is lost if you go up to fourteen or sixteen an acre. I had proved this by simpler arguments, but few took any notice. Floreat Scientia!

AMENIA, NEW YORK   6 October 1956

Dear F. J.

I am in arrears, as to correspondence, once more and I am a little disheartened to find that I haven't yet answered yours of September sixth, with its useful comments on *Man's Role* and my role in *Man's Role*. As to the geographic picture of urban development, I find it still pretty sketchy though the sketches, so far as they go, may be true. The geographers of the older generation were better in describing geography's effect upon man rather than man's effect upon the earth, which at first glance seemed negligible. The science that deals with man's disturbance of the climate is a very recent one indeed, though it now begins to seem as if the amount of combustion we are producing has definitely

---

[1] R. H. Best *and* J. T. Ward, *The Garden Controversy*, Ashford (Kent), 1956.

added to the carbon dioxide in the air, abetted of course by our destruction of vegetation which in turn may be making the climate in more civilised areas warmer—though after last winter you probably doubt it. But I agree that the need to give Man a sense of his moral responsibilities to the earth and all its creatures is more necessary than finer estimates of the damage or benefits he has brought about in the past. Your point about cities always tending to grow first where population and agriculture flourish is correct; but if you look close at the early part of my essay you'll find that I made note of it, and even suggested that urban man might have had some edge over his rural neighbour by reason of his more abundant and mixed food supply. (As Mr Dooley observed, 'If you want good food, you mustn't go to the place where it's grown but the place where it's sent to'.)

That was a silly slip of mine to make about Stamp's name, but the very fact you have just referred to seems to me to give other justification than Stamp supplies to the observation that the city in the past, by its growth, ate away the best agricultural land, that is, the rich silt of the bottoms; and it is only in old cities that did not grow, or in new ones that are built with low densities, that this is not true. You surely wouldn't suggest that Battersea, which was once rich with market gardens, increased its yield by becoming a brick desert? That was all I was referring to.

As for whether the growth of the big city uses more land than organised decentralisation, I think a good case could be made for this, if put in a slightly different fashion. Namely, that through the operation of land values, it sterilizes and prematurely puts out of agricultural use a far greater area than need be treated in this fashion. Seeing what is now happening in the Bay Area of San Francisco, Stein has recently been writing a memorandum suggesting ways in which the permanent balance between rural and urban uses might be achieved there, through a different taxation and land acquisition policy. The failure to tackle this as yet even in England, except in the negative form of the 1932 Act, seems to me a weakness in the New Town policy up to now, since the local greenbelt does not take care of the wider problem of balance.

AMENIA, NEW YORK   4 November 1956

Much has been happening to both ourselves here and the world, dear F.J., since you wrote your last letter to me just a month ago; but perhaps I had better begin by dealing with the local situation, since that is more simple. After putting off our trip three or four times Sophy and I began to get a little embarrassed when we wrote to the Cunard Line, so just a fortnight ago, after much vexatious debate with ourselves, we finally decided to postpone our trip till next March. This means giving up our long held dream of a whole winter of leisure and peace in Europe, ensconced on the Janiculum at Rome: a period I had looked forward to with especial eagerness at this moment of my life, because I had felt that the ancient city might somehow call forth from my depths some fresh work not yet visible in these familiar surroundings, as my trip to Europe in '53 certainly helped to bring forth the unexpected *Transformations of Man*. We are rather glad, on the whole, that we made up our mind more than a week before the crisis in Egypt developed, for if we had turned back after that it might have given us an unpleasant feeling of being unduly anxious or even cowardly.

As for the present crisis, it is hard to tell as yet whether hell or heaven has been breaking loose; probably, as usual, a little of both. The foreign policy of the Eisenhower administration has been so muddled, so fantastically irresponsible, so irresolute, contradictory and wishful, that I hold our government largely culpable for what has been happening, and not happening, in the Near East. We are betrayed even by our well-meant shibboleths, for it is absurd to renounce force as such: what one should renounce is any use of force except as an instrument of justice; and our failure, these last ten years, to develop an adequate police force within the United Nations is the ultimate source of the present disturbance and unbalance in the East. I trust that there will be enough intelligence to perceive this moral now, but I fear that if Eisenhower gets in again the result may be an overwhelming swing, at least in his party, toward complete isolationism. I write to you before our election, and I find that I am almost alone in thinking that Stevenson still has a fighting chance of winning out. His recent speeches have been excellent and he has met with an unexpectedly favourable response from the public on the Hydrogen Bomb issue; but he began to take this more active line too late in the election—held back doubtless by bad advice from his professional advisers. Two years ago, in correspondence, about which I may have told you, I suggested to him that he make out a new foreign policy for himself, different from both Truman and Eisenhower, and that he centre this on our mistakes in relying upon nuclear weapons and a strategy of extermination, since the physiological results were already threatening even to ourselves and might soon be disastrous. I did not, at the time, succeed in convincing him and even now he has only made a beginning, but he at least has done a big public service in opening up the question of the Hydrogen Bomb and the Cobalt Bomb, and he has given the scientists the courage to speak up and the publicity they need to make their own opinions carry further. Even if he loses the election, he will have served his country well.

This is the first autumn Sophy and I have spent all through in Amenia since 1944, and it has enabled me to get caught up on a lot of pruning and planting that I could never manage to get done in the summer. I have not yet decided upon what particular work I shall start on during the next three months; but while I am making up my mind, or rather, letting my mind make itself up, as one must always do in such matters, I am wading fairly steadily through the sea of books about cities that have come out during the last eighteen years—some of which I have, until now, examined only in cursory fashion. Speaking of which reminds me to send you a little article that you might easily overlook, even if you saw the magazine in which it was reprinted, on a matter that now concerns us both—Housing for the Aged! There is nothing in it that will be particularly new to you, but I think it takes account of more factors than the people who usually deal with the subject handle, and tries to deal with them in a more normal and sensible way. We rejoiced in the happy report of your vacation with Margaret in Wales and we'll eagerly take you up on your suggestion of spending a couple of days on a joint expedition next spring— provided, of course, that we finally manage to carry through our so-often-broken plans.

WELWYN GARDEN CITY   15 November 1956

Dear Lewis
To your letter of 6 October I ought to have replied that your not mentioning my own contributions to the agricultural land use controversy was no grievance. It just happens to be a fact that I have for many years asserted the importance of garden produce almost alone. I have made sure that the authorities, and my opponents, knew of my arguments. The planning technicians here all identify this view as mine, but till now they have not taken the trouble to understand what I have been saying, though I have documented it again and again with the utmost clarity. I ought of course to have collected the arguments in some sort of printed memorandum of the kind that gets into research libraries, since no student can be expected to read the files of *T & CP* or other periodicals or conference reports. I have been too lazy, or too pre-occupied with immediate policy questions, to put a selection of the millions of words I have written into books. The belief I had that if you state ideas clearly anywhere they get somehow into currency is true, but my method makes the infusion too slow.

The Middle East and Hungarian affairs have caused new political alignments here and shaken us all up a lot in our thinking about the UN. Margaret and I find we can't go along with those of our friends who think there was no justification for the British-French action. What we are worried about now is whether the USA will give the UN a lead to effect a solution of the really critical Canal issue, or will merely work to return Israel and Egypt to the

Armistice line. For eight or ten years, till atomic energy alters the whole energy situation, the West depends on oil—and it does look as if there was a move by the USSR to break us up before oil ceases to be an absolute necessity. It looks also as if the USSR is in the gravest of trouble on its own doorstep, and because people in trouble act sometimes desperately this is not a source of hope but of greater anxiety. I have no doubt at all that Britain would withdraw its forces in Egypt if the UN really meant to settle the Canal problem on international lines. But the Afro-Asian group would leave that to 'negotiation' with Egypt on the futile lines that were being pursued before the British–French action, and I can't see France and Britain withdrawing with the prospect of the USSR continuing to support Egypt in a wrecking policy. We are therefore watching with great anxiety for the decision that Eisenhower is going to take. The belief in the USA that England is jingo or colonialist is simply wrong. Rightly or wrongly, our Government was in my opinion driven to its action by the conviction that things were drifting to a situation in which Russian mischief-making and Nasser's ambition would bring us to disaster. Eden is fundamentally a UN man, but he could not be a blue-eyed innocent as so many of the UNA supporters unhappily are. M.P.O., and remarkably enough Tom, just managed last night to stop our local UNA branch from a mere endorsement of the Gaitskell line, which fails to take account of the menace to this country and the West. It is certain that the Labour Party, if in power, could not have taken exactly this opposition line.

AMENIA, NEW YORK   26 November 1956

Don't talk about forgetfulness, dear F.J.: I have a feeling that I wrote you at least two letters without remembering, till after the letters were sealed, to say how sorry I was over the news of your having to undergo another eye operation. You are, in my memory, so much the very picture of the hale Englishman that each time some bit of surgery comes up I feel as if it were almost an insult to the Lord's handiwork.

I was glad to hear that you and Margaret have taken the stand you have toward the intervention in Egypt, dreadful bungle and fiasco as it has proved to be all round. I don't remember whether I fully expressed in my last letter what I think about it; but it seems to me that the people ultimately responsible for driving even timid Eden to desperation were Eisenhower and Dulles, and that my country bears the major share of the reproof for not having any firm policy about the near East to begin with, and for having built up the Egyptian dictator as far as we were able, only to turn him over without a protest to the Russians when they offered to supply him with weapons. If we had been interested in peace we would not have permitted an arms race to take place between Egypt and Israel; and once we took note of Russia's support we should have warned them that we would match it, plane for plane and tank for tank, with weapons for Israel. Our failure to do anything like this was partly due to our 'realistic' policy of placating the Arabs, partly, I have no doubt, to our over-commitment to atomic weapons, so that we had no ordinary infantry and tank equipment to spare—which would also account for our failure to back Britain up in a pinch, even if Eisenhower had had the courage and resolution to wish to do so.

True, I think that the Anglo–French intervention was badly conceived and badly timed; badly conceived because any move that might awaken a Russian response needed American backing if it were to be successful, and badly timed because they should have let the Israelis wipe out the Egyptian army and reach the Canal before making any military moves of their own. Yes, it was even badly executed because it should have been done more swiftly, with far greater force, or not done at all. But once one has granted that, one must add that Eisenhower's stupidity both before and after the event reached an all time high, and that is saying a great deal for such a resolutely uninformed and stupid man as Eisenhower actually is. The fact that my fellow-countrymen gave him such a resounding vote of confidence in this crisis, rewarding him as it were, for his errors, at first shocked me; but the fact is that his weaknesses mirror their own desires, for they wish to be assured that everything is going well when it is going badly, and the kind of leader they really admire is the sort of realist who can look facts in the face without recognising their existence! Though I took a private vow of silence when this mess began to develop I finally broke it the other day, to the extent of venting my feelings in a letter to the *New York Times*, and if they print it I will send you a copy.

You will gather from all this that I *don't* like Ike; but my negative attitude developed long before this crisis, from the time he turned his back on his old friend Marshall, who had been scurrilously attacked by McCarthy, and shook hands with McCarthy. Remembering that, it does not surprise me to find Eisenhower turning his back on the British and shaking hands with Nasser: it's all of one piece. The moral cowardice of a weak, self-righteous man, who is also stubborn enough to permit all the work in creating some sort of political and military solidarity in the West to be undone rather than to alter his own line of approach. If I were a British statesman at this moment I would bend every effort to establishing a United Europe, and, once I achieved this in some sort of rough working form, I would make it clear that the presence of American troops and installations in Britain was unwelcome. What is behind our short-sighted and mischievous American policy is something I have pointed out repeatedly on this side: the fact that Eisenhower as Chief of Staff and even more as President, has put all our military eggs into the nuclear extermination basket. (Neither Bradley nor Ridgeway, both better soldiers than Eisenhower, agreed with this policy. But, because the President is 'economy-minded' he overruled them and put himself in the hands of Radford, a 'total annihilation-ist'.) This puts us, willy-nilly, into an isolationist position: we have no equip-ment with which to counter Russian moves except the threat of wholesale retaliation, and when we get to that point our army strategists probably believe that allies would be almost as much liabilities as assets. Because Eisenhower, if not his military advisers, is unwilling to bring on a world catastrophe, he will continue to retreat, as he retreated after ineffective bluffing, from Korea, from Indo-China, and now from the Near East.

WELWYN GARDEN CITY   25 February 1957

Dear Lewis

I am glad to have your note of 18 February. I know I am not at my most effective just now as a correspondent or in any other capacity; in fact my state is such that I suspect senescence is at last making definite marks on me—though I have had the same feeling before and seemed to snap out of it, if at a somewhat lower elevation. I would like, if I had time, to philosophise about this in a series just running in a leading Sunday paper about survival after death: the line I would take (and I *haven't* time, so this is the only summary) is that it doesn't for me simplify the profound mystery of existence to believe in a conscious Creator, since that only pushes the problem of origins one stage further back, but that if I did believe in such a Creator I should regard the extinction of individuals as one of his best ideas. Tagore is the only poet I know of who beautifully expresses this idea: 'Life is not the one long journey; Brother, keep that in mind and rejoice'. I would add that almost as good an idea is that we do not know when Death is coming to us, and even can't be sure, unless we are very unsubtle, that other experiences don't await us after physical death—though that seems to me unlikely and unnecessary and a bit destructive of the extreme beauty of the first idea: 'The flower that once has bloomed', etc. We shouldn't value a flower, or personal life, in the same tragic way if we knew they lasted for ever. Probably all this will seem just banal to anyone who has been a natural philosopher all his life; but I'm a late developer and things don't dawn on me till fifty years after they are commonplace to people of deeper intelligence.

I am still deeply embroiled in the campaign for dispersal planning, which is held back by agricultural opposition and the treason of the architects—or rather the architectural writers—who have got themselves into key positions in the cultural press and in certain high-level political circles. I feel that every-body is against me, as they were against Roosevelt, except the electors. I can organise very effectively in the smaller circles—and therefore can produce a stalemate, which is better than a degringolade of planning—but I just don't know how to mobilise the 95 per cent of people who are, without any question, on my side in the matter of housing and town development standards. The situation is interesting at the moment, as there are new men in all the relevant Cabinet offices (except agriculture), and some at least are very definitely of our party. Sandys has gone 'up' to the major office of defence; he is a complete convert, and so is the new Minister of Housing; but Macmillan is more under agricultural influence, and after all, he's the big boss.

AMENIA, NEW YORK   3 March 1957

Your letter, dear F.J. was waiting for me yesterday when I came back after a week's absence in New Hampshire, talking to the young at their State University; and I write at once, not to respond to the many chords in yours that touched me, but on the off-chance that something in my own experience may throw a light on your present physical condition, which you attribute so gracefully to advancing age. Ever since my operation I have had recurrent periods of fatigue, inability to focus my thoughts, and depression. Half the time when this happened it turned out to be the result of an infected tooth, and I took for granted that this was the nature of the other attacks, too, though not so plainly manifested. But on a recent examination by a very able physician, he could find nothing wrong with me except a few white cells in my urine, the result of a low-grade infection which he told me—and he was the first doctor to do so—sometimes hangs on in the pocket left by the removed prostate. Instead of giving me an anti-biotic, he has prescribed an antiseptic, probably American, called Mandelamine, to be taken internally; and since taking it I have thrown off the lethargy that was again so drearily overtaking me. This may not be what ails you; but on the remote chance that it might be, since you had a prostate operation, too, I am passing the word on to you. With much sympathy for you both.

WELWYN GARDEN CITY   9 March 1957

Dear Lewis
Your very thoughtful letter came this morning, and as I think you may be lighting out for Europe any day now I reply to it at once. I doubt if there is really much wrong with me but the lifelong laziness that the smell of some interesting thing to chase more often than not puts into quasi-temporary abeyance. (I have been so much interested in so many things that observers

get the impression that I am naturally energetic.) I suppose I am a bit bored just now with the necessity of saying the same things again and again, which I have done for twenty-one years, and not being able to interest myself by thinking of a new way to say it. I did see my doctor yesterday, and told him I could find nothing specific wrong but a touch of rather persistent bronchial catarrh and this rise to the surface of my congenital laziness; but if he could take a score or so of years off my age it would be appreciated. Maybe what I really want is a priest or moral 'straightener' (*Erewhon*) of great experience of the ways of men, who can tell me (for instance) whether, when one feels tired in bed in the morning and yet is not sleeping, one should seek to relax more effectively or jump out of bed, have a cold bath and try to do some work. Medical men never seem to me to be interested in these, the real problems of health; and the psychologists seem to be mostly mad themselves. ('Mad doctors', as GKC said.) There should be medical men who double with medicine the undoubtedly necessary function of the priesthood—with a tenable cosmology as a background, not the Incarnation or any such witchcraft that a normal non-mystical person like me simply can't take.

I go to Venice for five days on 21 March—and I was childishly thrilled to receive a notice that the IFHTP Bureau meeting is in the Doge's Palace, Piazza San Marco. Venice bothers me: it is so overwhelmingly full of beauties, yet so silly as a piece of town development and so inhuman as a family environment. However, I won't blow it up.

WELWYN GARDEN CITY   25 March 1957

Dear Lewis

. . . I have just accepted a publisher's invitation to write (along with Arnold Whittick) an 'authoritative' book describing the British New Towns Achievement—real title not yet settled—for publication in 1958.

I am to be responsible for the account of the genesis of the idea, the prior experiments in planned estates and towns, and the character and economic and social significance of the new towns. Whittick, with some guidance from me, will do accurate detailed descriptions of the fourteen or fifteen individual towns in progress; and probably some shorter notes on projects overseas influenced by our towns. It is intended that the book shall be well produced with a lot of plans and photographs, so that it should be of practical value to governmental and municipal authorities, professional people and students in all countries.

Would you be willing to write the Introduction for this book? We have in mind a contribution of say 5,000 words, taking on some aspect of the subject that you would like to deal with, and perhaps stressing the international importance of the British adventure in this field.

BRUGES, BELGIUM [March–April 1957]

It was a great pleasure, dear F.J., to get your letter, along with the copy of *T & CP*. And I am delighted to learn of your proposed book. I take the invitation to write a foreword to it as an honour, almost a royal command, but I think 5,000 words might be heavy going and I'd not like to bargain for more than 3,000: anything above that would be accidental and gratuitous. Whatever arrangements you make with the publishers will be satisfactory to me.

As for inquiries about my availability. My main purpose in being in England is to get fresh material for *The Culture of Cities* and to edit the Branford papers: this will take up a good part of the five weeks I'll have there, if indeed I find I can stay till the first of August as now planned. I am already committed to an afternoon and evening at the TPI, and half committed to a lecture for Contemporary Arts. If something interesting turned up I might find time for it: so perhaps you'd better be neutral, or in the case of fuddy duddies, discouraging. I expect to be back in 1959 and will be able to get about more then. Did I tell you? Invitation to go to Cambridge University on a Fulbright Professorship. This should be kept secret, for it needs American confirmation in October.

WELWYN GARDEN CITY 8 April 1957

Dear Lewis
The death of Patrick Abercrombie is a sad blow to our section of the planning movement. My personal correspondence with him over the last twenty years would be of interest to a student of the development of the dispersal, green belts and new towns policy, but I am uncertain how far I could disclose it at present. For example, when he was a member of the Barlow Royal Commission I redrafted for him some of the key paragraphs of the majority report and drafted some of his own minority report—but it was all very 'hush-hush', and both of us were kept hard at this underground work by Mrs W. L. Hichens[1], who was in full agreement with the TCPA policy, and did much to press Abercrombie to take a more definite line when the Commission (and its Chairman) were taking a very vague one. She and Abercrombie did get the

---

[1] A member of the Barlow Royal Commission.

wording of the main recommendations considerably strengthened, but not enough to avoid the necessity of the minority report.

In fact, when the report was finally published I was in grave doubt for forty-eight hours whether to damn it as feeble, or to hail it (and interpret it) as a great Crossing of the Rubicon, because it could have been otherwise interpreted. Enthusiastic welcome, with some criticism of its wording, proved to my relief the right course. Barlow himself, with whom I maintained close contact in the subsequent campaign, moved very much in our direction after the Report, and after a time strongly supported our interpretation. Mrs Hichens thought Abercrombie was indefinite and weak; but the truth, I now think, is that he had not seen the whole issue in perspective before the Commission was set up, and being highly intelligent and humane he came to see it quite clearly during all that controversy. He became afterwards the most brilliant exponent of the dispersal policy in this country and because of his wide culture, literary ability, utter sincerity and extraordinary personal charm, exercised enormous influence. He was well aware that I thought he had compromised too far with Forshaw in accepting such vast areas at 200 and 136 persons an acre in the County of London plan, and he proposed much better standards in the later Regional Plan of 1944. But it was a matter of what he had found possible; he never fluffed the issue in his own mind. I can always forgive a planner for compromising with immensely powerful forces. What often offends me is that they proceed to idealise their compromises. Abercrombie never did that. He continued to evidence to me a 'conscience' about his compromise, though he manfully stood by it; and it has become binding in practice, to my regret.

LONDON   29 June 1957

Dear F.J.

I found that the letter I thought I had written you got no further, in the mad rush of London, than the envelope. By now you've at least received Sophy's thanks for all your varied hospitalities. To that I now add my apologies for bringing in your name on Thursday in a context where it might be misunderstood. When I prepared the talk in my mind it had never entered my head. 'Spontaneity' sometimes pays a heavy penalty: and I'm sorry if you were in any way the victim—though of course there *is* a long standing, unresolved difference between us on the subject of densities; and I think it's important for you to realise that many people on your side, in no wise attached to the *Architectural Review* attitude, do not accept your and Unwin's views as final on this subject. But the TPI meeting was no place to bring this matter up: so I abjectly and humbly apologise.

Dear F.J.

In looking over my correspondence file I came upon your invitation to write an introduction to your New Towns book, and it suddenly occurred to me that, though my views on density have not changed since I wrote the Howard Introduction, you may now feel that my open difference with you on this matter in a book on New Towns would, for you, invalidate or nullify my agreement on so many other matters. Since neither of us can expect to convert the other at this late moment I could well understand this feeling, so please don't feel any need to hold to your invitation. Our friendship is too old and solid to be shaken by such a matter, I trust. I may not have an opportunity to say this tonight: so I seize this moment.

Dear Lewis

Thanks for honouring the TCPA with your company at the House of Lords dinner, which was for everybody who met you and Sophy there a most delightful occasion.

I just have not had the leisure this week to write you about the differences of opinion between us. I am surprised that you should think I should be offended because you do not agree with my formulation of a standard of housing density. What did rather distress me at the TPI meeting was your accusing me of thinking a city was no more than a place for the growing of vegetables! A great many other people were shocked at that, too—but I am so used to being misrepresented in that very way that I was in fact only intellectually distressed, and I put on an act when I pretended to be emotionally affected.

I do think you are completely mistaken in the particular criticism you made of the new towns, and that it is extremely important for your own influence over here, as well as for the credit of the new towns, that you should really go right into this question with me—or if you prefer it, with Sir Thomas Bennett[1] or H. W. Wells,[2] who have been handling new town developments. In an hour or so I could show you exactly why I am sure—absolutely sure—you are wrong in this case. It is not a matter of a marginal difference of views on density figures.

Will you have time to talk this over before you go?

---

[1] Chairman of Crawley New Town Corporation.
[2] Chairman of the Commission for the New Towns.

Dear F.J.

I hardly know how to reply to your letter of the fifth. For one thing, it is hard
to understand that you should still be distressed over my playful and passing
allusion to our differences over density at the TPI; for that context showed
plainly that I was thinking only of density, and not implying that you weren't,
what everyone there well knew you to be, the tireless advocate of the new
town principle, with the accent on the whole town rather than the residential
area alone. I might counter your distress here by what might have been my
much deeper distress over your concluding remarks at the dinner you had
taken the trouble to organise. But the fact is that your shots fell so wide of
of the mark that the only thing I could feel was sadness over the fact that you
were not, at the moment, doing justice to yourself. But your notion that an
hour spent with you would put me right on the matter of density, seems to me
to betray a blindness that is almost as wilful as your suggestion that the
reason I did not agree with you about densities was that I didn't read what
you had written on the subject. Of course I have read what you have
written; and the reason I don't agree with you is that I do not accept your
premises.

   If I took as my starting point the lowest possible density for housing that
could be called urban housing at all, the highest possible standard of open
spaces for playing fields and parks, and the greatest distance necessary between
houses separated by a street meant for wheeled vehicles, then I would have to
agree that the only kind of town that could be built are those that the New
Towns actually are. But within limits, all these fixed requirements of yours are,
and should be, modifiable; and in that modification, balancing one factor
against another, lies the town planner's art. I reject your stereotype for
the same reason that I reject Le Corbusier: he makes a fetish of uniform
high density, you of uniform low density, and in that one-sidedness neither
of you do justice to the varied and complex requirements of city living.
This is not an abstract conclusion: it is the result of both living and
observation.

   What you would have me do, by your statistical demonstration, is to deny
the evidence of my eyes and the results of my own experience in urban living.
I find a suburb of three or four thousand people, at from four to twelve people
per acre, altogether charming physically, though I do not think that it suffices
for many important human needs: but to multiply that area by twenty and
call the result a new town because, by travelling by bus or car, one can reach
a factory centre or a community centre, is to remove the element of charm and
create something that—though better than most parts of most existing cities—

is still far less than would be possible through good design, which conceived of the city in other terms than openness alone. This is not a new position of mine: it has threaded through my whole work. But it has been clarified, during the last ten years, by discovering that the New Towns had not gone beyond the planning principles of Letchworth or Welwyn and had, indeed, been bound down by an arbitrary set of space standards to be nothing other than a more extensive and voluminous reproduction of these earlier efforts.

The position you have taken, dear F.J., seems to you an impregnable one because you simply can't imagine any reasonable man having another point of view than your own, or proceeding from a different set of axioms than those which seem to you self-evident. Therefore you identify New Towns with only one kind of urban design. In that, I think, you do a serious disservice to the cause that you have otherwise so powerfully aided; and you drive most of the people who differ from you into advocating density for density's sake. That kind of opposition can be easily disposed of, but you can't so easily dispose of mine; and since that is so it is easier for you to assume that I am 'uninformed', that I haven't really read your arguments, etc.

I am perfectly willing to argue all these matters out with you, at length; but the argument had better be about axioms and preconceptions, about standards and aims, for it is on these matters that we differ; and it is here that I have a more catholic and comprehensive view of what constitutes a city than you do.

I shall be in London, off and on, for the next three weeks; and I will be happy if you'll have lunch with me next week or the week after and talk things over further. I've been frank in this letter, as I was at the dinner, because I believe that the worst disservice one can do a friend is to withhold a criticism or a dissent on a matter of great importance to both parties. I have more than once expressed to you what I have said in this letter; but apparently I did not do it bluntly enough to make any impression. At least that error or weakness has here been overcome.

WELWYN GARDEN CITY   23 July 1957

Dear Lewis
I find I won't have time today to set out my theory of the root of our difference; I have only some minutes between the office and a rather unwelcome bit of community obligation—a presentation to a retiring local headmaster who is thought well of by lots of people. I can only sketch one or two points on which you must have misunderstood me.

I don't stand out for a uniform density whether people like it or not. I think conscious popular desires, when persistent, are important; I am even hesitant to resist them when I think them low or pernicious—though I admit a difficulty there. (I doubt if I am really a 'reformer'; but probably I get over the logical difficulty by taking refuge in a Chestertonian belief that common prejudices are almost invariably sound).

I see no conflict however between popular desires (in England) and what may be a lofty sociological belief in the value of a good family life. I was much in tune with your criticism of the LCC Plan of 1943–44—that it would push family life out of central London. It is my own experience as a housing manager, which I often check with present managers, that impressed on me the strength of the desire for the two-storey (or one- or three-storey) house with private garden. We keep checking the numbers who want this, and everywhere (in Great Britain) it comes out at something like 90 per cent. I can't see how this should be ignored for our country and our current programme.

I have not proposed the universal application of the maximum density standard, to which I am driven by simple calculation, for the garden-type low house. I certainly do suspect that it is latently desired in most European countries—but of course not by architects. I attach very little importance indeed to a consensus of opinion among technicians on a matter of this kind. I have so much direct evidence that they do not know what people like—or even what they *are* like. This is partly a class matter. One could develop a Marxist theory of the thing.

Second main point. I don't think I underestimate the complexity of modern civilisation. I have not until the last week or two doubted the necessity of fairly high degrees of population concentration to civilisation; and even now I only question it to save myself from dogmatism. But I can't think of a single element of civilisation or city 'culture' that depends on densities higher than I would regard as all right for family living. Except, of course, the architects' special value in visual enclosure; and this I like, but would not push against values that have a stronger and more general appeal.

Third point. You accuse me of thinking our new towns the only possible sort of town. Is it not you who pursue a stereotype by thinking them not even one of the possible sorts of town? I should make exactly the opposite criticism but it would be dangerous at the present stage of acceptance of the whole dispersal idea for me to criticise too strongly. You do more harm than you imagine by your own criticism. If you were right I should still think this; but as it happens I think your particular criticism was mistaken. We can discuss this; it is not a matter on which I should be at all inclined to be resentful of discussion.

Dear F.J.

When I didn't succeed in dropping around to see you once more, before leaving London, I promised myself to at least write you soon; but I was reckoning without the eighty odd letters that had piled up on my desk during my four months absence, though the supposedly more important ones had already been forwarded to me. Nor did I reckon with the ton of second class matter and books whose sorting and throwing away took the better part of two whole days. Now I have tunneled far enough through this litter to have at least a sense of release, though half the letters are still unanswered, and I turn to you, to thank you—you and Margaret—for all that you did to make the English part of our journey so exciting, so rewarding and so memorable. All in all, I never got so much out of any trip before; and this applies with equal force to all that happened to me in England, even apart from gold medals! Whether my revision of *The Culture of Cities* makes it a better book than the first one is a matter in the lap of the gods; all I can say is that I am infinitely better prepared to do a good job, for many reasons, than I was in 1935–37 when I wrote that book.

The two days that I spent, one going around with the LCC people to Roehampton and other places, and the other going over Hemel Hempstead with the director of the corporation and his architect, didn't resolve in my mind any of the issues between us: in neither place did I find, in the scheme as a whole, any adequate interpretation of what a city can and should be, though there were occasional spots in both plans that were admirable. I was tempted to write a little more about the subject in a *New Yorker* Sky Line, but when I looked back at what I had written in 1953 I found that four years had done little to modify my views; and that the points which shocked you in my speeches had already been expressed in those early criticisms.

The new towns have, oddly enough, lost the pedestrian scale; and since I am no enemy of vegetable gardens I think that the only way to restore it may be to group such gardens as they are traditionally grouped, in allotment gardens on the edge of the city, as part of the green-belt and not in the midst of it. I think there's reason to put a greater stress on the neighbourhood than you do as the essential unit out of which bigger units, including the city, emerge; and that the neighbourhood must have, within easy reach, all that mothers and children require for their sustenance, including many things not now provided, like a small nursing home. This intimacy allows for the small private flower garden, and plenty of space for playgrounds on the intimate scale, but not for the bigger sort of playing field, which again should be at the edge of the city. But I shall have to leave the supporting reasons for these views to fuller development in the book itself.

Hemel Hempstead did not have the effect of convincing me, as you had hoped, that I was wrong about all the wasted and functionless open space, for I was actually horrified at the loose way in which it had been used, quite as much as I was at Stevenage, for it did not have the greater architectural beauty of Harlow to redeem it. I was driven quite against my just counsels of prudence, to express my dismay over a plan their architect had concocted, with the aid of Jellicoe, to cut off their shopping centre from its parking lot by a watercourse, and thus spoil the charming bit of landscape that now exists there and which should have even greater uses as the centre grows more popular, in a way that an obstructive body of water could not. But I don't think that my protests registered.

WELWYN GARDEN CITY   6 January 1958

Dear Lewis

The partial recovery of my left eye from the cutlery of the surgeons imposed almost complete motionlessness for ten or twelve days, and perhaps an interval of a month in customary routine. But the business went according to plan and the hospital experience was on the whole interesting and not unpleasant. In Bart's one sees English energy, organisation and technique at its highest—not excelled anywhere—and in a general ward one is reassured about human courage and kindliness.

I hope *The Culture of Cities* is shaping satisfactorily. I am becoming almost Marxian in my view of the history of cities. If the underlying English country pattern is feudal, the urban pattern of Southern Europe begins to seem to me to reflect a worse pattern—that of Slavery. In all modern societies a large middle class has escaped to suburbs—but the masses are still largely in barracks and compounds; and the privileged seem only too ready to give them sanitary and sophisticated versions of the same things. The Anglo-Saxons destroyed the Roman cities. I suppose I am half an aboriginal Anglo-Saxon; but I am as much an optimistic Macaulay schoolboy infatuated with the potentialities of scientific progress. So I visualise Dispersal and New Towns as a means to the marriage of both worlds—exactly old Howard's inspiration, though he could express it in a beautifully non-highbrow manner to which no-one nowadays dare rise.

CAMBRIDGE, MASSACHUSETTS   12 January 1958

Your two letters, coming in quick succession, dear F.J., have somewhat allayed my anxieties as to how you were faring, though I am grieved to learn that you have had still another surgical ordeal to go through. If anyone is to be afflicted in such a fashion, however, he might well pray for your temperament and discipline in facing it. In that respect you've set me a standard that I will find hard to approach, at least in the minor ailments of life, for I have found that in the larger difficulties one can summon up unsuspected resources, at least for a time. At all events, I am happy to hear that you've been in good hands and that things have gone well: that your head is not very bloody and is still, happily, unbowed.

We have been here—I still write from Cambridge, for we don't go back to Amenia till the end of the month—since mid-September, occupying these generous rooms forming half of an old house, rented from a Harvard professor named Howard Mumford Jones. This is a professorial quarter of Cambridge, blessed with a dead-end street, so it is as quiet as Amenia; and right behind our house is the even more enormous 3-storey wooden house occupied once by the great William James and still held by his ancient son. My professorship at MIT calls for only a two hour seminar per week, plus occasional student conferences, and were it not for the fact that both Sophy and I have suffered, by turns, from the wicked, debilitating aftermath of what seemed a *mild* flu, without even a fever, we would count this as one of the happiest sojourns of our life, for we have pleasant neighbours, many good friends and a generally friendly and pleasant environment, just a few blocks from Harvard Yard. This arrangement is to be continued two more years, and I count myself extremely lucky for having drawn such an honourable sinecure. I had hoped to get down to work on my book by the first of November but my own good intentions have fared no better than yours. Partly, I've been loath to begin till I had delved even deeper into the earlier history of the city, and there's been so much interesting archaeological research and anthropological interpretation during the last generation that I've not before tried to come abreast of, that this has taken a good part of my time.

Besides this, I have been appalled at the childish attitudes of my countrymen since the launching of the Russian earth satellite, and the even more infantile policies, political and 'military', pursued by the American government, abetted by the leaders in both parties, even Stevenson. Our whole programme for 'containing' Russia has been based upon illusions that should have been discarded long ago. We are heading steadily and even rapidly toward total desecration, because it never has occurred to the rigid minds that have developed these policies that when one is faced with an impossible situation, the only wise course open is to retreat. Like our 'expanding economy' our military policy can move in only one direction, even if the final destination is total disaster. The fact is that we all live in a state of total insecurity; and there is no way of lifting this insecurity without renouncing the diabolical means that

10

have brought us to this pass: all our weapons of mass extermination. No course is half as risky and half as dangerous as that we are now following, in competition with Russia. If the people of Europe were half awake, they would exert even more pressure than they are now doing to force a prompt removal of our stategic air force; and so far from welcoming rocket bases would not accept them at any price. I have been trying to make some of these facts plain to my fellow countrymen; but except for a talk in Washington, where I had an invited cross section of official Washington to listen to me, including three Air Force Generals and the head of the Vanguard rocket project, I find that it is still almost impossible to publish such views, except in pacifist circles, where one speaks to the already converted.

What you observe about the upper classes escaping to the suburbs is horrifyingly true in America now, where, in cities like New York, the older parts are more and more dedicated to the underprivileged minorities; and in Washington, if the exodus continues, the core of the city will be simply one vast Negro slum. This has been going on, more or less, since the foundation of cities, with perhaps exceptional periods like the early middle ages when the best life possible was that in the still fresh and new cities, not yet crowded or overgrown. Space, with country or suburban living, has always been an upper class privilege. I'd go even further with your Marxian hypothesis and say that at the beginning the city took form as a military means of holding down an exploited population: hence the function of the inner citadel, walled against the town's own inhabitants, which one finds in the earliest cities. I hope to have some fresh things to say about this in my book: things I discovered through writing *The Transformations of Man*.

AMENIA, NEW YORK   8 May 1958

Dear F.J.

Your remarks about the betrayal of the Urban Renewal programme awakens very heartfelt echoes: all the more because, though you are the first person to notice the relationship, I feel a little guilty at having even invented a phrase that has lent itself to such perverse misuse. Perhaps one should always in future use that term in quotation marks. Fortunately others begin to share our doubts. In particular there is a young woman named Jane Jacobs, an associate editor of *The Architectural Forum*, who for the last two years has been making a series of devastating criticisms of our whole method of urban renewal, on a wholesale scale, massive in their common sense, shrewd in their perception of social and personal relations. As I predicted in 1940, some of our skyscraper housing projects have become filthy slums, even worse than those they replaced, because the social life that held the old quarters together at an elementary level of neighbourly morality has been disrupted: so they have a high number of juvenile delinquents and the very elevators get used as public lavatories.

From February on I've been at work at my book, which must now be called a successor to *The Culture of Cities* rather than its revision. Almost against my will, I found myself being pushed into new fields I had never fully explored and making fresh excursions; much to my surprise the book has taken command of me, as if my unconscious were resolved that I should not leave this subject for good without making a fresh contribution to it. As perhaps I've told you, I think I've discovered some fresh things about the origin of the city and its nature that people have never interpreted adequately before, and if I am right this will cast some light on the problems we face today. But all this takes time, and the manuscript I hoped to have finished in June will not be ready, even if things go smoothly, till next January at the earliest; and I may even have to take a brief trip to Europe next spring to check up on certain things I've not personally verified, and to explore a few matters that I've never bothered to look into.

WELWYN GARDEN CITY   1 August 1958

Dear Lewis

... I am, however, always at work; the minuteness of my output distresses me, and I wonder often whether I am just immoral or slowing up through senility (as diagnosed by the American Immigration Officer in 1947). Perhaps I have disorganised my work too much this year by travelling; I was in Germany for three weeks in the spring; and in May–June I had a month in the USSR and Poland. The prolegomena and aftermaths of travel absorb more time than I care to recognize; and probably at my age I am trying to take in and digest more than I shall ever have time to make use of. 'It never done no good to me, But I can't drop it if I tried' (Kipling). For on 26 August I am leaving, with Margaret this time, for another busman's holiday of a month: the Liège Congress and our study-tour of Jugoslavia. It is beginning to penetrate my stupidity that I must stay put for a year or so and do some real work. Though I write a condolence letter to the widow of a friend once a week, I still can't quite take it in that I am 73 myself—simply because I feel exactly the same as I did at 20, and much less mortal than I did at 17.

Administration is the thief of time, of course; and I have not yet shaken off the daily responsibilities of the TCPA and its monthly magazine; and I think this is genuinely because we are still actively in a battle in which we count, and the line will be a little weakened when I retire to base. A day in the office, the telephone, letters to be answered, staff to direct, and not unimportant at this season—visitors from many countries to entertain and inform, in return for many favours received abroad—such a day leaves me at 6 or 7 pm feeling I have done nothing whatever, and I go to my study desk at home and just potter ineffectively or write letters to sympathetic friends. The trouble is that I know what I am in fact doing is not quite useless; but it isn't what I want to do and think I ought to be doing in the small amount of time I have left. I sometimes wish I had a Father Confessor; but I know that if I had, I should only argue with him about his untenable theology. I have no gift of despair and therefore (I suppose) no capacity of self-salvation. Calvin would write me off as unjustified, and Swedenborg would tell me I am already in Heaven. And Darwin would tell me, much more plausibly, though I ignore the obvious truth, that I am just one of millions of ants destined to be sucked into the beautifully-adapted long snout of the Anteater.

I have had a lot of correspondence with the USSR Ministry of Construction. They have fully adopted the Dispersal and Green Belt and New Towns policy, which they think they can operate more logically than Britain. I found the prestige of the TCPA and FJO there disconcertingly high. And they now want a hell of a lot of information and advice; more work for me. I feel far from adequate in these relationships.

AMENIA, NEW YORK   10 August 1958

. . . It's good to hear of all your peregrinations and adventures: worthy of Tennyson's Ulysses. 'Old age hath yet its honour and its toil'. Your youthful zeal and energy turns me green with envy, though as a matter of fact, ever since I had an attack on my liver and cut down radically on the amount of fat I consume, I have felt immensely improved in all sorts of ways, and can do more physical work without tiring, at 62, than I was able to do at 12: so perhaps in time I may catch up with you, in everything except the capacity to travel.

As for the book, it got possession of me last February and try as I will I can't shake myself free of it; for it insists upon my running down all sorts of clues, on devious trails I would prefer not to follow, and it has made me raise questions about the origin and nature of the city, and about the actual nature of particular functions, I was prudent enough in my youth to side-step. So I have had to do much more work than I originally planned to do on this job, and instead of being the relatively compact and readable book I had hoped to write it has sprawled in every direction; and even though it will not, thank heaven, succeed in being exhaustive, it might as well be, for I am bound to think it will be unreadable. The historic portion of *The Culture of Cities* will lie embedded within the larger mass: four chapters, surrounded by eight others that begin with paleolithic man and reach forward apprehensively toward post-historic man! Those who originally liked *The Culture of Cities* will regard those four chapters as veritable jewels surrounded by a dull matrix, and perhaps they will be right. At least there were large parts of my early book that I found myself unable to improve. Even if my new discoveries and new insights are as good as I think they are—and there are times when they seem to me quite striking, almost revolutionary in their importance—I know in advance that they cannot hope to have the impact of my earlier work, feeble and superficial as that often seems to me now. For whatever the defects of the original, it had the advantage of coming out at the right moment; and no matter what year its successor comes out, it will, I fear, be the wrong moment and will encounter the same dull 'So what?' that my *Transformations of Man* encountered, even in England.

I am not surprised about the new Russian interest in decentralisation and dispersal. That was looked upon as a 'left deviation' back in 1930, but in 1947 I predicted that the Russians would meet the threat of atomic bombing much more effectively than we ever could by carrying out such a policy, and I have even conjectured that they might be building 'Potemkin villages' in imitation of Moscow, a hundred miles away from the real city, to tempt American bombers to waste their bombs on these fake targets. That might help account for travel restrictions no less than rocket bomb sites!

Did I ever thank you for the reference you made, months ago, to the current perversion of my old term, urban renewal? I had a vague remembrance that I might have invented that term, and your words confirmed me. But what has happened to it gives no cause for anything but shame and indignation. In America it has simply become a policy of lending government aid to assemble land for the private investor, who gets a further government subsidy in acquiring the land at a lower price than the market would demand. The whole business is scandalous: socialisation for the sake of the rich accompanied by the expropriation and the expulsion of the poor! This use of the term has made renewal a filthy word—like 'love' or 'creativity' in the mouth of an advertising copy writer.

WELWYN GARDEN CITY   25 October 1958

Dear Lewis
MPO and I had really a wonderful time in Yugoslavia with our TCPA party of twenty-four: a country, of course, of tremendous geographical variety and

a meeting-point of many cultures; also at the moment a crucible for experiments in methods of industrial governance differing from those in the USSR and its satellite countries. We hadn't time to begin to assess these latter; but we met historians and planners able to tell us far more than I could assimilate about the cities. You would have made more of these studies of Belgrade, Dubrovnik, Split, Sarajevo, Ljubljana and Rijeka (Fiume) than I could. I am still floundering in the flood of powerful impressions; and I know that when I seem to feel my feet again it will only be because the flood has, so to say, subsided into the sands of forgetfulness.

We had a day with Clarence Stein in Liège along with Mr and Mrs Broughton of the USA, whom you also know. I thought B and CS clashed a bit at first; but as the day went on B's honest enthusiasms thawed some resistance in CS and they fetched out hidden aspects in each other that it was nice to see. Met unexpectedly by me, Clarence seemed somehow shrunk and frail compared with my memory of him, but after a little he rounded and expanded a bit, or I corrected my memory—I don't know which. Of course we are all older; but beside him I, who think of myself as thin, felt quite porcine, gross, clumsy. I noted in him again, as ten years ago in New York at sunset, the ecstasy that essentially urban architectural effects give him—quite as acute, I think, as that of the aesthetes who edit the magazines. But like Unwin he is pulled two ways, having sympathy with the less sophisticated pleasure in simple surroundings, and perhaps he is more sensitive to natural beauty than Unwin, who wasn't deficient in that way. He is much less conscious of other men's thinking than you are, or even than I am; yet he seems to scorn nobody. If he is a bit self-centred it isn't through common egoism, but because of an almost unconscious sense of creative power—of a mission. And, I think, of partial disappointment that he will not allow to grow to a grievance. His mind, always looking for things to appreciate, obliterates bores, but I think doesn't recognize enemies. That is a slight criticism; I believe one should love one's enemies, but should know who they are. But Clarence is a noble person.

AMENIA, NEW YORK   21 December 1958

My correspondence has fallen as seriously in arrears, dear F.J., as yours, without I'm afraid half as much excuse; for a man whose only official duties are a two-hour seminar each week must be a weak character to fall so far behind, even if he takes on extra lectures in distant cities and finds himself sear and worn after a succession of dinner parties and such like entertainments. Actually, I've done a fair amount of quiet work, reading books that had escaped me before and reflecting on what I wrote last spring and summer. Though I will be hard put to it to finish my revision of the book this spring, I still prayerfully hope that this won't be impossible; and at all events I have the feeling that, even if I take a little longer, this book will possibly prove to be a classic work, in a sense that *The Culture of Cities* was not—and could not be. My framework is a purely historical one; I leave the future and its moulding to another book, whether I write it myself or someone else carries through the plentiful suggestions I hope to leave in my last chapter. As a result of my work in two independent fields, I think I have some fresh things to say about the origin of the city. The two fields where I got some of my new insights are technology and religion; and when I tried out some of my ideas at a symposium of Mesopotamian and Egyptian archaeologists a few weeks ago, at Chicago, I got an unexpectedly favourable reception. What I think I have discovered about the early form of the city—which remained, more or less, its constant form until the nineteenth century—throws a light on many of our present difficulties, especially those that arise out of the massing and conglomerate urban growth of large populations.

All this is a surprise to me, as I think I must already have confessed to you. My thoughts have been so little occupied with cities these last ten years, or rather so much more occupied with other matters, that when I began I had no sense of having anything new to contribute to the field, beyond a few minor revisions that might save my work from premature obsolescence. True: I've written a series of articles on cities that shed light a little further in some directions than I had done in 1938, but these were all concerned with contemporary matters, not with the more ultimate subject of how and why the city came into existence and what functions it performs or has failed to perform. I did not seek this new perspective, certainly, and would probably not have found it had I gone about it more consciously, but once it presented itself to me I saw its implications and have learned much in the act of following them through. I wish I could tell you more about the work, in detail, but that would take time, and a half-baked explication would be worse than none. So have patience and keep well—and in another year or so, perhaps, you shall see the finished work! If it should shake some of your present ideas I'll confess that some of mine have been shaken, too.

It was a great delight to me to get your impressions of Clarence Stein. I have been so close to him that I never quite know whether my own good opinions of him find any echo in others. In many ways his talents were as modest as his personality; but in his most creative period, from 1920 to 1930, he used them to the full and enhanced them by his capacity, which grew out of his modest and single-minded devotion, for using other people to the full and bringing out their best possibilities. Had he continued in health and vigour through the thirties the history of planning would be a different one, at least in America, than what it turned out to be; and it is ironic, indeed bitter, that the very opportunities of the thirties, which he helped to make, were not given to him. The very people he had brought forward, including Catherine Bauer, turned their back on him at a critical moment and went in for a more 'practical' approach to housing; though a little while ago, at a conference, Catherine openly declared that she would never have promoted Public Housing if she could have anticipated that it would become the monstrous caricature that it has actually become. By the same token, in reverse, Clarence's work, even at its most conventional, now seems much better and sound than most of what has been done since.

WELWYN GARDEN CITY   24 December 1958

Dear Lewis

I am very glad to have your letter of 21st, just to hand, with its evidence of the excitement of creative analysis. I shall look forward with much interest to reading what you are to say about the origin of cities, but I don't know enough about that subject to have any views to be shaken, or so in my uncritical ignorance I think. I suppose I haven't got much beyond the recognition that the specialisation of functions and the advance of technology 'naturally' tend to population clusters; that any cluster is a potential market for things and services and a pool of potential workers; that associated labour in workshops, and later mechanised factories, necessitates in a pedestrian age masses of dwellings near by; that individuals who want to trade or take things for sale go where they can find workers and people to sell to; that individuals who want work, or more remunerative work than they can get on the land, go where enlarging or new functions are to be found; and that until recently there was no governmental or other conscious regulation of the process of the growth of settlements, short of some crisis such as the lack of sufficient food to feed the local population.

I state all this very crudely, because I have never in fact attempted to bring my ideas from this sort of vague working back to beginnings, from facts that I know in the contemporary world (with perhaps a little influence not studiously considered from Plato and a hundred other such simple souls); and in doing so I see at once that my statement might well need a lot of correction. For instance, there may have been all sorts of social, religious or even unconscious governmental limiting forces at work, differing much from place to place. I would be interested in any news of these, of course. But would they substantially alter my vague general conception? That towns may at certain times have been imposed on an unwilling population by state policies, as collective farming was imposed on the USSR in our time, I can, of course, believe; but I would have thought that an incidental variant of a general process that has deeper causes. However, I chatter merely. All this may be quite beside the mark, and nothing to do with your discoveries, which I cannot doubt are significant.

I hope you will have a good look at my latest New Towns issue of *T & CP*, which I regard as the best yet. The unsigned writing in it is as usual mine, and I have taken a great deal of trouble to concentrate some very important facts and figures, and to summarise the sixty years' history of the new towns movement. I would much value a comment from you on the total effect. It is all done for the purpose of renewing the pressure for the dispersal and decongestion policy, which is so weak at present that Britain is once more drifting, if not as fatally as the USA.

PHILADELPHIA   4 April 1959

. . . Since the first of February we have been very comfortably settled in Philadelphia, in a remaining row house handsomely done up by the university for their visiting professors in the School of Fine Arts, and we've never found life in Philadelphia, which is far from our favourite American city, so satisfactory. None the worse for my present work, too, because I am just a thousand feet from the library and for once am finishing up a book with all the resources I need for checking and filling out weak points. The book still has me in its thrall and I have been working at it with utmost diligence; but it has been growing to alarming proportions, so, after I get the 'final' draft done, I will probably have to spend another month or so in cutting it down to reasonable size and preventing the reader from getting hopelessly bored by too conspicuous patches of erudition.

For all its details, for all its length, it will only be a sampling of the field of urban history, far from the whole story. Except in the case of the earliest Near Eastern Cities, I deal with nothing with which I am not reasonably familiar: so I confine my interpretation to Western Europe and North America, leaving out even parts of them, like Spain and Russia, to say nothing of your fascinating Jugo-Slavia, because I want to use as little material as possible that I have not had a chance of verifying with my own eyes. One can't hold to this principle too inexorably, but it is my guiding line. Incidentally, in my analysis of Roman city building I've come to the conclusion that Rome actually developed a new towns policy; for none of the settlements of the Republic or the Empire were for populations over 50,000 people; and they were much better examples of Roman municipal progress than was the great city herself. Somebody must have thought this out, in government or in the bureaucracy, but like so much that we want most to know about in history there is no record of all this, except the towns themselves.

WELWYN GARDEN CITY   27 April 1959

Dear Lewis

Margaret and I are just off to Austria for a three weeks holiday-study tour with a small TCPA party, and I have only time for a perfunctory reply to your letter of 4 April, glad as I am to have it.

My excitement is naturally rising at the prospect of new light from you on city history. And I am particularly interested in your discovery of a new towns policy in ancient Rome. It is a pity, I sometimes think, that no one seems to have examined the papers of Edward Gibbon with a town-planning pre-occupation. He spent a long time in Italy before starting *The Decline and Fall*, and I have not the slightest doubt that he had a very full knowledge of the development of towns. It is evident in his great work that he was 'planning-conscious' (as David Hume was also, with less knowledge of details—see his essay on *The Populousness of Ancient Nations*). But he would have no reason to think his public would be interested in physical development, as we are today. I wish some student could be put on to go through his papers from this viewpoint.

Margaret is still struggling with the arthritic affliction; but I hope the Austrian tour, though we shall travel a lot, will be much better for her than housework. I have had a set-back in my activities in the last two months through a touch of 'flu', which seemed mild, but has left me with a slightly erratic heart, so that I am advised to limit physical (not mental) exertion for an indefinite time. This and a lot of other work has obstructed progress with the New Towns book, and I have had to arrange another postponement of publication. However, I now see a possibility of resigning daily executive work for the TCPA, since younger people of real capacity have at last turned up, after twenty-five years of enchainment.

As to the international situation, Margaret and I follow it closely, and share your deep anxiety, though I don't think either of us could agree with such a venture of faith as unilateral nuclear abnegation. There is a case for absten-tion by Britain, of course, on the ground that the USA and Russia provide in fact a balance of threats. But I don't think our standing aloof is practical politics here and doubt its international wisdom anyway. But I appreciate your intense consciousness of the dangers. I think this is shared by responsible people in all European countries, including Russia; I don't know about China,

where the Revolution may not be so sure of itself, and some ruler might well
go reckless as well as, in your word, 'mad'.

AMENIA, NEW YORK   2 September 1959

Dear F.J.

. . . I had had a splendid bout of work in Philadelphia, almost too splendid,
in fact, for the presence of a secretary ready to make a fair copy of my typewritten scrawls prompted me to write almost 200,000 words between February and mid-May; and that would have been a killing pace, even if I were
twenty years younger. My illness interposed and partly counteracted this folly,
lest I continue it too long, but I can think of better and more rational, to say
nothing of more enjoyable, kinds of vacation. As I've probably told you before, my book is overcrowded with superfluous knowledge, which I take it is
one of the symptoms of old age. When I was young I could magnificently
condense and, what was better, I never was bothered by any deficiency of
knowledge: I either jumped over the open spaces or filled them up with
fabrications of the imagination. Those who knew better might be indignant
but they could hardly be bored. Now I find myself writing as if I were the very
creature I had sworn all my life not to be: a specialist, writing with the cir-
cumspectness of one courting the good opinion of rival specialists, and
nothing could be more fatal to literary felicity.

The fresh things in the book are all in the chapters dealing with antiquity:
when I come to the Middle Ages I have more to say, but for me at least it
lacks novelty and originality and it remains to be seen if I can recover any of
these qualities in the final chapters, where I treat the suburb and the metropolis as urban forms. Isn't it strange that no one has bothered to write a
critical history of the suburb, as such? There has been a spate of rather
shallow sociological analyses of the suburb in the United States but all of
these, like so much of 'scientific' thinking, are only one generation deep. Much
of the data on the form and contents of the suburb, which could have been
gathered easily a generation ago, has been overlaid by new growths, so that
we have almost forgotten one of the accidental but formative characteristics
of the pre-motorised suburb, strung along the railroad line: that it was a green-
belt community, with all the houses within walking distance of the railroad
station, leaving an open belt, still often farmland, between. Some of this will
be in my chapter, but for lack of previous work by other people or even myself it won't have quite the density I'd like it to have. All through the latter
part of the book I find that the chief obstacle to my writing is all that I have
already written in *The Culture of Cities*, for there is little that I said in 1938
that I would go back on now. Perhaps the matter on which my mind has

changed most is the section on The Death of the Monument, for I don't
think I paid sufficient attention either to memory of continuity in human
affairs—but on *everything* my angle of vision has shifted a little and I find it
hard to bring my early images and my present ones into a common focus. But
enough about my book.

You can't imagine what pleasure I have at the prospect of your verses
being put together in a book, for as both a humorist and as a deft turner of
phrase you are in a class by yourself, at least in this generation; and although
both of us have had to discard half a dozen possible careers in order to follow
the one that we finally settled to, I've always felt a little regret, knowing you
as I do, that you renounced a marriage with literature and settled for a more
fitful kind of attachment. I feel the same way about Catherine Bauer: no one
could guess the scope of her sensibility and imagination as a writer who had
not read the letters she wrote me, as a young woman, between 1930 and 1934,
when she finally decided to go in for Housing and Political Action in a big way.
But at least you did not turn your back entirely on this early love, and we are
all the richer for your sparkling sallies and mockeries.

The possibility of Clarence Stein's getting the Howard Medal gives me the
greatest pleasure. I don't think you could hit on a better candidate, or on one
who is more truly in the apostolic succession, so to say. The first thing he and
Wright did, when Sunnyside Gardens was in prospect, was to go to England
and visit both the Garden Cities and Unwin and Howard. From the first he
considered the work done in Sunnyside as a preliminary study for a garden
city; and though Radburn took the publicity title of 'A Town for the Motor
Age' it was, as you know, conceived as a garden city, with a green belt and a
prospective factory and business area. No one has worked more tirelessly
to implant the idea of the garden city in America than Stein, and though the
political climate has not been favourable to his plans, his reputation here
among architects and planners never stood higher than it does now. As for
his own attitude toward it, he would be deeply touched, as he was by the Gold
Medal the AIA gave him, which he keeps in a conspicuous place on an open
desk in his living room. At the end of one's life all rewards seem empty except
the good opinion of those competent to judge one's life work: don't you find
it so? You, of course, are the outstanding candidate for this award, but unless
your colleagues arrange it behind your back I well understand that it is a little
embarrassing to transfer the medal from the left hand to the right!

CAMBRIDGE, MASSACHUSETTS   26 October 1959

From the fact that I don't find any letter from you in my files, dear F.J., I
must conclude, to my great astonishment, that I wrote you before leaving

Amenia, which was over a month ago. This process of camping around in one city after another is very wasteful of my time, I find, and it breaks the connections in more senses than one: but despite many interruptions I've at last been able to write the Introduction, which I send you herewith. It's only virtue, I suspect, is that it arrives on time; for though Whittick was good enough to send me an outline of the book I'm afraid that I have said nothing that you haven't said better either in the main text or in the preface. If this is your own conclusion, *don't be embarrassed over leaving my little essay out*. It was a labour of love, and surely the one inviolable principle of love is that it mustn't become a burden to the receiver! I have done my best to avoid any issue on which there might be a difference of judgement or feeling between you and me: there will be plenty of time to go into that if I ever write an extensive critique of contemporary city planning.

I am glad that you are getting the whole story of the New Towns movement down, for that will not merely put the achievement in perspective but may awaken the slumbering fire in the new generation. Perhaps, if your immediate duties are less pressing and your health allows, you should write a more personal account of the whole business, within the context of your autobiography. I find that I am plagued, in giving my course on Architects and Planners of our Time at MIT, that I have no such account by Unwin, or by his predecessor in America, Olmsted. It would be invaluable, not merely in the appraisal of their own work but for the light it would throw upon a whole generation. With your sense of humour and your vivid characterisation of people, you should do a marvellously entertaining as well as instructive book.

We are settled here, more comfortably than ever before, at the far end of a cul-de-sac, with a beautiful Victorian gothic episcopal seminary on one side of us and our living room—and my study—facing the wide rear garden of the Longfellow house. Apart from the fact that there is too much glass wall for either our comfort or our delight—I still have an old fashioned preference for windows and think that glass walls should be used with great discretion, as one used to use French doors—the house is marvellously spacious and the shrubbery that fills one of the views from our living room has an almost tropical brilliance and richness of texture. So we count ourselves very lucky.

My book, as I probably told you before, is still three chapters from being finished, but I hope to get it done before leaving and have only a few finishing touches to make when I return from abroad. I would have liked to finish it earlier for publication on my 65th birthday next October, but that piece of sentimentality has been properly squashed by the overlong gestation of my certainly overlong manuscript.

WELWYN GARDEN CITY   29 October 1959

Dear Lewis

I must answer your letter of 26th at once because I am trying to go out of circulation within a day or two to write the chapters I have promised for *The New Towns* book. Your keeping to the date adds to my shame that I have not been able to get down to that work properly yet. I have a lot I want to say, but it now looks as if I shall not be able to live up either to your very fine introduction or to Whittick's hard and patient work. However, I won't let the book go forward unless the totality of it is at least presentable.

Excuses? Plenty. Half this year has been destroyed for working purposes by that February flu and its aftermath of heart weakness. I seem to have recovered but my output is still meagre, and I have not been able to shake off yet my administrative responsibilities for the TCPA, which has indulged in three times its normal activity owing to the New Towns Exhibition and the Diamond Jubilee Appeal for Funds, and many committees preparing policy memoranda. My successor-designate as Chairman has even more commitments than I have and can't take over for some further months. And a new Government is an occasion for a restatement of policy in which I must take some part, even though for the first time for twenty-four years I don't actually draft it. And I am still Editor of the *Journal* and badly in arrears with work on it. Strictly speaking all this ought to give me a nervous breakdown; it is only a deplorable induration of conscience that saves me from it.

Your Introduction, in content and expression, is better than we hoped for even from you, and it helps me with my own drafting. Of course I don't in the least object to what you say about 'open' planning, though I do not agree at all that the importance of compactness has in fact been overlooked by the New Town Planners. They all have a passion for the utmost compression, which is the fashion here. Some have carried it a bit too far, and have caused discontent. I may not have room or time to go into the pros and cons fully. But none of the towns is anything like as low in density as a typical suburb in GB or USA or anywhere else. Current New Town residential densities are from fourteen to eighteen houses an acre; the inter-war suburbs were at two to eight; Radburn, as you know, is at about eight. Some towns are finding they have left too little space for cars on roads and for garaging. No one here argues that playing-field and school space is too generous—or the allowance for industry. What else is there to economise space on? Really, it is *not* an accident of history and taste that the New Towns are 'open'—it is a genuine response to functional requirements in modern society, with perhaps too little regard for prospective rises in standards. Howard did not foresee the full effect of the car and cycle, but it was lucky that Letchworth was on the safe side in its original space estimates.

It is a problem in this country that, with the revival of owner-occupation housing, there is enormous pressure on green belts, and that the movement of office businesses to New Towns is made more difficult because they have started as high-density working-class towns in the main—except Welwyn in its earlier part—and plots offered for middle-class housing are small and ground-rents high. The pressure is for plots at something like eight an acre or less. Expensive flats in cities are largely occupied by well-off families who have some sort of country cottage or other retreat. Even in the New Towns some of the executive class settle in the surrounding rural areas; Welwyn holds more of these inside than the later towns. Estate developers cannot ignore demands without losing some classes of customers. It is useless to tell people that their desires are out-of-date. Many rising families are in a position to satisfy the demand for ample space for the first time; new classes are asserting this desire. This is not a time when you can generally *increase* residential densities; the secular trend is the other way.

The architects oppose the popular trend, and want to go up into the air or reduce frontages or yard-space. They are supported by the lucky people in country houses and parks who don't want their Arcadia invaded. They have succeeded to some extent, owing to the structure of our democracy. But they are overriding the inarticulate yet vast majority, for whom I am a lone and feeble voice.

I think the Establishment will very possibly smother my book of verses, *Can Man Plan?*[1], when it appears in December. In this case they may be, according to their lights, quite sincere, because I am consciously out of the current poetic convention and in one or two pieces even mock at it, though quite lightheartedly. I do think there are some things in the book that would amuse a number of people if it ever came to their notice, and there are serious satires that I very much desire to get across to sympathisers with and opponents of my views on planning and housing; otherwise I would not have allowed it to be published. But only about a quarter of the verses are about planning; some are about factory and office work, in which I have some experience, and some are about love, on which I am not regarded as an authority, having been consistently cryptogamic. If the book is in fact ignored my reputation in many fields will be saved. You have already been warned that you will get an early copy.

WELWYN GARDEN CITY   8 November 1959

Dear Lewis

A copy of my little book of verses will be sent you by the publishers in a week or two, and in preparation I enclose the first copy I have received of the

---

[1] London, 1959.

prospectus. Not often having had a book published, and this one being an entirely new break, I am in a state of trepidation about the venture, which may, if noticed, revolutionise many people's 'image' of me.

You will 'jalouse' (the Scottish and perfect word) from the prospectus the mixture of motives I have had in allowing this queer collection to go forth. I think a simple sense of fun has usually been the impulse in composition, but whether the fun will communicate itself to people outside my family (who certainly have responded to those they have seen, though there are others I haven't dared to show them, feeling sure they would successfully press for their omission), I haven't the least idea.

But the mixture of motives also included propagandist fervour, and a hope (with doubt) that readers will be influenced by my scorn for certain inhuman and fallacious views, especially on housing and planning. Along with these major motives there is, I suppose, a certain vanity. I do like to be thought 'clever', because I am not sure I am, and even like to be told so when it is not done too effusively.

One thing worries me a bit: I have had no advice whatever from 'literary' people, because I am not in touch with any. My publishers are good commercial philistines—very nice people but without any special knowledge of verse, which may be why they publish my book. All the highbrow publishers rejected it because my conventions are out of fashion—though some were very complimentary about some of the pieces. I have had to trust my own judgement; and who can be sure of that?

Dr Johnson's sole motive for writing—financial gain—has never been mine, and does not enter into this case either. If 2,000 copies are sold I shall make 280 US dollars. The normal sale of a book of verses in GB is 150 to 300. So if I sell 500 copies I shall be among the popular contemporary poets! Betjeman's *Collected Verses* sold more than 30,000, which has annoyed the obscure highbrows no end; I think this quite extraordinary success is due to two things: he is a well-known broadcaster, and his poems are entirely intelligible as well as having a note of their own. But he has the advantage, which I haven't, of being in the aesthetic camp that sneers at garden cities, new towns, and all that—and most of the literary critics are in that camp.

So I must expect neglect, or shocks, from reviewers.

1960-1970

In the years 1960–70 Osborn came to be regarded as a sort of Grand Old Man of British planning. In 1961, prompted by the emergence at last of enthusiastic and able successors, he resigned as Chairman of the TCPA Executive, thus ending 25 years of main responsibility for the Association's affairs. He gave up Editorship of its Journal four years later.

Retirement from these offices, however, did not diminish his interest or activities. He wrote, with Arnold Whittick, The New Towns: the Answer to Megalopolis (1963 and 1969), a definitive history and description of the British achievement. He prepared a new edition of Greenbelt Cities (1969) which was hailed as still having point and relevance. And through writing, lectures and broadcasts he actively carried on his work.

Increasingly his concern turned to the world-wide application of New Town principles, with hopes that other countries might profit from Britain's mistakes and experience. He was designated in 1965 as the recipient of the international greetings on World Town Planning Day. He arranged for the publication of French, German and Japanese translations of Garden Cities of Tomorrow. As a Vice-President of the International Federation for Housing and Planning he made further tours abroad and delivered papers to congresses and conferences. Honours, tributes, the Gold Medal of the Town Planning Institute and the Silver Medal of the American Society of Planning Officials, came his way. Visitors sought his advice, scholars his knowledge and universities his services. And in 1970 the celebration of the Golden Jubilee of Welwyn Garden City served to recall how much of the work of Osborn and his colleagues had come to fruition.

His friendship with Mumford, through their letters and through Mumford's English visits, became more close and affectionate, and as they moved into their late years intermittent illnesses and disabilities increased perhaps their intimacy and fellow-feeling.

For Mumford the 'sixties were possibly the most creative period of his life. Three massive books marked the years, books which led to his increasing recognition as one of America's foremost thinkers and public moralists. The City in History (1961) merged new archaeological discoveries into a radical re-interpretation of the growth of cities; The Highway and the City (1963) and

295

The Urban Prospect (*1967*) *were collections of his current thoughts on planning and urban design. His next work,* The Myth of the Machine (*1967*), *revalued man's early history, arguing against the over-valuation of man as tool-maker in favour of his more important creations: myth, symbolism, social organisation and language. This concern to make man, and not his implements and machines, central to life, he carried further in* The Pentagon of Power (*1970*), *which demonstrated how the 'megamachine' had undermined and supplanted traditional, man-centred values.*

The Pentagon of Power *was the most immediately successful of Mumford's books and was published when other things were moving in his direction. Chosen by the Book of the Month Club and serialised in part in* The New Yorker, *it reached an immense readership and indicated that Mumford's ideas were at last winning through on a popular level. All his most important works of forty years were still in print in paperback, and while the generations following his own had somewhat slighted or disparaged his writings, it now seemed that the young read him and saw in him a potential leader.*

This derived partly from his campaign against the American invasion of Vietnam, an undeclared war which he attacked with a passion and anger reminiscent of his opposition to Nazism, a parallel which he himself drew. And as the mischiefs of urban renewal became evident and most large American cities were faced with breakdown, so both Mumford's prophecies—once dismissed as pessimistic—and his more fundamental solutions, began to attract respectful attention.

During these years he wintered in Cambridge, Mass., where he had the library resources of Harvard at his disposal and frequent contact with some of the best minds of our age. It could not be said that he mellowed, for The Pentagon of Power *and his Vietnam statements were anything but acceptant; but with a great, acknowledged body of work behind him and with his causes now of general concern and seen in his terms, he could, like Osborn, draw satisfaction from having opened up a fresh approach to the problems of urban and industrial civilisation.*

WELWYN GARDEN CITY   31 January 1960

Dear Lewis

It is now pretty clear that my book of verses is to be ignored by all the literary reviews, and that my only chance of getting it even modestly into circulation is to do some advertising myself, in conjunction with the publisher, of course, but probably at my expense. I think this well worth while, but I want some phrases from reviews or other opinions to quote. Dare I ask you to send me, perhaps for our journal, a few words that might make readers curious about the book? The review by Clough Williams-Ellis said nothing quotable at all. It occurs to me that you might write a brief note supplementing Clough's review, and giving a brief Transatlantic impression, with one short valuation that could be used in an advertisement.

This is a most unblushing request, which I am now hesitating to send you. If I don't post this letter you will never know what I contemplated. If I do, I hope to be forgiven, whether you feel you can comply or not. I have to find some way of breaking through the Silence Barrier, because I am so sure I have a public if I can reach it.

Chuck Palmer[1] is interested in a private-enterprise new town project south of Atlanta, and has asked me to advise on it. Whatever its defects, I think the move may be of some importance. I have long thought there should be some private-enterprise new towns in the USA—more comprehensive than the old company towns, and more definitely based on local industry than the green-belt towns.

WELWYN GARDEN CITY   21 November 1960

Dear Lewis

As too often, my filing is in arrears, so that I am not sure whether there is an unanswered letter from you since your return to the USA. This letter is there-fore apropos of no particular happening, though I was pleased to hear in a note from Clarence Stein that you had taken part in a discussion on the new towns at an AIP meeting recently. Clarence seems to have taken another dose of monkey gland or something; at any rate I have had a stream of enquiries from him about new towns' experience and policy which necessitated copious replies.

In my latest letter to him I have again expressed my view, as a distant outsider, that there ought to be in the USA an organisation, however modest,

---

[1] Charles F. Palmer of Atlanta, USA. Property developer and pioneer of public housing.

to keep going the lobbying and propaganda needed to influence federal, state and city opinion towards a dispersal and new towns policy. No doubt I have said this to you before (old men don't know how often they repeat themselves), as I have to others. The fact that conditions in the USA are different from those here seems to me an additional reason for such a body—since there is a lot of thinking to be done about methods, and no doubt private enterprise would have to play a larger part there than even here—where the first two new towns were in fact private ventures, albeit with a pronounced claim to public purpose.

You will see in the December *T & CP*, that First Garden City Ltd. is at the moment under threat of complete commercialisation. I have felt it an obligation that the TCPA should butt in on this because of our historic connection with the project. So I have had to spend much time on press statements, pressure on the Government, and even a television talk (which I could hardly make effective in two-and-a-half minutes). It is ironic that the struggle by financial interests to get hold of the estate justifies old Howard's theorem of the surplus profits and increments of value arising from unified ownership of a whole town site. By the 1956 decision of the company to abandon its dividend limit, the town and its inhabitants have lost up to now at least £2 millions. The threat now is that it will be deprived also of the promise of ultimate public ownership. Really it is a scandal that a company of public-utility character can unilaterally, under our law, repudiate the promise on which people have been attracted to the town. I argue that this discredits private enterprise, which here has on the whole good ethical standards. But city and financial editors are scared of expressing this view, so though some are giving prominent publicity to the affair they put all the responsibility for the moral case on me, by quotation.

As I am quite sure of my facts, I am not in the least afraid of any action against me by the take-over bidders or the company itself (the directors of which are confused and weak—which of course I don't say publicly). But I still wish, and slightly hope, that the *Times* or the *Guardian* will come out openly on our side. If one of them does it may induce the Government to take some action—but I have little hope of this. In truth, though the town and its local authority are now thoroughly roused, I think we shall again lose the battle.

Can Man Plan? was unnoticed by the literary critics, and I think only about 750 have been sold of the 2,000 printed. The market for verse being small this is not a complete flop, and I am only mildly, not seriously, disappointed. With the egoism of the neglected genius I am sending copies to a few poets and critics personally. One of these was Sir Francis Meynell—the man who runs the fine Nonesuch Press and is blessed (or cursed) by being the son of

Wilfred and Alice Meynell and the godson of Francis Thompson, but really lives (handsomely) by being chief of one of the big advertising agencies. I have had from him the enclosed comment, at which at first I just chuckled, but which MPO says contains some valid appreciation. So for the moment I am half-convinced that I can say more than I mean.

PHILADELPHIA   19 December 1960

Your letter, which came this morning dear F.J., anticipated only by a few hours this one, which I have been meaning to write to you—though whether in return for one of yours or as a gratuitous expression of friendship I would not know. But almost from the moment we came back here in July I became involved in the final revision of my manuscript; and since the middle of September, when I handed it in, the gathering of illustrations and the reading of proof, to say nothing of the writing of many pages of letterpress, has absorbed all of my energies: indeed, I can't remember working so hard since I wrote *Faith for Living* in three weeks, back in 1940. If I'd ever taken pains to get together a good collection of photographs some of my more frantic moments this fall might have been spared; but in the main I've let the ravens feed me with such fare, since I don't do any lecturing with slides, and so I had a heavy job on my hands assembling sixty-four plates of meaningful illustrations. On the whole, I think I've done better than I deserve, but there are one or two pages that will vex me, I suspect, until I find better pictures to illustrate the points I am making. But the book, practically, is finished; only the page proofs and the index, a mere month of drudgery more, remain.

It's name is *The City in History: its Origins, its Transformations, and its Prospects*.[1] By the time it's put together it will be from seven to eight hundred pages in length, far too long, in the estimation of the author, for any book, and it will be out in April if all goes well: at all events, around that time I'll be sending you an early copy. My publishers are very sanguine about its prospects, but just to be perverse I am taking the opposite point of view. I think it is a good book: perhaps too solid, too heavily over-worked, but still, full of lively patches and with enough originality to set up a score of PhD's if they have wits enough to follow up the trails I've opened. I am eager for you to see it but I won't bias your judgement by saying anything further about it.

Sophy and I have both had to work so hard on this task that we've seen scarcely any of our friends in Philadelphia and by now we are both a little the worse for wear. But once we are back in Amenia and can spend a few

---

[1] New York, London, 1961.

weeks in the open, doing a little honest work and rambling around the perhaps snowy countryside, we'll be ourselves once again. I've cancelled the few lecture engagements I'd made this spring to ensure a complete rest, and when I get back I intend to crawl into my burrow and spend a few months looking back over my life so far—I am now 65, you know—and plotting out, so far as one can, what I mean to do with what years may remain. Your own years after 65 have, it seems to me, been very fruitful ones; and you've set a mark for me to hit at.

What a scandalous betrayal of Howard and all he stood for is this capitalisation of Letchworth's success, converting the original public ideals into private dividends! I can imagine your feelings and that of those who fought and sweated to make the garden city a reality. I am afraid that the forces in our society that are still dominant will befoul or pervert all the good things we have set out to do. Certainly none of us who pleaded for public housing in the twenties can feel happy over what has been offered to us under that banner during the last twenty years, in this country. It was with those consequences in mind that I wrote my very sombre final chapter of *The City in History*; quite different in tone from *The Culture of Cities*. Howard's ideas thread through my whole book from the very beginning, as you will see when you come upon my treatment of the Greek city, though his name enters even before that when I distinguish between the two great attributes of the city, that of the container and that of the magnet. There is a sequel to *The City in History*, dealing with the future, that ought to be written; but I don't know if I will have the heart, to say nothing of the time and the driving power, to write it.

I will close this letter without saying anything about either the election or the general political prospects, for I have nothing very hopeful to say. I voted for Kennedy, reluctantly and with serious misgivings (which I still have), but when one has nothing good to offer one had better keep one's mouth shut. But if I occasionally succumb to despair it is not because my personal life colours my judgement; like the British worker or for that matter the American, we have never had it so good, and next autumn we shall spend a semester at the University of California at Berkeley, on even more generous terms than we're spending this one here.

WELWYN GARDEN CITY   18 January 1961

Dear Lewis

I write this time to say how glad I am that the RIBA is giving you its Royal Gold Medal, which rejoices me all the more because there must have been influences in that body against anyone like yourself who puts humanity first and façades second or third. They are very right to select you from the world's writers and teachers on architecture; I think they add more to their own prestige than yours by doing so. Anyway, I'm delighted, and so are many members of the TCPA—which is taking a new lease of life just now, when I am on the point of retiring from the Executive chairmanship after my twenty-five years of responsibility for the work.

Some of our members want me to organise a luncheon or dinner for you while you are here in June, but I hesitate a bit about this, in fear of putting another burden on you, and also with a little apprehension that the RIBA might think we would be breaking in on their glorifications. But you are here so seldom that, if you don't strongly object, I would like to arrange some sort of gathering—perhaps of an inner circle of our really thinking and influential members. Would this much trouble you?

The big question arising here is how to increase the scale of our dispersal policy so as to make it really adequate to decent redevelopment inside the congested conurbations. We now expect a rise of population in the next twenty years of four millions, and in forty years of seven-and-a-half millions. The 'trend' of things is such that, unless there is a very drastic national control of the location of employment, the Greater London region will swell by two or three millions. Some planners, while believing these millions can be guided to new and expanded towns within thirty miles of the centre, think it is un-realistic to try to guide any large proportion further afield. I agree that it will be inordinately difficult, but hold that we must do all we can to try—and that if we accept the principle of a vastly increased regional population with short-distance dispersal, the result will be worse than if we fight for a more wide-spread dispersal—which is not impracticable and would have support from the rest of the country (except for the damned high-rise architects and the extreme countryside preservationists, who are in tacit unholy alliance), but requires a Governmental policy of a strength one can hardly as yet envisage.

It is interesting that London and the six other official 'Conurbations' have together fractionally declined in population since their peak in 1939: partly through organised dispersal coupled with the check on outward expansion by green belts, but more by the continued outward movement of owner-occupiers, who jump the green belt or go into the few spaces left for infilling within the belt. The larger-regional population continues to increase, and employment in the centres (especially of commercial kinds) grows.

The TCPA's gain is that the problem is at last understood by the experts in the Ministry and the county authorities. But Ministers themselves remain obtusely 'realistic' and opportunist, and high-density housing is increasing—at an enormous excess cost in subsidies. We have, however, all the argumenta-tive cards, and our present team is competent to play them effectively—whereas, working almost singlehanded, I don't think I was.

The eye trouble is certainly a handicap; the vision in my good eye is clear and precise, but getting dimmer as the lens clouds, so that I read and write more slowly. By years of habit I could see at a glance what a page of type or MS contained; now I have to peer along and up and down it, like any average reader does. But I am told the dimming may not progress at all rapidly; and at least I can still work accurately, if slowly.

So far we have lost the Letchworth battle. A financial group has succeeded in its takeover bid. The local council proposes to promote a Parliamentary Bill in November 1961, and has support in all parties. But I don't know how they can get an acquisition by a Trust financed. I have done all I can, anyway, up to this stage; and I am pressing the UDC to stick to its guns.

WELWYN GARDEN CITY   18 February 1961

Dear Lewis

I think it may amuse you to read the enclosed reprint of the address I gave at the ASPO Conference in Miami last May.[1] I wrote it in a Mexico hotel when I was immobilised by an injury to my leg, and was very dissatisfied with it at the time because it was so completely undocumented; and I thought the standing ovation with which a very large assembly received it was just American courtesy, to a foreigner who was a sort of guest of honour as recipient of the ASPO Silver Medal. But when I read it in print after an interval, it does seem to me rather a telling rehash of an old story I have told in different words in thousands of talks and articles.

Not without regret I am resigning the Chairmanship of the TCPA Executive at the Annual Meeting in April after twenty-five years of main responsibility for its administration. We at least have an extremely able group at the core of the Association, with lines out among the best elements in the professions and central and local government, so that I am sure the work will go on effectively, and with wide acceptance of the dispersal policy, which now needs to be applied far more resolutely and on a far larger scale. So I can retire with some confidence that the work will go on, more effectively than I as a tired veteran can do it. In fact the Executive, with the aid of sub-committees, is now getting out memoranda on regional applications of our ideas more comprehensive and fully documented than any I could have prepared when I had more energy and freshness of approach—quite remarkable, indeed revolutionary, yet practical memoranda—as you will see within a month or

---

[1] 'The Conqueror City', published in *Planning 1960. Selected Papers from the 1960 ASPO Housing Conference*, Chicago, 1960.

two. I think they maintain the British planning lead. It is exasperating that we set out on a good principle, and stop just when it is beginning to show that it is practicable and could be really useful.

AMENIA, NEW YORK   1 March 1961

I've almost gotten to the bottom of a pile of fifty or sixty letters that I'd put off answering whilst I was finishing my book, letters of the kind that needed something more than a perfunctory Yes, No, or Perhaps; so I have at last come abreast, dear F.J., of yours of the 18th January with its heart-warming words apropos my RIBA honour. How swiftly all one's neatly laid plans get unsettled! When I left England last July I was sure I would not be back for at least two or three years, and certainly I didn't contemplate such an extravagance as a mere six weeks trip; but if the honour did not entirely turn my head it's effectually turned my plans upside down, so we expect to arrive by the Queen Mary the first week in June and will come back on 14 July. I plan to spend the first two and a half or three weeks visiting friends, going as far north as Edinburgh and as far west as Wales, where, incidentally, I've never been; and I'm reserving the last few weeks for being in and about London and attending to all my more official calls and appearances *after* the RIBA Meeting on the 27th. If you wish to arrange an informal gathering of the TCPA stalwarts I certainly wouldn't treat it as a burden to me, but rather a privilege to meet them again while they were still under your wing: but please don't feel any duty to me, dear F.J., in doing this; for you have done enough, and more than enough from 1946 onward, in surrounding me with hospitality and friendly honours; and even though you are now stepping down from some of your offices you would do better to hoard your energies. It will be enough if Sophy and I have a good day with you and Margaret, if that be arrangeable in Welwyn, if not in London; and by that time I trust you will both have recovered from some of the illnesses that have been afflicting you.

Our autumn in Philadelphia, as I perhaps conveyed in my earlier letter, was one of incessant and unremitting work, the dotting of i's and the crossing of t's on whose doing or not doing the fate of a book sometimes depends. By the end of January, when we left Philadelphia, we were both tired, to put it mildly; in fact I was so thoroughly exhausted that I cleared my calendar of all engagements till the end of April. We came back to a snowy landscape and an arctic climate—the worst winter in fact in eighty years—but though our water pipes froze twice and we couldn't get our car out of the garage we were not actually driven away from home, and settled down to the peace and quiet of the place with great content, slowly unloosing all the knots that had gotten so tight during the final weeks of correcting the page proofs. By now we are sufficiently rested to enjoy something more than the resting itself; but it took a whole month to achieve this state. This week I hope to get bound copies of my book, and very soon one of them will be on its way to you. It won't be published in England till the autumn, so no public mention should be made of it—no review or comment I mean. I won't prejudge it for you, but from little indications that have come my way I judge it will have a difficult time with the reviewers, who will attempt to cover up their haste and ignorance by assuming that it is little more than a slightly expanded rehash of *The Culture of Cities*.

Actually, it deals only with the historic portion of the first book; and the four chapters in that book have become eighteen, while the 120,000 words of text have become something like 280,000. All this quite apart from quite important shifts in the whole framework. Unfortunately, the reviewer would have to know the field rather well in order to be able to appreciate my latest contributions: so I am steeling myself for a somewhat disparaging and patronising reception. Happily, the RIBA Medal will be a large jar of salve to apply to my wounded vanity! As you will see it is a colossal work; and if you want to get the essential smell of it, without the reading, I think the graphic sections, with sixty-four plates and some forty pages of letterpress, will serve quite adequately! But if ever there is another edition I should like to add some sixteen more plates with some of the pictures I wanted but had to leave out— in a few cases because official sources were so dilatory.

As for the political scene, it is a great relief to have the weak and muddled and mushy-minded Eisenhower out of the White House; and even Nixon would, I feel sure, have seemed an improvement after Eisenhower, who I think will go down as the weakest President we have had since Lincoln's immediate predecessor, Buchanan, and above all, as the executive that made the *least* of his great opportunities. He has left Kennedy with all the tough jobs undone, or rather worse than undone, in a state of almost irremediable disorder: a depressed economy, an obsolete and highly vulnerable military strategy that should have been radically altered during the last eight years, and a properly suspicious and vindictive Khruhschev, whom Eisenhower brazenly and wantonly betrayed—and then insulted by his boasts. But, as you must have read, Kennedy's inaugural address had all the qualities Eisenhower lacked: crisp, firm, clean, unboastful, marked by a readiness to acknowledge grim realities instead of trying to deny their existence, and to seek actively to solve hard problems. His summoning Robert Frost to the inaugural, like his invitation to 160 scholars, scientists, and artists to be his personal guests on that occasion, showed a quality of imagination that would have surprised one even in Woodrow Wilson. He is a trained and prudent politician, and given time he might not merely develop long-range plans that would alleviate our otherwise hopeless military and political situation, but would even make a bold positive move or two in the right direction. But with Africa in turmoil and Russia in a far more intransigent mood than she was a year ago— probably her rocket successes have gone to the heads of the ruling groups there —one can only pray for the poor man, and our country too, for the odds are against him—and us.

The scandalous conduct of the business world, whose leaders have been setting monopoly prices on their products by collusion, without reference to the costs of production or the buying power of the consumer—witness the recent General Electric jail sentences—show that they have learned absolutely nothing from the depression of 1929–39 but are repeating all the original mistakes. The Ford Motor Company, instead of lowering the prices of their cars, keep them at an arbitrary level and siphon off their extortionate profits into 'educational foundations' that do as much harm as good, if not more. This compounding of pocket-picking with philanthropy is far worse than old-fashioned business in its most rapacious days, and is harder to deal with because the small investor and labour and the universities have all been taken in and made accomplices. I myself happen to be a beneficiary of Ford Foundation money, which is the source of my handsomely paid research professorships, but I can't close my eyes to the dismaying state of things. It will take more than a good President to undo the many-sided mischief that has been done during the last fifteen years.

But I don't want to close the letter on this note. Sophy and I are, for the moment, in a state of idyllic contentment in which our most serious duty is that of feeding the chickadees and the cardinals and the woodpeckers every morning, or of poking the logs on the great fire in our kitchen fire-place where in the evening, as often as not, we broil our steaks or chops and near which we sit to play chess. Except for the few little chores that lie ahead, especially the writing out of the RIBA lecture, there is nothing that demands my attention or presses me to activity the way that the book did these last four years. This is a blessed interlude, which I shall devote mainly to 'A backward look o'er travelled roads', to use one of Whitman's titles, before I start on the final lap of my journey. You and Margaret, dear F.J., have earned in even greater degree the same kind of freedom; and I trust you'll give it to yourselves before Nature, in sterner fashion, thrusts it on you. But if I am proposing to free you from burdensome task, it's about time that I released you both from a long and meandering letter.

WELWYN GARDEN CITY   2 April 1961

Dear Lewis

This is just to say that a few days ago your *City in History* duly arrived from
your publishers, with your kindly inscription, and that I am reading it with
great excitement and pleasure. It will take me a long time to read it right
through, as my sight is now very dim and I am having a hard struggle to complete my part of the *New Towns* book (which I must get rid of before we leave
for Czechoslovakia on 9 May), and so both the intake and output of words is
tiresomely slow for my slapdash and skimming type of thought and expression. So I have, in addition to starting the systematic reading of your book,
looked over its general arrangement, been drawn to particular pages by items
in the index, and (as always with your big works) been fascinated by the
pemmican reviews in the bibliography. I did read, out of turn, the chapter in
which you place and characterise Howard, which is extraordinarily interesting to me, as your assessment of his position selects points slightly different
from my own assessment, which is of course a very high one. Perhaps I was
too close to him in his later years to get him into exact historical perspective.
You see depths in his intuition that I did not see, and I think perhaps miss
one cardinal point that I feel is the key point of originality in his scheme. But
I shall read what you say more carefully, and in context, before making any
critical comment.

Whether your writing has changed a bit, whether I have become more used
to your style, or whatever other reason, I must say that I find this book makes
a stronger impact on my understanding than *The Culture of Cities* did, greatly
as I admired it. I cannot doubt that it will be a success and add greatly to your
influence on the people interested in urban affairs. As usual, of course, I
boggle at your views on nuclear armament. The dilemma in which the Western
world is placed is to my mind a real and tragic one, but I cannot see a solution
either right or conceivably acceptable by general opinion, in unilateral absten-
tion from making the frightful things. On the one hand we have the quite
real hazard, but not the certainty, of a world catastrophe; and on the other
the *certainty* that we should all come under communist domination. Whether
the Western Governments are doing all they possibly can to reach an agreement with the USSR for nuclear disarmament I cannot be absolutely sure,
but I think they are, and I do really think this is the only moderately hopeful
course to pursue. I am sorry you raise this point in your book; but no doubt
it is fundamental to your criticism of society. If so, you had to include it.

I am not at all against your argument for Social or Regional Cities; in fact
the TCPA is developing the theme on its own lines in connection with its
latest statement on Metropolitan planning—just about to be issued after a

lot of work. But we have some here who doubt the viability of the small detached city—and under modern conditions I think such cities are possible and very desirable, since I don't think the whole civilised population needs to be metropolitan-minded, but rather that civilisation will be richer for some urban elements of another kind, just as it is richer for having some almost wholly rural populations. Actually, communications of all kinds have developed so much since Howard's days that one can now live in a mountain fastness and still be as much in the centre of art and thought as Jean Paul Sartre is in Paris. Whether that is a good thing or not can be doubted, but it seems to me to transform the problem of city and regional structure. No doubt I shall find you have fully dealt with this thought in your book, and either established or exploded it. I am looking forward to finding what you conclude.

I end my chapter of twenty-five years' responsibility for leadership of the TCPA on Wednesday 6 April, when Peter Self steps into my shoes. Along with much regret, there is also a feeling of relief, and a stronger one of pleasure that I have hung on, with misgivings, long enough to have collected a really able and devoted team, who will carry on the thought and the propaganda, I think, more effectively than I have ever been able to do. I had extraordinary luck in possessing just the right background of miscellaneous knowledge and practical experience to be able to make a contribution to the discussion of our great subject, that no one else was in a position or had the leisure to make. It was greater good luck for me than for the purposes into which I drifted by a series of accidents—because nothing could have been more congenial to me or more enjoyable than working on this subject. If I had had your discipline and power of concentration, of course, I could have done the job much better.

AMENIA, NEW YORK   7 April 1961

It was a pleasure, dear F.J., to get your first comments about my book: but in heaven's name don't strain your eyes to read all of it! The most *original* chapters are the first two, but it may take another generation before it will be clear if they are also sound! The *best* chapters—also rather original—are those on the Greek city. Since you've read *The Culture of Cities*, you can close your eyes after this till you reach the chapter on Suburbia—though you know most of what is in that. The last two sections of chapter 17, and the summing up, tell everything that modifies or enlarges my original views. But I believe in the balanced small unit more than ever, and hope I have made this clear.

You are right about the style. *The Culture of Cities* was written under great pressure and great emotional difficulties: in writing this last book everything was in my favour—up to the doing of the final chapter last summer. I won't argue the Nuclear Policy issue now—though I think it's eminently arguable. Enough that it gave me a clue to what went wrong at the beginning. Don't worry about your new book: there's nothing in mine, I'm sure, to cause you to change a sentence.

LONDON   21 June 1961

You have not been altogether out of my mind these last ten days, dear F.J., but we had a busy, rewarding—and exhausting!—time of it in Wales, Manchester and Edinburgh; and we were so done in by Sunday that we decided to by-pass Durham, where I had planned to stop off, and come directly back to London, which we did yesterday. We're now staying put till next Tuesday, collecting the scattered pieces and broken fragments of ourselves. More of all that when we visit you! I trust that you have continued to make steady progress in your recovery—but I also trust you won't overtax yourself again by premature exertions, such as coming up to London for my *T & CP* dinner. I'd rather you were well and distant than near and in jeopardy. You've done quite enough over the long years to honour publicly our private friendship, and if you came I'd feel bound to divert the purpose of the evening by giving the eulogy of your life and works I planned to give at *your* special dinner!

WELWYN GARDEN CITY   30 June 1961

Dear Lewis

It was most kind of you to write to me as well as to call and see me in hospital.

I was very sorry not to be at the RIBA Gold Medal presentation; but I hear it went off with an appropriate bang.

I am sorry also that my doctor will not let me come up for the little TCPA party with you on Monday next, which I would much have liked to attend. I understand there will be a fairly good selection of the inner core of the TCPA, though some of the very active and influential persons cannot be present.

Of course I regret not hearing what you were going to say about me at the dinner to me. I do take much interest in these advance or draft obituary notices, all of which are of course unduly flattering but all of which are wrong, as judged from my position as an inside observer.

WELWYN GARDEN CITY 26 July 1961

Dear Lewis

I was a bit disappointed with the first reported reactions here to your visit—
and I think I said so in a hand-written letter just after my escape from
hospital.

Later reactions, I am glad to say, seem to me to have done you more justice.
The broadcast discussion in which you took part did make more clear your
criticism of modern cities; and no doubt the broadcasts to come will further
clarify this. The enclosed cutting from the *Official Architect* is also much
better than the articles in the Sunday highbrow papers. Altogether you certainly caused a notable ripple in public consciences—especially when you
consider the worrying preoccupations of this time.

The above was efficiently typed for me; I resume on my own machine, but
can't see what I am writing so there will be lapses. I have recovered from the
tummy trouble, pleurisy, pneumonia etc., but am almost unable to work owing
to mental lethargy and this difficulty in seeing—and of course increasingly
distressed by my many unfilled commitments. It looks now as if I shall not
snap out of this state until I have had the cataract operation—and I don't
know how soon that can be permitted. Altogether this is a bad patch in my
normally complacent life.

AMENIA, NEW YORK 26 July 1961

I never had such a busy, eventful, stimulating and exhausting trip, dear F.J.,
as this last one; and by the time the last week came I was drained dry and I
needed the whole seven days of blankness and boredom on the ocean—for I
came back on the slow *Mauretania*—to recover my balance and my appetite
for fresh things. We came back to a steaming, tropical city, but as usual our
place in Amenia, though not immune to the heat, quickly restored us, and
thanks to the most kind and zealous of young neighbours even the garden I'd
planted before leaving was in good order, yielding a plenitude of lettuces,
french beans, zucchini and swiss chard, enough to keep us going for the rest of
the summer, until we leave for Berkeley in early September.

I've only just cleared out the Augean stable that my little study always
becomes, with heaps of advertising and literary manure, during even the
shortest absence; and I am not yet free enough from the weight of unanswered
correspondence to talk in detail about what I found in England. Perhaps some
of that must wait till I put it in the form of a few articles for *The New Yorker*.
What moves me to write so soon is to reprove you for feeling any sense of
personal defeat over what has been happening to the old Garden Cities and

to the New Towns programme. Far more than most men, you have actually
accomplished what you set out to do, carrying Howard's ideas from their first
tentative experimental stage to the second stage of becoming a national policy.
This is a permanent contribution, momentarily retarded by forces moving, for
the most part automatically and irrationally, in the opposite direction because
they offer huge rewards to the more canny and conscienceless leaders of our
society; but by now your work is so firmly established that it will outlast and
eventually, I am sure, triumph over these forces. No weakness of yours is
responsible for the present set-backs; no extra effort would, under the circumstances, have had any effect, unless you had been intelligently supported by an
ever-widening group capable of independently arriving at your own conclusions. The nucleus of that group seemed to exist during the war and made the
New Towns policy possible; but apparently the members lacked the resolution
to hold on and to initiate a second wave of planning. The collapse of the
Labour Party seems to me both a cause and a symptom of the things that
negated *your* work. You have had better luck, or perhaps more ability, in
enlisting the support of the younger generation than Stein and I have had in
America; but even here I do not despair about the long-term effort, because
I believe that the irrational forces that are now so active are self-destructive
and must in time give way to constructive control. Don't, dear F.J., let your
grievous illnesses and surgical ordeals poison your feelings about your life and
work. You have put your country—and all of us—in your debt, permanently.

WELWYN GARDEN CITY									31 July 1961

Dear Lewis
A mere bulletin this time, just to thank you for your letter of 26 July, which
crossed the ocean at the same time as one from me to you. It was a kindly
act to try and reassure me about the influence of the new towns movement,
but you need not have worried: at my age I can't be fluttered by flattery
(though I like it), nor either deterred or stimulated by opposition or mis-
representation. The Howard movement, under my leadership, has had a
limited *succes d'estime*, and a positive achievement of perhaps a score and a
half of real new towns at home and abroad—but relative to its political
possibilities (I don't mean conceivable or ideal potentialities) it has been a
failure. Cities have marched on, and living and working conditions have not
merely not kept pace with technological progress generally, but have over
an enormous field positively deteriorated. Worse, standards of endeavour,
especially in housing and housing environment, have fallen and are still
falling—as you will have seen at Cumbernauld, Hatfield, Peterlee, and of

course in the County of London. I don't despair of a future resumption of good ideals; but it would be silly for me to deceive myself. Wrong things are being done that will affect the lives of millions of families for a hundred years or more.

In the small field of our success I can accept, smilingly, recognition that things would have gone more wholly wrong if I had not existed and done what I could (being what I am). These dinners and medals and so on please an element of pride and complacency in my soul, since I had no ambition to be anything or do anything except as supporter and voter for what seemed to me socially good causes. But I always wanted fun and games for myself, and looked on any sort of work as a kind of moral payment for the great happiness that life has given me in ever so many ways. Not having any theological beliefs or any conviction that there is an ordained morality in this world, I have never been able to find a formula for adjusting the right of self-satisfaction to the obligation of service; so the balance between these has fluctuated with opportunity, idealist desires, and temptations. Yet I am convinced that an impartial observer, knowing the world and the facts about me, would think I have been too happy. I am not the stuff of which the powerful reformers are made. I didn't want to be. And I never got what Shaw called the 'work craze' for more than a few months at a time. Neither you nor any number of complimentary dinner speakers will cause me to deceive myself on this matter. But all the same, I gloat over and cherish my minute achievement. I can't get out of the habit of the pursuit of happiness.

BERKELEY, CALIFORNIA   24 September 1961

Dear F.J.

As has happened everywhere in the United States, public transportation is disappearing in this area, and the railroad train that once took one across the bridge to San Francisco in ten minutes has been replaced by the bus whose best time is half an hour. Though we have a car we find the clogged streets and expressways no temptation to use it. Fortunately, our house is only a mile from the University, a pleasant down-hill stroll going there, and a rather stiff uphill climb coming back from the library or one's class, which makes the single mile seem three. But the house itself is a great delight, a great roomy redwood structure, set against the side of a hill planted with all the flora of the region and dominated by some of the most magnificent pines one could hope to find anywhere, which give a real reason for the clerestory in the living room. In such a rural setting as this—we live among neighbours but have as little sense of their being present as in our place in Amenia, indeed have greater quiet and isolation right here—the style of this Bay Region house is exactly right and matches the informal, indoor-outdoor life that goes along with it. Sophy is so enamoured of all our surroundings, human and architectural, that for the first time she entertains fantasies of moving back here permanently—if permanence is a word one dare use, at our stage of life, and in such an unstable world.

I forget if you were ever here, and if you visited the Wursters, or indeed if they were living in their present house at that time; but they rented this house for us, and as it happens we occupy the land just below them. All very nice in short; and though I've been getting invitations from all over the state, I intend to sit here quietly for the next few months and make the most of what I find here. My concern over the international situation, which I went out of the way to broach in my RIBA address, has been well-justified by events; and even when I put it aside consciously from my mind, I find it keeps on nagging under the surface, like an inescapable toothache. But I said what had to be said fifteen years ago; and I have no hope whatever that anything I could add now would alter anything by a tittle, except in the remote fashion in which one's very breath alters the balance of oxygen in the atmosphere!

If I do not write you before the celebration of your Retirement Dinner in October, this will carry both my congratulations and my regrets that I shall not be present on that occasion, to say in person what you already must know in your heart—how much I value our friendship and how much I feel we are all indebted to you for your courageous leadership, your unflagging devotion to, and your clear exposition of the New Towns idea, and all that it implies for the improvement of normal human life. No one after Howard has done so much as you, and your influence will still be felt a century hence and more, if anyone is left to think and feel on this threatened planet.

WELWYN GARDEN CITY   4 October 1961

Dear Lewis

Thanks for your letter of 24th September. I am still not able to read or write and therefore this letter, which is dictated, will be brief.

We have heard on the BBC your interview with Shankland[1], which was much better than the reports of your previous speeches in this country, but we regretted that Shankland did his best to counteract some of your chief points in favour of dispersal. This man is typical of the architectural group that almost monopolises the press and BBC in this country.

---

[1] Graeme Shankland, architect and planner.

Some reviews of your book have appeared but unfortunately we have not been able yet to arrange for a review in *Town and Country Planning*, as we have not received a review copy from Secker and Warburg and I do not want to send my copy to a reviewer as I am looking forward to reading it when I recover my sight. However, we have now asked for a copy.

The operation on my right eye has been successful but it will be another two or three weeks before I can have glasses that will enable me to read and write.

I am very sorry about the change of date of the dinner—now 25th October —to celebrate my retirement from the TCPA. The speakers will be the Minister, Sir William Hart, who was Clerk of the London County Council and was general manager of Hemel Hempstead, and Desmond Donnelly, MP, with Lord Salter in the Chair. So I shall once more receive three or four drafts of my obituary notice.

WELWYN GARDEN CITY   3 November 1961

Dear Lewis

Since I recovered my sight for reading and writing a week or so ago, I have written many letters to people who organised, spoke at, or wrote to me about the TCPA Dinner on the 25th October. As you must know from similar experiences, one has, in order to remain a normal human pin-head, to discount the cumulative effect of four or five draft obituary notices ingeniously assembling all that can be said in one's favour. All the same, one is pleased at the kindly exaggerations; and in this case I was even more delighted at the unmistakable evidence of warm friendship inside the Association, and the regard in which it is held by governmental and local authorities from all over the country. About 250 people were there, and the members gave me a really beautiful carved onyx marble bowl and a magnificently bound copy of the Oxford Dictionary of Classical Mythology etc: two valuable heirlooms. Simultaneously with the Dinner I appeared on a television programme that seems to have been seen by everybody I know who was not at the Dinner; this was film-recorded an hour or two before. Quite a day!

But after four or five months of lizard-like repose I find it nearly impossible to resume work; and I begin to wonder whether I will ever get back to my 50 per cent standard of activity. Luckily, the TCPA is now in the hands of a very energetic as well as thoughtful and able group; I resigned at just the right time. I couldn't do what they are doing, anyway.

Our national economic situation is very trying, but fundamentally I feel it can be dealt with, though as a *rentier* I am made to feel considerably less rich owing to the fall in security values. If I die in the near future my family will save a lot in death duties, as compared with what it would have cost them if I had not just escaped in May. Yet dividends have contracted much less, so far, than capital values. The world situation is of course a much greater headache. It is not yet clear what Krushchev is really up to; but pretty evidently he's contending with extremist believers in the inevitable clash—in China and in his own party. But who would ever have believed ten years ago that Stalin would be disembalmed? This is surely one of the outstanding peripeties of history, and must have terrific repercussions.

BERKELEY, CALIFORNIA   6 November 1961

I haven't yet answered the letter you wrote a month ago, dear F.J., but what a pleasure it was to get your letter of 3 November this morning and learn of the recovery of your site (what a bit of town-planning Freudianism), along with the happy festivities of the 25th October. Don't devalue any of these encomiums: They were well-aimed and well-deserved. I'd find it hard to pick anyone since Raymond Unwin who has done less harm and more good than you. I'll write at length during my first breathing spell, which may not be for another month, since my university duties have been piling up. This is just a whoop of joy over your recovery.

BERKELEY, CALIFORNIA   3 December 1961

I've been meaning, dear F.J., to follow up my first breathless response to the good news of your recovery from your operation; but a bout with the flu these last two weeks—one of those hide-and-seek affairs, down with a temperature one day, up the next, and then down again a little later—has put me out of commission and given me, incidentally, a well-earned rest. For some reason I can hardly fathom I accepted more invitations to talk and lecture here than I usually do, partly perhaps out of vanity, because there was such wide and eager interest in what I had to say. I could have managed it all nicely, I think, but for the fact that the University added a few extra burdens to the load, requests that I couldn't very well refuse and indeed did not want to refuse. One of them was to examine the Campus for a new university at Santa Cruz, about ninety miles south of Berkeley: a handsome wooded site of some three thousand acres at the edge of a little provincial town. As it happens the University here has, belatedly, arrived at a new towns policy of its own. Though it has allowed its two great campuses at Berkeley and Los

Angeles to grow too big, it has at last put a top limit of some 27,000 students on their growth and has founded, or is now founding, five other campuses in other parts of the state to take care of the present and future population.

This is a wonderful precedent, and at a meeting of the American Institute of Planners of Northern California I suggested that this was the first step for a similar policy in municipal colonisation. One of my friends here has already taken the initiative in putting the plan before the Governor. At the same time a Wisconsin congressman named Henry Reuss has introduced a bill in committee in Congress which takes the first step toward decentralising all the Government Agencies in Washington that could, with profit, be placed in other cities, in order to control Washington's growth and conserve its character; and in backing up his proposal by letter I suggested the further step of building a girdle of New Towns around Washington, to set an example for the rest of the country. This item was actually given national circulation in the press. Clarence Stein was supposed to testify in person on behalf of these measures, but I've not yet heard from him how the hearings came off. Actually, our Regional Development Council had made a study of these possibilities more than a decade ago, so we were well prepared to step in.

The interview with Shankland came off better than I expected, especially since the man irritated me. On my side, none of it was prepared beforehand, and since I had no opportunity to go over the transcript I must say that the final result in print was quite a happy surprise. I've always been very sceptical of the radio as a medium for intelligent communication, but by now I am almost won over, at least on the terms provided by the BBC. I daresay that my radio and television appearances are all that have kept *The City in History* from being a complete failure in Britain. Apparently, my long honeymoon with the British press is over: never before has any book of mine been as neglected and as under-rated as this has been. As my publisher Warburg confessed, 'This was not so much a half-hearted reception as a quarter-hearted one'. This does not raise any doubts in my own mind about the book; quite the contrary, for I now think that it is by far the solidest and best and most original work I have done—but it raises a lot of other doubts about the quality of our intellectual life today. In America the book got a tremendous ovation from the ordinary newspaper reviewers throughout the country, but the appraisals from my scholarly colleagues have been dismayingly narrow, ignorant and offensively patronising; while the complete lack of response from most of my old personal colleagues leaves me bewildered. Even at 66 it seems that one has still a lot to learn about human nature.

WELWYN GARDEN CITY   24 December 1961

Dear Lewis

. . . I find your address at the University of California one of the most eloquent statements you have made on the present world dilemma. If you are right that there is a national state of ferocious bellicosity behind the American policy your denunciation is appropriate. There is no such national emotion here. Our people almost universally (I know of no exception in my personal contacts) detest the necessity they feel themselves under of continuing to make or hold nuclear weapons. The 99 per cent who are against unilateral abstention from doing so, are against simply because they accept the *risk* of the appalling catastrophe of a nuclear war in preference to what they think is the virtual *certainty* of world-conquest by communism. Through the centuries men have faced the risk of death in battle through the same preference for freedom or group self-determination, to subjugation by some other group. I find myself indignant beyond measure at the suggestion by men like Bertrand Russell or Toynbee, that everyone but the unilateral disarmers *want* war or are criminally indifferent to the frightful possibilities. Their self-righteousness seems to me an insult to their fellow-men and, I must add, to their responsible governments, who are after all struggling for an international agreement to abandon nuclear weapons. Your view, which is more plausible but which I don't think is right—that the American Government is not sincere in its declared policy, does not offend me in the same way. But if you extend it to the British Government and Parliament I am absolutely certain you are mistaken. Russell's brilliant literary gift, like Shaw's, enables him to make untenable positions plausible; he has racketed about from complete pacifism to advocacy of preventive war, with the intermediate stance that Britain should disarm because we are protected by the American nuclear power; whatever his rank as a philosopher of mental processes, he is a babe in political philosophy.

Now I am going to concentrate on the last chapter of my never-sufficiently-to-be-damned *New Towns* book, which being aimed at the ignorant-intelligent will exasperate you and the learned super-intelligent.

AMENIA, NEW YORK   2 February 1962

Dear F.J.

It was a happy experience in almost every way, this semester in California, but as usual I am glad that my period of talking is over and I can at last get back to my favourite element, which is writing. As to the treatment of *The City in History*, I think I must have expressed myself clumsily; for it was not the

American reception that disappointed me—on the contrary, it was unusually vivid and appreciative and warm—but the general dismissal of the book in the opinion of the present run of editors and reviewers in England! I admit that I haven't seen some of the reviews you mention, such as that in the *Architects' Journal*, but it would have to be pretty generous to make up for some of the others!

Meanwhile, don't let this discourage you from finishing your own book, weary though you may be of re-stating the ideas that you have so well stated for so long. I can understand your mood for I have the same feeling about restating my own views on nuclear policy, which I have elaborated during the last fifteen years. Even the most true and sincere statement seems hollow, and almost rings false, if one repeats it once too often; which is why, except for a foray or two in California, I now feel that my main work on this subject is done and I can now leave further efforts to those who come to the situation fresh. But about that policy itself: the choice is not between holding fast to nuclear weapons and unilateral disarmament. Nothing could be more misleading than to accept this as the real alternative. First of all, the main choice is between a reasonable policy, sufficiently flexible to meet fresh situations and sufficiently realistic to admit that the dangers of total annihilation are far worse than the dangers of 'subjugation', and the rigid, irrational policy, based originally upon the delusion of our having a permanent monopoly of nuclear power, which the American government still clings to. Khrushchev has proposed mutual disarmament, not unilateral disarmament by ourselves or total surrender. If the Pentagon were not encased in the obsolete strategy of extermination, we would make haste to leave East Germany to the Russians and would withdraw our support for Western Germany's dream of re-uniting the country, as Khrushchev has in turn already plainly given up the hope of uniting it under communism. While my government clings to its present strategy it cannot and will not move an inch toward disarmament; all the professions of peace are for peace on our own exclusive terms: hence our insincerity and our lack of realism. But I see that this is no topic to open up on this kind of stationery. So let me stop abruptly, and give our affectionate greetings to you both and my promise of a more leisurely letter anon.

WELWYN GARDEN CITY   25 March 1962

Dear Lewis
Not having the historical knowledge to accept or reject your theory of city foundation and planning in your book, I was rather disturbed by the review

of it in *Pratt Planning Papers*[1] by Professor Sibyl Moholy-Nagy, which has a super-authoritative air. I am always put at a disadvantage by displays of vast learning—including yours. I suppose my own thinking on city development is based on a sort of *histoire raisonnée* constructed backwards from what I feel I fairly well understand—that of the history since the Industrial Revolution and in my own lifetime. So I might easily be taken in by either you or such a critic as this Moholy-Nagy person.

However, after five columns of Ancient history she asks: 'Why does Mumford gloss over the fact that Letchworth, Welwyn and Hampstead Garden Suburb failed?' and pontifically replies that 'The discontinuation of the post-war New Town programme . . . rests on the same resistance to social and economic isolation that killed the Garden City movement'.

It amazes me that a professor who claims to know what happened thousands of years ago in remote and undocumented circumstances can be so utterly ignorant of what is happening in an English-language country in her own time. No one here, except myself, will see her article (I have a unique information service!), but if they did, by this passage she completely discredits her criticism of your book, and indeed anything she may say at any date. I can of course at once detect the school of thought from which she derives her outlook on the current city problems. We have it here, though it is not quite so unwary in its attack on my own school of thought.

One thing that has taken some time has been the fight for the Letchworth Garden City Corporation Bill now in the Commons. I have helped the UDC in the lobbying for this Bill. We had good hopes of it before the Second Reading on March 20; we thought we should just carry it at that stage. To our delighted astonishment it was passed by 246 votes to 13 and now goes to Select Committee, where on the facts we can undoubtedly tear the opponents to bits. Of the 246 in favour I understand 109 were Conservatives, and the majority of speakers in the debate, including the mover, were of that party. Though in principle opposed to public ownership of land on a large scale, the Conservatives have been touched by our argument that in this unique case the honour of private enterprise claiming a public purpose is at stake. I am sending you a copy of the Hansard containing the debate, because it shows the British Parliament at its best and most honourable.

I am now attempting, by a circular, to moralise the actual shareholders to support the Bill. Here I don't expect a similar success, but we have arguments that put the present commercial-minded directors in a bit of a fix, and there will be a lively shareholders' meeting on 6 April. I admit I am not confident of making a speech without spluttering and omitting key points in the argument. I am better with a pen than with a tongue. It took me years (decades)

---

[1] February, 1962.

of painful humiliation before I could put up any sort of an argument at a meeting. In writing I have to try three or more ways of saying what I want to say (and dozens of other ways tiresomely present themselves), before I choose one that still seems effective. I think I should have been a painter or carpenter, because in these techniques I am not bothered by so much uncertainty as to what to do.

AMENIA, NEW YORK   2 April 1962

Your answer to the review of *The City in History* in the Pratt Planning Papers has at last persuaded me to look at what the author of it had written. And I must say you did it rather more honour than it deserves[1] . . . .

There was heavy snow and deep ice on the ground only three weeks ago but the soil is now open enough to work and the snowdrops and winter aconite are brightly up, with the daffodils and squill on their heels. Once my lectures are over I mean to settle down quietly and look over my life, doing nothing for the next year except responding to what comes from within. No easy task when I get invitations to lecture in every mail; but my No is becoming stereotyped and automatic, and I hope to have this coming year the vacation that previous engagements and honours kept me from getting last year.

---

[1] Publisher's note: the remainder of this passage was deleted during the printing run at the Editor's request.

WELWYN GARDEN CITY   14 April 1962

(Interim letter—not in the fundamental sequence. Can be omitted from the Concise 3-vol. edn. of the Guggenfeller *Selection from the Amenia—Welwyn Correspondence: First 50 Years, 1925–1975*).

Dear Lewis

I break off in the middle of trying to edit into tidiness an article for *TCP* by a French lady on New Towns in France, which in too many words does convey a lot of information as to what is going on in that super-urban-minded country. (I can see now the olympian look on the face of some architect or municipal official as he said to me years ago: 'One does not grow salads in towns'; thereby once and for all disposing of Howard and you and me and all our sentimental nonsense.) In the same issue of *T & CP* I hope to publish M.P.O.'s review of a little book by Jacques Riboud, an oil-engineering magnate who has just caught up with the garden-suburb movement of 1901 and has set out to evangelise La France. But what a holy failure our sixty-year effort has been to connect up planning and town development logically with the human passion for the single-family house and yard! I am a noble knight and you are a revered Lama, but skyscrapers will be erected over our graves. Levitt has grabbed the suburban movement, and Mrs Rose of Hotel York has grabbed the First Garden City—as Shaw at the time of Howard's death predicted someone would.

Just to report. I sent you the Hansard of the Letchworth Bill debate, which should be read as evidence that political consciences are not all dead here. As further evidence: with eight other shareholders I asked all other First Garden City shareholders to join us in demanding that the directors withdraw opposition to the Bill. To my amazement I got proxies from 248 holders of about 260,000 shares—21 per cent of the total holdings. The commercial controlling interest, which has over 51 per cent, polled altogether 57 per cent—so that I got many more of the other shareholders than they did. This will stiffen Parliament, which is sure to pass the Bill for public ownership, though the town will have to pay far more for the estate than was originally intended. What is amusing is that on a show of hands at the company meeting I defeated the directors by forty to twenty-seven—so they had to demand a poll and deploy their mass vote. The arguments against us at the meeting turned me temporarily into a Marxist; the ugliest side of capitalism showed itself.

I enjoyed your account of the recoil of your disregarded female admirers; it reminds me of the Cheltenham girls epigram on Miss Beale and Miss Buss. My experience is utterly the reverse of that of he-men like Geddes and you. No female ever pursued me; dozens that attracted me went by with noses in the air, and the few that amused themselves with me, and gave me nothing, all remain extremely good friends. My compliments:

> P.G. and L.M.
> Were run after by them.
> How different from me,
> L.M. and P.G.!

I sense that one of your love-hate pursuers, who once applied unsuccessfully for a job as my research secretary, dislikes my humane housing ideas as much as I scout her ridiculous idea that houses can be fitted to families as gloves to fingers (see my poem 'They Must Move!'), but I have never suspected any emotional attraction—which is, as I say, outside my normal experience with ladies. The ones I have liked have all been too good: and I don't interest the other kind.

Resuming next day, I see the above is a travesty of the facts of my 'love-life' —as what you said was of yours. But it is true that without exception all the women who in any degree stooped to folly with me became (and remain, if alive) non-passionate friends. I have seen the fury of women scorned in many cases, but by luck it has never focused on me. Perhaps the unsuccessful pursuer is luckier than the unsuccessfully pursued.

AMENIA, NEW YORK 9 June 1962

The world would be poorer, dear F.J., without that massive collection of Amenia-Welwyn correspondence to which you referred in your last letter: and I feel that I've hardly been doing my duty in letting more than six weeks pass before answering it. This has been a strange spring in both our countries. I learn from the Canada film people, who have had camera crews all over Europe trying to get documentary evidence for their five films on *The City in History*, that the cold and the rain halted their work for weeks at a time. The only satisfactory material is that which has been obtained for the historic portions from the museums and libraries of Europe where, by putting a man on the job for three months, they seem to have gathered a better mass of material than any one has collected since Marcel Poete[1]: something to make all the pictures in my own book look meagre and second rate! As for the weather here, we've had almost eight weeks of drought with but two rainy days in that whole period, so that I have kept the garden going only by the most strenuous irrigation, and even with that the asparagus have come up sparsely and slowly. But I've not been able to resurrect our lawn, which last

---

[1] Author of *Introduction a l'Urbanisme*, Paris, 1929.

autumn's drought, plus the energetic moles, left with horrid mounds of bare soil that are still in that condition. Otherwise though, our spring here has been Elysium, ever since we've been able to tend our garden and had the pleasure of beholding all the spring bulbs we have so zealously been planting, without ever seeing, these last half dozen years. We welcome these unbroken days at home, and once I throw off the last few niggling jobs and promises left over from the winter I expect to bask in this amplitude of leisure and floral beauty—not to mention the seven varieties of lettuce and the five kinds of peas we hope to be eating soon.

My book has gone well enough over here to ensure a whole year of leisure without any serious need to add to my income—the first time this has happened since 1930 when my *Melville* was a Book Club choice. I was so preoccupied with my own disabilities during the winter that it seems now, when I look back in our letters, that I didn't show sufficient sympathy for the contrary plight you find yourself in, with a falling income and rising inflation. Over my own good luck I keep my fingers crossed: for if serious illness had overtaken me before 1957 I can't imagine how we would have survived a siege of more than a year, and even now, with no pension though with double the capital reserve I had earlier, one has to say a prayer or two to safeguard the future. In the past, a prudent man who didn't speculate could have some assurance about the future; indeed the financial calamities which ruined the adventurous brought down prices to the benefit of those who had only modest expectations; but now the situation has changed to *our* disadvantage and I am sorry that, for no fault of your own, you are now feeling this.

What little work I have done this spring, apart from the series of lectures I gave on the irrationalities of modern technology, has been mostly by way of writing introductions to various modern classics, among them Henry Adam's notable study of the Middle Ages called *Mont Saint Michel and Chartres*, on which I discovered that I had something fresh to say since seeing Chartres with my own eyes. But my greatest pleasure has come from editing and writing a new preface to my old study of Herman Melville, a book that had a momentary success at the beginning of the depression and then suffered sudden deflation and thirty years of neglect. My publisher is now putting it out in a paperback, and when it appears my first five books, including my very first, *The Story of Utopias*, will all be in print, though the latter goes back a full forty years. The fact that they are all alive gives me a certain satisfaction. None of them will last a century; but even a half century, as things go these days, is rather a decent showing. All this contrasts with the indecent showing that *The City in History* has made in England: never before has any of my books met with such outrageous contumely and even more outrageous neglect. Why, your own TCPA book centre doesn't even include it among the list of new books for sale! The one exception is the article in the *Town Planning Review*[1] in the last number: by far the most perceptive and understanding review the book is likely to get anywhere; for the writer appreciates the departures in method as well as the more original contributions I have made in opening up hitherto uncovered ground. I should have felt that this one review counterbalanced all the patronising and contemptuous reviews that have so far been published in England but alas!, that pleasure is denied me, for the author is an American, teaching at MIT.

To go back to personal matters, which I shall soon be dealing with in another form in at least one chapter of my 'intellectual' autobiography. I have been singularly fortunate in my women friends: with one exception, with whom I nevertheless remained on speaking terms, a warm feeling on both sides survived the disattachments of their marriage or their other intimacies; and in the case of those I knew most intimately this has in two cases been the beginning of a warm friendship with Sophy, too: indeed, in one case Sophy now feels closer than I do! All these feminine friendships still nourish me in memory, even though one by one the people themselves have dropt below the horizon, claimed by death or disability or distance.

WELWYN GARDEN CITY   7 July 1962

Dear Lewis

... I have had for some months to give a lot of time and thought to the Parliamentary struggle for the Letchworth Garden City Corporation Bill, which retrieves for the town public ownership of the intact freehold estate, though not the surpluses of revenue and land-value increment that it was solemnly promised by the company. In fact the town will temporarily suffer a charge on its local taxes, which rankles with me: but there is a prospect of recoupment and substantial financial benefits in the long run when the 99-year leases fall in. It has been a historic fight, in which both Houses of Parliament have behaved in a way that fills me with a glowing pride in our democratic institutions; the Commons even improved the Bill in the interest of the town, and neither House was in the least shaken by the arguments that it is an outrageous attack on the rights of private enterprise. The Commons voted for the Bill by 246 to 13 (111 Conservatives in the majority), and the Lords and both Select Committees, after long hearings (in which I gave evidence for the TCPA as the sponsor of the scheme in 1903), approved it unanimously. It now goes back to the Commons for final approval, which is a formality at this stage.

---

[1] John Friedman, 'The City in History', *Town Planning Review*, April, 1962.

The data prepared for the case amounts to a complete documentation on which the extraordinary history of it can very easily be written, and I am hoping some historian will write it after the public acquisition has been effected at the end of this year.

This affair has interfered with my completion of the last stages of my *New Towns* book, but it is now almost done and I am already feeling a sense of relief in the fact that it has taken shape. Only bits and pieces such as tables, captions on pictures and plans, and a short bibliography have to be added, and these are far less painful to do than the arguments and historical account which makes the bulk of my part of the book. I don't anticipate that you will think much of my treatment, which by your standards is childishly amateur, but there *is* an argument against city concentration that may cause an intelligent layman to stop and think, if it ever gets to him through the likely barrage of contemptuous reviews.

I am very glad to hear that your own publications have been a success in spite of British neglect, and that you are free of cash worries. Let me, however, disclaim any need of sympathy for my own financial 'plight'. I am not a professional writer; my tiny receipts for books and journalism wouldn't pay one per cent of my paper and typing costs. The millions of words I have written in *T & CP*, in pamphlets, in lectures and articles, have been written (like Robert Burns' and my own verses) 'for fun'. And that this has been possible has been due to the fact that, by luck in business and investments, I have become sufficiently a *rentier* not to have to worry about enough for my wife and myself to live on if we live to 100—as we shan't by all present indications of senescence. In fact I would like to make modest gifts for useful purposes before I die if I could think of anything effective within my means. But as I come on both sides from proletarian rural families, I find a curious illogical reluctance to part with savings, which I think is due to some 'dungbeetle' instinct more than to fear of inflation. I don't approve of it, nor will St Peter if and when I apply for admission.

WELWYN GARDEN CITY   8 October 1962

Dear Lewis

There are many words in slang dictionaries to name what I feel like just now— especially if I think of the treatment under my editorship of *The City in History* . . . washout, dud, foozler, galoot, muff, lubber, looby; or to be more current, drip or creep. I have told you of my failure to keep the first reviewer up to scratch and of how, after a year or more, I passed the book to the very intelligent Brooke Taylor of Hemel Hempstead. His review is now in proof and will appear in the November *T & CP*, and it proves to be merely respectful and admiring, without anything like the study and critical appreciation I had hoped for from both these chaps. I have now read the book myself, and though I could not have done justice to it by any means I feel I could have given a better idea of its weight and scope. Don't forgive me; just write me off as a 'no count' boy! But realise I realise it.

I am, in other as well as editorial ways, in a poor and unproductive phase, and at my age it would be foolish not to entertain the thought that this is possibly the onset of senescence at last; yet of course I don't intend to assume that; I am studying my ways in the hope of a further spell of moderately useful (and interesting) activity. (I was never one of the saints who can labour without a degree of pleasure in doing so.)

My part of the *New Towns*[1] book now being virtually complete, it is being set up and I have a good hope of publication in the Spring of 1963, before the IFHP conference at Arnhem in June, where I am to open what I think may be a major discussion on the Garden City Idea, to advance which the Federation was founded fifty years ago. High-level highbrow opposition is being mobilised; but it is a real chance, if I can live up to it.

I remain worried about what you will think of my part of the book. Obviously, in view of your own learning and style, you must always regard me as naive and simple-minded. I suspect that to you I am something like the little girls Wordsworth used to find in the Lake District 'among the untrodden ways beside the springs of Dove'. But in my effective days I was not really an innocent idealist; I was a demagogic politician taking part in a revolutionary agitation and trying (despite my own highbrow literary tendencies) to employ an understood vernacular. I rather think the time has gone by for that; the world is now, more than in the eighteenth and nineteenth centuries, run by technicians contesting for supremacy in specialised jargons. I doubt if Tom Paine or Cobbett—far superior to me in the vernacular—would have much impact on effective opinion today. I fear my book, which is a sustained argument in language addressed to the intelligentsia with hearts in the right place, will be out of range of the populace (by price as well as relative literacy), and out of the wavelength and current sympathy of the controlling classes; besides being altogether too simple-minded to be respected by your professional types, as Howard's book was to nearly all of that class.

All parties here are now competing in their programmes with promises of more new towns; three have been started in the past year and soon there will be a few more. This is a big change, largely due to the able group that have

---

[1] F. J. Osborn and Arnold Whittick, *The New Towns: the Answer to Megalopolis*, London, New York, 1963, 1964.

taken over the TCPA from me, and the considerable number of Ministers who passed through our Executive Committee at one time or another.

AMENIA, NEW YORK   19 October 1962

. . . Apart from that, it was a broken summer for me, broken by many little tasks that I somehow couldn't evade because they were obligations of friendship; yet in spite of this and numerous visits to my New York dentist, I found when it was all over that I had written five more chapters of my autobiography, and that the first draft of the first volume—yes, there will have to be two volumes, no matter how stringently I abbreviate and cut!—is now done, and in a little while I shall begin work on the final draft. It has been a ticklish and teasing job, this going back over one's past life; and many interesting problems, literary, moral and political have to be faced, some of them quite vexing problems. And yet, in my present elation over what I have written, I think that I have done the most difficult parts of the job rather brilliantly; and I look forward with a good appetite to the even more difficult task of rounding out and filling up the bare patches and scaling off the superfluities. Fortunately, as I have probably told you at least three times before, *The City in History* has gone so well here that I can settle down to this work without even a passing cloud of financial worry, as long as my publisher doesn't go bankrupt through all his immense undertakings. For the first time in my life I can devote myself wholly and unreservedly to a purely literary task. But this, I find, makes me a little superstitious: I don't like to tempt fate. So just to prove that I could get along anyway I have written five articles on the nature and form of the city for the *Architectural Record*, articles which will appear during the next five months. *And* on top of that I have done something no one else has seriously attempted; I have grappled with Jane Jacobs' stimulating and awful book[1] and have written such a lengthy analysis of the conditions she is attacking, as well as her manner of attack and its solutions, that it may well daunt the editors of *The New Yorker*, to whom I have submitted it. I enjoyed your deft dismissal of the lady in this month's *T & CP*, but she has been so active here and has gotten so much publicity for her work that I felt it was high time to comment on it. I held my fire for a whole year; so this is no sudden reaction. But I can't pretend that I didn't enjoy giving her an awful walloping on the soft part of her carcass that she had so carelessly exposed. If it's ever published I'll send you copies *seriatim*.

---

[1] Jane Jacobs, *The Death and Life of Great American Cities*, New York, London, 1961, 1962.

I have not yet seen the Italian edition of Howard's book, but it happens that the other day the editor of the same publishing house asked me for permission to translate my *Story of Utopias*, and I seized the occasion to berate him for cutting out our introductions to Howard, saying that I fully shared your resentment and indignation, the more so because *our* views represent the best city planning thought today. On such occasions, one gains nothing by being humble: the high handed editing called for an equally high handed reply.

WELWYN GARDEN CITY   16 October 1962

Dear Lewis

Again I am jealous of your power of work as illustrated by your progress with a copious autobiography, which I hope to survive long enough to enjoy. I had thought of writing some partial autobiography myself; for which there is a perfect title: *Escaped Londoner*. But the sort of difficulties you mention are in my case almost impossible to overcome. Without the frankness of Cellini, Rousseau, Casanova, or even Augustine the story would be dishonest; but with it too many people still alive would be hurt or offended. Another thing is that I think (after the most critical examination and continual re-examination of the facts) that I personally have been a decisive factor in the evolution of the new towns policy and that this evolution is extremely important historically. I mean no less than that without my fanatical conviction and persistent work in writing, lecturing and especially lobbying, the New Towns Act of 1946 would not have come about, at any rate at that period. (Nor would it have come about without the concentration on the matter for a time by Silkin, an extraordinarily dynamic, even ruthless, politician. But he did it under my influence, and for him it was a political episode rather than a passionate conviction, and he has since lost much of his interest in it). How can one possibly state such facts or claims in an autobiography? It could only seem outrageously egoistic and immodest—however severely one also exposed one's weaknesses and vices. Also it goes against the grain with me, with whom modesty is not entirely a pose. I know that what I was able to do was due more to chance opportunity than sheer talent or strength, but saying that would, in an autobiography, just look like mock-modesty. So I now think there's no solution for me. And I can't regard it as important if my particular experience of life, like that of multi-millions of others, goes unrecorded. Which doesn't mean that I don't want to know yours.

Autumn here is late; trees are hardly yet in full colour; dahlias and clematis in my garden are simply dazzling, and roses are making a second rich display.

But, as all my life, I am conscious that 'Man comes and tills the field and lies beneath', without Tithonus's complaint of immortality.

WELWYN GARDEN CITY   20 October 1962

Dear Lewis

I was rather amused by a report in some paper in the last few days of an assessment of the numbers of minutes that known persons could speak without referring to their own personalities. I didn't make a clipping, but I think the period varies from fifteen minutes to a few seconds. It made me realise that if judged by my last few letters to you I should get a very low rating; and with this evidence that it is still low I announce an intention to reform. Point made.

The papers for the TCPA Conference on October 23–24 reveal with extraordinary force and clarity that a second Planning Revolution is now in progress in this country, and that the First, brought about by the Planning Act of 1947, was decisive and put us far ahead of any free-enterprise country. I have therefore asked that the papers should be sent to you for reference. One is by the Labour Party's 'shadow' Minister of Housing (which includes Town Planning), Michael Stewart, who is a member of the TCPA Executive, and shows the extraordinary advance in political thought that is taking place. Though he expresses it more clearly than his parallel in the Government, the advance is common to both the great parties and to the staff of the Ministry, and is taken up also, with less complete understanding so far, by the newly challenging Liberal Party. The present Executive of the TCPA has had a considerable part in this advance in thought.

The conference is to be concluded with an address by the new Minister of Housing, Sir Keith Joseph, a very bright person likely to have understood the current arguments since he is briefed by his Chief Planning Officer, J. R. James—but he will of course be very conscious of political resistance and will do some tightrope-walking. If his paper is available it will be sent to you with the others. We await with much interest an indication of his *emphases*, because in practice much depends on these. The obsession with 'saving land', though based on a defective sense of scale, is still influential. But it is in conflict with a rising realisation that space standards in urban development have been unduly cut down, and growing doubts of the tower-flat and Hook-Cumbernauld theses. Everyone now sees that the drift to the south-east menaces the London Green Belt and decently low housing density standards; but there are varying views as to how far it can be checked. Slum clearance and central redevelopment are both to be stepped up, and both raise the major issues of population and industrial distribution, now the subject of intelligent discussion.

You are two letters ahead of me now, dear F.J., but though that's a good reason for writing you so promptly, the real reason is that I want to tell someone about the unprecedented snow-storm that suddenly descended upon us this morning, as ravishing in its effects upon the still leaf-hung bushes as it is entirely unexpected. Flurries of snow we occasionally have as early as October, but I can't in all my life remember a snowfall at this time that covered the ground in half a day, instead of promptly melting into the earth; and though it makes one cower a little lest it be a sign of a long white winter, it also makes me feel as excited as I used to feel as a little boy when the first snow fell.

This morning my royalty cheque came in, and that was another sort of snowfall, or rather windfall, enchanting in another way because it frees my time for writing books and increases the possibility of my getting over to England next autumn. Don't feel that there is any need for personal apology over the tardiness of the review of *The City in History* in the *T & CP*. By itself, it is a purely individual accident, which I could not possibly take ill; but the strange thing is that it is part of a collective pattern of rejection, indifference, or vilification of that work in England which, as I have told you already, has puzzled me because it seemed to indicate a sudden change in the direction of the wind, as regards my own position in England. This is counterbalanced— and that puzzles me no less—by an equal sharp change in my favour here in America; though I have done nothing to gain either except state more effectively the things that I've said a hundred times over these last twenty years. The older one grows the more mysterious life becomes, for I have no explanation for either change.

What you say about the slowness of book publishing nowadays in England corresponds to my own experience here. I forget if I sent you the paperback edition of *The Story of Utopias* that recently came out here, but in my new introduction I recalled that I finished that book at the end of May and had read page proof on it by the 20th of July, before Sophy and I sailed for Europe, in 1922. In 1940 the pace was even faster. At the end of May I proposed *Faith for Living* to my publisher and in the next three weeks wrote and rewrote that book, handing it in on the 24th June. By the tenth of August I had *bound copies* of the book—and a book 80,000 words or so long at that. I have attributed most of the slowdown to trade union regulations, similar to the change in the output of bricklayers in the United States, from 2,000 bricks a day in 1930 to 500 today. But there is also a bureaucratic slowdown that is equally formidable: whereas my copy used to be sent directly to the printer without anyone's reading it till it was set up, now half a dozen people paw over the script and make typographical changes that I have, sometimes at my own expense, to undo. I suspect that the same tricks are being played in your country, for this is the fashionable style of life, the bureaucratic one.

As for your half-formed intentions of writing a 'partial' autobiography, damn both your modesty and your egotism and go ahead with it. If you tell the story straight, other people will deduce the moral and pin the necessary roses on you, or at least strew them over your grave. You have been an eye-witness to, as well as a promoter of, the garden city movement, next only to Howard in importance; and if *you* don't tell this story no one else will be able to tell it as well, or even fill up the few vacant spaces you may leave in the narrative. I've always admired your equable treatment of Purdom after his pointed attempt to efface your name from his record, so I'd trust you to tell the whole story. In the case of the really great and inventive American town planner, Olmsted, who had anticipated some of Unwin's best discoveries back in the seventies, I am convinced that he exercised only a tithe of the influence he might have because, after 1870, he wrote almost nothing about his activities or his plans or his ideas. This is something of a personal puzzle in his life, because in his younger days he was a copious writer and his travel descriptions of the South before the Civil War have long been classic. For this reason I kept urging Stein to gather together his own contributions for his book on *New Towns for America*; and though he was not such a creative mind as Olmsted's, he'll probably have a greater impact on later generations because what he did know and do is available in his book. So don't, dear F.J., flinch from this task; you'll find that such autobiographical writing is one of the least troublesome forms of literary composition, and that all one need guard against is undue garrulousness, or to put it in more kindly terms, copiousness: my own besetting sin, I find. This task is all the more essential just for the happy reason you state in your second letter: the extraordinary success that TCPA ideas—to speak of it in its collective form—are now having. As I said in my *City in History*, the 'failure' of the New Towns is a queer kind of failure indeed: the danger is that it may soon sweep the world like wildfire. . . .

On all this, I have come back to another attack on the opposition in a series of articles now being published in the *Architectural Record*,[1] and as they appear I'll send you clips. If I never live to write the complementary second volume of *The City in History*, on the potential cities of the future, this handful of articles will present in skeleton form some of my ideas, although for that matter a knowing eye could extract them from the first book; and I have no doubt that within the next generation some knowing eye actually will, unless the folly and intransigence of the present heads of government gets so completely out of hand, finally, that nothing is left of our civilisation.

---

[1] 'The Future of the City', in the *Architectural Record*, Oct., Nov., Dec. 1962, Jan., Feb. 1963.

As to what is happening here now, with relation to Cuba and Russia, I hesitate to write, for again my worst fears are being outdone by actual events. It was clear even before his election that Kennedy had no real grasp of the basic errors of our national policy and military strategy since 1945: on the contrary, as soon as he took office he demonstrated that he thoroughly subscribed to them and would, if anything, pyramid all the mistakes of his predecessors, as he is now doing. He is still dealing with Russia as if he were the head of a powerful nation, armed with a absolute weapon, facing a weak nation that lacked such weapons: an illusion that should have been cast overboard after 1949 at latest, since there is no doubt that each nation can largely destroy the other, and with it the possibilities of anything but a maimed, crippled, and finally doomed life for the rest of the world. But until both sides abandon their delusions about their own strength and their illusions about each other, nothing can be done. My only hope all along has been that at the last moment there would be, on the brink of a visible catastrophe, a decisive revulsion and a complete change of mind: more or less what happened in England after Dunkirk. The question is: Has that moment at last come, and will the revulsion take place? With that I leave you.

WELWYN GARDEN CITY   8 February 1963

Dear Lewis
At long last *The New Towns* has reached the galley-proof stage. I don't think your very fine introduction is in the least out-dated by the lapse of time since it was written; but I send you a proof so that you can make any revision that you now consider essential. Let me have the proof back within a couple of weeks if you can.

As to the British new towns, the only point on which my view appreciably differs from yours is that of the validity of the house-and-garden norm. The adoption of this pattern in the garden cities and new towns was *not* 'an accident of history and taste', or in any way an 'oversight' of the planners; it was a response to the immensely strong and stable preference of the incoming inhabitants. Many of the architect-planners of the Government new towns started with the fashionable-theoretical bias for 'urbanity', higher densities and more flats; and all, even Harlow and Hatfield, had to yield to the popular demand or, when specially obstinate, to compromise with it by raising densities from the acceptable maximum of fourteen houses an acre to eighteen or rather more.

It is true that social changes (the car, the smaller family and the lessened economic importance of garden produce) have reduced the acceptable area of the average garden and increased slightly the percentage of households who prefer flats. Hence the change from Unwin's ten houses a net acre to the new towns norm of about fourteen—which, when you allow for more garages, very considerably reduces the average garden size, but still admits of a modicum of privacy.

There are powerful pressures here (as everywhere) for further increases of density. They come (a) from the shortage of land in old cities, (b) from the architectural obsession with the phony concept of 'urbanity', coupled with the artists' boredom or love of 'gimmicks', and (c) from the agricultural and country-preservationist obsession with 'saving-land'. They are unpopular. More and more working-class families are buying houses, and want plots of four, six and eight an acre. The prevalence of much higher densities in the new towns is making them relatively unattractive to the owner-occupier, who tends to build in villages outside the towns and in the green belts around cities, so far as planning policy permits.

Believers in the new towns have always wanted them to have a balanced population of income-groups, and to bring this about many of them are now allocating sites for owner-occupiers of areas up to an acre (more often a quarter or half acre). Surely one of the main reasons for keeping towns reasonably small is that people can have the amount of space they like without long distances to work?

This is merely a personal explanation to you of the line I take myself. I do not ask you to alter your draft, which is based, I know, on a considered judgment. But I do draw attention to a misapprehension of the thinking of the new-town planners. There was no 'oversight'. They were well aware of all the arguments. Some held firmly to the known popular demand, some compromised between this and their own preferences, and others have made all sorts of experiments in housing layout to deal with the problem of the car, or under the influence of a vast amount of theoretical discussion.

AMENIA, NEW YORK   13 February 1963

I am glad, dear F.J., to find that *The New Towns* book is now in galleys, if only because this would seem also to indicate that your own energies have been adequate to the task. Remembering the pressures that year when I wrote my Introduction, I marvel that it does not call for more radical changes than those I have made. These are for the most part niggling ones, to avoid unseemly repetitions—I should have said 'nagging' ones—and to state this or that a little more clearly.

As to our differences over housing densities, they first came out, you will remember, in a discussion prompted by your new edition of Howard back in 1945. I am as sorry as you can be that further debate, after eighteen years, hasn't brought us closer together! But there we are, two stubborn men, neither of us moved by the fashions of the moment, both of us appealing to his own (but different!) experience and observation! I won't answer your point about 'oversight' by any changes in the text. But I have a much more massive answer, in the form of five articles that have been coming out in *The Architectural Record*, which I'll send you as soon as the last one appears. I don't for a moment suppose that this will convince you either: but it will show the reasoning behind my criticism. As a matter of strategy, I believe your book will have all the greater appeal because it openly admits such differences on matters of detail as our respective essays disclose.

What a bitter winter you have been through: it makes our own grim weather—sometimes twenty below zero with high winds—seem playful: at least here in our own home, though some of our neighbours, without our triple source of heat (wood, electricity and oil), suffered severely. I have gotten more than half-way through the second draft of my autobiography; and what is even better, have finished my part of the job on the six half-hour films the National Film Board of Canada has been producing. When it turned out impossible to put *The City in History* into a documentary, the Director decided to call it 'Lewis Mumford on the City'. The BBC television will probably put it on, sometime after April.

I'm rather glad, in view of my present work, that I cancelled my commitments to go to London last June or to Geneva this month: and I now fear that I won't be able to count on a European vacation till the spring of 1964—by which time I hope to have my biography revised and a little book on Technics I have been making notes for perhaps ready for the printer.

I forget if I've written you since we became grandparents: but in December Alison brought forth a big and beautiful little girl, named Elizabeth, and she has been thriving—both 'she's' in fact—ever since, for Alison has taken to motherhood as the proverbial duck to water.

WELWYN GARDEN CITY   15 February 1963

Dear Lewis

I have read your critique of Jane Jacobs in *The New Yorker*, but too hurriedly. My impression is that you have been too respectful and kind to her. But I intend to read your piece again as I know it is unlikely that you wouldn't get her into true perspective.

In the February *Architectural Review* there is an article on her book by a writer I hadn't heard of—Ivor de Wolfe—who is obviously young but has a cheeky journalistic talent (tabloid style). He says the book is 'a far more important work than Lewis Mumford's portentous *The City in History*', and is a *must* 'for all who believe the urban consequences of those odd bedfellows, Ebenezer Howard and Le Corbusier, to be the spawn of the devil working through his chosen vessels'. It is interesting that the godlike Le Corb is now in the doghouse along with Eb.

The line the reviewer takes is that Jane J's prescription of 'multiple use' confirms the *AR*'s philosophy (since that journal first invented the phrase). He seems to think with her that it is only in a crowded city that people run into each other and chat about everything and nothing (I do that in Howardsgate, WGC—never in Covent Garden). But he chews to pieces her view that the street is safe against thugs because there are so many eyes about—or rather he supports her in this but says that the danger from traffic is far greater than that from thugs. His solution, which he advances as new (it is his 'gimmick'), is to slow down cars to pedestrian pace—not, except in rare cases, to resort to separate pedestrian precincts.

In general Jane's book has had far more approval from the architect-journalist lizards than yours did. It is certain that mine is going to be torn to shreds, unless it is considered better tactics to ignore it completely. It becomes increasingly clear to me that the criterion of merit in planning thought is departure from whatever was thought last month. One might prepare a graph to work out when Howard and houses and gardens at twelve an acre will again be the only wear, and the *Forums* and *Reviews* publish reverent photographs of your grave and mine—or of the weeds growing in our abandoned gardens before a national fund to reclaim them has been employed.

To my complete surprise the TPI has just decided 'unanimously' to endow me with its Gold Medal—the fifth in the list of which you are third. Knowing how Knighthoods and Medals are awarded I don't over-rate the significance of such things. Yet one has to admit that they do make a difference to one's repute and influence in this credulous world. I feel perfectly sure that the award results from the initiative of the present President, D. W. Riley, a very able and wholly sincere county planning officer who has, by quiet persistence, done a marvellous job in getting his council and a number of towns in Staffordshire to provide for overspill from the Birmingham conurbation. The TPI is intensely profession-conscious and suspicious of amateurs like me because many members simply can't conceive that we have any other motive but to horn in somehow as paid planners. But when a President like Riley proposes my name and sketches my activities on the sidelines for fifty years, I surmise that no one on the spur of the moment can think up a reason for passing me over in favour of any other specific person. So it goes through. And I express my sense of the enormous honour from a body for which my respect amounts to awe. Please don't think me cynical; I am merely, as a chronic satirist, much amused. No, not 'merely'; irrationally I am flattered and pleased.

AMENIA, NEW YORK   28 February 1963

This is just a return bulletin, dear F.J., to answer the request in your last. I suggest that you hold off sending the book to any United States journals until we explore the possibility of getting it published here. Yesterday, lunching with Catherine Bauer Wurster, as she's now known over here, I found that she independently confirms my own suspicion that the younger generation of planners are beginning to flock to the New Towns standard—without of course having heard of you or Stein or myself. Your book could not be more timely over here, and since my publisher has a very warm spot in his heart for things English I wish you'd send it to them. If they turn the book down I'd be happy to show it to a few other publishers who might consider it. Don't send galleys, though: wait till it's at least in bound sheets.

As for the Jane Jacobs review, your impression of over-kindness is quite correct, but the reason is amusing. I'd written three long articles in which I had drawn and quartered and performed an autopsy on the lady; but the editors felt I'd been a little too rough and more than a little too long, so in cutting them down to a single article I unfortunately was compelled to leave in too much of the Introduction, whose only purpose was to counterbalance the ferocity of what followed. The result of this was that she was flattered rather than hurt by my criticism, and asked me to help her oppose an absurd crosstown expressway that the 'experts' were unanimously in favour of; which I did; and what with one thing and another the expressway was indefinitely shelved. (Gnashing of teeth by Mr Moses, my old enemy!).

I'm delighted over your long-delayed and eminently deserved TPI Gold Medal but I all too well understand your mixed feelings. They were mine too when I was recently made President of the American Academy of Arts and Letters, an institution I have always regarded with subversive and not always polite skepticism.

WELWYN GARDEN CITY   4 March 1963

Dear Lewis

I must send you this further interim note just to thank you for your advice about publication of *The New Towns* in the USA, and your generous offer of help in interesting publishers. I will tell our own publishers what you say about waiting till sheets can be sent.

I wish I had started the book fifteen years ago, when I knew more and could write more subtly and engagingly. I am gravely dissatisfied with it and I know it will be sneered at by many academicians and writing architects as naive or simple-minded. But it does make a little contribution to the history during my own part in it, and it does have a lot of plans and photographs that must amount to a fair description of what has actually been done in Britain.

Lloyd Rodwin will have as much fun with my book as I had with his brilliant and well-documented study. And I would be terrified of a review by you as the author of *The City in History*, with a hope however that you might be as soft with me as you were with Jane Jacobs. The truth is that I don't write for your sort of expert at all—but for a quite different sort of reader, not unlike myself, who exists in vast numbers but will probably never see the book. Fundamentally, I am still a housing manager going round collecting rents from tenants of weekly-rented houses, and transmitting their reactions to architects, city councillors and borough treasurers. I can't get off the ground into the aesthetic and intellectual stratosphere. So I am despised by the gods and unknown to my fellow-groundlings. Such is fate.

AMENIA, NEW YORK   7 March 1963

. . . Your modest 'doubts' about your book, dear F.J., do not fool me in the least. You know quite well that you've done exactly what you meant to do— and that nobody but yourself could pull it off so neatly and with such authority. I approve the new title—especially *The Answer to Megalopolis* as a subtitle. It's just as well that the world should *not* think of New Towns as a special English monopoly, as inimitable as a Rolls-Royce motor. All that you add about its contents makes me that much more eager to see it.

AMENIA, NEW YORK   11 March 1963

Dear Lewis

Thanks for yours of 7th and your welcome reassurance about the title of *The New Towns* book.

Let me insist that I am really a bit doubtful about the way I have handled our great subject in it. You are perfectly right in detecting that I make a public pretence to be more modest than I essentially am, or have become in maturity and old age. I know well it is a weakness, and also that such poses do not take in observant people like yourself—especially if they are exposed in correspondence in all one's moods. I must say I like better people who retain the childish unconsciousness of their balance between cleverness and stupidity, self-importance and negligibility, than I like myself for *affecting* to retain it.

But you haven't experienced old age and the growing consciouness that you can't keep up with the thought of other people (some cleverer, some stupider or less clever) in your own sphere of interest and study and statement. In this book I argue about the state of great cities and the necessity of dispersal to more and smaller towns much as I would have argued about them twenty years ago, and did argue about them within the Reith Committee of 1945–46, the reports of which represent almost exactly what I would have put forward if I had written the book at that time. Then I go on to discuss the resistances the policy of new-town building encountered from architects without social understanding, countryside preservationists, farmers and other 'land-economisers', city fathers with pride in size, governments reluctant to take drastic action, and so on; and how we gradually partially overcame these resistances. All this is necessary, because the resistances are still powerful, and I had to try to undermine them. Probably these are the most interesting parts of the book to those already familiar with the main argument, which isn't new.

But what worries me is that I haven't been able to deal with the immense amount of thinking in the last decade about possible forms of regional complexes—for instance Myles Wright's prescription or that of Washington's Year 2000 'corridor towns' concept, or even Saarinen's concept—to deal with which would have taken far more re-reading and judicious analysis than I now have energy for. I get all the writing from all the countries, much of it in languages I can't read; and I feel that, though my ideas are probably still pretty sound, I can't now place them in perspective with current discussions and proposals, some of which at least are worthy of respect, while others need care in critical rejection. I just don't like seeming to some extent unaware of what is being said and thought; and I know I must seem so in this book. I shall appear even more ignorant than I am, since I have never learned to assemble the data of which I have notes so as to make use of them when I am writing. My views are in fact incessantly modified by what I read and hear; but I haven't either the memory or the system to quote the sources. (I just don't know how you do this so copiously.)

Obviously I feel I have a contribution to make to the world problem of cities; vanity alone wouldn't be enough to make me write books or endless articles. But I have told you before: make the most of your years under 70.

I wish I could be 40 instead of nearly 78 at the present stage of development, with a similar but up-to-date combination of personal experiences.

Also I wish I hadn't started this round of self-criticism, which discloses a degree of egoism of which I am genuinely ashamed; my pose of modesty is due to a profound admiration for that virtue.

WELWYN GARDEN CITY   5 April 1963

Dear Lewis

It is thoughtful of you to send me your five articles on *The Future of the City*. A hurried reading of them is sufficient to make it clear that they amount to your most powerful statement of your prescription for urban arrangement; and to make me feel that my own prescription in the book now going through the mill is just a timid country practitioner's anti-biotic. There is of course a great deal in what you say with which I profoundly agree; but my own practical experience of the space requirements for what I think of as the end-product of social accumulation and daily exertion—human living, in and reaching out from the family home—compel me to differ from you about patterns of layout and density standards. What annoys me is that in my book I have not stated in adequate scientific language (such as you are far better able to employ) my slightly different accent on the *possibilities* of the town. I am entirely with you (and Howard) in seeing that marriage with the country must not be carried to the point of loss of the sense of being in a 'town' with its immensely important function of compelled and unchosen contacts. But I just don't see that the 'architectural' (by which surely you imply the visual) character of an environment has very much to do with the degree of community sense that arises. I am myself highly architecture-conscious; I enjoy beautiful buildings in compact groups, dramatic effects and all that; but prolonged experience has proved to me that I am in a tiny minority on that matter. I also have a terrific delight in trees, grass, flowers, light, views to a distance, and all that; and here I find I am one of an enormous majority. So while I can enjoy Venice as a visitor, I should feel as unhappy in one of its typical dwellings as the American in *The Aspern Papers*. However, I know well that in the present state of the decision-making power in society (which still consists of two nations no less than in Disraeli's time), Cabinet ministers and architects are likely to continue to live in green suburbs themselves and to build compounds for the other nation, despite my spluttering; and your influence will take them half-way to humanity, which justifies you completely and leaves me where I am as an impossiblist idealist.

Another thing I regret about my book is that I did not read Galbraith's

Affluent Society till after I had completed it. He puts the case for my 'end-product' in the sort of language that academics take notice of, which I don't because I can't. To conciliate what he calls the 'conventional wisdom' I couple, more than once, home satisfaction with efficiency of production as twin objectives, and only once hint that some sacrifice of productive efficiency might be justified in the interest of good environment. I would have made more of this point if I had read Galbraith before this week. (I am never up-to-date with fashionable literature).

WELWYN GARDEN CITY   16 May 1963

Dear Lewis

I have just heard from my publishers that Harcourt Brace have decided against taking the American rights for *New Towns*: *The answer to Megalopolis*. I am sorry, but not surprised. Proofs have now been sent to McGraw-Hill, with whom apparently my publishers already have connections. It is a good job I am not handling the matter myself, as whenever I get a rejection from an editor or publisher I am convinced my offering is no good and don't send it out again. However, this habit won't affect the British production, which is going through its mechanical phases and is due to appear in September.

After a very severe winter we have had here the most marvellously floral spring. In my own little garden an extraordinary display by daffodils is now followed by a competitive demonstration by flowering trees and shrubs—magnolia, snowy mespilus, crab and fruiting apples, forsythia and viburnum. And only about two things have succumbed to the frosts; perhaps because for long periods the ground was covered by a thick mantle of snow.

I suggest you should read the paperback *Honest to God*, by an Anglican Bishop (Robinson), which has had an enormous sale here, along with a pamphlet in comment by the Archbishop of Canterbury. To my mind they both tie themselves up in theological knots, and leave a rationalist as well as a fundamentalist baffled as to what their belief really amounts to. But I have always thought that of all the churches the Church of England was most likely, sooner or later, to become for all practical purposes Humanist and to interpret its ancient formulae in a Pickwickian sense. I will send you copies of these booklets if you are interested in the revolution they imply and they are not available in the USA. Robinson largely follows the German theologians, Tillich, Boenhoffer and Bultman, who re-locate Heaven and God—but whether they disperse or super-concentrate these I can't quite make out.

I am not sending you my 'address' at the TPI Gold Medal presentation because it will duly appear in the TPI *Journal*. Though I tried to reassert the main principles that I think should inspire planning, I just couldn't treat the occasion with entire solemnity. I can't get it out of my head that a bunch of people form themselves into an organisation, for good practical reasons, and in time feel that an afflatus has descended upon it which justifies them in giving medals to each other with a strange assurance, shared by the outside public, that such awards are evidence of approval from the gods. As a recipient I am egotistically gratified, and yet I want to laugh both at the givers and myself.

AMENIA, NEW YORK   10 June 1963

The recent *T & CP* has come, dear F.J., with your flattering references to my new paperback. I thank you both for your kind words and for the fact that you didn't make it a formal review, for Warburg—despite my warnings—is going to publish it, or at least the non-American essays, in England. Everyone is so relieved that this is not a big book like *The City in History* that they are inclined to over-rate *The Highway and the City*[1]: it goes down so easily! I don't complain: periodicals that never review paperbacks at length here have done it the compliment of full-scale reviews. A little while ago I saw the completed films—'LM on the City'—and found they turned out much better than I had any reason to hope. They will probably be on BBC television, but smaller groups and institutions can rent them for local showing. You may find some of them useful as propaganda.

As with you our formidable winter, despite the arid spring that followed, brought forth an explosion of flowers; and our year-round habitation here has rewarded us with the best flower-garden we've had in twenty years. A few weeks in the garden has, as usual, restored me to top physical form.

WELWYN GARDEN CITY   13 June 1963

Dear Lewis

Your letter came just in time to stop me from writing or commissioning a proper review of your paperback, which I had been reading more carefully after my hurried note on it in Planning Commentary. Now I shall of course await the English publication. You are at your most brilliant in your critique of modern architecture—for instance in your study of the Unesco building and the Guggenheim Museum. I am out of my depth in these waters, never having closely followed the developments; I am conscious of an intense

---

[1] New York, London, 1963, 1964.

emotional-aesthetic response to much of Lloyd Wright and Saarinen and a mild pleasure in the elegance of some of Mies van der Rohe, and a revulsion against the essential accent of Le Corbusier—as against that of the later Picasso. But even where I respond to the sheer creative expression of an architect I cannot find any excuse for inhuman or self-indulgent disregard of function, situation or cost. I find a great deal of modern painting and sculpture ugly, trivial, pointless, and some of it viciously quasi-sensational; but that doesn't worry me much, since I don't have to buy it or live with it. But it is a calamity when architects think they are free creative artists, with as much right as Edgar Allen Poe (whom I adored in my adolescence) to wallow in their morbid fantasies. Guggenheim is the Pit and the Pendulum in my garden, where I most definitely don't want it—even if I hadn't grown out of the juvenile craving for horror.

All the same, I wish you would withdraw your attack on the new towns for being too open. Most old small towns in England and the USA had in 1900 an overall town density of about ten persons an acre. The British new towns vary from about fourteen to fifteen an acre overall. Your support of the local (English) addicts of 'urbanity' and saving land does a lot of harm both to the prestige of the present new towns and the prospect of decent standards in those to come—because both the 'urbanitarians' and the land-savers are still perniciously active. They have no support among actual residents of the towns.

AMENIA, NEW YORK   3 July 1963

The *Journal of the Town Planning Institute* came yesterday, dear F.J., and Sophia and I both enjoyed your witty, caustic, light-hearted and altogether brilliant response to the presentation of the Gold Medal.[1] It was all done in your best style; and except for your own references to your age it corresponded exactly to the image of the youngish middle-aged man whose face accompanied the address. Only a man who could give that kind of speech could have had the influence you have actually exerted upon contemporary England, the influence that gave you, deservedly if belatedly, the Institute's Gold Medal. I only wish that I could have been present to add to the chorus of applause.

But I have a private reason for being grateful for your speech since in it, more clearly than I have ever seen you express it before, you stated the real difference between your point of view about cities and my own, in that you make the 'end product, for which almost everybody makes any effort, is life in and centering on the home'. I don't think you do complete justice to yourself in holding to this position, for if this is all you want Los Angeles, rather

---

[1] June, 1963.

than the New Towns, should be your goal, or that even more spread-out suburban nightmare which we find growing up in the rural no-man's land of Megalopolis. In contrast with your position I regard home, neighbourhood, city and region as on a parity with regard to their purposes and functions. I won't go into our differences in detail because I have expressed my view in many places, best perhaps in an essay in the *Town Planning Review on* 'Planning for the Phases of Life',[1] and once more, of course, in *The City in History*. But this explains why we differ over the matter of a low and uniform density for the New Towns.

What I have to account for to myself is not why I criticise the over-extension of the New Towns now, but why I didn't *warn* against it at a much earlier stage—though from the beginning I was extremely dubious about the great park wedges that separate the New Town neighbourhoods. My explanation is that the last time I visited Letchworth and Welwyn, in 1932, neither was much bigger than a large neighbourhood unit: therefore every part was still within walking distance. I was not sufficiently alert to see that an increase in size even up to 30,000, and still more to 60,000 population, required a change in the pattern of density if the essential virtues of a small city were still to be preserved and furthered. As soon as I began to walk around the New Towns with Sophia in 1957 I discovered what was the matter, though if you will recall I had already made this point, without the empirical evidence of the New Towns themselves to back me, in the introduction to *Garden Cities of Tomorrow*, in my reference to the densities that Howard proposed. That was the beginning of our disagreement, though it has taken much debate between us fully to clarify it.

At this late stage in our lives, dear F.J., I have no hopes of converting you; indeed, I have serious doubts if I could have done so at any stage of yours! Nor do I even wish to: that there should be differences between friends and that these differences should be unresolvable, as long as each is true to his character and his convictions, is a fact of natural history and the best justification of the whole democractic process of give-and-take. On most issues, including high rise buildings and Jane Jacobs, you and I will be fighting side by side, with the same gold medals ringing on our chests!

WELWYN GARDEN CITY   7 July 1963

Dear Lewis
I value your appreciation of my Gold Medal address more than anybody's: perhaps especially because the philosophical range and rich documentation

---

[1] April, 1949.

of your writing makes me very conscious of the ankle-deep thinness of my own. Yet as an organisation man having taken part in the dishing-out of medals myself, however conscientiously, I cannot take such awards with solemnity—as the world surprisingly does. Councils of institutes and societies seem to me like the Three Tailors of Tooley Street masquerading in neck-chains and togas; just as Queen and Princesses are simple shop-girls looking top-heavy with crowns; and Knights are Cockney clerks adventitiously picked out of a hat by Permanent Secretaries, to encourage millions of others to scorn delights and live laborious days, or to take care (*pace* Profumo) only to sport with Amaryllis in the shade. I am amazed and amused to find that I am flattered and delighted to be one of the chosen as well as a conspirator in a process that fundamentally I don't respect or approve, and that I revolted against in my iconoclastic and puritan youth. I have to admit that it has taken me a lifetime to get halfway to commonsense in these matters. Even in 1946 I was theoretical enough to decline the honour of a CBE, which in this strange country amounts to about a third of a knighthood. As I may have told you before, declining any honour is considered here an affront to the Monarchy, and the convention is that one is never offered another. In my case it was only the insistence of Minister Duncan Sandys (a ruthless hatchet-man whom I had years before converted to the new-town concept when he was out of office), that broke through the convention and elevated me to 'the lowest form of knight-life'. I see now that in practice this decoration, and gold and silver medals, definitely enhance one's influence nationally and internationally, and this being so it is just stupid for a propagandist to refuse to accept them. But the sense of irrationality remains.

Your assessment of the difference between us about the density of new towns is ingenious, but it is wrong. I entirely repudiate the suggestion that in placing personal and family home surroundings as the primary end-product I lessen the importance of the neighbourhood or the community. My view on this is more fully explained in the forthcoming book. Certainly I hold that if we had to choose between the suburb-and-commuting solution and the high-density solution (flats near cultural concentrations), I would take the former as the lesser of two frightful evils—as in fact millions do. It is just because I value the community plus the good home that I want smaller towns. And just because I value a high civilisation that I want these towns to be well grouped in regions. We don't differ on this in the least.

The difference between the older English towns and the new towns is that the former contain a much larger percentage of upper and middle class houses on plots from half an acre to several acres. In the outer suburbs of London, as of Philadelphia and Washington, there are many such houses. Even in Radburn the typical density is about eight houses to the acre, including the inner park spaces. The high density of the new towns is causing the executive types to seek houses in the surrounding country. But we found in Welwyn that it was possible to retain most of the executives in the town by providing residential areas at four to eight an acre, with a few larger plots. The sections at twelve to fourteen an acre, however, when well planned, seem to satisfy a very large number of people; those at higher densities (at Hatfield and Harlow up to eighteen an acre) are regarded as inferior, though under present conditions of housing shortage few are able to move to the areas considered more agreeable. Every effort has been made by the corporations to provide variety and to mix types of dwellings as far as practicable; but no town has found a demand for more than 5 to 10 per cent of flatted dwellings. With the continued rise of 'affluence' the demand for space both inside and around dwellings grows. And no one even suggests the reduction of the present standards of space for parks, playing fields, schools or factories.

Purdom is eighty on 15 October, and as his contribution to Garden City history has been under-recognized, I have written short birthday notices for *T & CP* and the International *Bulletin*, the draft of which he checked for facts and dates. Arising from this I took him to dinner and had a heart-to-heart talk for four hours—as I did just after the publication of his autobiography. These are the only two exercises in my lifetime in the role of priest or guru. As before, he was undoubtedly shaken; but I think my moralizing will have little lasting effect. He is a most interesting and extraordinary character, and I *think* he is really trying all the time to be honest in thought, and in fact that there is always an element of justification in his low opinion of almost everybody he has worked with, which has again and again led to his being kicked out of good positions. He can't see the offsetting merits in people, nor his own deficiencies of intelligence and knowledge, which to me (my own deficiencies being different) are very evident. In politics, for instance, he is a baby, and in religion a mystagogue. Yet on some things he has a strong grip, and he has a disciplined energy that I admire and envy.

P.S. While I deplore your attacks on the openness of the new towns, because they injure standards by encouraging the high-density fringe here, you mustn't think I *resent* a clash of opinion. The simple explanation of our difference is that I am an experienced practical producer highly aware of what ordinary people like in houses and surroundings, whereas your accent is that of a religious reformer more concerned for what would be good for their souls. It is a matter of accent. I never doubt that you are interested (though too mildly) in people's likings. But I claim that I am as much concerned for their souls as you are. I think their conscious interests and less apprehended needs can be almost fully reconciled.

... Now to your latest letter. I am glad to learn that McGraw-Hill are considering your book: they are the best possible publishers for such a work. Recently they absorbed the big Dodge company, which publishes *The Architectural Record*, the only professional magazine I write for; and the McGraw people were very anxious to bring out the series of articles on The Future of the City I sent you. But I regard those articles as a mere trial flight for the more comprehensive book that I might write if my wits and body hold together for a few more years, and I don't want to spoil that opportunity by premature publication. As it is, I view with misgivings my mounting pile of published work, for I have long held that the only authors who will be remembered a century hence are those who took the pains to write only half a dozen solid, first-rate works, and on these terms I'm already a forgotten man, even though I have the consolation of knowing that all of my first six books, going back more than forty years, are in print.

I am smothered by the work of preparation I find myself having to do for the book on Technics I've been planning. I had hoped I could do a rather neat little book on the origins of the machine and the present prospects of our machine-driven, machine-ridden civilisation: a book that would not need any more knowledge than, after thirty years rambling in this field, I could draw on readily without lifting a finger or a book. But one can't live like a *rentier* in the world of thought; I find I must earn some current income if the book is to be as fresh a contribution as I want it to be and hope to make it. Hence my preoccupation. I think I am on the trail of some important ideas about the early life of man, including his slow development to tools, which no one has yet explored, but I don't dare even hint at the notions I'm playing with now till I see if there is any substance in them. The better a hypothesis, the more necessary it is that its hopeful author should remain only half-convinced! But I must share with you my subjective excitement.

About the account of your meeting with Purdom and your proposal to honour his eightieth birthday. Purdom is a strange man: there is much in both him and his work that I admire, yet I have never felt drawn to him. There is even a kind of underlying affiliation in our careers: each of us has fallen short in two or three possible careers by not being willing to settle for one portion of experience or thought alone. With both of us a strong urge to write separated us, at critical moments, from our interest in cities and planning, and yet we could never be permanently divorced. Fate has not, I think, dealt quite as kindly with his career as it has with mine; yet perhaps he hoped for more than I did, and thus was doubly disappointed. He is not a great mind, not even a great man manqué; yet he would have liked to be one and at times must have thought, with all his abundant talents, that he really was. After his treatment of you in his revised *Building of Satellite Towns*, or rather his non-treatment, your four hour confab with him was—I purposely embarrass you with this characterisation—a work of pure Christian charity, or, if you prefer military terms, above and beyond the call of duty. Bravo! You yourself had some of the same potentialities as Purdom and myself, but perhaps because you hated mere highbrows you followed a narrower line and now you can say, looking at Purdom and me, there but for the grace of God might have gone F.J.! I could keep on chatting with you all afternoon, dear F.J., but you need a rest, if I don't.

WELWYN GARDEN CITY   23 September 1963

Dear Lewis

Our exchange of personal confessions, of which yours of 28 August is the latest item, is unique in my existence, and I find it seductively interesting as well as evidential of the difficulty any two beings have in understanding each other. Perhaps they have to live together for a long time before they get anywhere near that achievement. Habitual writers probably can't help building up a picture of aspects of themselves that they want understood, which if they are honest writers is true as far as it goes, but is very far from the whole truth. Even in private diaries, I think, most people control their features a bit, as they do when they know they are being photographed. And when clever and ruthless photographers catch their involuntary grimaces they don't really like it.

As an example of partial understanding, I am amused by your crediting me with Christian charity in my (again unique) role as priest or guru vis-à-vis Purdom. Really my motives are two: scientific and historical. I think I have still a slight resentment of his treatment of me: I did suffer a lot of anxiety and frustration when he was Finance Director of WGC and I was nominally estate manager; and of course I don't forget that he left me out of his account of WGC and libelled me in his autobiography[1] rather harmfully. But I don't forget either that in the 1917–19 period he, more than anybody, revived the garden city movement; that I as a new boy in 1912–16 learned a lot from his Letchworth experience; that he was an extraordinarily valuable member of the WGC team, because of his experience at Letchworth; and that he also revived the ideals of the International Federation when Hon. Treasurer and Secretary of it in the 1920–28 period.

And reflecting on the whole story, I am *more* conscious that his part in this

---

[1] C. B. Purdom, *Life Over Again*, London, 1951.

great movement has been under-recognised than concerned about his concealing that I also was a factor in the revival, and that he was greatly influenced by me in the formulation of a political policy for new towns—a side on which he is very weak and unpractical. I have had all the recognition I could possibly think I am entitled to; and of course he resents that, since there is no doubt at all that he sincerely believes that I merely reverberated *his* ideas.

Chance has made us both the chief contemporary historians of the two garden cities and the movement. He is a more laborious worker than I am, and his contributions to history are very important and in large measure strictly factual. They are indispensable; and yet they are seriously defective because of his scornful attitude to almost all his colleagues at Letchworth and Welwyn. Therefore in my own contributions to history I am always in the difficulty that I have to indicate his serious biases as well as to appreciate his own services.

But though I am moderately sympathetic, my motive was not simply 'Christian'. I have a strong streak of scientific curiosity: the 'desire to know'. Once my attention is drawn to a thing I have to study it, take it to pieces, try to see how it works, like any normal schoolboy. It annoys me that mechanisms have in my lifetime become so complex that I have had to give up this habit. I did understand the working of the early internal combustion engine and the thermionic valve, and I am distressed to accept that I have to give up the electronic computer as beyond my ken. I admit it is odd that I still hope to understand another human being—a far more complex mechanism. But it's the same impulse essentially. . . .

As to what you say about our initial 'potentialities', I could as Henry James would put it, expatiate. In my teens I decided to be (my phrase at the time) 'a specialist on things in general', and it isn't character or decision, but accident, that has caused me to specialise on commercial administration, accountancy, and on writing almost exclusively on one big subject. I could have been a cinema pianist, a playwright, a novelist, a painter, an engineer or architect, a sociologist, an economist, or a politician or trade-union official. I could never have been an athlete, a soldier, a parson, a mathematician, or a successful swindler the latter because I wouldn't have had the nerve.

I would like to know how you came to decide early to be a writer on historical-sociological subjects, and whether you or your mentors envisaged a 'career'. My parents and teachers did not; their idea was that good boys did their duty in the place to which God would call them. I was fundamentally a writer, and I think I vaguely dreamed, between about 12 and 14, of fame in that honoured field (unduly honoured, I now think). But after leaving school at 15 I was for twelve years a clerk/book-keeper of the Bartleby type, but in soft jobs that gave me a lot of time for reading; and I started and ran all sorts of amateur societies, including branches of socialist organisations, and was so much concerned with reforming society that I never even thought about how to get enough income to marry, and though intensely heterosexual I was pathologically shy, rather ugly and very shabby, and had no adventures with girls—though of course I day-dreamed about them. Besides reading enormously I attended evening classes and lectures in commercial subjects, economics, music and the arts, French and German, etc., and in debating societies and the Fabian Society and other socialist bodies got pretty well educated in left-wing politics—though I was always the secretary and organiser, never the prospective candidate for elections—I was too shy and almost inarticulate as a public speaker, though I had a lot that I couldn't say.

This was really my 'university' period; but it was one without professors or tutors. If I had gone to an ordinary university where the professors advised students what to do with themselves, I think my fate would have depended on which of two of my obvious propensities they were themselves interested in. One type would have started me on a noble poverty-stricken career as a literary critic, essayist and minor poet—perhaps a dwarf Matthew Arnold. But the other type, realising that I wouldn't have an inherited fortune, would have sent me into law or the civil service, in which I would certainly have attained the level at about 50 of an Under-Secretary and earned a C.B., and after retirement would have served on Commissions to consider Decimal Coinage or the Age of Consent or the Taxation of Bachelors.

What actually did happen was the accident of applying for and getting the job of secretary and manager of the Howard Cottage Society at Letchworth, for which as clerk and book-keeper I was fitted; but I found my amateurish interest in nearly everything under the sun adapted me to town development in general, of which I hadn't seen the major importance for social welfare until I had lived for some time in Letchworth. . . .

I write all this, not only as an officious attempt to correct your own comparisons of three people, but in order to clarify my own interpretations, which continue to develop and will never reach finality, and may even get less accurate as I come to accept my own crystallisations and build upon them, though I hope they won't. Writing is a dangerous business. Thoughts are subtle and almost as fluid as dreams; one struggles to catch them and formulate them; but when written they are stiff and angular and not *quite* true. Later thoughts suffer by the influence of those one has already formulated and fixed in words.

It is my habit to ask myself every day whether what I thought yesterday is true; and it is my experience that on most important things the answer is usually YES. Does this mean that I thought rightly, or that I have ceased to be capable of real thought at all? The architectural lizards would give the second explanation. In my acquired self-confidence I tend to the first; and when I read what I wrote on planning during my prime I am amazed at the literary resource and lucidity that I then possessed, and can't believe that what I write now is as effective. MPO, however, says that in that assumed 'prime' I thought the same about my past and current writing. Yet at some point, as Wells at 50 said of his future at 65, one must 'slacken and decline'. And I wonder if one knows it when that point has been reached. Wells didn't. . . .

You remember the obscure character in Boswell's *Johnson* whose single recorded remark is that he had tried to be a philosopher but 'Cheerfulness would keep breaking in'? Well, we treasure in our family as equally profound the remark of a Miss Potter: 'I sometimes think to myself, I think, "Well I dunno"'. I am saving this as a motto for my own autobiography—which however is very unlikely ever to be written. . . .

MIDDLETOWN, CONN.   17 October, 1963

Never, dear F.J., do I read an unsolicited manuscript the very moment I receive it; and almost never do I answer a friend's letter within a few hours of getting it: yet this is what has happened today, and I am none the worse for breaking my usual habits. I would not have wanted to miss your masterly summation of Howard's career: all the more because I have attempted this more than once myself and know how difficult it is to treat as freshly as you have a subject that, by dint of repetition, has necessarily lost some of its pristine bloom. No one will ever do him and his ideas better justice than you have done; and I suspect that after this demonstration very few will try it. Thank you not merely for writing this lecture, but also for sending it on to me. Friendship must not take too much for granted. In the book on Technics I have just begun all over for the second time—it keeps widening its horizon and making my original approach seem provincial—I am going to scotch the belief in the inevitableness of the inevitable, and in the kind of mind that believes this sort of automatic thinking 'scientific'—so I thank you for giving this attitude a sound, thumping, preliminary kick. Mine, I hope, will be fatal and leave a lot of pseudo-scientific corpses strewn over the landscape . . .

I am having my own difficulties in getting the material for my lecture on Raymond Unwin together, for I have mislaid *Nothing Gained by Overcrowding* and the library at Wesleyan University, where I am in residence this autumn, has not even a scrap of Unwin's writing. His daughter, Peggy Hitchcock, has, however, sent me on some interesting material and I have just discovered for the first time that he began his career as a mining engineer.

Nobody ever breathed a word about that in my presence before. But the burning of his papers was a great loss, and I kick myself at never using such opportunities as I had to ask him about his career, for he wasn't a man to talk about himself otherwise. Unfortunately, thirty years ago, I didn't know the right questions to ask, even though I appreciated his work. Lyon says he regretted not having read Camillo Sitte before he planned Letchworth; but in *Town Planning in Practice*, in 1909–10, he was quoting Sitte. What I'd like to know is how much he was influenced by the Cotswold villages. There's a group of houses in Bibury I came across in 1953 that looks exactly as if Unwin had designed it—two or three centuries ago! And did he know anything of Olmsted's work? Probably not, because Olmsted, though a copious writer before the Civil War, published almost nothing about his methods, probably because he could hope to have no readers: yet Unwin re-invented some of Olmsted's best tricks, including the super-block and the inner park. My irreparable ignorance here is vexing.

Now to personal matters. I think I must have told you that I am this autumn a Senior Fellow at the Centre for Advanced Studies at Wesleyan, a liberal arts university that has outgrown its original denominational limitations. I have a study in a nasty new air-conditioned building I enter only to get my mail, and we have a big, comfortable, traditional house at the edge of this fairly compact New England town, on what is almost a blind road that is actually quieter than our rural home because none of my Middletown neighbours sport tractors or power motors. The honorarium is a full professor's salary, plus a whole list of perquisites that include rent and a chauffered car to take me to the railroad station at Meriden, twelve miles away. In the middle of the nineteenth century Middletown was a prosperous industrial centre and a sailing port, too, because it is on the broad Connecticut River, which the cretinous highway engineers have now, of course, effectively barricaded from the town. But it has kept the great arcades of trees that characterised the old New England town, long before anyone had heard of suburbs or garden cities, and I have never, outside the Chiltern Hills, come upon more magnificently grown beeches, easily a century and a half old. . . .

Postscript. But I see I musn't send away this letter without answering the question you put to me in your extremely interesting letter of 23 September. How I came to decide early to be 'a writer on historical-sociological subjects', and whether my mentors envisaged such a career? The fact is that I never decided: life made the decision for me. Do you remember Samuel Butler's note about this, that a man may well decide what colour of tie or what kind of suit to wear, but when it comes to anything big, like choosing a wife or a career, he'd better leave the decision to providence. I reached the goal that now seems chosen by elimination. My earliest decision was to be a newspaper reporter but I never got beyond a copy boy. Then I decided to be an academic philosopher, but ill-health threw me out of college and kept me from getting a degree. Then I wanted, or rather all along I wanted, to be a novelist or a playwright, and I almost succeeded in the latter effort before I was twenty-three and kept on writing plays till I was thirty two; one real stage production success would have confirmed my resolution, but it never quite came and I lacked the temperament to battle Broadway. If I had had overwhelming ability I wouldn't have been daunted; but actually I was emotionally too immature, till I was forty, to have been anything but a clever, superficial fellow like Shaw. So I could go on. What really prepared me for my career was a negative decision: I didn't want to be a specialist. In this I had Geddes's encouragement and my own very wide interests made this easy. Nothing pushed me in any one direction, and that is what finally gave me the very wide field I now occupy. But it wasn't till I took a Rorschach test that I became fully conscious of the fact that I had an unusual ability, amounting to genius, for bringing widely separated observations together into a meaningful pattern: I got more out of one particular blot than the tester had ever found anyone else doing! Fortunately, I had no academic ambitions—in university harness I would have been frustrated or have committed intellectual suicide. In short, my path was an uncharted one. There were no shortcuts; I followed the currents of life where they took me. Fortunately I had a small inheritance, four thousand dollars, which helped me to endure a long apprenticeship and many rejections without actually starving. By the time the money was gone I had arrived!

WELWYN GARDEN CITY   21 October 1963

Dear Lewis

. . . First a word of thanks for your most encouraging appreciation of my Hamburg lecture. I don't think it is as good a study of Howard as the one I wrote for the *TP Review* October 1950, of which I think I sent you an offprint and which contained more complete biographical facts; but this time I emphasised more his Macaulayan attitude to scientific and mechanical progress. I am highly delighted that you like this little tilt at the Juggernaut worshippers, and that you are going to sweep up their corpses in your next book.

I wish I could send you in time for your Pennsylvania University talk proofs of the articles on Unwin in the November *T & CP*, but I don't think we have spare prints. Feiss's is a long study of his work and influence in the USA (of which I have to hold over half to December). May recalls his time in Unwin's office in Hampstead. Both these speak of Unwin with great technical respect and with deep affection for his fatherly interest and guidance. Rasmussen, who never worked under him, has immense respect for his blend of technical and social considerations. Purdom writes of Unwin's very short residence in Letchworth, regrets his early departure for Hampstead, admires his work and cultural-religious interests, but thinks him cold and aloof in personal relationships; in this last he differs entirely from the other three. . . .

Unwin never forgot the Garden City idea; in many lectures, including some brilliant ones at IFHP Congresses, he amplified the theme with a wealth of allusions to many cities. Some of these addresses ought to be reprinted and I am still looking for someone to do this. You will have noted Pevsner's[1] rediscovery in the *Architectural Review* of his *Town Planning in Practice. . . .*

I have to speak at the Unwin Centenary celebration at Hampstead Garden Suburb on 2 November—a ticklish assignment as I shall be preceded by Cleeve Barr, the Architect of the Ministry of Housing and Local Government, and followed by Pevsner, who recently described the Garden City as an off-shoot of the Garden Suburb!

MIDDLETOWN, CONN.   8 November 1963

Last Monday, dear F.J., we had a ceremonious meeting at the University of Pennsylvania, with a lecture hall that holds 500 crowded to the doors. Your letter was the first to be read, and after Holford, Williams-Ellis and Stein's were read I talked for a solid hour and a half about Unwin. In preparing the talk I discovered to my surprise that Unwin had begun as a mining engineer, and I dug up an old book he and Parker had published in 1901[2], which I'd never come upon before. In analysing his approach to the alternatives after the First World War: 100 garden cities (you) or better housing in Town Extensions, I concluded he was caught in a mathematical trap. Having proved that twelve houses to the acre was an economic and salutary method of planning, he used a circle to demonstrate that you could double the number of houses and the total area without widening appreciably the radius of the circle. That's a property of circles that made it easy for him to sanction town extension: but it took no account of the complexities of town growth—though on other occasions he was quite aware of them . . .

---

[1] Nikolaus Pevsner, historian of art and architecture.
[2] Barry Parker and Raymond Unwin, *The Art of Building a Home*, London, 1901.

WELWYN GARDEN CITY   12 November 1963

Dear Lewis

. . . I enclose a copy of the address I gave on 2 November at the Unwin Centenary meeting at Hampstead, from which you will see that I place the Unwin-Parker influence on modern domestic architecture much higher than the 'established' critics.

I also exonerate Unwin from the charge that he was complacent about the further suburban expansion of great cities. I had much correspondence with him in 1938–39, when he wrote a preface to my TCPA pamphlet on London planning, and advised me also on the draft of the National Planning Basis. At that time there was a tendency to resort to excessive flat-building, and Unwin, who was very firm about limiting housing density (though not dogmatic about twelve to the acre), used his mathematical argument to show that reasonably low density did not greatly increase town diameters.

I pointed out to him in one of my letters the danger of that argument as applied to London or any city already overgrown, and he replied agreeing that London should not be extended as a continuously built-up area. He was misunderstood on this point. The fact is that he was equally concerned for safeguarding the house-and-garden standard, and for regional planning; and saw that the two could only be reconciled by a dispersal and new-towns policy, in places where there was already overgrowth.

Essentially the argument about the effect of density on diameters is valid, and I use it in my new book as applied to towns of moderate size. But I think Unwin was incautious in applying it theoretically to the London region. He certainly did not want further suburban extensions to London. . . .

WELWYN GARDEN CITY   26 November 1963

Dear Lewis

The New Towns (Osborn–Whittick) is published at last, and I understand that some copies are being sent to you at once. The USA edition won't be out before about the end of January 1964.

Reading over my own chapters, I am again relieved. Though the attack on great cities is thoroughgoing, it seems to me more plausible, wary of comebacks and cogent, than I feared it might seem. Nothing could be more different from your own treatment of the same subject, but it takes all sorts of readers to make a public and there will, I think, be some, incapable of grasping your overwhelmingly documented argument, who may be influenced by my amateurish simplicity.

My anxiety is that the reviewers will not let what I say get through to the sort of people I address, who are numerous but have to be caught almost physically by the ears to listen. The look of the book, with its many pictures and plans, may give the impression that it's just another architectural compilation; too many editors here are likely to pass it to the established lizards who infest our most influential papers. Possibly here and there it will get through—but you never know.

As you may have noticed, there is an almost revolutionary advance in political thinking about regional distribution of industry and urban development in political circles here—largely the result of some excellent detailed work by the TCPA since I left. It is still a bit inchoate, but there is no doubt at all that it is an important breakthrough. The complacency about city growth has gone for good in this country; and there is now a flood of books, pamphlets and political speeches on the whole subject. But the pains for which the doctor is invoked are traffic congestion in one limb and economic anaemia in another; my effort is to prove that the loss of decent living conditions is an even bigger drain on vitality. The delusion that we haven't any space obstinately remains.

And owing to a bad system of accounting even the managers of the new towns still think they are 'in the red'—whereas those in England (not yet in Scotland) show collectively a handsome annual surplus—a point I may get across, if the book is read.

Grief and worry about the Kennedy tragedy is genuine over here. I don't need to say what M.P.O. and I feel.

MIDDLETOWN, CONN.   3 December 1963

Your letter came, dear F.J., in the very mail that brought the leaflet about your new book, and I am ready to congratulate you in advance over what will prove to be, I am sure, not merely a noteworthy but an influential work; for it could not have come, as you yourself indicate, at a better time. It should give you not a little satisfaction to realise how a certain John Bull-cum-bull-dog tenacity of yours has, in the long run, outlasted, and seems about to triumph over all the more flashy kinds of opposition that expressed the fashionable ideas of the moment; it is not so much the detailed work of the TCPA since you left, as the broad, solid barrage of ideas that you have so steadily laid down, that has had its effect and made the special contributions of your juniors acceptable. Many a good man has gone to his grave with no hope that his ideas would ever be accepted, often indeed driven there prematurely by despair, whereas your own work is ripening before your eyes, and that is as near to heaven, I suspect, as it is possible to get.

I wish my own work had anything like the same impact in this country, but only the other day your old enemy Lloyd Rodwin—who curiously was partly responsible for my being invited to MIT for three years!—in a pseudo-review of *The Highway and the City*, went out of his way to say that my ideas had had absolutely no influence on professional theorists and planners, who have no use for either my methods or my goals. He is right, of course: even my one-time friend and disciple, Catherine Bauer, is in Rodwin's camp, not mine. On the other hand, though Rodwin probably does not acknowledge it, I've had a certain *negative* influence, preventing bad things from being done, though always in small matters. Just the other day someone recalled my attention to a public letter I had written attacking Robert Moses's effort to put a four-lane avenue through Washington Square: one of the most coruscating pieces of criticism, I found when I re-read it, that I have ever written. The local groups that were opposing Moses's plan were willing to settle for a two-lane road, so that Fifth Avenue buses might continue to use the Square as their terminus. No one had dared to suggest what I did, that the Square be closed off entirely to traffic and the buses re-routed. My suggestion gave them the courage to ask for what they should have demanded in the first place; so today the entire Square has been reclaimed for pedestrian use and the bus route, which Moses said could not be changed, *has* been changed. I put that minuscule triumph alongside my blocking the Port Authority's attempt to make a jet airport in New Jersey, in a suburban area that would have been completely devastated by such traffic. (So much for the 'impractical idealist' who doesn't face realities!). But in the long run, after we have done many worse things here, I expect to catch up with you even in my own country.

As for the reviews, I can well understand your trepidation. I have never before been the object of such a brief, contemptuous sneer as *The Times Literary Supplement* reviewer gave *The City in History*. Speaking of reviews, if you do *The Highway and the City* for *T & CP* please use the English edition: not merely because it omits American material, but because I've added a special preface emphasising the importance of maintaining public mass transportation, above all the railroads, if all your cities, big and small, are not to be bulldozed out of existence by the motor car . . .

As for the event that has cast a shadow on all our lives these last two weeks —it has revealed both the best and the worst aspects of my countrymen. Kennedy was not in any sense the man that Roosevelt was, yet the grief over his death was as genuine and as deep, partly perhaps because it represented an unconscious hope that youth might save us from the follies that age and habit had committed us to—and yet with an unconscious fear, just as deep, that a single mad act by one or more conspirators, such as that which killed Kennedy, might suddenly put an end to all our hopes, if not to mankind itself.

Mrs Kennedy, as you perhaps saw—this was the great triumph of television—behaved with a queenly dignity that redeemed the thousand vulgarities of our life; but nothing could redeem the publicised violence to which the Dallas police force was a willing, indeed probably an active, accessory: so that we fully earned, by our world broadcast of this event by Telstar, the contempt that the Russians properly heaped upon us, even in the midst of their sympathy. But the majority of Americans, outside the South, lived through death and sorrow as they had never lived before; it had the appearance of a great national purgation which has been confirmed, in a way, by President Johnson's high-minded words and acts: so one hopes that some ultimate good may flower from this evil.

WELWYN GARDEN CITY   29 December 1963

Dear Lewis

. . . In the first month only two reviews of *The New Towns* have appeared in the national press—in the two papers that I would have hoped to be exceptions from a general attitude of disdain or hostility. *The Guardian*, formerly the most enlightened of English papers on planning (when Derek Senior was its correspondent on the subject), dismissed the book patronizingly as 'grinding the axe of the garden city movement' and 'fundamentally anti-urban'; it said that the authors 'had no time for improving the condition of the existing cities'—though in a dozen or more places in the book I had made it daylight clear that that is the primary purpose of the dispersal and new towns policy. *The Economist* printed a half-column notice following a two-column one on Spanish history in the fifteenth to seventeenth centuries. Neither was really a 'review' in the sense of telling the reader what our book is about. Both substituted for this a parade of the reviewers' own very conventional opinions, without any hint that the book deals very fully with, and tries to demolish, just these. It is obvious that neither writer had really done more than glance perfunctorily at the book. When a few more notices have appeared I am going to defy convention and write an article for *T & CP* on the present state of reviewing in this country.

I had a card from Catherine Bauer in which she says; 'At long last New Towns are becoming a fashionable idea in the USA! Achievement is another matter however'. As to Rodwin, you will see I have another tilt with him in the new book.

I think you are wrong in thinking your influence has been slight. Your sort of writing gradually sinks into academic thought and practical policy. But both of us should really have been writing in the eighteenth century, before the damage was done. Now we can only suggest ways to pick up some of the pieces for the existing cities. But we shall affect the cities of the twentieth century.

WELWYN GARDEN CITY   27 February 1964

Dear Lewis

... Debates in both Houses of Parliament this month on the latest New Towns Bill showed unanimity in support of the new towns policy, many demands for more energetic pursuance of it by the Government, and strong condemnation of the Minister's proposal to extend Stevenage from 80,000 to 140,000.

Another interesting thing this week is a scientific book by Lord Taylor and another[1] on the influence of environment on neuroses and psychoses; out of which the new towns came triumphantly. I am taking the risk of having it reviewed by Young or Willmott, who started the 'new town blues' myth and have, I am told, now recanted.

The TCPA has arranged showing in London on four evenings next week of your six films (three at a time). M.P.O. and I are going up to see them. Very rare thing for M.P.O. to go to London twice in a week.

At a quick glance Donald Foley's book on British planning[2] looks fairly intelligent and perceptive. It is about the first that notices that I have had some influence. A huge, brilliantly presented and illustrated tome by Paul Ritter[3], on the other hand, omits any reference whatever to the existence of the TCPA. And books from the USA that have just passed through my hands on the way to reviewers are equally unconscious of Stein, Henry Wright, Tugwell, Mumford or the Green-Belt towns. Future historians of this period are going to have a difficult job.

WELWYN GARDEN CITY   6 March 1964

Dear Lewis

Another damned letter, hard on the last! Sorry, but it's the burden of authorship, even when unpaid. Holmes Perkins is editing a reader in Civic Design, one of eight to be published for the Institute of Urban Studies. He asks Faber & Faber for permission to include in it, from Howard's *Garden Cities of*

---

[1] S. J. L. Taylor *and* S. Chave, *Mental Health and Environment*, London, 1964.
[2] D. Foley, *Controlling London's Growth*, Berkeley, Cambridge (UK), 1963, 1964.
[3] Paul Ritter, *Planning for Man and Motor*, New York, Oxford, 1964.

To-morrow, your Introduction and Howard's Chapter 1, 'The Town-Country Magnet'; and they refer the matter to me, as the TCPA owns the copyright of Howard's book. . . .

Should I agree (if you do)? I feel pretty sure that the series as a whole will parade the present 'conventional wisdom'. Would the extracts from *Garden Cities of To-morrow* be just submerged in that megalopolitan flood; or would it be a useful Trojan Horse within the citadel? As the readers will go out anyway I see some case for the Trojan Horse. But really, there ought to be in such a series some of the contemporary thinking of our own school. Have you been asked for anything else? I haven't, of course. Nor I think has Peter Self.

Gossip column (needing no comment). Reviews of the Osborn–Whittick volume are now appearing. *The Times Literary Supplement* was better than expected: respectful, and exposing the cloven hoof (? J. M. Richards) very warily. And this week they publish in a prominent position a letter from me which for advertising purposes is as good as a favourable review. We were mildly rebuked for not being 'objective and balanced' but 'polemical' and 'tendentious'. My letter asks on what principle of judgement is that wrong in a book on a controversial subject: 'Does one have to sit firmly on the fence in order to be considered "balanced and objective"?'.

And this week there is an even more favourable review in *The Times Educational Supplement*, which has a far larger readership—though perhaps not the same hallowed status with librarians.

The TCPA showed your six films to about 140 people, three each on four nights this week. You personally come over extremely well, and the photography is good, and the stimulus to thought valuable. I don't think it is a destructive criticism that your prescription is less telling than the diagnosis. You could have got more than perhaps you yourself realise from shots in our new towns. More on this later, perhaps.

AMENIA, NEW YORK   12 March 1964

Your letter about the Howard permissions came yesterday, dear F.J., and I find myself a little surprised that Perkins had not breathed a word about this project to me: possibly because he does not intend to include anything else of mine and was afraid that I might object to this particular selection. But I am quite willing to have it included and I think that you need have no hesitation to give permission to have Howard's chapter included too, for so far from taking away any sales of the book it will, if anything, add a few possible readers. These urban 'readings' books reach a very wide audience in the colleges, including classes in sociology as well as planning. Not merely that, but this is a timely moment to bring Howard to American attention again: even President Johnson vaguely advocated something that could be recognised as a sort of 'free enterprise' New Towns policy—the free part of it being the enterprises' free use of government aid and the governmental right of eminent domain, for the sake of ensuring his private gains. *But do not hesitate to ask the usual fee* for permission to use material of such length: one hundred dollars for each. Martin Meyerson, the general editor of the series, is now Dean of the School of Environmental Design at Berkeley; originally, he was influenced by my work and in 1952 he even assisted me in giving a course at the University of Pennsylvania; but he has long outgrown my influence and he has become one whose ambitions will always tend to put him on the side of whatever is immediately open to achievement.

Still, I don't think that Howard's contribution will necessarily be swamped in the proposed book for it is quite likely that they will be including a slice of Stein's *New Towns for America.*

I was glad to get your comments on the *City* films, in which my performance on the screen seemed to me extraordinarily wooden, partly because I was using a new medium, the teleprompter, without practice, and partly because they didn't have sense enough to show me a rush of my own part so that I could have discovered, in time, what was wrong. But as for the theme of the film itself, you must remember the occasion of it to see why there is so much diagnosis and so little prescription. From the beginning the Director wished to build his film on *The City in History*, a book which is all diagnosis and description, except in so far as the descriptive parts emphasise the elements that must go into any valid present day prescription. MacNeill, the director, naturally found that the book was far too complex and difficult to be translated into even three hours of film, so what is left is a combination of the original idea with such emphasis on the contemporary scene as would prepare the viewer for the book that I have still to write and the films that might be based on it. For all that, I insisted at the start that the positive lessons of the New Towns should be one of the culminating points in the series, and MacNeill, who was most faithful in his effort to interpret my ideas, fully understood this and sent one of his crews to England and another crew to Vallingby for this purpose. But it just happened that fate made the winter and spring that was given to this job quite the vilest season, as far as the weather was concerned, that you had known in many years; so despite all their honest efforts, most of the film they came back with wasn't good enough to show. That is why the new towns play such a small part in the film. I would have felt even more unhappy about this were it not for the fact that the last two films seem to me to contain important material that should be assimilated by the planners of new towns as well as rehabilitators of old ones. And so I was content, after the final film had been twice re-made, to give my imprimatur to the whole job.

Though I was consulted at every phase of the preparation of the script, and though I wrote and re-wrote a large part of the narration both on and off screen, the film primarily remains MacNeill's work and demonstrates what a sympathetic director was able to utilise by way of ideas and images from *The City in History*. If I knew as much about motion pictures as he does and had been appointed to the job, I would doubtless have made a quite different presentation of my ideas; but I think he did as well as anyone could reasonably demand, especially when one remembers that he had nothing of mine of the positive side to go with except the hints in the last chapter and a handful of illustrations. My *Architectural Record* articles on the forms of the contemporary city began to appear only when the film was almost finished. So much for history.

Since I am a subscriber to the *TLS* I noted with pleasure their respectful review of your book: likewise your very apt reply. The reviewer's attempt to rule out controversy was comic: what it really meant was—'Don't annoy me by trying to persuade me to change my mind'. On the whole, I think your book has fared better with the British reviewers than my *Highway and the City*. The reviewer in *The Observer* chose the neatest possible way of causing people to ignore my book, by saying flatly that it was out of date because it had been published in America in 1953; when the fact is, of course, it was first published in 1963 and nine of the fifteen essays were written in 1960 and 1961. All but three of the rest were published in 1957, facts which were plainly indicated by the dates after each essay. I've long suspected that reviewers don't read words, but now I find that some of them can't even read figures. . . .

AMENIA, NEW YORK   27 March 1964

The New Towns came, dear F.J., the day before yesterday and I was immensely pleased by the first impression it made. I am sure that when I begin reading it page by page that pleasure will deepen, and my admiration over the way you have coped with this mass of complex information will keep pace with it. The fine illustrations you've used reveal both the quality of the New Towns performance in building, and the remarkable individuality of their development, now far more obvious than in the earlier stages when the abstract plans dominated and the buildings were still meagre. No matter how Review Editors ignore this book or play it down, it will outlast all sneers and disparagements— a permanent landmark. My thorough reading of the book will have to wait till I finish the first draft of my present work, but I already see that I will have to draw heavily on *New Towns* when—or if!—I finally settle down to write the contemporary companion volume to *The City in History*.

Despite all the letters and notes I've written you the last four months, I wonder if I remembered to tell you that we hope to spend five or six weeks in England beginning in September: at least we have steamer reservations!

WELWYN GARDEN CITY   1 April 1964

Dear Lewis

It is late in the evening, and I am late in delivering my editorial on the Government's revolutionary (but not quite adequately revolutionary) *South East Study*[1], and I am mentally tired after writing to *The Times* a terse letter of as high as possible content to be understood of babes and sucklings— in reply to an incredibly stupid one by a very influential economist (Sir Geoffrey Crowther).

So I relax at your expense by this unnecessary reply to your letter of 27 March to hand today. It is really kind of you to reassure me that *New Towns* makes a good impression on you in advance of reading. So it did on me, and when I read over my own part of it I found it less incompetent than in the long interval of publication I had begun to fear. You may not; but the book isn't written for such as you and the high angels. It is written for Babbitt and Borough Councillor Jorkins and John Dumdrudge MP, who might have borrowed it from the public library if the reviewers had given them the least reason to be interested. As a reference book it will, as you encouragingly say, survive, but it is also a fighting and topical book, and as such, except in some professional circles, it has missed the boat here. But through the long campaign of the TCPA, through your work and that of a few others, half the philosophy has got through already to the political decision-makers here, as the *South East Study* shows. Half a policy, I suppose (to console myself), is better than no shred. But to change the metaphor, sitting now on the sidelines I wish I had a beer-bottle, or at least a cushion, to throw at the centre-forward.

When you read my review of *The Highway and the City* in the *Journal of the TPI*, you will think I am a cantankerous old devil, because I was provoked by your 1953 critique of the first new towns to a critique of your aesthetic approach. But perhaps you will detect that my main aim was to incite the 'lizards', who are in some reaction against you at the moment, to get and read

---

[1] Ministry of Housing and Local Government, *The South-East Study, 1961–1981*, London, 1964.

the book. A bit of shadow-boxing between us two old squares will, I hope, cause the teenagers to see that we can still put up a show. I think if there were world enough and time for us to argue things right out we should find ourselves, for all practical purposes, in agreement, though I should still feel by comparison with you a philosophic child. I haven't any bootstraps by which I could lift myself up, and on the verge of 79 it is too late to acquire any. . . .

I am in a miserable condition of unlit lamps and ungirt loins, unable to decide which parts of my unfilled programme to choose for the very limited remainder of my years and energy. Yet an incorrigible Cockney optimism prevents me from taking my position seriously. I sleep most of the night and part of the day, and my conscience sleeps too. Mildly I regret that I never learned to work.

AMENIA, NEW YORK   6 April 1964

I have reached a halfway point, dear F.J., in the writing of my book on Technics, at which for many different reasons I must pause: one of the reasons being to write a short biographic notice of old Geddes for the new *International Encyclopedia of Social Sciences*, and another to go to Chicago to give an opening talk (on the Automation of Knowledge!) to a conference of University presidents. So, though your letter came only this morning, I'm answering it now to take advantage of my breather; and even more, to anticipate the review you have written of *The Highway and the City*. I've never regarded intellectual or political agreement as a *sine qua non* of friendship: rather the reverse, in that a friend is a person for whom one has such a strong attachment that one may quarrel freely with him without any fear that the hottest kind of difference will do violence to the relationship; and by now that's the state that, thank heaven, we are in.

I do not even have to read your review in order to answer it, for on numerous occasions I have been aware of the curious breach that divides us, a breach that, by your particular, somewhat condescending 'correction' of my position, might lead to hot resentment on my part if it came from anyone else, but which by now I regard with a detachment that anesthetises umbrage. What puzzles me is the fact that your attitude on the subject of density in town building so oddly contrasts with your other outstanding traits: your solid empiricism, your common sense, your tolerance, your unwillingness to let the kind of planner you dislike impose his alien standards on you. But on this one subject you are as dogmatic, as absolutist, as Le Corbusier: for you, there is only one tolerable density, and therefore only one kind of 'ideal' town: that which, though it has all the other desirable attributes of a genuine city, is laid out on the pattern of the best nineteenth century suburbs. This is a pattern which was an acceptable, indeed a delightful and admirable, pattern for a suburb of five to ten thousand people, as it was equally for the small agricultural and industrial towns of New England in the first half of the nineteenth century. But when the scale of the city changes, the pattern itself, I hold, must change too: not to the point of accepting densities of over 125 or so people per acre for the entire residential area, but with many variations in form and density to accommodate the greater variety of tastes and interests one gets in the bigger urban unit. For those who love to cultivate their gardens, there would still be parts of the town on the outskirts of a ten-houses-per-acre density; but for those who are willing to forgo private gardens provided there are still open spaces and amenities, there might be higher densities that would not violate either sanitary or esthetic or social decency.

This flexibility, this readiness to meet a diversity of human needs, this tolerance of variety, is for me the very essence of urban life; and to forgo it because F.J.O. likes only one kind of environment seems to me the height of absurdity. No standard, however good, is as good as that, and you of all people should be the first one to say so. 'You can't plan man'. But in having only one pattern for the ideal city, your own, dismissing everyone else's notions as mere estheticism or Bloomsburyism, you are actually trying to do just that—and thereby proclaiming yourself the most obstinate of Utopians. As a result, you closely follow Thomas More's prescription: for he said that he who knew one town in Utopia knew all of them, they were so alike.

When, in 1953, I pointed out that the New Towns were overspaced, I was only reporting that the fears I had in 1947 when I looked at the first of the New Towns had been corroborated: that far too much internal space, important for pedestrian circulation, had been sacrificed to excessively wide streets, verges, front gardens, playing fields and to great wedges of park that over-separated the neighbourhood units. This misuse of urban space seemed to me to sacrifice the social character of the new town to empty asphalt and empty verdure. And with houses planned at fourteen to the acre, with a green belt surrounding the whole community, this sacrifice was gratuitous, indeed quite mad; for the planners were taking steps to compensate for non-existent crowding when they should have been moving in just the opposite direction— to increase variety and sociability and to overcome the smug isolationism of suburban life, itself justified only by the foul congestion of the big city.

My judgement on all these matters did not, as you've sometimes covertly implied, spring from any desire to be on the fashionable side: in this case, on the side of *The Architectural Review*. At what point in my whole career have I ever done anything to be in fashion? It was rather based on residence— not just tourist visits—in a wide variety of cities, from small country towns

like Hanover, through suburbs, like Olmsted's faculty suburb for Stanford
University, to old urban quarters, like those of Greenwich Village and
Brooklyn Heights in New York, to the heart of big cities like New York and
London, including four winters on the twentieth floor of a high-rise slab in
Philadelphia, which last, apart from the Turneresque views of sunsets, I
abominated. The closeness and intimacy of life in a well-designed city, like
old Amsterdam or old Florence, would be, I should agree, bought at too great
a price if that closeness is so excessive that it destroys open spaces, wipes out
all gardens and obstructs even the view of the sky: and it is still too high
when, as in American 'urban renewal' projects and in much post-war County
Council building in London, the Le Corbusier formula for over-crowding in
high-rise buildings, with only visual open space, has been followed.

On such matters I am on your side, fighting for a humane scale and a reasonable density. But when you hold that only *one* density is tolerable throughout
the town, and that only one set of architectural solutions, namely those that
conform to your personal taste, are enjoyable, you seriously damage the case
you make out for the New Towns—a sound, well-reasoned case—by attempting to make it a case for F.J.O.'s private judgements, as if you had descended
like Moses from Sinai with a tablet revealing divine authority for only one
kind of town.

Your attitude on this subject, dear F.J., would indeed be only a cause for
my personal distress—or even perhaps my amusement—were it not that it
has a public side that is serious; for while one part of you has with magnificent
persistence done more than any other one person of your generation to bring
the New Towns into existence—and whatever their minor shortcomings may
be, that is a memorable achievement—the other part of you, with something
that must be called blind stubbornness rather than persistence, has kept aloof
from or actively alienated many who should have been powerful allies; has
confused the real issues before us even in matters like density; and has helped,
along with Ministry of Transport regulations and other similar impedimenta,
to keep the architects and planners of these New Towns from inventing all the
many variations that are possible within this general pattern.

Though I see grave faults in the design of both Cumbernauld and Hook,
I welcome both as attempts to break away from a now too rigid pattern.
What you regarded as an indefensible folly or heresy on my part, has, in
some degree, kept people's minds open about the value of New Towns and
made them aware of all the further social and political innovations that will
be necessary before they will be able to compete, in their own right, with the
attractions of the present metropolis, congested, sordid, confused, over-
extended as so large a mass of London, New York, Paris or Rome actually is.

There, dear F.J., is my answer to your unread review! And though I haven't yet read my words over, and would doubtless be able to improve my argument by re-writing, I am willing to let you print it in its present form, if you think such a stirring up of controversy would be valuable for the common cause we both, each in his own way, serve. Nothing that I have said, or that you may say further, can abate my feeling of affectionate friendship, coupled with admiration for your fruitful public career. With blessings from us both, for you and Margaret . . .

WELWYN GARDEN CITY   12 April 1964

Your manifesto of 6 April demands a considered reply. Here is only a short interim comment . . . You have guessed wrong about my review in the *TPIJ*, intended to induce planners to read *The Highway and City* . . . I am far too much in awe of you to be 'condescending' . . . I think you underrate the first new towns, most of which will in fact develop into good urban units in sub-regional complexes. Their centres are already far livelier than you imagine. At this stage it is most important not to depreciate them.

I *don't* think there is only one kind of 'ideal' town or tolerable density, nor am I concerned for 'my own taste'. I think, as resources grow, many people will want a transfer from privately-maintained to public garden space—but that this does not imply higher densities . . . Cars and public transport facilitate contacts without compression, till the size of a town causes a central parking problem (Buchanan[1] puts the prospective limit at 70,000). Maximum density is a matter of judgment. The new towns all strove for higher maxima than mine, and under public demand compromised between the two. Some architects and country preservationists press for higher densities; the growing class of owner-occupiers want much lower ones; the new towns have to meet this unless they are to be enclaves for the under-privileged—their present damaging reputation.

I have never suspected you of following fashion. *Au contraire*, you are one of the few who make it. I do think you are highly sensitive to art fashions, which I think represent the state of soul of small coteries rather than society at large, and don't so much worry about. I feel the vast majority are untouched by them. On this I may be wrong, but in any case I admire the persistence with which you debunk decadent art and coterie pretensions. Don't resent it if M. Jourdain's tendency to scoff will out. I have a sense of inferiority without a complex.

---

[1] Professor Colin Buchanan, author of *Traffic in Towns*, London, 1963.

I am all for city variety within the limits of sanity and common human acceptance. But there are extremes (e.g. Eliot Paul's Paris Street) that I would exclude. I have never said that *nobody* should live in flats or dog-kennels. I merely oppose the provision of types of accommodation of which there are demonstrably too many already. I think it is a sociological fallacy that people are more neighbourly when their elbows are sticking into each others' sides. It would be absurd to suppose that all the thousands of new towns to be built in the world are likely to be carbon copies of our first fifteen. These have in fact much variety; but even what they have in common represents, I think, the best kind of manufacturing town yet produced. They have nothing of the 'smug isolationism of suburban life'—really, that is a curious travesty, coming from you. Don't you open yourself to the suspicion of being intolerant of one broad variety of town, because it isn't some other variety that you might prefer?

When someone produces another attractive pattern that meets economic, family and social requirements I shall rejoice. But Hook and Cumbernauld simply don't. They make some effort (not a very clever one) to grapple with the central car-assembly problem. But in housing layouts they are a sad falling-off; look at the housing plans in *New Towns*! There is an enormous variety of far better Victorian layouts at densities of four to twenty an acre.

Another subject I just mention. I have a request from Prof. Sherman Paul of the University of Illinois for a contribution to a book about Lewis Mumford. I'm scared of adventuring into that much admired but transcendent world, where I feel like Mark Twain's *Innocents Abroad*. Also it means time and effort, and I am increasingly work-shy. Yet I'm attracted, too.

AMENIA, NEW YORK   26 April 1964

This week, dear F.J., I came back from a weary trip to Chicago—cold, blustery, raining—where I addressed a huge gathering of University officials on the 'The Automation of Knowledge', dehorning most of their sacred cows, and I am paying for my audacities by being confined with a cold to my bed.

Even though this is only a stopgap letter, I must tell you how pleased I was to find that my 'Reply' hasn't widened the distance between us, but if anything has narrowed it. I felt like reciting the old lines Sophia and I have often repeated after a quarrel: 'The falling out of faithful friends renewing is of love'. It is the suppression of grievances or anger that taints human relations, as Blake put it in *his* famous quatrain.

By now you've probably heard from Professor Paul that I've called off his well-meant but ill-timed collective biography—that is something that must wait till I and a lot of other people are dead. Strangely, those who knew me least were most eager to contribute, while my most intimate friends were deeply disturbed over the whole enterprise. Behind their feeling was something else—their sense that such a public exposure was not in keeping with my character. How I came to overlook this at the beginning I still can't quite account for. I'm afraid I was at first seduced, like any silly girl, and forgot that the consequences of this seduction would be a very strange baby indeed! . . .

WELWYN GARDEN CITY   21 May 1964

Dear Lewis
You will have seen by this time my review of *The Highway and the City* in the TPI *Journal*, and I really do hope you will see it as favourable and likely to send people to the book.

I have only seen today the review by Reyner Banham in last week's *New Statesman*, which seems to me vicious and slightly vulgar. I at once phoned Secker and Warburg, but Warburg is away and therefore I couldn't speak to him personally. His secretary, however, promised to send you a copy by airmail at once, as you may think it worth a reply. I am making this comment in our own *Journal*, at the end of a note on the controversy about the proposed Gothic extension of the Houses of Parliament:

'Anyone who doubts the fluidity of fashion in architecture should read Mr. Reyner Banham's review of *The Highway and the City* in the *New Statesman* (15 May). Mumford's "Case Against Modern Architecture", he says, "represented a position that most younger architects had reached, or left behind, by the time it came out in 1962". We now await with excitement the Autumn fashion of 1964.'

There could be no more convincing demonstration than this review that modern architectural criticism has gone to pieces—more so, I feel, than architecture itself. The modern office block is frightfully dull externally, but it is not very bad functionally, in the sense that it provides well-lighted floor-space and is constructionally economical; and sometimes the interiors are very pleasant and attractively decorated. I am not so often offended as bored by the uniformity of the egg-boxes. And I do not get the pleasurable kick out of the shapes of the windows that I constantly get from those of the Georgian, the appeal of which is so strong that I think there may be fundamental laws of shape after all—though I never understand the classical theories of shape. However I don't intend to become an aesthetic theorist. . . .

AMENIA, NEW YORK   22 May 1964

I came back from New York yesterday, dear F.J., to find your *TPI* review
waiting for me. It gave me the first real laugh I've enjoyed for more than a
month: but the laugh was on *me*, not on you! For I could imagine your own
puzzled amusement over my gratuitous explosion over a review you had never
written, when in fact the actual review was almost too kind and flattering to
be swallowed by the author. It was your *warning* about its contents that put
me off—as if I could be so thin-skinned over our differences on aesthetics!
But I confess one sentence *does* puzzle me for it seems, on one reading, to
imply that I admire Mondrian, Mies, and Buckminster Fuller, when in fact
I have been their consistent enemy. But no matter. This is a trivial point. All
that's left is to thank you for such a laudatory review and to apologise for my
absurd explosion. . . .

WELWYN GARDEN CITY   27 May 1964

Dear Lewis

. . . I'm glad to be 'out of the dog-house' as a reviewer of your book. If you
look again at that passage about the Mondrians etc. you will see that I was
far from suggesting that you admired them: what I did suggest was that you
perhaps took them too seriously as representative of Our Time. I know so
many more people, intelligent, hard-working, enthusiastic about healthy
things, or devoted to their families, harmless sports or hobbies, without either
social idealisms or ambitions, than I know people who read the current
equivalents of Ezra Pound, Gertrude Stein or Kafka, or ever knew about or
enjoyed (as I did) the Picassos and Matisses when they were really rich and
revealing, that I can't see the modern literary or art movements as having
anything like the social importance that Shakespeare, Wordsworth, Tennyson, Dickens, Ruskin etc., had in their times. My Mother had a Tennyson:
her present parallel would not possess Eliot or Auden. My teen-age friends
read Shaw, Chesterton, Belloc, Conrad and Galsworthy with intense appreciation. My children don't so inevitably read Miller, Sartre or Scott Fitzgerald—and wouldn't even know the names of the novelists and philosophers
reviewed in the literary weeklies. Nor would they buy reproductions of typical
abstract painters. Tom came back from the USA with a huge reproduction of
a Renoir with sweet young things sitting on a grassy bank—from the Metropolitan Museum—*not* the one of Modern Art, which merely exasperated him,
whereas it would slightly interest as well as exasperate me, since I am half-
way to your understanding disapprobation.

The men I know in hundreds include a large minority of the normally vicious who would make love to other men's wives or to call-girls; and among the women I know is a smaller minority who wouldn't mind if I made love to them in a normal way. But I can't see that the standard of behaviour is nearly as casual or depraved as it would seem to have been in Restoration England, if one could believe the dramatists. Anyway, I just doubt if literature and art reflects the society of its time; it is just as likely that its interest is that it paints so different a world. But one should be aware of the percentage of people who follow it; and that in my own experience is small. I'm not dogmatic about this: I just doubt. I don't doubt at all that vast numbers of people gamble on horses, ball games and bingo; but that's a quite different order of depravity. Vast numbers play games, garden, love children, are remarkably loyal to wives they are tired of at times—the true pathos and sublime of human life, as in the age of Burns. Maugham's *Of Human Bondage* still seems to me truer to more life than Fitzgerald's *Tender is the Night*.

The Society of Authors Dinner was a bore. We met nobody we knew. We are not ourselves in the 500 who are known, or the 5,000 who are known *of*, but perhaps just in the 50,000 who can be found in reference books, so we were seated among others of the 50,000 (not amusing ones) in sight of two or three of the 500 or 5,000 and listened to dull speeches by Lord Radcliffe, S. J. Perelman (an American we couldn't place, who was perhaps entertaining but didn't articulate clearly enough for us), a French writer, and a young, conceited pup who had just received a Somerset Maugham Award (God knows why). Opposite us, but on the top table, was old Compton Mackenzie, with a sharp, bearded, inscrutable mask of a face; and some way along the table T. S. Eliot, a wizened little man leaning over his plate and gazing fixedly at it and listening to the speeches with a rare indulgence in a half-smile. Adjoining M.P.O. and me were semi-dumb authors neither interested nor interesting, and their more talkative but not very interesting wives and women companions. Old Stephen King-Hall was unfortunately two places away, and talking very little to his neighbours; but I made a date to meet him some time or other, which we'll probably both (to my regret) fail to follow up. The only amusing people we met were a couple of press reporters, one of whom was an enthusiast for Hemingway and had himself published a history of the American Civil War—but he had never heard of Stephen Vincent Benet!

This is a lazy letter by a tired old man (79 yesterday) who after an evening out can't work. Put it in the WPB.

AMENIA, NEW YORK   10 June 1964

. . . I'm pleased by the readiness of the MIT press to publish *Garden Cities of Tomorrow*, both for the sake of what's in the book, and perhaps quite as much for the way that the tide is turning in its favour, thanks to you and Stein—and no doubt partly to me—for holding our own when all the bright young things were dismissing us as mossbacks for suggesting that New Towns were not a faded dream but a dawning reality. At least the subject is now discussable in fashionable circles, and it may take root there even after they have taken up with a later fashion. . . .

You're good to have been so concerned about the Reyner Banham review; but long before I discovered that he didn't like me I discovered that I didn't like him, or rather, his cocky, half-baked interpretations of modern architecture. Warburg's secretary fell down on the job of sending me the review, but that was all right since, even if I could have found the time, I long ago resolved never to answer reviews: all one does by so doing, apart from spending valuable energy, is to publicise opinions that would otherwise die as soon as they were uttered. For people who take the trouble to know one's work, it is itself always the best answer to an unfavourable review; and if one's book does not perform that job, then it would prove that, after all, the reviewer was right. But I am human, and I've often been tempted! The private answer that I frame in my mind is always so blistering that it would stand little chance of publication, even if I were foolish enough to write it down. . . .

As for our sexual morality, I don't think that heterosexual attitudes toward sex are much different than what they have always been, though they are more openly acknowledged and more overt and unashamed than in Victorian times. By the same token, I find among the young that all sorts of corrective inhibitions of the Victorian kind are coming back again, as they did in fact in England around 1840 in reaction against Georgian looseness. But at the same time homosexuality has been increasing to a surprising degree in my country where it never, thanks to the absence of the public school system, was as rife as in England; and this change, which threatens serious damage to permanent heterosexual relations, seems to me to be encouraged by a general attitude of permissiveness which has at its roots a general deflation of meaning and purpose. I've given a more elaborate explanation of this in a long essay on Jung and Freud I've written for *The New Yorker*[1], but I have no intention of inflicting this masterpiece on you—though it's attracted a lot of favourable attention here, at least among those who in some degree share my views. . . .

AMENIA, NEW YORK   6 August 1964

Your letter, dear F.J., awakened pangs of guilt over my failure to say anything about *The New Towns*, so I soothed my conscience at once by sitting down with the book and perusing the first part of it with care, leaving the detailed report

---

[1] 23 May 1964.

on the towns themselves for next year, when I shall use them as a guide to my further explorations. The introductory chapters are masterly and on every page they show your masterly hand. They completely dispose of all the piddling criticisms the New Towns have evoked from the academic people over here, and the book will serve as a landmark of the movement's progress, even as Howard's book serves to mark its beginning. What has happened to it at McGraw-Hill I can't guess, for if they had sent out review copies I would have gotten one automatically from *The New Yorker*, so the theory of your English publishers about an internal communications breakdown is probably correct.

This is a by-product of something you might not even suspect: since good stenographers over here must be paid from a hundred to a hundred twenty-five dollars a week, someone has discovered that it's cheaper to phone, even long distance, than to write a letter, and the custom of letter writing has unfortunately almost disappeared. This is no high faluting explanation of mine: my own publisher tells me that he can't get any answer by mail from his colleagues in other publishing houses: and though he himself writes letters I suspect that his subordinates don't.

This is a weird world; but it looks as if both of us may have the last laugh at it, you with the re-emergence of the garden city idea, Stein and I with a similar renascence of the regional idea. You of course know about Reston, the new upper class New Town planned for 75,000 people seventeen miles from Washington, purely as a speculative enterprise: a sort of suburban Bath, twentieth century model. The man behind it, R. E. Simmons, has expressed a desire to meet me, so in a dim way our work may have influenced him. After being dismissed for a whole generation as old hat, the garden city is now in danger of being embraced and caricatured as the latest thing. Something like this has happened with the movement for regional planning: just the other day the Office for Regional Development of the State of New York published a report, based solidly on the final report drafted by Henry Wright three years ago, on a plan for decentralising housing and industry in the state of New York. What is more, it went a step farther than we were prepared to go in 1926 and advocated the division of the state into ten regions, each of which would be the focus for all the national, state, and local agencies concerned with planning. After forty years our ideas have sprouted again, showing that the need itself was vital. At the moment I am attempting to write an exhaustive critique of the New York Report, bringing out all its good points but also showing its shortcomings, some of which are serious, now that the moment for action seems close at hand. Only a little while ago the younger sociologists were dismissing my chapters on regionalism in *The Culture of Cities* as an idle dream.

My failure to read *The New Towns* was not due to indifference but to total absorption in my own difficult book on technology: at the end of a day's writing I seek not instruction but literary entertainment—and not too much of that! After spending June and July writing about 250 pages I found myself getting stale, partly because the weather was almost as trying as my subject, with alterations of oppressive tropical heat and almost autumnal cold. I hope to get the first draft of the book done by the end of the summer and the second, if I am lucky, by next April, when we hope to sail for a two or three months stay in Europe, the last six weeks probably in England. It will be the last time we shall have the opportunity to live in the Holfords' flat in Cambridge Terrace for the building is to be converted into some sort of bureaucratic menage. I've always liked living in London, whether in Pimlico, Bloomsbury or Kensington, but I confess I never could hope for better diggings there than the ones we occupied the last three times, four storeys above Regents Park, almost level with the tree tops. . . .

WELWYN GARDEN CITY   23 August 1964

Dear Lewis
. . . Visits here in the past week by Professor John Reps, who is I think making very useful contributions to history in our field (modern history in this case), and by Professor Jack Meltzer, who is authorised by Chicago University and its Press to commission a competent historical graduate to work on my papers and to prepare, or assist me to prepare, a book on *my* contribution to modern planning—biographical or autobiographical. My books and papers are in such a state of confusion (I keep too many papers and letters) that I see great difficulties. Also my repute here (despite gold medals and things) is so obscure that I can't believe my 'personality' is of sufficient interest outside a tiny circle to justify a book—though if I ever wrote an autobiography I could, like any other tricky writer, present myself as more interesting than I am, and I have entertained this as a seductive project. However, I am not dismissing without some thought the Chicago proposition. . . .

WELWYN GARDEN CITY   7 November 1964

Dear Lewis
Though M.P.O., my son and I have mixed feelings about the new Labour Government here, we have unmixed pleasure in the defeat of Goldwater, who as we see him stands for a streak in your nation's collective philosophy that

has worried us. It looks to me as if it is really in recess. Tom says: after all, 26 millions did vote for Goldwater. Yes, but almost certainly the majority of those just couldn't shake off long-held party loyalty; while very many are seriously afraid of the non-White vote, especially in the South, and yet do not retain the anti-social-welfare obsession—the view that those who cannot survive in a competitive society have the 'right to perish'. There is in my opinion no doubt that in this country the vast majority has become quite pragmatic about the sphere of public vis-a-vis private enterprise; but there is a hard-core of nationalisers on principle in the Labour Party, as of anti-nationalisers in the Conservative Party. The two main parties are numerically equally balanced in votes as well as in seats, and though the Liberals have only nine seats they had over 3 million votes in this last election, and no very distinctively different outlook.

I am no enthusiast for Wilson, whose inner drive is to me obscure. I don't know whether his cultivation of his Left wing derives from socialistic sympathy with the under-privileged, mechanical neo-Marxism, or astute tactics in marshalling his forces. I tend to this last assessment; he is, like Johnson, an expert politician. In his position of enormous responsibility, surrounded by experienced advisers and with a very narrow parliamentary majority, he cannot yield very far to his extremists without being out on his ear in a few months. Yet he is making a show of dynamic energy which, if he doesn't do anything really silly or unpopular, will strengthen his position—as there is certainly a feeling that this country has been 'drifting' in recent years. It is also very interesting to see how quickly the unknown men in his team have an impression of strength, ability and power of expression.

The first steps in our own field of town and regional planning, taken with remarkable speed, are encouraging; notably the decision to stop at once the building of further offices in London. This is an event of world importance, and of course it implies a new wave of new towns—though the Government is not less subject than the last to architectural and country-preservation (land-saving) fashions that will probably cause the new towns to be larger and at higher density than I think desirable. However, there is also to be an advisory regional set-up which may assist in working out the difficult problem of town-clusters—the concept of which, in various forms, is now much discussed.

Several TCPA boys are in the new Government—one of them, Michael Stewart, who has been on our Executive for many years, in the Cabinet. He was the Opposition spokeman for housing and planning and we expected that he would be Minister for that function. We don't know why Wilson has made him Minister for Education and Science, while Richard Crossman, who spoke for Education in opposition, has been made Minister for Housing and Local Government. Stewart is a most able man who thoroughly understands the planning issues. He may have been thought too definitely committed to TCPA policy; or possibly Crossman, a senior personality, may have been thought better for the intended major housing drive. Wilson's first idea was to separate town planning from housing and place it with the new ministry for Land and Natural Resources, which will handle the proposed Land Commission Bill. But after departmental arguments the MHLG succeeded in retaining the planning administration; and it will in fact be dealt with by the Parliamentary Secretary to Crossman, MacColl, who was on the Hemel Hempstead New Towns Corporation and knows something of our policy. He is not in the Cabinet, but Stewart is, which is important. . . .

It looks as if *The New Towns* book is even less of a success in the USA than here. I have seen only two or three reviews, all except O'Harrow's in obscure journals and written by lazy reviewers from the dust-cover blurbs. When I last heard, only 700 had been sold. I think I am not at all clever in choosing the right form for my books. Having worked with some very successful operators (in business) for whom I could perform services beyond their own scope, I have come to accept that I am a fairly competent writer but a poor operator. I ought in this case to have written a book with a longer argument, more historical and literary documentation and no pictures or plans. Even the reviewers who get past the blurb don't get beyond the illustrations. Only two reviewers have noticed that there is a bit of historical-economic-sociological argument in my chapters. I am wondering whether I should try again with a more up-to-date and more complex yet simply-written book of the *New Towns after the War* type, readable by the ordinary elector and yet not easily dismissable by the academics. Or whether I should drop the subject and write a book on the technique of English versification. Time is running out for me, but I may have another year or two of articulateness.

I have now had the seventh and last of Albert Mayer's articles in the *Architectural Record*[1]. These seem to me on the whole very good. But I think Mayer makes a mistake in thinking the Architect as such is the primary planner; by vocation he is apt to be obsessed by the final visual result and to underplay the social and economic factors. Men like Unwin and Stein are rare; they are far more alive to fundamental considerations than an architect in general can be expected to be, or even needs to be. Unwin started with a primarily visual conception in his great planning book, but he was simultaneously a great housing reformer deeply interested in common lives; and later he also came to terms with industrial and other economic considerations. Mayer in turn

---

[1] 'Architecture as Total Community', in the *Architectural Record*, March–October, 1964. These articles formed the basis of Mayer's book *The Urgent Future*, New York, 1967.

thoroughly grapples with the 'social-physical-spiritual meaning'. But is he right in thinking that the architect-planner should normally endeavour to do so, and does he himself successfully attain to that depth and breadth, while thinking all the time of the ultimate visual expression? Can we hope for a sufficient supply of university-trained Leonardos? I feel there is a better hope of trained regional planners who know how to engage and direct the expressive genius of designers, while they have the political and administrative ability to control and coordinate the innumerable practical pressures that influence actual development. My experience of the person of the creative-artist type makes me feel that he is extremely unlikely to possess that particular sort of talent.

AMENIA, NEW YORK   13 November 1964

I've just come back from two days at Princeton, dear F.J., where I gave a lecture on The Future of the City to a crowded hall and a very receptive audience, which contained both a large sprinkling of towns-people, chiefly lawyers, doctors and the like, and a good showing of students from the non-architectural departments. I made my usual blistering analysis of the destruction of the city by the automatic processes of our technology, which produce the nonentity Gottmann calls Megalopolis, that inaccurate term for Geddes's fifty-year old term, conurbation. The audience was very responsive—all except the architecture and city planning students, who for the most part are trained to connive at the irrationalities of our age.

Princeton, incidentally, is a wonderful argument for the New Town principle. I have been going there off and on for the last thirty years or so, from when it was only a suburban townlet with a university. Now it is a genuine little city with about 11,000 people and a student population of 5,000. Except for a few hideous and inept new university buildings, caricatures of modern architecture, the town has improved both in architecture and in planning: motor cars have been banished from the campus and the car parks for the shopping area have been placed well-behind the main street. The whole town has become so attractive that people of means prefer to live there, even though their main activities are in New York and they must spend a whole hour each way commuting. As a result land-values have sky rocketed, so it's lucky that outlying estates and university land form, for the present, a green belt that the planners of Princeton are trying to preserve. Since there is also a sprinkling of industries on the outskirts, toward the railroad, two miles away, it is becoming a balanced community, though it unfortunately doesn't make any public provision for workers' housing. But in future I intend to use it as an example of what an American New Town might be. We need such concrete examples here, now that serious talk about New Towns is heard everywhere: much to the embarrassment of all the planning authorities who were pooh-poohing them a few years ago.

Don't be discouraged by the sale of your book. The middle generation, the people who habitually dismiss you and Howard, are in the saddle for the moment; and even if book review editors send them your book they are likely to quietly overlook it. Stein's *New Towns for America* met the same fate; yet it has survived. Above all, don't blame yourself for the *kind* of book you wrote: its format and treatment were exactly right; and the young—the generation I've had a hand in forming—will come around to it in good time.

At last I begin to see the results of my own work. Though I am far from being a public figure, am never interviewed and never appear on television, the motor car people openly denounce me as public enemy number one, or even, somewhat more subtly, profess to come around to my position by saying, as the President of the Chrysler Corporation the other day said, that both cars *and* public transportation are needed: so he doesn't want the subject discussed any more! And yesterday the *New York Times* came out with an editorial entitled The Auto versus the City, which demanded that public authorities should stop enticing more private cars into the city by building more parks and garages. You might have thought I had written the editorial; and in a sense I did, for no one else has been saying the same thing so consistently, or even at all; but the publication of *The Highway and the City* in *two* paperback editions has had an effect, and the showing of my films on the city may have helped too. Incidentally, I was naturally very pleased with the generous review Self gave to the British edition of *The Highway and the City*. Please convey him my thanks, if you happen to remember. And did I tell you that *The City in History* is coming out as a Pelican book next July? You might even be interested, apart from any concern with my personal welfare, in the American sales of the book to date: to wit, 20,000 regular edition, 5,000 textbook, 30,000 Book Find Club, in other words 55,000 copies, though the book was so shabbily treated in the British press that, unlike *The Culture of Cities*, it sold only something under 5,000 copies in the regular edition. Even the President's wife—whom I met in September when I went to the White House as one of those receiving the 'Medal of Freedom'—had read the book and seemed impressed at meeting the author!

Your comments on the American election were very welcome. The advocates of Goldwater were rich, noisy, rancorous and all too often lost to any sense of reality; but though they made me uneasy, particularly when the Negro rioting became ominous last summer, I never really thought they represented any large section of the country. Goldwater wouldn't have gotten even 26 million votes without the aid of Southerners, normally democrats, who on the subject of race have become brutal and desperate; and even more, without the loyalty of many people to the party, no matter who the candidate may be. Superficially, many of the anxious things he said about the over-centralisation of government and the need for recapturing local initiative and local responsibilities appealed to many sensible people, who see that many of the essential attributes of freedom have, often for good immediate purposes, as short cuts, been whittled away. But Goldwater's analysis of our weakness and corruptions were undermined by a purely nineteenth century ideology which made private property sacred, and which ignored that not a single one of his criticisms against big, centralised government was not equally applicable to the business bureaucracy; which has done quite as much to wipe out small, local enterprises as the most regimented government programmes—or rather, infinitely more. Worst of all, Goldwater was not, in any sense of the word, a conservative: he was ready to scrap our oldest and firmest institutions to suit his caprice. The American people distrusted him, properly, despite his winning personal manners, as they did not distrust even Huey Long, our earliest fascist. The election was plainly a decision against Goldwater and all he stands for, though not to the same degree an affirmation of Johnson, for many people, like myself, voted for him reluctantly, as indeed I would have voted with similar misgiving for Kennedy—whose death has given him a factitious name and glory that he had not in fact earned. I don't like the temper and tone of the whole Kennedy family, beginning with their fascist minded father and not excluding the over-ambitious and ruthless brother, whom I did *not* vote for. But my personal prejudices here are not important: the voice of our people was clear, and it shows what a misleading picture the few indignant letter writers, who reproved *Punch* for its anti-Goldwater comments, could draw of the temper and spirit of the whole country.

I am very glad to have your report on the Labour government. The only member of it I have met is Patrick Gordon Walker, whom I liked even before I discovered that, as an historian, he knew my work quite well. Like you I am mystified by the Steel Nationalisation Policy. It seems to me that this drastic measure should be applied only to industries that are essential to national prosperity and are being badly run, or, like the motor car industry, are being over-run and over-sold to the detriment of many other major public interests. The mere establishment of Nationalisation, as the Railway Unions must have found out, is not a guarantee of improvement . . . On this matter I fear that the Labour Party is still governed by the ghosts and demons of the nineteenth century, and has not been sufficiently disillusioned by the realities of our own time. I am particularly glad to learn of the measures that have been taken to protect London from more skyscrapers; and I trust that the Minister of Transport is equally enlightened and has already come across the ideas I set forth in the last two articles in *The Highway and the City*. Even your great traffic expert Colin Buchanan, though quite intelligent, has fallen too completely for American technology in handling the motor car and is insufficiently critical of the results—dismissing my suggestion that our mistakes should be heeded. . . .

We are both in reasonably good shape, I perhaps a little better than Sophia because I'm capable of doing more manual work, while she still shows an undue susceptibility to colds, perhaps an aftermath of her long pneumonia last spring. But we've had a lively and rewarding autumn, our first full autumn for a long while; and we've had the pleasure of seeing some of the bushes we planted in their autumn glory for the first time. I shall always regret that you've never seen this place: it's as though a whole vital sector of my life had been concealed from you. People are always a little surprised at it when they find that the things I stand for in my writing are also visible in the way we live. They expect an elegant country house, I suppose, and then find, as only Holford suspected, that it is really most like a modest country parsonage, and like it, unexpectedly short on the little conveniences everyone has! (Oh, yes, we have a bathroom and three toilets; but no way of keeping the guest room in summer from turning into a black hole of Calcutta under the afternoon sun). . . .

AMENIA, NEW YORK   22 December 1964

. . . Meanwhile, our plans for going abroad have undergone repeated revision: For a while I thought I'd make a brief six week trip by myself, but the other day the Academic Senate of the University of Edinburgh informed me that they proposed to bestow an honorary doctorate on me in July, and that settled matters. We now plan to sail for England late in June and stay, mostly in Britain, till the end of August. I've probably told you before that I have, on principle, turned down a whole series of honorary degrees in America, and even one in England; but somehow my old association with Geddes broke down my resistance in this case, all the more easily because my original reason for refusing degrees no longer seems as convincing at 70 as it did at 40, and is now only an empty gesture.

You have doubtless heard about Catherine Bauer Wurster's death: It was a purely accidental event, due just to stumbling and falling while hiking alone on a mountain trail and hitting a rock that stunned her into unconsciousness, and which then, since she was not found for thirty-six hours or so, brought on death by exposure, seemingly without any recovery of consciousness for she was lying in the peaceful attitude of sleep. Until this happened it was her husband, now in an advanced stage of Parkinson's disease, that everyone pitied and feared for. She and I visited you in Welwyn in 1932, when we were doing a study of European housing that appeared in *Fortune*: that, incidentally, was the first time I laid eyes on *you*. I had met her when she was advertising manager of Harcourt's and got her interested in housing and planning: she is almost the only student in those fields I ever had particular reason to be proud of. For a while I saw much of her, for she had better insight into both my actual work and my capabilities than anyone else in her generation, and *I owed quite as much to her as she to me*. But after 1934 our ways parted: by then she wanted practical political results and dismissed me, increasingly, as a theorist, so at the end we could hardly talk to each other on the subjects we had once held closely in common. But our family friendship thickened as our personal and professional one thinned, for Sophy and Catherine liked each other, as Bill and I did, too, and the autumn we spent at Berkeley in 1961 in a house on a hill just 50 ft below theirs counted, I think, as a happy memory for all of us.

In the early thirties she had taken my place in helping Clarence Stein to develop his ideas on paper, and had she lived I think she would have been a great influence at the University, though more as a skilled administrator who knew how to use other people to best advantage, than as a producer of fresh ideas. In becoming a 'houser' she *buried, long ago, a genuine literary talent*, as the world will some day see if the letters we exchanged constantly over the first four years of our friendship are ever published. In an unexpurgated edition, incidentally, they would shock many people who have a quite different image of Lewis Mumford than the person revealed in that correspondence. I chuckle at the prospect; but by the time they *can* be published I suspect that no one will be shockable, or what is even more probable, no one will have the slightest interest in our hilarious interchanges.

Since this letter is fast descending into mere gossip, let me add one more gossipy item: my present involvement in the new traffic plans for Oxford. The Dean of Christ Church, prompted perhaps by Dr Demant, who knows my views about the Christ Church Meadow 'relief road,' asked me if I would testify against the present plans at the final Local Government Board Enquiry. I said 'No' to that of course, partly for lack of time, partly because, after seeing one witness after another made a fool of in the St Paul's Enquiry on the Holford Plan, by your fiendishly clever barristers, I resolved I'd never be caught in such a trap. But I eased my conscience by preparing a memorandum analysing the folly of the present half-baked plans and carrying much further the counter-proposals that have been made, even to the point of introducing into the kingdom of Nuffield the highly touchy subject of moving much of

Oxford's industry out into a New Town. This is all *sub rosa* for the present for I don't yet know how the memorandum will be presented, if at all. The Treasurer of Christ Church is flying over for a conference with me next week— though since I'm sure we could handle the whole subject satisfactorily by correspondence, he's probably killing half a dozen other birds with the same stone.

One more note to indicate how the winds of opinion are changing over here. Just today I received *Occasional Paper No. 1 on The City*, published by the Centre for the Study of Democratic Institutions at Santa Barbara. It's written by Bernard Weissbourd and introduced by the Mayor of Oakland. The author is now engaged in the construction of city apartments, hotels and office buildings, so though he began as a chemist on the Manhattan project, he is evidently no idle dreamer. He not merely observes that the English New Towns programme is sound but he *proposes to carry it out on a large scale in America*, as the only way to rebuild the interior of our big cities and keep them from turning into vile proletarian slums. I wonder what Rodwin will have to say to that? And who, now, are the dreamers, the impractical schemers, the old fashioned theorists?

WELWYN GARDEN CITY   29 December 1964

Dear Lewis

. . . I have had all the facts about Catherine and I have written a short appreciation for *T & CP*—which will be out late. I liked her, and much admired her intellect and literary skill. We well remember your simultaneous appearance on our doorstep in 1932.

I am glad to hear of the rising interest in new towns in the USA and look forward to having the CSDI paper No. 1. Rodwin's book did a lot of harm. You will find in the February *T & CP* a review, by me, of a book by a Professor of Tulane University[1] that contains a contemptuous dismissal of Howard, and no sign that he had read him, you or me. All his information came from Orlans and Rodwin—neither of whom understands how practical things happen in this world. But I have to admit that their books are more copiously documented than mine. . . .

Carl Feiss had a good review of our *New Towns* in the *AIA Journal*. But I have seen no other reviews in papers of large or important circulation. Obviously the book hasn't set the Potomac or the Hudson on fire. I had a hope

---

[1] Leonard Reissman, *The Urban Process: Cities in Industrial Society*, New York, London, 1964.

that it would do better. There *are* thoughts in it that should have aroused academic interest or criticism; but perhaps they were expressed too simply.

Intending to work during the Christmas recess, I had a bad attack, after a long interval of immunity, of verse-making, which began as an easy recreational attempt to make something of discarded drafts of years ago. It was just as if the Sorcerer's Apprentice had turned on a tap; I couldn't turn it off, day or night, for half a week. It is very curious that, once I had started, all sorts of ideas for new verses sprang up—some of which I just had to worry at. The satiric or facetious ones I could handle: I fear that is my vein; but I got very seriously bothered with one or two that contained inexpressible emotions. I think my temperature is now nearly back to normal.

AMENIA, NEW YORK   20 February 1965

Thank you, dear F.J., for your tribute to Catherine in *T & CP*; you struck the right note and said the right things. On that I am a good judge, that is, an impartial one, for the temperamental gap between us became so wide with time that neither of us could read what the other wrote, even when we agreed with the ideas. But I always respected her integrity and her sense—rare in men and even rarer in women—that the job was more important than her own ego. I smiled, of course, at your allusion to 'accidentally' meeting us on the same day. But I was pleased to have our association noted there. As I told you, she was my gift to the housing movement: but thirty years later even she had forgotten that fact. . . .

WELWYN GARDEN CITY   28 March 1965

Dear Lewis

Thanks for sending me the proof of your review of Howard's book for the *New York Review*. It's a good stroke both for the circulation of the book and for the new towns concept as it is now catching on. No British journal is likely to publish so long a review, or one by a contributor to the book; I am glad the *NYR* editor has so much sense.

One or two points for your future use. The Fabian criticism was not in a tract, but in its monthly sheet of December 1898, and it is initialled 'E.R.P.' (E. R. Pease, the famous secretary of the Society, who is very amusingly described in one of H. G. Wells's books). In *Fabian News* of October 1899 there is another note:

'J. Bruce Wallace and H. O. Thompson are members of the Council of the

Garden City Association, which has been formed to establish in England the geometrical cities projected by Mr E. Howard in his volume *To-morrow*, reviewed in these columns some months ago. We fear it is futile to wish success to a project so impracticable. No less than twelve sub-committees have been appointed to carry on the work. . . .'

I think you underestimate Howard's literary quality. The book had an inspirational effect on a great many people at that time, and created an appreciable popular movement without which I think the practical men who started Letchworth would not have acted. All the same, the real programme of the Garden City was the entirely realistic prospectus of First Garden City Limited in 1903. Neville[1] and the industrialists pruned out Howard's more-far-reaching social idealisms, and fastened on his essential common sense. Actually, of course, his idealisms were not silly, but they were ahead of the time. The first emigrants to Letchworth included a good many 'idealists', and though they were an embarrassment to the practical promoters, probably the scheme couldn't have been started without them.

Things are moving fast here; many more new towns are projected, and the concept of 'clusters' rather than big continuous units is gaining ground; also there is a partial reaction against the architectural pressure for high-density 'urbanity'. But Cumbernauld and its skilful propagandists have done a lot of harm to the housing standards of the later new towns.

As I shall (probably) reach 80 on 26 May 1965 I am planning to give up the editorship of *T & CP* as soon as I can find a successor who will on the whole maintain our mission; with a diminishing hope of being able myself to tackle some other writing work I have long had in mind. But I have aged a lot in the last two years. . . .

AMENIA, NEW YORK   17 April 1965

I came back here a few days ago, dear F.J., after a fortnight's absence in New York and Washington where I was attending a conservation conference, to find as usual a whole mountain of letters clamouring for my attention: and I have solved the problem of dealing with them by first turning to your two letters of March, for which a reply is now well overdue. But meanwhile I must tell you our family news: Alison, on 25 March, gave birth to a gargantuan son, three weeks too late and three pounds too heavy, for he was almost ten pounds at birth. The last week was a little harrowing and the little lad had such broad shoulders that his collarbone was broken in the last stages of his

---

[1] Sir Ralph Neville, Q.C., first Chairman of the Garden City Association and of First Garden City (Letchworth) Ltd.

emergence: but everything has turned out well, and if he turns out to be half as charming as his sister our grandparental cup will be full to the overflowing. Sophia, who looked after Alison's household for three weeks, is now recuperating from that strenuous ordeal. . . .

As to your comments on my review, I am of course grateful for your corrections. You convict me of never having seen the first edition of *To-morrow*, and if the book is in your possession I'll ask you to show it to me when we meet. Whether Howard got the idea of limiting town size from Buckingham, the fact is that Buckingham did set a limit of ten thousand, though for that matter the need for limitation is taken for granted by most utopian writers from Plato onward. But these are small differences. I still think it was the quality of Howard's mind and character, not his *literary* charm, that gave his book itself power to persuade; but perhaps you and I are using different words for the same thing. By literary quality I mean the power of using words in such a fashion that they compel interest even if one despises the writer's character and rejects his ideas—as in my own reaction to T. S. Eliot. You would be surprised, incidentally, as I was, at the sort of people who complimented me upon my Howard review and who said they were eager to get hold of his book: to me this indicates nothing about the review itself but rather the fact that the garden city thesis has at last taken on—perhaps because so many people are disillusioned over Le Corbusier's Brave New World, within whose New York apartment houses no woman now dares enter an elevator without a lurking fear of being raped! . . .

I am glad that the impulse to write more verse has seized you again: do not resist it but throw all other duties aside and give yourself to it. If I had your ability to write verse I would follow the same counsel myself; for there is far too much that in my busy life I have left unsaid, partly because I've turned to verse only when driven, as Yeats said, by 'lust or rage', but then I am usually too choked with emotion to achieve the fresh line and the newly minted image, since too much emotion leads to mere rhetoric, not poetry. Have you, by the bye, ever looked at Yeats' correspondence with Lady Wellesley[1], which I have just been reading? It tells much about him as both a poet and a man; and though the man does not attract me very much more than Eliot did, I like the poet, still practicing his craft, still learning, even when battered by all manner of age-wearied illnesses. He and Dorothy had a sort of spiritual liaison but one can tell by repeated references in his letters that he was disappointed in her slim, boyish body, and to recover the erotic feeling he harboured, wished himself into a girl, so that he might enjoy it! . . .

---

[1] W. B. Yeats and Dorothy Wellesley, *Letters on Poetry*, . . . London, New York, 1964.

WELWYN GARDEN CITY   23 April 1965

Dear Lewis

Yours of 17 April is particularly interesting. First, M.P.O. and I felicitate
you enviously on your second grandparenthood and ask you to convey good
wishes to Alison. Second, I am glad to hear you are bucked by the shaping of
the new book. And third, it rejoices us to know that you really are visiting this
hemisphere soon: we may be away in Sweden, Finland and possibly the
USSR at the end of June, but should be back here not later than 18 July. If
possible, do please save time for a couple of leisurely talks, either here or in
London. Let me know if there is anybody you would like to meet as it is very
easy for me to arrange a lunch or dinner at my club; and you would be good
bait for me to use in hooking someone I might hesitate to invite on my own
account.

I am interested in your opinion of Howard's writing. I find it eloquent in an
entirely established style, but of course it has no literary originality, no unique
character of its own—as you say, no compelling 'power of using words'. But
he is very resourceful in sentence arrangements without ever resorting to
elegant variation, and I do find charm in much of his eloquence. . . .

What you say about my own verse is what I would like to think, and at
times *do* think. The established critics, however, have entirely ignored it, and
the published book sold only 800 copies of 2,000 printed. Sometimes I contemplate a wide distribution of some of the surplus copies, because I think
there must be a lot of people in the world who share my interest in the development of traditional verse form and would be tickled by my tricks, if not moved
by my lightly expressed emotions. But I funk such an egoistic enterprise, and
anyway I am always too busy or lazy. Occasionally I send a new piece to some
journal, but it comes back, and I do not send it out a second time. Momentarily
I always agree with the editor.

Like you, I distinguish between poetry (even comic poetry) and mere
rhetoric. If I can make a copy I will send you a sonnet I wrote some time ago,
making this distinction, which Sir Francis Meynell, the only person who has
ever encouraged me to write serious verse, wants to publish in an anthology.
I don't think it is one of my good ones, but he does. So I have agreed.

WELWYN GARDEN CITY   24 April 1965

Dear Lewis

Since you have more than once expressed interest in my verses (I must
believe sincerely, though I am always suspicious about the friendliness of

friends), I am, after hesitation, sending herewith several attempts in serious and semi-serious vein.

When I read, after an interval, my light or comic verses, some of them do seem to me highly competent, and occasionally really witty—and I am amazed that I could ever have thought of them.

But I do not have the same reaction to my more serious experiments, either at the time of writing or when I have forgotten the process of composition. Perhaps because I am under the influence of the modern reaction against classical forms (though I like very few of the works of contemporary poets, which for me are *too* formless), I feel my serious 'poems' lack something essential. Either the emotion is too commonplace or the form irritatingly jog-trot.

I have not spent much of my lifetime writing verse, but the impulse seizes me at intervals; not to write for the sake of writing, but only on the infrequent occasions when my unconscious throws up what seems a good idea. If it is a comic (satirical, nonsensical, or entirely metrical) idea I can usually, with concentration, make something of it that at the time pleases me. If it is inspired by an experienced or conceived emotion (it is by no means always autobiographical) I struggle with it, but can very rarely express it in a way that satisfies my critical sense. I am sure verse-writing adds to one's vocabulary for prose purposes; but it also gives one a resourcefulness in alternative ways of saying anything that is embarrassing in prose writing, and slows up output, whether or not it improves the product.

One thing I have learned by publishing a book of verses is how few people have any critical appreciation of prosody as such. You would hardly credit the obtuseness of some of the suggestions my publishers made for improving my verses. So many people entirely fail to see what one is up to prosodically that I am extremely wary of expressing my own lack of appreciation of some modern verse—and read a thing many times over a period before I become sure it is weak or worthless. I do become quite sure of this in many cases, but I have no platform from which to demonstrate my criticism, except my own notebooks, which may be there for the Guggenheimer scholar's thesis on twentieth-century Squares.

AMENIA, NEW YORK   20 May 1965

Next Wednesday, dear F.J., the calendar reminds me you will reach your eightieth mile-stone. Whatever your own feelings about such occasions, this event is a blessing for your friends: they can, for once, drop the casual note of everyday life and tell you, to your face, how much they love you, and what a debt they owe you, not only for the bolder virtues of fortitude and probity, but for your unflagging wit and your inner cheeriness. I know hardly anyone else, not even Ebenezer Howard himself, who has lived to see so many of his hopes and proposals come to life, in a form so close to his original intentions. As for myself, I know that a great hole would be made in my life if ever our correspondence were to cease. So here is a congratulatory embrace for the 26th from both Sophia and me. May many more good years lie before you!

WELWYN GARDEN CITY   31 May 1965

Dear Lewis

Such is my nature and habitude that I receive all praises and congratulations with a mixture of smug self-satisfaction and realistic scepticism, and respond with a mask of modesty that anybody can see through. However much I discount the terms of your letter of 20 May it does give me great pleasure and some reassurance, and I thank you warmly for it—and Sophia for her concurrence in the 80th anniversary greeting.

The sensation of ageing, by the way, is not altogether pleasant, but it is interesting. A local manufacturer, Andrew Skarsten, a Norwegian who invented the Skarsten Scraper, sold it for some years in the USA and then settled in WGC and made it an international necessity for house-painters, told me recently that he had been '27 for 42 years'. I understand this perfectly; I was 27 for about 50 years, and then suddenly became almost 80. There was a marked slowing up and weakness physically; and though no obvious degeneration mentally, a certain sloth, disposition to sit in chairs and rest after meals, lessening of output in things like writing, and (more tiresome) forgetfulness of very recent happenings, and the beginnings of a tendency to repeat thoughts and observations. (Almost certainly this latter tendency will have appeared in my letters, though I fight against it.) And one is amused and slightly irritated by being told by everyone that one looks far younger than one really is.

Rightly or vainly, I think I write as lucidly and cogently as ever, but it takes longer. And I find it more and more difficult, in writing about planning, to take full account of current thought and practice—partly because the literature is now too copious for me to follow all its ramifications. This is why I have decided to resign as Editor of *T & CP*, with much regret because the necessity of writing something monthly does compel me to read snatches of the current literature, and because I still feel the desire to write corrective matter on the subject, and don't see anybody in sight who will maintain just my balance of humanism and technology. I console myself with the thought that a man can live only one life and that there will be plenty of successors to do what is necessary and valid. . . .

This business of retirement is a bit painful. I announced at last week's Welwyn Drama Festival my coming resignation as Chairman after thirty-six years and thirty-one Festivals. Dozens of people are trying to dissuade me, honestly or out of kindness; but I realise that the time has come. It was rather pleasant to be the hallowed patriarch of an annual event that has given pleasure and illumination to many hundreds of people known to me. And I don't really like becoming a back number who will soon be quite forgotten. Yet, as I have too often said, I think death and replacement, with its uncertainties of timing, was one of creation's best ideas. The mistake was that so many people go through a long period of useless and distressing senility—and this I strongly disapprove of.

AMENIA, NEW YORK   31 May 1965

The stand I've taken against our Vietnam policy—you may have seen a report of it in your *Times*—has involved me in such a mass of correspondence with people who are on my side that I'm bankrupt as far as other letter writing is concerned, dear F.J.: so your last two letters, and poems, will have to wait for a face-to-face meeting for an answer!

WELWYN GARDEN CITY   12 June 1965

Dear Lewis

I have not seen reports of your intervention in the Vietnam affair, but there are many about USA disquiet. I don't know enough about it to take a line. I was very sure we were wrong in refusing a negotiated peace in World War I, and very sure we were right in going to war with Hitler. Realising that national boundaries and spheres of influence have historically been determined by military power or readiness to defend, and that hopes that the United Nations would replace this process have so far failed, I cannot be sure that Johnson is not justified in the Formosa and Vietnam policies, or in Dominica. (In main principle, anyway, if not in the raids on N. Vietnam, for which one can see the case if N. Vietnam is supporting the 'rebels' in S. Vietnam.) Clearly Michael Stewart, who is a good man, is supporting the USA —but I don't know how far this is due to the necessity of the American alliance to this country.

But don't waste precious time writing to me about this. If I had the knowledge I haven't the energy to enter into the discussion here. You may be sure there is equal anxiety in this country, and that for every reason (including strong feelings inside the Labour Party) our Government must be striving for peace negotiations at the earliest possible moment. . . .

WELWYN GARDEN CITY   5 October 1965

Dear Lewis

I have just heard from Jack Meltzer that his Centre for Urban Studies is negotiating for the appointment of Dr Roy Lubove to concoct a volume on FJO's part in the New Towns movement[1]. It isn't certain yet that he will be invited to do it by the University of Chicago, or whether he would accept. In any case he would not start here till October 1966 —which suits me—if I last out—because I would have to do a lot of sorting out of my papers beforehand anyway.

Reading his book on the Regional Planning Association of America, which you kindly sent me in March 1964, I think he has much of the desirable background knowledge, and his work seems to be careful and scientific, and competently written. I imagine he might be very much interested in comparing our New Towns movement here with yours in the USA. So I have told Meltzer that I would think he is a good choice for the job. If you agree with this, please don't trouble to reply. On the other hand, if you want to raise an alarm, or propose a curfew, send me a six-line message soon.

I am sure that if I could get into a book a good collection of passages from my past occasional writings, I could be made to appear quite bright, and sometimes entertaining and argumentatively forceful (You have to read things you have forgotten before you can judge your own literary effects). But how to put the best of one's work into an integrated book, especially in collaboration with someone else, I doubt if I know.

At times I am quite convinced that my writings, endless talks, and persistent lobbyings have had an effect on urban policy; even that without my efforts the New Towns legislation would not have happened as early as 1946. But I know I have enough vanity and egoism (detestable qualities as these are) to *wish* to think so. At dinners and places where they bleat I have heard many people say so, and I dishonestly deprecate and inwardly welcome such flatteries. And as one recedes into the shadows one welcomes a polite and kindly resuscitation. At the same time I wish one didn't; for what the hell does anyone's relative part in historical events matter?

Much more important, I think some of my past writings state a case, of

---

[1] This project did not materialise.

public importance, that the vast majority of people have never taken account of, in simplified terms that would convince many if they encountered them. But I have never found out how to reach that larger public which I am certain would understand my sort of language. And this to a certain extent annoys me, because writers who do reach the public don't say the right things.

AMENIA, NEW YORK   8 October 1965

Just a line, dear F.J., not to raise any embarrassing questions about Lubove, but to settle your doubts. I think he would do an excellent job by your life-work: all the better because he is not an original mind and will therefore be more likely to listen to you and draw heavily on your writings. I found him a little stubborn about clinging to his preconceptions about the RPAA doctrines; but after I had gathered together the documents that showed him he was wrong he proved open to reason and revised his text. (If you look at his appendix you'll see how heavily he drew on my letters to him.) Meanwhile he has been learning steadily: so I can't think of a better candidate for this task. All the things that you modestly deprecate in praise of your work and influence are true! and a good book will pass this on to the *next* generation—who will probably be in rebellion against the people who now underestimate you or reject you. So, whether or not Lubove gets appointed, do gather together your papers, writings and important correspondence, to prepare the ground for your biographer—and incidentally confirm the good opinion you *justly* have of your own work.

AMENIA, NEW YORK   23 October 1965

. . . A few days ago (on 19 October) I became 70; and celebrated the occasion in my usual fashion by doing a stiff morning's work on my book, whereof I've almost finished the first draft. I am a little frightened by the originality of my arguments and no less so by my publisher's unheard-of enthusiasm about its prospects; but I see now that the book will have me in its grip well through next summer, and my plans for spending a couple of months in Europe next spring have become very dim indeed.

In a new book *The Miracle Ahead*, by the poll-taker George Gallup, I've found an item, from a bit of research he doesn't identify, that may amuse you, since it backs up 'scientifically' a position you and I have always taken. In a sampling of people to find out who is 'happy', they found that the happiest group liked gardening, reading and quiet pleasures, while the unhappy ones were those who needed excitements and stimuli of every kind. So too, people who lived in smaller towns were happier than those who lived in big cities: and of all classes the unhappiest were industrial workers, confined to dull, manual jobs, who lived in big cities. All this is not news to us: but it may be useful in putting a quietus upon your loudest opponents.

WELWYN GARDEN CITY   28 October 1965

Dear Lewis

Thanks for yours of 23rd with notice of your change of address—another piece of evidence of American mobility. How you can work in so many places remains for me a mystery. M.P.O. and I lived for some days in a multi-storey apartment overlooking the Charles River, while the usual occupier, a distinguished planner, was elsewhere. It had every convenience, but no sign that literate intellectuals had ever lived in it. The only book (and I still wonder how that got in) was the 1862 edition of *The Travels of Baron Munchausen*, with coloured plates by Alfred Crowquill. Does an American carry his reference library around in a lunch-tin? I could get no clue from Munchausen. How does he produce his words of learned length and thundering sound without an encyclopedia and a thesaurus?

Naturally, if you are frightened by the originality of your emerging argument, I am full of curiosity and awe. And I envy your capacity to plan ahead for years of work on such a book. It now takes me sometimes several days to write an editorial of 900 words, and though I do often think afterwards that the product is forceful, compact and bright, I rarely have any evidence that anyone reads it. I have had a thought of publishing half a hundred of them in a volume in fairness to a possibly more appreciative posterity; but undoubtedly it would have to be at my own expense in cash and spirit. Johnson said no one ever wrote for anything but money. He forgot vanity.

I've just drafted a four-minute talk for the BBC on Eb. Howard, to be broadcast on World T-P Day (8 November). It is supposed to be a personal impression; but it's impossible to characterise Howard for an ordinary listener without a historical background. So you will rightly guess it is a thin, Thurberish sketch, but not amusing.

Glad to have the excerpt from Gallup's book. I just wonder by what criterion he measures human happiness, though I am sure he is right in fixing its main locations. Are you happy? I think I am. I like gardens, reading etc., but I also like excitements and stimuli, of which I get less and less. . . .

Dear Lewis

. . . As 'President' designated by the faithful widow of Prof. della Paolera of Buenos Aires, I have just run the Celebration of World Town Planning Day, of which GB is this year the focus. The fifty telegrams I received show that the Day has caught on most in the Latin countries, many of which are pretty backward in planning. For *T & CP* and another planning journal I collected articles on the policies in other countries for metropolitan planning, location of industry etc., and I have learned a lot from this exercise, which cost me a lot of work. If you have time, the articles are worth a look at. Dr Robert Weaver's[1], though well composed, is disappointingly complacent, like some others. But I have a hope that my comparisons may have some political-educational value. I managed to keep all the articles short, and most get straight to the main points.

Our own central Celebration at London County Hall was certainly remarkable. About eight or nine present and past Ministers of the Crown attended the Luncheon and the Reunion, which is most unusual. And among the large crowd of bigwigs were all the heads of the Greater London Council, the Lord Mayor of London, and the Argentine Chargé d'Affaires. I was able to say that, unlike the Rt Hon. Chairman of the Council—(who is a provincial) and the (then) Lord Mayor (who was a former Lord Provost of Edinburgh), I am a born Londoner, though I escaped fifty years ago. I recalled that thirty-five years or so ago I tried to get the LCC to build new towns, and offered to do one for them if they would lend me the product of a 1*d* rate. As they wouldn't bite we 'parted brass-rags'. But in recent years London had completely changed its policy, so my youthful pride as a Londoner had been resuscitated, and I now went about the world bragging of London's lead to more backward cities! This I thought was a good piece of propaganda without excessive solemnity. They took it very well: old, old men can get away with this sort of serious joke, as you may find in another ten years. . . .

Sophia and I salute you and Margaret, dear F.J., at the beginning of the New Year: may all possible blessings envelope you! The afternoon with you both at Welwyn remains one of the highlights of our otherwise disappointing and frustrating trip to England. When we left I hoped to remove the bad taste by

---

[1] Economist and public official. Secretary of the US Department of Housing and Urban Development, 1961–68.

going over again in April, thinking my book would be the better for a change of scene and a little quiet reflection before I plunged into the final draft. But though I've worked steadily on the ms, and half of it is in good shape, I now see that I mustn't leave it if it's to be ready for the printer by mid-September, as I have promised. Even apart from the promise, every big book is an incubus that sucks the life-blood out of its author: and there comes a moment in the writing of it when one must, at any cost, throw the dreadful monster off!

You asked me a little while ago if I'd like a few extra copies of *Can Man Plan?* and I now answer gratefully: 'yes: I'd be happy to have half a dozen'. You are in good company. Of the first thousand copies of *Walden*, as I remember, Thoreau got back 900. I am still puzzled by the fact that such a witty, finely turned lot of verses did so poorly. Perhaps the original error was in giving it such a forbidding, non-poetic title. I know the good reason you had: this was one of your best poems!

Sophia and I have had a highly stimulating and socially rewarding time here in Harvard, from whence I write: and in many ways we'll be sorry to turn back to Amenia at the end of this month. We're both essentially sociable people, despite my solitary ways as a writer: so we remain thirsty for just those meetings and mixings that a university community like this still gives.

But in another few years this place, like Boston, will be ground to dust under the wheels of motor cars, and become one vast congested parking lot. But such gloomy thoughts are no way to usher in the New Year!

WELWYN GARDEN CITY   3 January 1966

Dear Lewis

You may like to see this quotation from a lengthy and flowery 'Message' issued by the Planners of Mexico at their meeting to celebrate World Town-Planning Day on 8 November:

'On this occasion we render world homage to Sir Frederic James Osborn, of England, whose contributions to the well-being of the human race are known throughout the entire world. Simultaneously we send our best greetings to our fellow town planners in Great Britain.

'In the English speaking world there exist other distinguished town planners, among them the notable figure of Lewis Mumford, to whom we pay a tribute of recognition for his important work.

'The works of Sir Frederic Osborn and of Lewis Mumford have been luminous guide lines (*guias luminosas*) for many planners in wide-spread regions of the earth'. . . .

It is mentioned that Lisbon was originally designated as the centre for 1965, but ceded its turn to GB on the ground the FJO had reached the age of 80 in 1965! I had no knowledge of this till I received the Mexican extravaganza. I have met old Sā-e Mello, who was the chief planner for Portugal till recently, many times in Lisbon and other places, and have much affection for him, though he is almost impossible to converse with as he doesn't speak English, has a throat affliction that makes him almost inaudible, and is as taciturn as William the Silent. But when MPO and I have been with him and his young planning associates in Portugal, we have been struck by the fact that his briefest whispers receive the respectful attention of commandments from Sinai. It was the same at IFHP Bureau meetings, where he seldom spoke. I don't understand why we all respected him so much; still less why he respected me, who never said anything he could understand beyond 'Bon jour' and 'Au revoir'.

WELWYN GARDEN CITY   11 January 1966

Dear Lewis
Is my letter really necessary? NO. But it is a pleasure to have New Year greetings from Sophia and you, and to return them from M.P.O. and me— who both cherish memories of our meeting last year and wish we had had more time together.

I have had to spend several days revising the TP and New Towns articles for a new edition of Dent's little *Everyman's Encyclopedia,* and I'm so short-winded nowadays that I'm sick to death of this tiny and tricky job, in which I try to compress a hogshead into an egg-cup. But it has been a reminder of the second planning revolution in GB since the war. Every day now the papers and the radio report proposals for or protests against new towns or development projects all over the country. Tonight, for instance, comes news of the Greater London Council's schemes for two new towns of 40,000 as far away as Devonshire. And last week Crossman[1] declared that in the S.E. there must be new towns to take another 1 million of London overspill. There are similar proposals for all the major conurbations; I can't keep pace with them in my aged and decrepit state of absorption.

However, J. R. James, the MHLG's chief planner, in reply to my congratulations on his New Year Honour (CB), tells me he is 100 per cent for the new town policy, and when he retires (a long way off yet) is going to replace me as cheer-leader on the sidelines. And I have another letter today from Dennis

---

[1] Rt. Hon. Richard Crossman, Minister of Housing and Local Government, 1964–66.

O'Harrow to say he is definitely slated for the next President of the IFHP—a choice I had wirepulled for when on the Bureau, and regard as internationally important. He is very able, energetic and articulate, and fundamentally sound on the 'new towns' philosophy while realistic on strategy. He will keep the Americans in the Fedn., and is as likely as any other personality to get the Russians in, which I have been trying to do for years, though I only got them about half-way. And he can make an address that gets across, which no President since since Howard could do.

Thanks for your encouraging words about my poems; I am sending the six copies to Amenia. I am pretty sure that if one accepted critical pundit had noticed the book, it would have done much better. Whatever its right level is, I think it will find it sooner or later. In the meantime I am just giving away copies to anyone who *might* have my sense of humour or social outlook. Versifying has been a small factor in my life, and has given *me* some fun, if few others.

Never having consorted with the intellectual elite, I have to envy you in your university sojourns, all the more because you do not seem to have suffered from the intelligentsia's ignorance of ordinary folk. I've just re-read E. M. Forster's *Howard's End*, which has something of that weakness; and I begin to see it as a factor in the development of the 'Bloomsbury' cult and the attitude of our cultivated middle-class to the city and countryside issues. Forster's London clerk, whose love of Thoreau-Borrow-RLS-Jeffries-etc. he despises as half-baked or a pose, is less real to me than Dick Swiveller; and having worked among London clerks, and being one, I know there are thousands of varieties of the species with their own gusto and capacity for infinite forms of culture. And many who are as capable of getting drunk on Beethoven or Wagner as Forster's middle-class dilettanti.

No more Forster for me, though I much liked *Passage to India* many years ago. I am now trying to re-educate myself, and starting with Julian Huxley on *Evolution in Action*. How necessary—by Gosh—that is at 80!

WELWYN GARDEN CITY   20 January 1966

Dear Lewis

I have just received Dr Robert Weaver's new book *Dilemmas of Urban America* (Harvard University Press), the main theme of which is 'New Communities' in relation to urban renewal and the race question.

He discusses at length whether the British new towns have any relevance to the American situation, mentions our book *The New Towns* etc. as 'an impressive study of the new towns movement in GB', and quotes your preface.

His conclusion is that the British and European circumstances are so different that they don't help the USA much, but he does think many 'new communities' (the term he prefers) should be built around, sometimes well away from and sometimes contiguous with metropolitan areas, by private enterprise. His information about the British new towns is not quite correct; he has for instance swallowed the most misleading MHLG statement about 'New Town Blues', and does not realise that we are all well aware here of the 'town cluster' principle, with which in fact most of our first new towns, by accident or design, do comply; and which is certain to govern the siting and planning of the many further towns under consideration by the Government.

Oddly enough, while he makes a big point of the fact that the British towns are promoted and financed by Government corporations, which he thinks inconceivable in the USA, later he agrees that Federal assistance to 'new communities' is necessary and desirable, and that the fear that this will prejudice the assistance to existing cities is unjustified. He rightly wants your new communities to have a spread of income groups, which necessitates housing subsidies for the poorer classes. But he doesn't seem to know that the British NTs have a fair mixture of classes, and that only the low-rent houses are in fact subsidised, and the proportion of owner-occupied houses is increasing—and is the deliberate policy of the Labour Government. Actually there is a large amount of private investment in the NTs, mainly in factories, but also in houses. We are consciously now a 'mixed economy', and Labour Ministers almost flaunt the term.

If you have any influence in getting Weaver's book reviewed, it might help the circulation of our book.

Tactically, Weaver, in his position (now that of Cabinet Minister) is probably wise to discount the influence of the British precedent. His outlook on the issue is far ahead of any British politician's before the New Towns Act of 1946. Up to then, and even now, there is no book supporting the new towns idea by a Minister or high civil servant.

AMENIA, NEW YORK   30 January 1966

We are back here again in Amenia, dear F.J., after an extremely stimulating and rewarding sojourn in Cambridge; but with the usual accumulation of books and magazines awaiting us, to say nothing of a big file of unanswered letters, I do not expect to be settled sufficiently to resume writing on my book till the end of the week. When my correspondence gets hopelessly in arrears, I find that the best way of handling it is to begin at the top of the pile, on the theory that those who have waited six months for an answer won't notice the passing of another month: the New Testament principle that 'the first shall be last'. And on those terms, your two letters of January come first, even though the number of mistakes I've been making in my typewriting tells me, as it has probably already told you, that I am still tired from the tensions of packing and unpacking, to say nothing of the journey down, with the snow and mud from the sanded roads freezing on the windshield after each spattering. But we are both in good health: Sophia being much better than she has been at any time since last Spring, thanks to an excellent physician she found in the Harvard University Health Clinic, and we look forward to the lonely days here, after three months of being wined and dined and petted, with a pleasure that will be sharpened by the contrast. But my book demands more time than I was originally willing to give it; so the prospects of my being able to get over to England this year look exceedingly dim, though they seemed quite vivid only six months ago.

Our careers seem to be converging. Just a little while after you were revising your articles on Town Planning for the *Everyman Encyclopedia*, I was revising my new article on The City (forms and functions) for the new edition of the *Encyclopedia of Social Sciences*. For a person of my temperament and training, this kind of article is about the most difficult possible assignment, and I feel like something of a fraud when I try to put my ideas in a form that would be swallowed by the kind of academic mind that consults such an encyclopedia—though I must admit that the editors, so far from being frightened by heresies, actually insisted that they were needed, to round out the more orthodox views of other contributors. As for my getting mentioned in the same breath as that which delivered the well-deserved 'world homage' to you, dear F.J.—the only thing that this testifies to is the fact that since my books have come out in Spanish and Portuguese, I occupy a place in the Latin consciousness out of all proportion to the part I have played in the planning movement. We both, of course, can smile over the fact that it is ourselves, rather than the trained professionals, who have supplied the 'luminous guidelines' for town planning: though some of that smile must disappear when we remember that an even greater influence has been exercised by another amateur, Le Corbusier, to the great embarrassment of everything that we have stood for and promoted. Still, I am glad we are coupled together, even if I can't claim a tenth of the credit that properly comes to you.

When I look at what has happened in both architecture and planning during the last generation here in the United States, I must honestly confess to myself that I might as well never have written a word: the tide has been entirely against me. There is only one concrete testimonial to my actual influence: the fact that the city of New York has begun to build small neighbourhood parks, of half an acre or less, a suggestion I made first in a

Sky Line a dozen or more years ago, later re-printed in *From the Ground Up* and then repeated in another article in *The Highway and the City*. That one little sensible suggestion did get lodged in fertile soil and sprouted: but of course the people who are planning the parks haven't the faintest notion that I planted the seed. There is a sense in which, despite all the honours that have come my way, I am a forgotten man in my own country. And though my Open Letter attacking Johnson's Vietnam Policy last March started the whole-sale protest that has grown ever since—including the teach-in movement—this whole episode is now critically discussed without a mention of my name. I might as well be orbiting in space for all that the newspapers or the television know about my existence: or rather, if I *were* in orbit, they'd pay attention to me! Still, there is one great compensation: my time is my own, as it wouldn't be if I were a Public Figure.

AMENIA, NEW YORK   5 February 1966

Your letter about Robert Weaver's book, dear F.J., reached me only today, through some carelessness or capriciousness about the way my mail is for-warded from Cambridge: indeed, I don't see why it shouldn't have reached me before we left on the 27th, but maybe the bad winter weather disrupted the air mail service. What you say about the book makes me realise how deeply I have been sunk in my own book: so that I have tossed aside, quite automatically, all reading that does not [in some way] concern it. I suspect that Weaver's book may be lying in the bottom of a box of books on cities and architecture that I cleaned out of the book-case in my study, which I reserve for new books, in order to relieve the suffocation of unwanted reading matter that somehow, when I am trying to keep my mind clear, makes me feel as if I were trying to swim in a pond full of slimy weeds or tentacular water lilies. I don't even promise to look up Weaver's book till I am finished with my own, though I realise from your description that I should welcome it and that, if I were free to, I should even try to review it. I am annoyed at the fact that he tosses the New Towns idea aside as if it were not for the United States.

When I reviewed the New York State Regional Council's Report last year —surely I sent you a copy?—I pointed out that the time was past for that kind of timidity. A government that can spend fantastic sums of money on super-fluous highways that gouge out the heart of American cities, can well spend even greater amounts on supplying funds for New Towns which would alter the whole pattern of traffic distribution, whose present layout duplicates the centralizing tendencies of the railroad age, repeats all those early mistakes and creates gratuitous problems in daily transportation that cannot be solved on any terms—except by changing the pattern. What Weaver, of course, is stupidly suggesting is that private enterprise may be tempted to build new towns on the same indecently profitable terms it has been doing 'urban renewal' projects. But for reasons you know even better than I, private enterprise cannot afford the capital needed to launch a new town and keep it going until it is built up. I have no enthusiasm about Reston: it is a fake. All that it is, all indeed that it ever started to be, is an upper class suburb dressed up to *look* urbane rather than suburban: a conversation piece, not a serious effort at town-building. Knowing how Washington operates, I suspect that Weaver's book was ghosted by some smart young professor who took his information about New Towns from the Orlans–Rodwin wing. And yet, as you say, the fact that Weaver goes as far as he does is a hopeful sign, though I am not at all convinced that President Johnson's seemingly dynamic policies may not, by their *inherent superficiality* and their lack of any plans for underlying changes, do as much harm as our Highway Building policy, whose very dynamics only increased the velocity of its mistakes and the area of its damage.

But you must, I need not perhaps warn you, allow in my judgement of these immediate affairs for my outrage over Washington's continually mounting blunders—and worse than blunders—in Vietnam. Johnson is not a man to be trusted on any account, for he is neither a New Dealer nor a Fair Dealer but a Double Dealer. He is now in the act of wrecking the lives of the whole younger generation, because he has neither sufficient intelligence nor sufficient courage to admit the obvious—that our whole Vietnam policy, from the time we refused to countenance a general election there in accordance with the Geneva Agreement, has been a succession of increasingly ghastly errors; and that the only honorable course open to us is to admit these errors, to apologise for them and try to repair them, and to make a start on this long road by withdrawing our military forces completely. A great nation could make such a reversal of its course without any loss of dignity, indeed with a great gain, if we had a President great enough to utter the appropriate words, beginning with the frank admission that we have suffered a complete moral defeat by the atrocities we have inflicted upon the Vietnamese peasants, and a military defeat at the hands of the Vietcong. Ours is the story of David and Goliath all over again: the little, unarmed shepherd with his sling shot has brought down the Giant, appropriately armed in brass, according to the Bible, and— also appropriately—slain by a shot in his weakest spot—his head. The whole thing is a nightmare, and the only thing that relieves the horror of it is that the opposition to the Goldwater-Johnson policy has been growing steadily, ever since I wrote my Open Letter to the President at the end of last February, which, in a way that surprised me, helped to trigger the reaction. Never did our country fight a more unpopular war to justify such a senseless policy.

You must forgive this tirade, dear F.J. Usually I manage to confine it to those hours when I prematurely awaken from sleep, and if I allow it to creep into this letter—possibly gallop would be a better word than creep!—it is because this infamy lies so heavy on the hearts of all decent people in this country now—though I will admit that there are 'decent' people on the other side, still living in the dream world of my country's supposed humanity and love of freedom. I have lost the ability to exchange letters with a few people whom I once counted friends. Some day, I believe, they will be sickened by the Pentagon's calculated brutality and by Johnson's lying and hypocrisy; and then they may, if we're still alive, apologise to me, as more than one honorable person apologised for attacking my pro-war policy in 1938, when they regarded me as a madman for suggesting that Hitler might be a menace to the world, that France would be his first victim, and that we must be ready to fight him alone.

Meanwhile, you have doubtless received the brief letter I wrote you on coming back here, and looking back on it, I think I may have overplayed the part about my being neglected by my own countrymen. I should have remembered that last June, at the AIA meeting in Washington, a Hawiian state planner told me that my report on Honolulu was now their Bible, and that they were beginning to carry out and even carry further its recommendations. While just a few months ago, the secretary of the Longshoremen's Union in San Francisco wrote that his union was concerned about the possibility that Hawaii might be ruined by avaricious realtors, and he wanted to know if I would consider going back there for a month and preparing a report to guide the union in formulating a policy. It is true that Hawaii is nearly as far from the mainland as Europe: still, that's not neglect! As for the review of the New York State planning report, it was circulated in a conference of Local Authorities held by the Council of Europe, and has made a stir in those circles. While an enterprising young Frenchwoman—at least I hope she is young—is planning six 'emissions' on radio and television, based largely on *The City in History*. Who am I to complain? As for the inordinate length of this letter, that's something for you, dear F.J., to complain about!

P.S. Your obituary on Purdom in the *Bulletin* was delicately and justly done.

WELWYN GARDEN CITY   18 March 1966

Dear Lewis

Hazel Evans, now editor of *T & CP*, has shown me the proof of what you are to say about me in the April issue, which along with a number of other flatteries by eminent personages, would cause me to blush if I still could. The effect is that of a series of obituary notices—*nil nisi bonum* perforce—and though I discount the tributes (and considerably disagree with their assessments of the subject) I have to admit that I like being praised, mostly because of my vanity, but also because some people are impressed and this adds to my influence in public affairs. So let me thank you.

I mustn't argue with you about Vietnam, not only because I don't know enough, but also because I don't want to be ex-communicated. I am much shaken by what you say about your President, yet hope you are not entirely right about him. I am influenced by the views on the Cold War now held by my friend Desmond Donnelly, MP, as developed in his *Struggle for the World* (1965) after his visits to the USSR and China, and his patient and relentless discussions with leaders in those countries and with Western statesmen such as Eden and Acheson. And I am quite sure that our present Foreign Secretary, Michael Stewart, who was for many years on the TCPA Executive when I was its Chairman, is sincere as well as highly intelligent. We shall be having a thorough talk with Donelly after the election, in the course of which I hope to move towards a better understanding of the GB–USA relationship on Vietnam—which of course cannot be disentangled from the whole question of European defence. But I can't think Stewart is a handful of nickels in Johnsons' pocket. The British policy, which is bi-partisan, is to get the antagonists to the conference table; and I must say it looks to me as if the obstacles to this are in Hanoi and Peking rather than in Washington. Behind it all, of course, is the question whether US intervention in Vietnam is a wanton interference with a local revolution, or a necessary resistance to Communist aggression. You are surer than I am which it is.

As to the US strategy for New Towns, is it not possible that you should accept a stage of private-profit projects with public encouragement by designation and compulsory acquisition of sites, subject to conditions as to size, structure, planning and housing standards, and provision for local employment? Does it matter fundamentally if there is private benefit by the increment of overall land value, for which well-financed commercial companies might be prepared to wait, as in the Country Club estate in Kansas? Could not planning control look after the zoning of green belts, and a system of planning restrictions and encouragements guide new industries to preferable places, while leaving much freedom of choice to firms? Does a town-planning idealist as such have to be anti-capitalist? Capitalism has frightfully ugly features, but isn't Communism in practice worse? Isn't the best hope for a balance of productiveness and freedom to be looked for in a 'mixed economy'? And is not America certain to go that way, as Britain now does—consciously? And isn't it politically dangerous to be biased against either public controls or enterprises, or enterprises based on the quest of personal profit? Or even to be rigid about where the boundary comes? Don't we have to preach tolerance and commonsense to Leftists as well as Rightists?

You (and I) have given credit to old Howard for prescience in many important matters. I think we might add that he was a prophet of the 'mixed economy', in which the proportions of public and private enterprise must be for ever pragmatic and will differ in different societies. Lenin's New Economic Policy was only temporary, but there seem to me to be signs of a return of it in a more lasting form—e.g. in the recognition that a rate of interest on capital expenditure is necessary for wise allocation, and that the profit test is indispensable in state enterprise. The market test is also necessary once you rise above subsistence; and it may soon be discovered that an element of speculative or adventurous enterprise is necessary for the emergence of new products. East is East and West is West, but it is a fallacy that never the twain shall approach.

AMENIA, NEW YORK   10 April 1966

I think I know how you feel about tributes, dear F.J., though there wasn't an ounce of marshmallow fluff in mine to you: but perhaps we shy away from them for different reasons. What usually annoys me, when I get any such citations, is that no matter how fulsome and glowing they are, they always seem to concentrate on matters that don't seem to me either characteristic or important, and don't come within miles of touching more essential matters. But there's no modesty about me, though some people seem all too easily taken in by my gentlemanly self-effacement, which I achieved by reacting against Shaw, the hero of my youth. When I had finished *The City in History* I said to Sophy: it will take ten years before anyone fully understands what an original book this is; and about my present book I say to myself, it may take half a century before people understand, much less accept, what is in it. When a man feels this way, he'd better close his ears to what his contemporaries are saying about him, and that is what I try hard to do. But even when one's dead one is not safe. The MIT press has just showed me the outline and Introduction to the book of selections from Raymond Unwin's works they are going to publish: my suggested alternative to trying to get out *Town Planning in Practice* in a new edition. The selections are all right but Creese, the editor, for all his admiration for Unwin, manages to say the wrong thing about him again and again, rising to a climax of misinterpretation by drawing a lengthy comparison between him and Bernard Shaw, more or less on the basis that they both had known William Morris and were both Socialists. I wish now I had had the time to do this job myself. Incidentally, the MIT press has just published a paperback edition of Stein's *New Towns for America*. . . .

I don't know what I could have written you about the American New Towns that made you so completely misinterpret my attitude toward the present proposals as anti-capitalist. My chief objection to them is that they are merely suburbs, set further out from the central city, usually, than before, and dressed up to look like cities but without the industries and the mixed populations that would make them anything but what they are now: swank residential establishments. Furthermore, I don't think that, in a country as big as the United States, the financing of the New Towns by the Federal Government will prove any less of an obstacle to sound regional development than the subsidising of the National Highway Programme has been: on the contrary, it will only add to the existing sprawl and untidiness, until a regional framework, embracing a whole state or a group of states, is put together by the States themselves. I am all for a mixed economy, on both practical and philosophic grounds; but I look with mistrust on every evidence of a totalitarian economy, whether governmental or capitalistic, and I see every reason to fear that the American new towns programme, if it does not sink into suburbanism, will prove as dreary in its results as our high rise housing projects.

As to our Vietnam fiasco, which gets deeper and deeper, precisely as I predicted a year ago, I'll say nothing further except to report on a poll taken by our local country newspaper, among this representative rural population. Ninety-five per cent of the people were in favour of putting the matter in the hands of the United Nations, five-sixths were in favour of a negotiated peace, three-quarters judged our intervention to be morally objectionable, while only one-twelfth were in favour of Johnson's policy. (Some of these items of course overlap). The protests against the war continue to rise, not merely against our tactics and strategy, but against the false assumptions upon which they have been based. Don't think that my position or preaching has had any effect on the people of Amenia! They are so little aware of my existence that they don't even consult me when a problem of planning or school architecture comes up —though the Longshoremen's Union of the Pacific Coast asked me if I would be willing to spend a month reporting for them on the better planning of Hawaii! . . .

AMENIA, NEW YORK   30 June 1966

I forget, dear F.J., when you and Margaret were supposed to come back from your Tokyo jaunt: but if you are back, I trust that you have emerged from that adventure—to me it would be an ordeal!—not too much the worse for wear. Time flies quickly for us over here, between working in the garden and working on my book. Although the spring was raw and windy, so all growth was delayed or set back, we've had heavenly weather, punctuated by equally heavenly rain these last six weeks, and our garden has never burgeoned so riotously in years. As for my book, that's been burgeoning, too; and as with a purely vegetable overgrowth I've had to cut it back. Or rather I decided to break it in half at a natural dividing place in my theme; and I am now hoping to have volume I ready for the publisher by September—and follow with volume II a year later. The chief trouble about writing a book when youth is past is that one knows too much, has too many second thoughts, makes too many footling and unnecessary corrections, which then have to be re-corrected; and, in short, one does the simplest thing in the hardest way possible. Even being aware of these pitfalls doesn't help much; and if I didn't have Sophy to decipher my hieroglyphics the book would never come out. But the nice thing is that at the end it all turns out to be quite clean prose, which looks as if it had smoothly rolled off one's mind!

The best part about being so absorbed in my book is that it keeps my mind off the political folly, military imbecility and moral abomination that Johnson has, to the eternal disgrace of my countrymen, perpetrated in Vietnam. Even so, like King Charles' head it keeps on breaking into my writing—as here! . . .

WELWYN GARDEN CITY 6 July 1966

Dear Lewis

Yours of 30 June arrived today. We have been home from Japan for some weeks, but the memories of that extraordinary experience remain vivid, especially as they are reinforced by making notes for one or two talks and studying and selecting my colour slides, and reading again your Ambassador Reischaur's truly brilliant little book *Japan Past and Present* and Lady Murasaki's *Tale of Genji* (11th century), as well as the guide books and special publications issued by the Japanese hosts for our Congress. The palimpsest of Western (USA) modernisation and oriental background culture make a quite fascinating if bewildering blend, even if we can't by any means take it all in. One might (to use Henry James's word) 'expatiate' at length, but one couldn't improve on or correct Reischaur—who should be read by anyone interested in Japan. . . .

Of course we were de luxe tourists living mostly in Hilton-type hotels, and as it happened the two Osborns were treated as hallowed, ancient monuments of the Garden City movement, under the influence of Issei Inuma, the much-honoured *doyen* of Japanese planning, who with his charming wife travelled with us most of the time in comfortable cars provided by the governments of cities and prefectures. He also insisted on my preaching the New Towns gospel on TV, at a crowded public meeting in central Tokyo, and at a private 'audience' with the Crown Prince and Princess. (For the public lecture I was delicately remunerated, not by cash, but by costly presents of a gold and pearl brooch for MPO and similar jewellery for me).

Thus we did not dig deeply into the seamy side or the poverty of the country. But from external observation and the excellent surveys and statistics I got a fairly clear view of the economic situation, and of the existing housing and the standards of rehousing—the latter of course being of the 5-storey walk-up with very small floor areas by European comparisons.

Regional planning and a big redistribution of population are seriously contemplated, but powers and politics are not yet very advanced. Leading planners are in the main closer to AIP thinking than TCPA thinking. I have no illusion that we are winning in the world at large. However, like Old Man River, I just keep rolling along. Probably I have shot my little bolt. (A significant senile mixture of metaphors.)

How pleasant to hear of the progress of your work! You at any rate have bolts still to shoot.

WELWYN GARDEN CITY   31 August 1966

Dear Lewis

I'm in a cribbed and cabined state of mind this week through defying the rebukes of all sorts of papers on my desk, in order to alternate between taking part in family celebrations of our 50th wedding anniversary (yesterday) and Margaret's 77th birthday (today), and reading for review Creese's book about the garden city movement[1]. We succeeded in keeping the dated events secret from everybody but our own four and Lesley's husband and MPO's brother's family, and a celebration dinner at a local restaurant and visits by these relatives were easy and pleasant. Creese however was work, because I had made up my mind to study him in detail and to try to assess for once exactly what an outside observer of the GC movement sees in it. I thought this might help me in any necessary correction of my own perspective, since I continue to think of contributing to the record. . . .

My difficulty is to define just where Creese goes wrong in his estimate of Unwin—and of Morris. Like Pevsner, Summerson, and almost all architectural and aesthetic critics, he entirely fails to understand the social reformer

---

[1] Walter Creese, *The Search for Environment*, New Haven, London, 1966.

who is *also* an artist or a man of intense appreciation of visual beauty. It would be very hard to say whether Morris was primarily an aesthete of high creativeness in visual art and words, with a passionate desire that everybody should share his delights, or primarily a deep sympathiser with deprived humanity who wanted everybody to have the fullest possible life in every way *including* his own special cultural pleasures. I would put him and Ruskin in this latter class. And unquestionably I would put Unwin there, and give him much higher marks for a sense of the politically practicable and therefore as a force for actual reform. He had also the quantitative sense (which covers dimensions as well as finance), and it was this, along with his aesthetic sensibility, that made him unique as an originator in town planning. I don't think he was in the class of Voysey or Parker or C. H. James as a sheer (or mere?) architectural designer, but he was a first class judge of design, and it is this, and Parker's ability to learn from Unwin about the wider planning considerations, that accounts for the brilliant success of the partnership.

I would say that Creese at moments sees this, but his mind is not (what is the word?) autonomous (?); he has read far too much purely aesthetic criticism, and most of the time he sees successive physical developments as façades or vistas, and tries to classify them or affiliate them stylistically as Queen Anne or Georgian or 'modern'—without, it seems to me, even realising, as the aesthetic critics usually do, that many industrial villages and housing schemes are not consciously stylistic, but are in a builders' vernacular of the moment as governed by unconsidered habit, economy, and byelaws. The row houses at Saltaire, and even the first few at Bournville, seem to me to have no importance whatever in stylistic history. The importance of Unwin and Parker is surely that they took up the real break in style represented by Voysey's, Baillie Scott's and Curtis Green's houses for well-off clients, and by a combination of good taste, economic realism and new forms of group layout, 'democratised' it and made it practicable on a large scale—internationally. Curt Behrendt seems to me to be close to the mark on this—but no one ever mentions his book[1]—except you—and me.

Creese often quotes me, but he hasn't a clue as to my contribution (such as it is) to the movement. Though I know he is aware of the Osborn–Whittick book, which contains some information as to the political evolution of the New Towns Act, he never mentions it, and is almost unconscious of the sort of sustained campaign that such things require. Howard and I to him are earnest propagandists, by inference irrelevant to the major issue of urban 'design'. The vastly important historic chance that Unwin and Parker in their career were drawn into the garden city movement, by Howard, and that

---

[1] *Modern Building: Its Nature, Problems and Forms*, New York, 1937.

Unwin at once grasped its significance and became one of its greatest proponents, he misses altogether. I certainly, like Howard, started from the social reform angle, and it was by sheer chance that I got a job as housing manager at Letchworth in 1912. But I was captivated at once by the sheer beauty of Letchworth housing and landscaping, and, like Howard, I have always coupled the aesthetic with the social and economic arguments for decentralisation to new towns. I spent a great deal of time and effort in the publicity of Welwyn persuading a public, then indifferent, to accept as a value the 'look' of a town and the importance of architectural control—the latter against much opposition from anarchistic architects as well as their clients. (I could have qualified for the RIBA Gold Medal on that ground). Architects nowadays have no idea how difficult that was, or how dependent the harmony of WGC was on the remarkable strength and judgement of de Soissons' partner A. W. Kenyon. One of my publicity slogans was: 'You live only inside one house, but outside all the others'.

However, this is an egoistic side-issue. Back to Creese's essential outlook. I shan't say this, but he is a patient student, over-influenced by very limited aesthetic writers, anxious to be thought thoroughly modern-minded, and not adapted to hard critical thinking. Yet he half-sees, or senses at times, that the established critics are unfair to Unwin and Parker. He wants to rehabilitate them without being written off as a 'square' himself. Therefore he tries to imitate their critics' pseudo-learned and pseudo-philosophical language in the hope that they will respect his writing and revise their estimates of Unwin, Parker and Co. I think they are clever enough to do neither. But we shall see. . . .

AMENIA, NEW YORK   20 September 1966

Your two letters, dear F.J., written within a fortnight, deserve a far more generous and leisurely response that I shall be able to give them; for they find me in the act swiftly gathering together the illustrations for my book, which I handed in to the publisher last week, while tidying up my garden for the winter and preparing for the trip to Cambridge next week, where we'll be in residence until next February. But first, before I say anything else, let me give Margaret our congratulations on her seventy-seventh birthday, and you both on your fiftieth wedding anniversary. I don't know how you both feel about it, but I find I am incredulous over 'old age' suddenly bursting upon one, a boring, uninvited guest whose only virtue is that he won't stay too long: and as for golden weddings, they are a little ironic, despite the sweet, reassuring sense of being, temporarily speaking, 'home', and I feel as if

Sophy and I must get ready for that, too, for if luck holds it's only half a dozen years away. Meanwhile, we embrace you both, and wish we could have peeped at the celebration dinner to add our good wishes then and there.

Your description of your qualms and misgivings over Creese's book tallies with my feelings, though as usual you are a more generous and forgiving opponent. I didn't have time to read the book from cover to cover when it came, nor have I yet had time; but I dipped into the parts that interested me most, and again like you felt that he had done a very good job on the whole, not by Howard, but by Unwin and Parker, in rescuing them from neglect and contemptuous—and contemptible—misunderstanding, and bringing out their important contributions. Though I had partly caught up with the biographic data about both men when I gave a memorial lecture at the University of Pennsylvania, which I've unfortunately never written out, Creese had still many little things to tell me. For this part of his work, I claim, secretly, a little credit; for when as a young man he decided to pursue his studies in England, I told him not to overlook Hampstead Garden Suburb, or the work of Unwin and Parker, who had been unfairly passed over. And of course at the same time I told him about you and suggested that he see you, as I gather from you he must have done, though the book shows he was not capable of learning very much. We were in touch with each other from time to time, though I have never met him, and our relations, up to the time I last wrote him, were always friendly. In that letter I praised his work warmly, for just the things I have been saying to you, and then I told him what I thought about his sins of omission and commission: the latter his giving so much place and weight to people like Giedion, who have a complete blind spot about the garden city idea and what it implies, and on the score of omissions, passing over the fact that Howard's idea was kept alive during the twenties and especially the thirties by two men whom he barely refers to in this regard—F. J. Osborn and Lewis Mumford. You are the more important figure, certainly, for the political impact and practical effect your advocacy had in England; but I gave the ideas international circulation, or at least restored that circulation at a time when to speak of garden cities was to label oneself a back-number in both communist and conservative circles—especially among the so-called advance guard. Stein would have made a third as an advocate but for the fact that from 1935 to 1945, and even later, his ill-health put him out of the running. This seemed to me an inexcusable oversight, not because either of us need 'recognition' but because it fails to account for the results of this campaign, the New Towns themselves and the spread of the movement once more during the last ten years: so that Creese's account makes it seem as if the fashionable opponents had said the last word, and the movement had died. I am afraid my criticism shocked the life out of him: indeed, I meant it to.

I should by now be used to being treated as the Invisible Man, and seeing other people getting credit for work I did long before: but after a while I find myself wondering whether I have not paid rather heavily by doing my work without any thought for publicity or any immediate reward; whether, in fact, I am not in the same position, largely for the same good and amiable reasons, that Unwin and Parker were in; and that my sole compensation will be that a generation hence another Walter Creese will dig me up and restore me, while forgetting equally important later contemporaries! I knew my letter would end our correspondence; indeed I made it easier by telling him that I expected no answer; and of course no answer has come. So you can imagine with what impatience and with what eagerness I am looking forward to your review. I am delighted, too, with your new Eureka and the staggering universes it opens up at both ends of the scale: this is part of the playfulness that I note in all good minds in their old age, when they lift their eyes from the work they have attended to so assiduously and look around them, with the smiling wonder of a child, much in the mood one has when one quits at the end of a day's work and goes out to look up at the sky. I have a few such queer cronies, too, and cherish them. But incidentally, and quite by accident, I have an answer to your mathematical speculations in my book: in which, by taking a different measure than time and space, I present a picture of man which shows him, by my criterion, far more interesting and more important than our whole solar system, and quite respectably weighty even when put alongside the visible universe. . . .

My autobiography, I confess, still teases me; and I would like to get this monstrous opus on Technics and Human development off my shoulders, so that I may go back to my life story and finish it before it finishes me. A little while ago Catherine Wurster's husband, after much hesitation, gave me back my letters to her, which covered a period from 1930 to her death—though the most interesting—and unpublishable—ones cover the first four years. Her own letters to me are often better than mine; and if they could be published within the next decade, before we are both forgotten, they would make an interesting contribution to contemporary history in more than one area. But they are too intimate to be opened up, and though I shall draw on them for my autobiography some of the best parts will be killed by discretion. My correspondence with Van Wyck Brooks, which will come out a year or so hence, will be a poor substitute!

I have rambled on, this grey afternoon, dear F.J., and as I look over the letter I find it disgracefully full of pride, spite, and malice, probably too long suppressed. Discount it, as a subterfuge for concealing something far more

hurtful, my feelings of animosity against President Johnson for the disgrace
and degradation his Vietnam war has wantonly inflicted on my country.
That I cannot forgive and will never forget. But this is a bad note to end on:
so I raise my eyes from the typewriter—and smile!

WELWYN GARDEN CITY   27 September 1966

Dear Lewis

I save 3*d* (3·49 cents) by replying to your letter before 3 October, when the
air-letter rate goes up by 50 per cent to 9d, so you must bear with my precipi-
tancy and feel no call to emulate it. What you say about Creese's book is of
course very interesting and has caused me to look again at my review and the
last two letters I wrote to you, in which I fancy now I more nearly expressed
what I think about the book than in the review. It is natural, and legitimate,
in letters between friends, to be a bit egoistic about the difference between
what the world thinks of us and our part in events, and what we think ourselves. But I couldn't, and didn't, in my review of Creese, complain of his
under-estimate of the political influence of consistent and persistent advocacy
of the new towns idea by you and me and Stein, and the indispensable
organisation of the campaign in GB by the TCPA, with a small staff to pour
out for years and years memoranda and speeches into the eyes and ears of
inattentive technicians, journalists, economists, sociologists, and governmental decision-makers. (As you know, I have felt that the USA has lacked a
TCPA to reverberate the thoughts of Mumford, Stein, Tugwell and the rest
of your very able group.) Creese, as an academic with an elect-aesthetic
outlook, has no real grip on the way things are brought about in the political
field. Stein certainly has a gift for politics, equivalent to Unwin's (and
perhaps I might add, mine); I was much impressed by his methods in lobbying
'on the Hill'. But he would have been much more influential with a small
political organisation behind him. Without the TCPA and its Mr Justice
Nevilles, its Lord Harmsworths and Lord Salters, and its semi-articulate
army of enthusiasts, Howard, Unwin and their articulate successors would
have spluttered ineffectually in the void. Wire-pullers like me have to have
coils of wire to throw out before they can pull them. Webb was probably the
most influential spider in political history; but he had to spin the real Web,
the Fabian Society, before he could catch any flies. . . .

I find I did meet Creese while he was at Liverpool, when I went there to
give a lecture to the students. But he never called here to see my Howard,
Unwin and Parker papers, which seems odd. . . .

We moved up here, dear F.J., just a few weeks ago, and are still in the sort of unsettled state that is unfavourable to work, if only because our nine bags and boxes, sent in advance ten days ago, have not, in the current state of transportation efficiency, arrived. So I write you during this brief pause, knowing that in a few days illustrations and galleys and letterpress for the pictures will be demanding all my attention—when I am not digging further into the second part of my book. I've had exceptionally good luck in assembling my pictures, however, and the somewhat bigger apartment we now occupy is as near to heaven on earth as I ever expect to get in a big city. From the eleventh floor, facing south and west, we take in a marvellous panorama of river and sky, and the city of Boston is just far enough away to be dimly enchanting, or at least not as obnoxious as it is now at closer view, with its monstrous new insurance company skyscrapers. This is home for us far more than New York has ever been since the nineteen-thirties: so to say were are happy about it is sheer understatement.

There is a point in your last letter that I'm tempted to write you about now, for it may never get into my autobiography, even if I finish it, and I feel it ought to be somehow, somewhere, on the record. You are right in saying that our influence in the United States was less that it should have been: but this is true only after 1932. In the twenties, we did have the makings of a TCPA in the Regional Planning Association of America; and we did our best to widen it by suggesting to our colleagues in other cities that they start similar groups, since this country is too big to have a single center serve as the core of a movement on a national scale, and every attempt to do so leads to the most sterile kind of bureaucratic organisation. Even though we never got this response, and even though our Association remained small, we would have continued to widen the scale of the activities we began in the 1920's but for two things: the depression and the fact that subsequent government work scattered our best members, McKaye, Henry Wright and Catherine Bauer; and what was worse, after 1932 a serious breach took place between Stein and Wright. Someday I will have to write about that breach, for I suppose I am the only one left who knew what happended; but though I remained friends with both men, I felt then and still feel that Stein was at fault. It was because of this breaking of their association that Albert Mayer, Wright and I founded the Housing Study Guild, to perform the immediate task of preparing the younger generation to do the large-scale public housing that, in 1932, loomed ahead as the next step.

During the worst period of the depression, the Guild—thanks largely to Wright's leadership—trained most of the good planners of the next generation, as well as some who turned out not so good. But we lacked one of the essentials that Stein had always, because of his ample means, provided us with, a commodious room in which as many as twenty people could comfortably meet; something we could not afford to hire and for which, for that matter, a hired room would hardly have been an adequate substitute. The final blow came with the breakdown in Stein's health in 1935, caused partly by his enforced separation from his wife, who spent half the year acting in Hollywood and who then earned fifty thousand dollars for such a period, partly by disappointment in not getting government jobs, and partly, I am convinced, by inner conflicts caused by Wright's bitterness over what had happened between them. His repeated breakdowns, physical and mental, have diminished his influence ever since; but this was particularly critical during the period between 1932 and 1948, by which time he was once again well enough to resume active leadership, with me and Mayer, of the Regional Development Council (the old RPAA reorganised and re-named). Had he remained in top form this might have been effective; but in addition to his repeated disabilities, the younger men whom we had drawn in did not take things into their hands, as Catherine and I (even earlier) had done with the Regional Planning Association. That was a great disappointment, and this whole effort petered out in the fifties. You did a far better job than we, dear F.J., that is plain; but there were extenuating circumstances in our case. Catherine's going off to Washington after 1934 completed the debacle, for she had taken my place as Stein's intellectual collaborator. He was an excellent judge of men and ideas and a fine organiser, quiet but very firm and persistent; but he needed someone to supply fresh ideas and expand his own; and after 1934 he lacked them. So much for our sad tale. This interweaving of personal events and impersonal conditions is what, I find, makes current history so fascinating.

WELWYN GARDEN CITY   8 October 1966

Dear Lewis

I reply to yours of 4th while some important points of it are still fresh in my mind. I had no thought of claiming credit for inventing the TCPA. It was created by Howard and developed by Thomas Adams, Culpin and others long before my time, as an instrument of propaganda or education. When I got interested in the subject and wrote *New Towns After the War* (1918), I probably assumed that published thoughts got into circulation more or less automatically and would be adopted or not adopted on their merits, though of course I did welcome the immediate acceptance by the GC & TP Association of our group and the book as a reinforcement, and when asked I wrote and lectured for the Association. But between then and 1936, when I became the Hon. Secretary of the Association, most of my own thought and educational effort went into sporadic articles in the press and single lectures to organisations who invited them. It was not until I found myself wearing the mantle of the organisation that what I thought and expressed had any appreciable effect. Moses tumbled to this trick when he put his ideas forward as Tables from Sinai. The Editor of *The Times* is only Sir William Haley, but when he writes a leading article he is the Thunderer and multitudes hearken with awe. There is no mystery about this; it's merely that a loud-speaker reaches a bigger crowd than one weak human voice, and that an institution is regarded (often credulously) as having some sort of collective wisdom.

I see your point about the continental scale of the USA. But in fact the TCPA was, and still is, primarily a London organisation, generalising from London experience. It failed for many years to establish regional branches, and those it did start lapsed into heresies (I had to exterminate one). Two founded during my chairmanship (for Scotland and the West Midlands) have been most effective; they were helped by the fact that they could use the monthly review and the flow of documented thoughts from our centre. Would not an Atlantic Seabord association be similarly useful to societies in other regions of the USA?

I think probably I and Gilbert McAllister[1] developed the TCPA as a political (constructively legislative and lobbying) body, on the lines pursued for a few years from 1919 by Reiss and Purdom, but though Reiss was, like Stein, a quite realistic politician, he was not radical enough and set his sights rather short perhaps, whereas Purdom was not good at political proposals or persuasion and tended to a kind of idealistic impossibilism and belief in a 'New Order'—which Howard, for all his rosy idealism, never did. I suppose my special contribution was due to my having a balance of idealism and political realism that happened to suit the moment, and some practice in writing popular propaganda and political memoranda that didn't seem ridiculous to wary statesmen. . . .

WELWYN GARDEN CITY   10 January 1967

Dear Lewis

. . . As for F.J.O., I have like Wells' Mr Lewisham, prepared a *Schema* for 1967 which begins with the revision of the big book on NT's, and includes a serious account of the Foundation and Early Development of WGC—an

---

[1] Labour Member of Parliament. Secretary of the Town and Country Planning Association, 1936–38; Editor of *Town and Country Planning*, 1936–42.

obligation, since I am the only survivor of the team and my evidence will be necessary for any future historian. Purdom left for the official archives an account that libels all the others, including to my surprise his faithful supporter Chambers; so I have found it necessary to deposit my own account of the crisis of 1928, and that of Purdom's personal assistant Pelly, which is far more damaging to Purdom than mine—since I have to make it clear that Purdom made a great contribution both to the movement and to WGC. So did Chambers, the great Caliph to whom Purdom was Grand Vizier. I think I can be completely objective about both; but I feel a sense of having a mean advantage in being their survivor; also in having a trickier trick of writing.

Next after these two projects comes some sort of Autobiography of F.J.O., preferable I now think, to a study by a Chicago University 'scholar', who hasn't appeared anyway since Lubove dropped out. But I funk it a bit; autobiog. is an impossible art. I had a trial run last week with a fifteen-minute talk on the BBC, *Escaped Londoner*, on which I have had many compliments, though some people said I played down too much my own part in the NT achievement. I had to be light-hearted and amusing; I suppose I take myself seriously, but I can't, as I rather think you can, take myself solemnly. My main purposes in this talk was to open the eyes of London listeners to their situation in London and the possible way out; and to do this along with a sketch of my own career was difficult in fifteen minutes. However, it seems to have come off. The BBC have asked me to talk some more, which is the best compliment; but I am at present far too busy arranging my records for the immediate writing work of the *Schema*. By an extraordinary stroke of luck I am having the help of the young Librarian of this district, who is most enthusiastic and far more energetic and systematic than I could ever be. He really enjoys browsing over my past articles, lectures and correspondence, which I must admit seem to me far more interesting than anything I write nowadays. I suppose I am folding up—not surprising at $81\frac{1}{2}$. . . .

WELWYN GARDEN CITY   29 January 1967

Dear Lewis
Don't reply to this unless you have an instantaneous and compelling reaction of warning or approval. I write because I have a decision to make and must think: and I can only think with a pen or type-keys at work under my fingers. That Chicago University project for a book about the GC Movement has come alive with a letter from Asst. Professor Stanley Buder of the Illinois Institute of Technology, proposing to come here in September 1967 for a

year to work with me on 'a history of the GCM'. He is BA, City Coll. NY, and MA 1960 and PhD 1966 of University of Chicago, all in History. His PhD thesis is on 'Pullman: an Experiment in Industrial Order & Community Planning', to be published 1967 by Oxford University Press—of which he sends me an abstract, which seems to me sensible but not distinguished in style or wit, giving me an impression not negative but neutral.

Meltzer's original proposal was for a book about F.J.O.'s part in the GC movement, apparently largely biographical. As I said in my last to you I boggled at this, because I fancy I could handle my own record more interestingly (and usefully) than any other writer could—if, which is unlikely, I could ever make myself do it. But egoistically I was tempted. The project as defined by Buder is for a history of the movement; and I think, in view of the desirability of such a history, I should agree to cooperate in such a work when a responsible academic body offers to undertake it.

So what? My view at the moment is that I accept—on the assumption that what is meant is a general history of the GCM and not a special study of F.J.O.'s part in it—though I make my personal records available for the study. I think I must assume that the man is reasonably competent. If I refused, no comparable offer to do the history might come while I am still able to assist—and after all, I am now the only survivor of the active and articulate participants in the GCM in its most important period.

I am starting on my own record of the details of the Foundation and Early History of WGC, of which I hope to do the main part before September. In this I now have the active help of the young Librarian of WGC, who has made a considerable collection of the local records. Obviously the two works can be coordinated to exclude tiresome overlaps. . . .

AMENIA, NEW YORK   1 February 1967

Yours of the 29th came this morning, dear F.J., and since my reaction to your decision is hearty approval, I write you forthwith. Professor Buder may not be an inspired scholar, but I know of very few good minds working in this field. A lot of decent, earnest people; but as I cast my mind over the younger generation I can detect few with any promise of originality. One must make the best of what is offered. I have no doubt that you'll have a chance to set much of the record of the GC movement straight, before the facts are lost or hopelessly distorted; your own story will inevitably enter into this—and meanwhile you can handle your personal memoirs in your own way. On such matters of these—at our age—it would be foolish to wait for an ideal collaborator; if he hasn't appeared yet, he doesn't exist! As you see, I am only mirroring your own thoughts: but sometimes, as in shaving, a mirror is useful!

WELWYN GARDEN CITY 5 February 1967

Dear Lewis

... Don't think I told you that MPO and I had dinner recently with Lord and Lady Reith at his club (Athenaeum of course); most interesting to both of us, MPO not having properly met Reith, and neither having talked with his wife, a modestly charming person. I think I am probably the only person who has ever told him very nearly the truth about himself; it certainly is not because of this that he has some peculiarly high regard for me, while at the same time looking down on me as a tycoon looks down on a bank clerk. I rather think it is analogous to Leverhulme's regard for Howard—seen from the world of power and ambition we stand for a suppressed streak of social conscience or idealism. Reith's idealism is all mixed up with his superb and unalterable egoism; but he wants to justify himself to God by concentration on good works in his post-ambition period. Never having really thought about philosophy, he reverts to his father's traditional faith; and as Rector of Glasgow University he is making some really fine pronouncements of traditional morality—which on the whole I welcome. I hope some day to write my own assessment of a man with a character of real greatness and very curious defects.

WELWYN GARDEN CITY 30 April 1967

Dear Lewis

I have recently arranged through Faber and Faber for French and German editions of Howard's book, and am negotiating hopefully for a Japanese edition and one in Spanish (probably from Mexico). These will all include your introductory essay and my preface of 1945, with my foreword to the 1965 paperback edition, making it clear that these have now to be read, like Howard's book, 'in historical perspective'. You will remember that I mentioned the change in the population prospects referred to in your essay.

Last time we exchanged letters you were recovering from bronchitis and I was debating with myself about the coverage of the proposed book on the GC movement. I trust you have since been in full health and able to get your Volume 2 far enough on to permit of your visit to Europe in June—in which month our only obstructions to welcoming visits are the six evenings 5th to

10th, when we are locked up in our Drama Festival. As to that GC book, in the end I concluded that I could not be both an object and a joint transitive verb; so we have agreed that Professor Buder will be the sole author and the topic F.J.O.'s part in the movement, as originally proposed by Chicago University.

As usual I am all behind with work commitments, especially the revision of the Osborn–Whittick book on *New Towns*. This has to be done by September, when Buder comes, and I think will be. But I have fallen for a temptation by the BBC to give a series of about five autobiographical talks in August–September—so seductive to my egoism and propaganda obsession that I simply couldn't turn it down, though I can't see how the blazes I can do the work. It arises from a 'listener research' report that a short talk I gave in December was outstandingly well received. It was a very light-hearted sketch of my life story as an 'Escaped Londoner'; and it looks as if that label is going to be fastened on me, which disturbs me a bit, though I invented it myself.

WELWYN GARDEN CITY   18 May 1967

Dear Lewis

Thanks for yours of 2 May and for the Senate Committee statement, which arrived today. On a first reading this looks to me like a revolutionary Anti-Megamachine Manifesto comparable to the Anti-Capitalist Manifesto of 1848. Curious that it coincides in time with the British effort to enter the Common Market, the underlying philosophy of which is a faith in Bigness (of productive organisations firstly, and secondly of states). On the Bigness issue I don't really know where I am now; I was all for Roosevelt's TNEC at the time. But I have since come to think, or hope, that organisational Bigness could be combined with locational or geographical Smallness. Even if the United Nations concept ultimately developed into World Government the human race might be able to distribute its components, controls and habitations in such a way as to reconcile productive cooperation with individual enjoyment. I await your fuller development of the idea.

Have you noticed at all the research now going on in France under the auspices of Canaux's CRU? (*Les Pavillonnaires*, etc). This looks to me like a profound reaction against Le Corbusier and CIAM, so I am rather plugging it in *T & CP* (from the July issue). The demographers and sociologists are astonished to discover that the French, by a 'Majorité considérable', unshakably prefer 'la maison individuelle', and are making exhaustive inquiries into the reasons for this queer fact. A wealthy oil tycoon, Jacques Riboud, is experimenting with small communities, as a step towards new towns in regional groups ('en grappe') and writing about the new town idea in a very intelligent and practical way.

Dear Lewis

This Epistle to the Columbians should creep across the Atlantic almost in your wake. It is to say how much Margaret and I enjoyed meeting with Sophy and you and the signs of your blooming health and unabated vigour. I am very conscious of the acceleration of time and that we cannot often meet again, and of a certain feeling that we didn't get down to exchanges of philosophy in the way that I always half-hope we might, and never do. I think I was in an abnormal physical state just then. Forced concentration on drafting those autobiographical talks for the BBC in September has been bad for me, at least temporarily, in that the attempt to find significance in happenings to me has disclosed too clearly their insignificance; yet I can't help dwelling on them to the amusement or boredom of others. You must forgive this, and Sophy must forgive my extraordinary mis-recognition of her at the TCPA party. This much disquieted me as another piece of evidence of senescence, but on reflection I am less worried though not less apologetic. Partly it was due to defects of sight, but also partly to the social ambience of the occasion. In a TCPA circle I would not be surprised to see Lady (Evelyn) Sharp, but I would be astonished to see Sophy, and though I had invited you (and by implication Sophy) I had not expected you would have time to come. My central sight is almost perfect, and my power of visual discrimination between persons as certain as my sense of the spelling of words. But I am confused in the street or in any surroundings where much is moving on the peripheries. Looking straight at a face I could not possibly mistake one known person for another. There is no close resemblance between Sophy and Lady Sharp. All they have in common is a kind of handsomeness that for me is (in a way, and I can't hit on the right adjective) awe-inspiring. Having half-seen Sophy I noticed that you were with her, and supposed you must, as was possible, have met Lady Sharp beforehand or on the way in. And (this really does show a touch of senescence) it took half a minute for the penny to drop. And of course longer for me to recover from the shock of my awful gaffe. This elaborate explanation is not a lame attempt at a plausible excuse: it is the truth.

I am reading with great interest and some intellectual stretching *The Myth of the Machine*[1]. I don't yet follow you in your analysis of the pre-language ages,

---

[1] New York, London, 1967.

but I do understand the chapters about ancient mass-organisation, when Men

> 'were lost, like slaves that swat,
> And in the stars of morning hung
> The stairways of the tallest gods
> When tyranny was young'. (GKC or course)

I find the thought of pyramid building unbearable, and don't see how any life-acceptant philosophy can really accommodate it. But while I can understand the methods of enslavement, or mass organisation, by the cash-wages system, I am still puzzled as to how thousands of men could be controlled by say ten per cent of overseers armed only with staves or whips. What was the sanction for the overseers? And how did the top men prevent mass revolts by the slaves against the overseers, during work hours or mealtimes or rest times, or some getting together between the mass and the overseers? I suppose the answer is that there must have been a force nearby ready to enforce discipline by killing, as in a modern military force? But I can't take in the ruthlessness (and the sheer courage) necessary for such operations of power, since the love and gentleness necessary for family life must have been going on pari-passu. Perhaps I shall see it all more clearly when I have read the whole book.

My only criticism so far is that I think tactically you too often refer to the topical issue of nuclear armament and Vietnam, which for some readers will have a 'King Charles's Head' effect. I see that your view is that rocket-building is an exact modern equivalent of Pyramid-building. But is it so 'exact' an equivalent? Pyramids no doubt had a similarity as enterprises of Prestige, but they had no competitive defence element. When the world is divided between two colossal power-groups, neither of which can assume that the other will not at some point exercise its power, can either refrain from seeking to maintain a 'balance' of deterrence until the other is willing to accept some sort of world order? The United Nations is failing, not only because of its one-state-one-vote composition, which makes its decisions unreal, but because in a changing world the formula of maintenance of the status quo of boundaries is insufficient—yet there cannot be for a long time a consensus of world opinion as to the right revisions or a common force to impose them.

You appear to me as a prophet formulating a new and essentially right Religion. What I can't see is the World Statesman who will initiate and carry through the governmental system that will permit of the adherence of the citizens of the world to that religion.

Enough for now. You help me to see the Destination, but not the Way.

Dear Lewis

The part of my last letter (17 July) about *The Myth* was more than usually feeble. Forget it. I have now read through the whole book, and I can at least take in what you are saying in the later chapters, though I am utterly at a loss in the prehistoric stages of the mind of Man. I shall never know enough to judge whether your analysis of the evolution of capitalism is entirely correct, but it is most exhaustively and interestingly documented, and written in your very best style, with a resourcefulness in vocabulary and analogy that I can only envy. I wish I were more intelligent and less aged, so that I might study and note it and see whether I can get the thought into my head and weigh it up. That won't now be possible. But I realise that you are proposing a philosophy of history and of the conduct of personal and social life that is, in relation to the wisdom of today, revolutionary. I am still in doubt how you would resolve the dilemma of responsible statesmen that I rather crudely described in my last; but I see you are taking the long-term view, and asking for a change in thought that would eventually produce, if you are right, the possibility of a totally different attitude between states. I'm left wondering whether, in view of the immense revolution you are contemplating, it is tactically wise, or fair, to condemn so unequivocally the present American international policy, and by implication that of Britain. Vietnam is a special and certainly debatable case of the logic of the defence of existing boundaries. But as I understand it your argument questions the whole theory of defence, and yet you don't seem to take a pacifist (non-resistant) policy, as some of the Axial religions did in principle, but their home-states never did.

Concurrently I've just read Bertrand Russell's *Autobiography*, volume I, which comes up to 1914. I find it interesting in detail but on the whole disappointing. I share his three major passions—for love, knowledge and social reform—but I don't follow his complaint of loneliness, even if by love he means, as he seems to mean, sex-love. The letters show that he has had very many deep friendships, with men as well as women, with intense sharing of interest and reciprocal affection; and yet he says he has never found peace or escaped loneliness till he found his fourth wife Edith. This doesn't seem intelligible to me at all. Relatively to him I have never had a close friendship in the sense of intimacy plus warmth with anybody except MPO, but I have never felt lonely. I have had hundreds of pleasant, admired, admiring, and mentally interesting acquaintances, and have never wanted to reveal my inner thoughts to them—though I have been coolly and scientifically curious about theirs, and this and our common activities have been the subjects of our intercourse. And of course I have had terrific sex-obsessions, but love in this sense doesn't imply mental intimacy, though it can in some cases lead to that. I understand Matthew Arnold's 'We mortal millions live alone', because I'm that sort of reserved and secretive chap, but that doesn't make us 'lonely' in any distressing sense.

Thirdly I have read with close attention and making full notes Le Corbusier's *Radiant City*[1], just published by Faber for the first time in (American-) English, and I have written a brief review of it for *T & CP* (August–September). I have reviewed his earlier books before, and very carefully, and like you, have regarded him as a pernicious influence. But I hadn't realised till now how fundamentally *stupid* he was. What is extraordinary is that an architect should have such a lack of the sense of scale and of the *feel* of surroundings. He was dominated by a desire for striking visual effects and by a Macaulayan belief in technology, and left out everything else. As a writer he has the Ruskinian gift of invective, without the superb language, and the controversial manners of a ranting political columnist. And as a pseudo-sociologist-economist he is a babbling baby. . . .

AMENIA, NEW YORK   10 August 1967

Don't be alarmed, dear F.J., at this quick response to your letter: for I meant to write you today anyway, and your words only turned my intention into an act. I have not yet swung back into my usual routine of work, partly because Alison and her two little ones have been with us for the last two and a half weeks, and much as we love having them, the young, whether they are thirty or three, are a little distracting—all the more because yesterday, when Alison was on the point of flying back to Montreal, the kids came down with some local virus and the journey has been postponed for another few days. There couldn't be a better moment than this to write you, accordingly; and if I waited till next week I might be absorbed, once more, in my book—though I hesitate to make that plunge, knowing that once started on it I shall have to stay under water and ice like a submarine in the Arctic Ocean, till I have reached my distant destination.

Your apologies about *The Myth of the Machine* are quite needless: you have really grasped my ultimate intentions in writing that book, though I did not start out with them in mind and might have flinched from the effort if I had realised in advance all that would be demanded of me. The American reviewers, few in number, thick-headed, churlish for the most part, have not the faintest conception of the book's quality: but you have had the insight

---

[1] New York, London, 1967.

to grasp at once what most people may not be able to do for at least a decade
—namely, that this is, as it turns out, a radical reinterpretation and revision
of human history, as now known; and if it should become generally accepted,
in time it might have the same role in the future that Bacon's *Advancement of
Learning* and Galileo's *Dialogues* had—but slowly!—on subsequent generations. I can now see clearly, as I could not and dared not at the beginning,
where the second volume is leading: that is, I can now see it in detail, not as a
vague intuition, and I realise all the ways in which my view of both the past
and future has come to differ from the ones that have increasingly prevailed
during the last century or two. This is big talk, of course, and possibly it will
turn out to be foolish talk, too: I allow for that. So I would not utter this
judgement on my own work to anyone but an old friend, who may be tempted
to burn this confession lest it do harm to my future reputation!

My original intentions were very modest but the success of *The City in
History* made me realise that, so far from completing my life work with
the last volume of the Renewal of Life Series, I now had the task, and as it
turned out, the privilege, of going beyond that achievement to pull together,
in the light of all that I had seen and observed, a great mass of evidence that I
was either ignorant of back in 1932, or incapable of interpreting intelligently.
The groundwork for my present views was laid in *The Transformations of
Man*: but now, as you alone have so far seen, I am ready to build up, or at
least to lay out, a more adequate philosophy which shall take full account, not
merely of our great human achievements, but also of our irrationalities, our
frustrations, our perversions; and by which, because for the first time we have
the means of becoming fully conscious of our hidden past, we may ultimately
overcome the forces and institutions that have so far bedevilled human
development. I may fail in this effort, even if I don't stupidly die before I
accomplish it, as many a good fellow has done before me; but at least it has
given a fresh point and meaning to this part of my life, when I had thought,
ten years ago, I would be living effortlessly on my intellectual capital, writing
readable condensations of my past discoveries and mulling over new chapters
in my autobiography! How modest I was then, and how immodest I have
become since! though if anything should reduce the swelling of my head the
scurvy reviews *The Myth* has received from my own countrymen, indeed from
my old colleagues, should serve that purpose. *The New Yorker*, where I am a
member of the family, has not even deigned to review the book. Yet this
unusually bad reception, worse than has been accorded to any other work of
mine, only convinces me that this time I have really said something important—though I'll not live long enough to see whether this is an illusion or will
turn out to be a fact.

I understand your uneasiness about my allusions to American policy in

Vietnam: even my British publisher, Warburg, thought this might have hurt the book in the United States. But I could no more keep Vietnam out of this book than Mr Dick could keep King Charles's head out of his Address: this, like our hideous nuclear and bacterial preparations, bears witness to the external pressures under which the book was written. A book that is meant to last must be nourished partly by the ordure its own period produces. But I have another private reason for these allusions: when I have attempted to use the usual channels of the press and magazines in making my views known I have found those channels blocked: so a book is my only outlet, and I am confident that the future historian will vindicate my views, which an ever-growing number of Americans now hold. We have been morally disgraced and militarily defeated by this disastrous policy; and Johnson's only way of wiping out the odium this callousness and stubbornness earned will be to widen the scale of extermination by a World War that will annihilate his own country, and his critics as well. The present government has lied to *itself*, as well as to its people: it multiplies its errors because it cannot admit that its initial premise was false and all the nice calculations it based on that premise have turned out to be wrong. England was not able to conquer Ireland in almost a thousand years, and in the USA the North was not able to conquer the South, though in both cases the weaker party seemed forced to submit. By now it should be plain that whilst we *can* destroy Vietnam and all its people, they cannot be conquered, and even if they surrendered, as Lee's army was forced to do, they would not in their hearts submit. Meanwhile the acts of violence and the human atrocities we have committed in Vietnam have had their terrible echoes in our own cities, where a minority of the Negro population now proposes to conduct a similar guerilla warfare indiscriminately against all whites. The only consolation I have is that the minority who protested against this infamous policy will, if Johnson persists, become a majority, and will reverse, though they may never be able to repair, all the damage he has done both to the Vietnamese and to his own countrymen. As you see, dear F.J., I feel more strongly than ever on this subject; and that explains why I didn't excise those references in *The Myth of the Machine*. At least those who read the book will know (what the editors of the *New York Times*, the *Washington Post* and others kept their readers from knowing) about my opposition to Johnson's policy, uttered the very day he decided to make the North Vietnamese beg for terms by bombing them.[1]

---

[1] Mumford wrote an Open Letter on Vietnam to the Associated and United Press Agencies, to *The New York Times*, *The Washington Post*, *The Christian Science Monitor*, *The St. Louis Post-Dispatch* and *The San Francisco Chronicle*. Only the latter two newspapers published or reported on the letter.

A day has passed, and Alison and her young ones are flying back to Montreal this evening: not an easy thing to arrange these days, with our railroads in even more absurd shape than yours and the nearest airport at Albany, seventy-five miles away: too long a drive for Sophy to make nowadays, except at a heavy price in fatigue. So I come back to the rest of your letter, and first to say that I agree at every point with your judgement on Le Corbusier. I made a similar judgement, as it happens, in the address I gave at Rome when I received my doctorate, pointing out the parallelism of our careers and the much greater success he had achieved, precisely because of his defects—fitting our technical and bureaucratic methods. If it gets printed here I'll send a copy for your amusement. For precisely opposite reasons, I regard both him and Jane Jacobs as a menace; and I'd put Doxiadis[1] as a close third.

I haven't read Russell's *Autobiography*, but though his little Home University Library book on *Philosophy* was almost the first book on philosophy I ever bought, I never cottoned to his thought, nor have I had much respect for his practical judgements, even as a younger man. He tried to get me to join his so-called Tribunal on American War Crimes in Vietnam; and though, as you know, I was as deeply disturbed as anyone about both our political strategy and our military tactics, the whole conception of such a tribunal seemed to me a folly, since it could not pretend to command the evidence or to give an impartial verdict based on it. We had a little correspondence over it; but even before that happened I saw that he was being used by his secretary—whom both Sophy and I disliked the one time we visited Russell, though we didn't then know the extent of his influence. As for Russell's loneliness, that seems to me a sentimentalism that echoes the stoic sentimentalism of his early essay on *A Free Man's Worship*. I of course knew something about Russell's sex life by hearsay, as well as by his open proclamation; and I find myself interested by your own confession about friendship, for there our experience seems to differ almost as much as it does in relation to sex and love.

Friends seem to have occupied the place in my life that sexual companions have done in yours, though for a different purpose. My sexual life has been a rich and abundant one; but only four women besides Sophia have had any part in it; and though I have been as open to temptation—and even to assault!—as anyone, I've never gone to bed with a woman I wasn't in love with, indeed sufficiently in love to marry. This greatly increased marital

---

[1] Constantinos Doxiadis, planner and theorist of urban affairs. Originator of Ekistics, 'the science of human settlements'.

tensions, of course, in the middle decade of my life when these encounters took place, one after another. But my marriage stood firm and was even enriched and benefited by all but one of these loves. . . . Each of these affairs had a tragic side; so less and less did they encourage repetition. One of them, as you probably have guessed if I did not tell you, was with [Kay], and our correspondence, if it could be published, would probably be a best seller— though before her death she was incredulous, when I showed her the chapters I had written about our relations, that she had ever written me in the fashion she did: so even in the disguise of fiction I won't be able to tell this story in my lifetime. But if my loves were few, my intimate friendships were many; and though I rarely exposed my whole life to men, more than one woman knew fully at least a part of it, besides those with whom I had sexual intimacy. With a few men I was less reserved; but my friendships with women, which always had a sexual under-current, perceived and acknowledged on both sides, made up for the lack of those final intimacies which I kept, more because it was my nature than by any deliberate intention, for those with whom I was deeply and fully in love. The full story of anyone's life is hard, almost impossible, to tell: I can remember one or two trivial but shameful episodes I would like to erase—though perhaps an outsider would regard them as quite venial sins, like not giving a sufficient tip to a waiter. But when I read in James Cozzens' novel *By Love Possessed* the passage in which the virtuous but bereft hero secretly makes love in a kind of blind animal lust with the wife of his respected law partner, I said to myself: I might have done that too, and actually once or twice did something I'd now consider its moral equivalent. . . .

AMENIA, NEW YORK   20 August 1967

. . . If your first letter had come earlier I could have spared you any further misgivings about not recognising Sophia at the TCPA party: for a few minutes afterward still another person, presumably with normal eyesight, addressed her as Lady Sharp, so apparently the resemblance is real. It was really our turn to be embarrassed, because when I got back to Park Square and looked again at your invitation, I realised that Sophia had not been included and I had not even had the decency to ask you if, since it was our last-night-in-London-but-one, she might come. I know how disturbing it is, even before old age breathes down one's neck, to make such little mistakes. As for old age, I find myself often, in my typewriting, making ominous substitutions of words with similar sounds, just as Emerson did when his mind faded and he would call an omnibus an obelisk; and if I haven't already done so, I may find myself making the same slips in speech. But these weaknesses come and go, I have learned: they are increased by tension, and then may disappear entirely. I think you keep up remarkably well, and hope I do as well if I ever reach your present age.

Still, I know what you mean by your feelings about our last meeting; and I will not try to console you by what a sage Hindu I knew used to say: 'Treat every meeting with your friend as if it were a first encounter, and every parting as if it were forever'. That's a counsel of perfection. I too have been conscious as I saw some of my old friends this time that, whether *I* went first or *they*, this might be our last time together. But that doesn't improve conversation: it's like trying to say something magnificently fitting when one says good-bye to a friend at the docks. Nothing important ever gets said at such moments; though once a person is gone, I have repeatedly found, one regrets that one had never seized the hour—or recognised it—for saying what lay deepest in one's heart. With a few people, you among them, I have at least expressed in some fashion my gratitude or my admiration, sometimes both, but still there is always a great deal unsaid, much of it by way of biographic details, particularly before we made each other's acquaintance.

I find myself, lately, constantly regretting that Catherine [Bauer] Wurster and I parted, in letters, on such a sour note. I knew she had increasingly come to disagree with my opinions: this she had expressed freely after 1939; while I in turn found myself less and less attracted to her own kind of thinking, to her easy pragmatism, her overemphatic hard-boiledness, her indifference to the larger world crisis. But, significantly, she remarked to Meyerson a little while before she died, discussing my 'pessimistic' interpretations: 'Do you know, after all, Lewis may be right!' But sometimes I have been troubled with the thought that the chapters I had written about our life together may have awakened feelings that had long been savagely repressed, so that now she even denied their existence; and that this inner turmoil may have contributed to a debility actually sufficient to make her stop teaching for a term, and perhaps, in the end, to have deviously led to her death. This may seem an egoistic interpretation on my part; but it is slightly substantiated by one bit of evidence. Back in the early thirties, on the basis of her letters to me, I felt that she had remarkable literary abilities which her growing specialised interest in housing was threatening. Almost as if in defiance of my valuing this side of her, she developed a strong inhibition against writing, and never even did justice to her concern with housing after writing a book she planned and wrote while we were still intimately associated. But just a few weeks before her death, and a year after she read my autobiographical chapters, she said to her mother out of a clear sky: 'What I'd like to do now is to write a novel'. . . .

I had hoped to begin work on volume II soon after getting back; but I was too depressed to do more than gather my travel notes together, in an article I'll send to you if it's published. I haven't started on the book even now but at least a few days ago I found myself writing, with a little of my old vigour, a preface to a book of essays on the city which I am talking over with my publisher this week. Most of the essays date since 1961; and the purpose of the preface is to explain why none of them deal with the urban problems of segregation and violence and wholesale destruction, and why, despite current illusions still held by many people in government, none of these symptoms will be cured by better housing and Urban Renewal projects: indeed, are likely to be aggravated by these remedies, which the slum dwellers who are displaced actively hate. To write even this preface I have had to go rapidly through a whole shelf of books I had never even peeped at while writing *The Myth of the Machine*. I am still not sure whether I want to publish a book on urbanism at this time, even though the essays are still alive and easy to retrieve. Now that I am in a mood to work, I feel obliged to attend exclusively to the next book—all the more because the professional reviews of *The Myth* that I have so far read are a disgrace to American scholarship, since the anthropologists, who do not feel sure enough of their position to criticise my data or even to suggest alternative interpretations, have fallen back on the simple device of trying to discredit me as a person.

As to your question about pyramid and rocket building—these seem to me precisely equivalents; but this does not mean that the contemporary megamachine is not radically different from the original type, if only because it commands far more perfect mechanical—and in addition—electronic resources. The original machine could not have worked without the aid of religion: so one of my tasks is to find out if this is necessary today, or if in fact already exists. But God keep me from founding a new religion! Actually, I see the means more clearly than the end: but probably neither will be accepted!

WELWYN GARDEN CITY   24 August 1967

Dear Lewis

I must just acknowledge your letter of 20th, here today; but briefly, because I am clearing the decks for the repainting of my study while I am in Germany next week, and all my papers and books are in such a state that when I return it will probably take me weeks to catch up with correspondence. And how I am to cope with Mr Buder from Chicago, who arrives on 15 September, I don't yet see.

I am honoured by your confidences, and as usual shaken by their confirmation of my own lightness of moral and philosophical weight and my facile ability to remember my follies and humiliations, with some acceptance that that is the poor sort of guy I am, and that it is useless to repine like Hoffman over eyes that shine, even to the extent of drowning one's loss or self-reproach in wine. Once only I took an overdose of whisky, and as it destroyed all my illusions, and showed me the skeleton under the rounded contours of the world, I have not repeated the experiment. I could, like you, take retrospective pleasure in a few unlawful fixations, but I couldn't resent my partners' repressions of the memory of them—which is probably due to their sense of conflict with other and more permanent loyalties. I am pretty sure that they would wishfully think that I was the seducer and they the seduced; and also that they were in fact only egoistically flattered rather than emotionally overwhelmed. Probably also they retain a certain mild gratitude for any reassuring episode of admiration.

Contemptible complacency, you may think; a confession of likings rather than deep, unshakable affections or loves. I feel inferior to you in this respect —an admiring awe. Yet I feel that you, like me, have a deep-seated tendency to monogamy.

I have had for review Creese's new book on Unwin[1], which contains a very useful selection of his writings. Coming hard on the heels of Le Corbusier's *Ville Radieuse* and a CRU study of *Tony Garnier*[2] by a young Polish architect whom I met some years ago in Cracow, it is a breath of humanity and common sense. I should have added Edmund Bacon's *Design of Cities*[3], of which I have also written a brief review; a gorgeous picture book showing that the charming Ed B. has a real love of classical and decorative architecture, and regards Le Corb as a disaster to architecture. But he is ambivalent in his taste and as much impressed by Paul Klee, as was Giedion, for his insight into the nature of SPACE. To my mind Klee, Picasso and their followers have simple-mindedly exploited the sometimes pleasing but confusing effects anybody gets from bi-focal spectacles. It was a gain to understanding when we rationalised perspective, not a loss. I don't particularly want to go back to the vision of a 1,000 eyed beetle.

CAMBRIDGE, MASSACHUSETTS   15 October 1967

More than a month has passed, dear F.J., since your last letter, with its delightful colour-prints, came to remind us of that memorable afternoon we

[1] Walter Creese, *The Legacy of Raymond Unwin*, Cambridge (USA), London, 1967.
[2] C. Pawlowski, *Tony Garnier*, Paris, 1967.
[3] New York, London, 1967.

spent with you and Margaret. And while you have been off in Berlin I have been putting together a new collection of my cities essays, topping them off with a lengthy postscript upon the present urban situation in America. The book will be called *The Urban Prospect*[1], and should come out next spring. I had held off republishing some of these essays, which are practically unknown even in planning schools, because I had planned to use them in the second volume of *The City in History*, dealing with the present and immediate future; but Heaven knows if that book will ever be written, at least by me: so I thought I'd better seize the present moment, when our common ideas are now conspicuously in the limelight, to bring these essays before a wider public. At the moment the tide seems to be running ever more swiftly in our direction: by 'our' I mean yours and mine and Stein's direction. Just the other day a Finnish Radio director interviewed me for a programme in my honour they will soon put on in Finland; and next week an American radio interviewer is seeking me out for a talk on the new cities programme. In one sense it's an inopportune moment for me, since my mind is mainly centred on the sequel to *The Myth of the Machine*; and in the last few years I've made no effort to keep abreast of current American legislation or further proposals. But luckily for me Albert Mayer's *The Urgent Future*[2] has just come out, and it turns out to be an excellent digest of past efforts, as well as a useful prospectus, for Mayer has more or less succeeded in bringing together the useful ideas in planning and housing of the last half-century. We have never been very close personally, though he and I and Henry Wright founded the Housing Study Guild back in 1930, and even went on to write a series of articles about a fresh housing programme, which we have no reason even now to be ashamed of. But I thought well enough of his book to write a long review of it for the *Architectural Record*[3], even though I had to steal time from my own work to do it.

As you see from the address, we are back in Cambridge again, in our eleventh floor eyrie overlooking the turrets and towers of Harvard, feeling very much at home again, and very regretful that this will be our last winter here, since these facilities are for Visiting Scholars—that is my official title— and not for permanent occupancy by Aged if not Indigent Scholars who would like to prolong their stay here indefinitely.

Before leaving for Cambridge I had, apart from writing, an immense amount of work to do scything weeds and clipping bushes, for the vegetation had grown to jungle density during the rainy spring and early summer, and in every direction we began to feel choked with leafage and hemmed in, unable

---

[1] New York, London, 1967, 1968.
[2] New York, 1967.
[3] December, 1967.

even to see the ten acres of open meadow that stretches behind our home acre. We lingered on a few days longer than we had planned, enjoying the soft Indian summer, and hacking down perfect mountains of branches and leaves: but at least I can now face the spring growth without feeling oppressed. You don't know how often I have wished that you and Margaret had seen us in our country home. Since you never did it's as if you hadn't seen one side of our character, the simple rustic side; for our home has a kind of down-to-earth character that often shocks our more elegant friends, who know I could afford something better—or who go away distressed over the suspicion that I can't—which latter isn't true any more, though of course it was in 1929 when we acquired the place. But, battered and shabby though the place is, it fits us like a glove; and we find that the young, at least, are delighted with it.

Feeling a little tired after I had put together my Cities book, I 'rested' from my labours by writing an Introduction to a book of Emerson's essays I am selecting, to be published by the Literary Guild. Emerson was perhaps the freest mind in the nineteenth century, and though he and I are quite different in our intellectual capabilities—he had no gift whatever for organising his thoughts, even in the span of an essay—we are temperamentally blood brothers, and in the course of growing older I have come even closer to him: partly because his *Journals* have, these last twenty years, been my constant companions. I value the *Journals*, as they stand, more than any other work of his: indeed, they were the sources of most of his essays; but the image of Emerson left by the *Journals* is a truer and more interesting revelation of his character, for it has more of his humour in it, and of his slashing personal criticisms of the corrupt politicians and timid, genteel ninnies of his own day. This editing is a labour of love, before I settle down to the real work of the winter. . . .

WELWYN GARDEN CITY   18 October 1967

Dear Lewis

That I answer your letter at once is no sign of energy; it is the reverse. I am struggling off and on with the revision of *The New Towns*, which is *work*, whereas a letter just received, under its stimulus, is indulgence in the garrulity that now grows on me. At the same time your report of the work you do so systematically hits me in the midriff. I know I have made a mistake in not getting more than a tiny percentage of my writing into book form.

I much admire the steadiness of your assessment of your own work, due I think neither to conceit nor illusion, but to sense of responsibility for rightful thinking and a strong conviction that you are adding to it with some effect. As you certainly are. I have wondered whether you ever have my experience. Five minutes after writing a piece I feel it is fairly well done but that I have only said about a third of what I had hoped to say. Next day I think it is not only thin in content but lame in some way—in humour, moral force, or choice of phrase. Ten years later I find it, and think 'How could I ever have written a thing as good as that!', and regret that I never published it. A possible explanation is that years have diminished my 'reach' (in Browning's sense) and made me more complacent about my 'grasp' when in my usual easy-going state. I could expatiate on the theme of the happy amateur who thinks he could have been a respected professional. But I am writing to a professional who developed and employed his talents, not merely for literary display but for great things that matter for humanity.

I am glad to hear of your enthusiasm for Emerson; I had thought, from some comment of long ago, that you were severely critical of his philosophy and influence. I have had for fifty or sixty years his collected essays, and have read them from time to time with dazed admiration—though I have never sized up the Transcendentalist movement. The Whites' *Intellectual versus the City*[1] now throws some light, but I confess it irritates me by a strange failure to see that most critics of the evils of cities are not 'anti-city'. They don't even mention Howard, and I feel they caricature you.

MPO and I enjoyed your sketch of your rustic retreat, and of course wish we could have seen you both in it. We're too citified for scythes and too pastoral for jungles. The marriage of town and country—both I suppose tamed or domesticated—saves us from alternating between Stuyvesant Town and Maine. I guess both the Town Mouse and the Country Mouse would regard us as degenerate pets.

CAMBRIDGE, MASSACHUSETTS   18 November 1967

It is precisely a month, dear F.J., since you wrote me. At that time you were struggling with the revision of your *New Towns*, and here am I, similarly struggling with an even more drastic version of the first draft of the second volume of Technics and Human Development—as I shall call the combined volumes after the second appears. I am also, it happens, struggling with suppressed rage over a scurrilous review of *The Myth of the Machine* which recently came out in the TLS: a particularly annoying performance because the writer accuses me of suppressing two quite imaginary intellectual debts and presumptuously corrects me for being inadequately informed on matters

---

[1] M. *and* L. White, *The Intellectual Versus the City*, Cambridge (USA), 1962.

where I, not he, have the latest data. But I long ago realised that one wastes energy in replying to such attacks: so I console myself with a quite handsome and sympathetic appreciation that has come out in *The New Statesman*. I have the further consolation of knowing that the book has attracted prompt and adequate attention, which is more than happened in my own country. Yet in the long run, how much do reviews matter? Very little, I suspect. Despite American neglect of *The Myth* it sold better the first two months than *The City in History*. The worst effect of bad or absent reviews, at least in America, is that once the booksellers are out of stock they are reluctant to re-order.

My experience with my own writings is very similar to yours: so much so that I've learned to distrust my immediate reactions, whether elated or dismal. In the end, the only works of mine that give me *no* pleasure a few years later are those that I have written under pressure, or under the call of duty. They lack ease and spontaneity: tend to be 'rhetorical'. With your special talents you could obviously have had a full career as a writer, but I don't know whether this would have made your actual life richer; probably not. About 'genius' there is no choice: but that is a deadly gift that the good fairies spared us from at birth!

How strange that you should have misinterpreted my feelings about Emerson. Why! he plays the same part in my life that Robinson Crusoe did for the old butler in Collins' *The Moonstone*. I carried a World's Classics edition of his essays in my middy-blouse when I was in the Navy in 1918—right here in Cambridge, as it happened. And when I made a selection from Emerson's *Journals* for my present edition that task, which might have taken a good month, was performed in a morning, because over the last twenty years of reading and re-reading those ten volumes I had already marked every desirable passage. For me he is the central American writer: our whole literature, apart from the novel, flows downward from that mountain spring. Have you, by the by, read Harold Nicolson's *Diaries*[1]? I am just starting on the second volume, edited with incredible tact, sympathy and skill by one of his sons. I have never liked Nicolson: indeed he is the quintessence of all the things in upper class England that I detest. And yet there is another side to him, a kind of honesty and courage, that gives the lie to his weak face: and I find his account of those fifteen terrible years, 1930–45, altogether rewarding. If we'd ever met I am sure he would have been aloof, supercilious and politely rude: but in the pages of his *Diary* I find nothing to rouse my personal dander: if anything he awakens a kind of brotherly affection!

---

[1] Sir Harold Nicolson, *Diaries and Letters, 1930–39*; . . . *1939–45*, London, New York, 1966, 1967.

CAMBRIDGE, MASSACHUSETTS   22 December 1967

... Christmas is almost upon us, dear F.J., and I haven't yet answered your letter of a month ago. But before I do anything else, let me on behalf of both of us embrace both you and Margaret and whisper into your ears all our wishes and hopes and blessings for the New Year, hoping that there is enough magic left in the world to bring about exactly the transformations and fulfilments that you would enjoy. However futile these wishes, the impulse behind it, which they record, is what matters. In many ways, this has proved to be one of the best years in our lives, and not the least precious part of it was the day that we spent at Welwyn in your company—though we remember, with pleasure, too, the *T & CP* party that we 'crashed' on almost our last afternoon in London! We've done the latter so rarely that it gave us a double enjoyment.

Yes: I've seen some of the snooty and sneering reviews of my book in the British papers, but there have also been some good ones; and since I don't expect that many people will realise how many fresh things I've said and *how radically I've altered old perspectives* till at least another ten years have gone by, I don't feel too bad about the reception, except for the people at Warburg's, who exerted themselves in every possible way to make a go of the book. Had my American publishers been half as zealous, it would have made a great splurge over here; and strangely enough, despite the weak response from the reviewers, and the total neglect from the papers I write for, *The Myth of the Machine* actually did better in its first two months than did *The City in History*—though I suspect that those original sales were derived in part from the success of the former book. No matter; I've already completed four chapters of my volume II, if one can use the word 'complete' about a second draft which will have to be re-written a third time. Meanwhile, I have just read proofs on the book we're getting out this spring, *The Urban Prospect*, a collection of my city planning papers, mostly from the last ten years: though I am using as preface an article I used in the Regional Planning number of the *Survey Graphic* in 1925. Though it has a few slightly obsolete allusions and omissions—I mention radio and do not refer to television—I'll warrant that most readers won't realise till they reach the end that it was all written more than forty years ago. My little joke.

I can sympathise with your tribulations over the future form of *T & CP*, for the *Journal of the RIBA* has undergone a similar transformation, and though the advertising pages flourish as never before I find myself repelled by the whole effect and often have to force myself to look at the articles. We sacrifice too much to bigness and numbers. And the proof of this to me is what happened at the fifteenth Anniversary of the American Institute of

Planners. Have I already told you about this? They handed out some ten or a dozen awards; and three of them went to members of the Regional Planning Association of America, a body that in its heyday never embraced more than eighteen members, and was chiefly the vehicle of half a dozen in the inner circle. The awards went, incidentally, to Stein, Catherine Bauer and myself; though as far as I know their journal never asked anyone of us, except perhaps Catherine, for an article. That makes this kind of acknowledgement a little hollow: as if the planners thought they would salve their consciences by voting for the right thing and continuing in practice to ignore it or flout it.

All friends of England over here have been shocked and saddened by the economic plight you are in, since it is a consequence, largely, of the great sacrifices you were forced to make in prosecuting the Second World War, and then of repairing the ensuing damage, at a time when you were also trying to improve the lot of your industrial population and raise the general conditions of life. France's behaviour, at least De Gaulle's, is an example of the blackest ingratitude; and it makes the whole situation doubly bitter. But I needn't talk about France, since the tactics used by the American air forces in Vietnam, now fully documented *with the aid of the Air Force itself*, are those of cold-blooded genocide, with whole villages being burned without provocation to give inexperienced airman practice in 'pressing the button' on more dangerous military tactics. Our country has been degraded and dishonoured, as Germany was by the extermination camps, though here, I am happy to say, a growing number of people have been sickened by the spectacle and have joined together to denounce it to the United Nations. What a nightmarish world in which to wish a Merry Christmas! These thoughts poison one's most innocent pleasures. May heaven punish the wicked men in the Pentagon and the White House who have devised or sanctioned this hideous barbarism. Forgive me, dear F.J., for uttering these curses in your letters. . . .

WELWYN GARDEN CITY   2 February 1968

Dear Lewis

. . . And why are so many people so stupid about new towns? I have just had a friendly letter from a man on the *Washington Post* telling me he heard 'a very distinguished architect' say at a meeting that the British new towns are horrible and have the highest suicide rate in the country, and asking me for statistics. Notoriously, suicide rates are higher in big cities than in the country, but there have been no official statistics of the incidence in new towns, so this quite fantastic impression is difficult to dispose of off the cuff. . . .

As you know, I disagree with your view that the first new towns in GB are too open—and Robin Best's *Land for New Towns*[1] has shown conclusively that the density standards of our new towns are rather higher than those adopted for the development plans of Britain's urban areas generally. The new towns' space standards are in fact very similar to those of existing large towns, most of which are planning to *reduce* their density. Some of the latest new towns are planning higher densities than the old county boroughs, conscious of over-compression—which I think very sad. Business executives and better-off families therefore tend to live outside the towns, which makes it more difficult to get a balance of classes and incomes inside.

CAMBRIDGE, MASSACHUSETTS   5 February 1968

... It was a pleasure to get your letter of the second, dear F.J., not because you were under any obligation to even up our output of letters; but because it told me that you had survived both the bitter frosts of December and the bitter—I suppose even more bitter—devaluation of the pound. As for the muddle you are in with your new drafts for the fresh edition of *New Twons*, I can match that experience: for I have made so many preliminary notes and sketchy drafts of the sequel to *The Myth of the Machine* that I find myself frantic to the point of stupefaction, trying to bring them all together: I sometimes spend hours trying to recover the thread of what I originally intended to say. Though half of this second draft is now written, I am as usual so dissatisfied that I foresee I may still be working on a third or even a fourth draft next autumn, when we come back here. This is depressing enough by itself, without having all the arrogance and folly that has brought on our current humiliations in Vietnam to confront us in the newspaper every day. If President Johnson were Prime Minister in a responsible cabinet government he would not survive another week, for the tide of disillusion and disgust, to say nothing of righteous indignation, has been rising steadily among my fellow-countrymen. Johnson has been hoping to unify the country by enlarging the present crisis; but he has actually succeeded in disintegrating it further; and it is hard to see through whom or at what point recovery can take place, since those in power have made miscalculations and blunders so huge and irremediable that they are unable to face them, much less publicly acknowledge them and seek a new course. I feel today the way decent Germans must have felt under Hitler, who somehow knew all about Auschwitz and Buchenhausen: but I am just as helpless as they were to do anything about it. The one thing that consoles me, slightly, is that millions of

---

[1] London, 1964.

Americans feel the same way and constantly make themselves heard—
though as yet without any effect. Forgive this sad tirade: somehow this is a
nightmare that haunts my days as well as my nights, lowers my vitality and
robs me of some of the energy I need for work. And yet if I bottle it up
entirely I am worse off than ever.

Now for a word about my Introduction, which so happily prompted your
note. As you see I am not returning it, for to my great surprise and my no
little delight I cannot find a word or a punctuation mark, to say nothing of a
statement, that I feel any need to change. On the old matter of densities and
open spaces I might easily add a page or two in the hope of healing our
differences or at least defining them more closely; but this is not the moment
to do that. If I had made urban planning my exclusive speciality there are
many matters which I should have written on at length, and this was one of
them, gathering together ideas I have dropt by the way but did not take pains
fully to develop. But life is short, and as you know I have chosen to keep my
interests broad, rather than concentrated. Now that I must begin to count my
days I sometimes feel regretful over the things I have neglected to do, or, in
terms of my present observations, have done badly. But at this state such
regrets are frivolous. . . . But this brings me back to the venomous and
libellous statements that are made about New Towns. There is something in
a well-balanced, healthy, normal, or simply beautiful object or person or city
that seems to frighten and exacerbate our sick contemporaries. I have come
upon this from time to time in reviews of my own work, and never more so
than in some of the English reviews of *The Myth of the Machine,* which
record, not intellectual dissent, but sheer poisonous hatred for the man who
utters ideas that disagree with the reviewer's. It's an alarming symptom of
our times. Catherine Bauer, when she was young, used to say to me: 'You're
good for me, because you are so healthy,' and whatever else I did for her, I
think perhaps I kept her from becoming a neurotic and disintegrated intellectual, a mere esthete of the 1930's—though Heaven knows that Catherine
at her worst was infinitely saner than the best of the present breed. . . .

WELWYN GARDEN CITY   5 March 1968

Dear Lewis
I suspect I have had another letter from you since that of 5 February; my
papers are in more of muddle even than customary. Neglected letters, like
forgotten misdeeds, always show their heads sooner or later, even after the
injured parties have faded away. . . . I am still struggling with the last of my
chapters of *The New Towns,* which I had hoped would give a general sketch of

the 'new towns' in other countries, with the background planning policies in representative cases. But there is now such a vast literature on planning that it has taken me, at my slow pace, far too long to read a selection of it, and I now find that unless I make written notes or abstracts as I read, the information goes into my one usable eye and out through the back of my neck, and the more or less interesting thoughts they rouse in my brain bury themselves deep down in my unconscious and only come up when I can't possibly use them. So I am becoming a mere columnist, writing ephemeral notes for *T & CP* instead of books and serious essays.

Dr Stanley Buder, who is here starting on the history of the garden city movement and the TCPA, is of course overwhelmed by the mass of documentation that exists, of which my own collection is, for its period, the most complete—but is filed in such miscellaneous ways, and sometimes mixed with my personal correspondence on a thousand other things, that he won't be able to complete his abstractions in the year. He now expects to go back to the USA and read accessible books there for at least another year, and to come back here for a third year. By which time, if I deteriorate at the speed of the last few, I won't be of much use as a check on his assessments. However, I have been able to guide him a bit in the first stages of his study. He is very conscientious and exact about facts and dates; but it must be as difficult for him to get the NT movement and its personalities and influences into perspective as it would be for me to size up Franklin Roosevelt's New Deal.

It becomes clear to me that the situation at any moment of time is so complex, and its changes from minute to minute so subtle, that only a contemporary witness can have any intelligent view of events. But as contemporary witnesses, whether involved in action or not, have their own prejudices or preconceptions, loves and hates etc., they will vary enormously in the truth of their recordings. Accepted history is based on the witnesses who are cleverest at publicity and are therefore believed by historians—who probably are much influenced by the cast of mind of their favourite witnesses.

I am not able to discuss the Vietnam horror with you. But for your intense conviction I would have leaned to the belief that Johnson is a reasonably decent politician caught on a hook from which he can't extricate himself; and that Vietnam, like Korea, is a frontier of Western defence against the communist world's revolutionary determination. I couldn't myself see him as in the least in the Hitler class. MPO and I often speculate whether in the 1860's we (and you) would not have been opposed to Lincoln's resolution to fight to a finish. Would the North have followed him to the limit had there been war correspondents and television bringing home Appomatox to everybody? I just don't know. We were sure World War I should have been stopped by negotiation; and equally sure that World War II had to be won.

I understand your feeling about your duty to concentrate on broad issues in planning; but I must say that if you had gone right into the density question (as I had to when a housing manager dealing directly with tenants and purchasers), you would have been nearer to me in judgment. In practice the standards applied are fairly satisfactory when developers are faced with owner-occupiers and not so when housing the masses in a time of shortage. Councils and architects are at a distance from their real clients, for whom I have to fight with all the odds against me. I would have liked stronger support from you. . . .

WELWYN GARDEN CITY   6 May 1968

Dear Lewis

One of our local journalists mentions you this week in a leading article about the Howard Memorial Medal, so I send a copy for your biographical files. You'll be amused to note that the presentation was made by Duncan Sandys, the TCPA's rightest-fringe VP—quite a wise choice to demonstrate the all-party composition of the movement for new towns, but criticised by our liberal and mid-road members because he is nearer to Powell than to Luther King. Lord Reith was our first choice and he wanted to do it, but had only just come out of hospital with a permanent electric pacemaker for his heart. Sandys, when Minister of Housing, didn't build any new towns, but I had got him quite enthusiastic about the policy some years before, and I am sure he would have tried to compete with Edward I and Silkin if the Cabinet had let him; but it was then dominated by Macmillan's 'land-saving' obsession.

And now I have to start on some one of the many tasks that this job has interfered with—and don't quite know which to choose. Stanley Buder has done a lot of research for his book, which is now to be on the history of the new towns movement generally, rather than on my part in it. He is a very careful and objective scholar, but goes into so many details so exhaustively that I think he already has enough material for three books, which will take him three or four years to write—and I wonder if any publisher will take it. I have supplied him with abstracts of all Howard's correspondence with his wife; her writing is so difficult that no one else would ever have deciphered it. There is some content of anecdotal interest, but of course no important new light on his personality, which I have already fairly well described, I think. But Buder is fascinated by his studies of the social movements and atmosphere in which Howard developed his ideas. He even goes and wanders about the parts of London in which Howard lived. For you and me this will have a mild interest, but whether he can make it interesting to the general or technical reader remains to be seen.

MPO did benefit appreciably by her five weeks in hospital, but nothing could be done about the muscular or structural disablements of arthritis—which chemicals however keep to some extent from rapid worsening. She continues full house-keeping activity. I also continue the habit of reading, thinking, formulating revised ideas, and writing, but I get slower and slower of course. The process of ageing is interesting, but not exactly thrilling.

I have still half an intention to attend the IFHP Congress in Philadelphia at the end of June, if I can get the necessary official permission to spend a bit more than the £50 travel allowance inside the USA. I asked Carl Feiss if he could get some authority to write and say my visit might be regarded as useful—but he hasn't replied, which must mean that he hasn't found one that is so simple-minded. In any case I am not sure that I could stand up to the exertion and still say something useful at the Congress. I feel that so long as I am a Vice-President I have a duty to attend Congresses. So I may resign instead. Though I have had a long run, I am somehow reluctant to retire into the shadows for good and all. But the time must come.

I hope you are having pleasure in the spring in Amenia. The beauty of WGC is overwhelming. How can people bear to live between walls and on concrete?

AMENIA, NEW YORK   10 May 1968

. . . My little collection of essays, called *The Urban Prospect*, has just come out: at the moment I can't recall whether I told you about it. Most of the essays were written during the last decade, and besides my testimony before the Ribicoff Committee last spring (1967) it contains a long essay on the present dismal urban situation over here. All in all it seemed to me a very timely book, bolstered by fresh ideas I had never put in book form before. So, for once, I was confident that it would make a splash and reach a wider public than my usual one; so confident, indeed, was I that I even overcame my dislike of publicity and agreed, without too much persuasion, to appear on three national television programmes. Added together, all these things would ordinarily be enough to launch a book handsomely, but instead it has hardly caused a tremor of interest, and the few reviews that have come out are tepid and condescending, if not quite as hostile as those that *The Myth of the Machine* evoked. . . .

What you say about Duncan Sandys is interesting to me, all the more because I find, in the light of the wholesale seizure of the big cities of the North by the Negro and Porto Rican invasions, that I feel more on the side of Enoch Powell than I would have done a dozen years ago. We Western peoples

are now beginning to pay for our original sins: we in America for our acceptance of slavery and our failure to rescue the Negro population from quasi-
slavery after 1870, closing our eyes to the fact that we in the North had taken
no adequate steps to secure the 'freed' negro from economic exploitation or
political disenfranchisement. You in turn are suffering from your early
successes in Imperialism, which made you retain the shadow of imperial
power, in the form of grants of equal citizenship in the commonwealth, even
after the solid reality was gone. And, contrary to all our liberal expectations,
the answer in neither case to the present situation is desegregation, except in
areas of regular daily intercourse. The Black community in America has
found, just at the point where desegregation was being effectively practised,
that it does not want to mingle with the white community but to retain its
own identity—with an immediate grant of all white privileges and advantages
in addition! And faced with a black community that is self-contained, self-
conscious and increasingly hostile, the white population is leaving the big
cities for the suburbs at a faster rate than ever. The attitude of the Blacks,
and their present dilemma, is very much like that of the orthodox Jews
throughout history: only for those who wish to mingle with the dominant
community, the Jews have it much easier since in a generation or two they
become physically unrecognisable. We shall have to re-think our whole
position on these matters. There is nothing *per se* wrong with asserting one's
racial or national or religious or cultural identity, providing one doesn't
claim that this special fact gives one superiority over other nations or races.
In fact, in the present world, this is perhaps the one human trait that may
save us from complete submission to the sterile forces of mechanisation and
dehumanisation that I've been dealing with in my fresh analysis of technics.
Indeed, I am proud to say that as early as 1934, in *Technics and Civilisation*,
I pointed out that nationalism and regionalism were perhaps the most
effective means available for achieving this. But what a sad joke this is: that
Britain should be suffering now from what one must call 'racial counter-
imperialism', and that it is the working class that now is rallying, despite their
theoretic convictions, to keep Old England from changing its colour! . . .

WELWYN GARDEN CITY   21 July 1968

Dear Lewis

The enclosed introduction of Dr Stanley Buder is not for immediate concern;
but just for you to note *if and when* he and you are in the same region, he
suggests a meeting, *and* you have time and inclination to meet him. I would
add that he is a quite exceptionally sincere, modest and likeable man. He and

his charming and pretty young wife have been living next door but one to us, with their little girl, now just 2, and have endeared themselves to all the neighbours. We are very sorry that they have left us now for a short tour in Europe.

I think his history of the GC–NT movement will prove an important, perhaps definitive, contribution; but it is a larger subject than he expected, and may take him several years. He goes very thoroughly into the written records and seems to know how to organise his notes (as you do and I don't—though I have a vast accumulation into which he has so far only been able to dip). He has come to regard our subject as of immense social importance and intends to specialise on it, both as university teacher and as writer, the combination of which is essential to his temperament.

Having been brought up in New York and lived in apartments all his life, he says the experience of living in a small house with a garden for nine months has revolutionised his ideas and assumptions.

I was able to arrange for him to meet Silkin, Reith and others who took part in the political developments in our field, so he will have had a unique insight into our branch of history. He also had access to all the TCPA records and Howard's correspondence from the 1870's to the end.

You may have noticed an incredibly imperceptive article on the origins of the GC idea by W. Peterson in the AIP Journal[1]. I have briefly dealt with this in my Planning Commentary in the next *T & CP* and Peter Self may do so in the JAIP. The charge that Victorian intellectuals were 'anti-city' is about as absurd as to say that being 'anti-slum' is to be 'anti-housing'. We were respectfully shaken by the questioning of ultra-commercial assumptions by Dickens, Kingsley, Carlyle, Ruskin *et al*, but I doubt if any English writer (even Morris) was 'anti-progress' or Jeffersonian or Thoreauist—except perhaps Richard Jeffries, who had no political influence whatever. Certainly Howard was almost as uncritical a believer in mechanical and scientific progress and in the town as Macaulay. It was just for that reason that he believed in the practicability of humanised towns. Early letters of Howard show that he was as enthusiastic about the marvels of London and Chicago as I was in a later generation.

I am in a state of acute consciousness of declining energy and decision about how to make the best use of my remaining time—even how to get my papers into such order as to be of use to some conceivable future student. I know the goblins may pounce at any moment, yet I don't fully 'realise' my impermanence. The flow of my circulation (aided daily by digitalis) masks my abstract knowledge of the facts. Probably I need a guru or priest to keep

---

[1] 'The Intellectual Origins of Britain's New Towns', *Journal of the American Institute of Planners*, May 1968.

me up to the potential mark; but none appears, and I would laugh at him if
he did. The gift of irresponsibility from my fairy godmother will not be shaken
off. (This statement could be misleading. I hold that I have personal responsibility and some elasticity of will, though I simply cannot understand why
the primitive particles or waves of the universe went in for Life and Repro-
ductive Organisms, nor believe that there is a Life Force with definite purposes. Yet if I took responsibility entirely seriously, obviously I should go
mad with worry. But I have a much thicker spiritual or moral skin than the
saints, even the sane saints; and of this relative insensitivity or complacence
I do not entirely approve. In other words, I mildly criticise myself but don't
reform.)

With misgivings I have taken on a commission to write two articles for a
special number on NT's for the London *Times* (10 September), which I have
to write by 10 August and which I can't, at present, see how to make appropriate, respectable, or interesting. I have said the same things so many
hundreds of times in different words that no new words seem left. But you see
I had to accept, because it is an important opportunity to reach thousands of
readers in many countries that I can't get at through other media.

WELWYN GARDEN CITY   27 July 1968

Dear Lewis
Brief note to thank you for the offprints of your articles in the *Int. Encyc. of
Social Sciences*, which I have found interesting and valuable. 'And still the
wonder grew That one small head could carry all he knew'. Thanks for
patting me on the back. . . .

The more I learn about city history the more the absence of governmental
control of sheer size over the centuries astonishes me, and especially the fact
that even after the Industrial Revolution no one (except perhaps Ruskin in his
airy-fairy way) suggested it for nearly 150 years, and no government took it up
for over 200 years (1946, Silkin's NT Act). I may be overlooking some contrary facts; but it seems to me that all the reformers and political philosophers
from Godwin & Shelley, the Chartists, Socialists (or Populists) up to the
Social Democrats and Communists of this century were obsessed with the
maldistribution of wealth and political power, and quite ignored the maldistribution of people and industry over the face of the earth. The practical
urban reformers all seemed to think the evils of great cities could be cured by
bye-law regulations. Even Marx (and his prompter Engels) opposed any
attempt to abolish the distinction between town and country or the evils of
the great city until after the Social Revolution, since great cities were a

symptom of capitalism. The loss to civilised man of the failure to attend to the control of the *size* of cities, is incalculably grievous.

How odd that spotting this enormous neglect had to be left to the unlearned simple-minded Howard! Others had proposed new towns, but almost all as a reaction against individualist capitalism, not as part of a redistribution of urban fabrics. . . .

AMENIA, NEW YORK   31 July 1968

I have been meaning, dear F.J., to respond to your earlier letter, and this explains why I am answering yours of the twenty-seventh on the very day of its arrival. The curious slip about Unwin's name did not puzzle me: it enraged me! It is one of *six* errors that the editors of the *Encyclopedia* made on their own initiative, without referring the problem to me, after I had given the final OK on the copy. I had left out Unwin's first name on the assumption that anyone who was in the least acquainted with town-planning would be able to identify him; but the ignoramus who checked my copy was unable to and so substituted the barely plausible name of an English economic historian. They have meekly apologised for their errors and promised to correct it in another printing; but it is highly unlikely that any such edition— or such an expensive series of corrections, will occur. This is not the first time some editorial monkey has made a monkey out of me by correcting a statement which was correct when it left my hands. Once a checker on *The New Yorker* eliminated my reference to a bicycle path that used to run alongside the bridle path on Riverside Drive: he had phoned some minion of the Park Department for verification and had learned from him, out of *his* ignorance, that no such path had ever existed. I fume over such matters because they are uncorrectible by the victim; and in the case of an encyclopedia such high-handed editing is unforgivable. I don't expect such a work to be without errors; but I think one is justified in demanding that the errors should be made by the writers, not the editors.

Once I got my garden planted and recovered from the benign fatigue of manual work, which always reduces my mental activity to a minimum, I set to work on the ms. in good earnest and have managed to pull together in fairly coherent form the jumble of earlier drafts and notes. If *The Myth of the Machine* enraged the more shallow reviewers, the new volume will cause them to burn me at the stake for blasphemy against their machine gods and for heresy to all the fashionable and long accepted doctrines about the role of technics. They will be all the more outraged because the themes I have developed are so well fortified with evidence and because, far from over-stating my case against our runaway technology, I show how much more beneficial its real improvements will be once we get control of the whole system, and use it for our purposes, instead of letting the megamachine use us for *its* purposes. As to the megamachine, the threat that it now offers turns out to be even more frightening, thanks to the computer, than even I in my most pessimistic moments had ever suspected. Once fully installed our whole lives would be in the hands of those who control the system, much as the life of an American conscript is now in the hands of the Pentagon and the White House, and no decision from birth to death would be left to the individual. The joke of the whole business is that this miscarriage of technology has been the ideal goal of almost all utopias, notably that of Edward Bellamy; and my demonstration of this fact turns out to be one of the most brilliant chapters in the book, though, like many of my most brilliant ideas, the facts have been staring at everyone all the time without being noticed. . . .

I haven't had time to look at Peterson's article on *The Origins of the Garden City Idea*; but I am glad you are sailing into it, for a studious ignorance, not merely of the garden city but of the city itself, is almost the chief qualification for American scholars or planners to write about the history of the whole movement. An American philosopher, Prince, who has written about the subject, even accuses me of being anti-city. The ground for this nonsense is that they acknowledge, as a city, only one kind of city, namely a very big one, preferably a modern one. People like Morton Prince talk as if Thomas Jefferson was a sentimental reactionary because he feared that the urbanisation of America would bring on all the evils he had found in European cities; and, as it happens, this is exactly what occurred. When Jefferson predicted that urbanisation would result in a greater incidence in disease and in crime, he was saying what every honest statistical investigation has been demonstrating ever since. I find that I have less and less patience with these smug academic minds: one of them last spring, in the face of the outbreaks of disorders that has enveloped the whole American scene in violence, dared to say that there was nothing more than usually wrong with the American city today. Did I say one? There were three of 'em at the symposium I attended, and all three said the same thing. This is what is known as scholarly objectivity . . .

As for the symptoms of old age, I have been keeping a wary eye on them for some time, and know that though there are some fluctuations up and down one can't hope for any permanent improvement, or rather one must expect something worse, in as philosophic a mood as one can summon up. I count among the lucky people those who die suddenly of heart failure when their major work is finished. But who knows when that moment is, or even what *is* one's major work! I find that I can still do much the same work I used to do, but it takes more out of me; I drop and misplace words more frequently than I used to; I forget recent occurrences far too easily, and so on and so on. But as long as one can smile to oneself, instead of being fretful and irritated, one still keeps 'a hand uplifted over fate'—and 'shall not loveliness be loved for ever?' Which is only another way of saying what you have said. But the final words are Emerson's, which I must have quoted more than once before. 'Old Age—an indignation meeting proposed . . .'

WELWYN GARDEN CITY   20 August 1968

Dear Lewis

. . . I have replied, too briefly perhaps, to Petersen's article in the *JAIP*, using much the same words as in *T & CP* July–August. The Editor says he has two other comments, they won't appear till Spring 1969. . . . The incident caused me to read the White's *Intellectual Versus the City*, which I had received in 1963 but had unaccountably neglected. I now find its documentation of American writers really valuable, as I had only read one or two works of most of the writers quoted, and didn't know any work of Howells, Park or Dewey. With all their learning the Whites don't convince me that they have really understood what they call the intellectual's 'traditional hostility to the city'. Apart from the special cases of Thoreau and perhaps Melville, with extraordinary sensitivities to other than social or community satisfactions, none of the writers studied seems to me to be fundamentally against 'the town'. They have various bugbears: ugliness, poverty, squalor, cultural crudeness, lack of history, unfriendliness, immorality, conformity, unconformity, etc.; and some (most in fact) detect that the cause of what they don't like is excessive *size*. One or two have the all-too-common habit of putting their evils down to 'capitalism' or blind pursuit of quantitative material wealth. Few of them have any sense of physical arrangement, and those who go utopian, such as Howells, have no physical planning intuitions. If you look at Hawthorne's twenty-nine criticisms of Rome, you will see that every one of them was quite sane (except perhaps 'hard pavements') and could be applied to WGC or Radburn. Henry James' objections are 100 per cent sound, though lots of people don't want the intermediate degree of ultra-culture and chatty ease that he couldn't find in Paris, London or Boston. 'Where is fancy bred?' For him only in Rye, Sussex—which is WGC plus relics of the historic past.

However, I have learned a lot from this book, though I think the authors are themselves remarkably blue-eyed about the virtues of the big city, and utterly wrong in thinking that planners have been deterred from tackling their evils by 'traditional anti-urbanism'. What they suffer from today is the traditional belief that the peculiar form of city growth is inevitable and there-fore 'somehow good'—much more characteristic of USA literature and popular opinion than the intelligent doubts of a few great minds, and a few eccentrics with a specially acute moral or aesthetic sense. I belong myself to the torpid-souled masses, who are touched by poets and philosophers now and then, but can't be roused to their heights or depths. So you probably think naive my belief that a different arrangement of the urban fabric could be beneficial to the masses, whatever the economic structure or culture of society may be or become.

I am conscious of a bias for giving priority to the quality of the immediate surroundings of living, as against maximum productivity of artifacts and services—certainly as against the mechanism of the 'higher' culture, much as I value that. But it wouldn't over-trouble me if Henry James or Santayana could not find within a stone's throw the society of Appolinaris, Sartre, Proust, Bertrand Russell, Emerson, Thomas Aquinas, Henry Miller, T. S. Eliot, Ezra Pound, L. M. and F.J.O. First things first. A different lay-out of towns will produce a different culture. But it wouldn't be less varied and rich, given Freedom. As to that, Bigness of Cities does not advance it. And neither Bigness nor Smallness will guarantee it.

WELWYN GARDEN CITY   19 September 1968

Dear Lewis

Various people have pressed me from time to time to get *Greenbelt Cities* (1946) republished, and I certainly wish it were not out of print, since it is probably my best statement of the case. Faber and Faber have declined to do it because they think the sales could only be small (with which I agree). But a smaller, new and ambitious firm, with some American publishing associates, has spontaneously made an offer to reissue it by some photo-graphic process which precludes any changes in the text—even numbered references to notes at the end of the book. Bringing it up to date would have to be done, therefore, by an author's preface and notes at the end giving page references only; both additions could of course be made quite interesting in view of happenings and controversies since 1946. They propose no pictures. . . .

My own egoistic feeling is that I would like the book to be available as evidence of a certain historical priority in stating things that are now obvious to many; and that its manner of presentation would convince some readers who cannot be influenced much either by highly learned, or academic, or by highly journalistic treatments—the class that in my opinion really brings political reforms about. But I doubt if a 1946 book reissued in mid–1969 would reach many such readers. Still, if a publisher wants to have a go, should I discourage him? . . .

In my view from a distance, *Title IV* of the USA Act of 1968[1] is a forward move of real historical importance. Carl Feiss has asked me for some documents describing actual procedure in GB, a mass of which I have sent him.

AMENIA, NEW YORK   24 September 1968

Your letter about the republication of *Green-Belt Cities* has reached me, dear F.J., at the best possible moment. After a long summer's work, which brings me within three chapters of the end of my book—but they are the hardest!— I have decided to leave off for a few weeks to recover my waning energies, tidy up the garden, read a few books I don't want to carry with me to Cambridge, and tend to other unfinished chores. In this mood, writing a brief note about your book would not be a burden but a pleasure, and without further ado I shall do so, if possible during the next fortnight. Your book should never have gone out of print; and in the United States, if not in England, it will be a timely contribution, for even the planners and the 'urban-institutes-of-research' people are beginning to talk about new towns, though they remain secretly miffed over the fact that their own special interests have not been nearly as fruitful, and do their best still either to ignore us or put forth our ideas as if they themselves had independently come around to them. Unfortunately, the people who are advocating New Towns here have the hallucination that this can be done solely by private capital; and you might do a service if you pointed out how essential government aid has been, and how retarded the development of Letchworth was by the heavy first costs. Robert Simon started Reston without understanding this, and paid the penalty. I never troubled to accept his invitation to discuss Reston with him, for I felt that he had come to me too late to get the sort of advice he really needed; and alas! that proved correct. My own contribution will be brief; but I should like to make a reference to your *New Towns After the War*, to show how cogent and foresighted your ideas were. Did you do this by yourself, or were you expressing the ideas of a whole group? I daresay if I hunted hard enough I could answer the question for myself, but perhaps you could save me time, when you register your assent or rejection.

In your letter of August twentieth you mentioned White's book on *The Intellectual Versus the City*. It is a specious work and unworthy of a philosopher, for he makes out his case without inquiring what grounds there were for the

---

[1] Which authorised Federal Aid for the establishment of 'New Communities'.

early rejection of the city. . . . To hold that those who pointed out the ills of the city were against the city, is as much as to say that a physician who diagnoses the ills of the human body is against the body or opposed to its normal growth. To tell the truth, I have so little respect for such thinking that I haven't bothered to examine White's text carefully, though I am sure he has influenced many of the younger people against me. One of the jokes life has played on White, though he doesn't seem to know it, is that all the evils that Jefferson prophesied would come in with the big city have, in fact, arrived!

WELWYN GARDEN CITY   27 September 1968

Dear Lewis

. . . *New Towns After the War* was written by me at the instance of the other members of the group of four (Howard, Purdom, F.J.O. and W. G. Taylor, a close friend of Purdom and a director of Dent & Sons, who got this firm to publish it) which called itself the National Garden Cities Committee. At a meeting we discussed my draft, but the only amendments were of a minor textual character. We agreed on its being signed 'by New Townsmen' because I was in 1918 an absentee from the army, having refused service and not being exempted, because I could not say I was a non-resister; I took the same line as Ramsay Macdonald, that Britain should offer peace by negotiation. (I am by no means sure now that that was a tenable position, but facts are facts).

Purdom was undoubtedly the prime mover in the formation of our group, and had considerably influenced my thought on the possibilities of a national garden cities policy between 1912 and 1916 when I was a housing manager in Letchworth. I had become an enthusiast for the GC idea through living and working in the town, and Howard had developed a belief in me as a possible continuator of his campaign. I was in almost daily contact with him during my absenteeism in London, which I spent for a whole year studying the history of community projects in the British Museum Library (my theory being that the best way to hide was to be conspicuously visible, which I learned from Poe's 'Purloined Letter'). I had had a fairly good education in economics and politics as a socialist organiser and a member of the Fabian Society, but knew nothing about the garden city idea till I went to Letchworth; and I learned a lot about actual development from my experience there and from Purdom, who had been on the staff (as junior clerk and then accountant) from the start in 1903; and also from Howard himself, though neither had much talent for politics.

In 1917, after some discussion with me, Howard restarted the campaign by letters to the press, and Purdom wrote and had printed a pamphlet advocating the inclusion of new towns in the post-war policy, on the draft of which I, as a politician, gave him some advice. It was Purdom who pushed me into writing *New Towns After the War*, which, however, expressed my own ideas of the time and, I think, made some advances in the theory.

I am sorry to bother you with this long statement. For the present purpose what matters is that *New Towns After the War* was as much a book by one author as any book can be.

CAMBRIDGE, MASSACHUSETTS   21 January 1969

Hail! to thee, Blithe Spirit! I am glad to have at least one friend who can look about the world today with his own head unbloodied and unbowed, no matter how many others may be cracked open. I often find myself tearing up letters after a few sentences because the things I am saying are so discouraging, even to me, who nevertheless is driven to say them. To preserve the serenity necessary to go on writing my book I resort to cheap dodges such as never listening to radio and only skimming through the newspaper; but even that isn't very effective.

As far as the election goes, dear F.J., I was heart and soul for McCarthy, though I was never quite sure that *his* heart was entirely in the fight, and as it turned out I stood by him longer than he stood by me: his conduct since the election, almost disowning both his cause and his followers, is inexplicable and indicates a weakness that would have been disastrous had he been elected. But I could not stomach either Humphrey or Nixon: so I voted for neither, and didn't bother to sit up to hear the election returns. I don't think Nixon can be worse than Humphrey, and since politicians always go back on their pre-election pledges, as Johnson notoriously did, if Nixon goes back on his with equal vigour he may even make a good president, perhaps a remarkably good one. I like the fact that he called in his inaugural speech for lowered voices and calm manners. The young have taken to screeching, and their elders have not been far behind. The fact that Nixon has taken the level-headed and imperturbable Moynihan as his urban adviser is a good sign; for Moynihan has the courage to speak out on many issues where his fellow liberals, out of a fear to annoy or hurt the feelings of minorities, are far too discreetly silent. . . .

If my writing career had been based on the hope of finding an immediate audience and popular acclaim I would be tempted to shut up shop right now, without bothering to finish my new book. *The Urban Prospect* was completely neglected by the press in both the United States and England, though there are things in it that people will begin to discuss a dozen years from now, as they are now, in effect, discussing my *Survey* essay, the fake 'preface' which I wrote in 1925. Except for a brief but intelligent review of the book in the *Birmingham Post*, there is no indication that anyone in England thinks that I am still alive. For all that, Volume II is at last taking shape, and by the middle of the summer I hope to have it ready, or almost ready for the printer. Unfortunately, it has gotten a little too long, and therefore tedious, for the same reason that Plato's *The Laws* is not so good as *The Republic*—old age, with its surplus knowledge and uncontrollable loquacity. . . .

WELWYN GARDEN CITY   13 February 1969

Dear Lewis
Many signs of renewed interest in Howard and New Towns policy. I have had copies of the Japanese edition of *GC of T*—an exquisite production; and of the German edition—with a well-illustrated historical introduction by the translator, Julius Posener. Unfortunately I can't read German or Japanese, so I have asked both for English versions of their essays. Ours are included in both editions. If you have not received copies and want them for your collection, let me know.

My friend Prof. Waclaw Ostrowski of Warsaw has written a very competent book for CRU: *L'Urbanisme Contemporain; des Origines a la Charte Athenes*[1]. The 'origins' are Soria and Howard, to whom and to Unwin he is highly respectful and reasonably critical. He gives of course much space to CIAM and Le Corbusier, but seems to be more critical of them; he quotes you on 'La folie de Marseille'. It is a learned, highly documented book, written in French intelligible even to me.

At first glance *Matrix of Man* (Sybil Moholy-Nagy)[2] looks super-learned, and certainly has interesting pictures; but what it says about Garden Cities, still here to see, is so stupid that I am not disposed to take as correct its interpretations of cities lost in the past. And Anselm Strauss's *American City: Sourcebook of Urban Imagery*[3], seems to be oblivious of the vast literature that the Whites are aware of, even though they misunderstand it. . . .

Dr Stanley Buder, who went back to Chicago in September, has sent me an essay[4] on the development of Howard's thought before 1898, which contains

---

[1] Paris, 1970.
[2] New York, London, 1968, 1969.
[3] Chicago, London, 1968, 1969.
[4] 'Ebenezer Howard: The Genesis of a Town Planning Movement', *Journal of the American Institute of Planners*, November 1969.

much hitherto unpublished matter about his contacts with the reform movements of that time. To a slight extent he modifies my account in my *TP
Review* article on E.H., but I don't agree with his interpretation. For instance
he thinks Howard's importance is that he asserted the value of social integration as against city impersonality and anonymity, rather than his spatial
organisation. But Howard said very little about social disintegration (much
less than you or I have, or the sociologists). He saw the city as the social
place and the country as the unsocial place. I gave Buder some extracts from
Howard's early letters in which he is exalted by the crowds and vitality
of the city (London, NY and Chicago). It never occurred to him that
country villages, whatever their deficiencies in other ways, had a greater
sense of community than big cities. He was inherently a townsman, wanting
to remain a townsman when the town had married the country. I'm the
same; it would never occur to me to live in an Amenia, though I would
prefer a barn to a dustbin, or a Levitt-town to a multi-storey flat. And I'm
convinced I am the average sensual man. . . .

CAMBRIDGE, MASSACHUSETTS   25 February 1969

Since yesterday, dear F.J., this city has been blanketed in snow, and of
course there is no better time for writing letters since, though I have been
outdoors, the underfooting is hazardous, and the chance of being sideswiped
by a skidding car, if not run over, is too high to be shrugged off. Yes—to
begin with the beginning of your letter—I received the Japanese edition of
Garden Cities of Tomorrow, and my gratitude for it is mingled with vexation;
for most of my books since 1945 have been translated into Japanese, and the
only thing I can read in any of them is my own name, if I am so lucky as to
find it: so my storeroom, where the overflow of books goes, along with my
files, is lined with unreadable and unsellable and unbestowable Japanese
books—to say nothing of *The City in History* in Arabic! So I am glad you are
going to get an English version of both the Japanese and the German introductory essays.

What you say at a later point in your letter about Howard's excitement over
the vitality of cities is very important both biographically and historically;
and I wish I had known about it when I was wopping Jane Jacobs over the
head in *The Urban Prospect*—though I never believed that Howard hated
London or wanted to wipe it out. Strangely, there's a whole group of people
who so dislike anyone who likes gardens or country living, who, if they find
that one doesn't agree with them that the existing city is the finest possible
environment in the world, are convinced that one wants to destroy it and
retire to the country. Sybil Moholy-Nagy is one of those: though I think in

addition that she has, for some obscure reason, a special grudge against me personally, and she certainly is highly successful in misunderstanding my position, quite as much so as Jane Jacobs. But Mrs Moholy-Nagy actually did a remarkably interesting book on primitive housing of all sorts, mostly in rural communities, like those villages of conical houses in southern Italy which, to my regret, I have never seen. While we are on Howard let me ask you a question I have repeatedly wanted to put to you, and perhaps already have. Did you ever see the actual plan offered by Lethaby and his associate for Letchworth, in competition with Unwin and Parker, and if so, was it ever reproduced? Since I am a great admirer of Lethaby and even wrote an Introduction to the Oxford edition of *Form and Civilisation*, I should like to see it.

As for my living in Amenia, in a little hamlet, I have never regarded this as a universal solution; but it happens to be an excellent one for a writer when he wants to concentrate on the writing of a book. Actually, I spent the first forty-one years of my life in New York; and after that, except for perhaps half a dozen years in the forties and early fifties, I have spent half of each year in a city, usually a big city; so, like the old British aristocracy, I have had the best of both worlds. The only place I have never lived in for as much as a week is a suburb—unless I count the Stanford campus which, though it was in fact an integral part of the little town of Palo Alto, is separated from it by Olmsted's pre-Howardian greenbelt, one mile wide. (The walk from the railroad station along a drive lined with date palms and hedged with cotoneasters is still one of my loveliest memories.)

Don't give a second thought to *The Urban Prospect*: the complete neglect of that book by friend and foe, coming on top of the vilifications of *The Myth of the Machine*, convinces me that the President of the Immortals was teaching me a lesson in humility, preparing me for worse to come when I died. The only person who appreciated my fresh contributions in *The Urban Prospect* was Patrick Moynihan[1], and fortunately I had formed my good opinion of him before he wrote about it. There comes a time in every writer's life when he suddenly realises that he is being put on the shelf. Emerson avoided this by writing his little poem Terminus at the age of 63, and ceasing thereafter to produce any fresh work, even before his mind gave way. I, on the other hand, wrote probably my best work, *The City in History*, when I was 65, and had the illusion that I would produce an even more original and important one when I began *The Myth of the Machine*. I still retain that illusion, but I am sure no one else shares it; and yet some devil in me drives me, despite many discouragements, to finish the second volume. . . .

---

[1] American government official and specialist on urban affairs. Assistant to the President for Urban Affairs, 1969–70.

WELWYN GARDEN CITY   28 February 1969

Dear Lewis

. . . In GB the regional concept of planning, and of government, has become
a topic of major political concern, and will for a long time be highly controversial. The Report of the Royal Commission on Local Government should
be issued next month, and will have at least one minority report (by a TCPA
member, Derek Senior). As you must be aware, regional government, which
must come, can include elements of centralisation and enlargement of
political units as well as decentralisation. There is another government
committee here on Public Participation in Planning, and of course for many
authoritarian thinkers Participation means Mobilisation of Consent. We are
beginning to think about the fundamental problem of democracy in large
states; the economy and staff efficiency of the bigger unit versus the sensitivity
to popular desires and influence of the small unit.

You accuse me, unjustly, of being indifferent to the neighbourhood unit,
whereas I want it but find it tends to disappear because of the propensity of
people to a complex of associations, over a too-wide area for ward 'community consciousness'. I have always wished we could find some worthwhile
political function for the small precinct—such as we had for a few years during
the war in the Air-Raid Protection service, which compelled frequent meetings of everybody in a street or group of streets. One part of Guessens Road
has middle-class owner-occupied houses, the other part ninety of the lowest-
rented houses in the town. We don't normally mix much. During the war we
patrolled or sat in shelters in different chance combinations, and were a
neighbourhood. Since, we have reverted to segregation, except in so far as a
few attend the same Labour Party ward meetings, or a church or a football
club—in which there are also, of course, members from other parts of
the town. Thus there is to a genuine extent a town community, but not
much sense of a ward or neighbourhood unit community. I have somewhere
stated this as a fact, not I think as desirable or inevitable. It was the 'face-
to-face' experience in Letchworth that made me an enthusiast for the
garden city, when the town had about 8,000 people but no appreciable sub-
communities.

I am glad to hear your book progresses, but sorry that its delay may prevent
your visit to England next spring, when we have the Golden Jubilee of WGC,
for which extensive plans are in hand. I am supposed to write a booklet on
the Foundations and Early History, but am now doubtful of having the time,
energy and inspiration to do this decently. It looks as if the Goblins are at
last pouncing on the Osborn menage: an experience more interesting than
enjoyable.

WELWYN GARDEN CITY 4 March 1969

Dear Lewis

... I have asked for translations of the Japanese and German pieces in Howard's book, to send you when they come. Also I will get my extracts from Howard's letters about London, Chicago and New York typed. Buder has used some of my extracts in an article he is writing for some planning journal—but I have asked him to correct his view that Howard was primarily a socialist utopian. More true to describe him as a matter-of-fact utilitarian inventor. I made the mistake for years of affiliating him to Owen, Fourier *et al.*—of whom he knew in fact almost nothing. I can see now that what appealed to him in Bellamy was his combination of Christian 'Socialism' (the 'somehow good' Victorian assumption) and his firm Macaulayan faith in scientific and material progress. He had no belief in 'the State', and though he had a belief in the essential goodness of human nature, he didn't expect that any environmental change would turn us all into angels. Remember for instance what he said about workers being just as greedy as land-owners, if given the chance. Sheer realism! But he did see, as you and I see, that poverty and environmental squalor is degrading.

The plan for Letchworth by Lethaby and Halsey Ricardo is printed in C. B. Purdom's *The Letchworth Achievement*[1], which surely was sent to you. If not, I'll get a copy for you. Of course I share your appreciation of Lethaby.

WELWYN GARDEN CITY 18 April, 1969

Dear Lewis

To own up promptly and thus to hope for early absolution I enclose my review of *The Urban Prospect* from the April *T & CP*, just published.

The last paragraph is an immature expression of a thought that in my old age continually recurs. I suppose I am still in a Tennysonian state of shock about the Darwinian revelation of Nature red in tooth and claw, with a congenital or indoctrinated disposition to see the universe as somehow good, and human love, if unable to conquer all, capable of advancing its frontier appreciably. Some Victorian labelled this line of philosophy 'conative meliorism'—as a position between optimism and pessimism. There are some horrors of existence that could perhaps be removed by human effort; but many that never can be. And the thought persists: would any human being be desirous that the universe should have been an order of ease and content— a paradise of milk and honey and the ever-pleasing music of harps? ...

---

[1] London, 1963.

This worry is of course nothing new to me. I could be acceptant of, might even approve, a world in which pain and joy alternated, because I doubt if either is conceivable without the other—which would justify Creation—but as a fundamental equalitarian I can't easily accept the fact that for many persons there is an adverse balance on the life account. Which leaves the film at the point at which I came in. . . .

There are some hopeful developments on the New Towns front. Very surprising, indeed inexplicable so far, is that the Greater London Council has appointed Dr David Eversley as Strategic Planner for London, and is bragging of this appointment as a new break in their effort to lead regional planning for the South East. Now Eversley is about the most intransigent academic advocate of TCPA policy in this country; he claims to have learnt his philosophy from me, and under my influence started the Midland New Towns Society, which has had substantial effects in the highly conservative and possessive Birmingham conurbation. For the last three years he has been Reader in Population Studies at Sussex University and his books have been treated with great respect. . . .

Another: PEP is publishing this week a booklet claiming that the New Towns round London are 'a howling success', and with a mass of statistics and graphs destroying all the accepted 'myths' (their word) about them—including the myth of unbalanced social composition, and that of lack of comparative 'self-containment'. PEP has great academic and political repute and it says what we have been saying for years with a far greater wealth of documentation, based largely on the Sample Census reports for 1966. I think it may have a massive effect on public and press opinion. Its constructive proposals include a much increased decentralisation of office business from London, which the GLC has lately begun to oppose. You should see this booklet, *London's New Towns*, by Ray Thomas (whom I had not heard of). Opening words: 'London's New Towns are the brightest stars in the firmament of British planning'. . . .

AS OF AMENIA, NEW YORK   3 April 1969

. . . My soul has been lightened a little because my book is now approaching the end of its long tunnel and I can see daylight ahead. Sophia is at the point of typing the next to the last chapter, and on viewing the clear text I see that it is not such a bad job, though it is somewhat over-prepared and therefore overwritten, which means that I shall have to cut out some 25,000 words before sending it to the printer. It is probably the most original book I have written, and if it should prove as sound as it is original it should have a fairly long life—provided it awakens sufficient response to curb the forces of destruction that are now actively in operation. What people like to call my pessimism is an attempt to awaken a reaction sufficient to prevent my worst forebodings from coming true. Unfortunately, all too often, I have been dismally right. Catherine Wurster originally thought that I had exaggerated the evil results of metropolitan growth and thought my characterisation of both the old and the new Romes was exaggerated. But a few weeks before she died she said to a common friend, 'I begin to think that Lewis after all was right!' As a man and a citizen nothing would please me better than to have turned out wrong, so long as the world I feared for was saved.

As to the neighbourhood principle, it has been coming to mind spontaneously here in America, without any help of mine and much to the embarrassment of the planners who had dismissed it as a leftover from a simpler culture. I have never thought of the neighbourhood as in any sense a self-sufficient or all enclosing unit, any more than I have thought of the New Town as such. Our problem is to organise in an effective working unit the immediate and local with the remote and universal; and this problem greets us at every level, from city to nation, from nation to world organisation. The thinking physicians in this country are at last beginning to realise that they cannot run their big, well equipt, centralised hospitals efficiently unless they establish smaller hospitals over a wide area to take care of most of the local cases that do not need special facilities and the highest degree of surgical skill. I have been preaching this for a long time; and somehow the idea has at last leaked through—though I don't flatter myself as being responsible for this. . . .

The German edition of Howard has come and though I've done no more than glance at the Introduction, it seems sympathetic: likewise the Japanese, which of course is all Greek to me, but the French has still to arrive. Your Auzelle is the man who edited a really first-rate graphic *Encyclopedia of Urbanism*[1], with plans and photos. I met him in 1960 at a dinner party at the apartment of Lavedan, the historian: you couldn't have found a better editor.

I am somewhat pleased, impishly, at the fact that you mentioned the terrible Kennedy fiasco and said nothing about the moon landing, for despite the fact that all the resources of publicity were on hand to magnify our great feat of technological exhibitionism, Kennedy's meteoric plunge, once the landing was accomplished, drew attention away from it and dampened the enthusiasm. The *New York Times*, in preparation for the great event, asked people of note all over the world to give their reactions in advance, and on

---

[1] Paris, 1950–.

21 July devoted two whole pages to their replies. Most of these replies were conventionally awe-struck and nation-proud: not a few of them were downright silly, like the biologist who hoped that the astronauts would return from the moon with a new religion. And I have heard since, from a friend who talked with Harrison Salisbury, one of the Editors, that a large number of replies were so feeble and fatuous that the Editors—mistakenly I think—did not publish them, though they were hard put to it to explain to the disappointed authors why they suddenly lacked space to do so. As you will see from the enclosed, I did not share the enthusiasm: like the hero of *The Wild Duck* I am still thirteenth at table. Your guess about the Kennedy affair is I am afraid all too accurate: but then I never liked *any* of the Kennedy's, from the Nazi-minded Joseph onward. I make no exception for the dead—falsely characterised as the 'martyred'—President, for we have John F. Kennedy to thank for the Bay of Pigs disaster, for total involvement in the Vietnam war and for the thirty billions already wasted on the moon shots—though he almost cancelled out these thanks by bringing on an interchange of nuclear genocide with Soviet Russia. There are far better men available for the Presidency than any we have yet chosen since Roosevelt; but somehow they don't get into politics, or, like Averill Harriman, don't survive there. . . .

AMENIA, NEW YORK   21 April 1969

Your letter and review of *The Urban Prospect* came this morning, dear F.J., and I can't for the life of me understand why you were so anxious about it. You couldn't have written a more understanding or more generous account of either me or the book: if you'd added another word of praise you'd have cheapened both of us. . . . It is not our attitude toward good and evil that is so different: I've never thought that evil could or even should be entirely wiped out. As I said long ago, evil is a tonic in grains but a poison in ounces, like arsenic, and the problem is to reduce it to humanly tolerable amounts—with good having eventually the upper hand, to a greater or lesser degree. The real difference between us is actually one of historical perspective; for I regard this as one of the worst periods in human history, despite its immense scientific and technological advances, indeed in many ways *because* of them: more threatening in every way to mankind's future than the bitterest centuries of the Ice Ages, which never for a moment had the possibility, as ours does, of mankind's being completely wiped out. My own temperament is on the whole a buoyant one: it is the facts themselves that are gloomy. When a doctor says of a patient, he has an incurable disease, you do not accuse the doctor of being 'gloomy'. You may properly say that his diagnosis may be wrong; or you may say, also properly, that the body sometimes shows amazing capacities for self-restoration and that the patient may after all recover. Certainly, the doctor must be on the side of the patient, not the disease. One of the reasons that writing the second volume of Technics and Human Development is so difficult is that the evidence I draw together there is so dismaying; and every day the chances for our facing mankind's present predicament seem to grow smaller. If I didn't think that there was indeed a chance for recovery, given enough time, I would throw up the whole job: in so far as I continue to write at all I still, if not an optimist, have faith. Possibly obscure factors, already in operation, will save us, and in fact some of the things that are now happening, like the revolt of the youth against war, point in this direction—though alas! undermined too often by ignorance and psychotic hatred. But I won't go into this here: I needed two long chapters in the new book to make even a half-adequate analysis of the situation. You will find the beginnings of this analysis in *The Condition of Man*, but it needed the experience of the last quarter century both to mature my own thought and to confirm, indeed over-confirm, my prognosis. . . .

I am delighted to learn of the good things that have been happening to you—your portrait bust, and your name on a school. Things are really coming your way now, as they have been coming to my friend, Benton MacKaye, the man who conceived and largely carried through the Appalachian Trail, and who invented the 'townless highway' much as Howard invented the Garden City. Now people are even beginning to say of me: if people had listened to him thirty years ago we'd not be in such a mess. Small consolation that!

WELWYN GARDEN CITY   24 July 1969

Dear Lewis

When I can't do real work, of which daunting arrears lie on my desk, I write unnecessary letters to understanding friends. Whether they are bored or not, this is a moral delinquency on my part. I have just seen a young doctor (a locum for my regular one) and when I told him I am chronically tired and sit in chairs for much of the day when I ought to be working, he said 'you are entitled to at 84, and you are lucky to have a normal young blood pressure and a heart that jumps but doesn't stop, and no special organic troubles'. If I want to work, well, that's up to me; nobody else can help me with pep pills or any other dopes. He is right; I do occasionally work when I get enticed to do so by some very interesting job; but mostly I just laze about and shuffle my papers in different orders and leave most of them in new states of disorder. He obviously didn't think this matters. I think it does, and decide every night to be a different man tomorrow. And on the morrow, new letters and papers arrive with incitements to additional tasks, some of which, if short, I do; but the accumulation of undone tasks still grows. No doubt I need a priest, not a medical man. . . .

One of my publishers is playing with the idea of asking you and me to consent to a book of extracts from our correspondence. I doubt if this is yet possible, and certainly it would require very expert editing, probably by someone nominated by you. But you might tell me if you would entirely veto such a proposal if it is made. No one has seen any of the letters, of course, but our local librarian knows they exist and that I have all yours and copies of nearly all mine.

Plans are going ahead here for a big celebration in 1970 (about May) of the 50th anniversary of the physical start of WGC. Are you likely to be over here at the time?

Letter from Slayton[1] with copy of Urban America Inc's *The New City*[2]. I addressed a big party of its members in WGC last month and found them very tough but surprisingly receptive to my arguments. . . .

WELWYN GARDEN CITY   30 July 1969

Dear Lewis

This is an addendum to mine of 24th, since when I have had a definite proposal from the firm who have just published *Green-Belt Cities*, for a volume of the Mumford–Osborn correspondence.

They argue that 'such a work is done more economically and more expeditiously in England', and that 'it would be a great help to all of us to have the help of Mike Hughes'—the young WGC Librarian who has, in fact, given me an immense amount of help, voluntarily, in organising my records and planning correspondence for the local historical archives. He must have, after these two or three years of working with me on this and on my publications, a pretty good idea of the garden city movement (and of me), and he is a most sincere and enthusiastic personality, with a considerable knowledge of English literature and a lively interest in public and social affairs.

Margaret is even more doubtful than I am as to whether the time is ripe for a selection of our letters; she thinks such things should normally await the writers' demise. But then she has none of the vanity or desire for notice that occasionally, though mildly, afflicts me, and which I rather hope (for

---

[1] W. L. Slayton, Executive Vice-President, Urban America, Inc.
[2] Donald Cantry, *editor*, *The New City*, New York, London, 1969.

reassurance of normality) touches you also. Let me know, however, if you think we should give a firm NO to the proposition, either because you are against it in principle, or because you have thoughts of some other editor or agency in the USA. . . .

The latest Kennedy tragedy has created immense comment here. I have (rightly or wrongly) a feeling that there is a streak of the Scott Fitzgerald world in the Kennedy circle. The dynastic, almost royalist, prestige the family has acquired is a phenomenon that as an old republican democrat I have never been reconciled to in any country, including ours; and all the more surprising when I think of the character of the old patriarch Joseph (surely one of the worst Ambassadors to Britain?) But it has to be reckoned with in political philosophy. After all, I did accept two taps of the sword from Elizabeth II, and duly kowtowed and walked away backwards.

AMENIA, NEW YORK   3 August 1969

By now, dear F.J., I am three letters behind you, the first of yours being dated 7 June: I won't bother to make excuses for you can easily guess all the pressures, inner and outer, that have delayed me; but lest you are unduly alarmed about my physical difficulties, let me say that, despite a succession of misadventures with my dentists—so many that my frustrations became almost farcical—I am again in good physical shape; and best of all, thanks to my extraordinarily good New York eye doctor, a woman, my eye difficulties have been overcome, through a new vascular dilator untried by my other doctors. This last was so quick and so complete that it even surprised my ophthalmologist as much as it surprised and pleased me. Sophia has begun to keep Margaret company in her arthritis, which handicaps her gardening; but otherwise we are in good health and in as good spirits as this wicked world allows one to be.

And now let me begin with last things first: the interesting possibility that your last two letters have opened up: the publication of our correspondence. For quite a while I have realised that our interchange of letters these last thirty years might have more than purely personal significance, though that, too, has its interesting aspects, not merely as revealing two quite different and equally positive characters pursuing many of the same ultimate goals, not without strong differences; but also as throwing a light, quite incidentally, on certain national differences, just as clearly as did the Carlyle–Emerson correspondence. So I am pleased, rather than shocked, over the fact that others feel the same way about our correspondence. Fortunately, to cover Margaret's apprehensions about premature publication, the letters are so lacking in allusions of a private and personal nature that no one, not even ourselves, need be embarrassed by their publication—which is something I could not say about all my steadfast correspondents.

There does, however, remain a question that I find myself raising about many other matters: namely, are we not—'we' meaning here our overproductive and over-manifolding civilisation—giving permanent form and wide distribution to records whose very abundance will either smother our successors or prove utterly self-defeating, since no one will look at them? I've asked this question about my own writings; and I have answered it by limiting the number of books I have written, to date only seventeen, which is a small output for a man living out of his earnings as a writer, not to be compared with the sixty or eighty volumes that Wells left behind him. For the same reason, I've tried to make my collections of essays ephemeral by publishing three of them only as paperbacks, marked, at least in my mind, as good for this year or decade only. Yet like you, dear F.J., I am human too; and just this year I have allowed a Bologna publisher to translate my *Story of Utopias* into Italian, though if judged on its merits it should be allowed quietly to die. But these are large public reasons for continence in publication, all publication, and they do not necessarily invalidate this particular project if the material to be published is inherently interesting. I have no record of my own letters for I keep copies, for safety's sake, of only my angry letters or purely business transactions; and as I remember it, there is very little anger in our correspondence, even when we differed sharply. But I know your letters are lively and extremely intelligent; and I hope that a sufficient number of mine are, too. But there must be some repetition of well-worn themes, and these a good editor would judiciously eliminate.

As you see, I am inching slowly toward agreement with your publisher's proposal; and if I haven't yet given a wholehearted Yes, it is because of my recent experience with the preparation of a volume of my correspondence with Van Wyck Brooks[1]. I agreed to this, when approached, taking the word of the Professor (an old colleague at Pennsylvania) who proposed to edit it as to its significance. But I found that he had a quite different interest in our relationship than I had and the letters, when I finally saw them in Xerox, turned out to be disappointing; so that I am not sure that my reputation will be brightened by their publication. This has made me cagey about giving permission sight unseen: but I am willing in this case to trust your judgement. The fact that the young editor, Mike Hughes, is established in WGC, and is closely acquainted with your work, is reassuring; and the positive interest of your publishers also counts in favour of the object and especially of its being

---

[1] Robert E. Spiller, *editor, The Van Wyck Brooks Lewis Mumford Letters ... 1921–63*, New York, 1970.

edited and published in England. So, after all this beating around the bush, I find myself saying—*Nihil obstat!* I gladly leave you to handle the terms of the contract. All blessings on your adventurous publishers, who stand to lose more than we do if it doesn't pan out.

WELWYN GARDEN CITY   7 August 1969

Dear Lewis

. . . Since I wrote I have read *The New City*, published by Urban America Inc. It catches right up with our Barlow and Reith reports of the 1940s. And there is a Foreword by Vice-President Agnew that could have been written by a reincarnation of Eb Howard or by F.J.O. or L.M. I wonder if Spiro Agnew has read it himself! William Slayton writes me letters, and contributes to this book, in terms that indicate that he is all the way with us on the new towns policy. He says that the big UAInc party that visited WGC in May was immensely impressed with my own talk; and he has now written to the Ministry of H & LG demanding that the next two parties, in September and October, shall also visit WGC and be received by F.J.O. The composition of the committee that sponsored the book consisted mainly of Senators, Congressmen, Governors and Mayors of Cities. Again I wonder if they realise what they have committed themselves to. But the publication is none the less very encouraging. . . .

AMENIA, NEW YORK   29 September 1969

A week ago, dear F.J., I turned the final ms. of my new book over to my publisher—all but the crucial final chapter, which I'll keep fussing over till the last possible moment—to undergo the usual pawing and processing that now takes place in every American publishing office. . . . It's an original and powerful work, but unfortunately it would be unconvincing without a considerable mass of evidence, so it is overlong, almost as big as *The City in History*, and will be even more difficult to read. I found myself in the same predicament as Darwin when he wrote *The Origin of Species*. He could have stated his thesis in a pamphlet, but since in neither of our cases was anything like positive proof possible, we both had to pile up and distribute the facts so that the various parts would support and confirm each other. In it you'll find in detail why I cannot share your optimism about our present state or our future prospects, unless we undergo a far more swift and radical change than seems—barring a miracle—possible. What keeps us within speaking distance, however, is that I have always granted the scientific possibility of miracles, as I long ago pointed out in *The Conduct of Life*; and in some sense, the growing cries of dismay and alarm, not merely from the young people but from a growing body of their elders, there is perhaps a hint that the miracle is already at work—the great miracle of waking up to the true nature of our situation.

You are ahead of me in your reading *The New City*, for I look at nothing outside my immediate concerns, except for relaxation. I'm an old lover of Dickens and for the first time in my life I've been reading *Bleak House*: on one hand, a repulsive mass of sentimental goo, but on the other, a masterpiece of descriptive prose, in its opening pages, and of flashing anger and pity in his revealing the plight of the Victorian poor. . . .

AMENIA, NEW YORK   10 October 1969

Your report of Margaret's condition, dear F.J., has given us much concern, and we can imagine how disturbing it has been, in different ways, to both of you. We've both, as you know, sent messages to her, and though you may well be too burdened to be able to keep us informed, perhaps Tom might be willing to send us a brief word now and then.

Last week Sophia became 70, that ancient milestone, and both of us feel Old Time breathing down our necks, though Sophia, I am happy to report, finds her arthritis more bearable if only she dolefully assents to giving up her gardening. She's had a dull summer, with very little human company other than my preoccupied self. . . .

You are right, I think, in choosing Columbia rather than Reston[1], though I have been so preoccupied with my book that I have seen neither and have barely examined their literature. Neither is a genuine New Town, even though both profess to provide for industry, for they are distinctly purely middle class communities and workers in the lower ranks will have to live elsewhere, like those in the Morris works at Oxford. Reston, from the beginning, was only a new kind of suburb, dressed up to look like a smart urban community; and if the promoter had consulted me at the beginning I would have advised him against undertaking it without heavy government aid. Columbia, with its dispersed villages, is in one sense an up-to-date version of the Amana communities in Iowa, one of the finest pieces of industrial, agricultural and urban planning done in the nineteenth century; but inhabited only by Hutterite true believers. In another sense, Columbia goes back to the old Egyptian or

---

[1] A reference to a proposal to 'twin' Columbia or Reston with Welwyn Garden City during the latter's Golden Jubilee Year.

Mayan urban pattern, but the villages are just for residence, not an out-growth of agriculture. Incidentally, a Gallup poll in 1965 showed that most Americans prefer either a small town or an open country environment to that of a big metropolis or a suburb; and a re-take in 1968 showed an even greater percentage now expressed this preference. So much for the megalomaniacs with their megastructures and the megalopolis!

There's a long article, incidentally, in the *Journal of the American Institute of Planners*[1], professedly on my urban contributions. But though it is quite friendly, the writer spends most of his time giving in detail the opinions of those who regard me as an enemy of the city—as if their perverse and false interpretations of my work were actually more important than what I myself had plainly written. The professor who wrote this probably thinks I should be flattered by his willingness to defend me; instead I am enraged over his thinking it necessary to do so, except by taking the trouble to examine what I have actually written and showing what idiots my critics have turned out to be!

WELWYN GARDEN CITY   14 October 1969

Dear Sophia and Lewis (in order of your letters to M.P.O.)
First to thank you both, at the request of Margaret, for your two kind letters, which she appreciated highly and wants to acknowledge herself as soon as she is able to do so.

Second, to say that she has much improved in condition in the last few days. The gastritis, or whatever it was that sent her into hospital, has entirely disappeared; the affliction of the eyes that is probably associated with her arthritis seems to be diminishing a bit, though she is still unable to read books or to write; and generally she is returning to the state that preceded hospitalisation about a month ago. She is terribly thin and weak, and Lesley, Tom and I, and the doctors, all think she really must give up attempts at housework and have daily help—the necessity of which, however, she herself refuses to accept, and the personnel for which is extremely difficult to recruit in this factory town. I have mobilized the 'monstrous regiment of women', voluntary welfare enthusiasts who dominate the life of this town, to find her the help required, and at least one nominee has emerged—but it is a toss-up as to whether M.P.O. will accept her. I plead and sputter in Meredithian terms; 'This woman, O this agony of flesh!', and Tom and Lesley add to the bullying in their own ways; but M.P.O. is a law unto herself. . . .

---

[1] Park Dixon Goist, 'Lewis Mumford and "Anti-Urbanism," ' *Journal of the American Institute of Planners*, September 1969.

WELWYN GARDEN CITY   18 December 1969

Dear Lewis

I read your letter of 14th to M.P.O. this morning, and she asks me to reciprocate your greeting for the season and for the New Year, and especially to express sympathy with Sophia in her new misfortune and a hope that this one is quickly curable.

M.P.O. remains in bed, unable to read or write, but just capable of crossing the bedroom for meals and natural necessities—often with my help, though she won't, in spite of my entreaties, call me out at night. She is mentally as good as ever, but curiously placid in the long hours of wakeful inactivity, rarely even wanting to listen to radio programmes, though she must have the weather forecasts, which leave me deaf, and generally likes to hear news bulletins twice a day, a habit I share, though I also read the papers at length to myself, and some bits of them to her. I also read a short story or a classic essay now and then, but she doesn't want a lot of such reading. . . .

The domestic situation makes it almost impossible for me to pursue my writing programme; but I am becoming quite a fair cook, housekeeper and nurse. Our national welfare service proves of considerable benefit; we get Meals on Wheels twice a week, provided by local manufacturers' canteens to the Women's Voluntary Service at less than cost, and charged to us at the ridiculous price of 2s 6d a person (equivalent to a local restaurant meal of at least 8s) and so large that we have to divide it over two days! Thus I am able to keep us both well fed by providing lighter meals myself at supper time and at breakfast. And M.P.O. is really feeding remarkably fully and well. When necessary we also get (free) the services of a District Nurse. And as an Old Age Pensioner I get a discount of 25 per cent on the commercial Laundry bill and 6d off the normal price of a haircut.

CAMBRIDGE, MASSACHUSETTS   New Year's Day 1970

Sophia and I, dear F.J., have had just enough personal experience of what you and Margaret are now going through, backed by anticipatory forebodings, to sympathise adequately with you in the situation you are in. And it is no comfort to realise that this is part of the lot of man, and only those who have not been lucky enough to live as long as we have are able to escape it. Margaret's gallantry all along, despite the pain we knew she suffered, has made us think more lightly about our own ills; but it is a pleasant surprise to find that you, too, with none of the conventional American training in household duties, have been able to rise to the occasion and do all the tedious chores that running a household, even on the sketchiest lines, entails. I am glad to realise that the social services of your country are so well organised and so helpful: but though we have the beginnings of the same kind of care over here in many states, notably New York, I doubt if we have yet a sufficient staff to carry it through well.

We too have faced the problem of finding the right things to read aloud; for that has become, during the last half dozen years or more, a nightly habit with us. The best books for reading aloud are not always those one enjoys most for other reasons, but there are times when these two purposes mix. My favourite reading, by all odds, are the stories of Frank O'Connor, perhaps because I fancy my Irish brogue, which is not at all like his own voice on a phonograph record; but even more because they are written as a good story is told, face to face. Dickens' *Great Expectations* I found marvellously good: but then it's my favourite novel of his. *David Copperfield*, which I liked when I was young, proved a great bore; and even some of the famous scenes, like Micawber's denunciation of Uriah Heap, fell quite flat. Dickens' reputation has come back in academic circles but, as one might expect of current taste, the dons favour his worst books. Since *Bleak House* is one of the few novels of his I never read, I tried it a while ago and found it in- credibly bad—though it opens with one of the finest descriptions of London and a London fog to be found anywhere. The good girl of the story, Esther Summerson, who tells part of it, is so sickeningly smug that I dropt the book when half through it; though as usual, some of the minor characters bring the novel to life every time they appear for a single page. Our most surprising discovery is that Virginia Woolf's novels—at least the three I have always liked best, *Mrs. Dalloway*, *To the Lighthouse*, and *Jacob's Room*—need to be read aloud in order to be fully appreciated; for her pauses and silences are essential to the effect, and if one reads only with the eye one reads too swiftly to be impressed. You will make me try Anatole France again: a delight of my youth which I have forsworn for at least forty years or more, though I keep a vivid memory of his elegant, straightforward, lucid prose.

As for my personal life, I shall skip the more dreary parts of it, since our roubles are not to be mentioned in the same breath as your own. Enough to say that I have been so continually dogged by interruptions that the last chapter of my book is still unfinished, though the rest of the manuscript has been corrected by me and even copyread at the publisher's. If no more interruptions come I hope to finish it by February, though that means it will not be ready for publication till the spring of '71. Our final decision is not to change the main title but to call it *The Myth of the Machine*, volume II—and defy all the nasty reviewers who snarled and yapped over volume I. I suspect it will prove to be an important book, though I am too near to it to have the right to say so; but by the same token I do not expect it to be appreciated or understood until a good while after I am gone. Among the bothersome interruptions was, of course, one I had voluntarily accepted: doing a series of articles for Whittick's *Encyclopedia*[1]. I am not at all happy over the longest article and hope to revise it once more before the ms. goes to the printer. But it was the best I could do under the circumstances. How well I can understand the difficulties you've been having with your own work!

If I were a praying man, I'd say a very special prayer for you and Margaret: particularly, at this moment, for Margaret. To have known her, even so distantly and occasionally, has been one of the precious blessings of life for Sophia and me; and the vibrations of her life will remain with us and pass in widening circles from soul to soul, giving courage and hope to those who are touched by them.

CAMBRIDGE, MASSACHUSETTS   15 February 1970

I realise, dear F.J., that you and Margaret know quite well how we feel about both of you, whether in fair weather or foul: so I respect your admonition to say nothing further. All I'll let myself say, since life is closing in on us, too, is that we trust we'll both summon up the same pluck to face our difficulties as you have shown. For the moment our own news bulletin turns out to be happier: whatever the cause of Sophia's 'bad knee' it seems to be disappearing, so she can get around without crutch or cane and with a gradual abatement of pain, too, if she doesn't walk too far or stand too long. As for myself, I finally, to my immense relief, handed in the ms. of my new book to the publisher at the beginning of last week; and except for an unrevised Epilogue and a few odd illustrations, my main work is done—unless one is honest enough to count proof-reading as 'main work' too. To my great satisfaction Harcourt seems inclined, if the presses are not too crowded with work, to get the book out next fall, instead of the following spring; and this would please me greatly, for there is a sense in which the grand theme of my book—the necessity to get control over our runaway technology—has suddenly become a popular one, and there is just a chance that this might prove that tide in the affairs of men that leads on to fortune. In many departments the popular mind, and even the academic mind, is catching up with me; and people are now constantly telling me: 'But you said all this thirty years ago'—though it is only now that they realize how realistic my analyses were. The promised early publication of my book has ruled out all thoughts of

---

[1] Arnold Whittick, *editor*, *Encyclopaedia of Urban Planning*, for publication during 1970–71.

running over in May to witness the Welwyn Garden City celebrations, or even to making a brief visit in September. So I shall have to follow those doings at a distance, cheering from the sidelines the present consummation of Howard's—and your—efforts. . . .

I have a long chapter on Utopias and Science Fiction in my new book and you will be amused, I think, to find that I now regard utopias as instruction of What *Not* to Do, or What to Avoid, since all the classic ones are static and authoritarian! There is one good utopia that I didn't discover until after I had written my own juvenile book, namely, that by Herzl, the founder of the Zionist state. It was never translated from the German and even Zionists don't seem to know about it; but it was a remarkable document in many ways, as I remember, not least because Herzl pointed out that the Jewish colonization of Palestine would be successful only if one condition were observed: that the Arabs were treated as co-partners in the government of Palestine! (Its title was *Altneuland*.)[1]

As usual, we shall be leaving here around the middle of April, by which time, I imagine, my galley proofs will be in full flood. In May I am to receive another Gold Medal, which amuses me for reasons I'll tell you about later, when the source can be disclosed. The joke about Gold Medals is that one can't keep them at home without being uneasy about their being stolen—a situation that gets alarmingly worse in this country where, in the mid-nineteenth century, Daniel Webster boasted without exaggeration that no one in Massachusetts needed to lock his door at night, and where, at least in small towns, no one in fact did. The other joke about medals in general is that the only person one can show them to without embarrassment is one's grand-daughter—who is also perhaps the only person really interested. . . .

WELWYN GARDEN CITY   19 February 1970

Dear Lewis

. . . I doubt if any of us will ever get old Howard quite right. Buder calls him a 'visionary', which in OED or Webster is shockingly wrong. He was certainly influenced by the welter of reformist and revolutionary argument going on in London in the 1880's–90's—socialistic and land-increment minded—but except in so far as some of these were interested in utopian thinking, he wasn't influenced by either the generalist utopias or the community utopists. Fundamentally he was a simple inventor, much nearer to the practical colonisers like Wakefield than to the Mores or the Owens.

Just a warning about terminology. Maurice Beresford and others use the word 'organic' for the natural or spontaneous growth of villages into towns,

---

[1] Translated into English as *Old-New Land*, 1941.

and 'planted' for deliberate foundations. Beresford's *New Towns of the Middle Ages*[1] is such a magnificent historical work that his usage can hardly be ignored, though I would not have chosen the adjective myself.

Buder has let me down, perhaps rightly from his own point of view. He was to write the history of the GC Movement with special attention to F.J.O.'s part in it; and I arranged for his accommodation for a year in WGC in 1968 and gave him access to all my papers, on which I and the local Librarian, Michael Hughes, did a great deal of work while Buder was here—and since. Now Buder has taken on a two-year assignment to write a history of American cities for a certain period. So he is off my subject, for an interval of three or four years from 1968. He had then got up to about 1893 in his study of Howard. It is improbable that I will ever be able to make a serious contribution to the history of the movement as a participant. Nor do I think my voluminous records will be effectively used by a historian without my help, though they are being assembled for the local archives, for what they are worth.

I have not read Herzl's book, though I know about his work and have visited Herzlia. I have a long list of utopias, including a few not named by you or Kauffman etc., and many notes on the well-known ones; but I think my study of these in 1918 was an extravagant use of time, because the GC Movement was never much influenced by either type of utopists.

In my own iconoclastic period (pretty crude it was) I was a 'state socialist' under the inspiration, first, of Bellamy, then of H. G. Wells and very soon after of the Fabian Society, which I joined about 1906, and which was dead against Owenite 'communitarianism'. I at once accepted Webb's *Socialism: True and False* (1894) as the milk of the gospel. I fear that if I had read Howard's book I would stupidly have dismissed it as Pease did, and probably Webb did; fortunately I hadn't read it before taking the job as manager of a housing society at Letchworth in 1912. It was living and working in that town that made me an enthusiast for Garden Cities. But I might have been attracted by the GC idea if I had read in 1903 or a bit later the prospectus of First Garden City Ltd., which was probably drafted by Sir Ralph Neville, a down-to-earth Chancery Lawyer and Liberal land reformer.

CAMBRIDGE, MASSACHUSETTS   19 March 1970

Your letter, dear F.J., with its good news about Margaret, at least lifted the natural load of anxiety we had felt about you both: indeed it almost had the effect of that scene in *The Devil's Disciple* when the hero is about to be

---

[1] London, New York, 1967.

executed, and a horseman gallops up waving a paper: *Reprieve!* (At least that's how I remember it after fifty years, though if you know your Shaw better than I do you will mentally correct me.) What an example of both psychological and physical vitality you both set. ... At the moment I am enjoying the first real vacation, with my mind totally unoccupied, that I have had in years; for ten days ago, even as my book was on the way to the printer's, I finished the last pages of the Epilogue I found it necessary to write, and now I have a fortnight ahead of me before the proofs begin to roll in. The last fifty pages were the hardest: chiefly because the publishers, for obscure reasons, suddenly decided that my book was a timely one and should come out next fall. Since it now takes longer to produce a big book over here than it does a baby, it meant a very concentrated last month on my part; and I don't yet know whether it was wise or foolish of me to go along with this new schedule, though I do know I am heartily sick of the whole job since there are certain chapters that I must have read twenty times and revised at least six, and therefore will never again enjoy, even if they should happen to turn out well. But the illustrations are, I think, going to appear amusing; and I shall come to them fresh.

I haven't yet got around to reading Buder's article on Howard, but from your allusions to it I am sure that I shall be as dissatisfied with it as you are. To call Howard a visionary is a misuse of language, for that word is properly applied only to people whose visions never become realities. The fact is that most planners and planning professors are jealous of the success of people who do not use their methods or respect their shibboleths; and they can't understand that their utter failure to put forward new proposals about cities that have any relevance, or even to make timely corrections of the mistakes that have been made, cast disrepute upon their favoured methods. I haven't read Beresford's work yet, but since I apply the word organic to the kind of plan that Howard put forth, you can see that I don't think that planting and organic are antithetical terms. The New Towns of the Middle Ages, and earlier of Roman colonisation, were geometric in plan at the beginning. Some of them never became organic, for even when they were well planned they corresponded to the needs of life only at the time of their foundation; but others, like Florence for instance, became organic, adding fresh institutions and different street patterns. This has already happened in the central area of Welwyn, as you showed me on a recent visit; and I would take it as a mark of effective planning if more such changes took place in the course of time, to meet new needs that the first planners could not anticipate.

As things have turned out here, I am glad I didn't make any firm plans for attending the Welwyn Garden City celebration, for I shall be devilling over proofs and illustrations till well into mid-summer, I suspect. As for writing a few appropriate words of the occasion, I shall try to compose them soon: but I'd rather write a five thousand word article than a fifty word statement of that kind. My consolation will be that nobody, except perhaps a few survivors from your generation, will even be conscious of anything missing if I don't manage to find the right words. For all that, the work you and Howard have done is at last beginning to tell over here; and I myself am now being hailed as a pioneer in ecology and the 'great' philosopher of the environment. There is going to be a nationwide 'teach-in'—a stoppage of work at universities—to consider plans for combating the destruction of the habitat, which is now frightening even conservatives; and I received at least seven invitations to speak on this occasion. I have accepted the one that came from my old University, Pennsylvania, where a fine Scot named McHarg, whom I hope you have met, has been doing a very effective job in showing what is implied by environmental design. . . .

WELWYN GARDEN CITY   2 April 1970

Dear Lewis

I was about to write to you to say don't bother about a jubilee 'message', when yours of 30 March arrived this morning enclosing a magnificent manifesto. I can't now honestly say I regret having bothered you, since this is a document of which wider use can be made than just a reading at the conference.

M.P.O. has been home for a week now after an absence of thirteen weeks, for which return we both rejoice. She is still of course disabled, but can with my help get downstairs, where she now has meals with me and sits for part of the day in a chair and sorts out some of the mass of accumulated papers (letters, accounts, greeting cards, reports of societies, etc., etc.). She is now able to read again, which for some months she couldn't, and is just beginning to use a pen to sign things and make a few notes. One very surprising thing is that she can eat food cooked by me with quite a good appetite, as well as the 'meals on wheels' brought to us twice weekly by the Women's Royal Voluntary Service. District Nurses call every other day and help her in ways I can't, though she has a wired buzzer through which she can call me in the night or day, if necessary to be helped out of bed for natural necessities.

I am glad to know that your book is scheduled for early publication; I envy your power of concentration. I simply cannot make progress with my own very small projects, yet I obstinately won't accept my situation as an extinct 'Old Faithful' geyser, and try to believe that I have merely declined in height and frequency.

You should certainly look at Beresford's *New Towns of the Middle Ages*: a fine piece of scholarship. I am rather ignorant about social history, and I am bound to say that this book enabled me to grasp the broad picture of the feudal system as I had never been able to do before. You may already have known of the enormous number of 'planted' towns of the past. I think you will be interested to note how many of those in England were *not* laid out on the Roman pattern, but are similar to the ribbon street fashion of the natural village.

The design for the memorial garden to Louis de Soissons[1] at the top end of Parkway, [Welwyn Garden City] included a long wall about 4ft high, which was built, and roused a storm of local protest. The matter was referred to the Royal Fine Arts Commission, which supported the objectors, and the wall was instantly demolished and a new plan prepared, which has to be very quickly acted on, as the Queen Mother is opening the garden on 30 May.

AMENIA, NEW YORK   4 June 1970

Two whole months have passed, dear F.J., since you wrote me; and though you and Margaret have often been in my thoughts, this is the first week in which I have had a chance, or been in the mood, to write anything but business letters. There were many reasons for my silence; but the chief one was the necessity for reading proof on my book[2]. . . . There were weeks during the last year when I feared that the book would be a failure, or at all events, that I would not have the energy or the ability to write the last two chapters that were necessary to tie the whole book together. And till I finally saw the whole work in cold print I had serious doubts about the whole performance. But now that I have read it and re-read it in page proof, my doubts have vanished; it is perhaps the most original work I have ever written and worthy to stand beside *The City in History*. This may seem like the usual euphoria of a vain author once he sees his work in print; but happily it has been shared by others who have seen the book, for The Book of the Month Club—which heretofore has turned down all my other works—accepted it promptly for publication next March, and the editor of *Horizon* quarterly, who is printing most of the Epilogue, said that he found it one of the most important books he had ever read. This means, among other things, not only that my income is guaranteed—barring a runaway inflation or the bankruptcy of my publishers! —for another five years: but, more importantly, that it will have a circulation

---

[1] Planner and principal architect of Welwyn Garden City.
[2] *The Pentagon of Power*, New York, London, 1970, 1971, being Volume Two of 'The Myth of the Machine'.

of possibly a hundred thousand, larger than any other book of mine has achieved in a whole lifetime. In that sense, our cup runneth over. The only serious problem I face is that of preventing too large a share of this windfall going to the United States government for the continuance of its atrocious policy in Vietnam and Cambodia!

There are a hundred things to write about the situation over here, which goes, politically and morally, from bad to worse. Living in Cambridge, we saw the breakdown in the Universities taking place before our eyes; and from the windows of Leverett House even watched an outbreak of violence in the street below, an organised move by so-called leftists, only partly black, which resulted in the systematic destruction by stones and fires of a variety of buildings around Harvard Square. A grim spectacle, and a possible prelude to an even grimmer reaction from the so-called Silent Majority of the right —far from silent, though, and probably not a majority, though large enough as an inert mass to be politically formidable. But I won't go into all this: you probably get enough of it through newspapers and television; and there's very little one can do about it, I am afraid, except to hold one's breath and pray—two responses that I am not very skilled in making!

But I am eager, dear F.J., to hear about what has been happening to Margaret and you; and I trust that by the time you get this you will have recovered some of the energy that the great New Towns celebration must have taken out of you. I find it a miracle that you have kept on going so well; for both Sophia and I notice that, despite all efforts to circumvent it, the slowing down process has already begun. I remember with a wry smile how I used to say to my mother, when she complained about her looks or some other mark of old age, 'But mother: you are seventy, and you can't expect to feel as young as you did at thirty'. Unfortunately, one *does* expect to; and in spite of all foreknowledge, the facts of old age remain astonishing. After I had let two bottles I was about to pour from, last year, slip out of my hands, I suddenly realised that there was meaning in the phrase: 'The old man is losing his grip'! ! So now I consciously take care to grip bottles a little more firmly. Next October I shall be seventy-five, and Sophia is already seventy: so it's high time I took my own advice to my mother—incredible though the need for it is! . . .

WELWYN GARDEN CITY   8 June 1970

Dear Lewis
. . . Our affairs are in a state of suspended animation from which we can at the moment see no practicable return to a workable regime. M.P.O. has had a

series of falls which completely immobilised her for some weeks, involving daily visits by nurses; first in this house, later in our magnificent local hospital, and now in a nursing home ten miles away. I was part of the nursing corps, which involved attending to her many times at night. And one day, about two-and-a-half weeks ago, I found myself in the same hospital with her, and under treatment for what I can only suppose was the onset of senile debility. How we got there I am not yet quite clear, but I was released in about six days and am now living in a small hotel five minutes' walk from home, and creeping from one to the other two or three times a day, opening and reading letters and telegrams about the WGC Golden Jubilee and my 85th birthday and adding them to the tumbling heap of papers, without answering any but yours of 4th.

M.P.O. had to miss all the brilliant Jubilee celebrations, but I was just able to take a feeble part in most of them, with the most generous help in transport and guidance by the city authorities, neighbours and friends, who have made the most extraordinary fuss of me as the only survivor of the founders of WGC. At the time of my collapse I was writing a brief history of *The Genesis of Welwyn Garden City*[1]; and three days before the main events Hazel Evans drove me to the printers, where I just managed to patch it into shape for publication. This is a poor thing by my intended standard, but it is regarded by the intelligentsia as a success and has been popular with the masses.

The Jubilee doings included the opening of a Memorial Garden for Louis de Soissons by Elizabeth the Queen Mother, who stayed three hours and talked with hundreds of people in the most understanding and friendly way. Even an inveterate republican had to admire this superb performance; and press photos make me look as if I was enjoying the meeting with her as much as she did—and it is her job to look like that.

There were 150 visitors for the TCPA International Conference and Tour of New Towns, and I had a number of sessions with the party, which was undoubtedly enormously impressed by WGC, looking at its best in the summer sunshine. The climax of their visit was a banquet at the Old Palace of Hatfield, at which I presided as President of the TCPA, and made a speech recalling that fifty-one years ago I, as secretary of WGC Ltd., bought part of the land for the town from the present Marquess of Salisbury's father, who was at the time President of the Association! If anyone had predicted fifty-one years ago that I would some day entertain the Marquess and Marchioness of Salisbury in their own Palace I would have been incredulous....

---

[1] London, 1970.

WELWYN GARDEN CITY   21 June 1970

Dear Lewis

Your warmly sympathetic letter of 17th has just arrived and I hope to read it to Margaret tomorrow. I have just had a telephone talk with her doctor at the Nursing Home, who tells me that she is slowly declining and that it will be impracticable for me to make adequate arrangements for her in our own home, and that we ought to reconcile ourselves to her remaining where she is. . . .

I have in fact advertised for a Resident Housekeeper-Nurse, but it now looks as if this is not a possible solution, and that our quite wonderful fifty-four years companionship in a delightful home has come to its end—a thing as hard to realise as to bear. (One still retains a half-hope of a miracle).

I am living in a small hotel near by, but may move back home soon, and get one or two meals out daily. It is a very easy house to run, and I can get some Meals on Wheels and the service of Home Helps for cleaning and dusting. There is still a lot to do in arranging and indexing my historical documents, which could never be removed to another dwelling and certainly not to the geriatric institution in which I am likely to end up.

My garden this year is more beautiful than it has ever been, and it is a deep grief that M.P.O. has not been able to see it in its present glory, which is seen only by me, passers-by, and an occasional rare visitor. I have a childish pride in it as my single exploit in landscaping; and this year, for the first time, I have a succession of flowers throughout all the seasons—at times quite dazzling. It is as fine a garden as any in this town of wonderful gardens. . . .

WELWYN GARDEN CITY   1 July 1970

Dear Lewis

This modifies and supplements my remarks about the L.M./F.J.O. letters in mine of 21 June.

Michael Hughes definitely offers to select and edit the letters, indeed would like to do this. He has helped me for years on my records and is familiar with the interests you and I share, besides being in touch with me for consultation during the process. . . .

The publishers write me that they are much interested but of course want to see the correspondence before deciding. If they accept they could not publish (in England and USA) before autumn 1971—which is anyway the earliest practicable date for editing and approval by you and me.

I enclose a typescript of my speech when presiding at the Banquet at Hatfield Palace on 1 June. Its content was influenced by the fact that the audience was mainly the party of tourists from all over the world visiting WGC and other new towns under the auspices of the TCPA. I sent a copy to the present Lord Salisbury, who writes a most charming, indeed almost affectionate, letter, showing 'nostalgia' (his word) for the events of 1919 and great enthusiasm for WGC as by far the best of the new towns.

WELWYN GARDEN CITY   1 July 1970

Dear Lewis
M.P.O.'s condition remains much the same and the doctor holds out no hope of recovery. I think she has no severe pains, but she necessarily suffers much discomfort, and she is now sometimes mentally confused: thinking for instance that she is in bed in her own house and giving me instructions about matters on which, as the responsible head, she doubts my competence. Possibly her intense sense of responsibility and inability to exercise it causes her more distress than her own sufferings. Curiously enough, along with temporary delusions, her memory remains intact. If I report a letter from a friend far away and not heard of for years, she will recall characteristics and incidents that I had almost forgotten, and she seems to know what is going on in the world (through listening to radio news) and comments on them as intelligently as ever. It is a sad situation. . . .

WELWYN GARDEN CITY   11 July 1970

Dear Lewis
It is generous of you to send me the Brooks/Mumford Letters by airmail so promptly. It greatly helps me and Michael Hughes to consider how the Mumford/Osborn letters might be handled.

I have read a number of the early B/M letters and most of the introductory comments and biographies, and with the incitement of the index have dipped into many of the later letters. I am of course vastly interested in the revelation of your characters and relationship, and especially impressed by the seriousness with which you take yourselves and each other and the thinking and aims you share. The breadth and depth of your reading and your power of absorption of past writers' views and philosophies, and the clear retention of your assessments you both possess, stagger and humiliate me. My own reading, up to a few years ago, was pretty extensive and diversified, but in general I retain only vague impressions of temporary and partial assessments of views and philosophies; Brooks and you make me feel like a moth floating from flower to flower but with no capacity for storage in any sort of honeycomb. If anything I read told me I had been wrong in my view about anything, I corrected myself; but I could never remember the source of the correction. . . .

It astonishes me that over a considerable period you could carry on simultaneously such a radically different correspondence with the unphilosophical F.J.O., whose work in life has been to put over a very simple idea to the populace and its elected authorities, with some resourcefulness in literary trickery. I quote myself: 'Beneath the rule of men by no means great, the Pen is mightier than the Brain.' In my prime I was clever rather than intelligent. Since May 1970 even my cleverness has diminished. And my energy and discipline, never up to much, have fallen almost to zero. . . .

I have to face the fact that my beloved Margaret is lost to me and her devoted Tom and Lesley. She is slowly sinking physically and hardly able to communicate mentally, though there are signs that her lifetime memories remain. I have always dreaded this kind of ending. Creation's worst mistake.

WELWYN GARDEN CITY   19 July 1970

Dear Lewis

This is just to tell you that Margaret died in the Nursing Home on Friday 17 July at 7 a.m.

The end was peaceful and expected, as she had obviously been sinking for some weeks, and though not in severe pain she had been in some discomfort and unable to communicate with us, though she seemed to be aware of our visits and appreciative of the attentions of the extremely good nurses who were attending her day and night.

We have arranged an entirely private cremation on Tuesday 21st with no ceremony of flowers—nothing but the playing of Schubert's A minor Moment Musicale by a pianist friend of whom she was very fond and who was very fond of her. This would have been Margaret's own wish, and was also desired by Tom and Lesley.

AMENIA, NEW YORK   22 July 1970

Greetings, dear F.J.! Don't talk to me about your fading powers! You are a good three letters ahead of me in your correspondence! True, I am supposed to be enjoying a vacation from all pressures, responsibilities and strenuous efforts: but so far my relaxation has proved to be mythical. . . .

This week my time has been entirely broken up by the visitation of a Librarian from Cleveland who has engaged himself to do a bibliography of my writings, and who has now found out what a huge task he has wished on himself—and incidentally on me, since he needs my help in identifying and verifying innumerable items. If I'd known in advance how much work it would involve on my own part I think I'd have called this enterprise off; but thoughtlessness and vanity have let me in for it. All in all, it's a thankless task; and though its achievement may give the bibliographer status, I feel he deserves an extra award in heaven for all the tedious hours he must spend on it. . . .

As for the Brooks–Mumford Correspondence, dear F.J., don't forget that both of us had to earn our living by our writing, and until we were both past forty-five that was no easy matter and meant that we had to devil at it constantly. The *New York Times* critic who said that we live a sheltered life must have meant that we hadn't hob-nobbed with gangsters! But perhaps the Brooks–Mumford letters performs one service to the present generation: it shows that men of letters, once upon a time, could write elegant English without flaunting their sloppy thinking and feeling as a testimony of their 'democracy'. Also that decent people can quarrel over honest differences without losing their respect for each other. *Our* correspondence, as I think back on it, will tell the same story. . . .

Your latest news about Margaret, dear F.J., deepens our sadness; but she is oblivious by now to her condition, happily, so our greatest feelings of sadness and sympathy are for you. And for ourselves, in anticipation, as our days lengthen. 'There but for the Grace of God . . .'

AMENIA, NEW YORK   23 July 1970

The letter I sent you yesterday, dear F.J., was almost an answer to yours this morning. All that need be said between two old friends has already been said. Margaret's death dims our light as well as yours. I know no other woman, not even Sophia, whom I admired more: the epitome of courage, clear-sightedness, and magnanimity.

We both embrace you.

WELWYN GARDEN CITY   7 August 1970

Dear Lewis

This is a letter out of any sequence just to say how delighted I am to see the review of the Brooks/Mumford Letters in the *Washington Post*[1]. As I have

[1] 26 July 1970.

long been a fan for 'the major American line of Emerson, Whitman and William James', I am thrilled to see you placed as the fourth in line by a critic in a leading journal—which may make other critics jump, howl or cheer, but will certainly make the reading public take notice.

What a perfectly beautiful drawing accompanies the review! I don't think the artist—whose name I can't read—has got your portrait quite right, but it is an interesting interpretation and a very sensitive one, and technically exquisite, as is also that of Van Wyck Brooks. In these days of the abstract and gross caricature, it is a joy to see a pair of portraits of such gravity and truthful intention.

AMENIA, NEW YORK   23 August 1970

... You are right about the drawing that accompanied the *Washington Post* review. But the joke is that it was done from a very bad photograph: proving that the human hand and eye are often better—even more accurate!— than a machine. Did I tell you that *The Pentagon of Power* was taken by the Book-of-the-Month Club, and will be out in November instead of March. Even without any extra readers our coffers will be overflowing: but some of our pleasure in this is tainted by the thought that this windfall would have been far more useful twenty years ago! As usual Warburg will bring the book out in England next March, and he is *un*usually enthusiastic about it. What the reviewers will say is another matter: but though I expect a hostile reception I don't think *The Pentagon* will be ignored, as the first volume was. ...

AMENIA, NEW YORK   18 September 1970

Your letter of the fourteenth has just come, dear F.J., and everything about it pleases us except the news of your health. As to that, we too have had the first premonitory symptoms of the state you find yourself in now, and can sympathise with you all the easier. The one disturbing thought that has haunted us for many a year, certainly for the last decade, is that one of us might go and leave the other behind. After a long life together, with such mates as your Margaret and my Sophia, this is a sadder prospect than death itself. I am glad that your children have stept in to ease your physical diffi- culties, and the plan for a housekeeper seems to me a very sensible one. In a way, we've already had to make parallel re-arrangements here, in order to make it possible for one of us to look after the other when he or she is ill; and to that end we have created a bedroom on the ground floor with an adjacent bathroom; and in a pinch my little study, scarcely more than a cell, could be turned into another bedroom. So now the carpenters and the steam-fitter and the painter are taking over. Though there is no pressing need to do this, except for the fact that Sophia's knee keeps her from climbing stairs often, we dare not wait for a crisis before making such a change. How often, incidentally, have I wished that you had seen this place when you were over here! I am sure it would have given you a sharper and perhaps even more favourable impression of our whole life. And now, in its wilder way, it is almost as beautiful as your own place; for this home acre has turned into a park, with a garden, a shrubbery, a woodland walk, a meadow, and a grove of locust trees, while the boundary is marked by a palisade of maples, elms, and locust trees. . . .

. . . Stemming from what has happened to my new *Pentagon of Power*: Not merely did the Book-of-the-Month Club accept it for their list, to come out in December, but the editor of *The New Yorker* was so extremely enthusiastic about it that he made the unprecedented decision to print about 100,000 words in four instalments during October, over sixty columns each number!: something never done on that scale since Ross, the founding editor, threw out all the advertisements and printed John Hersey's book *Hiroshima* in a single number. My long Epilogue has already been printed in *Horizon*. . . . As you can guess, we are flabbergasted: almost more flabbergasted than delighted. Even if *The Pentagon of Power* is received unfavourably, as maliciously as the first volume, the reviewers still won't be able to cut me off from the enormous body of readers the Book Club provides: so I can sweetly thumb my nose at them. Ironically, this huge windfall comes at a time in our lives when we are quite sufficiently provided for; because for the last thirty years my total earnings have never been less than that of a full professor at Harvard—sometimes more. This is one of those strange practical jokes that life sometimes plays on one. I'd trade all the money that's coming in for ten years of undiminished energy, even at the lower level of this last decade. But that's a vain wish. As I wrote my English publisher, Warburg—who also has been overwhelmed by the book, and looks on it as a crowning feat in my and his career—'I am fortified against neglect, disparagement and even poverty; but I have no armour against riches and will have to improvise some sort of defence, since spending, in the manner of those used to affluence, does not amuse either Sophia or me'.

I go back to your own plight, dear F.J., whose rough edges I know no formula for dulling. Yet it should be a consolation to you that during the last ten years, at the summit of your life, you have won the recognition and evoked the admiration, and brought forth the open expressions of affection and love that were long due to you; and that for a good part of this time Margaret was able to share in this and enjoy it, as you both did for instance in Japan. Most lives come to an end without reaching such a happy climax; and I hope you will let your mind dwell on these good days. You have left your mark on your country and at last on the world: and it is a brave mark, worthy to leave its imprint beside Howard's and Unwin's and their Victorian forerunners, Morris and Ruskin. When your letters are published Margaret will again share in this, in the minds of those who come after. . . .

WELWYN GARDEN CITY   3 October 1970

Dear Lewis

I was very grateful for your letter of 18 September, but at present I can only reply briefly as I am still in a poor state physically and mentally. I have on my desk a vast pile of letters to answer and informative printed matter to read— but I fear I am in a final state of senescence, and won't ever be able to get a grip of the world again. But one never knows. As I have no definite physical troubles, except some deterioration of eyesight, recovery is not impossible. . . .

I rejoice to hear of the effect on your finances of the placing of *The Pentagon of Power* and the assurance of a wide readership that goes with it. My own income from writing has been almost negligible; but I have been lucky in business, and am very conscious of the advantage of adequate means in one's old age.

Mainly for the entertainment of my housekeeper I have installed a colour television set produced by the company of which I was a director for twenty years—Murphy Radio, now taken over by the Rank-Xerox combine. I am amazed at the enormous variety of the programmes and the quality of the colour and photography. TV must be revolutionising the general view of the natural as well as the organised world. But I missed the programme on Patrick Geddes in which I am told you had a part.

I am sorry to hear that you and Sophia are still afflicted by health troubles, but hope you will be well enough to come across the Atlantic next year.

WELWYN GARDEN CITY   18 October 1970

Dear Lewis

I feel I have a lot to say to you, but start with a queer reluctance because I am doubtful of being able to express myself or to maintain the effort for more than a few minutes. One thing I want to say is that I have read every word of the Brooks–Mumford Letters and quite a lot of *The Myth of the Machine* in the past week, and this has aroused a feeling, which cannot be wholly right, that I have never properly read any of your books before and that I am utterly incompetent to evaluate your work. Yet you say I have reviewed some of them intelligently! I have not read any of Van Wyck Brooks' work at all, and therefore must have lost a vast amount of understanding of the great American writers. What impresses me about Brooks and you is the capacity you both have to remember and size up the philosophies of all the writers you have read. I have read scores of American writers with interest and enjoyment, but I retain only the vaguest notion of their characters and messages. I think that if a selection of our correspondence was published I would appear to be an almost illiterate lightweight. But I admit that I forget what we wrote about in those 1,100 pages of letters and 450,000 words. . . . I look back on F.J.O. with a tepid, proprietary interest, less conceit than depreciation, as clever, grossly self-indulgent, implacably scientific and objective in his own thoughts, and extraordinarily lucky in his opportunities for work of social value, of which he made use far below his capacity through lack of discipline and a curious lack of self-confidence, and a pathological fear of being *thought* self-pushing. Like Hazlitt, he had a happy life, but he won't like Blake, 'die singing', because I can see now that he bought his happiness at a high price in potential work and influence.

As an ancient monument I get many visitors, and spend some time answering questions about the history of the GC movement and the foundation of WGC, which gives me a certain amount of pleasure and hope. Did you receive, by the way, the booklet I wrote on *The Genesis of WGC*? This now seems to me quite a good and useful little work, which puts the episode in correct perspective. I would have liked your brief comment on it. One curious thing is that the TCPA, which is faced with an almost insoluble financial problem owing to changes in its premises and enlargement of its staff, makes some money as a travel agent, by arranging tours of the new towns for people from other countries. I am called in to address these parties and am listened to as if I were the Lenin of the Marx–Lenin sequence, or the only survivor of the 12 Apostles. I confess to being pleasantly flattered by these signs of respect. But I have ceased to develop my thought on planning, and I simply cannot follow the continuing evolution of policy either here or abroad. . . .

I must insert here, shamefully, a good but tasteless joke made at a men-only dinner of the Abbey National Building Society by my late friend Sir Harold Bellman, then its Chairman. Boasting that the Society is the second largest Building Society, he said 'Washington was described as "First in war, first in peace, and first in the hearts of his countrymen". But he married a widow. Which shows you can't be first in everything!' In England that story could not have been told in the presence of ladies, but the men would all tell it

afterwards to their wives; and M.P.O. appreciated it as much as I did. You
and Sophy may not; I wonder. . . .

Here we are once again, dear F.J., back in Leverett House, probably
for the last time, though not we hope the last time in Cambridge for the
winter: we've been here in fact for just nine days, and so familiar has the
scene become that it seems almost like nine months. In the meantime I
celebrated my *75th birthday on October 19*, at a private dinner given by one of
my scientific friends, at which three of the five males present were Nobel
prize laureates—and very entertaining company, too. . . .

. . . Don't think that there is anything strange or unusual about your
forgetfulness: you haven't a single symptom that I haven't already experienced
in some degree. I am amazed in writing my autobiography how much of my
life has become a blank. When I look through my correspondence files I
discover people whom I seem to have met and exchanged letters with, whom
I can't account for; and many interesting things I did have disappeared too.
Sophia, for the last dozen years or so, has kept a rough personal record of
where we went and what we did; and both of us are amazed and pleased to
find how rich our life has been—and dismayed to find how much has vanished
from our minds. As for books, we have the same experience as you have had
and suspect that it is universal: old age, I find, does make little quantitative
changes, so that the annoying trick of forgetting names, which can occur
even in youth, occurs a little more frequently; and what is worse, one becomes
more conscious of these lapses. Incidentally, your account of the quantity
of our correspondence is nothing less than apalling: how is it that we had
time to do or write anything else? Four hundred and fifty thousand words is
the equivalent of four good-sized books: so there's room for a lot of judicious
deletion, thank heaven. Such a lively exchange of letters is more in the style
of the eighteenth century than the twentieth. . . .

I find myself under the necessity of giving some thought to what shall
become of my unpublished manuscripts and my correspondence: above all
the intimate correspondence that I have had with some half a dozen people,
beginning of course with Sophia. Some of this, especially with three other
women, is very intimate indeed; and I am not at all sure that I want it to
get into the hands of a possible biographer, still less to be published. Not
because there is anything disgraceful in these letters: just because they are
intimate. In the case of Catherine Bauer they are too good as literature to be
destroyed; if they could be published along with my letters—her husband

happily surrendered mine to me a few years after she died—they would I am sure be a great *succés de scandale,* for we were unsparing in our comments about the people we knew, and our personal affairs were complicated enough to serve almost as in informal novel. But they can't alas! be published in my lifetime, and may of course never be published at all. Yet even now I sometimes, when in a low mood, take them out to read just for the pleasure of remembering those exciting days.

As for the naughty story of Sir Harold Bellman's you passed on, Sophia and I were both greatly amused over your qualms about our reception of it: you have no idea what a bawdy pair we are. But I can give you an inkling; for one of our household expressions is 'just a Nun', to characterise some disappointing thing. This comes from a story that the Chinese novelist Lin-Yutang once told us. It's about a venerable Buddhist abbot, known for the purity and piety of his life, who lay on his deathbed. All the young monks were gathered about him; and to comfort him they asked whether there was something he would greatly like at this sad moment, which they could give him. Yes, he confessed, there was one thing. All his life he had wanted to see a naked woman. The brothers were a little disconcerted by the request, but they rose to the occasion by sending for the town prostitute. And when she came into the abbot's chamber she proceeded to take off her clothes and show herself. The abbot rose in his bed to look at her and sank back wearily. 'What a disappointment! *What* a disappointment! She's just like a nun'.

I've managed to write a whole letter, dear F.J., without saying a word about the grim state of the world: so you see that I have taken my seventy-fifth birthday as a moment to detach myself from any further responsibility for keeping the world straight. My final effort to that end is embodied in *The Pentagon of Power*: but please don't feel any obligation to read it to the end: or rather, since it has, in the Epilogue, a happy ending, at least as happy as I can honestly make it, it might be well to jump to the end and forget about the rest of the book. Where would *I* be if I tried to read all my friends' books?

WELWYN GARDEN CITY   7 November 1970

Dear Lewis
I had a brain stroke last week, and was carted from the floor beside my bed to the magnificent Queen Elizabeth II Hospital for four days, and was dosed with phenobarbitone, the continuance of which is expected to preclude a continuance of the habit of dying temporarily. This is the second experience this year, so you never know. I am back home, a little feebler but just able to read and write. . . .

I am not at present working to any appreciable effect. I have found it quite troublesome to attend to the settlement of Margaret's estate on which, however, I have had competent professional advice. She left a considerable sum on which I receive the income during my lifetime. Thus I am myself well enough off to be able to make some useful grants to the T & CPA, now that I can't do any useful work for it. This I regard as inordinate good luck, since I never paid much attention to earning or gaining money. The main source of our fortune was the Radio Company of which I was Financial Director for many years, after being dismissed by Welwyn Garden City Ltd. in 1936, which was taken-over by Rank-Xerox at a high price. I had invested in it only the one-year salary of £900 which WGC Ltd. paid me on my dismissal.

You misunderstood my doubt about your response to a naughty story; I never suspected you and Sophy of prudery—only of a kind of superiority to such trivialities. Thanks for the Lin-Yutang story, which is a classic. M.P.O.'s favourite story, which she told me before our marriage, was about the Scottish Minister's warning to his flock: 'Ah, ma frens, when ye are in Hell, sufferin' the torments of the flames an' thinkin' of the sins that brought ye there, wi' never a drap of watter to moisten the tip of yr tongues, ye will cry upon the Lord, "Lord, Lord, I didna ken it would be like this!" And the Lord, in His infinite maircy, will say, "Well, ye ken noo!".'

There are so many different accounts of the results of the USA elections that I find it difficult to assess their effect; but one senses that they do not imply any great change in the balance of forces. Our own economic position is terribly serious; the rises of wages and salaries are outpacing the growth of production to such an extent that there is a continuous inflation of prices that more than cancels out the earnings increases; and no one can see how to stop the process. There was a time (in fact during most of my adult life) when I had views as to what was happening and what should be done. Now I can't take in the facts, can't understand their full significance, and can't prescribe any remedy. And I don't like being so unintelligent and helpless. I have become an ancient parasite. If I could quietly accept that situation I suppose it would be justifiable, but somehow I can't. I still have a quarter hope of resuming understanding and interest in the world's affairs.

I am sorry to write to you such a miserable letter. Obviously I am at a stage when a mighty moral resolve to transform myself is called for, even if I have no confidence in its possibility. One should either be alive in full or decently dead.

It does give me great pleasure to hear of your literary successes and further projects. You have had an international influence beside which my own is thin and pale. But as it happens we have both been associated with a practical constructive movement of colossal human importance, which will continue on its own momentum.

Our letters, dear F.J., seem to have been crossing in the air lately; but they are none the worse for that. Please don't feel a personal obligation to read *The Pentagon of Power*: least of all consecutively. I can tell you in advance that it has a 'happy ending', but I am afraid most of our contemporaries will regard it as both unhappy and impossible, since it calls for changes they are very reluctant to make in their own lives, and what is more, it does not promise that any of the things worth doing will come easily or quickly. I can think of no better formula for unpopularity, at least while I am still alive: for though the young have begun to belatedly take to my writings, I seem to arouse an almost vicious response from the generation just after mine—or at least from reviewers of that generation. . . .

Do not be disturbed too much over your present mental sluggishness, or lay the blame too heavily on your age. Don't forget that you are taking phenobarbital, which is a sedative; and even if you were half your age your brain wouldn't function at its usual level under such medication. This is one of many cases in which, in order to restore function to a threatened organ, a doctor may have to neglect the effect on some other part of the body. When my own heart was misbehaving thirty years ago, I had the same experience. As for being baffled by the present state of the world, and without a solution for its economic problems—who isn't baffled, and who is so silly as to think that there is some made-to-order solution? If you were confident that you had the right answer for our present difficulties, I should be alarmed!

Thanks to a young American scholar who has been writing a thesis on my old master, Geddes, I discovered that the National Library of Scotland had a complete file of my letters to Geddes and Branford[1]. Quite to my astonishment they had not merely been preserved, but had found their way to a library with a Xerox service: so that I now have facsimile copies. It's nothing less than treasure trove for me now, as I begin preparations to continue my autobiography, for these letters recall all sorts of odd events I had quite forgotten. Moreover they have provided a wonderful tonic for my ego, for they show that, between the ages of 25 and 30, I had an astonishingly firm notion of what I wanted to do and how to set about doing it; and I already knew that despite my admiration for Geddes, I could never be the kind of

---

[1] Victor Branford, Secretary of the British Sociological Society.

faithful, doglike disciple that he would have liked in order to carry out his own unfulfilled ideas and schemes. What is even more remarkable is that these letters show, sometimes in only a few sentences, that most of the important themes of my books were already present in the germ at a much earlier moment than, off-hand, I would have supposed.

After going through the almost finished chapters of my autobiography, and looking over a great pile of notes that have meanwhile accumulated, I have pretty well decided that I shall have to postpone its publication until after my death. If I were hard up toward the end of my life I might, like Chateaubriand, consent to an earlier publication: but otherwise not. Instead I mean to pave the way for the consecutive account of my life by putting together a Mumford Miscellany consisting mostly of unpublished, or barely published work (like my verses), along with extracts from my Random Notes and from such of my letters as have been preserved. The idea of this came to me suddenly, last summer, while engaged in the almost hopeless task of tidying up my files, for I found the stuff I was unearthing quite fascinating. This will reveal a great deal about me which would only impede the flow of the kind of biography I am writing. When the time comes, I will doubtless find letters in *our* correspondence that should have a place in this Miscellany. And what a proper joke on me it would be if, after writing a long list of highly organised books, I should finally become known to posterity only as a writer of letters—who obviously didn't have anything more important to do than to write to his friends.

Did I tell you that more than one reviewer of the Brooks–Mumford letters was openly surprised at the fact that he and I both wrote literate—I do not mean literary!—English, in coherent and consecutive sentences? Not fashionable today, when confusion and unintelligibility are treated as evidence of honesty and sincerity. How often I congratulate myself on having been born earlier and having made my way as a writer under better literary auspices. One of the privileges of having been born so early, and of having stuck to a single publisher for more than forty years, is that I have had a hand in the design of all my hardback books, including the jackets, since 1934: so I modestly take to myself some of the praise you have given the publisher for the appearance of *The Pentagon of Power*. . . .

CAMBRIDGE, MASSACHUSETTS   16 December 1970

This supposedly cheery Christmas season, dear F.J., makes us feel acutely the misfortunes of our old friends . . . and not least with your having to face these days without the comforting presence of dear Margaret. There are no adequate words of consolation for such misfortunes, and any cheery words are little better than an outright insult. So all we can offer you is our silent sympathy, knowing well how we would feel under similar circumstances.

This last year, as I have perhaps too often told you, has been a grim one for us, too, in many ways, though not to be compared with your ordeals. But one of its brighter features, as I look back on it, is the sense that I have of our friendship becoming solider and closer: not more so perhaps than in the past, but in a more open way. The publication of our letters will be public recognition of this fact, and the thought of this gives me real pleasure. I only wish I had been able to make up my own mind to this proposal, which you indeed broached earlier, while Margaret was still alive, for I know she would have been pleased by it, too. Though I haven't yet looked at any of your letters since answering them, and can do no more than remember the tone of mine, I have a feeling that they will mean something to many people who are not our contemporaries, and who have no special interest in town planning or new towns development. For a future generation they will convey something that does not easily find its way into history books, or even into formal biographies—the sense of the impact of immediate events and experiences upon two knowledgeable and well-balanced minds. If these letters do nothing else, they will show that well-balanced minds still actually existed, even in our distraught and crazy age. . . .

Index